Winchester Bibliographies of 20th Century Writers

GEORGE ORWELL
A Bibliography

FOR

VIRGINIA

)

GEORGE ORWELL
By courtesy of the Orwell Archive

GEORGE ORWELL
A Bibliography

by Gillian Fenwick

ST PAUL'S BIBLIOGRAPHIES · WINCHESTER

OAK KNOLL PRESS · NEW CASTLE · DELAWARE
1998

First published in 1998 by St Paul's Bibliographies,
West End House, 1 Step Terrace, Winchester, UK
as part of the *Winchester Bibliographies of 20th Century Writers Series*

Published in North and South America by
Oak Knoll Press, 414 Delaware Street,
New Castle, DE 19720, USA.

A CIP Catalogue record for this book is available from the British Library

Library of Congress Cataloging-in-Publication Data

Fenwick, Gillian.
    George Orwell : a bibliography / by Gillian Fenwick.
       p.   cm.
    Includes bibliographical references and index.
    ISBN 1-884718-46-9
       1. Orwell, George, 1903–1950--Bibliography.   2. Satire, English--
    Bibliography.   3. Dystopias--Bibliography.   I. Title.
Z8647.F45   1997
[PR6029.R8]
016.828'91209--dc21   97-35454
                                                                           CIP

ISBN (UK) 1 873040 05 9   ISBN (USA) 1 884718 46 9

Printed in Great Britain by Alden Press, Oxford

Contents

Note: The Footnotes to Sections A, B, C, D, G & H are at the end of the relevant Section.

Preface

I am pleased to thank the people who helped me write this Bibliography. It began in 1990 as my postdoctoral research project, and in 1991 I was awarded a two-year Postdoctoral Fellowship for it from the Social Sciences and Humanities Research Council of Canada. Simultaneously, I was awarded a Metcalfe Fellowship at Victoria College, University of Toronto, and I moved into a quiet little office in Northrop Frye Hall. I am grateful to Michael Millgate (University Professor Emeritus, University of Toronto), Patricia Fleming (Professor of Information Studies, University of Toronto), and Richard Landon (Director of the Thomas Fisher Rare Book Library, University of Toronto) for their support in my doctoral fellowship applications, and I thank Michael Millgate again for his advice throughout the project. I thank all my colleagues and friends at Victoria University in the University of Toronto, particularly Principal William Callahan, Professor Aubrey Rosenberg, Professor Michael Laine, Professor David Blostein, Professor Jay Macpherson, Professor Kenneth Thompson, and the late Professor Laure Riese. I am grateful to Dr Robert Brandeis, Librarian of Victoria University in the University of Toronto, and the staff of the E.J. Pratt Library there, especially Irene Dutton, Lisa Sherlock, Linda Oliver and David Brown. In 1994 I was appointed to the Department of English at the University of Toronto, and I moved to Trinity College. I am pleased to thank the Fellows there, and in particular former Provost Robert Painter, for warm support, and former Dean of Arts, Professor Christopher McDonough, for his advice and encouragement.

In England, I thank Ian Willison, whose 1952 study was the original backbone of this bibliography. His enthusiasm was a major factor in my decision to begin the work. Gillian Furlong, Archivist of the Library at University College, London, and her staff at the Orwell Archive have been infinitely painstaking, thorough and professional, and a pleasure to work with. I thank Mark Hamilton, Barry Bloomfield and Peter Davison for their interest and for so generously sharing materials. I met him at the Orwell Archive, so I take the opportunity here to thank Michael Shelden, Orwell's most recent biographer, for his interest in my work, and for generously sharing information. And most especially I would like to express my gratitude to Ann and Ian Angus. They have welcomed me into their home with the warmest, most generous hospitality. I could not have produced this bibliography without Ian's wealth of knowledge on Orwell, his private collection, and his scholarship. I am sad to record final thanks to the late John Garrod, former Bursar of Clare Hall, Cambridge. Although this is an opportunity once again to thank the Master and Fellows of Clare Hall, it was John to whom I always felt a particular debt of gratitude. Michael Collie, Professor Emeritus at York University, Toronto, is now in England, and I once again thank him for years of sound counsel and friendship, and this time for inside information on Barnhill, Jura, where he recently spent a summer.

I am grateful to Barry Walfish (University of Toronto Library) for help with Hebrew translations; Philip Oldfield (Thomas Fisher Rare Book Library) for extensive help with eastern European translations; and Dr Solomon Nigosian (Victoria College) for help with Persian and Farsi. I thank my friend Professor Leslie Howsam (Department of History, University of Windsor, Ontario) for her sympathy and encouragement, and her diligence in clipping odd, obscure references for me. Special thanks to Dr Carl Spadoni, Research Collections Librarian at McMaster University, Hamilton, Ontario, who kept me and Orwell in mind, with news of editions, sales and new material, at times when I was flagging, and who always gives me sound practical advice. I am particularly grateful to Professor Eva Kushner, former President of Victoria University in the University of Toronto, for all her help, encouragement and support. I also owe a great deal to her assistant and my dear friend, Ann Lewis. I am once again happy to acknowledge my profound thanks to Professor Jane Millgate (University of Toronto), whose commonsense continues to be one of my greatest sources of help. Beginning this bibliography in 1990 was easy, and something I happily undertook under my own steam, but I could not have finished it without Virginia and Umberto, and to them no thanks are great enough. No-one can write a bibliography that has any soul, without a deep sympathy for the subject. I came to Orwell liking a few of his books, knowing a few of his essays, admiring him as a writer. I finish this bibliography with a deep respect, a love for the man, for his intelligence, his integrity, his humanity, his ordinary English decency. He was a good bloke.

Introduction

Personally I am satisfied ... because I have been lucky, at any rate during the last few years. I had to struggle desperately at the beginning, and if I had listened to what people said to me I would never have been a writer. Even until quite recently, whenever I have written anything which I took seriously, there have been strenuous efforts, sometimes by quite influential people, to keep it out of print. To a young writer who is conscious of having something in him, the only advice I can give is not to take advice. Financially, of course, there are tips I could give, but even those are of no use unless one has some kind of talent. If one simply wants to make a living by putting words on paper, then the BBC, the film companies and the like are reasonably helpful. But if one wants to be primarily a *writer* then, in our society, one is an animal that is tolerated but not encouraged – something rather like a house sparrow – and one gets on better if one realises one's position from the start.[1]

George Orwell (1903–1950) is not only a major figure in twentieth-century literature but, more than forty years after his death, he remains a best-selling author. Much of his work is still in print. In 1984 there were more than thirty new editions or reissues of his most famous novel, *Nineteen Eighty-Four*, in at least sixteen languages. The new *Complete Works of George Orwell* is under way, with nine volumes published and the next eleven in preparation. Recently there have been important new biographies and works of criticism. The Orwell Archive at University College, London, continues to expand, with new acquisitions of manuscript materials, writings about Orwell, copies of editions and reissues of his works, and publication records of his books and journalism.

From the early 1930s until his death in January 1950 Orwell earned an income as a novelist, editor, essayist, journalist, reviewer and broadcaster. He wrote novels, essays, contemporary social history, reviews, and even poetry. Eric Blair's and, later, George Orwell's writing life ranged from unpublished letters to his mother from his Eastbourne boarding school in 1911, to his first publication in 1914 – a stirring, poetic call to arms, 'Awake! Young Men of England', to essays anthologised and eulogised a thousand times, such as 'Politics and the English Language', 'Shooting an Elephant', and 'The Prevention of Literature', to his best-known works, *Animal Farm* and *Nineteen Eighty-Four*, the novel he completed as he was dying. His words have become part of the English language – 'Newspeak'; 'Big Brother is watching you'; 'All animals are equal, but some animals are more equal than others'. In 1946 Orwell wrote that 'the English language is in a bad way', and that, 'Probably it is better to put off using words as long as possible.' He offered a set of maxims on word use, though concluding, 'Break any of these rules sooner than say anything outright barbarous'. Orwell cared passionately about his writing and taught himself to write well.

Terry Eagleton has written about what he terms the literary phenomenon known as George Eliot. George Orwell is, I suggest, a similar case. A writer, the sum of whose work, together with a name, somehow outshadows the components, the individual books and essays. George Orwell was unique and he was also Everyman. He spoke for himself, and yet what he wrote often put into words ideas of universal concern. He wrote about contemporary issues, and yet his ideas had a permanence, relevant 50 or 60 years later: *Nineteen Eighty-Four* didn't disappear from the shelves, the curriculum, or everyday vocabulary once the year was gone.

If George Orwell had been born half a century earlier than 1903 he would have been labelled a man of letters. He would have written for *The Saturday Review*, *The Cornhill Magazine*, the *Encyclopaedia Britannica*. He might have edited a monthly magazine, given

1 'The Cost of Letters', *Horizon* (September 1946). *CEJL* IV 202–203.

public lectures on literary or political topics, had a long association with a publishing house. Perhaps he would have stood for Parliament, still keeping his hand in with his writing. His novels, one every three or four years, would have been serialised in popular magazines; his essays collected into volumes every decade or so.

Had George Orwell been born half a century later than 1903, it would have been more difficult to find a single label for him. He might well have been a bright young thing at Wadham College, Oxford, writing poetry in avant garde magazines, speaking at the Union, active in student politics, his first novel published when he was 23 or 24. He might have chosen a career in broadcasting, working on documentaries, producing arts programmes for television, appearing on a late-night discussion show, eventually hosting his own: a popular media figure. He might write screenplays for movies, a regular column in a left-wing magazine, an occasional long article in *The Atlantic*, publish books on travel, local history, a novel every two years, more or less good but guaranteed to sell for his name alone.

If what I describe sounds stereotypical, perhaps like Leslie Stephen or Melvyn Bragg, it's because both then and now it was and is possible neatly to categorise a writer, journalist, novelist, public speaker, broadcaster, in ways which didn't apply in the years between, say, 1910 and 1960. Orwell was at Eton, but Cambridge wasn't an option for him. His family didn't have private income. He had to work. He didn't have the stimulus of Oxford, the contacts with writers and publishers. He had to go to Burma. His writing career was, therefore, something which began late, something which, even if it was a burning ambition, he had to put on hold for several years. It wasn't immediately possible for him to make a living as a writer. Instead he was a policeman, a tutor, a dishwasher, and, by choice admittedly, a tramp. Orwell very deliberately turned himself into a writer, choosing to live a fairly pinched life, needing the supplement of his wife's income in order to get by. Bit by bit, it worked. He taught himself to write well, and yet recognition was very slow to come. His modest broadcasting career did nothing to enhance his reputation or fame, indeed it actually slowed down and reduced his writing output. Although his books sold reasonably well, it wasn't really until the mid 1940s with the publication of *Animal Farm* that he achieved major success, and not until the publication of *Nineteen Eighty-Four* in 1949 that he became famous. And then within a few months he was dead. Thereafter, his reputation flourished and the royalties poured in. But being a writer in the 1930s and 1940s, through the Depression and the Second World War, wasn't easy; making a real income from writing was hard.

It is worth looking at what Orwell thought about writing as a career, and what the basic necessities of a writer's life should be. Responding to a *Horizon* questionnaire to writers in 1946, he wrote:

> The *best* income for a writer ... at the present value of money – is about £1000 a year. With that he can live in reasonable comfort, free from duns and the necessity to do hack work, without having the feeling that he has definitely moved into the privileged class. I do not think one can with justice expect a writer to do his best on a working-class income. His first necessity, just as indispensable to him as are tools to a carpenter, is a comfortable, well-warmed room where he can be sure of not being interrupted; and, although this does not sound much, if one works out what it means in terms of domestic arrangements, it implies fairly large earnings. A writer's work is done at home, and if he lets it happen he will subjected to almost constant interruption. To be protected against interruption almost always costs money, directly or indirectly. Then again, writers need books and periodicals in great numbers, they need space and furniture for filing papers, they spend a great deal on correspondence, they need at any rate part-time secretarial help, and most of them probably benefit by travelling, by living in what they consider sympathetic surroundings, and by eating and drinking the things they like best and by being able to take their friends out to meals or have them to stay. It all costs money. Ideally I would like to see every human being have the same income, provided that it were a fairly high income: but so long as there

is to be differentiation, I think the writer's place is in the middle bracket, which means, at present standards, round about £1,000 a year.[2]

By this time, 1946, he was more comfortably off than he had ever been. *Animal Farm* had brought him good royalties, and a certain measure of acknowledgement.

Today Orwell is probably as famous and his works as revered as he, or they, have ever been. Even people who don't regularly read novels will recognise his name, the name of *Nineteen Eighty-Four*, the name Big Brother, the catchwords. A few of his essays are held up as examples of brilliantly turned words, economic prose, precision and wit, anthologised in dozens of school and university textbooks. Most of his major books are still in print – novels, essays – and available in reasonably cheap paperback editions: people are still reading Orwell. The definitive biographies have been written. His major books have appeared in collected editions. There have been movies, plays, cartoons of some. There are collections of essays, journalism and letters, and more are planned. There are rudimentary checklists of works by and about his writing and broadcasting. There are a few doctoral dissertations, though not as many as might be expected, and there is not a growing body of critical material: Orwell has never become an "industry", like Virginia Woolf or James Joyce. There are no annual Orwell conferences, societies, meetings, no electronic bulletin board or web page.

Why not? Why is this the first Orwell bibliography? It seems to me that when the twenty-first century looks back on the previous one, it will surely identify Orwell as one of the major literary figures, along with Joyce and Woolf, more important than Waugh or Forster or Greene; not a great poet like Eliot or a movement-shaper like Pound, though of their literary stature overall. It is, perhaps, a self-perpetuating phenomenon, a syndrome: Orwell is just famous enough to be famous, but not so famous that he's very famous. He has never quite taken off, as it were. Perhaps graduate students aren't working on him in great numbers because there isn't a huge body of critical work on him. Perhaps scholars are not working on Orwell because there has been no guide to his whole publishing life. Orwell has undoubtedly missed the boat where the great age of literary criticism is concerned. But perhaps there is still hope: might not the range of his work – novels, social criticism, political writing, reviews of by now undoubtedly dated books, reviews of long-forgotten B-movies, arts broadcasting to the colonies – lend itself perfectly to that burgeoning field, cultural studies? Because if Orwell was a half century too late or a half century too early in some respects, he falls into what is surely one of the hottest areas of cultural studies interest, the 1930s and 1940s. And the way in which *Nineteen Eighty-Four* in particular quickly became part of popular culture is itself a fascinating phenomenon, although undoubtedly Orwell would have been horrified by the misrepresentation of his ideas it has involved.

So here is a bibliography of Orwell's working life as a journalist, reviewer, essayist, novelist, broadcaster – with a few interesting, peripheral items like juvenilia, movies, tape recordings and T-shirts. My emphasis is on the years when Orwell was alive, although, inevitably, since he died so young and with his reputation at its height, the bibliography covers important posthumous editions of works already published. A bibliography of Orwell which stopped in 1950 would not reflect the importance of his work. And yet nor have I been neurotic in tracing every single paperback reissue of, say, *Animal Farm*, or every anthology containing 'Literature v. Politics'. Such items may be of interest to collectors, but this is not intended as a work for them: it is a work to enable scholars to identify the whole range of Orwell's publishing life, and, taking it from there, to advance Orwell scholarship in new directions.

No bibliography is ever definitive. Every bibliography has limitations. This one appears at a time when electronic texts are daily springing up. A librarian called me recently and asked if I had seen an extract from *Animal Farm* on the world wide web. No I hadn't. So I did a search and found it. Is it, therefore a text? It was there that day, but will it be there tomorrow? A few years ago I was in China. In Tianjin there were two bookstores just

2 'The Cost of Letters', *Horizon* (September 1946). *CEJL* IV 201.

around the corner from each other. One was 'The Friendly Corner' – the name reminded me of Orwell's 'Booklovers' Corner' – and indeed the staff was friendly and the books were interesting, though the selection was mainly limited to Chinese authors. The other was called, in English, 'Foreign Language Bookstore'. This was not a friendly corner. In the window was a hand-written sign: 'NO FOREIGNERS'. Why not? I asked. My guide from Nankai University hummed and hawed and changed the subject. Later, American students teaching English as a second language told me that foreigners aren't allowed in that store because it sells pirated editions of English and American copyrighted texts which we aren't supposed to know about. I imagined the shelves full of unauthorised editions of Orwell. It occurs to me that somewhere in the world such a new edition of, say, *Nineteen Eighty-Four* is no doubt in the press even now. And, as Orwell's publisher and literary executor told me, even where authorised translations of Orwell's books are concerned, keeping track of what is actually published isn't easy. He might well give permission for, say, a new Farsi edition of *The Road to Wigan Pier* to be published in Tehran, but that is no guarantee that the book actually will be produced. Foreign publishers occasionally send copies back to the executor or to the Orwell Archive at University College, London, but that is an act of goodwill, and not a stringent requirement in the granting of permission to publish. My coverage of foreign language editions is, therefore, undoubtedly spotty, depending heavily on foreign-language catalogues of publications and on the scrupulousness of the publishers. No bibliography is ever definitive.

* * *

Eric Arthur Blair was born in Bengal in 1903, the son of a civil servant. In 1904 the family came to England, although Eric's father returned to work in India. Eric attended the local Anglican school, and then, when he was eight, St Cyprian's, a private boarding school in Eastbourne. At eleven, two of his poems were published in a local newspaper: interesting juvenilia and wartime patriotism. In 1917 he went to Wellington College and the same year to Eton, where he wrote for school magazines. He left in 1921, and the family moved from Henley-on-Thames to Southwold, Suffolk. He did not go to university. He joined the Indian Imperial Police in Burma in 1922 and served until his 1927 home leave.

He began to seek out experience of how the poor and exploited lived, first in London, and then, in the spring of 1928, in Paris. He published his first professional articles later that year, in translation, in French papers. By the middle of 1929 his work was also appearing in English papers. He had written two novels which he couldn't get published and which don't survive. He returned to Southwold at the end of 1929, occasionally working as a private tutor, occasionally tramping in London. By October 1930 he had completed a version of *Down and Out in Paris and London*. He was writing regularly by now, and his articles and reviews were published even if his early novels and stories were thrown away. By 1932 he was serious enough about his writing to employ an agent, Leonard Moore. That didn't immediately guarantee him publication, however, and both Jonathan Cape and Faber & Faber rejected *Down and Out in Paris and London*. Not until he had revised and reduced it was it finally accepted by Gollancz in August 1932. By that time he had also written *Burmese Days*. He was working as a teacher in private schools near London, although he had to give it up because his health was poor. This time it was pneumonia: his lungs were a perennial problem. In early 1934 he was back at Southwold, writing *A Clergyman's Daughter*. He still had not found an English publisher for *Burmese Days*: like his later novels, it held the potential to offend. It was, therefore, first published in the United States, by Harpers. He moved to London, living in Hampstead and working part-time at Booklovers' Corner.

The pattern continued into 1935: flats in London, finishing a novel – *A Clergyman's Daughter* – publishing it after last minute alterations for fear of libel, writing a novel – *Keep the Aspidistra Flying* – *Burmese Days* published, with revisions, in England, regular journalism for a pittance. And so on into 1936. But by now he had moved to Wallington, Hertfordshire, and then he went north to collect material for what became *The Road to Wigan Pier*, and then he married Eileen. By now, his journalism was more regular and a little more profitable. In December 1936 he enlisted in the Workers' Party of Marxist Unification,

POUM, in the Spanish Civil War, later joining the Independent Labour Party contingent. He was wounded in the throat in May 1937 and back in England by July. He immediately started writing what he considered his best book, *Homage to Catalonia*. He was planning to go to India to research for another book, but he fell ill with tuberculosis early in 1938. In the autumn he went to Marrakech to recuperate and began *Coming Up for Air*, although from now on his writing was often interrupted by ill health. He returned to Wallington in March 1939 having completed the book. Now he concentrated on the essays which became *Inside the Whale*. It was a difficult time for him. He was doing little journalism. He was frustrated at being turned down for active military service in the war. He projected a long, three-part novel, which he never started. He was ill again. Eileen was working in London.

Then in 1940 he moved to London to join her. He began to contribute regularly to *Tribune*. He was reviewing books and films regularly for *Time and Tide*. He became editor of the new Searchlight Books series, writing the first volume himself, *The Lion and the Unicorn*. It was a special series, concentrating on war-time problems and suggesting solutions. In 1941 he began his regular contributions for the American *Partisan Review*, and later that year he joined the British Broadcasting Corporation as a Talks Assistant and later Talks Producer in the Indian Section of the Eastern Overseas Service. His salary of £640 a year was the largest regular money he had ever earned. The work cut into his writing time, although it was the larger projects, the novels, which went by the way, and he managed to keep up his regular journalism throughout his time at the BBC. He took on more journalism once he left the BBC in November 1943, becoming literary editor of *Tribune*, writing for *The Observer* and later the *Manchester Evening News*. And he started writing *Animal Farm*. Within three months *Animal Farm* was finished. Orwell wrote *The English People*, a commissioned book, just as quickly. He and Eileen adopted a baby, Richard.

But then there were new difficulties. Their flat was bombed and for more than three months they were without a home of their own. Gollancz, Cape, and Fabers all rejected *Animal Farm* on political grounds. Orwell gave up the editorship of *Tribune* and went to France as a war correspondent for *The Observer*. While he was there, Eileen died under anaesthetic in a fairly routine hysterectomy.[3] Orwell returned to his work in Europe, returning to cover the British General Election. In these circumstances, in July 1945, he began to write *Nineteen Eighty-Four*.

It was a new phase of his life. After a year and a half of setbacks, *Animal Farm* was published in August 1945. Orwell went to Jura in the Hebrides, nominally to write *Nineteen Eighty-Four*, although there were enough distractions in the roughness of the life to distract him. He returned to Jura in 1946, having decided to give up journalism for six months to concentrate on the novel. *Animal Farm* was published in the United States, including a Book-of-the-Month Club edition of more than half a million copies. For the first time in his writing life, Orwell need not worry about money. From now it, it would be fair to say, whatever he wrote, he did because he wanted to and not just to make ends meet. But now his health began to fail. Late in 1947, with only a first draft of the new novel finished, tuberculosis of the left lung was diagnosed and he was hospitalised.

As he recovered, he continued to supervise the revisions and publication of the Uniform Edition of his works for Secker & Warburg. He began a new draft of *Nineteen Eighty-Four* in May 1948, and did a little journalism. But by the end of the year he was seriously ill again and was hospitalised at a sanatorium in Gloucestershire. At times in 1949 he was too ill to write, although he corrected the proofs of the novel more or less to his satisfaction, realising that in the circumstances it was as good as he could make it. He projected a new novel set in 1945, a long short story called 'A Smoking Room Story', and a long essay on Joseph Conrad, but he wrote none of them. *Nineteen Eighty-Four* was published in June 1949. It was a Book-of-the-Month Club choice. Orwell was too ill to leave hospital. He was transferred to University College Hospital, where he married his second wife, Sonia, and died on 21 January 1950 at forty-six.

---

3 Eileen Blair is buried in St Andrew's and Jesmond Cemetery, Newcastle upon Tyne. Orwell composed the text of the simple headstone.

Chronology

1903
25 June   Eric Arthur Blair born at Motihari, Bengal

1904   Moved to Henley-on-Thames, England with mother and sister

1911
September   Entered St Cyprian's preparatory school at Eastbourne

1914
2 October   First publication, 'Awake! Young Men of England'

1916
December   Left St Cyprian's

1917
January   Entered Wellington College
May   Entered Eton College

1921
20 December Left Eton

1922
June   Took India Office examination
October   Appointed Assistant District Superintendent of Police
27 October   Sailed from Liverpool for Rangoon, Burma
29 November Arrived at Provincial Police training school, Mandalay

1924
January   Posted to Myaungmya
June   Posted to Twante
December   Posted to Syriam

1925
26 September Posted to Insein

1926
April   Posted to Moulmein
December   Posted to Katha as headquarters assistant

1927
June   Left Katha
14 July   Sailed from Rangoon
August   Disembarked at Marseilles
September   On holiday at Polperro, Cornwall
       Announced decision not to return to Burma
autumn   Moved into lodgings in Portobello Road, London
       Spent time in the East End with tramps
       On the road, sleeping in workhouses

1928
1 January   Resigned commission in Indian Imperial Police
spring   Went to France, stayed at 6 rue du Pot de Fer
6 October   Published first article as professional writer, 'La Censure en Angleterre', in *Monde*

29 December	First professional article in England, 'A Farthing Newspaper', in *G.K.'s Weekly*

1929

February	Ill with bronchitis
7 March	Admitted to Hôpital Cochin with pneumonia
22 March	Left hospital
March	L.I. Bailey, a London literary agent, agreed to look at his work
April	Met Bailey in Paris
autumn	Dishwasher in Paris
December	*The Adelphi* agreed to publish his article on tramps, 'The Spike'
	Returned to 3 Queen Street, Southwold

1930

	Reviewer for *The Adelphi*
	Tutor to boy at Walberswick, Suffolk
early in year	Writing *Down and Out in Paris and London*
	Tutor to three Peters boys 1930–1931
from April	Occasional tramps in London and the home counties
October	Completed a diary version of *Down and Out in Paris and London*. Sent to Jonathan Cape. Rejected
	Began or resumed work on *Burmese Days*

1931

January	In London, staying with Francis and Mabel Fierz at 1b Oakwood Road
April	'The Spike' published in *The Adelphi*
summer	Submitted revised typescript of *Down and Out in Paris and London* to Jonathan Cape
August	At Golders Green
25–28 August	Tramping in central London
28 August	Set out for Kent
2–19 September	At Mereworth, Kent, hop-picking
	In Bermondsey, London
	Cape again rejected *Down and Out in Paris and London*
October–November	In lodgings at 2 Windsor Street, Paddington
autumn	Began *Burmese Days*
November	Contacted Leonard Moore, a literary agent
14 December	Submitted *Down and Out in Paris and London* to T.S. Eliot at Faber & Faber
	In police custody for two days for drunkenness

1932

February	Faber & Faber rejected *Down and Out in Paris and London*
April	Teaching at The Hawthorns, private school in Hayes, Middlesex.
July	revised *Down and Out in Paris and London*
August	signed contract with Victor Gollancz for *Down and Out in Paris and London*
summer	in Southwold writing *Burmese Days*

1933

9 January	*Down and Out in Paris and London* published
30 June	American edition of *Down and Out in Paris and London* published
September	Teaching at Frays College, private school in Uxbridge, Middlesex
December	Completed final version of *Burmese Days*
	Ill with pneumonia
	Gave up teaching

1934

mid-January	Went to live in Southwold
	Began writing *A Clergyman's Daughter*
	Gollancz rejected *Burmese Days*
spring	Revised *Burmese Days* for Harpers in New York
3 October	Finished *A Clergyman's Daughter*
mid-October	Moved to 3 Warwick Mansions, Pond Street, Hampstead
	Part-time job at Booklovers' Corner, 1 South End Road, Hampstead
25 October	*Burmese Days* published in New York

1935

February	Began writing *Keep the Aspidistra Flying*
	Altered proofs of *A Clergyman's Daughter*
March	Moved to 77 Parliament Hill, Hampstead
	Met Eileen O'Shaughnessy
11 March	*A Clergyman's Daughter* published
24 June	Revised edition of *Burmese Days* published by Gollancz
August	Moved to 50 Lawford Road, Kentish Town
	Began reviewing for the *New English Weekly*

1936

January	Finished *Keep the Aspidistra Flying*
	Gollancz commissioned book on working class conditions
	Gave up job at Booklovers' Corner and flat at Lawford Road
31 January	By train to Coventry
1 February	On foot and by bus to Birmingham and Stourbridge
2 February	On foot and by bus to Wolverhampton, Penkridge and Stafford
3 February	By bus and on foot to Hanley and Burslem
4 February	On foot and by bus to Macclesfield and Manchester
5 February	In common lodging house
6–10 February	At 49 Brynton Road, Manchester
10–15 February	At 72 Warrington Lane, Wigan
16 February–	
1 March	At Darlington Road, Wigan, over tripe shop
17 February	Gollancz asked for more changes to *Keep the Aspidistra Flying*
24 February	Went down Crippen's coal mine
25–26 February	In Liverpool
2–4 March	At Wallace Road, Sheffield
5–13 March	At 21 Estcourt Avenue, Leeds
6 March	Visited Haworth
9 March	Visited Middlesmoor
13–26 March	At Agnes Terrace, Barnsley
19 March	Went down Wentworth coal mine
21 March	Went down Grimethorpe coal mine
26 March	Returned to Leeds
29 March	Returned to London
2 April	Moved into The Stores, Wallington, Hertfordshire
20 April	*Keep the Aspidistra Flying* published
early May	Began writing *The Road to Wigan Pier*
	Began reviewing for *Time and Tide*
9 June	Married Eileen O'Shaughnessy at Wallington
12 June	Submitted 'Shooting an Elephant' to John Lehmann
18 July	Outbreak of Spanish Civil War
17 August	*A Clergyman's Daughter* published in New York
15 December	Sent ms of *The Road to Wigan Pier* to Moore

| | Went to Spain |
| 30 December | Enlisted in POUM in Barcelona |

1937
January	At the front at Alcubierre
end January	Transferred to Independent Labour Party contingent on Aragon front, later at Monflorite
February–March	Eileen Blair in Spain
8 March	*The Road to Wigan Pier* published
end April	On leave in Barcelona
10 May	Returned to front
20 May	Wounded in throat
14 June	Collected discharge papers
20–22 June	In Barcelona, running from Communist police
23 June	Crossed into France
July	Back in Wallington
mid-July	Began *Homage to Catalonia*
	Gollancz said he would not publish *Homage to Catalonia*
	The *New Statesman and Nation* rejected Orwell's review of *The Spanish Cockpit*
	Resumed writing for the *New English Weekly* and *Time and Tide*
1 September	Signed contract with Fredric Warburg for *Homage to Catalonia*
6 December	Told Leonard Moore he was planning *Coming Up for Air*
end December	Desmond Young offered him job on Lucknow *Pioneer*

1938
mid-January	Finished *Homage to Catalonia*
8 March	Lung haemorrhage
March–August	In sanatorium at Aylesford, Kent
25 April	*Homage to Catalonia* published
13 June	Joined ILP
July	Projected *Coming Up for Air*
summer	Turned down offer to write *Poverty in Practice* for Nelson
	Accepted loan of £300 to go to warm climate to convalesce
1 September	Left sanatorium
2 September	Sailed for Morocco with Eileen
12 September	Arrived in Marrakech
September–March	In Morocco
late September	Began *Coming Up for Air*
December	Completed first draft of *Coming Up for Air*

1939
early January	At Taddart in the Atlas Mountains
27 January	Returned to Marrakech and was ill again
26 March	Sailed from Casablanca
30 March	Arrived in London, went to Southwold
end March	Submitted ms of *Coming Up for Air*
11 April	Returned to Wallington. Tended animals and vegetables
May	At 24 Crooms Hill, Greenwich, Eileen's brother's home
24 May	Returned to Wallington. Began *Inside the Whale*
12 June	*Coming Up for Air* published
28 June	In Southwold, present at death of his father
24–31 August	Stayed at L.H. Myers's home in Ringwood, Hampshire
3 September	Outbreak of war

September	Eileen moved to Greenwich to work
	Left ILP
mid-December	Finished *Inside the Whale*
late December	At Greenwich with Eileen

1940

early January	At Wallington
30 January– 13 March	At Greenwich. Ill with influenza
February	Began contributing to *Horizon*
March	Began contributing to *Tribune*
11 March	*Inside the Whale* published
April	Projected long novel in three parts, never written
May	Moved to 18 Dorset Chambers, Chagford Street, Regent's Park
	Joined Local Defence Volunteers, London Home Guard in St John's Wood
18 May	First theatre criticism for *Time and Tide*
August–October	Writing *The Lion and the Unicorn*

1941

3 January	Began contributing 'London Letter' to *Partisan Review*
19 February	*The Lion and the Unicorn* published
3 March	*The Betrayal of the Left* published
April	Moved to 111 Langford Court, Abbey Road, St John's Wood
18 August	Joined British Broadcasting Corporation as full-time Talks Assistant, later Talks Producer
22 November	Lecture, 'Culture and Democracy', to the Fabian Society

1942

8 March	Began contributing to *The Observer*
15 May	*Victory or Vested Interest?* published
summer	Moved to 10a Mortimer Crescent, Maida Vale
end June	Fishing holiday at Callow End, Worcestershire

1943

19 March	Mother died
November	Began writing *Animal Farm*
18 November	*Talking to India* published
23 November	Left Home Guard on medical grounds
24 November	Resigned from BBC
end November	Literary editor of *Tribune*
3 December	First 'As I Please' article in *Tribune*
9 December	Began reviewing for the *Manchester Evening News*

1944

February	Finished *Animal Farm*
May	Finished *The English People*
14 May	Future adopted son born
early June	Eileen gave up work to look after adopted baby, Richard
28 June	Maida Vale flat bombed
	Moved to Inez Holden's flat, 106 George Street, Baker Street
by July	Gollancz, Cape, and Faber rejected *Animal Farm*
early October	Moved to 27B Canonbury Square, Islington
	Signed contract with Fredric Warburg for *Animal Farm*
October	Projected *Critical Essays*

1945

22 January	Sent ms of *Critical Essays* to Moore
early February	Finished 'In Defence of P.G. Wodehouse', and added it to *Critical Essays*
February	Gave up literary editorship of *Tribune*
15 February	Went to Paris as war correspondent for *The Observer* and the *Manchester Evening News*. Stayed at Hotel Scribe
late March	Went to Cologne
29 March	Eileen died in Newcastle
	Returned to England
8 April	Returned to Paris, then to Nuremberg and Stuttgart
8 May	VE Day. In Paris
mid-May	In Austria
24 May	In London
June-July	General Election correspondent for *The Observer*
3 July	Contract for four long articles in *Polemic*
	Told Moore he was writing *Nineteen Eighty-Four*
August	Vice-chairman Freedom Defence Committee
17 August	*Animal Farm* published
10–22 September	On Jura, Hebrides
late September	Resumed writing for *Tribune*, *The Observer*, and the *Manchester Evening News*
Christmas	In North Wales, at Arthur Koestler's house, with Richard

1946

14 February	*Critical Essays* published
mid-April to mid-October	Gave up journalism
29 April	American edition of *Critical Essays, Dickens, Dali and Others* published
3 May	His sister, Marjorie, died
mid-May	At Biggar, near Edinburgh
23 May	On Jura
early July	Went to London to bring Richard to Jura
early August	Writing *Nineteen Eighty-Four*
26 August	American edition of *Animal Farm* published
August	American Book-of-the-Month Club edition of *Animal Farm* published
13 October	Returned to London
November	Gave up writing for the *Manchester Evening News* and *The Observer*
	Began writing for *Tribune* again
29 December	Returned to Jura to plant fruit trees

1947

8 January	Returned to London
early April	Ill
April	Finished regular journalism
11 April	Returned to Jura
spring	Writing 'Such, Such Were the Joys'
31 May	Finished 'Such, Such Were the Joys'
August	*The English People* published
September	Gave up The Stores, Wallington
September–October	Ill with lung inflammation
October	Corrected proofs of Uniform Edition of *Coming Up for Air*

late October	Finished first draft of *Nineteen Eighty-Four*
December	Tuberculosis diagnosed
20 December	Admitted to Hairmyers Hospital, East Kilbride

1948

late January	Reviewing again
April	Corrected proofs for new edition of *Burmese Days*
13 May	First volume of Uniform Edition, *Coming Up for Air* published
May	Began second draft of *Nineteen Eighty-Four*
28 July	Returned to Jura
August–November	Writing *Nineteen Eighty-Four*
September	Suffered relapse
November	Retyped *Nineteen Eighty-Four*
15 November	*British Pamphleteers* published
4 December	Sent *Nineteen Eighty-Four* to Moore
December	Gave up Canonbury Square flat

1949

6 January	Admitted to Cotswold Sanatorium, Cranham, Gloucestershire, seriously ill with tuberculosis
during 1949	Wrote synopsis of 'A Smoking Room Story', but only ever wrote four pages
	Projected long essay on Joseph Conrad, never written
mid-February	Began article on Evelyn Waugh, never completed
March	Corrected proofs of *Nineteen Eighty-Four*
9 April	Submitted last completed article for publication
April	Projected novel set in 1945, never written
June	*Nineteen Eighty-Four* published in London and New York
July	*Nineteen Eighty-Four* Book-of-the-Month Club choice
August	Projected book of reprinted essays
3 September	Transferred to University College Hospital, London
13 October	Married Sonia Brownell in hospital

1950

January	Plan to transfer to Swiss sanatorium
21 January	Died at University College Hospital
26 January	Buried at All Saints churchyard, Sutton Courtenay, Oxfordshire

The Sections of the Bibliography

Section A Books contains Orwell's major book publications. Each of his major works is introduced here with a narrative account of the pre-publication history of the book, and notes on the text. These accounts are drawn chiefly from Orwell's own writings about the books, mainly from his letters. They attempt to reconstruct the process of his writing the books and his efforts to have them published. His letters in particular are often the only surviving contemporary account of the genesis of the texts. The nine major works are:

Down and Out in Paris and London
Burmese Days
A Clergyman's Daughter
Keep the Aspidistra Flying
The Road to Wigan Pier
Homage to Catalonia
Coming Up for Air
Animal Farm
Nineteen Eighty-Four

I have included full descriptions and notes on editions and important reissues published within Orwell's lifetime, as well as important editions since his death. What I have not attempted to do is to describe and account for every edition and reissue of the major works. Particularly once a book is in paperback format, it becomes difficult to keep track of reissues. In the case of Orwell's most popular and most published books, *Animal Farm* and *Nineteen Eighty-Four*, not even copyright deposit libraries are keeping every copy. Nor have I attempted to trace every study edition for schools and students. In the case of *Animal Farm* and *Nineteen Eighty-Four*, there are so many of these that their numbers would obscure the important editions of real textual significance.

Each entry begins with a quasi-facsimile titlepage transcription, details of collation, contents, binding, and jacket, and then a section of notes on other details of publication. This is followed by a brief list of some important contemporary reviews. I have then noted usually two or three easily-accessible locations for every copy. Typically these are Cambridge University Library and the Orwell Archive. While I have been compiling this bibliography, book-retrieval time at the British Library has been slow and I really cannot recommend, for example, the two or three day wait for out-housed Penguins. I have also experienced difficulties in obtaining multiple copies of individual titles.

Bibliographical convention requires that this section also include minor works. My sense is that they tend to draw attention away from the significance of the cohesive body of work the nine books represent, the close connection between them, and the way in which they illustrate the growth of Orwell's professionalism and skill as a writer. When Orwell mentioned "my book" in correspondence, it was almost always one of these nine to which he was referring. And, of course, the minor works often represented far less time, work and writing than books to which Orwell contributed or which he edited. The three minor works here, *Inside the Whale*, *The Lion and the Unicorn*, and *The English People*, in some cases contain essays previously printed elsewhere, and these instances are noted. But by and large these were books which Orwell wrote as books, and they therefore differ from the essay collections in Section D.

The numbering within the section works in a conventional way, so, for example, A.10a is the first edition of *Animal Farm*. A.10b and A.10c are important reissues of the first edition. I have chosen to number some reissues separately because often the reissue is of equal or even greater significance. For example, A.10d is the first American edition and

A.10f the Book-of-the-Month reissue of the American first edition which sold more than half a million copies, ten times more than the first American edition.

Following the main editions is a miscellaneous section of some related materials. This section makes no claims to comprehensiveness, since, particularly in the cases of *Animal Farm* and *Nineteen Eighty-Four*, the peripheral materials might well have taken over the bibliography. The miscellaneous items are identified by the letter M following the book's identification number. So A.10.M1 is the animated cartoon version of *Animal Farm*.

I have grouped all the translations of a particular book in a section following miscellaneous items. The translations are arranged alphabetically by language: in the case of *Animal Farm* the section begins with Afrikaans, followed by Basque, Catalan, Danish and so on. I have numbered the translation section as follows: A.10.T1 is the Afrikaanse edition of *Animal Farm*. A.10 is the number for *Animal Farm* throughout the bibliography, the T identifies a translation, and the number 1 following it shows that it is the first language within that translation section. So Basque is 2, Catalan 3, Danish 4, and so on. Where there is more than one edition of a translation, I have appended a letter after the translation number. So, in the case of the Danish *Animal Farm*, there are 3 editions, 1947, 1963 and 1981. These are numbered A.10.T4a, A.10.T4b and A.10.T4c. In some cases there are foreign editions of books, in English, often with foreign-language introductions and notes, and I have included these with translations. I have followed the same system for miscellaneous items and translations in other sections of the bibliography, as appropriate.

Section B, Contributions to books, books edited by Orwell, and works reprinted in anthologies, contains work Orwell did in his lifetime and then a selection of items anthologised after his death. But this section by no means attempts to account for every reprinting of an article, essay or review by Orwell. Most of these anthologised essays are easily found in the standard collections of Orwell's essays, and the reprinted texts are of no particular bibliographical significance. Certain essays and extracts, notably 'Shooting an Elephant', 'Politics and the English Language', and 'The Principles of Newspeak', are repeatedly anthologised, for example in the *Little, Brown Reader*, and *The Norton Anthology*, and they are not included here. Nor are the many students' editions, particularly for students of English as a second language. On the other hand, Orwell's earliest publications, two poems, recently included in a selection of various writers' juvenilia, are listed here, since they are less accessible in earlier formats. In this section, as well as in Section C and Section D, I have included notes on the publication history of some items with references to them from Orwell's letters.

Section C is Orwell's Contributions to periodicals. It ranges from his first newspaper publication, a poem in a local newspaper when he was 11, to the last articles he wrote in 1949, and then continues with items published posthumously. Many of the latter are reprints of previously-published pieces, and also some translations of his writings, and there are also a few collections of letters.

Section D is Essay collections. These include collections on which Orwell worked in his lifetime, as well as posthumous collections, some in collected editions of Orwell's works, such as the Uniform Edition. Very significant here is the four-volume *Collected Essays, Journalism and Letters of George Orwell*, hereafter abbreviated to *CEJL*, which, until the publication of the final volumes of the *Complete Works*, remains the most comprehensive and textually reliable collection. Users should note the similarity of many collection titles, and also the changing titles of some collections: *Inside the Whale* is a title which has been given to more than one collection; and yet other collections with different titles have the same contents, notably the 1946 *Critical Essays*, published in the United States as *Dickens, Dali & Others*. Miscellaneous items here include a few letters, private printings of individual essays, and English-language editions produced in non-English-speaking countries usually for students' use. I have grouped all the translations together, rather than trying to connect them to a particular British or American edition, because, most often, they are independent of any English edition. The numbering system in Translations in this section works as follows. Translations and foreign edition are arranged within an alphabetical list by language. Each book is identified by the letter D, the section letter for Essays; T, which identifies a translation; and then a number – 1 is Danish, 2 Dutch, 3 French, and so on. Where there is more than one collection in a particular language, the items are arranged chronologically and the letters a,b,c etc are appended.

Section E is Orwell's Radio broadcasts, including his own broadcasts as well as talks which he wrote but which were broadcast by others. It covers the period before he was a full-time BBC employee from August 1941, as well as the period up to November 1943 when he was a Talks Assistant and later Talks Producer. There are also a few items listed after 1943, including productions of *Animal Farm*.

Related to this section is Section F BBC talks organised by Orwell. These are radio talks initiated, arranged, organised or produced by Orwell, although not with his input in the form of a written script or actually broadcast by him.

Section G is Orwell's Published letters. The bulk of Orwell's letters published to date are in the *Collected Essays, Journalism and Letters of George Orwell*, although the new *Complete Works* volumes will include many more. There are also letters and fragments of letters in biographies and secondary sources as noted. In this section, I have added explanatory notes about recipients on the first appearance of their names. Many occur elsewhere in the bibliography, but this is the only section in which they are identified.

Section H is Orwell's published Poems. A few of his poems were published in his lifetime, and these are cross-referenced to the Periodicals section. Subsequent biographies, collections and secondary works of criticism have sometimes reprinted poems and fragments, as indicated in the notes to individual poem entries.

Section I is Unpublished materials. These are letters from Orwell for the most part, although there are also some poems, preliminary sketches and unpublished notebooks. The Orwell Archive has a comprehensive collection of unpublished Orwell manuscripts and letters, which will be included in the *Complete Works*. In anticipation of those volumes, I have identified unpublished items with Peter Davison's enumeration.

Throughout the bibliography, manuscript and typescript materials, as well as proofs are noted after details of first publication, or in Section I Unpublished materials.

I conclude with a list of books and articles about Orwell and his writings. This is by no means a comprehensive list of secondary materials on Orwell, but rather books and articles which I have found interesting and useful while writing this bibliography. The books and articles I list generally, although not exclusively, include materials of bibliographical and biographical significance, rather than works of critical interest. They range from obituaries published in the weeks immediately after Orwell's death, to reminiscences which several of his friends published in the early 1950s, then to scholarly works and early checklists, and, more recently, to scholarly biographies. Not included here are contemporary reviews of Orwell's major works, which are listed immediately after the edition to which they refer in the main part of the bibliography.

A: Books

A.1 DOWN AND OUT IN PARIS AND LONDON

... please see that it is published pseudonymously, as I am not proud of it.[1]

Composition and publication

I lived for about a year and a half in Paris, writing novels and short stories which no one would publish. After my money came to an end I had several years of fairly severe poverty during which I was, among other things, a dishwasher ... [2]

In the spring of 1928 Orwell had gone to Paris to live cheaply while he wrote. Over the next year, although he earned 'scarcely twenty pounds',[3] he published a few articles and wrote various stories and even two novels. Through his aunt he was in touch with L.I. Bailey, a literary agent with the McClure Newspaper Syndicate in London. On 17 February 1929 Orwell wrote to Bailey about his writing. Bailey's reply indicates what at least one of the books, written or projected, was about: 'I should not be sanguine about the Tramps and Beggars book, but one never knows. Maybe at some future time you will shoot it across to me, though of course if it is political, that would be rather against it.'[4] He stayed on in Paris, writing and giving English lessons, but by the autumn he was forced to take a job as a dishwasher, and at the end of December he returned to Southwold. Through the spring and summer he tutored local boys, wrote reviews for *The Adelphi*, and collected his Paris experiences into a novel in diary form. In November 1930 he thanked Max Plowman, co-editor of *The Adelphi*, for passing on his manuscript to John Middleton Murry, founder of *The Adelphi*, adding, 'I hope he understands that there is no hurry & I don't want to be a nuisance to him.'[5] But nothing came of this or either of the versions he later submitted to Jonathan Cape. All these early versions were rejected.

In April 1931 *The Adelphi* published 'The Spike', which Orwell then revised and used as Chapters 27 and 35 of the final version of *Down and Out in Paris and London*. By November 1931 he was in touch with another literary agent, Leonard Moore of Christy and Moore, who became his permanent agents, and in April 1932 he outlined to him the history of the manuscript, 'Days in London and Paris':

About a year and a half ago I completed a book of this description, but shorter (about 35000 words), and after taking advice I sent it to Jonathan Cape. Cape's said they would like to publish it but it was too short and fragmentary (it was done in diary form), and that they might be disposed to take it if I made it longer. I then put in some things I had left out, making the ms you have, and sent it back to Cape's, who again rejected it. This was last September. Meanwhile a friend who was editor of a magazine had seen the first ms, and he said that it was worth publishing and spoke about it to T.S. Eliot, who is a reader to Faber and Faber. Eliot said the same as Cape's – i.e. that the book was interesting but much too short. I left the ms you have with Mrs Sinclair Fierz and asked her to throw it away, as I did not think it a good piece of work, but I suppose she sent it to you instead. I should of course be very pleased if you could sell it, and it is very kind of you to take the trouble of trying. No publishers have seen it except Faber's and Cape's. If by any chance you *do* get it accepted, will you please see that it is published pseudonymously, as I am not proud of it.[6]

Orwell had been in touch with T.S. Eliot at Faber & Faber in October 1931, offering his services as a translator of French novels.[7] Later that year, he submitted a version of *Down and Out in Paris and London* to them, shown in their register for 14 December 1931 as

'A Scullion's Diary'.[8] On 17 February 1932 he telephoned Eliot about the manuscript, as a postcard the same day confirms:

> Dear Mr Eliot,
> I rang up today about a ms of mine, & you were kind enough to say you would have a look at it shortly. I forgot to say, if you are writing any time before <u>Saturday</u>, could you please send it to the above address [Westminster Chambers, Westminster Bridge Road].[9]

Eliot replied,

> Dear Mr Blair,
> I am sorry to have kept your manuscript. We did find it of very great interest, but I regret to say that it does not appear to me possible as a publishing venture. It is decidedly too short, and particularly for a book of such length it seems to me too loosely constructed, as the French and English episodes fall into two parts with very little to connect them.
> I should think, however, that you should have enough material from your experience to make a very interesting book on Down-and-out life in England alone.
> With many thanks for letting me see the manuscript.[10]

By the summer of 1932, Moore had offered the manuscript to Victor Gollancz and then arranged a meeting between the publisher and Orwell, on which Orwell reported:

> I went & saw Mr Gollancz at the time named, & he gave me a full account of the alterations he wants made in the book. Names are to be changed, swearwords etc cut out, and there is one passage which is to be either changed or cut out [Charlie's story, Chapter II]. It's a pity as it is about the only good bit of writing in the book, but he says the circulation libraries would not stand for it. I am going to let him have the ms back in about a week. I did not say anything about the book having no commercial value as he seemed to think fairly well of it, so perhaps you will be able to get good terms from him.[11]

He wrote again on 6 July:

> I am sending herewith the ms which I told Mr Gollancz I would let him have back in about a week. I have made the alterations of names etc that he asked for, & I think there is now nothing that can cause offence. The passage between pp. 6 and 13 that was objected to cannot be altered very radically. I have crossed out or altered the phrases that seemed to show too definitely what was happening & perhaps like this it might pass inspection. If not, I think the only thing to do is to remove Chap II in toto, as Chap III follows fairly consecutively from Chap I.[12]
> As to a title (Mr Gollancz said the present one will not do) I suggest putting at the start the quotation
>
> "The Lady Poverty was fair
> But she hath lost her looks of late"
> (Alice Meynell)
>
> calling the book "The Lady Poverty" or "Lady Poverty". If this will not do I will think of another title.
> I think if it is all the same to everybody I would prefer the book to be published pseudonymously. I have no reputation that is lost by doing this and if the book has any kind of success I can always use the same pseoudonym again.
> Perhaps you will be kind enough to tell Mr Gollancz all this? [13]

In August 1932 Orwell agreed contract terms for its publication with Victor Gollancz, and an advance of £40.[14] He received the proofs on 14 November 1932. He wrote to Moore:

> Many thanks for your letter & the two sets of proofs which arrived yesterday. As there are *two* proofs, I do not fully understand whether I am intended to correct the one bearing the reader's objections with a view to answering those objections, & the

other for misprints etc, or whether I need only correct one. I have begun doing *both* corrections in the copy with the reader's remarks, & hope this will do. I will let you have the proof back in abt a week – I can't manage it before as I am terribly rushed at present.

I have no objection to the title, but do you think that "X" is a good pseudonym? The reason I ask is that if this book doesn't flop as I anticipate, it might be better to have a pseudonym I could also use for my next one. I leave this one to you and Mr Gollancz to decide.[15]

In a letter to Eleanor Jaques on 18 November 1932, Orwell said that he was

suffering from a devilish cold, & correcting proofs. My book is to come out in early Jan., I think. Gollancz wants to call it "The Confessions of a Down & Out". I am protesting against this as I don't answer to the name of down & out, but I will let it go if he thinks seriously that it is a taking title.[16]

The next day he returned the first proof:

I sent off the proof with the printer's queries on it yesterday. I made a few alterations and added one or two footnotes, but I think I arranged it so that there would be no need of "over-running". I will send on the other proof as soon as possible.

As to a pseudonym, a name I always use when tramping etc is P.S. Burton, but if you don't think this sounds a probable kind of name, what about

Kenneth Miles,
George Orwell,
H. Lewis Allways.

I rather favour George Orwell ...

PS. As to the *title* ... Would "The Confessions of a Dishwasher" do as well? I would rather answer to "dishwasher" than "down and out", but if you and Mr G think the present title best for selling purposes, then it is better to stick to it.[17]

The advance copies arrived on 23 December 1932. Orwell wrote to Moore, asking that a copy be sent to *The Adelphi* for review:

I think the get-up is very nice, & they have shown extraordinary cleverness in making it look quite a long book. What does "a recommendation of the Book Society" on the cover mean?[18]

The book was attacked in a letter in *The Times* from a restauranteur and hotelier, Humbert Possenti, on 31 January 1933. Orwell described it to Moore as a 'rather snooty letter', adding, 'It would have been most damaging to let it go unanswered.'[19] In his reply, published in *The Times* on 11 February 1933, he objected to the attack on the truthfulness of his book, maintaining he merely reported the circumstances at an hotel known to him. This attack was followed by one which he deemed 'beneath answering' in the *Licensed Victuallers Gazette*, 17 February 1933.[20] The letter to Eleanor Jaques says that by this time the American rights had 'been disposed of to Harpers ... & I should think they are pretty good people to deal with.'

In 1934 he wrote to Moore:

I know that Harper's owe me a few royalties – not much, I am afraid, but about £20 or £30. Do you think it would be possible to get anything out of them say next month? It doesn't matter now, but I may be getting rather hard up in a month or two.[21]

A 1936 letter to the American novelist, Henry Miller, confirms that the American sales were small:

I am glad you managed to get hold of a copy of *Down and Out*. I haven't one left and it is out of print, and I was going to send you a copy of the French translation ... Yes, it was published in America too but didn't sell a great deal. I don't know what sort of reviews it got in France – I only saw about two, either because the press-cutting people didn't get them or because I hadn't arranged to have copies sent out with flattering letters to leading critics, which I am told you should do in France.[22]

By 1938 he told Jack Common, the writer and, from 1935–1936, editor of *The Adelphi*,

... the Penguin people are making moves towards reprinting one or other of my books, and I hope they'll do so, because though I dont suppose there's much dough in it it's the best possible advert. Besides it's damned annoying to see your books out of print. One of mine, *Down and Out*, is so completely out of print that neither I nor anyone else known to me except my mother possesses a copy – this in spite of the fact that it was the most-taken-out book in the library at Dartmoor.[23]

A.1a   *First Edition, 1933*

DOWN AND OUT IN | PARIS AND LONDON | by | GEORGE ORWELL | "O scathful harm, condition of poverte!" | CHAUCER | LONDON | VICTOR GOLLANCZ LTD | 14 Henrietta Street Covent Garden | 1933

Collation [Ao]–So⁸; 144 leaves (19.5 × 12.3); [1–4] 5–288

Contents [1] halftitle: DOWN AND OUT IN | PARIS AND LONDON [2] blank [3] titlepage [4] imprint: *Printed in Great Britain by* | The Camelot Press Ltd., London and Southampton | *on paper supplied by* Spalding & Hodge Ltd. | *and bound by* The Leighton-Straker Bookbinding Co. Ltd. 5–288 text, on 288: THE END

Binding Black calico-textured cloth on boards. Off white endpapers.

Front and back covers Plain.

Spine Stamped in yellowish-green: DOWN AND OUT | IN PARIS | AND LONDON | BY | GEORGE ORWELL | GOLLANCZ

Paper
Cream esparto antique wove

27 lines per page
11 pt Baskerville

Notes
Published 9 January 1933
8s 6d
1,500 copies

Although the official publication date was 9 January 1933 copies are catalogued as received by the library of the British Museum on 22 December 1932 and by Cambridge University Library on 28 December 1932.
Part of Chapter 35 was first published as 'The Spike' in *The Adelphi* (April 1931) 24–33. Signed: Eric Blair

In connection with Chapters 36 and 37, see 'Common Lodging Houses', *New Statesman and Nation* (3 September 1932) 256–257 [See C.048].

For references to his discovery of Brenda Salkeld's copy of the first edition, annotated by Orwell, see Michael Shelden 132, and 'Jilting Mr Blair', *The Daily Telegraph* (16 September 1989).

Contemporary reviews
Times Literary Supplement (12 January 1933)
C. Day Lewis *Adelphi* (February 1933)
W.H. Davies *New Statesman and Nation* (18 March 1933)

Locations
British Library – rebound. Acquisition 22 December 1932.
Cambridge University Library. Acquisition 28 December 1932.
London Library – rebound.
Orwell Archive

REISSUES

A.1b   Reissue of First Edition, 1933

A reprint of 500 copies, issued later in January 1933.

A.1c   Reissue of First Edition, 1933

As first edition, A.1a, but imprint on [4] begins: *First published January 1933 | Second impression January 1933 | Third impression January 1933*

Notes
A reprint of 1,000 copies, issued in January 1933.
Type distributed 13 February 1934

Locations
Orwell Archive

A.1d   First American Edition, 1933

DOWN AND OUT IN | PARIS AND LONDON | BY | GEORGE ORWELL | "O scathful harm, condition of poverte!" | CHAUCER | [ornate device of flaming torch passing from hand to hand within an oval wreath, 1.8 × 1.4] | HARPER AND BROTHERS PUBLISHERS | NEW YORK AND LONDON | 1933

Collation There are 19 unmarked gatherings of 8 leaves each: [A–T]^8; 152 leaves (20.4 × 13.9); [i–vi] 1–292 [293–298]

Contents [i] halftitle: DOWN AND OUT IN | PARIS AND LONDON [ii] blank [iii] titlepage [iv] imprint: DOWN AND OUT IN | PARIS AND LONDON | [short rule] | *Copyright, 1933, by | Eric Blair | Printed in the U.S.A.* | [short rule] | FIRST EDITION | F–H | *All rights in this book are | reserved. No part of the | text may be reproduced | in any manner whatsoever | without written permission. | For information address | Harper & Brothers.* [v] halftitle: DOWN AND OUT IN | PARIS AND LONDON [vi] blank 1–292 text, on 292: THE END 293–298 blank

Binding Pale purple calico-textured cloth on boards. Elaborately printed green, pale green and black endpapers depicting six portraits of human heads against a background of London and Paris street scenes.

Front cover Stamped in purple in bottom right is a rectangle depicting a flaming torch being passed from hand to hand.

Back cover Plain.

Spine Stamped in purple are nine broad stripes, between which is stamped in purple: DOWN | AND OUT | IN PARIS | AND LONDON | GEORGE | ORWELL | HARPERS
Jacket As endpapers, with the Paris scene on the front and London on the back.
Front DOWN | *and* [cursive script] | OUT | IN PARIS | *and* [cursive script] | LONDON | *by* [cursive script] GEORGE ORWELL. | [printed in green against black strip at foot]: HARPER & BROTHERS ESTABLISHED 1817
Spine Within yellowish green top panel: DOWN | *and* [cursive script] | OUT | *in* [cursive

script] | PARIS | *and* [cursive script] | LONDON | *by* [cursive script]/ [and within green bottom panel]: GEORGE | ORWELL | [printed in green against black strip at foot]: HARPERS
Front flap [Extracts from contemporary reviews, and at foot]: No. 2414
Back flap [Biographical notice of Orwell, and at foot]: No. 2413 [sic]

Notes
Published 30 June 1933
$2.50
1,750 copies
Type distributed 13 February 1934
383 copes remaindered
Text as First British Edition, A.1a

Contemporary reviews
F.T. March *Books* (30 July 1933)
H. Gorman *The New York Times* (6 August 1933)
The Nation (6 September 1933)
James T. Farrell *The New Republic* (11 October 1933)

Locations
Orwell Archive

A.1e   First Penguin Edition, 1940

DOWN AND OUT IN | PARIS AND LONDON | BY | GEORGE ORWELL | "O scathful harm, condition of poverte!" | CHAUCER | [device of dancing penguin, 2.0 × 1.8] PENGUIN BOOKS | HARMONDSWORTH MIDDLESEX ENGLAND | 41 EAST 28TH STREET NEW YORK U.S.A.

Collation [A]–F¹⁶; 96 leaves (17.9 × 11.0); [1–4] 5–184 [185–192]

Contents [1] halftitle: DOWN AND OUT IN | PARIS AND LONDON | BY GEORGE ORWELL | [two paragraphs of extracts from reviews in the *Evening Standard* and *Bystander*] [2] [publisher's note on mailing list] | [photograph of Orwell] | caption: GEORGE ORWELL | [biographical note on Orwell] [3] titlepage [4] imprint: Published in Penguin Books 1940 | MADE AND PRINTED IN GREAT BRITAIN FOR PENGUIN BOOKS LIMITED | BY R. & R. CLARK, LIMITED, EDINBURGH 5–184 text, on 184: THE END [185–192] advertisements

Binding Paper bound.

Front cover Broad orange stripe, 5.6, above broad off white stripe, 7.1, above broad orange stripe, 5.2. Within the top stripe is a rounded white diamond, outlined in black, within which is printed: PENGUIN | BOOKS [Within the middle stripe is printed]: DOWN AND OUT IN | PARIS AND LONDON | GEORGE ORWELL [and printed laterally in orange to each side]: FICTION [Within the bottom stripe is printed]: COMPLETE [penguin device in black and off-white] UNABRIDGED

Back cover Illustrated advertisement for Pear's Jif shaving stick.

Spine The three broad stripes are wrapped around from the front cover. Printed laterally [in top stripe]: GEORGE ORWELL [in middle stripe]: DOWN AND OUT IN PARIS AND LONDON [and vertically in black and off white in the bottom stripe]: [penguin device] | 297

Notes
Penguin Book number 297.
Published 18 December 1940.
55,000 copies
Type distributed after printing

Peter Davison suggests that this edition served as the copy text for the 1949 Uniform edition, A.1f.

Although the edition announces itself as 'unabridged', several expletives are omitted.

Contemporary reviews
Daniel George *Tribune* (24 January 1941)

Locations
British Library has a rebound copy with original covers bound in at the back.
Cambridge University Library. Acquisition 30 January 1941.
Orwell Archive

A.1f   *Uniform Edition, 1949*

DOWN AND OUT IN | PARIS AND LONDON | BY | GEORGE ORWELL | "O scathful harm, condition of poverte!" | CHAUCER | LONDON | SECKER & WARBURG | 1949

Collation [1]–12^8 13^4 14^8; 108 leaves (18.2 × 12.2); [1–4] 5–213 [214–216]

Contents [1] halftitle: DOWN AND OUT IN | PARIS AND LONDON [2] [list of books by Orwell] [3] titlepage [4] imprint: Martin Secker & Warburg Ltd. | 7 John Street, Bloomsbury, London, W.C.1 | *First published (Gollancz), January 1933* | *New edition, reset, 1949* | MADE AND PRINTED IN GREAT BRITAIN BY | MORRISON AND GIBB LTD., LONDON AND EDINBURGH 5–213 text [214] at foot: W.791 [215–216] blank

Binding Pale green linen grain cloth on boards. Off white endpapers. Purplish red topped leaves.

Front and back covers Plain.

Spine Stamped in purplish red: [pyramid of six lines] | DOWN & | OUT IN | PARIS & | LONDON | [small ornate device of circled dots] | GEORGE | ORWELL | [inverted pyramid of six lines] | SECKER & | WARBURG

Notes
Published 15 September 1949
7s 6d
3,000 copies
Although the official publication date was 15 September 1949 a copy was catalogued as received by the library of the British Museum on 24 August 1949.

This was the third volume of Orwell's work to appear in this Uniform edition. Its code number is W.791.

Reissued December 1950, 3000 copies. February 1951, price increased to 8s 6d, and in February 1952 to 10s 6d.

Distributed in Canada by Secker & Warburg's agent, Saunders.

Locations
British Library
Cambridge University Library. Acquisition 31 March 1950.

A.1g   *American Reissue of Uniform Edition, 1950*

Notes
Published in New York by Harcourt, Brace on 19 January 1950.
$2.75
3,000 copies

Printed by photo-offset-litho from the English Uniform Edition. The prelims have reset type, including a new titlepage, with the quotation from Chaucer printed on the rector of an otherwise blank leaf before the first page of text. There are 7 unmarked gatherings: [A–E]¹⁶ [F]¹² [G]¹⁶; 108 leaves

Red binding stamped in gilt.
Glossy jacket. Designed by Jack Moment. Inside front flap is a brief summary and quotation from *Nation* review.

A.1h   Reissue of Uniform Edition, 1951

A reprint of 3,000 copies issued in January 1951.
The price was increased to 8s 6d in February 1951, and to 10s 6d in February 1952.

As A.1f, but with additional imprint line on [4]: *Reprinted, 1951*

Jacket Front and spine green, otherwise off white.
Front [Two off-white panels outlined in black] [Top panel]: DOWN AND OUT | IN PARIS | AND LONDON [bottom panel]: GEORGE | ORWELL [and in off-white at foot]: UNIFORM EDITION
Spine DOWN& | OUT IN | PARIS & | LONDON | [leaf motif] | GEORGE | ORWELL | SECKER & | WARBURG
Back List of Orwell's works published by Secker & Warburg.
Front flap Extracts from reviews, and at foot: *Second Impression* | 8s.6d. | W.791 NET
Back flap | [within a frame]: [publisher's advertisement]

Locations
Orwell Archive

A.1i   Second Reissue of Uniform Edition, 1953

As A.1h, but with additional imprint line on [4]: *Reprinted, 1953*

Jacket As 1951 reissue, but glossy green and glossy off white, and the following differences:
Back Advertisement for *Nineteen Eighty-Four*.
Front flap Extracts from reviews, and at foot: 10s.6d. | NET

Locations
Orwell Archive

A.1j   Permabooks edition, 1954

Down | *and* | *Out* | *In Paris and London* [cursive script] | PERMABOOKS | A DIVISION OF DOUBLEDAY & COMPANY, INC. | GARDEN CITY, NEW YORK

Collation 120 leaves in a perfect binding, unsigned (17.8 × 10.4); [1–8] 9–233 [234–240]

Contents [1] [review excerpt and extracts from the text] | [2] [list of books by Orwell] [3] blank [4] [opposite and continuation of titlepage]: A NOVEL BY | *George Orwell* [cursive script] [5] titlepage [6] imprint: PERMABOOKS EDITION 1954, | by special arrangement with | Harcourt, Brace and Company | PRINTING HISTORY | Harper edition published 1933 | Harcourt, Brace edition published January, 1950 | 1st printing . . . October, 1949 | Permabooks edition published January, 1954 | 1st printing . . . December, 1953 | Copyright, 1933, by George Orwell | PRINTED IN THE UNITED STATES [7] "O scathful harm, condition of poverte!" | CHAUCER [8] blank 9–233 text [234–240] publisher's advertisements

Binding Paper bound. Red edged leaves, except at top.

Front cover Yellow stripe at top, 2.0, within which is printed: [black square, within which is a red and black circle, within which is printed in red on black]: A | PERMA | BOOK | [and in black on red] DOUBLEDAY | P267 [to the right of the circle, printed in black against the yellow background]: The strange, savage world of forgotten | men ruthlessly exposed by one of the | greatest writers of our day [to the right of which is printed]: 35¢| IN CANADA 39¢ [Beneath the yellow strip is a coloured painting of Paris street scene depicting a man in a crumpled suit, a street walker turning to look at him, and a man with a bicycle. Overprinted in white]: *Down and Out in | Paris and London* [cursive script] | [in yellow]: GEORGE ORWELL | *author of* [cursive script] | "1984" | [in white]: COMPLETE AND UNABRIDGED

Back cover Vertical yellow strip at left, 2.9, within which is printed in black: [prices as on front cover] | [and vertically]: PERMABOOKS [in the remaining off white section of the cover]: [printed in red and black]: [review extract and plot summary] | [publisher's device as on front cover] | THE BEST IN FICTION | AND NONFICTION | Wherever Books Are Sold | PERMABOOKS | A DIVISION OF DOUBLEDAY & COMPANY, INC. | GARDEN CITY, NEW YORK

Spine [against a yellow background, printed in black]: [prices as on front cover] | [laterally]: Down and Out in Paris and London [printed in red]: George Orwell | [printed horizontally]: PERMA | P267

Notes
This edition follows the text of the Uniform Edition.

Locations
Orwell Archive – two copies

A.1k   *Berkley Edition, 1959*

GEORGE ORWELL | down and out in Paris and London | [publisher's device of striped shield and fleur de lys] | A BERKLEY MEDALLION BOOK | Published by BERKLEY PUBLISHING CORP.

Collation 80 leaves in a perfect binding, unsigned (17.8 × 10.4); [i–iv] [1–4] 5–155 [156]

Contents [1] plot summary and review extracts [2] blank [3] titlepage [4] imprint: COPYRIGHT © 1933, BY GEORGE ORWELL | *Published by arrangement with* | *Harcourt, Brace and Company* | BERKLEY MEDALLION BOOKS are published by | *The Berkley Publishing Corporation* | *101 Fifth Avenue, New York 3, New York* | Printed in the United States of America [i] "O scathful harm, condition of poverte!" | CHAUCER [ii] blank [iii] halftitle: DOWN AND OUT IN PARIS AND LONDON [iv] blank 5–155 text, on 155: THE END | (Please turn page) [156] publisher's advertisements

Binding Paper bound.

Front cover [against a red background is a painting of a street landscape, overprinted]: BERKLEY | MEDALLION [above and below publisher's device of striped shield and fleur de lys, all printed in white] | by the author of 1984 [printed in yellow | [within a yellow framed red rectangle]: BG535 | 50c [printed in black] | GEORGE ORWELL [printed in white] | down and out in | Paris and London [printed in blue] | COMPLETE AND UNABRIDGED [printed in white]

Back cover Against a red and black background: [plot summary and review extracts]

Spine [against a solid red background]: BG535 | [laterally]: DOWN AND OUT IN PARIS AND LONDON *Orwell* | BERKLEY | MEDALLION [above and below publisher's shield device]

Notes
Published in August 1959. Reprinted June 1961
This edition follows the text of the Uniform Edition.

A.1l   Reissue of 1950 American Reissue of Uniform Edition, 1961

DOWN AND OUT | IN PARIS | AND LONDON | A NOVEL BY | GEORGE ORWELL | *New York* | HARCOURT, BRACE & WORLD, INC.

Collation There are 7 unmarked gatherings: [A–E]¹⁶ [F]¹² [G]¹⁶; 108 leaves (20.1 × 13.7); [i–ii] [1–4] 5–213 [214]

Contents [i] halftitle: DOWN AND OUT IN PARIS AND LONDON [ii] [list of books by Orwell] [1] titlepage [2] imprint: COPYRIGHT, 1933, BY | GEORGE ORWELL | © 1961 BY S.M. PITT-RIVERS | *All rights reserved, including | the right to reproduce this book | or portions thereof in any form.* | PRINTED IN THE UNITED STATES OF AMERICA [3] imprint: "O scathful harm, condition of poverte!" | CHAUCER [4] blank 5–213 text [214] blank

Binding Reddish brown linen grain cloth on boards. Off white endpapers.

Front and back covers Plain.

Spine Stamped in gilt: GEORGE | ORWELL | [15 gilt rules] | DOWN | AND | OUT | IN | PARIS | AND | LONDON | Harcourt, Brace | and Company

Jacket Glossy red and greyish pink front and spine, otherwise glossy white.
Front Red stripe across top, across which is a white flash, printed with a black shadow to resemble a piece of torn paper, on which is printed: GEORGE ORWELL [In the lower, greyish pink area is an indistinct black and white photograph of a tea towel against which is printed]: *Down and Out | in Paris | and London | a novel by the author of* [cursive script] | NINETEEN EIGHTY-FOUR [in the bottom right is a line drawing in white of an irregular staircase and two rubbish bins]
Spine [laterally][in red stripe]: GEORGE | ORWELL [in greyish pink stripe]: *Down and Out in Paris and London Harcourt, Brace | and Company* [cursive script]
Back [reviews of *Nineteen Eighty-Four* and list of books by Orwell]
Front flap [plot summary and publisher's address]
Back flap [advertisements for *Coming Up for Air* and *Burmese Days*.]

Notes
A reissue of the 1950 Harcourt, Brace reissue of the Uniform Edition.

Locations
Orwell Archive

Reissue
This American reissue was itself reissued in the Harbrace Paperbound Library in 1961, and again in 1968. The text is identical to the 1950 American reissue and thus to the 1949 Uniform Edition. Its code number is HPL 54. In 1968 it sold for $1.75.

Locations
1968, Orwell Archive.

A.1m   Second Penguin Edition, 1963

DOWN AND OUT | IN PARIS AND LONDON | GEORGE ORWELL | *O scathful harm, condition of poverte!* | CHAUCER | PENGUIN BOOKS | *in association with Secker & Warburg*

Collation 81 leaves in a perfect binding, unsigned (17.9 × 10.9); [1–4] 5–188 [189–192]

Contents [1] halftitle: PENGUIN BOOKS | 297 | DOWN AND OUT IN PARIS AND LONDON | GEORGE ORWELL | [biographical note on Orwell] | [publisher's device of penguin in oval frame, 1.5 × 1.0] [2] blank [3] titlepage [4] imprint: Penguin Books Ltd, Harmondsworth, Middlesex | AUSTRALIA: Penguin Books Pty Ltd, 762 Whitehorse

Road, | Mitcham, Victoria | [short rule] | First published by Gollancz 1933 | Published in a new uniform edition by Secker & Warburg 1949 | [short rule] Published in Penguin Books 1940 | Reprinted 1963 | [short rule] | Copyright © George Orwell, 1933 | [short rule] | Made and printed in Great Britain | by C. Nicholls & Company Ltd | Set in Monotype Baskerville | [copyright clause] 5–[189] text [190] blank [191] stamped in black is the publisher's device of a penguin, 1.5 × 1.0 | *Some other Penguin books by George Orwell* | *are described overleaf* [192] publisher's advertisements

Binding Paper bound.

Front cover Broad orange stripe at top, 5.4, above black and white photograph of a wine bottle and crumpled newspaper, printed on an orange background. Within the orange stripe is printed: [penguin device in black and white] a Penguin Book 3/6 | DOWN AND OUT | IN PARIS | AND LONDON | George Orwell

Back cover Against an orange background is printed: a Penguin Book [penguin device printed in black and white] | [book summary and review excerpt] | *For copyright reasons this edition is not for sale in the U.S.A.* | Cover photography by Fletcher/Forbes/Gill | [photograph of Orwell] | Vernon Richards

Spine Against an orange background is printed [penguin device printed in black and white] | [printed laterally]: George Orwell [printed in white] Down and Out in Paris and London [printed in black] | [printed horizontally]: 297

Notes
Copy received at British Library 23 December 1963.

Reissues
This edition was reprinted in 1964; reissued as a Penguin Modern Classic in 1966; and thereafter reissued in 1968, 1969, 1970, 1971, 1972, and 1973, with many variations in cover design and illustration. The same setting of type was used for the 1974 reprint, which also incorporated material from the author's proof,[24] although not all the variants, and a note on [190] by Victor Gollancz on the bowdlerisation of the text; this reissued was reprinted in 1975, and again in 1977, 1978 (twice), 1979, 1980, 1981, 1982 (twice), 1983, and 1984.
1989 Twentieth Century Classics edition, based on the Complete Works edition.

1969 has a detail from the painting, 'Bank Holiday in the Park', by William Roberts.
1975 has photograph of a tramp's calloused hands with one mitten around a cup. Photograph by Hymphrey Sutton.

Locations
1963, British Library – rebound with original covers bound in.
Cambridge University Library. Acquisition 13 January 1964.
Orwell Archive
1974, Cambridge University Library. Acquisition 28 July 1975.
Orwell Archive – two copies
1984, Cambridge University Library
Orwell Archive

A.1n *Third Reissue of Uniform Edition, 1969*

A new printing of the 1949 Uniform Edition, A.1f. Text, titlepage, collation and contents are as for A.1f, except that the titlepage is undated; the list of books by Orwell on [2] is expanded; the imprint on [4] is: MARTIN SECKER & WARBURG LTD., | 14 Carlisle Street, Soho Square, | London, W1V 6NN | *First Published (Gollancz), January 1933* | *New edition, reset, 1949* | *Reprinted 1969* | 436 35004 1 | REPRODUCED AND PRINTED BY | REDWOOD PRESS LIMITED, TROWBRIDGE & LONDON; and the code number, W.791 is removed from [214].

Binding Green paper on boards, embossed to resemble calico textured cloth. Off white endpapers.

Front and back covers Plain.

Spine Stamped in gilt: [pyramid of six lines] | DOWN & | OUT IN | PARIS & | LONDON | [small ornate device of 3 circles and 2 dots] | GEORGE | ORWELL | [inverted pyramid of six lines] | SECKER & | WARBURG

Jacket Dull brown.
Front [Printed in silver]: GEORGE | ORWELL | [and in dark brown]: DOWN AND | OUT IN PARIS | AND LONDON
Back Plain.
Spine [laterally] [in silver]: ORWELL [and in dark brown]: DOWN AND OUT | IN PARIS AND LONDON | [horizontally in silver]: SECKER & | WARBURG
Front flap [in dark brown][extracts from reviews] | [bottom left]: Jacket design by | Format [bottom right]: 30s net | £1.50 net
Back flap [in dark brown] 224 pages | SBN: 436 35004 1

A.1o   *Undated American edition*

Down and Out in Paris and London | GEORGE ORWELL | *Author of "1984"* | *Complete and Unabridged* | AVON PUBLICATIONS, INC. | 575 Madison Avenue – New York 22, N.Y.

Collation 96 leaves in a perfect binding, unsigned (16.1 × 10.5); [i–ii] [1–4] 5–188 [189–190]

Contents [i] [quotation from text and plot and character summaries] [ii] [opposite and continuation of titlepage]: Down and Out in [1] titlepage [2] "O scathful harm, condition of poverte!" | – CHAUCER | Copyright, 1933, by George Orwell. Published by arrangement with | Harcourt, Brace and Co. Printed in the U.S.A. [3] halftitle: *Down and Out in* | *Paris and London* [4] blank 5–188 text [189–190] publisher's advertisements

Binding Paper bound.

Front cover Against a gold-coloured background: [narrow red rule] | GEORGE ORWELL'S savage portrait | of the lower depths [and in the top right corner adjacent to these two lines]: AVON | [printed in white within a red rectangle, publisher's code and price]: 35¢ | T–121 | [red rule] | [printed in white against a black background]: DOWN and OUT in | PARIS and LONDON | [red rule] | [within a white frame is a smaller version of the painting on the front cover of A.1k] | [broad red rule within which is printed in white]: AN AVON RED AND GOLD EDITION . COMPLETE AND UNABRIDGED

Back cover [black rule] | [broad red stripe within which is printed in black]: *Avon Red and Gold Library* [cursive script] | [black rule] | [against a gold-coloured background is printed a red and white box within which is printed a publisher's advertisement for this book] | [extracts from reviews] | Printed in U.S.A.

Spine [against a gold-coloured background]: [black rule] | [printed laterally in white against a red background]: GEORGE | ORWELL | [black rule] | [laterally]: DOWN AND OUT IN | PARIS AND LONDON | [black rule] [against a red background is a broken black circle within which is printed]: AVON [and beneath]: T-121

Notes
This edition follows the text of the Uniform Edition.

A.1p   *The Penguin Complete Longer Non-Fiction of George Orwell edition, 1983.*

Harmondsworth: Penguin, 1983, 488pp

The edition consists of:

Down and Out in Paris and London 7–153
The Road to Wigan Pier 155–299

Homage to Catalonia 301–467
Looking Back on the Spanish War 469–488
Paper bound
£3.95

A.1q   The Complete Works Edition, 1986
THE COMPLETE WORKS OF | GEORGE ORWELL | VOLUME ONE | Down
and Out | in Paris and | London | 'O scathful harm, condition of poverte!' |
CHAUCER | SECKER & WARBURG | [short rule] | LONDON

Collation There are nine unmarked gatherings: [A–D]^{16} [E]^8 [F–I]^{16}; 136 leaves (23.3 ×
15.4) [i–vi] vii–xxxviii [xxxix–xl] 1–[216] 217–[230] [231–232]

Contents [i] halftitle: THE COMPLETE WORKS OF | GEORGE ORWELL. ONE |
DOWN AND OUT | IN PARIS AND LONDON [ii] blank [iii] publisher's note [iv] blank
[v] titlepage [vi] imprint: [selective publishing history of editions and reissues] | [copyright
notices] | [British Library Cataloguing in Publication Data] | ISBN 0-436-35023-8 | Typeset
in Monophoto Bembo by | Northumberland Press Ltd, Gateshead, Tyne and Wear |
Printed and bound in Great Britain by | Richard Clay (The Chaucer Press), Bungay, Suffolk
vii–xxxix general introduction to the first nine volumes [xl] blank 1–[216] text, on 216:
THE END 217–[230] textual note [231–232] blank

Binding Blue paper on boards, embossed to resemble calico textured cloth. Black endpapers.

Front and back covers Plain.

Spine Stamped in gilt: [double rule] | GEORGE | ORWELL | [rule] | Down and | Out in |
Paris | and | London | [double rule] | SECKER & | WARBURG

Jacket Smooth dull black. Flaps white.
Front [in white]: GEORGE | ORWELL | [in blue and white]: DOWN | AND OUT | IN
PARIS AND | LONDON
Back [in white, note on *The Complete Works of George Orwell* and extracts from reviews.
ISBN code and bar strip within a white rectangle.]
Spine [laterally] [in white]: GEORGE ORWELL | [in blue and white]: DOWN AND OUT
IN PARIS AND LONDON [horizontally in white]: Secker & Warburg
Front flap [biographical note, plot summary, and note on this edition. At foot]: Jacket
design by David Quay | £12.95 | net
Back flap [biographical notes on Orwell and Peter Davison]

Notes
This edition, edited by Peter Davison, incorporates all Orwell's textual changes and
restores previously omitted words. In his textual note, Davison says that for this edition,
the first edition, the first American edition, the first French translation, the Uniform
edition, the 1940 Penguin edition and the page proofs have all been collated.^{25}
Reprinted 1996

Locations
Cambridge University Library
Orwell Archive, with jacket

MISCELLANEOUS

A.1.M1   Down and Out in Paris and London
Stage adaptation, 1992
Adapted by Nigel Gearing.
Produced at the Riverside Studios, London.
Reviewed in the *TLS* 27 March 1992, 18.

A.1.M2   *Pages from a Scullion's Diary.*

Harmondsworth: Penguin, 1995.
Extracts from *Down and Out in Paris and London* published in the *Penguin 60s* series, on the occasion of Penguin's 60th anniversary.
32 leaves. paperbound. 60p

TRANSLATIONS

All Orwell Archive unless otherwise noted

CZECH

A.1.T1   *Trosecnikem v Parizi a Londyne*, 1935

Praze: Sit
Translated by Karla Krause
Cloth on boards

DANISH

A.1.T2a   *Elendighedens London og Paris*, 1954

Kobenhavn: Det Schonbergske Forlag
Translated by Michael Tejn
Paper bound

A.1.T2b   *Elendighedens London og Paris*, 1960

Kobenhavn: Hans Reitzel
Translated by Michael Tejn
kr. 6.95
Paper bound
A new edition of A.1.T2a

A.1.T2c   *Paris og London pa vrangen*, 1975

Pa dansk ved Birte Svensson
Kobenhavn: Gyldendal
Translated by Birte Svensson
Paper bound

A.1.T2d

As A.1.T2a, but cloth on boards. A book club edition, published in 1976 by Gyldendals Bogklub in Copenhagen

DUTCH

A.1.T3   *Aan de grond in Londen en Parijs*, 1970

Amsterdam: Meulenhoff
Translated by Joop Waasdorp
Paper bound
Reissued in 1983

FINNISH

A.1.T4   *Puilla Paljailla Pariisissa ja Lontoossa*, 1985

Helsinki: Werner Söderström Osakeyhtiö
Translated by Jukka Kemppinen
Paper, embossed to resemble calico grain cloth, on boards

FRENCH

A.1.T5a   *La Vache Enragée*, 1935

Paris: Gallimard, Editions de la Nouvelle Révue Française
Translated by R.N. Raimbault and Gwen Gilbert
Published 2 May 1935
15 francs
5,500 copies
Paper bound
With an Introduction by Orwell, translated into French, dated London, 15 October 1934, in which he confirms the authenticity of the story.

Peter Davison describes this translation as being 'of considerable importance in the establishment of the text' in part because of the footnotes, some of which he attributes to Orwell (see the *Complete Works* edition, 217–218). In 'Notes on Translations' Orwell describes this as a good translation, as opposed to *Burmese Days* which he considered very badly translated. Even more than the proofs, this French edition indicates what Orwell had been obliged to omit from the English first edition. A note on page 238 says:

Ce mot e les mots en italique qui suivent sont figurés par des tirets dans l'édition anglaise; nous les rétablissons ici en toutes lettres d'après les indications de l'auteur.

The *Complete Works* edition incorporates Orwell's notes into the text, in English, and the translators' notes, in French, in its textual notes [See A.1q] .

Ian Willison's copy is now in the Orwell Archive. He notes that this copy has "dixième édition" on the titlepage and cover, although the publishers say there was only one "tirage".

A.1.T5b   *Dans la dèche à Paris et à Londres*, 1982

Translated by Michel Pétris
Paris: Editions Champ Libre
A new translation by Michel Pétris, published in Paris in 1982
Paper bound

This edition is more closely related to the first English edition than to the 1935 translation and it omits almost all the notes, however it does have a few additions from the proofs, not included in the earlier editions

GERMAN

A.1.T6   *Erledigt in Paris und London*, 1978

Aus dem Englischen von Helga und Alexander Schmitz
Zurich: Diogenes
Translated by Helga and Alexander Schmitz
Paper bound
Reissued in 1983

ITALIAN

A.1.T7a   *Senza un Soldo a Parigi e a Londra*, 1966

Verona: Arnoldo Mondadori
Translated by Isabella Leonetti
Medusa volume 71
Printed in Italy 9196 QDM
November 1966
Cloth on boards

A.1.T7b   *Senza un Soldo a Parigi e a Londra*, 1981

Milan: Mondadori
Translated by Isabella Leonetti
October 1981
Lire 4,000
Paper bound
A reissue of Isabella Leonetti's translation, with an added introduction and bibliography.

NORWEGIAN

A.1.T8   *Pa bunnen og blakk Uteligger i Paris og London*, 1970

Oslo: H. Aschehoug
Translated by Torstein Bugge Hoverstad
Paper on boards, with cloth around spine

SERBIAN

A.1.T9   *Nitko i nista u Parizu i Londonu*, 1984

Zagreb: August Cesarec
Translated by Maja Novoselic
Published by arrangement with Harcourt, Brace & Company, Berkeley edition, August 1959
Paper, embossed to resemble calico textured cloth, on boards

SPANISH

A.1.T10   *Sin blanca en Paris y Londres*, 1973

Barcelona: Ediciones Destino
Translated by José Miguel Velloso
Paper on boards
Reissued: Ediciones Destino, March 1983

SWEDISH

A.1.T11   *Nere for rakning i Paris och London*, 1973

Stockholm: Rabén & Sjogren
Translated by Olof Hoffsten
A Trend Pocket Book
Paper bound
Reissued as a Moon Pocket Book 1983
Paper bound

A.2 BURMESE DAYS

I wanted to write enormous naturalistic novels with unhappy endings, full of detailed descriptions and arresting similes, and also full of purple passages in which words were used partly for the sake of their sound. And in fact my first completed novel, *Burmese Days*, which I wrote when I was thirty but projected much earlier, is rather that kind of book.[1]

[Burmese Days] had to be pedalled from publisher to publisher [since it] attacked another vested interest, British Imperialism.[2]

Composition and publication

Orwell had made a start on *Burmese Days* by the autumn of 1931. In April 1932 when he was working as a schoolteacher, he told his agent, Leonard Moore,

> ... there is a novel I began some months ago and shall go on with next holidays, and I dare say it will be finished within a year: I will send it to you then.[3]

He was still working on an early draft of *Burmese Days* in September 1932. He was not pleased with it. He told Brenda Salkeld that he was 'reading through the rough draft of my novel, which depresses me horribly.'[4] By October, he had a clearer idea of what needed to be done with it,

> My novel is making just a little progress. I see now more or less what will have to be done to it when the rough draft is finished, but the longness & complicatedness are terrible.[5]

In November 1932 he told Moore,

> The novel is not getting on badly in the sense that I am fairly pleased with what is now done, but it moves slowly as I have practically no time to work. I did a good deal to it during the holidays & some at the beginning of the term, but at present, besides teaching, I am kept busy producing a school play, which means making costumes etc besides rehearsing. I *hope* to get the book done by the summer, but can't promise.[6]

And, indeed, four or five days later, he was reconsidering, as he told Moore,

> I would rather not promise to have [*Burmese Days*] ready by the summer. I could certainly do it by then if I were not teaching, but in this life I can't *settle* to any work, & at present particularly I am rushed off my feet.[7]

He told Moore he hoped that over the school Christmas break he would be able 'to polish up a fair chunk of the novel to the point where you can form an opinion on it.'[8] In January 1933, he sent Moore the opening chapters, and by 1 February he was telephoning him at his office on a Saturday, 'on the off chance of finding you there'. He continued,

> I wanted to know what you thought of the first 100pp of my novel, that is if you had had time to look at it. I know that as it stands it is fearful from a literary point of view, but I wanted to know whether given a proper polishing up, excision of prolixities & general tightening up, it was at all the sort of thing people want to read about. I should think that [the] fact that it is about Burma and there are so few novels with that setting, might offset the lack of action in the story – it is mostly description, I am afraid; there are to be a murder and a suicide later, but they play rather a subsidiary part.[9]

By the end of the month he was promising the second hundred pages by the end of the school spring term,[10] and presumably he stuck to that schedule since in June 1933 he told Brenda Salkeld,

I sent you about two thirds of the rough draft of my novel yesterday. I would have sent it earlier, but it has been with my agent all this time. He is quite enthusiastic about it, which is more than I am; but you are not to think that when finished it will be quite as broken-backed as at present, for with me almost any piece of writing has to be done over and over again. I wish I were one of those people who can sit down and fling off a novel in about four days.[11]

In July 1933 he told Eleanor Jaques, 'I have finished my novel but there are wads of it that I simply hate, & am going to change. They say it will be soon enough if it is done some time at the end of the year.'[12] The process dragged on into November 1933. Orwell told Moore,

I finished my novel some time back and have been typing it out in what spare time I can get in this place, and I think I can get it all typed by Saturday.

I am very dissatisfied with the novel, but it is all about up to the standard of what you saw, and of course I have made all the necessary corrections and tightened it up as well as I could. It will be about 375pp. – allowing for the fact that I have used wide margins, about 85,000 words. That seems awfully long to me. If the publisher said he would take it subject to cutting I would know where to cut it, but I'd rather not have to, as I am sick of the sight of it. Let's hope the next one will be better.[13]

Later in the month Orwell described Moore's attitude as 'hopeful'.[14] Moore had taken it to Victor Gollancz, but he rejected it at a first reading for fear of libel, as did at least two other publishers, Heinemann and Cape. Orwell commented to Moore, 'It is disappointing about Heinemann's – however, if we can find *somebody* to publish the book, no matter.'[15] It turned out to be easier to arrange American publication and by the end of January 1934 Moore and Orwell were meeting with Eugene Saxton of Harper Brothers, New York. He at first asked for cuts and alterations, although he eventually agreed to publish it with only minor modifications. Orwell wrote to Moore, thanking him for his 'exertions' over the novel,

As soon as I get the ms from you I will go over it very carefully and make the necessary alterations, which should not, I think, take more than three or four days at most. But with regard to Mr Saxton's remarks about the last two or three pp. of the novel, I am sorry to say I don't agree with him at all. I will cut these out if it is absolutely insisted upon, but not otherwise. I hate a novel in which the principal characters are not disposed of at the end. I will, however, cut out the offending words 'it now remains to tell' etc.[16]

Harpers were clearly seriously concerned, as Orwell's letter to Moore in April 1934 makes clear: 'I suppose you haven't heard from Harper's whether their solicitors thought the novel was all right?'[17]

It was published in New York on 25 October 1934. Orwell saw the *Herald Tribune* review, 'Rather a bad one, I am sorry to say – however, big headlines, which is I suppose what counts.'[18] He had already told Brenda Salkeld,

My novel about Burma made me spew when I saw it in print, & I would have rewritten large chunks of it, only that costs money and means delay as well.[19]

In January 1935, with *A Clergyman's Daughter* about to be published by Gollancz, Orwell asked Leonard Moore:

I wonder if you can persuade him, if he puts "Books by the same author", or words to that effect, on the front page, to mention *Burmese Days*. He probably won't want to, as it was published in anomalous circumstances and not by him, but I want that book, if possible, not to be altogether lost sight of.[20]

British publication was delayed while Gollancz ensured that he would not face legal action for libel or defamation. On 16 February Orwell told Brenda Salkeld,

Gollancz, who has re-read *Burmese Days*, wrote enthusiastically about it & said he was going to have it thoroughly vetted by his lawyer, after which the latter was to cross-examine me on all the doubtful points. I hope the lawyer doesn't report against it as he did last time. You notice that all this happened a year ago, & I do not know what has made G change his mind again. Perhaps some other publisher has wiped his eye by publishing a novel about India, but I didn't seem to remember any this year … I hope G <u>does</u> publish *Burmese Days*, as apart from the money (& my agent has tied him down with a pretty good contract) it will tide over the very long interval there is going to be between *A Clergyman's Daughter* & the one I am writing now [*Keep the Aspidistra Flying*].[21]

Orwell and Gollancz met to discuss possible publication on 22 February 1935. The same day, Orwell wrote to Moore,

I saw Gollancz and his solicitor this afternoon and had a long talk, and you will be glad to hear that they are quite ready to publish BURMESE DAYS, subject to a few trifling alterations which will not take more than a week.[22]

On 28 February Orwell returned Gollancz's copy of the novel with his list of the alterations he had made, based on Gollancz's suggestions. Orwell no longer had a typescript from which to work at this stage, but Moore had kept one and he took it to Gollancz. Orwell was pleased to note that Moore had made 'very good terms' for it with Gollancz.[23] The alterations included changes to proper and place names and descriptions of topography. In addition, before publication, Orwell wrote the Author's Note, emphasising the fictitious nature of the work and adding, 'I have thought it better to sacrifice a little probability than to risk seeming to caricature individuals'. Nonetheless, it was this British edition which Orwell later described as 'garbled' and unsuitable as a copy text for a possible new edition.

It was published by Gollancz on 24 June 1935. In 1936 Orwell told Henry Miller that the novel had been published in America before it was published in Britain

because my publisher was afraid the India Office might take steps to have it suppressed. A year later my English publisher brought out a version of it with various names etc altered, so the American edition of it is the proper one. That is the only one of my books that I am pleased with – not that it is any good qua novel, but the descriptions of scenery aren't bad, only of course that is what the average reader skips.[24]

The 1944 Penguin edition is based on the first American edition, A.2a, however Orwell read the proofs of this new edition and made changes to the text to remove racial descriptions. He had finished correcting these proofs by 21 November 1943. In an article in *Tribune* in December 1943, Orwell discusses racial discrimination and refers to his proof-reading of the new Penguin edition, 'I have just recently been going through the proofs of a reprinted book of mine, cutting out the word "Chinaman" wherever it occurred and substituting "Chinese".'[25]

For the January 1949 Secker & Warburg Uniform Edition, Orwell made changes to the text at the publisher's suggestion, but also some of his own. These are noted in the Textual Note to the *Complete Works* edition. The Secker & Warburg Uniform Edition is the first to correct an error which Orwell *said* had existed in all editions to date – 'sat' for 'knelt' [Chapter XXIV], although in fact he *had* corrected it in the Gollancz edition, p.300. Otherwise it uses the 1944 Penguin edition as its source. An unmarked proof of this edition is in the Orwell Archive. The *Complete Works* edition uses the American first edition as its copy text with changes 'adduced to be those Orwell wished to introduce into later editions' [313].

Writing about the novel as he corrected the Uniform Edition proofs, Orwell said,

I wrote [it] more than 15 years ago & probably hadn't looked at [it] for more than 10 years. It was a queer experience – almost like reading a book by somebody else. I'm also going to try and get Harcourt Brace to reprint [*Burmese Days* and *Coming*

Up for Air] in the USA, but even if they do so they'll probably only take "sheets", which never does one much good. It's funny what BFs American publishers are abt reprints. Harcourt Brace have been nagging me for 2 years for a manuscript, any kind of manuscript, & are now havering with the idea of doing a series of reprints, but when I urged them to reprint *Burmese Days* immediately after they had cleaned up on *Animal Farm*, they wouldn't do so. Nor would the original publishers of *BD*, though they too were trying to get something out of me. Apparently reprints in the USA are done mostly by special firms which only take them on if they are safe for an enormous sale.[26]

There are 19 pages of manuscript at the Orwell Archive. They are not early drafts of the novel, either singly or collectively, but rather preliminary sketches for the novel. The manuscript consists of five parts:
'My Epitaph' 1p
'I said at the end of the last chapter' 2pp
'Autobiography' 4pp
'Incident in Rangoon – "Here for a while"' 10pp
'A rebuke to the author' 2pp

A.2a   First Edition, 1934

BURMESE | DAYS [printed in green] | A NOVEL BY | GEORGE ORWELL | AUTHOR OF | "DOWN AND OUT IN | PARIS AND LONDON" | *"This desert inaccessible* | *"Under the shade of melancholy boughs."* | –AS YOU LIKE IT. | [printed in green is a publisher's device of a flaming torch being passed from hand to hand, within a laurel wreath, 1.4 × 1.1] | PUBLISHERS | HARPER & BROTHERS | NEW 1934 YORK [date printed in green]

Collation There are 23 unmarked gatherings of 8 leaves each and a final unmarked gathering of 6 leaves: [A–Z]⁸ [2A]⁶; 190 leaves (20.6 × 13.8); [i–vi] 1–371 [372–374]

Contents [i] halftitle: [two short rules] | BURMESE DAYS | [short rule] [ii] blank [iii] titlepage [iv] imprint: BURMESE DAYS | *Copyright, 1934, by Eric Blair* | *Printed in the United States of America* | *All rights in this book are reserved. It may not be* | *used for dramatic, motion- or talking-picture pur-* | *poses without written authorization from the holder* | *of these rights. Nor may the text or part thereof be* | *reproduced in any manner whatsoever without per-* | *mission in writing. For information address: Harper* | *&* *Brothers, 49 East 33rd Street, New York, N.Y.* | FIRST EDITION | I–I [v] halftitle: BURMESE DAYS [vi] *All* | *characters* | *in this book* | *are fictitious* | [flower and leaf motif, 0.4 × 0.4] 1–371 text, on 1: [row of 22 flower and leaf motifs as on [vi] | BURMESE DAYS | [two rules] [and on 371]: THE END [372–374] blank

Binding Orange calico grain cloth on boards. Dull yellow and off white floral swirl endpapers.

Front cover Burmese | Days | GEORGE | ORWELL

Back cover Plain.

Spine Burmese | Days | GEORGE | ORWELL | HARPERS

Paper
White wove

Notes
Published 25 October 1934
$2.50
2,000 copies

In his literary notebook, Orwell described this as 'the true first edition', as opposed to the first British edition which he considered 'a garbled version and should NOT be followed' for any new edition. Nonetheless, there are misprints in the American first edition, such as 'hismelf' for 'himself' on 127.

Contemporary reviews
M.C. Hubbard *Books* (28 October 1934)
The Boston Transcript (1 December 1934)

Locations
Orwell Archive
Cambridge University Library

A.2b   Reissue of First Edition, 1934

As A.2a, but on [iv]: SECOND EDITION | K–I
Presumably issued on or before 11 December 1934 (see Locations)
Type distributed 16 February 1935
976 copies remaindered

Locations
British Library has a copy autographed by Orwell. Autograph on verso of front free end-paper: Presented to the | British Museum | by | George Orwell 11 12|34 | rule | [two dots] Received by British Museum Library 12 January 1935.

A.2c   First British Edition, 1935

BURMESE DAYS | *A NOVEL* | by | GEORGE ORWELL | "This desert inaccessible | Under the shade of melancholy boughs" | –*As You Like It* | LONDON | VICTOR GOLLANCZ LTD | 1935

Collation [AD]–UD⁸; 160 leaves (18.2 × 12.2); [1–5] 6–318 [319–320]

Contents [1] halftitle: BURMESE DAYS [2] Publisher's advertisement for *A Clergyman's Daughter* [3] titlepage [4] author's note, and at foot imprint: *Printed in Great Britain by* | The Camelot Press Ltd., London and Southampton [5]–318 text, on 318: THE END [319–320] blank

Binding Black calico textured cloth on boards. Off white endpapers.

Front and back covers Plain.

Spine Stamped in yellowish green: BURMESE | DAYS | BY | GEORGE | ORWELL | GOLLANCZ

Jacket Yellow with black printing unless otherwise noted.
Front [in pink, geometric design] by George Orwell | BURMESE | DAYS | by the author of | A CLERGYMAN'S DAUGHTER | [broad rule] | [narrow rule] | A CLERGYMAN'S DAUGHTER: | [extracts from reviews of *A Clergyman's Daughter* | [pointing hand symbol]
Back Publisher's advertisements.
Spine BURMESE | DAYS | by | GEORGE | ORWELL | 7|6 [not a line break] | NET | [publisher's geometric motif] | GOLLANCZ
Front and back flaps Extracts from reviews of *A Clergyman's Daughter*

Locations
British Library
Cambridge University Library, with jacket. Acquisition 18 June 1935.
London Library – rebound.
Orwell Archive – two copies.

Contemporary reviews
Sean O'Faolain *The Spectator* (28 June 1935)
Times Literary Supplement (18 July 1935)
G.W. Stonier *The Fortnightly Review* (August 1935)
M. Sayers *The Adelphi* (August 1935)

Notes
Published 24 June 1935.
7s 6d
2,500 copies
50 bound copies were sent to the Ryerson Press for distribution in Canada.
There was a second printing of 500 copies.
Type distributed 5 May 1936

A.2d   *Penguin Edition, 1944*

BURMESE DAYS | A NOVEL BY | GEORGE ORWELL | *"This desert inacces-sible* | *"Under the shade of melancholy boughs."* | –AS YOU LIKE IT. | [dancing penguin motif 2.1 × 1.7] | PENGUIN BOOKS | HARMONDSWORTH MIDDLESEX ENGLAND | 245 FIFTH AVENUE NEW YORK U.S.A.

Collation [B.D.–1]^{16} B.D.–2^8 B.D.–3–B.D.–8^{16}; 120 leaves (17.3 × 10.8); [1–4] 5–239 [240]

Contents [1] halftitle: BURMESE DAYS | BY GEORGE ORWELL | (456) | [publisher's note about war-time production difficulties] [2] photograph of Orwell | THE AUTHOR | [biographical note] [3] titlepage | [4] imprint: First Published in 1934 | Second Edition 1934 | Published in Penguin Books 1944 | BURMESE DAYS | *Copyright* 1934, *by Eric Blair* | *Printed in the United States of America* | [copyright notice] | imprint: MADE AND PRINTED IN GREAT BRITAIN BY | HAZELL, WATSON & VINEY, LTD., LONDON AND AYLESBURY 5–[240] text

Binding Paper bound in orange and white.

Front cover Broad orange stripe, 5.6, above broad off white stripe, 7.1, above broad orange stripe, 5.2. Within the top stripe is a rounded white diamond, outlined in black, within which is printed: PENGUIN | BOOKS [Within the middle stripe is printed]: BURMESE | DAYS | GEORGE | ORWELL [and printed laterally in orange to each side]: FICTION [Within the bottom stripe is printed]: COMPLETE [dancing penguin device in black and off-white] UNABRIDGED

Back cover Illustrated advertisement for Greys Cigarettes.

Spine The three broad stripes are wrapped around from the front cover. Printed laterally [in top stripe]: GEORGE ORWELL [in middle stripe]: BURMESE DAYS [and vertically in black and off white in the bottom stripe]: [penguin device] | 456

Locations
British Library has a rebound copy with the original covers bound in.
Cambridge University Library. Acquisition 14 June 1944.
Orwell Archive has two copies including a review copy with a publisher's slip indicating that publication was due on 11 May 1944.

Notes
Published 11 May 1944. British Museum Library copy received 10 May 1944.
60,000 copies
Penguin Book number 456.

A.2e   Uniform Edition, 1949

BURMESE DAYS | *A Novel* | BY | GEORGE ORWELL | *"This desert inaccessible* | *"Under the shade of melancholy boughs."* | –AS YOU LIKE IT. | LONDON | SECKER & WARBURG | 1949

Collation [1]–18⁸; 144 leaves (18.2 × 12.2); [1–4] 5–287 [288]

Contents [1] halftitle: BURMESE DAYS [2] list of books by Orwell [3] titlepage [4] imprint: Martin Secker & Warburg Ltd. | 7 John Street, Bloomsbury, London, W.C.1 | *First published by Harper Bros. (New York) 1934* | *First published in this edition 1949* | MADE AND PRINTED IN GREAT BRITAIN BY | MORRISON AND GIBB LTD., LONDON AND EDINBURGH 5–287 text [288] at foot: W411

Binding Green calico grain cloth on boards. Off white endpapers. Purple topped leaves.

Front and back covers Plain.

Spine Stamped in purplish red: [pyramid of six lines] | BURMESE | DAYS | [small ornate leaf device] | GEORGE | ORWELL | [inverted pyramid of six lines] | SECKER & | WARBURG

Contemporary reviews
Malcolm Muggeridge *The World Review* (June 1950)

Locations
British Library
Cambridge University Library. Acquisition 4 February 1949.
1955 Orwell Archive

Notes
Published January 1949. British Museum Library copy received 7 January 1949
9s 6d
3,000 copies, 200 bound immediately
Second printing February 1951
3,000 copies
Price changed to 8s 6d in March 1951 and to 10s 6d in February 1952
Copies distributed in Canada by Secker & Warburg's Canadian agent, Saunders.

Uncorrected proof in Orwell Archive.
Reprinted December 1950 [imprint reads 1951], July 1955, March 1961, February 1966

A.2f   Second American Edition, 1950

BURMESE DAYS | A NOVEL BY | GEORGE ORWELL | *"This desert inacces-sible* | *"Under the shade of melancholy boughs."* | AS YOU LIKE IT | *New York* | HARCOURT, BRACE AND COMPANY

Collation 9 unmarked gatherings of 16 leaves each arranged: [1–9]¹⁶; 144 leaves (19.7 × 13.3); [1–4] [5]–287 [288]

Contents [1] halftitle: BURMESE DAYS [2] list of books by Orwell [3] titlepage [4] imprint: COPYRIGHT, 1934, BY | GEORGE ORWELL | FIRST PUBLISHED, 1934 | NEW EDITION, 1950 | *All rights reserved, including* | *the right to reproduce this book* | *or portions thereof in any form.* | PRINTED IN THE UNITED STATES OF AMERICA [5]–287 text [288] blank

Binding Green calico grain cloth on boards. Off white endpapers.

Front and back covers Plain.

Spine Stamped in gilt: GEORGE | ORWELL | [15 rules] | BURMESE | DAYS | Harcourt, Brace | and Company

Jacket
University College, London copy:
Front Green stripe across top, across which is a white flash, printed with a black shadow to resemble a piece of torn paper, on which is printed: GEORGE ORWELL
The rest of the front is printed in shades of green to resemble a straw blind against which is stamped in black: *BURMESE | DAYS | a novel by the author of NINETEEN EIGHTY-FOUR* [script to resemble handwriting] In bottom right is stamped in white a drawing of a table with three legs on which are two glasses, a sun helmet and two small boxes.
Back Publisher's advertisements and reviews of books by Orwell.
Spine Green areas as front cover. Laterally, stamped in white: GEORGE | ORWELL [stamped in black]: *BURMESE DAYS | Harcourt, Brace | and Company* [script to resemble handwriting]
Front and back flaps Publisher's advertisements for works by Orwell.

Locations
Orwell Archive

Notes
The text is based on the 1949 Uniform Edition.
Printed by photo-litho offset from the Uniform Edition.
Published 19 January 1950
$3.00
3,000 copies
Reprinted 5 April 1951
2,000 copies

A.2g   *Paper bound reissue of Second American Edition, 1962*

BURMESE DAYS | A NOVEL BY | GEORGE ORWELL | *"This desert inacces-sible | "Under the shade of melancholy boughs."* | AS YOU LIKE IT | *Harbrace Paperbound Library* | [publisher's monogram device in rectangle, 0.9 × 0.6] | HARCOURT BRACE JOVANOVICH, INC. | NEW YORK

Collation 144 leaves in a perfect binding, 18.2 × 10.3; [1–4] [5]–287 [288]

Contents As hard bound American Second Edition, A.2f, with expanded list of books by Orwell on [2], new imprint page [4], and list of Orwell's books available as paper bound editions from Harcourt Brace Jovanovich on [288].

Binding Paper bound.

Front cover Overall pattern of red mosquito netting against an orange background, against which is depicted in green mosquito netting against a lighter green background the silhouette of a man's head wearing a tropical helmet. Stamped in black: HARBRACE PAPERBOUND LIBRARY . HPL 62 . $2.25 | [stamped in white]: *George | Orwell | Burmese | Days* [elaborate script] | A NOVEL BY THE AUTHOR OF | NINETEEN EIGHTY-FOUR

Back cover White. In top left is a man's head in sun helmet in green. Stamped in black: Fiction | [stamped in red] *Burmese | Days* | [stamped in black] *George | Orwell* [elaborate script] | [plot summary and extracts from reviews] | HARBRACE PAPERBOUND LIBRARY | HARCOURT BRACE JOVANOVICH, INC. | [stamped in grey]: *Cover design by Karen Braren* | [stamped in black]: 0–15–614850–1

Spine Red mosquito netting pattern as on front cover. Stamped in white, laterally: *Burmese Days . George Orwell* [elaborate script] | [stamped in pink horizontally against a black background]: [publisher's monogram] | [stamped in black]: HPL | 62

Locations
Orwell Archive

Notes
The text is that of the 1934 Harper's First Edition.

A.2h   *Third American Edition, 1962*

BURMESE DAYS | George | Orwell | With a New Introduction | by Malcolm Muggeridge | [publisher's monogram device in a rounded rectangle, 0.7 × 0.9] TIME Reading Program Special Edition | TIME INCORPORATED . NEW YORK

Collation 144 leaves in a perfect binding, 20.1 × 13.1; [X1–X2] [i–v] vi–ix [x–xi] xii–xv [xvi–xviii] [1]–263 [264–268]

Contents [X1–X2] blank [i] halftitle: BURMESE DAYS [ii] blank [iii] titlepage [iv] imprint [v]–ix Editors' Preface [x] photograph of Orwell [xi]–xv Introduction [xvi] blank [xvii] epigram: This desert inaccessible | Under the shade of melancholy boughs | AS YOU LIKE IT [xviii] blank [1]–263 text [264] publisher's note [265–268] blank

Binding Paper bound with thick brown-backed paper. Across the front and back covers and spine is depicted in greens and browns a jungle scene with dense trees, cut trunks, elephants, men and undergrowth and a single white figure.

Front cover Stamped in red: BURMESE DAYS George Orwell

Back cover In bottom left is a publisher's monogram device in rounded rectangle.

Spine Stamped in white laterally: BURMESE DAYS George Orwell

Locations
Orwell Archive

Notes
The text is based on the 1934 First Edition.

A.2i   *American Signet Classic Edition, 1963*

BURMESE DAYS | A Novel by George Orwell | *"This desert inaccessible | Under the shade of melancholy boughs."* | AS YOU LIKE IT | With an Afterword by | Richard Rees | [publisher's monogram device] | A SIGNET CLASSIC | PUBLISHED BY THE NEW AMERICAN LIBRARY

Collation 128 leaves in a perfect binding, 17.7 × 10.7; [1–6] 7–254 [255–256]

Contents [1] drawing of Orwell and biographical summary [2] blank [3] titlepage [4] publisher's note and imprint [5] halftitle: BURMESE DAYS [6] blank [7]–244 text 245–154 afterword by Richard Rees [255] selected bibliography [256] publisher's advertisements

Binding Paper bound.

Front cover Within a green border and a three-quarter white frame is a painting of a jungle scene in green, brown, black and white with two men and a woman by the artist James Hill, over which is printed: [publisher's monogram around which is printed]: SIGNET | CLASSICS [and] CP194 60c | [printed in white]: *Burmese Days* | [printed in black]: *George | Orwell* [script to resemble handwriting] | [artist's signature]: James Hill | A SIGNET CLASSIC

Back cover Burmese Days | *George* | *Orwell* [script to resemble handwriting] | [plot summary] | [printed in blue]: With an Afterword by Richard Rees | [printed in black]: PUBLISHED BY THE NEW AMERICAN LIBRARY

Spine [publisher's monogram in a black square] | CP | 194 | [printed laterally]: BURMESE DAYS *George Orwell*

Locations
Orwell Archive

Notes
Published in December 1963 @ 60 cents. Based on 1950 Second American Edition. Also available in Signet Classics are *Animal Farm* [#CP121] and *1984* [#CP100] @ 60c [publisher's advertisements p 256].

A.2j   *Heinemann Educational Books Edition, 1967*

GEORGE ORWELL | [rule] | *Burmese Days* | WITH AN INTRODUCTION BY | MALCOLM MUGGERIDGE | [publisher's device in oval frame, 1.5 × 1.0] HEINEMANN | LONDON

Collation [A]–I^{16} K^6; 150 leaves (18.3 × 12.3); [i–iv] v–xiii [xiv] [5][sic]–287 [288–290]

Contents [i] halftitle: *The Modern Novel Series* | BURMESE DAYS [ii] list of books in the series [iii] titlepage [iv] imprint v–vi biographical note vii–xiii introduction by Malcolm Muggeridge [xiv] epigram: *This desert inaccessible* | *Under the shade of melancholy boughs.* | –AS YOU LIKE IT [5]–287 text [288–290] blank

Binding Green calico-textured cloth on boards. Off white endpapers.

Front and back covers Pattern of irregular lines printed in black. On the front cover is printed an irregular white rectangle within which is: [black stripe within which is printed in white]: THE MODERN NOVEL SERIES | [beneath which is printed in black]: GEORGE ORWELL | *Burmese Days* | introduction by | Malcolm Muggeridge | [irregular black line]

Spine On a white panel amid black, green and white stripes is printed in black laterally: GEORGE ORWELL | *Burmese Days* | [and horizontally in white]: [publisher's device and initials]: H.E.B.

Locations
British Library. Acquisition 10 July 1967.
Cambridge University Library. Acquisition 2 August 1967.
Orwell Archive

Notes
Series also includes *Nineteen Eighty-Four*.
This edition is a reprint of the 1949 Uniform Edition, as indicated by the pagination of the text which begins on page [5].

A.2k   *New Penguin Edition, 1967*

George Orwell | Burmese Days | 'This desert inaccessible | Under the shade of melancholy boughs.' | –*As you like it*. | Penguin Books | in association with | Martin Secker & Warburg

Collation [1]–4^{12} 5–8^{10} 9–12^{12}; 136 leaves (17.9 × 10.9); [1–4] 5–272

Contents [1] biographical note [2] blank [3] titlepage [4] imprint 5–272 text

Binding Paper bound.

Front cover [penguin motif top left, price top right]: 5|– [In an orange strip at the top]: BURMESE | DAYS [printed in blue] | GEORGE ORWELL [rest of cover has a photograph of a seated buddhist monk in saffron robes, sitting behind a white sun helmet on which are Union Jack sunglasses]

Back cover [plot summary] | Cover photograph by John Goldblatt [printed in white] | [photograph of Orwell] | Vernon Richards | For copyright reasons this edition is not for sale in the U.S.A.

Spine not seen

Locations
British Library – Micawber Street, Science Reference Library. Acquisition 2 June 1967.
Cambridge University Library. Acquisition 14 June 1967.
Cambridge University Library has a 1975 reissue and two 1984 reissues of the 1967 Penguin edition. The first, received 28 July 1975, has a cover photograph of boats on a muddy tropical river. The first 1984 reissue, received 25 October 1984, has the same illustration. The second, received 31 January 1985, but with the 1984 imprint, has a painting of a tropical scene with fields, palm trees, field workers in straw hats, and oxen.
Orwell Archive has 1982 and second 1984 issues.

Notes
Based on the 1949 Uniform Edition.
Reprinted 1969, 1972, 1973, 1975 (twice), 1977 (twice), 1978, 1979, 1980, 1981, 1982, 1983, 1984 (twice).
Reissues have a penguin motif on the titlepage.
Many variations in cover design and illustration.
1982 reissue has a photograph of boats on a muddy tropical river by Robert McFarlane.
1984 reissue has cover illustration of a painting of a tropical village scene by Christopher Corr.
1989 Twentieth Century Classics edition, based on Complete Works edition.

A.2l   *Larger format reissue of Uniform Edition, 1968*

BURMESE DAYS | *A Novel by* GEORGE ORWELL | *"This desert inaccessible* | *"Under the shade of melancholy boughs."* | –AS YOU LIKE IT. | SECKER & WARBURG . LONDON

Collation and Contents as A.2e, with *The Road to Wigan Pier* and *A Clergyman's Daughter* added to list of books by Orwell on [2] and addition to imprint on [4]

Binding Blue paper to resemble calico grain cloth on boards. Off white endpapers.

Front and back covers Plain.

Spine Stamped in silver: [pyramid of six lines] | BURMESE | DAYS | [small ornate leaf device] | GEORGE | ORWELL | [inverted pyramid of six lines] | SECKER & | WARBURG

Jacket Dull brown.

Front [Printed in silver]: GEORGE | ORWELL | [and in dark brown]: BURMESE | DAYS
Back Plain.
Spine laterally [in silver]: ORWELL [and in dark brown]: BURMESE | DAYS | [horizontally in silver]: SECKER & | WARBURG
Front flap [in dark brown][extracts from review] | [bottom left]: *Jacket design by* | BARTHOLOMEW WILKINS | Format [bottom right]: 30s | net

Back flap Continuation of review from front flap.

Locations
British Library – Micawber Street, Science Reference Library.
Cambridge University Library. Acquisition 30 December 1968.
Orwell Archive, with jacket.

A.2m   *Octopus Edition, 1976*

For titlepage transcription see *Animal Farm* A.10s

Burmese Days is one of six Orwell novels in this compendium volume. The other novels are *Animal Farm*, *A Clergyman's Daughter*, *Coming Up for Air*, *Keep the Aspidistra Flying*, and *Nineteen Eighty-Four*.
Published by Secker & Warburg|Octopus, 1976.
Burmese Days is on pp.69–249.
Hard bound with jacket.

Locations
Cambridge University Library. Acquisition 7 January 1977.

A.2n   *The Penguin Complete Novels of George Orwell Edition, 1983*

(Harmondsworth: Penguin, 1983) 925pp

A compendium edition of the following novels:

Animal Farm
Burmese Days
A Clergyman's Daughter
Coming Up for Air
Keep the Aspidistra Flying
Nineteen Eighty-Four

Paper bound
£4.95

Locations
Orwell Archive two copies

A.2o   *The Complete Works Edition, 1986*

THE COMPLETE WORKS OF | GEORGE ORWELL | VOLUME TWO | Burmese Days | *A Novel* | This desert inaccessible | Under the shade of melancholy boughs. | AS YOU LIKE IT | SECKER & WARBURG | [short rule] | LONDON

Collation There are 11 unmarked gatherings: [A–E]¹⁶ [F]⁸ [G–L]¹⁶; 168 leaves (23.3 × 15.4); [i–viii] 1–[300] [301–302] 303–[322] [323–328]

Collation There are 11 unmarked gatherings: [A–E]^{16} [F]^{8} [G–L]^{16}; 168 leaves (23.3 × 15.4); [i–viii] 1–[300] [301–302] 303–[322] [323–328]

Contents [i–ii] blank [iii] halftitle: THE COMPLETE WORKS OF | GEORGE ORWELL . TWO | BURMESE DAYS [iv] blank [v] publisher's note [vi] sketch map [vii] titlepage [viii] imprint: [selective publishing history of editions and reissues] | [copyright notices] | [British Library Cataloguing in Publication Data] | ISBN 0–436–35024–6 | Typeset in Monophoto Bembo by | Northumberland Press Ltd, Gateshead, Tyne and Wear | Printed and bound in Great Britain by | Richard Clay Ltd, Bungay, Suffolk 1– [300] text, on [300]: THE END [301] blank [302] key to sketch map 303–308 appendix 309–[320] textual note [321–326] blank

Binding Blue paper on boards, embossed to resemble calico textured cloth. Black end-papers.

Front and back covers Plain.

Spine Stamped in gilt: [double rule] | GEORGE | ORWELL | [rule] | Burmese | Days | [double rule] | SECKER & | WARBURG

Jacket Smooth dull black. Flaps white.
Front [in white]: GEORGE | ORWELL | [in orange and white]: BURMESE DAYS

Back [in white, note on *The Complete Works of George Orwell* and extracts from reviews. ISBN code and bar strip within a white rectangle.]
Spine [laterally] [in white]: GEORGE ORWELL | [in orange and white]: BURMESE DAYS [horizontally in white]: Secker & Warburg
Front flap [biographical note, plot summary, and note on this edition. At foot]: Jacket design by David Quay | £12.95 | net
Back flap [biographical notes on Orwell and Peter Davison]

Notes
This edition, edited by Peter Davison incorporates all Orwell's textual changes and restores previously omitted words. Reprinted 1996

Locations
Orwell Archive
Cambridge University Library
Robarts Library, University of Toronto

TRANSLATIONS

All Orwell Archive unless otherwise noted

DANISH

A.2.T1   *Burma dage*, 1976

København: Det Schønbergske Forlag
Translated by Michael Tejn
Paper bound

In this series *Kammerat Napoleon* [*Animal Farm*], *1984, Hyldest til Catalonien, Det engelske folk og andre essays.*

DUTCH

A.2.T2   *De jaren in Birma Roman*, 1975

Amsterdam: Meulenhoff
Second edition, 1983
Translated by Anneke Brassinga
Paper bound

Also in this series:
Aan de grond in Londen en Parijs
De jaren in Birma
De domineesdochter
Houd de sanseferia hoog
Happend naar lucht

FRENCH

A.2.T3a   *Tragédie birmane*, 1946

Paris: Les Editions Nagel
Translated by Guillot de Saix
Paper bound
190 fr
Published August 1946
7,800 copies
In the series *Les Grands Romans Etrangers*

A.2.T3b   *Un histoire birmane*, 1984

Paris: Editions Gérard Lebovici
Translated by Claude Noel
Paper bound
90 fr

GERMAN

A.2.T4   1982

Zurich: Diogenes
Translated by Susanna Rademacher
Paper bound
DM 9.80

Diogenes Taschenbuch series

Also in the series:
Farm de Tiere
Im Innern des Wals
Rache ist sauer
Mein Katalonien
Erledigt in Paris und London
Auftauchen, um Luft zu holen
Das George Orwell Lesebuch

Reissued 1983, 1984

ITALIAN

A.2.T5a   *Giorni in Birmania*, 1948

Milano: Longanesi
Translated by Giovanna Caracciolo
Paper bound
Published 6 October 1948
600 L
3,012 copies

A.2.T5b   *Giorni in Birmania*, 1975

Milano: Longanesi
Translated by Giovanna Caracciolo
With an Introduction by Gianni Zanmarchi
With two other stories by Orwell, "A Hanging" and "Shooting an Elephant"
Paper bound
L 3,000
Reissued in 1981

A.2.T5c   *Giorni in Birmania*, 1983

Verona: Oscar Mondadori
Translated by Giovanna Caracciolo
With an Introduction by Mario Maffi
Series Editor: Arnoldo Mondadori
Published under licence of Longanesi

March 1983
Paper bound
L 4,500

JAPANESE

A.2.T6   1980

Hard bound

NORWEGIAN

A.2.T7   *Dager i Burma*, 1975

Trondhjem: J.W. Cappelens Forlag A.S.
Translated by Kari and Kjell Risvik
Paper bound

PORTUGUESE

A.2.T8   *Dias na Birmânia*, 1983

Rio de Janeiro: Editora Nova Fronteira
Translated by Newton Goldman
Paper bound
Second printing, labelled second edition, 1983

SERBIAN

A.2.T9   *Burmanski Dani*, 1984

Zagreb: August Cesarec
Hard bound
Prijevod: Nada Soljan

SWEDISH

A.2.T10   *Dagar i Burma*, 1975

Uddevalla: Raben & Sjogren
Translated by Olof Hoffsten
Hard bound
Reissued in Legenda Pocket paperback, 1985

A.3   A CLERGYMAN'S DAUGHTER

That book is bollox, but I made some experiments in it that were useful to me.[1]

Composition and publication

In January 1934 Orwell went to stay with his parents in Southwold and he began to write *A Clergyman's Daughter*. The idea for the novel had been with him for a while before, although his teaching commitments and his revisions to *Burmese Days* prevented him starting it earlier. In December 1933, with *Burmese Days* in Moore's hands, he told Brenda Salkeld, 'The next one will be better I hope, but I don't suppose I shall be able to start it before the holidays.'[2] But just before Christmas 1933 he was admitted to Uxbridge Cottage Hospital with pneumonia, and from there he wrote to Moore with the news that he was giving up teaching:

> It is perhaps rather imprudent, but my people are anxious that I should do so, as they are concerned about my health, & of course I shall be able to write my next novel in 6 months or so if I haven't got to be teaching at the same time.[3]

By April 1934 he told Moore, 'My novel is not getting on badly, and I have done more than I expected to do in the time, though of course very roughly as yet.'[4] But it was not a book that gave him satisfaction. In July 1934 he told Brenda Salkeld, 'I am so miserable, struggling with the entrails of that dreadful book and never getting any further, and loathing the sight of what I have done. *Never* start writing novels, if you wish to preserve your happiness.'[5] By the end of August, the book was almost finished, 'I am going up to town as soon as I have finished the book I am doing, which should be at the end of October.'[6] But the final stages of the work were, if anything, more difficult. He told Brenda Salkeld:

> My novel, instead of going forwards, goes backwards with the most alarming speed. There are whole wads of it that are so awful that I really don't know what to do with them. And to add to my other joys, the fair, or part of it, has come back and established itself on the common just beyond the cinema, so that I have to work to the accompaniment of roundabout music that goes on till the small hours.[7]

He managed to obtain a copy of Joyce's *Ulysses* at a second attempt, though somewhat to his regret:

> I rather wish I had never read it. It gives me an inferiority complex. When I read a book like that and then come back to my own work, I feel like a eunuch who has taken a course in voice production and can pass himself off fairly well as a bass or a baritone, but if you listen closely you can hear the good old squeak just the same as ever.[8]

But he pressed on, telling her in the same letter, 'I most particularly want to get this novel done by the end of September, and every day makes a difference.' And by 3 October it was finished. He wrote to Moore from Southwold:

> I am sending my novel *A Clergyman's Daughter* under a separate cover. I will register it and trust it will arrive all right. I am not at all pleased with it. It was a good idea, but I am afraid I have made a muck of it – however, it is as good as I can do for the present. There are bits of it that I don't dislike, but I am afraid it is very disconnected as a whole, and rather unreal. Possibly you will be able to find a publisher for it. I should be interested to hear your reader's opinion, and what publisher you intend to try it on. In case the point should come up, the school described in Chapter IV is totally imaginary, though of course I have drawn on my general knowledge of what goes on in schools of that type.[9]

Moore took the novel to Gollancz, who, not to Orwell's surprise, raised objections. Orwell told Moore:

> I knew there would be trouble over that novel. However I am anxious to get it published, as there are parts of it I was pleased with, & I dare say that if I had indicated to me the sorts of changes that Mr Gollancz wants, I could manage it. I am willing to admit that the part about the school, which is what seems to have roused people's incredulity, is overdrawn, but not nearly so much as people think. In fact I was rather amused to see that they say "all that was done away with 30 or 40 years ago" etc as one always hears that any particularly crying abuse was "done away with 30 or 40 years ago". As to this part, it is possible that if Mr Gollancz agrees, a little "toning down" might meet the bill. I don't want to bother you with details about this, however.

As to the points about libel, swearwords etc they are a very small matter & could be put right by a few strokes of the pen. The book does, however, contain an inherent fault of structure which I will discuss with Mr Gollancz, & this could not be rectified in any way that I can think of. I was aware of it when I wrote the book, & imagined that it did not matter, because I did not intend it to be so realistic as people seem to think it is.

I wonder if you could be kind enough to arrange an interview for me with Mr Gollancz? I should think it would take quite an hour to talk over the various points, if he could spare me that much time.[10]

The negotiations were successful and in January 1935 Orwell told Moore, 'Naturally I am very pleased to hear that you have made such good terms with Gollancz for *A Clergyman's Daughter*. I am afraid he is going to lose money this time, all right. However we must hope for the best.'[11]

He made last-minute revisions to the proofs at Gollancz's request, once again because of the publisher's worries about libel suits. The novel was officially published on 11 March 1935, although Orwell had his copies a few days in advance and sent one to Brenda Salkeld with a note that,

I sent off your copy of *A Clergyman's Daughter* last night. As you will see, it is tripe, except for chap 3, part 1, which I am pleased with, but I don't know whether you will like it. It is billed to come out on Monday next, so don't show it to anyone before that, will you?[12]

As he had expected, Gollancz was unwilling to risk legal action for libel by publishing Orwell's original typescript. Gollancz had recently faced legal action over another fictional account of private schooling, in Rosalind Ward's *Children be Happy*. This made him particularly cautious over *A Clergyman's Daughter*. Orwell was willing to compromise, because he was anxious to see the novel published. So, for example, in a letter to Gollancz, he noted:

In general, throughout this school part I have toned down, but not cut out altogether, the suggestion that private schools of this type are apt to be more or less of a swindle, existing only to make money and not giving much more than a pretence of education. What I have done in effect is to make the standard at the school somewhat higher than I made it before. I have not altered the character of Mrs Creevy, the proprietress, except in so far as was necessary to fit in with the other changes.[13]

In 1944, when Leonard Moore was trying to arrange Penguin publication of *Keep the Aspidistra Flying*, Orwell told him that he could not allow it, or indeed *A Clergyman's Daughter*, to be reprinted. He told him, 'They are both thoroughly bad books and I would rather see them go out of print ... It wouldn't do me any good to have those two books revived.'[14]

The problem for the modern editor is that the original manuscript does not survive and so cannot be restored. The *Complete Works* edition makes the most comprehensive attempt to date, using Orwell's December 1934 letter to Gollancz, 'Notes on alterations in "A Clergyman's Daughter"', and subsequent correspondence in January and February 1935. Davison includes as comprehensive a list of alterations as the correspondence allows, although he has to rely on the 1935 edition as the copy text. His notes are of special interest in that, wherever possible, he has used Orwell's own descriptions of the changes to the typescript: 'I have not altered except in minor details ...', 'I have greatly toned down ...', 'I have cut out the suggestion ...', and finally 'In the final chapter I have made minor alterations, but have not changed the general trend of it. I had myself thought it a very weak ending ...'[15]

A.3a   *First Edition, 1935*

A CLERGYMAN'S DAUGHTER | by | GEORGE ORWELL | Author of | *Down and Out in Paris and London* | "The trivial round, the common task." | *(Hymns A. and M.)* | LONDON | VICTOR GOLLANCZ LTD | 1935

Collation [AD]–UD⁸; 160 leaves (18.2 × 12.4); [1–5] 6–317 [318–320]

Contents [1] halftitle: A CLERGYMAN'S DAUGHTER [2] extracts from reviews of *Down and Out in Paris and London* [3] titlepage [4] imprint: *Printed in Great Britain by* | The Camelot Press Ltd., London and Southampton [5]–317 text, on 317: THE END [318–320] blank

Binding Black calico-textured cloth on boards. Off white endpapers.

Front and back covers Plain.

Spine [stamped in yellowish green]: A | CLERGYMAN'S | DAUGHTER | BY | GEORGE | ORWELL | GOLLANCZ

Paper by Spalding & Hodge, cream esparto antique laid
33 lines per page
Baskerville 10 pt

Jacket Yellow with black printing unless otherwise noted.
Front [in pink, geometric design] a novel | A CLERGYMAN'S | DAUGHTER | by | GEORGE ORWELL | This is a novel by the | author of "Down and Out in | Paris and London." That was | truth, and this is fiction: and the fiction | is more – almost terrifyingly – vivid than | the fact. To make mention only of one | part of the book, the 'night out' in Trafal- | gar Square is quite unforgettable. [pointing hand symbol]
Back Publisher's advertisements.
Spine A | CLERGYMAN'S | DAUGHTER | By | GEORGE | ORWELL | 7/6 [not a line break] | net | [publisher's geometric motif] | GOLLANCZ
Front and back flaps Extracts from reviews of *Down and Out in Paris and London.*

Notes
Published 11 March 1935
7s 6d
2,000 copies
Type distributed 20 March 1936

There is an error on p188: Blask Mass [for Black Mass]
50 bound copies were sent to the Ryerson Press for distribution in Canada.

Contemporary reviews
L.P. Hartley *The Observer* (10 March 1935)
V.S. Pritchett *The Spectator* (22 March 1935)
Peter Quennell *The New Statesman and Nation* (23 March 1935)
Times Literary Supplement (11 April 1935)
Michael Sayers *The Adelphi* (August 1935)

Locations
British Library
Cambridge University Library, with jacket. Acquisition 5 March 1935.
London Library
Orwell Archive – three copies

A.3b   *First American Edition, 1936*

A CLERGYMAN'S DAUGHTER | by | GEORGE ORWELL | Author of | *Down and Out in Paris and London* | "The trivial round, the common task." | *(Hymns A. and M.)* | HARPER AND BROTHERS | New York and London | 1936

Collation [AD]–UD⁸; 160 leaves (18.2 × 12.4); [1–5] 6–317 [318–320]

Contents [1] halftitle: A CLERGYMAN'S DAUGHTER [2] blank [3] titlepage [4] blank [5]–317 text, on 317: THE END [318–320] blank

Binding Blue calico textured cloth on boards. Off white endpapers.

Front cover In bottom right is stamped a pink rectangle, 1.9 × 1.6, in which the publisher's monogram: HB and a flaming torch passing from hand to hand and depicted from the blue background.
Back cover Plain.

Spine Stamped in pink: [zigzag] | [rule] | The | Clergyman's | Daughter | GEORGE | ORWELL | [rule] | [zigzags] | [rule] | HARPERS | [rule] | [zigzag]

Notes
This is in fact a reissue of sheets of the British first edition, with a new titlepage and altered prelims. The error on p. 188 is the same.

There is a further error in the binding, the spine being stamped: The Clergyman's Daughter

Published 17 August 1936.
$2.50
Ian Willison notes that Gollancz said that 500 copies were shipped, but that Harpers claimed it was 1000.

Contemporary reviews
Geoffrey Stone *Commonweal* (18 June 1937)

Locations
Orwell Archive – two copies

A.3c   *Uniform Edition, 1960*

A | CLERGYMAN'S | DAUGHTER | BY | GEORGE ORWELL | LONDON | SECKER & WARBURG | 1960

Collation [A]–K¹⁶; 160 leaves (18.2 × 12.0); [1–5] 6–320

Contents [1] halftitle: A CLERGYMAN'S DAUGHTER | [2] list of books by Orwell [3] titlepage [4] imprint: MARTIN SECKER & WARBURG LTD., | 7 John Street, Bloomsbury, | London, W.C.1 | *First published (Gollancz) 1935* | *Uniform Edition 1960* | *Printed and bound in Great Britain by* | *The Camelot Press Ltd., London and Southampton* [5]–320 text, on 320: THE END

Binding Green calico-textured cloth on boards. Off white endpapers. Purple topped leaves.

Front and back covers Plain.

Spine Stamped in gilt: [pyramid of 6 lines] | A CLERGYMAN'S | DAUGHTER | [small ornate device of half circles and a dot] | GEORGE | ORWELL | [inverted pyramid of 6 lines] | SECKER & | WARBURG

Jacket Front and spine beige, green black and off white, back green, flaps off white.
Front [and wrapping around spine] Drawing of Church with a woman and a bicycle. In the upper third: A clergyman's | daughter | [and in white]: George Orwell | [in lower left]: Denis Piper.
Back List of books in Orwell Uniform Edition.
Spine [laterally]: A clergyman's | daughter [and on the same line in white]: George Orwell [and in black]: Secker & | Warburg
Front flap [plot summary] | Jacket design by | DENIS PIPER 18s | net
Back cover [at foot]: APT/V140

Notes
18s 0d – later increased to 21s 0d.
Although this is clearly a new edition and a new setting of type, the error noted in the previous editions is maintained. Here Blask Mass occurs on page 191.

Although this is announced as the Uniform Edition, the binding is not exactly uniform with other books in the set.

Locations
British Library
Cambridge University Library. Acquisition 12 May 1960.
Orwell Archive, with jacket.

A.3d   Second American Edition, 1960

A | Clergyman's | Daughter | By GEORGE ORWELL | [publisher's monogram device] | HARCOURT, BRACE AND COMPANY | NEW YORK

Collation Ten unmarked gatherings of 16 leaves arranged: [A]–K¹⁶; 160 leaves (18.2 × 12.0); [1–5] 6–320

Contents [1] halftitle: A CLERGYMAN'S DAUGHTER [2] list of books by Orwell [3] titlepage [4] imprint: Library of Congress Catalog Card Number: 60–10943 | Printed in the United States of America [5]–320 text, on 320: THE END

Binding Green calico-textured cloth on boards. Off white endpapers.

Front and back covers Plain.

Spine Stamped in gilt: GEORGE | ORWELL | [rule] | A | Clergyman's | Daughter | [rule] | HARCOURT, BRACE | AND COMPANY | [publisher's monogram device]

Jacket Front green, otherwise off white.
Front In upper two thirds of right is a four-paned window outlined in black. The top right and bottom left panes have purple and black curtains, the bottom right a black and white sketch of a woman waving, and in the top left: A | *Clergyman's* | *Daughter* [elaborate script] | GEORGE | ORWELL
Back List of books by Orwell [stamped in purple] and extracts from reviews of *Nineteen Eighty-Four*.
Spine A | *Clergy-* | *man's* | *Daughter* [elaborate script] | [and laterally]: GEORGE [stamped in green] | ORWELL [stamped in purple] | [horizontally]: HARCOURT, | BRACE | AND COMPANY | [publisher's monogram device]
Front flap [plot summary] | *Jacket design by Seymour Chwast* | *Harcourt, Brace and Company* | *750 Third Avenue, New York 17, N.Y.*
Back flap [biographical note on Orwell] | [extracts from view of Orwell] | [publisher's address]

Locations
Orwell Archive

Notes
This is printed from the same plates as A.3c, and is therefore in fact really only a reissue, however the error on page 191 is corrected.

A.3e   First Penguin Edition, 1964

George Orwell | A CLERGYMAN'S | DAUGHTER | [penguin motif in oval frame, 1.1 × 0.8] | PENGUIN BOOKS | IN ASSOCIATION WITH | SECKER & WARBURG

Collation [T–A.C.D.–A] – T–A.C.D.–D¹⁶ T–A.C.D.–E⁸ T–A.C.D.–F – T– A.C.D.–I⁶; 136 leaves (17.9 × 10.8); [1–4] 5–262 [263–272]

Contents [1] notes on Orwell's life and works [2] plain [3] titlepage [4] imprint: Penguin Books Ltd, Harmondsworth, Middlessex, England | Penguin Books Pty Ltd, Ringwood | Victoria Australia | [short rule] | First published by Gollancz 1935 | Published by Secker and Warburg 1960 | Published in Penguin Books 1964 | [short rule] | Copyright [copyright symbol] the estate of Eric Blair, 1935 | [short rule] | Made and printed in Great Britain | by Cox and Wyman Ltd, London, | Reading, and Fakenham | Set in Monotype Baskerville | [copyright clause] 5–[263] text [264] blank [265] [penguin motif] | [publisher's advertisement] [266] blank [267–272] publisher's advertisement for books by Orwell

Binding Paper bound in orange.

Front cover [penguin motif] a Penguin Book 3'6 | [rule] | A Clergyman's | Daughter | [rule] | George Orwell [in white] | [drawing of woman's head and shoulders, repeated in negative]

Back cover [penguin motif] a Penguin Book | [rule] | [plot summary] | Cover design by Fletcher|Forbes|Gill [all one line] | *For copyright reasons this edition is not for sale in the U.S.A.* | [photograph of Orwell] | Vernon Richards

Spine [laterally]: George Orwell [in white] A Clergyman's Daughter | [horizontally]: [penguin motif] [in white] | 1877

Notes
3s 6d
Reprinted 1966, 1967, 1971, 1972, 1974, 1975 (twice), 1978, 1979, 1981.
Several cover designs: 1971 has a drawing of a woman holding an accounts book, in green, black, pink and blue.
1975–1981 have a tinted photograph of the front of a bicycle against stone wall background, the bicycle basket containing a Bible, fruit, flowers and a brown paper bag.
1989 Twentieth Century Classics edition, based on the Complete Works edition.

Locations
British Library – rebound, with original covers bound in. Copy received 8 May 1964.
Cambridge University Library. Acquisition 22 May 1964
Orwell Archive

A.3f   Reissue of 1960 Uniform Edition, 1969

A | CLERGYMAN'S | DAUGHTER | BY | GEORGE ORWELL | LONDON | SECKER & WARBURG

Collation and Contents as Uniform Edition, A.3c, but with new imprint on [4]: MARTIN SECKER & WARBURG LTD., | 14 Carlisle Street, Soho Square, | London, W.1 | *First published (Gollancz) 1935 | Uniform Edition 1960 | Reprinted 1965, 1969 | Printed in Great Britain by | Fletcher & Son Ltd, Norwich*

Binding Green paper on boards, embossed to resemble calico textured cloth. Off white endpapers.

Front and back covers Plain.

Spine Stamped in gilt: [pyramid of 6 lines] | A CLERGYMAN'S | DAUGHTER | [small ornate device of 3 circles a dot and lines] | GEORGE | ORWELL | [inverted pyramid of 6 lines] | SECKER & | WARBURG
Jacket Dull brown.
Front [Printed in silver]: GEORGE | ORWELL | [and in dark brown]: A CLERGYMAN'S | DAUGHTER

Back Plain.
Spine [laterally] [in silver]: ORWELL [and in dark brown]: A CLERGYMAN'S | DAUGHTER | [horizontally in silver]: SECKER & | WARBURG
Front flap [in dark brown] [plot summary] | [bottom left]: Jacket design by | Format [bottom right]: 35s. net | £1.75 net
Back flap [in dark brown] SBN: 436 35010 6

Notes
The text is identical to 1960 Uniform Edition, including the error on page 191.

Locations
Orwell Archive

A.3g   *Paper bound reissue of Second American Edition, no date*

A | Clergyman's | Daughter | By | GEORGE ORWELL | HARBRACE PAPER-BOUND LIBRARY | Harcourt, Brace & World, Inc. | New York | [publisher's monogram device]

Collation 160 leaves in a perfect binding (17.9 × 10.50); [1–5] 6–320

Contents [1] halftitle: A CLERGYMAN'S DAUGHTER [2] list of books by Orwell [3] titlepage [4] imprint: Library of Congress Catalog Card Number: 60–10943 | Printed in the United States of America [5]–320 text, on 320: THE END

Binding Paper bound. Front cover pale blue, spine and back off white.

Front cover Against a background depicting plain blue cloth: HARBRACE PAPER-BOUND LIBRARY HPL 37 | $1.45 | [stamped in blue in an arc]: GEORGE ORWELL | [in brown, black, red, yellow and green is a picture of a woman riding a bicycle] | [in blue] [short rule] | [and in black]: A Clergyman's | Daughter | [and in blue] [short rule]

Back cover FICTION | [plot summary] | [in blue] [extracts from reviews] | [in black]: HARBRACE PAPERBOUND LIBRARY | HARCOURT, BRACE & WORLD, INC. | [in blue]: *Cover design by Paul Bacon Studio*

Spine Laterally, stamped in blue: A Clergyman's Daughter [and in black] George Orwell | [horizontally]: [publisher's monogram device] | HPL | 37

Notes
This is a paper bound reissue of the second American Edition, A.3d, itself a reissue of the British 1960 Uniform Edition.

$1.45

Locations
Orwell Archive

A.3h   *Octopus Edition, 1976*

For titlepage transcription see *Animal Farm* A.10s

A Clergyman's Daughter is one of six Orwell novels in this compendium volume. The other novels are *Animal Farm, Burmese Days, Coming Up for Air, Keep the Aspidistra Flying,* and *Nineteen Eighty-Four.*
Published by Secker & Warburg|Octopus, 1976.
A Clergyman's Daughter is on pp253–425.
Hard bound with jacket.

Locations
Cambridge University Library. Acquisition 7 January 1977.

A.3i *The Penguin Complete Novels of George Orwell Edition, 1983*

(Harmondsworth: Penguin, 1983) 925pp

A compendium edition of the following novels:

Animal Farm
Burmese Days
A Clergyman's Daughter
Coming Up for Air
Keep the Aspidistra Flying
Nineteen Eighty-Four

Paper bound
£4.95

Locations
Orwell Archive two copies

A.3j *The Complete Works Edition, 1986*

THE COMPLETE WORKS OF | GEORGE ORWELL | VOLUME THREE | A Clergyman's | Daughter | The trivial round, the common task. | HYMNS A. & M. | SECKER & WARBURG | [short rule] | LONDON

Collation There are 10 unmarked gatherings: [A–K][16]; 160 leaves (23.1 × 15.4); [i–viii] 1–297 [298] 299–306 [307–312]

Contents [i] halftitle: THE COMPLETE WORKS OF | GEORGE ORWELL . THREE | A CLERGYMAN'S DAUGHTER [ii] blank [iii] publisher's note [iv] blank [v] titlepage [vi] imprint: [selective publishing history of editions and reissues] | [copyright notices] | [British Library Cataloguing in Publication Data] | ISBN 0–436–35025–4 | Typeset in 13|14 pt Monophoto Bembo by | Northumberland Press Ltd., Gateshead, Tyne and Wear | Printed and bound in Great Britain by | Richard Clay, (The Chaucer Press) Ltd., | Bungay, Suffolk [vii] [editor's note] [viii] blank 1–297 text, on 297: THE END [298] blank 299–302 list of pre-publication revisions, 1934–5 303–[307]: textual notes [308–312] blank

Binding Blue paper on boards, embossed to resemble calico textured cloth. Black endpapers.

Front and back covers Plain.

Spine Stamped in gilt: [double rule] | GEORGE | ORWELL | [rule] | A | Clergyman's | Daughter | [double rule] | SECKER & | WARBURG

Jacket Smooth dull black. Flaps white.
Front [in white]: GEORGE | ORWELL | [in orange and white]: A | CLERGYMAN'S | DAUGHTER
Back [in white, note on *The Complete Works of George Orwell* and extracts from reviews. ISBN code and bar strip within a white rectangle.]
Spine [laterally] [in white]: GEORGE ORWELL | [in orange and white]: A CLERGY-MAN'S DAUGHTER [horizontally in white]: Secker & Warburg
Front flap [biographical note, plot summary, and note on this edition. At foot]: Jacket design by David Quay | £12.95 | net
Back flap [biographical notes on Orwell and Peter Davison]
The Orwell Archive also has a variant jacket with the coloured printing on the front cover and on the spine in yellow.
Reprinted 1996

Locations
Orwell Archive two copies

Cambridge University Library
Robarts Library, University of Toronto

TRANSLATIONS

All Orwell Archive unless otherwise noted

CATALAN

A.3.T1   *La Filla del Clergue*, 1985

Barcelona: Libres a mà, Edicions Destino
Translated by Carles Alier i Aixalà and Roger Alier i Aixalà
Paper bound

DUTCH

A.3.T2a   *De domineesdochter*, 1972

Amsterdam: Meulenhoff
Translated by Elizabeth Stortenbeker
Paper bound

Reissued 1983

A.3.T2b   *De do neesdochter*, 1979

Amsterdam: Pranger
Translated by Elizabeth Stortenbeker
Paper bound

GERMAN

A.3.T3   *Eine Pfarrerstochter*, 1983

Zurich: Diogenes
Translated by Hanna Neves
Paper bound

Reissued 1983

ITALIAN

A.3.T4a   *La figlia del reverendo*, 1968

Milan: Garzanti
Translated by Marcella Bonsanti
Hard bound
Published 5 December 1968

A.3.T4b   *La figlia del reverendo*, 1976

Milan: Garzanti
Translated by Marcella Bonsanti
Paper bound reissue of A.3.T3a
Published 4 June 1976

PORTUGUESE

A.3.T5a   *A Filha do Pàroco*, 1966

Lisbon: Editora Ulissia
Translated by M. Marques da Silva
Paper bound
Published February 1966

A.3.T5b   *A Filha do Reverendo*, 1985

Rio de Janeiro: Editora Nova Fronteira
Translated by Alvaro Cabral
Paper bound

SPANISH

A.3.T6a   *La Hija del Reverendo*, 1970

Madrid: El Libro de Bolsillo, Alianza Editorial
Translated by Emilia Palomo de Valente
Paper bound

A.4   KEEP THE ASPIDISTRA FLYING

I want this one to be a work of art, & that can't be done without much bloody sweat.[1]

Composition and publication

In the middle of October 1934, soon after completing *A Clergyman's Daughter*, Orwell left Southwold and went to live in London. He took a part-time job as an assistant in 'Booklovers' Corner', a bookshop in Hampstead, and rented a room nearby. By February 1935 he had begun to write *Keep the Aspidistra Flying*. A letter to Brenda Salkeld written at this time describes his day, with periods for 'writing' or 'work' as he also labelled it around his time in the shop:

> My time-table is as follows: 7 am get up, dress etc, cook & eat breakfast. 8.45 go down & open the shop, & I am usually kept there till about 9.45. Then come home, do out my room, light the fire etc. 10.30 am–1 pm I do some writing. 1 pm get lunch & eat it. 2 pm–6.30 pm I am at the shop. Then I come home, get my supper, do the washing up & after that sometimes do about an hour's work. In spite [of] all this, I have got more work done in the last few days than during weeks before when I was being harried all day long ... I want this one to be a work of art, & that can't be done without much bloody sweat.[2]

He moved to another room, on Parliament Hill, Hampstead, in March. In the same month he met Eileen O'Shaughnessy, his future wife, a graduate student in Psychology at University College London. In August 1935 he rented a flat in Kentish Town. With many interruptions to his regular writing, he told Rayner Heppenstall, 'I shall be glad to get back to my good old novel where one has plenty of elbow room. I have three more chapters and an epilogue to do, and then I shall spend about two months putting on the twiddly bits.'[3] A month later he wrote, 'I am very happy to have got back to my novel, which is going not badly.'[4]

In a letter to Moore written on 17 January 1936 Orwell reports that he gave the MS to Gollancz on 15 January and that Gollancz was 'sending it to be vetted by his solicitor'. Gollancz subsequently called for revisions. Orwell made changes to the MS. Publication was scheduled for the beginning of March 1936 and proofs were prepared. Orwell had received two copies by 13 February when he sent one to Moore. By this time he was in lodgings at Wigan: 'I am correcting the proofs of my novel, which should be out in about a month ... otherwise not doing any work, as it is impossible in these surroundings.'[5] At this stage either the publisher's staff or perhaps the printer read the novel more closely and saw the possibility of libel. On 17 February Norman Collins of Gollancz called for further changes which Orwell reluctantly made: 'I will do what I can short of ruining the book altogether'.[6] This was followed by a request from Gollancz to change the advertising slogans. Orwell wired from Wigan: 'ABSOLUTELY IMPOSSIBLE MAKE CHANGES SUGGESTED WOULD MEAN COMPLETE REWRITING'.[7] By 24 February Orwell had corrected the proofs, making further alterations and trusting 'it will now be all right'.[8] By the end of the month he was able to tell Richard Rees:

> My novel ought to be out in a few weeks. There was the usual last-minute stew about libel, this time, unfortunately after it was in proof so that I had to spoil a whole chapter with alterations. This business of libel is becoming a nightmare – it appears that there now exist firms of crook solicitors who make a regular income by blackmailing publishers. However I hope I may get an American edition of my novel printed unmutilated.[9]

In March he told Jack Common, editor of the *Adelphi*:

> My next novel ought to be out shortly. It would have been out a month ago only there was one of those fearful last-minute scares about libel and I was made to alter it to the point of ruining it utterly. What particularly stuck in my gizzard was that the person who dictated the alterations to me was that squirt Norman Collins. Do you want a copy sent to the Adelphi? If you think you could get it reviewed I will have them send a copy, but not if you haven't space to spare.[10]

Common wanted it reviewed, so Orwell promised, 'I'll see that the Adelphi get a copy of my novel. It ought to be out in a few weeks and would have been out a month ago if it had not been for all that bollox about libel.'[11] Just before the publication date, he wrote to Richard Rees about the copy for the *Adelphi*, adding,

> I also sent a copy to Mrs Meade because I had promised them a copy and M asked me privately to send it to his wife, but this is troubling me because I fear she might think herself obliged to read it and it might bore her. If you are with them you could drop a hint to the effect that presentation copies are not meant to be read.[12]

Keep the Aspidistra Flying was published in London on 20 April 1936. The reviews were mixed, as a letter in response to a complimentary letter from Anthony Powell indicates: 'Yes, the reviewers are awful, so much so that in a general way I prefer the ones who lose their temper & call me names to the silly asses who mean so well & never bother to discover what you are writing about.'[13] In 1944 Leonard Moore tried to arrange for Penguin publication of the novel, but Orwell wrote to him,

> I had not realised you were in negotiation for a Penguin of 'Keep the Aspidistra Flying'. I don't think I can allow this book to be reprinted, or 'A Clergyman's Daughter' either. They are both thoroughly bad books and I would much rather see them go out of print ... It wouldn't do me any good to have those two books revived.[14]

It was not published again until the 1954 Uniform Edition. The first American edition, for which Orwell had expressed such hopes, was not published until 1956. In a letter to Henry Miller, Orwell wrote that

> [it] won't I imagine be published in America, because it is a domestic sort of story with an entirely English theme and the American public are getting restive about what I believe is called 'British sissy-stuff'. I noticed also when I worked in the bookshop that it is harder and harder to sell American books in England. The two languages are drifting further and further apart.[15]

The copy text for the *Complete Works* edition is the British first edition with 'restorations' noted in the files of Victor Gollancz Ltd.

A.4a First Edition, 1936

KEEP THE ASPIDISTRA | FLYING | by | GEORGE ORWELL | LONDON | VICTOR GOLLANCZ LTD | 1936

Collation [AF]–UF⁸; 160 leaves (18.3 × 12.2); [1–7] 8–318 [319–320]

Contents [1] halftitle: KEEP THE ASPIDISTRA | FLYING [2] review of Orwell's work [3] titlepage [4] imprint: *Printed in Great Britain by* | The Camelot Press Ltd., London and Southampton [5] Quotation adapted from I Corinthians, Chapter xiii [6] blank [7]–318 text, on 318: THE END [319–320] blank

Binding Blue calico textured cloth on boards. Off white endpapers.

Front and back covers Plain.

Spine Stamped in blue: KEEP THE | ASPIDISTRA | FLYING | BY | GEORGE | ORWELL | GOLLANCZ
Paper
Cream esparto antique laid
33 lines per page
11 pt Baskerville

Jacket Yellow
Front [publisher's geometric motif in pink] by GEORGE ORWELL | KEEP THE | ASPIDISTRA | FLYING | by the author of | BURMESE DAYS | [double rule] | BURMESE DAYS: | [extract from review of *Burmese Days*] [pointing hand symbol]
Back Publisher's advertisements
Spine KEEP THE | ASPIDISTRA | FLYING | by | GEORGE | ORWELL | 7|6 | NET | [publisher's geometric motif] | GOLLANCZ
Front flap [continuation of review of *Burmese Days*]
Back flap Publisher's advertisements

Notes
Published 20 April 1936
7s 6d
3,000 copies
2,500 bound, 2,256 sold
Ryerson Press took 25 bound copies for Canadian distribution $2.00

Type distributed 1 May 1936
500 sets of sheets and the remaining 219 bound copies destroyed by German bombing 16 March 1942 484 bound stock issued at 3s 6d. 422 of these sold

Contemporary reviews
William Plomer *The Spectator* (24 April 1936)
Cyril Connolly *The New Statesman and Nation* (25 April 1936)
Times Literary Supplement (2 May 1936)
Richard Rees *Adelphi* (June 1936)
Kenneth Macpherson *Life and Letters Today* (Autumn 1936)

Locations
British Library. Acquisition 9 April 1936.
Cambridge University Library, with jacket. Acquisition 15 April 1936.
London Library
Orwell Archive – three copies

A.4b   *Uniform Edition, 1954*

KEEP | THE ASPIDISTRA | FLYING | BY | GEORGE ORWELL | LONDON | SECKER & WARBURG | 1954

Collation [A]–T⁸; 152 leaves (18.2 × 12.1); [1–7] 8–303 [304]

Contents [1] halftitle: KEEP THE ASPIDISTRA FLYING [2] list of books by Orwell [3] titlepage [4] imprint: MARTIN SECKER & WARBURG LTD., | 7 John Street, Bloomsbury, | London, W.C.1 | *First published (Gollancz) 1936* | *Uniform edition 1954* | *Made and Printed in Great Britain by* | *The Camelot Press Ltd., London and Southampton* [5] Quotation adapted from I Corinthians [6] blank [7]–303 text, on 303: THE END [304] blank

Binding Green calico textured cloth on boards. Off white endpapers. Purple topped leaves.

Front and back covers Plain.

Spine Stamped in purplish red: [pyramid of six rules] | KEEP THE | ASPIDISTRA | FLYING | [small ornate device of 3 circles and lines] | GEORGE | ORWELL | [inverted pyramid of six rules] | SECKER & | WARBURG

Jacket Front and spine green, otherwise off white.
Front [Two off-white panels outlined in black] [Top panel]: KEEP THE | ASPIDISTRA | FLYING [bottom panel]: GEORGE | ORWELL [and in off-white at foot]: UNIFORM EDITION
Spine KEEP THE | ASPIDISTRA | FLYING | [leaf motif] | GEORGE | ORWELL | SECKER & | WARBURG
Back List of Orwell's works published by Secker & Warburg.
Front flap Plot summary | 12s.6d. | NET
Back flap Continuation of plot summary, and publisher's advertisement

Notes
Although this is a new edition the error noted in the first edition is repeated in this edition on page 24. Other errors are introduced in this new edition, for example, on page 45 'bracket' replaces 'bracelet' in the first edition, page 47. Peter Davison lists other new errors in the Uniform Edition in the Textual Note to the new *Complete Works* Edition.

Locations
British Library. Acquisition 12 July 1954.
Cambridge University Library. Acquisition 22 July 1954
Orwell Archive

A.4c   *First American Edition, 1956*

GEORGE ORWELL | Keep the | Aspidistra Flying | HARCOURT, BRACE AND COMPANY | NEW YORK

Collation Eight unmarked gatherings of 16 leaves each arranged: [A–H]¹⁶; [i–vi] [1–2] 3–248 [249–250]

Contents [i] halftitle: KEEP THE ASPIDISTRA FLYING [ii] list of books by Orwell [iii] titlepage [iv] imprint: FIRST AMERICAN EDITION, 1956 | LIBRARY OF CONGRESS CATALOG CARD NUMBER: 56–5326 | PRINTED IN THE UNITED STATES OF AMERICA [v] Quotation adapted from I Corinthians [vi] blank [1] halftitle: KEEP THE ASPIDISTRA FLYING [2] blank 3–248 text [249–250] blank

Binding Green calico textured cloth on boards. Off white endpapers.

Front and back covers Plain.

Spine Stamped in silver: GEORGE | ORWELL | [stamped in yellow]: Keep | The | Aspidistra | Flying | [and in silver]: HARCOURT, | BRACE AND | COMPANY

Jacket
Front Against a background picture of white lace netting: George Orwell [stamped in black] | Keep the aspidistra flying [stamped in orange] | [stylised outline of aspidistra plant in green, in a black pot on a black stand, with orange colour filling the bottom right quarter of the cover]
Back Against an off white background is a list of novels by Orwell, the heading and titles in green and the extracts from reviews in black.
Spine Against white lace netting background, laterally: George Orwell [stamped in black] Keep the aspidistra flying [stamped in orange] | [and horizontally in black]: Harcourt Brace | and Company
Front flap Against a white background, stamped in black: $3.75 | [in green]: George Orwell's | Keep the Aspidistra Flying | [and in black, plot summary]
Back flap [plot summary continued] | [in green]: George Orwell | biographical note [in black]

Notes
Printed in November 1955
Published January 1956
Second printing March 1956
$3.75

Contemporary reviews
Anthony West *The New Yorker* (28 January 1956)
Henry Popkin *Commonweal* (23 March 1956)
Dorothy Van Ghent *The Yale Review* (Spring 1956)
Isaac Rosenfeld *Commentary* (June 1956)
Louis Simpson *The Hudson Review* (Summer 1956)

Locations
Orwell Archive
British Library

Reissue
This edition was reissued in 1969 in the Harbrace Paperbound Library. Titlepage, collation, contents and text are as for the hardbound issue, with amended imprints, and with publisher's advertisements on 249–250.

Binding Paper bound.

Front cover Against a blue background: [printed in yellow]: HARBRACE PAPERBOUND LIBRARY HPL 38 | $1.25 | [in white]: KEEP THE | ASPIDISTRA | FLYING | [short rule] | [in yellow]: GEORGE ORWELL | [in red, green, yellow, brown and white is a painting of a man reading a book, and a woman, in front of an aspidistra, window and lace hanging]

Back cover [against an off white background]: FICTION | [plot summary] | [in blue] [review extracts] | HARBRACE PAPERBOUND LIBRARY | HARCOURT, BRACE & WORLD, INC. | [in black] *Cover design by Paul Bacon Studio* (Rob Cobuzio)

Spine Against a blue background, laterally: [in white] Keep the Aspidistra Flying] [in yellow] George Orwell | [horizontally in black] [publisher's motif in square frame] | HPL | 38

A.4d   *Second American Edition, 1957*

A NOVEL | KEEP THE | ASPIDISTRA | FLYING | GEORGE ORWELL | AUTHOR OF "1984" AND "BURMESE DAYS" | [publisher's device in circle diameter 2.1, in which is printed]: POPULAR LIBRARY | *15th* | *Anniversary* | [wavy line and dashes] | INTEGRITY | LEADERSHIP | SERVICE | [device of branches, leaves and stylised tree] | POPULAR LIBRARY . NEW YORK

Collation 112 leaves in a perfect binding, 17.4 × 10.1; [1–6] 7–221 [222–224]

Contents [1] [plot extract and extract from review] | [within a rectangular frame is a biographical note] [2] [extracts from reviews] [3] titlepage [4] imprint: [publisher's advertisement] | [rule] | POPULAR LIBRARY EDITION | Published in June 1957 | First American Edition, 1956 | Library of Congress Catalog Card Number: 56–5326 | Published by arrangement with Harcourt, Brace and Company | [details of first edition and translations] | PRINTED IN THE UNITED STATES OF AMERICA | All Rights Reserved | [5] Quotation adapted from I Corinthians [6] blank 7–221 text, on 221: THE END | [rule] | [publisher's advertisement] [222–224] publisher's advertisements

Binding Paper bound. Green edged leaves.

Front cover Around a roughly coloured picture of a man lying on a bed and a woman entering through a doorway is printed against a beige background: [publisher's device of stylised tree in an oval frame surrounded by] POPULAR GIANT [and below and to the right]: G193 KEEP THE | ASPIDISTRA | FLYING | GEORGE ORWELL | Complete and Unabridged [in top right corner]: 35c | "The most powerful | novel he (Orwell) | has produced" | LOS ANGELES TIMES [at foot]: AN EXCITING AND MEMORABLE NOVEL BY THE WORLD- | FAMOUS AUTHOR OF "1984" AND "BURMESE DAYS".

Back cover Within a beige stripe: [publisher's device as on front cover] | POPULAR LIBRARY | THE WORLD'S LEADING PUBLISHER OF POCKET-SIZE BOOKS | [within a red stripe are extracts from reviews] | [within a white panel is a stylised coloured picture of a man against a woman's face and long hair, to the right is a plot summary] | Originally Published at $3.75 by Harcourt, Brace and Co. | [stylised coloured drawing of Big Ben clock tower and Palace of Westminster]

Spine Against a beige background: [publisher's battlement motif and rule in white] | G193 | [laterally] KEEP THE ASPIDISTRA FLYING [white line] POPULAR | GIANT [white line] 35c

Notes
Published June 1957
35c

Locations
Orwell Archive

A.4e   *Reissue of Uniform Edition, 1959*

Titlepage as A.4b, but with new date: 1959

Collation and Contents as A.4b with additional imprint line: *Reprinted 1959*

Binding as A.4b, but with spine stamped in silver.

This reprinting corrects the comma error on page 24, but retains the other errors noted by Davison.

There were further reprints of the Uniform Edition in 1962 and 1966.

Locations
1959 – Orwell Archive

A.4f   *First Penguin Edition, 1962*

KEEP THE | ASPIDISTRA FLYING | [short rule] | George Orwell | Penguin Books | IN ASSOCIATION WITH | SECKER & WARBURG

Collation [A]–D^{16} E^8 F–I^{16}: 136 leaves (17.9 × 10.9); [1–6] 7–263 [264–272]

Contents [1] PENGUIN BOOKS | 1698 | KEEP THE ASPIDISTRA FLYING | GEORGE ORWELL | [penguin motif] [2] blank [3] titlepage [4] imprint: Penguin Books Ltd, Harmondsworth, Middlesex | AUSTRALIA: Penguin Books Pty Ltd, 762 Whitehorse Road, | Mitcham, Victoria | [short rule] | First published by Victor Gollancz 1936 | Published in Penguin Books 1962 | [short rule] | Made and printed in Great Britain | by Richard Clay & Company, Ltd, | Bungay, Suffolk | [copyright notice] [5] Quotation adapted from I Corinthians [6] blank 7–264 text [265] [penguin motif and publisher's advertisement] [266] blank [267–272] publisher's advertisements

Binding Paper bound.

Front cover [within top orange stripe]: [penguin motif] a Penguin Book 3'6 | [within white stripe]: Keep the | Aspidistra Flying | [rest of front has set against an orange background a black and white photograph of a street scene of terraced houses and a cobbled street strung with drying laundry and a woman with a baby carriage and child. Across the upper portion is printed in white]: George Orwell | [rule]

Back cover Printed on an orange background: a Penguin Book [penguin motif] | [within a white stripe]: Keep the | Aspidistra Flying | [against an orange background is a plot summary and review extract] | *For copyright reasons this edition* | *is not for sale in the U.S.A.*

Spine [against an orange background] [penguin motif] | [laterally in white]: George Orwell [and laterally in black]: Keep the Aspidistra Flying | [horizontally]: 1698

Inside front cover [Photograph of Orwell and biographical note] | Cover photograph by Roger Mayne | [publisher's advertisement]

Inside back cover publisher's advertisements

Reissues
This edition was reissued in 1963 with an amended imprint page, and with different advertisements on [267–270]. The covers are also slightly different: the white stripes are removed from front and back, the title is in both cases now printed in white and George Orwell on the front in black. On the spine the penguin motif is at the bottom. In all instances on the covers and spine the penguin motif is now within an oval frame.

The edition has been reissued in different covers since 1963: 1965, 1966, 1968, 1970, 1972, 1973, 1974, 1975, 1977, 1978, 1980, 1981, 1982, 1983, 1984, 1985
1989 Twentieth Century Classics edition, based on the Complete Works edition.

1973 cover illustration is by Ken Sequin and is a coloured line drawing of a young man in brown jacket and tie against an aspidistra in a green pot. 40p
1980 and 1985 cover is black with a photograph of an aspidistra in a brass pot on a lace mat and against a lace curtain. £1.25

Locations
British Library – copy received 21 February 1962
Cambridge University Library – 1962, 1985. Acquisition 21 February 1962.
Orwell Archive – 1962, 1963, 1980

A.4g   *Reissue of Uniform Edition, 1969*

Titlepage as A.4b but without a date.

Collation and Contents as A.4b, but with expanded list of books by Orwell on [2] and new imprint on [4]: MARTIN SECKER & WARBURG LTD., | 14 Carlisle Street, Soho Square, | London, W1V 6NN | *First published (Gollancz) 1936* | *Uniform edition 1954* | *Reprinted 1959, 1962, 1966, 1969* | 436 35006 8 | Reproduced and Printed by | Redwood Press Limited | Trowbridge & London
THE END is omitted from 303
Leaf size 19.3 × 12.7.

Binding Green paper on boards, embossed to resemble calico textured cloth. Off white endpapers.

Front and back covers Plain

Spine Stamped in gilt: [pyramid of six rules] | KEEP THE | ASPIDISTRA | FLYING | [small ornate device of 3 circles and lines] | GEORGE | ORWELL | [inverted pyramid of six rules] | SECKER & | WARBURG

Jacket Dull brown.
Front [Printed in silver]: GEORGE | ORWELL | [and in dark brown]: KEEP THE | ASPIDISTRA | FLYING
Back Plain.
Spine [laterally] [in silver]: ORWELL [and in dark brown]: KEEP THE | ASPIDISTRA FLYING| [horizontally in silver]: SECKER & | WARBURG
Front flap [in dark brown] [plot summary] | [bottom left]: Jacket design by | Format [bottom right]: 35s net | £1.75 net
Back flap [in dark brown] [plot summary continued] | SBN: 436 35006 8

Locations
Orwell Archive

A.4h   *Octopus Edition, 1976*

For titlepage transcription see *Animal Farm* A.10s

Keep the Aspidistra Flying is one of six Orwell novels in this compendium volume. The other novels are *Animal Farm*, *Burmese Days*, *A Clergyman's Daughter*, *Coming Up for Air*, and *Nineteen Eighty-Four*.
Published by Secker & Warburg|Octopus, 1976.
Keep the Aspidistra Flying is on pp. 573–737.
Hard bound with jacket.

Locations
Cambridge University Library. Acquisition 7 January 1977.

A.4i   *The Penguin Complete Novels of George Orwell Edition, 1983*

(Harmondsworth: Penguin, 1983) 925pp
A compendium edition of the following novels:

Animal Farm
Burmese Days
A Clergyman's Daughter
Coming Up for Air
Keep the Aspidistra Flying
Nineteen Eighty-Four

Paper bound
£4.95

Locations
Orwell Archive two copies

A.4j   *The Complete Works Edition, 1987*

THE COMPLETE WORKS OF | GEORGE ORWELL | VOLUME FOUR | Keep the | Aspidistra Flying | Quotation adapted from I Corinthians | SECKER & WARBURG | [short rule] | LONDON

Collation There are 10 unmarked gatherings: [A–D]¹⁶ [E–F]¹² [G–K]¹⁶; 152 leaves (23.1 ✕ 15.3); [i–viii] 1–276 [277–278] 279–286 [287–296]

Contents [i–ii] blank [iii] halftitle: THE COMPLETE WORKS OF | GEORGE ORWELL. FOUR | KEEP THE ASPIDISTRA FLYING [iv] blank [v] publisher's note [vi] blank [vii] titlepage [vii] imprint: [selective publishing history of editions and reissues] | [copyright notices] | [British Library Cataloguing in Publication Data] | ISBN 0–436–35026–0 | Typeset in Monophoto Bembo by | Northumberland Press Ltd, Gateshead, Tyne and Wear | Printed and bound in Great Britain by | Richard Clay Ltd, Bungay, Suffolk 1–[277] text, on [277]: THE END [278] blank 279–[287] textual note [288–296] blank

Binding Blue paper on boards, embossed to resemble calico textured cloth. Black endpapers.

Front and back covers Plain.

Spine Stamped in gilt: [double rule] | GEORGE | ORWELL | [rule] | Keep the | Aspidistra | Flying | [double rule] | SECKER & | WARBURG
Reprinted 1996

Locations
Orwell Archive
Robarts Library, University of Toronto

TRANSLATIONS

All Orwell Archive unless otherwise noted

DUTCH

A.4.T1   *Houd de Sanseferia Hoog*, 1973

Amsterdam: Meulenhoff
Translated by Else Hoog
Paper bound
Reissued 1983

FRENCH

A.4.T2a   *Et Vive l'Aspidistra!*, 1960

Paris: Gallimard
Translated by Yvonne Davet
Paper bound
12F

A.4.T2b   *Et Vive l'Aspidistra*, 1982

Paris: Editions Champ Libre
Translated by Yvonne Davet
Paper bound
90F

GERMAN

A.4.T3   *Die Wonnen der Aspidistra*, 1983

Zurich: Diogenes
Translated by Nikolaus Stingl
Paper bound

Reissued 1983

ITALIAN

A.4.T4a   *Fiorira l'Aspidistra*, 1960

Milano: Mondadori
Translated by Giorgio Monicelli
Published September 1960

A.4.T4b   *Fiorira l'Aspidistra*, 1960

Milano: Club Degli Editori
Translated by Giorgio Monicelli
Published October 1960

NORWEGIAN

A.4.T5   *Vi Ma Ha En Aspidistra*, 1978

Trondhjem: J.W. Cappelens
Translated by Kari Risvik
Paper bound

PORTUGUESE

A.4.T6   *Moinhos de Vento*, 1984

Rio de Janeiro: Editora Nova Fronteira
Translated by Waltensir Dutra
Paper bound

SPANISH

A.4.T7   *¡Venciste, Rosemary!*, 1976

Barcelona: Ediciones Destino
Translated by José Domínguez

Reissued in paperback in May 1981 by the same publisher.

SWEDISH

A.4.T8   *Leve Aspidistran!*, 1975

Stockholm: Rabén & Sjögren
Translated by Olof Hoffsten
Paper bound

A.5   THE ROAD TO WIGAN PIER

> It is not a novel this time but a sort of book of essays, but I am afraid I have made rather a muck of parts of it.'[1]

Composition and publication

With *Keep the Aspidistra Flying* finished in January 1936, Victor Gollancz commissioned Orwell to write a book about the condition of the working classes and the unemployed in the north of England. His offer of a £500 advance, payable in instalments over two years when the contract was signed, the manuscript delivered, and on publication, convinced Orwell to take up the offer.

At the end of January he gave up his job at Booklovers' Corner in Hampstead and his flat at Lawford Road, Kentish Town, and on the 31st he travelled north by train to Coventry, and for the next five days by bus and on foot through Birmingham, Stourbridge, Wolverhampton, Stafford and Macclesfield to Manchester where he arrived on 4 February. He stayed with Frank Meade, a trade union official, from 6–10 February and then at Meade's suggestion went to Wigan where he stayed first with an unemployed miner and then in lodgings above a tripe shop until the end of the month. In the middle of the month he told Cyril Connolly:

> I am living here with a family of coal-miners, employed and unemployed. After staying a month in Lancs. I intend to go on to Yorkshire or Durham or both & have a look at the mines & miners there. I haven't been down any coal mines yet but am arranging to do so. The miners here are very nice people, very warm-hearted & willing to take me for granted. I would like to stay a good long time in the north, 6 months or a year, only it means being away from my girl & also I shall have to come back and do some work after about a couple of months.[2]

Writing was difficult in his squalid lodgings, although he managed to correct and revise the proofs of *Keep the Aspidistra Flying*. His letters at this time are full of descriptions of the trip. At the end of February he wrote to Richard Rees:

> I thought you might like to hear how I am getting on in partibus infidelium. Your introductions were of the greatest value to me, especially that to Meade,[3] who put me in touch with a friend at Wigan who was exactly what I wanted. I have been here nearly three weeks and have collected reams of notes and statistics, though in what way I shall use them I haven't made up my mind yet. I have been living and associating almost entirely with miners, largely unemployed of course. The lads at the NUWM [National Unemployed Workers' Movement] have been of great service to me and everyone has been most willing to answer questions and show me over their houses. I have gone into the housing question rather minutely, because it is a very urgent one here and I gather in most places in the north. I have only been down one coal mine so far but hope to go down some more in Yorkshire. It was for me a pretty devastating experience and it is a fearful thought that the labour of crawling as far as the coal face (about a mile in this case but as much as 3 miles in some mines), which was enough to put my legs out of action for four days, is only the beginning and ending of a miner's day's work, and his real work comes in between. Have you ever been down a mine? I don't think I shall ever feel quite the same about coal again.[4]

It was work which we would today label research, and even his letters must have been helping him to shape his ideas, although he told Rees in the same letter that 'work' was 'impossible, of course, in these surroundings.'

He moved on to Liverpool, Sheffield, and Leeds, where he stayed with his sister, and then to Barnsley, where he wrote to Jack Common,

> I have been in these barbarous regions for about two months and have had a very interesting time and picked up lots of ideas for my next book, but I admit I am beginning to pine to be back in the languorous South and also to start doing some work again, which of course is impossible in the surroundings I have been in.[5]

He returned to London on 30 March.

Orwell wrote a diary of his two months in the north, dated 31 January–25 March 1936. It is a typescript, which, along with other notes, forms the basis of *The Road to Wigan Pier*. But the diary was typed after he returned south, perhaps as a first draft of the final book and perhaps as an experiment with the format.[6] His other notes, some of which he used for the book, include facts and figures collected at the Wigan Public Library on conditions in the coal mines, mine accidents, housing and living conditions. Other notes include details of a communist meeting he attended in Liverpool and a fascist meeting in Barnsley where he heard Oswald Mosley speak.

On 3 April, back in the south of England at his new home, The Stores, Wallington, Hertfordshire, a village shop that he was thinking of re-opening, he wrote to Jack Common, somewhat modestly, 'I collected some interesting material for my new book while in Yorkshire and Lancashire, and only hope I shall be able to make use of it.'[7] The question of opening The Stores as a going concern was not unconnected with the trip north and with what he called 'this business of class-breaking'.[8] In the same letter to Jack Common he wrote,

> The working classes are very patient under it all. All the two months I was up north, when I spent my entire time in asking people questions about how much dole they got, what they had to eat etc I was never once socked on the jaw and only once told to go to hell, and then by a woman who was deaf and thought I was a rate-collector. This question has been worrying me for a long time and part of my next book is to be about it.

Actually writing the book demanded time and fundamental decisions. In mid-April he told Richard Rees, 'I haven't begun my new book yet but am all set to do so. It is not going to be a novel this time.'[9] And later that spring he told Geoffrey Gorer that he was about to marry Eileen, although 'it will always be hand to mouth as I don't see myself ever writing a best-seller. I have made a fairly good start on my new book.'[10] In 1938, writing to Jack Common, he confirmed the precariousness of his financial situation at this time: 'When Eileen and I were first married, when I was writing Wigan Pier, we had so little money that sometimes we hardly knew where the next meal was coming from, but we found we could rub along in a remarkable manner with spuds and so forth.'[11]

Later in the summer of 1936 he told Henry Miller 'I agree about English poverty. It is awful. Recently I was travelling among the worst parts of the coal areas in Lancashire and Yorkshire – I am doing a book about it now – and it is dreadful to see how the people have collapsed and lost all their guts in the last ten years.'[12] In October 1936 he told Jack Common, 'Things are prospering tolerably. I have just finished the rough draft of my book and begun on the revision, which will take me till some time in December. It is not a novel this time but a sort of book of essays, but I am afraid I have made rather a muck of parts of it.'[13]

Orwell sent the manuscript of *The Road to Wigan Pier* to Leonard Moore, on 15 December 1936, anticipating that it would not be included in Gollancz's successful new Left Book Club list, launched in May 1936, 'as it is too fragmentary and, on the surface, not very left-wing.'[14] But on the 19th Gollancz telegraphed Orwell, asking him to see him about making it a Club choice, and following the meeting Moore wrote to Gollancz on 29 December that he understood from Orwell that it was 'practically certain' to be a Left Book Club choice for March 1937.

The meeting on Monday 21 December 1936 was important also for the discussion that presumably took place about illustrating the book. A scrap of blotting paper survives with names and addresses of possible illustrators, in Gollancz's hand-writing.[15] Norman Collins, Deputy Chairman of Gollancz, wrote to people who might have suitable photographs, including the Rev Gilbert Shaw:

> Mr. George Orwell has written a new book (which we are making a future choice of the Left Book Club) dealing with life in the distressed areas. Any photographic material of this kind which you could let us have – either slum interiors or exteriors – would therefore serve a most useful purpose. We are going to make the book fully documentary, both as regards the text and as regards the pictures, and the finished work will probably contain some forty-eight plates.[16]

The book was illustrated with 32 photographs, without acknowledgements. Both the Left Book Club edition and the public first edition included the illustrations, as did the Left Book Club reissue of Part I, and the first American edition in 1958.

The book was published without having been proof-read by Orwell because by the time the proofs were ready he was in Spain, fighting in the Civil War. Although he had authorised Eileen to check the proofs in his absence, in the event she did not see them either, the haste to get the book out was so great. In January she wrote to Christy & Moore expressing satisfaction that the book appeared not to contravene libel and censorship laws and hoping that the in-house proof-correctors had not made too many changes. The *Complete Works* edition lists those changes including Gollancz's alteration of Orwell's 'copulating' to his own 'courting', and the compromise 'treading'. There is an uncorrected proof in the Orwell Archive.

From Spain in mid-February 1937 Orwell wrote to thank the novelist James Hanley for his appreciation of *The Road to Wigan Pier*: 'I am glad you found the book interesting. It is due out about March 10th I believe, but I shall probably still be in the line here when it comes out, so I shan't know how it gets on.'[17] The book was in fact published on 8 March 1937 in both a Left Book Club edition and a public edition. The reviews were mixed. From Monflorite Orwell wrote to Eileen: 'Yes, Pollitt's review was pretty bad, tho' of course good as publicity. I suppose he must have heard I was serving in the POUM militia [Partido Obrero de Unificacion Marxista – the Workers' Party of Marxist Unification]. I don't pay much attention to the Sunday Times reviews, as G [Gollancz] advertises so much there that they daren't down his books, but the Observer was an improvement on the last time.'[18] He wrote in more detail to Gollancz in May from Barcelona:

> I didn't get an opportunity earlier to write and thank you for the introduction you wrote to Wigan Pier, in fact I didn't even see the book, or rather the BC [Book Club] edition of it, till about 10 days ago when I came home on leave … I liked the introduction very much, though of course I could have answered some of the criticisms you made. It was the kind of discussion of what one is really talking about that one always wants and never seems to get from the professional reviewers. I have had lots of reviews sent on to me, some of them very hostile but I should think mostly good from a publicity point of view. Also great numbers of letters from readers.[19]

The title, *The Road to Wigan Pier*, created interest at the time of publication and continues to draw questions. In a 1943 BBC radio programme Orwell was asked, 'How long is Wigan Pier and what is the Wigan Pier?' His answer is worth quoting in full:

> Well, I am afraid I must tell you that Wigan Pier doesn't exist. I made a journey specially to see it in 1936, and I couldn't find it. It did once exist, however, and to judge form the photographs it must have been about twenty feet long.
>
> Wigan is in the middle of the mining areas, and though it's a very pleasant place in some ways its scenery is not its strong point. The landscape is mostly slag heaps, looking like the mountains of the moon, and mud and soot and so forth. For some reason, though it's not worse than fifty other places, Wigan has always been picked on as a symbol of the ugliness of the industrial areas. At one time, on one of the little muddy canals that run round the town, there used to be a tumble-down wooden jetty; and by way of a joke someone nicknamed this Wigan Pier. The joke caught on locally, and then the music-hall comedians got hold of it, and they are the ones who have succeeded in keeping Wigan Pier alive as a byword, long after the place itself had been demolished.[20]

The Orwell Archive holds Orwell's *Wigan Pier* notes and the diary, as well as peripheral material which he collected on the trip north. This includes the miners' pay slips on which he, incorrectly as it turns out, made his calculations about earnings.

A.5a   *First Edition, 1937*

THE ROAD TO WIGAN PIER | by | GEORGE ORWELL | With a Foreword by | VICTOR GOLLANCZ | LONDON | VICTOR GOLLANCZ LTD | 1937

Collation [AP]–HP⁸ [A–B]⁸ IP–QP⁸; 144 leaves (21.5 × 14.0); [i–vii] viii [ix–xi] xii–xxiv [1–5] 6–104 [105–136, numbered]: 1–32 [137]–150 [151–153] 154–264

Contents [i–ii] blank [iii] halftitle: THE ROAD TO WIGAN PIER [iv] advertisements for books by Orwell [v] titlepage [vi] imprint: *Printed in Great Britain by* | The Camelot Press Ltd., London and Southampton [vii]–viii list of illustrations [ix] halftitle: FOREWORD [x] blank [xi]–xxiv foreword by Victor Gollancz [1] halftitle: THE ROAD TO WIGAN PIER [2] blank [3] halftitle: PART I [4] blank [5]–104 text [105–136] illustrations [137]–150 text [151] halftitle: PART II [152] blank [153]–264 text, on 264: THE END

Binding Limp orange cloth. Off white endpapers.

Front cover THE | ROAD TO WIGAN PIER | by | GEORGE ORWELL | LEFT BOOK CLUB EDITION | NOT FOR SALE TO THE PUBLIC

Back cover Plain.

Spine THE | ROAD | TO | WIGAN | PIER | by | GEORGE | ORWELL | GOLLANCZ

Paper
White bulky esparto antique wove
34 lines per page
12 pt Baskerville

Locations
Cambridge University Library. Acquisition 17 April 1984.
Orwell Archive – four copies

Variant
200 copies were bound without the foreword. The British Library copy is one of these. The BL copy is dated 24 February 1937, ie before the publication date.

Contemporary reviews
A. Calder Marshall *Time and Tide* (20 March 1937)
Times Literary Supplement (27 March 1937)
Adelphi (May 1937)
Hamish Miles *New Statesman and Nation* (1 May 1937)

Notes
Left Book Club edition was 44,150 copies
2s 6d
Gollancz's Foreword is dated 11 January 1937
In some copies the illustrations are placed in the wrong order, 1–16 following 17–32.
A short extract was published in 'Presenting the Future', *News Chronicle* (10 June 1937) 6, the fourth of a five-part series illustrating the work of 'young writers already famous among critics, less well-known by the public.'[C.099].

A.5b *First Public Edition, 1937*

THE ROAD TO WIGAN PIER | by | GEORGE ORWELL | LONDON | VICTOR GOLLANCZ LTD | 1937

Collation [AP]⁸ CP–HP⁸ [A–B]⁸ IP–QP⁸; 136 leaves (21.7 × 13.6); [i–vii] viii [1–5] 6–104 [105–136, numbered]: 1–32 [137]–150 [151–153] 154–264

Contents [i–ii] blank [iii] halftitle: THE ROAD TO WIGAN PIER [iv] advertisements for books by Orwell [v] titlepage [vi] imprint: *Printed in Great Britain by* | The Camelot Press Ltd., London and Southampton [vii]–viii list of illustrations [1] halftitle: THE ROAD TO WIGAN PIER [2] blank [3] halftitle: PART I [4] blank [5]–104 text [105–136] illustrations [137]–150 text [151] halftitle: PART II [152] blank [153]–264 text, on 264: THE END

Binding Blue calico textured cloth on boards. Off white endpapers.

Front and back covers Plain.

Spine Stamped in yellow: THE | ROAD | TO | WIGAN | PIER | BY | GEORGE | ORWELL | GOLLANCZ

Locations
Cambridge University Library – rebound. Acquisition 3 March 1937.
Orwell Archive – two copies

Notes
This is really only a reissue of the first edition, without the foreword, with a new titlepage, and in a variant binding.
Published 8 March 1937
10s 6d
2,150 copies

Contemporary reviews
Walter Greenwood, *The Tribune*, 12 March 1937, p12.
Hugh Massingham *Observer* (14 March 1937)
Edward Shanks *Sunday Times* (14 March 1937)
Harry Pollitt, *Daily Worker*, 17 March 1937.
Arthur Calder-Marshall, *Time and Tide*, 20 March 1937, p382.
Harold J. Laski, *Left News*, March 1937, pp275–276.
Douglas Goldring, *The Fortnightly Review*, April 1937, pp505–506.
Hamish Miles, *The New Statesman and Nation*, 1 May 1937, pp724, 726.

A.5c   *Reissue of Part I of the Left Book Club Edition, 1937*

THE ROAD TO WIGAN PIER | by | GEORGE ORWELL | LONDON | VICTOR GOLLANCZ LTD | 1937

Collation [AP]⁸ CP–HP⁸ [A–B]⁸ IP⁷. The extra leaf IP1 is pasted in; 79 leaves (21.5 × 13.7); [i–vii] viii [1–5] 6–104 [105–136, numbered]: 1–32 [137]–150

Contents [i–ii] blank [iii] halftitle: THE ROAD TO WIGAN PIER [iv] advertisements for books by Orwell [v] titlepage [vi] imprint: *Printed in Great Britain by* | The Camelot Press Ltd., London and Southampton [vii]–viii list of illustrations [1] halftitle: THE ROAD TO WIGAN PIER [2] blank [3] halftitle: PART I [4] blank [5]–104 text [105–136] illustrations [137]–150 text

Binding Limp orange cloth. Off white endpapers.

Front cover THE | ROAD TO WIGAN PIER | by | GEORGE ORWELL | LEFT BOOK CLUB EDITION | ABBREVIATED . PART ONE ONLY

Back cover Plain.

Spine THE | ROAD | TO | WIGAN | PIER | by | GEORGE | ORWELL | GOLLANCZ

Notes
Published May 1937 as a Left Book Club Supplementary book
1s 0d
890 copies

Locations
Orwell Archive

A.5d   *First American Edition, 1958*

The Road to Wigan Pier | BY GEORGE ORWELL | WITH A FOREWORD BY VICTOR GOLLANCZ | *Harcourt, Brace and Company* [publisher's monogram device] *New York*

Collation Nine unmarked gatherings of 16 leaves, arranged: [A–I]¹⁶; 144 leaves (20.4 × 13.6); [i–vii] viii [ix] × [xi] xii–xxiv [1–5] 6–104 [105–136, numbered]: 1–32 [137]–150 [151–153] 154–264

Contents [i–ii] blank [iii] halftitle: THE ROAD TO WIGAN PIER [iv] list of books by Orwell [v] titlepage [vi] imprint: first American edition 1958 | Library of Congress Catalog Card Number: 58:10888 | Printed in the United States of America [vii]–viii list of illustrations [ix]–x publisher's note [xi]–xxiv foreword [1] halftitle: THE ROAD TO WIGAN PIER [2] blank [3] halftitle: PART I [4] blank [5]–104 text [105–136] illustrations [137]–150 text [151] halftitle: PART II [152] blank [153]–264 text, on 264: THE END

Binding Blue calico-textured cloth on boards. Off white endpapers.

Front and back covers Plain.

Spine Stamped in silver: *The* | *Road* | *to* | *Wigan* | *Pier* | [within a silver frame is a block of silver against which is picked out]: GEORGE | ORWELL | [and beneath in silver]: *Harcourt, Brace* | *and* | *Company* | [within a silver frame, publisher's monogram device]

Jacket Off white, except spine.
Front In black and blue is a drawing of a man on a railway line in front of a coal wagon. Across the top is printed in blue: GEORGE | ORWELL [and to the right of the wagon is printed in blue]: THE | ROAD | TO | WIGAN | PIER
Back [Extracts from view of Orwell] | HARCOURT, BRACE AND COMPANY | 750 Third Avenue, New York 17, N.Y.
Spine Against a black background is printed in white: ORWELL [and in blue]: THE | ROAD | TO | WIGAN | PIER | HARCOURT, | BRACE | AND COMPANY | [publisher's monogram device]
Front flap [extract from review and summary] | *Illustrated with 32 pages of photographs* | *Jacket design by Seymour Chwast*
Back flap [biographical sketch of Orwell and list of his books]

Notes
This is really only a reissue of the British First Edition with a new titlepage and prelims. The illustrations are reproduced from the first edition plates.

Contemporary reviews
Robert Hatch, *The Nation* 30 August 1958, pp97–98.
Philip Toynbee, *Encounter*, August 1959, pp81–82.

Locations
Orwell Archive

A.5e   *Uniform Edition, 1959*

THE ROAD TO | WIGAN PIER | BY | GEORGE ORWELL | LONDON | SECKER & WARBURG | 1959

Collation [A]–N⁸; O⁴ P⁸; 116 leaves (18.3 × 12.3); [1–7] 8–119 [120–123] 124–230 [231–232]

Contents [1] halftitle: THE ROAD TO WIGAN PIER [2] list of books by Orwell [3] titlepage [4] imprint: MARTIN SECKER & WARBURG LTD., | 7 John Street, Bloomsbury, | London W.C.1 | *First published (Gollancz) 1937* | *Uniform Edition 1959* | *Printed in Great Britain by* | *The Camelot Press Ltd., London and Southampton* [5] halftitle: PART I [6] blank [7]–119 text of Part I [120] blank [121] halftitle: PART II [122] blank [123]–230 text of Part II, on 230: THE END [231–232] blank

Binding Green calico textured cloth on boards. Off white endpapers. Purple topped leaves.

Spine Stamped in silver: [pyramid of 6 lines] | THE | ROAD TO | WIGAN | PIER | [small ornate device of circles and dots] | GEORGE | ORWELL | [inverted pyramid of 6 lines] | SECKER & | WARBURG

Jacket
Front Irregular beige stripe across top on which is printed in black: The road | to Wigan Pier | [and in white]: George Orwell [the lower part consists of a drawing in black, white and grey of three men idling outside a cottage and against a crumbling wall].
Back Against a grey background a list of the Uniform edition of Orwell is printed in black. To the right is a white stripe and the beige, black and white sections wrapped around from the spine.
Spine The spine is divided into a beige, a black and a white section, wrapped around from the stripe and illustration on the front cover. In the beige is: The road | to Wigan pier [in the black is printed in white]: George Orwell [with a continuation of the cottage drawing from the front and four hanging pieces of laundry in white] [and in the white section]: Secker & | Warburg
Front flap [summary] | Jacket design by | DENIS PIPER 18s | net
Back flap [summary continued | extracts from reviews] | APT|P605

Notes
This edition omits the foreword and the photographs.
18s 0d

Locations
Cambridge University Library. Acquisition 27 April 1959.
Orwell Archive, with jacket.

Reissues
Reprinted in 1965, by D.R. Hillman & Sons Ltd, Frome.
Bound in brown linen grain cloth on boards.
There are two copies at the E.J. Pratt Library, Victoria University in the University of Toronto.

Reprinted in 1969 and 1973, by Redwood Press Limited, Trowbridge, Wiltshire.
Bound in green paper, embossed to resemble bead-grain cloth, on boards.
Copy at E.J. Pratt Library.

A.5f   *Second American Edition, 1961*

GEORGE ORWELL | The | Road | to | Wigan | Pier | [publisher's shield and fleur de lys device] | A BERKLEY MEDALLION BOOK | published by | THE BERKLEY PUBLISHING CORPORATION

Collation 96 unsigned leaves in a perfect binding, (17.9 × 10.6); [i–iv] v [vi] vii–xvi [17–18] 19–191 [192]

Contents [i] book extract, and extracts from reviews [ii] blank [iii] titlepage [iv] imprint: *Published by arrangement with | Harcourt Brace and Company, Inc.* | All rights reserved | BERKLEY EDITION, APRIL, 1961 | *BERKLEY MEDALLION BOOKS are published by* | *The Berkley Publishing Corporation,* | *101 Fifth Avenue, New York 3, New York* | Printed in the United States of America v publisher's note [vi] blank vii–xvi foreword [17] halftitle: *THE ROAD TO WIGAN PIER* [18] blank 19–191 text [192] publisher's advertisements

Binding Paper bound. Red edged leaves.

Front cover In red, orange, yellow, brown, purple and black is a montage of drawings of a pit head, man in a cloth cap, miners digging, and a drawing of Orwell. At top left in white: Berkley | [shield and fleur de lys device] | MEDALLION | BG517 | 50c [across the top in yellow]: GEORGE ORWELL [and beneath in black]: The Road to | Wigan Pier | [and beneath in white is an extract from a review] | [in bottom left in white]: COMPLETE | AND | UNABRIDGED

Back cover In white against a blue background: [extract from review] | [in yellow]: $575.00 per year … | [and in white, summary | [in off white lower third is an advertisement for *Down and Out in Paris and London*]

Spine [against a blue background]: BG517 [and vertically, letter by letter]: THE ROAD TO WIGAN PIER Orwell | [horizontally]: BERKLEY [[shield and fleur de lys device | MEDALLION

Notes
Published April 1961
50c
Omits photographs

A.5g   *First Penguin Edition, 1962*

THE ROAD | TO WIGAN PIER | *George Orwell* | PENGUIN BOOKS | IN ASSOCIATION WITH | SECKER & WARBURG

Collation [T–R.W.P.–A]–T–R.W.P.–C¹⁶ T–R.W.P.–D⁸ T–R.W.P.–E – T– R.W.P.–G¹⁶; 104 leaves (17.3 × 10.4); [1–4] 5–203 [204–208]

Contents [1] halftitle: PENGUIN BOOKS | 1700 | THE ROAD TO WIGAN PIER | GEORGE ORWELL | [penguin device] [2] blank [3] titlepage [4] imprint: Penguin Books Ltd, Harmondsworth, Middlesex | AUSTRALIA: Penguin Books Pty Ltd, 762 Whitehorse Road | Mitcham, Victoria | [short rule] | First published by Victor Gollancz 1937 | Published in Penguin Books 1962 | [short rule] Made and printed in Great Britain | by Cox and Wyman Ltd, | London, Reading, and Fakenham | [copyright notice] 5–[204] text [205] penguin motif and publisher's notice [206] blank [207–208] publisher's advertisements

Binding Paper bound. Covers orange.

Front cover [top left in white is penguin motif] [in black]: a Penguin Book 3'– | [rule] The Road to | Wigan Pier | [rule] | George Orwell [in white] | [rule] | against a photograph of a pit head in grey is a black and grey drawing of a crowd
Back cover [top left in white is penguin motif] [in black]: a Penguin Book | [rule] | The Road to | Wigan Pier | [rule] | summary and extracts from reviews | *For copyright reasons this edition is not* | *for sale in the U.S.A.*

Spine Laterally: George Orwell [in white] [and in black]: The Road to Wigan Pier | [and horizontally]: [penguin motif in white oval] | 1700

Inside front cover [photograph of Orwell] | *Vernon Richards* | [biographical summary] | Cover design by Alan Fletcher | [publisher's notice]

Inside back cover Publisher's advertisements for books by Orwell

Notes
Omits photographs
3s 0d
Reissued in 1962, and in 1963, 1966, 1967, 1969, 1970, 1971, 1972 (twice), 1974 (twice), 1975 (twice), 1976, 1977, 1978, 1979, 1980, 1981, 1982, 1983, 1984 (twice), with a variety of jackets
1989 Twentieth Century Classics edition, based on the Complete Works edition.

Locations
Cambridge University Library – 1962, 1975, 1984. Acquisitions 26 February 1962, 28 July 1975.

Orwell Archive – 1962
> – 1981 – with photograph of man in flat cap
> – 1984 – with painting of miners in lift cage at pit head

A.5h   *Heinemann Edition, 1965*

George Orwell | The Road to Wigan Pier | WITH AN INTRODUCTION BY | Richard Hoggart | *Professor of English,* | *University of Birmingham* | [publisher's device of windmill and monogram] | HEINEMANN EDUCATIONAL | BOOKS LTD. LONDON

Collation [A]–G^{16} H^{16} (but H15 is the back free endpaper and H16 is the back pasted down endpaper); 126 leaves plus two leaves as back endpapers (18.3 × 12.1); [i–v] vi–xxvi [5–7] 8–119 [120–123] 124–230 [endpapers not included in collation]

Contents [i] halftitle: THE ROAD TO WIGAN PIER [2] blank [iii] titlepage [iv] imprint: Heinemann Educational Books Ltd | [list of publisher's locations] | Introduction [copyright symbol] Richard Hoggart 1965 | First published 1937 | First published in this edition 1965 | Published by | Heinemann Educational Books Ltd | 15–16 Queen Street, Mayfair, London W.1 | Printed in Great Britain by | Butler & Tanner Ltd, Frome and London [v]–xxvi introduction [5] halftitle: PART I [6] blank [7]–119 text of Part I [120] blank [121] halftitle: PART II [122] blank [123]–230 text of Part II, on 230: THE END [endpapers not included in contents]

Binding Grey and black paper, embossed to resemble linen grain cloth, on boards. Off white endpapers – front only; see note in collation on back endpapers.

Front cover Against a black background is printed in orange: George Orwell | [and in white]: The road to Wigan pier | Introduction by Richard Hoggart | [in orange against a black and grey background depicting the roofs of terraced cottages is a pithead]

Back cover As front without the names and title.

Spine Black and grey background wrapping from covers, on which is printed laterally in orange: George Orwell [and in white]: The road to Wigan pier | [and horizontally in white]: [publisher's device of windmill and monogram]

Notes
Omits photographs
The text of this edition is a reissue of the 1959 Uniform Edition.

Locations
Orwell Archive – two copies
Cambridge University Library

A.5i   *Reissue of Uniform Edition, 1969*

THE ROAD TO | WIGAN PIER | BY | GEORGE ORWELL | LONDON | SECKER & WARBURG

Collation Eight unmarked gatherings arranged: [A–F]^{16} [G]^{4} [H]^{16}; 116 leaves (19.4 × 12.2); [1–7] 8–119 [120–123] 124–230 [231–232]

Contents [1] halftitle: THE ROAD TO WIGAN PIER [2] list of books by Orwell [3] titlepage [4] imprint: MARTIN SECKER & WARBURG LTD., | 14 Carlisle Street, Soho Square, | London, W1V 6NN | *First published (Gollancz) 1937* | *Uniform Edition 1959* | Reprinted 1969 | 436 35008 4 | *Reproduced and Printed in Great Britain by* | *Redwood Press Limited.* | *Trowbridge and London* [5] halftitle: PART I [6] blank [7]–119 text of Part I [120] blank [121] halftitle: PART II [122] blank [123]–230 text of Part II [231–232] blank

Binding Green paper, embossed to resemble calico textured cloth, on boards. Off white endpapers.

Spine Stamped in gilt: [pyramid of 6 lines] | THE | ROAD TO | WIGAN | PIER | [small ornate device of circles and dots] | GEORGE | ORWELL | [inverted pyramid of 6 lines] | SECKER & | WARBURG

Jacket Dull brown.
Front [Printed in silver]: GEORGE | ORWELL | [and in dark brown]: THE ROAD | TO WIGAN PIER
Back Plain.
Spine laterally [in silver]: ORWELL [and in dark brown]: THE ROAD | TO WIGAN PIER [horizontally in silver]: SECKER & | WARBURG
Front flap [in dark brown] [summary] | [bottom left]: Jacket design by | Format | [bottom right]: £1.75 | 35s. | Net
Back flap [Continuation of summary from front flap] | 224 pages | SBN: 436 35008 4

Location
Orwell Archive

Notes
Omits photographs.
This is a reissue of the 1959 Uniform Edition.

A.5j   *The Penguin Complete Longer Non-Fiction of George Orwell edition
1983.*

(Harmondsworth: Penguin, 1983) 488pp

The edition consists of:

Down and Out in Paris and London 7–153
The Road to Wigan Pier 155–299
Homage to Catalonia 301–467
Looking Back on the Spanish War 469–488

Paper bound
£3.95

A.5k   *Complete Works Edition, 1986*

THE COMPLETE WORKS OF | GEORGE ORWELL | VOLUME FIVE | The Road to | Wigan Pier | SECKER & WARBURG | [short rule] | LONDON

Collation Eight unmarked gatherings arranged: [A–E]^{16} [F–G]^{12} [H]^{16}; 120 leaves (23.3 × 15.4); [i–viii] [1–2] 3–109 [110–112] 113–214 [215] 216–225 [226] 227–[232]. There are two gatherings of eight leaves each, with photographs, between gatherings [C] and [D] (between pages 88 and 89). These illustration pages are unnumbered.

Contents [i] halftitle: THE COMPLETE WORKS OF | GEORGE ORWELL. FIVE | THE ROAD TO WIGAN PIER [ii] blank [iii] publisher's note [iv] blank [v] titlepage [vi] imprint: selective publishing history of editions and reissues | [copyright notice] | [British Library Cataloguing in Publication Data] | ISBN 0–436–35027–0 | Typeset in Monophoto Bembo by | Northumberland Press Ltd, Gateshead, Tyne and Wear | Printed and bound in Great Britain by | Richard Clay Ltd, Bungay, Suffolk [vii] publisher's note [viii] blank [1] halftitle: PART I [2] blank 3–109 text of Part I [110] blank [111] halftitle: PART II [112] blank 113–[215] text of Part II, on [215]: THE END 216–225 appendix [226] blank 227–[232] textual note.
The appendix is Victor Gollancz's Foreword of the First Edition.

Binding Blue paper on boards, embossed to resemble calico textured cloth. Black endpapers.

Front and back covers Plain.

Spine Stamped in gilt: [double rule] | GEORGE | ORWELL | [rule] | The Road | to | Wigan Pier | [double rule] | SECKER & | WARBURG
Reprinted 1996

Locations
Cambridge University Library
Robarts Library, University of Toronto

MISCELLANEOUS

A.5.M1   *Short extract from The Road to Wigan Pier*

Published in *If all the Beats were Gone* ed. Christopher Cornford and John Norris Wood (London: Royal College of Art, 1977) 21–22.

TRANSLATIONS

All Orwell Archive unless otherwise noted

DUTCH
A.5.T1   *De Weg Naar Wigan*, 1973

Amsterdam: De Arbeiderspers
A Synopsis Book
Translated by Joop Waasdorp
Paper bound

FINNISH
A.5.T2   *Tie Wiganin Aallonmurtajalle*, 1986

Helsinki: Werner Söderström Osakeyhtiö
Translated by Leevi Lehto
Paper bound

FRENCH
A.5.T3   *Le Quai de Wigan*, 1982

Paris: Editions Champ Libre
Translated by Michel Pétris
80F
Paper bound

GERMAN
A.5.T4   *Der Weg nach Wigan Pier*, 1982

Zurich: Diogenes
Translated [and with a Nachwort] by Manfred Papst
Reissued 1983
Paper bound

ITALIAN

A.5.T5a   *La Strada di Wigan Pier*, 1960

Verona: Arnoldo Mondadori
Translated by Giorgio Monicelli
Hard bound

A.5.T5b   *La Strada di Wigan Pier*, 1982

Verona: Arnoldo Mondadori
Translated by Giorgio Monicelli, with an Introduction by Francesco Marroni
A reissue of A.5.T5a
Paper bound
L4500

NORWEGIAN

A.5.T6   *Veien til Wigan*, 1978

Oslo: Cappelen
Translated by Einar Schøning
Paper bound

PORTUGUESE

A.5.T7   *A Caminho de Wigan*, 1985

Rio de Janeiro: Editora Nova Fronteira
Translated by Glaucia Freire Sposito
Paper bound

SPANISH

A.5.T8a   *El Camino de Wigan Pier*, 1976

Barcelona: Ediciones Destino
Translated by Ester Donato
Hard bound

A.5.T8b   *El Camino de Wigan Pier*, 1982

Barcelona: Ediciones Destino
Translated by Ester Donato
Paper bound
Destinolibro 189
A reissue of A.5.T8a

SWEDISH

A.5.T9a   *Vägen till Wigan Pier*, 1976

Stockholm: Rabén & Sjögren
Translated by Lars Bäckström
4 pages of photographs
Paper bound

A.5.T9b   *Vägen till Wigan Pier*, 1983

Stockholm: Litteraturfrämjandet
Translated by Lars Bäckström
A new edition
Paper bound

A.6   HOMAGE TO CATALONIA

I greatly hope I come out of this alive if only to write a book about it.[1]

Composition and publication

In late December 1936, immediately after submitting the manuscript of *The Road to Wigan Pier* and finalising the arrangements for its publication, Orwell left for Spain. In *Homage to Catalonia*, Orwell wrote:

> I had come to Spain with some notion of writing newspaper articles, but I had joined the militia almost immediately, because at that time and in that atmosphere it seemed the only conceivable thing to do.[2]

And so he fought in the Civil War. On 30 December in Barcelona, he enlisted in the POUM militia [Partido Obrero de Unificacion Marxista – the Workers' Party of Marxist Unification], and in early January 1937 he went to the front line at Alcubierre. Before he left England Secker & Warburg had said they would take any book he wrote as a result of his experiences. He wrote to Victor Gollancz in May 1937 in part to confirm that he had not forgotten the book, even though he was at the front:

> I expect to be there till about August. After that, I think I shall come home as it will be about time I started on another book. I greatly hope I come out of this alive if only to write a book about it ... I hope I shall get a chance to write the truth about what I have seen. The stuff appearing in the English papers is largely the most appalling lies – more I can't say, owing to the censorship. If I can get back in August I hope to have a book ready for you about the beginning of next year.[3]

In fact he had already applied to be discharged from the militia, intending instead to join the International Brigade, but he was turned against Stalinist Communism by the Communist attempt to suppress the revolutionary parties at the beginning of May. On 10 May he was wounded in the throat by a fascist sniper. He was in hospital and recovering until 14 June. While there, he wrote to Cyril Connolly, 'Thanks ... for recently telling the public that I should probably write a book on Spain, as I shall, of course, once this bloody arm is right. I have seen wonderful things & at last really believe in Socialism, which I never did before.'[4] Then, while he was collecting his discharge papers, the Spanish government outlawed the POUM, forcing him to run to Barcelona and from there across the French border.

At the beginning of July he was back at Wallington. He immediately began to write the book about Spain, although, as he told Rayner Heppenstall, first Kingsley Martin, editor of the *New Statesman*, refused his article about the suppression of the POUM,[5] then they refused to publish his review of *The Spanish Cockpit*,[6] 'although they offered to pay for the review all the same – practically hush-money'. Then he realised:

> I am also having to change my publisher, at least for this book. Gollancz is of course part of the communist-racket, and as soon as he heard I had been associated with the POUM and Anarchists and had seen the inside of the May riots in Barcelona, he said he did not think he would be able to publish my book, though not a word of it was written yet. I think he must have very astutely foreseen that something of the kind would happen, as when I went to Spain he drew up a contract undertaking to

publish my fiction but not other books. However I have two other publishers on my track and I think my agent is being clever and has got them bidding against one another. I have started my book but of course my fingers are all thumbs at present ... I am just getting going with my book, which I want to get done by Xmas.[7]

He again discussed what he saw as the British press cover-up of the real situation in Spain in a letter to Geoffrey Gorer in August:

It is a real reign of terror, Fascism being imposed under the pretence of resisting Fascism ... The most disgusting thing of all is the way the so-called anti-Fascist press in England has covered it up. I wonder if you saw my review in *Time and Tide* of a book called *The Spanish Cockpit* ...? The author wrote and told me that I was the only reviewer who had mentioned the essential point of the book, i.e. that the Communist Party is now the chief anti-revolutionary party. But the interesting thing was that I had also reviewed it for the *New Statesman* and was, of course, able to treat it more seriously than for *Time and Tide*. But the *NS* having previously refused an article of mine on the suppression of the POUM on the ground that it would 'cause trouble', also refused to print the review as it 'controverted editorial policy', or in other words blew the gaff on the Communist Party. They then offered to pay for the review, though unprinted, then asked me by telegram to review another book. They were evidently very anxious to prevent me giving away the fact that they are covering up important pieces of news. However they will get a nasty jar when my book on Spain comes out, as I intend to do an appendix on the lies and suppressions in the English press.[8]

The British press continued to engage his attentions, to the point where, as he told Geoffrey Gorer in September,

The *Daily Worker* has been following me personally with the most filthy libels, calling me pro-Fascist etc, but I asked Gollancz to silence them, which he did, not very willingly I imagine. Queerly enough I am still contracted to write a number of books for him, though he refused to publish the book I am doing on Spain before a word of it was written.[9]

On 1 September 1937 he signed a contract with Secker & Warburg for the book on Spain. In October 1937 he was still writing the book, which was occupying most of his attention. Jack Common wrote suggesting that he write something, perhaps a short story, for Penguin:

I would like to do something for the Penguin people very much, only the devil of it is that at present I simply can't write about anything but Spain and am struggling with a bloody book on it which I have contracted to do by the end of the year. Of course I could detach something from the book – I think there is at any rate one chapter that would do – but that mightn't be the kind of thing they want and also I don't know that my publishers would want it. It is a devil of a business. It seems only yesterday that nobody would print anything I wrote, and now I get letters from all quarters saying won't I write something, and except for the thing that I actually have on hand I am as empty as a jug. Of course I never could and never have written short stories proper. This Spanish business has upset me so that I really can't write about anything else, and unfortunately what one has to write about is not picturesque stuff but a blasted complicated story of political intrigue between a lot of cosmopolitan Communists, Anarchists etc. Beyond the book I am not doing anything except the usual hack-work of reviews which I don't count as writing.[10]

He had completed the book by the middle of January 1938. In February he told Jack Common: 'My book thank God is done and gone to press. It ought to be out in March. I think the title will be Homage to Catalonia, because we couldn't think of a better one. I'm not starting another for a few weeks.'[11] The book he was planning was to have been about India, based on material he had hoped to collect while on a visit as a leader writer for the Lucknow *Pioneer*. But in early March he was ill with a tubercular lesion in one lung and by the end of the month he was in a sanatorium in Aylesford, Kent, expecting to be there for two months, although he was not eventually discharged until 1 September. There was, therefore, a long gap in his writing: 'The bore is that I can't work, & what with having slacked for abt 2 months on the strength of finishing my last book, my next … will be some time coming along.'[12] By April he was anticipating the publication of *Homage to Catalonia*. He told Stephen Spender:

> I really wrote to say I hoped you'd read my Spanish book (title *Homage to Catalonia*) when it comes out, which should be shortly. I have been afraid that having read those two chapters you would carry away the impression that the whole book was Trotskyist propaganda, whereas actually only abt half of it or less is controversial. I hate writing that kind of stuff and am much more interested in my own experiences … I don't know that I can give you a copy of my book because I've already had to order about 10 extra ones & it's so damned expensive, but you can always get it out of the library.[13]

Spender hoped to arrange to review it. Orwell told him, 'It's very kind of you to review my Spanish book. But don't go and get into trouble with your own party – it's not worth it. However of course you can disagree with all my conclusions, as I think you would probably do anyway, without actually calling me a liar.'[14]

Homage to Catalonia was published on 25 April 1938. The *Collected Essays, Journalism and Letters of George Orwell* includes his 'Notes on the Spanish Militias', which, the editors say, could well serve as an appendix to *Homage to Catalonia*.[15] He was now, as always, keen to have his colleagues and friends read the book and if possible to review it, even if they wrote adverse criticism. He asked Cyril Connolly, 'Did you manage to get my book to review, or did they give it to someone else? It came out on Monday.'[16] In similar vein he wrote to Jack Common:

> Isn't it a grand feeling when you see your thoughts taking shape at last in a solid lump? I don't know if Eileen remembered to send you a copy of my Spanish book, but if not she will when she gets back home on Monday. I don't know how it's sold, but I haven't had as many reviews as usual so I suppose it's been boycotted a bit. Of course apart from any political back-stabbing there is the usual reviewing ramp, i.e. the number & favourableness of the reviews you get is directly dependent on the amount your publisher spends on advertising. I think if I was a publisher I wouldn't even do it in such a roundabout way as that, but simply pay the leading hack-reviewers a monthly retaining fee to keep my books to the fore.[17]

And to Cyril Connolly, 'I'm glad you liked the book, & thanks for recommending it to people. I had better reviews than I expected but of course all the best ones in obscure papers.'[18]

In September 1938 he went to Morocco, for the climate, arriving in Marrakech on 12 September. *Homage to Catalonia* had not been a great commercial success – he told Jack Common, 'I don't believe my book on Spain sold at all'[19] – but he was still anxious to circulate copies among his friends and fellow writers. He told Frank Jellinek, 'I am … asking my agent to send you a copy of my book on the Spanish war. Parts of it might interest you. I have no doubt I have made a lot of mistakes and misleading statements, but I have tried to indicate all through that the subject is very complicated and that I am extremely fallible as well as biassed.'[20] He again emphasised his lack of popular success in another letter to Jack Common, 'My Spain book sold damn all, but it didn't greatly matter as my agent had got the money out of him [Warburg] in advance and the reviews were ok.'[21]

In 1944 when Leonard Moore was trying to arrange Penguin publication of *Keep the Aspidistra Flying*, Orwell rejected the idea, calling it a bad book, and suggesting instead *Coming Up for Air*, and noting, 'The other one that deserves reprinting is the Spanish book.'[22] In 'Why I Write', first published in 1946, Orwell wrote:

My book about the Spanish civil war, *Homage to Catalonia*, is, of course, a frankly political book, but in the main it is written with a certain detachment and regard for form. I did try very hard in it to tell the whole truth without violating my literary instincts. But among other things it contains a long chapter, full of newspaper quotations and the like, defending the Trotskyists who were accused of plotting with Franco. Clearly such a chapter, which after a year or two would lose its interest for any ordinary reader, must ruin the book. A critic whom I respect read me a lecture about it. 'Why did you put in all that stuff?' he said. 'You've turned what might have been a good book into journalism.' What he said was true, but I could not have done otherwise. I happened to know, what very few people in England had been allowed to know, that innocent men were being falsely accused. If I had not been angry about that I should never have written the book.[23]

Orwell made a list of errata for a possible revised edition. It included notes on the re-ordering of chapters:

> If reprinted, it would be better to put Chaps V and XI at the end as an appendix. The political parts of the books were deliberately concentrated into these two chapters so as to make them excisable at need, but Chap. XI in particular contains historically valuable material. The book if ever reprinted could do with a preface, preferably by a Spaniard.[24]

Lionel Trilling wrote a preface to the American edition in 1952, although the contemporaries that Orwell had in mind closer to the time of publication were, in 1939, Georges Copp, his Commander in Spain, and later, in 1947, André Malraux. There was only one edition in Orwell's lifetime. The *Complete Works* edition uses the first edition, Orwell's notes on a possible revised edition, his marked-up copy, and the 1955 French translation. Orwell was in correspondence with Yvonne Davet, who did the 1955 translation, in 1947 and those letters indicate other changes he wished to make. She had been translating the book as early as 1938, without the prospect of publishing it, and by 11 September 1938 Orwell had corrected the first six chapters of that translation, and chapters 7–10 by 19 June 1939. Those corrections, and the other changes he later wrote about, are clearly of textual interest. There is also an unmarked proof of the 1938 first edition in the Orwell Archive. The notes Orwell made for his literary executors are part of two sets of literary notes he made about his writings. Those about *Homage to Catalonia* are especially interesting when read along with his own marked-up copy of the book. He sent that copy to Roger Senhouse, then a director of Secker & Warburg, a few months before his death. But Senhouse did not make use of the noted revisions, even in the 1951 Uniform Edition, and when Senhouse died Orwell's copy of the book was sold, although Peter Davison was able to see it when compiling the *Complete Works* edition.

On the titlepage, Orwell included two biblical quotations. He told Frank Jellinek: 'On the title page of my book you will find two texts from Proverbs which sum up the prevailing theories of how to combat Fascism, and I personally agree with the first and not the second.'[25]

A.6a   *First Edition, 1938*

HOMAGE | TO | CATALONIA | by | George | Orwell | LONDON | *Secker and Warburg*

Collation [A]–U[8]; 160 leaves (21.6 × 13.8); [i–vi] 1–[314]

Contents [i] halftitle: HOMAGE TO CATALONIA [ii] list of books by Orwell [iii] titlepage [iv] imprint: *HOMAGE TO CATALONIA COPYRIGHT IN 1938 | BY MARTIN SECKER AND WARBURG LTD. OF | 22 ESSEX STREET, STRAND, WC2, AND PRINTED | BY WILLIAM BRENDON AND SON, LTD., AT | THE MAYFLOWER PRESS, PLYMOUTH | First Published April 1938* [v] halftitle: Answer not a fool according to his folly, lest | thou be like unto him. | Answer a fool according to his folly, lest he be | wise in his own conceit. | *Proverbs xxvi*, 5–6 [vi] blank 1–[314] text, on 314: THE END

Binding Green calico textured cloth on boards. Off white endpapers. Green topped leaves.

Front and back covers Plain.

Spine Stamped in gilt: HOMAGE | TO | CATALONIA | *George* | *Orwell* | SECKER & | WARBURG

Jacket Off white.
Front HOMAGE TO | CATALONIA | GEORGE ORWELL [decorative print with two capital E letters inside each letter] | AUTHOR OF "THE ROAD TO WIGAN PIER" ETC | [drawing in green and black of a clenched fist against a ruined building] [and in bottom left]: K
Back publisher's advertisement
Spine [green flash] | HOMAGE | TO | CATALONIA | GEORGE | ORWELL | [drawing of broken guitar against a green and black background] | [in white against a black background]: SECKER & | WARBURG
Front flap [summary] | [dotted diagonal rule] | 10s. 6d. | net
Back flap Plain.

Paper
Cream esparto antique rolled laid

31 lines per page
12 pt Wallbaum

Notes
Published 25 April 1938
10s 6d
1,500 copies
There is a printing error on p236, line 3 where a comma is omitted after "in fact".

Contemporary reviews
V.S. Pritchett *The New Statesman and Nation* (30 April 1938)
Times Literary Supplement (30 April 1938)
Geoffrey Gorer *Time and Tide* (30 April 1938)
John McNair *The New Leader* (London) (6 May 1938)
Philip Mairet *The New English Weekly* (26 May 1938)
A.W.J. *The Manchester Guardian* (14 June 1938)
Douglas Woodruff *The Tablet* (9 July 1938)
Stephen Spender *The World Review* (June 1950)

Locations
Cambridge University Library – binding repaired and reinforced. Acquisition 22 April 1938.
Orwell Archive – two copies, one with jacket.

A.6b Uniform Edition, 1951
HOMAGE | TO | CATALONIA | BY | GEORGE ORWELL | LONDON | SECKER & WARBURG | 1951

Collation [A]–Q⁸; 128 leaves (18.3 × 12.2); [i–viii] [1]–248

Contents [i] halftitle: HOMAGE TO CATALONIA [ii] list of books by Orwell [iii] titlepage [iv] imprint: MARTIN SECKER & WARBURG LTD., | 7 John Street, Bloomsbury, | London, W.C.1 | *First published April 1938* | *New edition, reset, 1951* |

Printed and bound in Great Britain by | *The Camelot Press Ltd., London and Southampton* [v] imprint: Answer not a fool according to his folly, lest | thou be like unto him. | Answer a fool according to his folly, lest he be | wise in his own conceit. | *Proverbs xxvi. 5–6* [vi] blank [1]–248 text, on 248: THE END

Binding Green calico grain cloth on boards. Off white endpapers.
Purple topped leaves.

Front and back covers Plain.
Spine Stamped in purplish red: [pyramid of six lines] | HOMAGE TO | CATALONIA | [small ornate leaf device] | GEORGE | ORWELL | [inverted pyramid of six lines] | SECKER & | WARBURG

Jacket Front and spine green, otherwise off white.
Front [Two off-white panels outlined in black] [Top panel]: HOMAGE TO | CATALONIA [bottom panel]: GEORGE | ORWELL [and in off-white at foot]: UNIFORM EDITION
Spine HOMAGE | TO | CATALONIA | [leaf motif] | GEORGE | ORWELL | SECKER & | WARBURG
Back List of Orwell's works published by Secker & Warburg.
Front flap [summary] | 10s.6d. | W.814 NET
Back flap | [within a frame]: [publisher's advertisement]

Notes
Published February 1951
10s 6d
This, and all other editions and reissues until the 1986 Complete Works Edition, follow the text of the First Edition.

Locations
Cambridge University Library. Acquisition 13 March 1951.
Orwell Archive

Reissues
Reissued with amended titlepage and imprint 1954 and 1959.

Reissued with amended titlepage, imprint and new binding – green paper, embossed to resemble linen grain cloth, on boards – in 1967 and 1971.
Jacket Dull brown.
Front [Printed in silver]: GEORGE | ORWELL | [and in dark brown]: HOMAGE TO | CATALONIA
Back Plain.
Spine [laterally] [in silver]: ORWELL [and in dark brown]: HOMAGE TO | CATALONIA [horizontally in silver]: SECKER & | WARBURG
Front flap [in dark brown] [summary] | [bottom left]: Jacket design by Format [bottom right]: £1.75 | 35s | net
Back flap [in dark brown] 436 35005 X

Locations
Cambridge University Library
Orwell Archive – 1959, 1967, 1971

A.6c   *First American Edition, 1952*

George Orwell | HOMAGE | TO | CATALONIA | Harcourt, Brace and Company | New York

Collation Eight unmarked gatherings arranged: [1–8][16]; 128 leaves (20.1 × 13.4); [i–v] vi–xxiii [xxiv] [1–3] 4–232

Contents [i] halftitle: HOMAGE TO CATALONIA [ii] list of books by Orwell [iii] titlepage [iv] imprint: COPYRIGHT, 1952, BY | SONIA BROWNELL ORWELL | *All rights reserved, including the right to | reproduce this book or portions thereof in any form | first American edition* | LIBRARY OF CONGRESS CATALOG NUMBER: 52–6442 | PRINTED IN THE UNITED STATES OF AMERICA [v]–xxiii introduction [xxiv] blank [1] halftitle: HOMAGE TO CATALONIA [2] halftitle: *Answer not a fool according to his folly, lest thou be like unto | him. | Answer a fool according to his folly, lest he be wise in his own | conceit.* | Proverbs xxvi. 5–6 [3]– 232 text

Binding Yellow calico textured cloth on boards. Off white endpapers.

Front cover Greenish grey diagonal flash in which is picked out: HOMAGE TO CATALONIA | [in bottom right in greenish grey is the silhouette of a bayonet fixed to a gun, crossed by a rose on a stem]

Back cover Plain.

Spine [laterally]: [within a greenish grey rectangle is picked out]: *George Orwell* [and stamped in greenish grey]: HOMAGE TO CATALONIA [and within a greenish grey rectangle is picked out]: *Harcourt, Brace & Co.*

Jacket Front and spine speckled green, otherwise off white.
Front Printed in red: *Joseph Low* | [within an off white flash]: *George Orwell* [cursive script] | [and beneath]: HOMAGE | TO | CATALONIA | [silhouette of a bayonet fixed to a gun, crossed by a rose on a stem] | [within three off white flashes]: *Orwell's personal story | of the Spanish Civil War | & the Communist betrayal* | [and within a red flash is picked out]: *with an Introduction by Lionel Trilling* [cursive script]
Back publisher's advertisements
Spine [Printed in red, laterally] [within an off white flash]: *George Orwell* [cursive script] | HOMAGE TO CATALONIA | [and within a red flash is picked out]: Harcourt, Brace & Co.
Front flap summary
Back flap assessments of Orwell

Notes
Published May 1952
$3.50
4,000 copies
Introduction by Lionel Trilling
Second impression of 3,000 copies in July 1952.

Contemporary reviews
T.R. Fyvel *The New Leader* (New York) (16 June 1952)
George Mayberry *The New Republic* (23 June 1952)
Herbert Matthews *The Nation* (27 December 1952)

Locations
Cambridge University Library. Acquisition 27 April 1984.
Orwell Archive, with jacket.

Reissues
Reissued in paperback by The Beacon Press, Boston, in April 1955, and thereafter in November 1955, April 1957, December 1957, and June 1959.

Titlepage and imprint revised; collation and contents as First American Edition.

Binding
Paper bound.

Front cover Black, with white stripe across top, within which is printed in red: "One of the most important documents | of our time." – *Lionel Trilling* | [publisher's monogram device] BEACON | $1.25 | [short rule] | BP5 [below the stripe is picked out in white]: HOMAGE TO | CATALONIA | [beneath which is a red, yellow and purple striped flag, and beneath this, picked out in white]: BY George Orwell | AUTHOR OF "1984" | Introduction by | LIONEL TRILLING

Back cover Yellow, with black printing: HOMAGE TO CATALONIA | By George Orwell | [extracts from reviews] | [publisher's monogram device] | *This title also available cloth-bound* | *(Harcourt, Brace) at your bookseller; $3.50* | BEACON PRESS . Beacon Hill, Boston

Locations
Orwell Archive – 1959

Reissued after 1968 by Harcourt, Brace & World, Inc. with revised titlepage and imprints, but otherwise as American first edition. Introduction by Trilling. Paperbound in yellow with a silhouette of a bayonet dripping with blood, and the title and author's name in concentric circles, like a target. A Harvest Book, HB162. Sold for $1.95. Cover design by Ken Braren. In Harvest's 'History' series.
Reissued by Harcourt Brace Jovanovich in 1980. As above, in yellow paper, $4.95.

A.6d   First Penguin Edition, 1962

GEORGE ORWELL | [short rule] | *Homage to Catalonia* | PENGUIN BOOKS | IN ASSOCIATION WITH | SECKER & WARBURG

Collation [T–H.T.C.–A] – T–H.T.C.–G^{16}; 112 leaves (17.8 × 10.9); [1–6] 7–[221] [222–224]

Contents [1] halftitle] PENGUIN BOOKS | 1699 | HOMAGE TO CATALONIA | GEORGE ORWELL | [penguin motif] [2] blank [3] titlepage [4] imprint: Penguin Books Ltd, Harmondsworth, Middlesex | AUSTRALIA: Penguin Books Pty Ltd, 762 Whitehorse Road, | Mitcham, Victoria | [short rule] | First published by Secker and Warburg 1938 | Published in Penguin Books 1962 | [short rule] | Made and printed in Great Britain by Cox and Wyman Ltd, | London, Reading, and Fakenham | [copyright notice] [5] halftitle: *Answer not a fool according to his folly, lest thou be* | *like unto him.* | *Answer a fool according to his folly, lest he be wise in* | *his own conceit.* | PROVERBS XXVI, 5–6 [6] blank 7–[221] text [222–224] blank

Binding Paper bound.

Front cover Top quarter orange, otherwise off white. Within the top quarter is printed: [penguin motif in white] a Penguin Book 3'– | [rule] | Homage to | Catalonia | [rule] | [and in white]: George Orwell [the rest of the front is a pencil drawing of a man's head and shoulders, with an orange neck band]

Back cover Orange. [penguin motif in white] a Penguin Book | [rule] | Homage to | Catalonia | [rule] | [summary] | *For copyright reasons this edition is not for* | *sale in the U.S.A.*

Spine [laterally] [in white]: George Orwell [and in black]: Homage to Catalonia [horizontally]: [penguin motif] | 1699

Inside front cover [photograph of Orwell] | *Vernon Richards* | [biographical sketch of Orwell] | Cover drawing by Paul Hogarth | [publisher's notice]

Inside back cover Publisher's advertisements.

Notes
3s 0d

Contemporary reviews
Hugh Thomas *The New Statesman* (20 April 1962)

Locations
Cambridge University Library. Acquisition 26 February 1962.
Orwell Archive

Reissues
Reissued in 1962 and 1964.

New edition, including 'Looking Back on the Spanish War' in 1966 (two printings), 1968, 1969, 1970, 1971, 1972, 1974 (twice), 1975 (twice), 1976, 1977, 1978, 1979, 1980, 1981, 1982, 1983, and 1984.
Cambridge University Library has first 1975 reissue. Acquisition 28 July 1975.
1989 Twentieth Century Classics edition, based on the Complete Works edition.

'Looking Back on the Spanish War' was first published in *Such, Such Were the Joys* and *England, Your England* in 1953 [See D.4 and D.5].

Locations
Cambridge University Library 1975
Orwell Archive 1980 and 1984 – covers have photograph of contemporary Spanish newspaper, part of a gun, ammunition, and a red cloth.

A.6e   Folio Society Edition, 1970

Homage to | Catalonia | by GEORGE ORWELL | With an Introduction by | BOB EDWARDS | THE FOLIO SOCIETY | London 1970

Collation [A]–M⁸ N⁴ O⁸; 108 leaves (21.4 × 13.9); [1–4] 5–11 [12–14] 15–211 [212] 213–214 [215–216]. There are eight additional leaves of photographs, unpaginated and with blank versos, bound around and sewn with gatherings A, D, H, M, and thus facing pages [1], 16, 48, 65, 112, 129, 177 and 192. These additional leaves in effect give the collation: A¹⁰ B–C⁸ D¹⁰ E–G⁸ H¹⁰ I–L⁸ M¹⁰ N⁴ O⁸

Contents (excluding illustration leaves) [1] titlepage [2] imprint: This edition is published by kind permission of | Martin Secker & Warburg Ltd | PRINTED IN GREAT BRITAIN | *Printed by Alden & Mobray Ltd at the Alden Press, Oxford* | *Set in 'Monotype' Times New Roman 10 point leaded 2 points* | *Illustrations printed by Westerham Press Ltd, Westerham* | *Bound by W & J Mackay & Co Ltd, Chatham* [3–4] list of illustrations 5–11 introduction [12] blank [13] halftitle: *Answer not a fool according to his folly, lest thou be* | *like unto him.* | *Answer a fool according to his folly, lest he be wise in* | *his own conceit.* | PROVERBS XXVI, 5–6 [14] blank 15–211 text [212] blank 213–214 index [215–216] blank

Binding Grey printed cloth on boards. Red endpapers printed with a map of Catalonia. Red topped leaves.

Front and back covers (and wrapping around spine) is a black and white photograph of a group of armed, uniformed men on a hill, looking over flat countryside.

Spine Across the photograph is printed laterally in black and gold: Homage to Catalonia

Slip case Red morocco grained paper on boards.

Notes
The Introduction is by Bob Edwards MP. The list of illustrations reveals that the cover photograph is a view of the battlefield near Belchite on the Aragon front.

Locations
Cambridge University Library. Acquisition 15 July 1971.
Orwell Archive – two copies, one with slip case.

A.6f   *The Penguin Complete Longer Non-Fiction of George Orwell edition 1983.*

(Harmondsworth: Penguin, 1983) 488pp

The edition consists of:

Down and Out in Paris and London 7–153
The Road to Wigan Pier 155–299
Homage to Catalonia 301–467
Looking Back on the Spanish War 469–488

Paper bound
£3.95

A.6g   *The Complete Works Edition, 1986*

THE COMPLETE WORKS OF | GEORGE ORWELL | VOLUME SIX | Homage to Catalonia | SECKER & WARBURG | [short rule] | LONDON

Collation There are nine unmarked gatherings: [A–D]^{16} [E]^8 [F–I]^{16}; 136 leaves (23.3 × 15.4) [i–viii] 1–[248] [249–250] 251–[261] [262–264]

Contents [i] halftitle: THE COMPLETE WORKS OF | GEORGE ORWELL . SIX | HOMAGE TO CATALONIA [ii] blank [iii] publisher's note [iv] blank [v] titlepage [vi] imprint: [selective publishing history of editions and reissues] | [copyright notices] | [British Library Cataloguing in Publication Data] | ISBN 0–436–35028–9 | Typeset in Monophoto Bembo by | Northumberland Press Ltd, Gateshead, Tyne and Wear | Printed and bound in Great Britain by | Richard Clay (The Chaucer Press), Bungay, Suffolk [vii] halftitle: Answer not a fool according to his folly, lest | thou be like unto him. | Answer a fool according to his folly, lest he | be wise in his own conceit. | *Proverbs xxvi*, 5–6 [viii] blank 1–187 text 188–[248] appendices [249–250] blank 251–[261] textual note [262–264] blank

Binding Blue paper on boards, embossed to resemble calico textured cloth. Black endpapers.

Front and back covers Plain.

Spine Stamped in gilt: [double rule] | GEORGE | ORWELL | [rule] | Homage | to | Catalonia | [double rule] | SECKER & | WARBURG

Jacket Smooth dull black. Flaps white.
Front [in white]: GEORGE | ORWELL | [in red and white]: HOMAGE | TO | CATALONIA |
Back [in white, note on *The Complete Works of George Orwell* and extracts from reviews. ISBN code and bar strip within a white rectangle.]
Spine [laterally] [in white]: GEORGE ORWELL | [in red and white]: HOMAGE TO CATALONIA [horizontally in white]: Secker & Warburg
Front flap [biographical note, summary, and note on this edition. At foot]: Jacket design by David Quay | £12.95 | net
Back flap [biographical notes on Orwell and Peter Davison]

Notes
This edition, edited by Peter Davison, makes changes to the first edition suggested by Orwell. This involves moving all but the first paragraph of the original Chapter Five, and part of the last paragraph of Chapter Ten and all of Chapter Eleven to the appendices. Orwell had written:

> The political parts of this book were deliberately concentrated into these two chapters so as to make them excisable at need, but Chap. XI in particular contains historically valuable material. (Complete Works Edition, p251)

Reprinted 1996

Locations
Orwell Archive – two copies, one with jacket
Robarts Library, University of Toronto

MISCELLANEOUS

A.6.M1   *Homage to Catalonia*

Braille edition, 1940
Published by the National Library for the Blind in 4 volumes.

TRANSLATIONS

All Orwell Archive unless otherwise noted

CATALAN

A.6.T1   *Homenatge a Catalunya*, 1969

Barcelona: Edicions Ariel
Translated by Ramon Folch i Camarasa
Cloth on boards
Published December 1969
Reissued in paperback April 1972, December 1982, and February 1984.

DANISH

A.6.T2   *Hyldest til Catalonien*, 1975

Copenhagen: Gyldendal
Translated by Birte Svensson
Paper bound
Reissued in paperback 1984

DUTCH

A.6.T3a   *Saluut aan Catalonië*, 1964

Amsterdam: N.V. de Arbeiderspers
Translated by A. Nuis
Paper bound
Reissued in paperback in Amsterdam in 1982 by Van Gennep.

A.6.T3b   *Afscheid van Catalonië*, 1975

Amsterdam: Synopsis
Translated by Aad Nuis

This is really only another paperback reissue of A.6.T3a by N.V. de Arbeiderspers, under
the Synopsis imprint, and with a new title.

FINNISH

A.6.T4   *Katalonia, Katalonia!*, 1974

Helsinki: Werner Söderström
Translated by Taisto Nieminen
Paper bound

FRENCH
A.6.T5a   *La Catalogne Libre*, 1955
Paris: Gallimard
Translated by Yvonne Davet

A.6.T5b   *Hommage à la Catalogne*, 1981
Paris: Editions Champ Libre
Translated by Yvonne Davet
Reissued in paperback in 1982

GERMAN
A.6.T6a   *Mein Katalonien*, 1964
München: Rütten & Loening
Translated by Wolfgang Rieger
Cloth bound

A.6.T6b   *Mein Katalonien*, 1975
Zurich: Diogenes
Translated by Wolfgang Rieger
Paper bound
Reissued in 1983

ITALIAN
A.6.T7a   *Omaggio alla Catalogna*, 1948
Verona: Arnoldo Mondadori
Translated by Giorgio Monicelli
Published December 1948
Paper bound
L. 550

A.6.T7b   *Omaggio alla Catalogna*, 1964
Milano: Il Saggiatore
Translated by Giorgio Monicelli
Paper bound
L. 600

A.6.T7c   *Omaggio alla Catalogna*, 1982
Verona: Mondadori
Translated by Giorgio Monicelli
Paper bound
L. 4,500

A.6.T7d   *Omaggio alla Catalogna*, 1984
Milano: Edizione CDE spa
Translated by Giorgio Monicelli
Paper on boards
Reissued as an Il Saggiatore paperback in 1984
L. 15,000

PORTUGUESE

A.6.T8a   *Lutando na Espanha*, 1967

Rio de Janeiro: Civilização
Translated by Affonso Blacheyre
Paper bound

A.6.T8b   *Homenagem à Catalunha*, undated

Lisboa: Livros do Brasil
Translated by Fernanda Pinto Rodrigues
Paper bound

SERBIAN

A.6.T9   *Kataloniji i Čast*, 1984

Zagreb: August Cesarec
Translated by Dragan Milković
Paper on boards

SPANISH

A.6.T10a   *Cataluña 1937*, 1963

Buenos Aires: Editorial Proyección
Translated by Noemi Rosenblatt
Paper bound

A.6.T10b   *Homenaja a Cataluña*, 1970

Barcelona: Ediciones Ariel
Translated by Carlos Pujol
Paper bound
Reissued as an Ariel Quincenal paperback in 1983, and as a Seix Barral paperback in 1985.

SWEDISH

A.6.T11a   *Hyllning till Katalonien*, 1971

Uddevalla: Rabén & Sjögren
Translated by Ingemar Johansson
A Trend Pocket Book
Paper bound

A.6.T11b   *Hyllning till Katalonien*, 1984

Malmö: Atlantis
Translated by Ingemar Johansson
Paper on boards

A.7   COMING UP FOR AIR

> One good effect the rest has had on me is that it has made me feel I can write a novel again, whereas when I came here I felt that my novel-writing days were over.'[1]

Composition and publication

At the beginning of December 1937 Orwell told Leonard Moore he was thinking of a new novel: 'It will not be about politics, and it will be about a man who is having a holiday and trying to make a temporary escape from responsibility, public and private. The title I thought of is "Coming Up for Air".'[2] But two factors put the project on hold. The first, at the end of December, was an unexpected letter from Desmond Young, editor of the Lucknow weekly journal, *The Pioneer*, offering him a job in India as his assistant editor and leader writer. Orwell reluctantly felt it was an opportunity he should seize. He hoped to get 'a clearer idea of political and social conditions in India ... [and] I shall no doubt write some book on the subject afterwards.'[3] He told Jack Common,

> Unless the India Office takes steps to prevent it, I am in all probability going to India for about a year quite shortly. It is a frightful bore and I have seldom wanted to do anything less, but I feel that it is an opportunity to see interesting things and that I should afterwards curse myself if I didn't go. I wish it didn't come at this moment, because I particularly wanted to vegetate for a few months, look after the garden etc and think about my next novel.[4]

In the event, his left-wing sympathies persuaded Young and the Government of India that he was unsuitable. A second factor, a lung haemorrhage on 8 March, led to almost six months in a sanatorium. On 14 March, still at Wallington, he told Cyril Connolly that he was relieved to have an excuse not to go to India, although his health, the doctors' ban on his working, and the political situation in Europe combined to depress him: 'I am writing this in bed ... This bloody mess-up in Europe has got me so that I really can't write anything. I see Gollancz has already put my next novel on his list tho' I haven't written a line or even sketched it out.'[5]

But a few days later he was admitted to the Jellicoe Ward of Preston Hall, a sanatorium in Aylesford, Kent, and until mid-July he was not allowed to write. He told Jack Common, 'The bore is that I can't work, and that 'my next [book], which Gollancz has hopefully put on his list, I see, will be some time coming along.'[6] On the other hand, he told Stephen Spender, 'I am to stay in bed and rest completely for abt 3 months & then I shall probably be OK. It means I can't work & is rather a bore, but perhaps is all for the best.'[7] Similarly, he told Cyril Connolly, 'I can't work of course, which is a bore & will put my next novel back till 1939.'[8]

In May he was still at the sanatorium. He told Jack Common,

> I suppose I shall be here another month or two months. It's a bore not being able either to work or to get home & try & salvage what is left of the garden after this bloody weather, but undoubtedly the rest has done me good & incidentally has made me keen to get started with my next novel, though when I came here I had been thinking that what with Hitler, Stalin & the rest of them the day of novel-writing was over. As it is if I start it in August I dare-say I shall have to finish it in the concentration camp. [9]

Eileen told Leonard Moore, 'the book seethes in his head and he is very anxious to get on with it'[10] and, as Orwell told Cyril Connolly in July, 'I still haven't done a stroke of work but keep toying with the idea of starting my novel. One good effect the rest has had on me is that it has made me feel I can write a novel again, whereas when I came here I felt that my novel-writing days were over.'[11] About to be released from hospital, he told his mother, 'I am anxious to get away and start working, which I can't here. My next novel will be very late of course, but I dare say I'll get it done in time to come out about next March.'[12]

On his release from the sanatorium on 1 September 1938 Orwell and Eileen travelled immediately to Morocco on 2 September, at first as tourists and then as short-stay residents until 26 March 1939. His period of rest had clearly stimulated him intellectually. He told Jack Common,

> much as I resent the waste of time it's probably done me good to lay off work for seven months. People who don't write think that writing isn't work, but you and I know the contrary. Thank God I've just begun to work again and made a start on my new novel, which was billed for this autumn but might appear in the spring perhaps. Of course if war comes God knows if the publishing of books will even continue. To me the idea of war is a pure nightmare. Richard Rees was talking as though even war couldn't be worse than the present conditions, but I think what this really means is that he doesn't see any peace-time activity for himself which he feels to be useful. A lot of intellectuals feel like this ... But I personally do see a lot of things that I want to do and to continue doing for another thirty years or so, and the idea that I've got to abandon them and either be bumped off or depart to some filthy concentration camp just infuriates me.[13]

In this mood, he started writing *Coming Up for Air* in Marrakech in late September 1938. Jack Common was meanwhile staying at The Stores, Wallington. Orwell wrote to him in October with various practical advice on running the house: 'I think we forgot to warn you not to use thick paper in the WC. It sometimes chokes the cesspool up ... if you find the sitting room fire smokes intolerably, I think you can get a piece of tin put in the chimney ... [and could you get] the vacant ground turned over sometime in the winter and preferably some manure (the goat's stuff is quite good if there isn't too much straw in it) dug in.' Keeping the house in good order was important to Orwell because, as he said in the same letter,

> 'I don't know what my financial situation will be next year ... and if I have to come back to England and start on yet another book with only £50 in the world I would rather have a roof over my head from the start.'[14]

In October he wrote to John Sceats, an insurance agent and left-wing writer, asking his advice on the work of an insurance agent for his portrait of George Bowling in *Coming Up for Air*. It is a lengthy request, but worth quoting for the light it throws on Orwell's determination for accuracy and the documentary background to his fictional works:

> I'm writing to you now for some expert advice. The chap in the novel I'm writing is supposed to be an insurance agent. His job isn't in the least important to the story, I merely wanted him to be a typical middle-aged bloke with about £5 a week and a house in the suburbs, and he's also rather thoughtful and fairly well-educated, even slightly bookish, which is more plausible with an insurance agent than, say, a commercial traveller. But I want any mention that is made of his job to be correct. And meanwhile I have only very vague ideas as to what an insurance agent does. I want him to be a chap who travels round and gets parts of his income from commissions, not merely an office employee. Does such a chap have a 'district' and a regular round like a commercial traveller? Does he have to go touting round for orders, or just go round and sign the people up when they want to be insured? Would he spend all his time in travelling or part of it in the office? Would he have an office of his own? Do the big insurance offices have branch offices all over the place (this chap lives in a suburb which might be Hayes or Southall) or do they only have the head office and send all the agents out from there? And would such a man do valuations of property, and would the same man do life insurance and property insurance? I'd be very glad of some elucidation on these points. My picture of this chap is this. He spends about two days a week in the branch office in his suburb and the rest of the time in travelling round in a car over a district of about half a county, interviewing people who've written in to say that they want to be insured, making

valuations of houses, stock and so forth, and also touting for orders on which he gets an extra commission, and by this time he is earning round about £5 a week after being with the firm for 18 years (having started very much at the bottom). I want to know if this is plausible.[15]

Sceats replied with the facts Orwell wanted. He replied to him:

Thanks so much for your letter and the very useful information about insurance offices. I see that my chap will have to be a Representative and that I underrated his income a little. I've done quite a lot of work, but unfortunately after wasting no less than a fortnight doing articles for various papers fell slightly ill so that properly speaking I've done no work for 3 weeks. It's awful how the time flies by. What with all this illness, I've decided to count 1938 as a blank year and sort of cross it off the calendar. But meanwhile the concentration camp looms ahead and there is so much one wants to do. I've got to the point now when I feel I could write a good novel if I had five years peace and quiet, but at present one might as well ask for five years in the moon.[16]

Just before finishing *Coming Up for Air* he speculated on his future as a writer:

I suppose after this book I shall write some kind of pot-boiler, but I have very dimly in my mind the idea for an enormous novel in several volumes and I want several years to plan it out in peace.[17]

He finished the first draft of the novel at the end of December 1938. He told Jack Common that the new novel was 'really a mess but parts of it I like and it's suddenly revealed to me a big subject which I'd never really touched before and haven't time to work out properly now.'[18] Early in January 1939 he told Herbert Read, 'I have had what is practically a wasted year, but the long rest has done me good and I am getting on with a new novel, whereas a year ago, after that awful nightmare in Spain, I had seriously thought I would never be able to write a novel again.'[19]

By mid-January 1939 he said that he was 'not displeased with parts of my novel.'[20] He told Geoffrey Gorer that he was taking a week off in the Atlas Mountains because 'I'd finished the rough draft of my novel'.[21] He had all but completed it by the time he left Morocco on 26 March 1939 and finished the typescript on the return voyage. He submitted the manuscript to Gollancz, according to the terms of the contractual arrangement Eileen had made with Gollancz during Orwell's absence in Spain in 1937. It gave him an option on Orwell's next three novels, and after reading the manuscript Gollancz hesitated to accept it. Orwell was not surprised, but he was determined not to bow to pressure from Gollancz to alter the book. He told Jack Common,

I finished my novel just before we got back & dumped it but haven't heard any repercussions yet. Gollancz was anxious that I shouldn't 'leave' him as they call it & by contract he's supposed to publish my next 3 fictions, but if he tries to bugger me abt I think I shall leave him, & then there'll be long complications abt who else to go to.[22]

He told Moore, 'I thought Gollancz might show fight. The book is, of course, only a novel and more or less unpolitical, so far as it is possible for a book to be that nowadays, but its general tendency is pacifist, and there is one chapter ... which describes a Left Book Club meeting and which Gollancz no doubt objects to.'[23] Orwell was determined not to alter the structure or to make any but the most minor changes, and Gollancz evidently accepted his terms. *Coming Up for Air* was published on 12 June 1939. It sold well and was almost immediately reprinted.

Leonard Moore tried to arrange for an edition of *Coming Up for Air* to be published in English in Europe by the Albatross Press in 1939. Their paperback series, the Albatross Modern Continental Library, was a model for Penguin Books when it began publishing in 1935. In August 1939 he wrote to Moore:

Naturally I'm delighted about the Albatross business. It was very clever of you to work it. I've always wanted to crash one of those continental editions. English people abroad always read the few English books they can get hold of with such attention that I'm sure it's the best kind of publicity.[24]

For the Albatross edition Orwell was prepared to make certain changes. In his 'Diary of events leading up to the war', he wrote that they, 'require excision of certain (though not all) unfriendly references to Hitler. Say they are obliged to do this as their books circulate largely in Germany. Also excision of a passage of about a page suggesting that war is imminent.' The contract with Albatross and Tauchnitz is dated 31 August 1939 and stipulated that the book was to be published not later than August 1940, but the war intervened and it was unpublished.[25] Orwell's list of changes for the Albatross edition, enclosed with his August letter to Moore, has not survived.

In 1944 when Leonard Moore was trying to arrange Penguin publication of *Keep the Aspidistra Flying*, Orwell rejected the idea of reprinting what he labelled a bad book. Instead he asked if Penguin could not instead do *Coming Up for Air*,

I should like that to be reprinted and I should imagine that from their point of view it would be a better speculation than the other.[26]

There was no new edition until 1948 when *Coming Up for Air* was the first volume in the Uniform Edition of Orwell's works. He received the proofs of the new edition on 7 October 1947 on Jura, returning them to Roger Senhouse on 22 October. He wrote, 'There are not many corrections. In just one or two cases I've altered something that had been correctly transcribed, including one or two misprints that existed in the original text', such as 'Boers' for 'Boars'. He adds, 'Did you know by the way that this book hasn't get a semicolon in it? I had decided about that time that the semicolon is an unnecessary stop and that I would write my next book without one.'[27] In November he told Anthony Powell, 'In the spring I'm reprinting a novel which came out in 1939 & was rather killed by the war.'[28] He wrote the same to Julian Symons in April 1948, adding that he hoped to persuade Harcourt Brace to reprint *Coming Up for Air* and *Burmese Days* in the United States, although 'even if they do so they'll probably only take "sheets", which never does one much good. It's funny what BFs American publishers are abt reprints. . . . Apparently reprints in the USA are done mostly by special firms which only take them if they are safe for an enormous sale.'[29]

In March he had written to Symons about the physical appearance of the series:

Fred Warburg . . . brought a blank of my uniform edition which we are starting this year. I was rather dismayed to find that he had chosen a light green cover, but maybe he'll be able to get hold of some darker stuff. I think a uniform edition should always be a very chaste-looking & preferably dark blue.[30]

The Uniform Edition *Coming Up for Air* was published on 13 May 1948. Orwell told Julian Symons that although the novel 'isn't much', he thought it worth reprinting because during the war it had been 'blitzed out of existence, so thoroughly that in order to get a copy from which to reset it we had to steal one from a public library.'[31] He responded to Symons's criticism of his technique:

Of course you are perfectly right about my own character constantly intruding on that of the narrator. I am not a real novelist anyway, and that particular vice is inherent in writing a novel in the first person, which one should never do. One difficulty I have never solved is that one has masses of experience which one passionately wants to write about, e.g. the part about fishing in that book, and no way of using them up except by disguising them as a novel. Of course the book was bound to suggest Wells watered down.

A corrected proof of the Uniform Edition survives, stamped '6 Oct 1947' by the printer, Morrison & Gibb, and with 'Received 7 Oct 1947' on the halftitle page. Peter Davison suggests that this corrected proof is in fact a 'house proof' and not Orwell's. He bases this on both Orwell's reference in the letter to Symons about the absence of semicolons, written after he had read the proof, and the marks in the proof: 'In fact, the surviving set of proofs ... and the Uniform Edition do include three semicolons. The deletion signs in these proofs are unlike those which can definitely be associated with Orwell about this time'.[32] Davison goes on to speculate that there may have been another set of proofs, although he concludes that it seems more likely that Orwell merely missed the three semicolons. Nevertheless, because he was adamant about the absence of semicolons, the *Complete Works* edition omits them, though with notes on the changes. He makes the note that, 'What is plain is that though we have a later edition [the Uniform Edition], the proofs of which were read by the author, we cannot always be sure that Orwell noticed all he might have been expected to note nor can we be sure that his practices were carried through by the printer and publisher.' And he questions, 'To what extent did Orwell note and approve, or acquiesce to, changes made?'[33]

The first American edition was not published until 19 January 1950, two days before Orwell's death.

A.7a   *First Edition, 1939*

COMING UP FOR AIR | by | GEORGE ORWELL | LONDON | VICTOR GOLLANCZ LTD | 1939

Collation [AA]–SA⁸; 144 leaves (18.2 × 12.2); [1–9] 10–41 [42–45] 46–173 [174–177] 178–213 [214–217] 218–285 [286–288]

Contents [1] halftitle: COMING UP FOR AIR [2] publisher's advertisements [3] titlepage [4] imprint: PRINTED IN GREAT BRITAIN BY PURNELL AND SONS, LTD. (T.U.) | PAULTON SOMERSET) [sic] AND LONDON [5] halftitle: *He's dead, but he won't lie down* | POPULAR SONG [6] blank [7] halftitle: PART I [8] blank [9]–41 text of Part I [42] blank 43 halftitle: PART II [44] blank [45]–173 text of Part II [174] blank [175] halftitle: PART III [176] blank [177]–213 text of Part III [214] blank [215] halftitle: PART IV [216] blank [217]–285 text of Part IV [286–288] blank

Binding Blue calico textured cloth on boards. Off white endpapers.

Front and back covers Plain.

Spine Stamped in blue: COMING | UP FOR | AIR | BY | GEORGE | ORWELL | GOLLANCZ

Paper
Spalding & Hodge
Cream esparto antique wove
34 lines per page
11 pt Baskerville

Jacket Yellow
Front [publisher's geometric motif in pink] GEORGE | ORWELL'S | new NOVEL | COMING | UP | FOR AIR | [pointing hand symbol]
Back THE FANFARE PRESS, LONDON
Spine COMING | UP | FOR AIR | by | GEORGE ORWELL | 7|6 | net | [laterally] BY GEORGE ORWELL | [horizontally] GOLLANCZ
Front and back flaps Extracts from reviews of Orwell's works

Notes
Published 12 June 1939
7s 6d
2,000 copies

Contemporary reviews
Times Literary Supplement (17 June 1939)
Margery Allingham *Time and Tide* (24 June 1939)
Winifred Horrabin *Tribune* (21 July 1939)

Locations
Cambridge University Library, with jacket. Acquisition 5 June 1939.
Orwell Archive – two copies, one of which is inscribed by Orwell. Inscription on front free endpaper in ink in Orwell's handwriting: Richard Rees | from | Eric Blair | [short rule]

Reissue
Reissued later in June 1939, with slight, unintentional differences of slipped type.
1,000 copies
Additional and corrected imprint on [4]: *First published June 1939* | *Second impression June 1939* | PRINTED IN GREAT BRITAIN BY PURNELL AND SONS, LTD. (T.U.) | PAULTON (SOMERSET) AND LONDON

Locations
There is an inscribed copy of this issue in the Orwell Archive. Inscription on front free endpaper in ink in Orwell's handwriting: Mabel Fienz | from | Eric Blair | [short rule]

A.7b   Uniform Edition, 1948

COMING UP FOR AIR | BY | GEORGE ORWELL | LONDON | SECKER & WARBURG | 1948

Collation [1]–14⁸ 15⁷; 119 leaves (18.1 × 12.1); [1–6] 7–237 [238]. In the final gathering, 15, there is in fact an eighth leaf, but this is pasted down as the back fixed endpaper. It is, therefore, not included either here or under Contents.

Contents [1] halftitle: COMING UP FOR AIR [2] list of books by Orwell [3] titlepage [4] imprint: Martin Secker & Warburg Ltd. | 7 John Street, Bloomsbury, London, W.C.1 | *First published (Gollancz) June 1939* | *Reprinted June 1939* | *New edition, reset, 1948* | MADE AND PRINTED IN GREAT BRITAIN BY | MORRISON AND GIBB LTD., LONDON AND EDINBURGH [5] imprint: *He's dead, but he won't lie down.* | POPULAR SONG [6] blank 7–237 text [238] blank

Binding Green calico textured cloth on boards. Off white front endpapers. No back endpapers, see Collation. Red topped leaves.

Front and back covers Plain.

Spine Stamped in purplish red: [pyramid of six lines] | COMING | UP FOR | AIR | [small ornate leaf device] | GEORGE | ORWELL | [inverted pyramid of six lines] | SECKER & | WARBURG

Jacket Front and spine green, otherwise off white.
Front [Two off-white panels outlined in black] [Top panel]: COMING UP | FOR AIR [and in space between panels]: *A NOVEL* [bottom panel]: GEORGE | ORWELL [and in off-white at foot]: *UNIFORM EDITION*
Spine COMING | UP FOR | AIR | [leaf motif] | GEORGE | ORWELL | SECKER & | WARBURG
Back Advertisement for *Animal Farm.*
Front flap [summary] | W.408 [only jacket seen had bottom corner of front flap torn off]
Back flap | [summary continued] | [within a frame is a publisher's advertisement]

Notes
Published 13 May 1948
9s 6d
5,000 copies

Price reduced to 7s 6d in February 1950
Price increased to 8s 6d in March 1951
Price increased to 10s 6d in February 1952

Saunders acted as distributing Canadian agents.

This was the first volume of the Uniform Edition.

Locations
Cambridge University Library, with jacket. Acquisition 27 May 1948.
Orwell Archive, with jacket.

Corrected proof
Orwell Archive [Box 5]
Corrected proofs of new edition of *Coming Up for Air*, Secker & Warburg 1948
Titlepage 1947 corrected to 1948
Proofs stamped 6 October 1947 Morrison & Gibb, Printers, Edinburgh and stamped
Received 7 October 1947 on halftitle
Sections stamped 6 October 1947, 7 October 1947, 13 October 1947, 14 October 1947, 16
October 1947.
Corrected by Orwell in ballpoint pen. Other corrections in another hand
15 unbound gatherings [1]–15
size varies from 19.0 × 12.6 to 18.3 × 12.3
Date stamped by Morrison & Gibb: 6 October 1947
Marked by Orwell: Received 7 Oct 1947
Described by Davison.[34]

Proofs of four leaves of first part of prelims of *Coming Up for Air* 1948, with corrections
made as marked by Orwell as above.

Contemporary reviews
Julian Symons *The Manchester Evening News* (19 May 1948)

Reissues
Reissued in 1954 with amended titlepage and imprint, and with the eighth leaf of the final
gathering free and a full set of back endpapers. Leaf tops plain. Jacket as 1948 issue, but
with publisher's advertisement for books by Orwell on back, and price added to front flap:
10s. 6d | NET
W.408 removed from front flap.

Reissued in April 1959 with amended titlepage and imprint. Reddish purple topped leaves.
Spine stamped in gilt. Jacket as 1948 issue. Orwell Archive jacket shows original price on
front flap as 9s 6d, printed out and amended to 8s 6d, and with two amending stickers
over showing price as 6s 0d and later 10s 6d.

Reissued in 1963, 1967, 1971, 1973 and 1978.

Orwell Archive has a 1971 reissue with jacket. The titlepage is undated, there is a new
imprint and a list of Orwell's books. The binding is green paper embossed to resemble
calico textured cloth.
Jacket Dull brown.
Front [Printed in silver]: GEORGE | ORWELL | [and in dark brown]: COMING UP | FOR
AIR
Back Plain.
Spine [laterally] [in silver]: ORWELL [and in dark brown]: COMING UP | FOR AIR
[horizontally in silver]: SECKER & | WARBURG
Front flap [in dark brown] [plot summary] | [bottom left]: Jacket design by | Format
[bottom right]: £1.75 | net
Back flap [in dark brown] [list of books by Orwell] | 436 35002 5

Locations
Cambridge University Library – 1971, with jacket. Acquisition 6 March 1972.
Orwell Archive – 1954, 1959, and 1971.

A.7c   First American Edition, 1950

GEORGE ORWELL | [short rule] | COMING UP | FOR AIR | [short rule] | HARCOURT, BRACE AND COMPANY | NEW YORK

Collation There are nine unmarked gatherings of 16 leaves arranged [1–9]¹⁶; 144 leaves (20.1 × 13.4); [X1–X6] [1–2] 3–36 [37–38] 39–166 [167–168] 169–206 [207–208] 209–278 [279–282]

Contents [X1] halftitle: COMING UP FOR AIR [X2] list of books by Orwell [X3] titlepage [X4] imprint: COPYRIGHT, 1950, BY | HARCOURT, BRACE AND COMPANY, INC. | *All rights reserved, including | the right to reproduce this book | or portions thereof in any form.* | B.5.60 | PRINTED IN THE UNITED STATES OF AMERICA [X5] halftitle: *"He's dead, but he won't lie down."* | POPULAR SONG [X6] blank [1] halftitle: I [2] blank 3–36 text of Part I [37] halftitle: II [38] blank 39–166 text of Part II [167] halftitle: III [168] blank 169–206 text of Part III [207] halftitle: IV [208] blank 209–278 text of Part IV 279–282 blank

Binding Grey calico textured cloth on boards. Off white endpapers.

Front cover Stamped in grey in bottom right is a drawing of a fishing rod and line, a hat, brief case, and glass of beer.

Back cover Plain.

Spine Stamped in grey: GEORGE | ORWELL | [rule] | [laterally]: COMING UP FOR AIR | [and horizontally]: [rule] | HARCOURT, BRACE | AND COMPANY

Jacket Front and spine green and blue, otherwise off white.
Front Against a coloured illustration of a lake and grassy tree lined shore with fishing rod and line, a hat, brief case, and glass of beer is printed in blue: *George Orwell's new novel* [cursive script] | [and picked out in white]: COMING | UP | FOR | AIR | [and beneath in blue]: *by the author of Nineteen Eighty-four* [cursive script] | [artist's signature]: hawkins
Back Publisher's advertisement for books by Orwell.
Spine Against a blue and green background wrapped from front is printed in blue: *George* | *Orwell* [cursive script] | [and picked out in white]: COMING | UP | FOR | AIR | [and in blue]: HARCOURT, BRACE | AND COMPANY
Front flap [in blue]: $3.95 | COMING UP | FOR AIR [in green]: By GEORGE ORWELL | [in blue]: [plot summary] | [in green]: HARCOURT, BRACE AND COMPANY
Back flap publisher's advertisements

Notes
Published 19 January 1950
$3.95
8,000 copies
Jacket designed by Arthur Hawkins

Contemporary reviews
John Cogley *Commonweal* (3 February 1950)
Irving Howe *The Nation* (4 February 1950)
Edmund Fuller *The Saturday Review of Literature* (18 February 1950)
James Stern *The New Republic* (20 February 1950)
Charles Rolo *The Atlantic Monthly* (March 1950)
Isaac Rosenfeld *Partisan Review* (May 1950)

Locations
Orwell Archive

A.7d   Second American Edition, 1950

[across two pages] [facing titlepage]: Coming Up [titlepage]: For Air | GEORGE ORWELL | *Complete and Unabridged* | AVON PUBLICATIONS, INC. | 575 Madison Avenue – New York 22, N.Y.

Collation 96 unmarked leaves in a perfect binding (16.1 × 10.3); [X1–X2] [1–4] 5–190

Contents [X1] extracts from reviews [X2–1] titlepages [2] imprint: Copyright, 1950, by Harcourt, Brace and Company, Inc. Pub- | lished by arrangement with Harcourt, Brace and Company, | Inc. Printed in the U.S.A. [3] halftitle: *Coming Up For Air* [4] blank 5–190 text, on 190: [within a frame]: *Also published by Avon* | DOWN AND OUT IN LONDON AND PARIS [sic] | By George Orwell

Binding Paper bound.

Front cover In red: GEORGE ORWELL'S | [in black]: GREAT NOVEL OF | ONE MAN'S TEMPTATION | [in blue]: COMING UP | FOR AIR [and in top right in blue]: AVON | [short rule] | 35c | [short rule] | T–144 | [cover illustration in colour of a man and woman embracing, overlooked by a man depicted in larger format than the couple and in black and white] | [in white]: By the Author of "1984" | artist's signature: Marchetti | [in yellow]: Complete and Unabridge [sic]

Back cover Across two red stripes and one white stripe: [extracts from reviews] | Printed in U.S.A.

Spine Against a blue background [laterally in yellow]: GEORGE | ORWELL [and laterally in white]: COMING UP FOR AIR | [horizontally in black]: [publisher's device]: AVON | T–144

Notes
35c

A.7e   Third American Edition, 1961

COMING | UP | FOR | AIR | by George Orwell | [publisher's monogram device in frame]: HB | A HILLMAN/MACFADDEN BOOK

Collation 96 unmarked leaves in a perfect binding (17.9 × 10.2); [1–4] 5–191 [192]

Contents [1] plot summary and extract from review [2] list of books by Orwell [3] titlepage [4] imprint: This book is the complete text of the hardcover book. | A HILLMAN/MACFADDEN BOOK ... 1961 | Copyright 1950 by Harcourt, Brace and Company, Inc. | Published by arrangement with Harcourt, Brace and World, Publishers | HILLMAN BOOKS are published by | BARTHOLOMEW HOUSE, Inc. | 205 East 42nd Street, New York, 17, N.Y. | PRINTED IN THE U.S.A. 5–191 text [192] publisher's advertisement

Binding Paper bound. Covers green. Yellow edged leaves.

Front cover Printed in white: GEORGE ORWELL | BY THE AUTHOR OF 1984 | [in blue]: COMING | UP FOR | AIR [and to the right in white]: 50–106 | [publisher's monogram device] | 50c [cents sign] | [coloured illustration of a village by a lake, with a man in the foreground in brown suit and bowler hat, carrying a rolled umbrella] | [in blue]: "'COMING UP FOR AIR' is by | any standards, a work of rare | vigor and imagination." | [in black]: – NEW YORK HERALD TRIBUNE

Back cover [in white]: [quotation, plot summary and extract from review] | [grey and white version of front cover illustration] | [in white]: A HILLMAN-MACFADDEN BOOK | PRINTED IN THE U.S.A.

Spine Printed in white: 50–106 | [laterally]: COMING UP FOR AIR GEORGE ORWELL | [and horizontally]: [publisher's monogram device] | 50c [cents sign]

Notes
50 cents

Locations
Orwell Archive

A.7f *First Penguin Edition, 1962*

George Orwell | COMING UP FOR AIR | [two short rules] | PENGUIN BOOKS | IN ASSOCIATION WITH | SECKER & WARBURG

Collation 120 unmarked leaves in a perfect binding (18.1 × 11.0); [1–6] 7–232 [233–240]

Contents [1] halftitle: PENGUIN BOOKS | 1697 | COMING UP FOR AIR | GEORGE ORWELL | [penguin motif] [2] blank [3] titlepage [4] imprint: Penguin Books Ltd, Harmondsworth, Middlesex | AUSTRALIA: Penguin Books Pty Ltd, 762 Whitehorse Road, | Mitcham, Victoria | [short rule] | First published by Victor Gollancz 1939 | Published in Penguin Books 1962 | [short rule] | Made and printed in Great Britain | by C. Nicholls & Company Ltd | [copyright notice] [5] halftitle: *He's dead, but he won't lie down* | POPULAR SONG [6] blank 7–232 text [233] [penguin motif and publisher's notice] [234] blank [235–240] publisher's advertisements

Binding Paper bound in orange.

Front cover [penguin motif in white] | a Penguin Book 3'6 | [rule] | Coming up | for Air | [rule] | [in white]: George Orwell | [black and grey photograph of top half of a man's head, with bowler hat, above which is a bubble cloud containing a photograph of a man fishing in a stream]

Back cover [penguin motif in white] a Penguin Book | [rule] | Coming up | for Air | [rule] | [plot summary] | *For copyright reasons this edition* | *is not for sale in the U.S.A.*

Spine laterally: [in white] George Orwell [in black] Coming up for Air | [horizontally] [penguin motif] | 1697

Inside front cover [photograph of Orwell] | *Vernon Richards* | [biographical summary] | Cover design by Alan Fletcher | [publisher's notice]

Inside back cover Publisher's advertisements

Locations
Cambridge University Library. Acquisition 26 February 1962.
Orwell Archive

Reissues
1963, 1965, 1967, 1969, 1970, 1971, 1973, 1974, 1975, 1976, 1977, 1978, 1979, 1980, 1981, 1983, 1984 (twice)
1989 Twentieth Century Classics edition, based on the Complete Works edition.

Locations
1965 – Orwell Archive [covers as first Penguin issue]
1979 – Orwell Archive [cover has coloured photograph of bowler hat and primroses on an old stone wall]
1984 – Orwell Archive, second 1984 issue [cover has painting of the upper torso of a man in a bowler hat, against a suburban scene, with military aircraft in the sky above]

A.7g   *Octopus Edition, 1976*

For titlepage transcription see *Animal Farm* A.10s

Coming Up for Air is one of six Orwell novels in this compendium volume. The other novels are *Animal Farm, Burmese Days, A Clergyman's Daughter, Keep the Aspidistra Flying,* and *Nineteen Eighty-Four.*
Published by Secker & Warburg|Octopus, 1976.
Coming Up for Air is on pp.427–571
Hard bound with jacket.

Locations
Cambridge University Library. Acquisition 7 January 1977.

A.7h   *The Penguin Complete Novels of George Orwell Edition, 1983*

(Harmondsworth: Penguin, 1983) 925pp

A compendium edition of the following novels:

Animal Farm
Burmese Days
A Clergyman's Daughter
Coming Up for Air
Keep the Aspidistra Flying
Nineteen Eighty-Four

Paper bound
£4.95

Locations
Orwell Archive two copies

A.7i   *The Complete Works Edition, 1986*

THE COMPLETE WORKS OF | GEORGE ORWELL | VOLUME SEVEN | Coming Up for Air | He's dead, but he won't lie down. | POPULAR SONG | SECKER & WARBURG | [short rule] | LONDON

Collation There are nine unmarked gatherings arranged [A–D]^{16} [E]^8 [F–I]^{16}; 272 leaves (23.2 × 15.4); [i–viii] [1–2] 3–247 [248] 249–[255] [256–264]

Contents [i–ii] blank [iii] halftitle: THE COMPLETE WORKS OF | GEORGE ORWELL . SEVEN | COMING UP FOR AIR [iv] blank [v] publisher's note [vi] blank [vii] titlepage [viii] imprint: [selective publishing history of editions and reissues] | [copyright notices] | [British Library Cataloguing in Publication Data] | ISBN 0–436–35029–7 | Typeset in Monophoto Bembo by | Northumberland Press Ltd, Gateshead, Tyne and Wear | Printed and bound in Great Britain by | Richard Clay Ltd, Bungay, Suffolk [1] halftitle: PART I [2] blank 3–247 text [248] blank 249–[255] textual note [256–264] blank

Binding Blue paper on boards, embossed to resemble calico textured cloth. Black endpapers.

Front and back covers Plain.

Spine Stamped in gilt: [double rule] | GEORGE | ORWELL | [rule] | Coming | Up for | Air | [double rule] | SECKER & | WARBURG

Locations
Cambridge University Library
Orwell Archive
Robarts Library, University of Toronto
Reprinted 1996

TRANSLATIONS

DANISH

A.7.T1   *En mundfuld frisk luft*

Translated by Poul Pedersen
Denmark: Gyldendal, 1977
Paperbound

DUTCH

A.7.T2   *Happend naar lucht*

Translated by Gerrit Komrij
Amsterdam: Meulenhoff, 1971, reissued 1983.
Paperbound

FRENCH

A.7.T3a   *Journal d'un anglais moyen*, 1952

Translated by Claude de Leschaux
Paris: Amiot Dumont
Paperbound
April 1952
Serialised in *Le Monde* August–September 1952

A.7.T3b   *Un Peu d'Air Frais*, 1983

Translated by Richard Prêtre
Paris: Editions Champ Libre
Paperbound

GERMAN

A.7.T4   *Das Verschüttete Leben*, 1973

Translated by Helmut M. Braem
Zurich: Neue Diana Press
Paper on boards
Reissued in a Diogenes paperback 1981, 1983, 1990

ITALIAN

A.7.T5   *Una Boccata d'Aria*, 1966

Translated by Bruno Maffi
Verona: Arnoldo Mondadori
July 1966
Cloth on boards
Reissued in paperback with an Introduction by Elena Croce, 1980

JAPANESE

A.7.T6   *George Orwell*, 1985

Edition in English
Kyoto: Yamaguchi Shoten
Edited with an Introduction and Notes by Koji Watanabe
Cloth on boards

Contents:
Coming Up for Air
Politics v Literature
Why I Write

PORTUGUESE

A.7.T7   *Na Sombra de 1984: Un Pouco de Ar, Per Favor!*, 1973

Translated by Maria Judith Martins
Sao Paulo: Hemus
Paperbound

SPANISH

A.7.T8   *Subir a por Aire*, 1972

Translated by Ester Donato
Barcelona: Ediciones Destino
Cloth on boards
Reissued in paperback, 1982

SWEDISH

A.7.T9   *Snappa efter luft*, 1975

Translated by Olof Hoffsten
Stockholm: Rabén & Sjögren
Paperbound

A.8   INSIDE THE WHALE

I find this kind of semi-sociological literary criticism very interesting.[1]

Composition and publication

Orwell began to write the essays for *Inside the Whale* on 24 May 1939, soon after his return to England. He told Geoffrey Gorer,

> We got back from Morocco in the spring & I began on another book, then I'm sorry to say my father died ... Then I got going on the book again & then the war threw me out of my stride, so in the end a very short book that was meant to take 4 months took me 6 or 7.[2]

By mid-December, following a fairly frustrating, unproductive period at the outbreak of the war, he had finished the book and sent to manuscript to Victor Gollancz. In January 1940 he explained the thinking behind it to Gollancz:

As to your remarks on my book, I am glad you liked it. You are perhaps right in thinking that I am over-pessimistic. It is quite possible that freedom of thought etc may survive in an economically totalitarian society. We can't tell until a collectivised economy has been tried out in a western country. What worries me at present is the uncertainty as to whether the ordinary people in countries like England grasp the difference between democracy and despotism well enough to want to defend their liberties. One can't tell until they see themselves menaced in some quite unmistakable manner. The intellectuals who are at present pointing out that democracy and fascism are the same thing etc depress me horribly. However, perhaps when the pinch comes the common people will turn out to be more intelligent than the clever ones. I certainly hope so.[3]

In April 1940 he wrote to Gorer,

You didn't I suppose see my last (*Inside the Whale*) which came out a few weeks back. There is one essay in it that might interest you, on boys' weekly papers, as it rather overlaps with your own researches. You remember perhaps my saying to you some years back that very popular fiction ought to be looked into & instancing Edgar Wallace. This essay was published first in a slightly abridged form in Cyril Connolly's monthly paper *Horizon*, & now the editor of *Magnet*, which you no doubt remember from your boyhood, has asked for space in which to answer my "charges". I look forward to this with some uneasiness, as I've no doubt made many mistakes, but what he'll probably pick on is my suggestion that these papers try to inculcate snobbishness. I haven't a copy left to send you but you might be able to get it from the library. There is an essay on Dickens that might interest you too. I find this kind of semi–sociological literary criticism very interesting & I'd like to do a lot of other writers, but unfortunately there's no money in it. All Gollancz would give me in advance on the book was £20![4]

In July 1940 he responded to a request from James Laughlin, the editor and writer, and American publisher of New Directions books: 'Yes, you may certainly reprint the Henry Miller essay ['Inside the Whale']. I'm not sure how my contract with my publisher stands, and I have written to him, but I know he won't object.'[5] [See B.3].

A.8a   First Edition, 1940

INSIDE THE WHALE | *and* | OTHER ESSAYS | *by* | GEORGE ORWELL | LONDON | VICTOR GOLLANCZ LTD | 1940

Collation [A]–L[8] M[6]; 94 leaves (21.6 × 13.5); [1–4] 5 [6–8] 9–188

Contents [1] halftitle: INSIDE THE WHALE | *and* | OTHER ESSAYS [2] list of books by Orwell [3] titlepage [4] imprint: PRINTED IN GREAT BRITAIN BY RICHARD CLAY AND COMPANY, LTD., (T.U.) | BUNGAY, SUFFOLK. 5 contents [6] blank [7]–188 text, on 188: THE END

Binding Black calico textured cloth on boards. Off white endpapers.

Front and back covers Plain.

Spine Stamped in yellow: INSIDE | THE | WHALE | BY | GEORGE | ORWELL | GOLLANCZ

Jacket Yellow
Front INSIDE THE | WHALE | [in purple] BY | GEORGE | ORWELL | [in black] note on Orwell and these essays | [in purple is a pointing hand]
Back THE FANFARE PRESS, LONDON
Spine INSIDE | THE | WHALE | by | GEORGE | ORWELL | 7|[not line break]6 | NET | [in purple is a publisher's triangular device and the letter]: G | [in black] GOLLANCZ

Front flap front cover notes continued
Back flap Plain

Paper White esparto straw, wartime wove

Notes
Published 11 March 1940
1,000 copies
7s 6d
'Boys' Weeklies' had appeared in a slightly shortened form in *Horizon* in March 1940 as an excerpt from the forthcoming book.
Several copies destroyed in an air raid

Contents
Charles Dickens
Boys' Weeklies
Inside the Whale

Contemporary reviews
Max Plowman *Adelphi* (April 1940)
V.S. Pritchett *New Statesman and Nation* (16 March 1940)
Times Literary Supplement (20 April 1940)
Margaret Cole *Tribune* (15 March 1940)

This is not the same collection as the Penguin *Inside the Whale and Other Essays*, a selection which was first published under the title *Selected Essays* [D.8].

Locations
Orwell Archive, two copies, one with jacket
Cambridge University Library

A.9   THE LION AND THE UNICORN

As I write, highly civilised human beings are flying overhead, trying to kill me.[1]

Composition and publication

In an autobiographical note written in April 1940, Orwell said,

> I am not at the moment writing a novel, chiefly owing to upsets caused by the war. But I am projecting a long novel in three parts, to be called either *The Lion and the Unicorn* or *The Quick and the Dead*, and hope to produce the first part by some time in 1941.[2]

But he abandoned the idea of writing it as fiction, using the title instead for the new essays he was working on. Orwell wrote *The Lion and the Unicorn* between August and October 1940, while living in London and working as a journalist. It was published on 19 February 1941 as the first of the *Searchlight Books*, a series started in 1940, and edited by Orwell and T.R. Fyvel. It was a special series, produced to war-time standards, and concentrating on war-time problems and possible solutions. Seventeen titles were originally projected, although only ten were published between 1940 and 1942.[3]

In his 'London Letter' to the *Partisan Review*, published as the July–August 1941 issue, but actually written in April 1941, Orwell responded to a question from his American editors: 'How do you explain what, over here, seems to be the remarkable amount of democracy and civil liberties preserved during the war? Labour pressure? British tradition? Weakness of the upper classes?' Orwell replied:

> "British tradition" is a vague phrase, but I think it is the nearest answer. I suppose I shall seem to be giving myself a free advert, but may I draw attention to a recent book

of mine, *The Lion and the Unicorn* (I believe copies have reached the USA)? In it I pointed out that there is in England a certain feeling of family loyalty which cuts across the class system (also makes it easier for the class system to survive, I'm afraid) and checks the growth of political hatred.[4]

Orwell was called on to account for the views he expressed in the book elsewhere. A Congregationalist minister wrote to him in April 1941, asking for amplification of certain points. Orwell wrote him a comprehensive reply,[5] admitting, 'Perhaps in one or two cases I expressed myself rather ambiguously'. Then in 1944 he wrote,

I believe very deeply, as I explained in my book *The Lion and the Unicorn*, in the English *people* and in their capacity to centralise their economy without destroying freedom in doing so.[6]

A.9a   First Edition, 1941

THE LION AND THE | UNICORN | Socialism and the English Genius | GEORGE ORWELL | SEARCHLIGHT | [searchlight motif] | BOOKS | LONDON | SECKER & WARBURG | 1941

Collation [A]–D[16]; 64 leaves (18.2 × 11.2); [1–8] 9–126 [127–128]

Contents [1] halftitle: THE LION AND THE UNICORN | SEARCHLIGHT BOOK No. I [2] THE SEARCHLIGHT BOOKS | *Edited by T.R. Fyvel and George Orwell* | [list of Searchlight Books] [3] titlepage [4] imprint: Martin Secker & Warburg Ltd. | 22 Essex Street, London, W.C. 2 | *First published 1941* | Made and Printed in Great Britain at | *The Mayflower Press, Plymouth.* William Brendon & Son, Ltd. [5] contents [6] list of books by Orwell [7]–[127] text [128] W3001

Binding Mottled grey linen grain cloth on boards. Off white endpapers.

Front and back covers Plain.

Spine Stamped in green, laterally: GEORGE | ORWELL | [double horizontal rules] | [laterally] THE LION AND THE UNICORN | [two horizontal rules] | S.B.

Jacket Off white and blue
Front THE LION AND | THE UNICORN | *SOCIALISM AND THE ENGLISH GENIUS* | [blue dot] | GEORGE ORWELL | [drawing of a searchlight in blue and white] | SEARCHLIGHT BOOKS
Back Publisher's advertisement
Spine [laterally] [against a blue background] THE LION AND THE UNICORN [and against an off-white background] *GEORGE ORWELL* | [horizontally] 2s. | net | S.B. | No. 1
Front flap [summary] | *Jacket design by Zec*
Back flap [biographical summary]

Notes
Contents: England Your England
            Shopkeepers at War
            The English Revolution

Published 19 February 1941.
2s 0d
5,000 copies

The type was destroyed in an air raid on Plymouth.
There were no separate American or Canadian editions. Transatlantic Arts and Saunders distributed bound copies of the British edition.

Reprinted in *CEJL* II 56–109.
Part of 'England your England' was published as 'The Ruling Class' in *Horizon* in

December 1940 [see C.224], and the essay was published in full in *Such, Such Were the Joys*, *England Your England*, and *The Orwell Reader*.

Contemporary reviews
Max Plowman *Adelphi* (April 1941)
Evening Standard (22 February 1941)
The Listener (6 March 1941)
V.S. Pritchett *New Statesman and Nation* (1 March 1941)
Times Literary Supplement (8 March 1941)

Locations
Cambridge University Library. Acquisition 19 May 1941.
Robarts Library, University of Toronto [rebound].
Orwell Archive, with jacket

Reissue
March 1941.
5,000 copies
Orwell Archive, two copies. Both copies are bound in mottled grey linen grain cloth, although one has the grain vertical, and the other horizontal.

A.9b   Uniform Edition, 1962

THE LION AND THE | UNICORN | Socialism and the English Genius | GEORGE ORWELL | LONDON | SECKER AND WARBURG | 1962

Collation [A]–C^16; 48 leaves (18.4 × 12.4); [1–8] 9–96

Contents [1] halftitle: THE LION AND THE UNICORN [2] list of books by Orwell [3] titlepage [4] imprint: MARTIN SECKER & WARBURG LTD | 14 Carlisle Street | London W.1 | ALL RIGHTS RESERVED | First published February 1941 | Reprinted March 1941 | Reprinted May 1962 in the Uniform Edition | *Printed in Britain by* | *Northumberland Press Limited* | *Gateshead on Tyne 8* [5] contents [6] blank [7]–96 text

Binding Green calico grain cloth on boards. Off white endpapers.

Front and back covers Plain.

Spine Stamped in gilt: [pyramid of 6 lines] | THE LION | AND THE | UNICORN [leaf motif] | GEORGE | ORWELL | [inverted pyramid of 6 lines] | *Secker &* | *Warburg*

Jacket
Front Broad red stripe at top in which is printed: The Lion | and the Unicorn | [in white] George Orwell | [Rest of front is grey with red line drawing of lion and unicorn and, to the right] Socialism | and the | English genius | [in red] Part 1 | England your | England | [in red] Part 2 | Shopkeepers | at war | [in red] Part 3 | The English | revolution
Back
Printed against a red background is a list of the books in the Uniform Edition of Orwell.
Spine Red and grey sections wrapped around from front. In the red stripe, laterally: The Lion | and the Unicorn | [in the grey stripe, in white, laterally] George Orwell | [horizontally printed in red is a line drawing of a lion and a unicorn] | [laterally in black] Secker & | Warburg
Front flap [description of contents] | Jacket design by | DENIS PIPER | 12s 6d | net
Back flap MP | G306

Locations
Cambridge University Library. Acquisition 2 November 1962.
Orwell Archive, with jacket.

Notes
There is a new Penguin edition, with an Introduction by Bernard Crick, published in 1982. Reissued 1986.

Locations
Cambridge University Library. Acquisition 20 May 1982.

1989 Penguin Twentieth Century Classics edition.

A.10 ANIMAL FARM

I do not wish to comment on the work; if it does not speak for itself, it is a failure.[1]

Composition and publication

Despite his plans to produce a grand-scale novel once *Coming Up for Air* was finished, it was an ambition Orwell failed to realise. In 1938 he had told Jack Common, 'I suppose after this book I shall write some kind of pot-boiler, but I have very dimly in my mind the idea for an enormous novel in several volumes and I want several years to plan it out in peace.'[2] And in early 1939 he wrote to Geoffrey Gorer,

> I have an idea for a very big novel, in fact 3 in series, making something abt the size of War and Peace, but I want another year to think over the first part. I suppose it's a sign of approaching senile decay when one starts projecting a Saga, but in my case it may merely be another way of saying that I hope war won't break out, because I don't think I could write a Saga in the middle of a war, certainly not in the concentration camp.[3]

He returned to England from Morocco at the end of March 1939. The house, the garden and The Stores demanded most of his time, although on 24 May he began writing the *Inside the Whale* essays and had finished them by mid-December. But war broke out on 3 September 1939 and he wrote almost nothing new – only seven published items, including five short reviews and two longer pieces already in preparation – in four months. He tried repeatedly to find war work, but his chest made him medically unfit for the armed services. His financial situation was so critical that Eileen took a job in London, in the Censorship Department, going home only at weekends. Although he kept on The Stores until 1947, in May 1940 he and Eileen took a flat near Regent's Park in London. Later in the war they moved to Abbey Road, and then to Maida Vale. He joined the Local Defence Volunteers, the Home Guard, as a sergeant, and began a regular theatre criticism column in *Time and Tide*. In August 1940 he began *The Lion and the Unicorn* for the Searchlights Books series on war-time problems, a series which he also edited over the next two years. In 1941 he began contributing to the *Partisan Review*. Over the next five and a half years he wrote 15 major articles for the journal. He continued his journalism, but on 18 August 1941 he joined the BBC, first as a Talks Assistant and later as a Talks Producer, at a salary of £640 a year, in the Indian Section of the Eastern Service. It was full-time work, although he continued to write for newspapers and magazines. On 23 November 1943 Orwell left the Home Guard, and on 24 November he resigned from the BBC, both on medical grounds. He became literary editor of *Tribune*. On 3 December, the first of his 'As I Please' articles appeared in the magazine, a column he continued until April 1947, more or less regularly. He also began a fortnightly column for the *Manchester Evening News*, which continued until November 1946, and a fortnightly *Observer* column, which continued until May 1946. And, also in November 1943, he started writing *Animal Farm*.

In December he told Philip Rahv, 'I have left the BBC after two wasted years in it and have become literary editor of the *Tribune* ... It leaves me a little spare time, which the BBC didn't, so I have got another book under weigh which I hope to finish in a few months if nothing intervenes.'[4] In February 1944 he told Gleb Struve, a teacher in Slavic studies, then at the University of London, 'I am writing a little squib which might amuse you when it comes out.'[5] It was very quickly written, and finished in February 1944. On 5 April, having received the anticipated rejection from Gollancz, he told Leonard Moore,

... we shall have great difficulty in getting this book published in England though it may be easier in the USA. Naturally I want it in print, and if all else fails I shall take it to one or other of the little highbrow presses I know of.[6]

On 15 April he suggested to Moore,

Faber's is *just* possible, and Routledge's rather more so if they have the paper. While Cape's have it I'll sound both Eliot and Herbert Read. I saw recently a book published by Eyre and Spottiswoode and I think they must be all right.[7]

While looking for an English publisher, Orwell also sent it to the Dial Press in New York. On 1 May he told Philip Rahv,

I dare say the Dial people will have got my MS by about now. As you say you're in touch with them, I wonder if you could ask them to let you have a look at it. I think you will agree it deserves to be printed, but its 'message' is hardly a popular one nowadays. I am having hell and all to find a publisher for it here though normally I have no difficulty in publishing my stuff and in any case all publishers are now clamouring for manuscripts.[8]

By July Gollancz, Nicholson & Watson, Jonathan Cape, and Faber & Faber had all turned it down on the grounds that the political climate of the time was unfavourable for such a book.

In early June Orwell and Eileen adopted a baby. At the end of the month their Maida Vale flat was hit by a bomb, and they moved into a friend's off Baker Street until they were able to find another, in Islington, in October. Orwell had sent the manuscript to T.S. Eliot at Faber & Faber at the end of June:[9]

This MS has been blitzed which accounts for my delay in delivering it and its slightly crumpled condition, but it is not damaged in any way.

I wonder if you could be kind enough to let me have Messrs Fabers' decision fairly soon. If they are interested in seeing more of my work, I could let you have the facts abt my existing contract with Gollancz, which is not an onerous one nor likely to last long.

If you read this MS yourself you will see its meaning which is not an acceptable one at this moment, but I could not agree to make any alterations except a small one at the end which I intend making anyway. Cape or the MOI [Ministry of Information], I am not certain which from the wording of his letter, made the imbecile suggestion that some other animal than pigs might be made to represent the Bolsheviks. I could not of course make any change of that description.[10]

But Faber & Faber also rejected it. On 13 July T.S. Eliot wrote to Orwell about the novel:

... a distinguished piece of writing; that the fable is very skilfully handled, and that the narrative keeps one's interest on its own plane – and that is something very few authors have achieved since Gulliver.[11]

A letter from Orwell to Moore in mid-July, however, indicates a couple of other possibilities:

... could you send me the copy of the MS that you have. Faber's replied in much the same sense as Cape's. Warburg again says he wants to see it & would publish it if he can see his way to getting the paper, but that is a big 'if'. If that falls through I am not going to tout it round further publishers, which wastes time & may lead to nothing, but shall publish it myself as a pamphlet at 2|–. I have already half-arranged to do so & have got the necessary financial backing. With the demand for books there is now, and the strings I can pull in one or two papers, I have no doubt we should get our money back, though probably not make much profit. You understand that it is important to get this book into print, & this year if possible.[12]

Fredric Warburg was slow to arrive at the decision to publish the book, but by the beginning of October they had agreed terms. Orwell began to plan the book which became *Critical Essays* and by 22 January 1945 he had sent Moore all but the essay 'In Defence of P.G. Wodehouse', which was not completed until February. Orwell had the page proofs of *Animal Farm* on 31 January 1945. He gave up the literary editorship of *Tribune* in February and on the 15th, about to leave for two months' work in France as a war correspondent for the *Observer*, he told Moore:

> I am sending back these contracts after some delay as I have been very busy ... I suppose I shall be away when Animal Farm comes out. I am sending Warburg a list of the people to send complimentary copies and special review copies to. I wonder if you could be kind enough to send my press cuttings and any other communications direct to my wife ... She has full powers to make decisions for me on any question that may come up.[13]

There were delays in publication, not entirely without their usefulness. In mid-March Orwell wrote to Roger Senhouse:

> I don't know whether Animal Farm has definitively gone to press. If it has not actually been printed yet, there is one further alteration of one word that I would like to make. In Chapter VIII (I think it is VIII), when the windmill is blown up, I wrote 'all the animals including Napoleon flung themselves on their faces.' I would like to alter it to 'all the animals except Napoleon.' If the book has been printed it's not worth bothering about, but I just thought the alteration would be fair to JS [Joseph Stalin], as he did stay in Moscow during the German advance.[14]

He continued to send articles back to the *Observer* and the *Manchester Evening News*. He anticipated being back in England at the end of April. In the event, he did not return until 24 May, having visited, among other places, Nuremburg, Stuttgart and Paris, where he was on VE Day, 8 May 1945. He did not return earlier despite Eileen's sudden, tragic death on 29 March: perhaps it made him prolong his time away.

He was now busier than ever, the only breadwinner, and with a young child in his care. In June and July he covered the London General Election campaign for the *Observer* and resumed regular, serious journalism. Then on 3 July he told Leonard Moore that he had 'recently started a novel': he was writing *Nineteen Eighty-Four*. The question of a publisher was clearly already in his mind, since, technically, he was still under contract to Gollancz for his next two novels. On 13 June he had told Fred Warburg:

> I will send the blurb [for *Animal Farm*] as soon as possible.
>
> As to a contract for a novel, I was in France when the two contracts reached me and I probably did not explain adequately why I did not sign the novel contract and struck out references to it in the other contract. To begin with, the novel referred to did not exist and does not exist yet. Secondly there was the question of my existing contract with Gollancz. I still have a contract to give Gollancz the first refusal of my next two works of fiction, but I have no intention of keeping this as he has not kept his contract with me in spirit nor, I think, in the letter. However, I want to remain within my rights and this involves something which I had explained to Moore but which he failed to understand. Gollancz was offered Animal Farm, which of course I knew in advance he would refuse, and he was only offered it on his own insistence. Having refused it he refused to regard it as one of the two contracted novels on the ground that it was too short. It appeared that these two novels, of which he was to have first refusal, were to be of standard length. I then tried to get Moore to get from Gollancz a statement of what amounted to standard length. Moore failed to see what I was driving at and simply said that standard length is a trade expression meaning about 70,000 words and that 65,000 words could be regarded as a minimum. I then decided that I would make my next two novels, if any, less than 65,000 words, which would get me out of this contract. It was for that reason that I did not want to sign

an ordinary novel contract with you, which might give Gollancz the chance to say I was defrauding him. If you like we can draw up another contract worded differently, but in any case you know I will bring you all my books except any which may be written for some special purpose.

I don't think the list of review copies needs adding to. I think it is best if you send them out, as your office will be able to do them more systematically than I can. Have you fixed a definite date for publication yet?[15]

Another letter, this one to Leonard Moore, is worth examining in detail since it makes clear the care he intended to take in future over contractual arrangements, having found himself in a difficult position with Gollancz:

I had a talk with Warburg about the contract position. He is quite satisfied with my assurance that I will bring him all my future work, subject to books of a special nature (e.g. that 'Britain in Pictures' book) being allowed to go elsewhere. He is not pressing for a hard and fast contract, but he would no doubt prefer to have one when the other business is settled.

The real trouble is with Gollancz. The contract to bring him my next two novels is still extant, and as he refused to regard Animal Farm as working off one of these, it looks as if he wants to keep to it. At the same time I frankly would prefer not to give or offer him any more books if we can get out of it. I have no quarrel with him personally, he has treated me generously and published my work when no one else would, but it is obviously unsatisfactory to be tied to a publisher who accepts or refuses books partly on political grounds and whose own political views are constantly changing. When I wrote Animal Farm, for instance, I knew in advance that it would be a very difficult book to find a publisher for, and having to submit it to Gollancz simply meant that much time wasted. This might happen over and over again, and judging by some of the things he has published during the past year or two, I doubt whether I could now write anything that Gollancz would approve of. For instance, I recently started a novel. Considering how much work I have to do elsewhere I don't expect to finish it till sometime in 1947, but I am pretty sure Gollancz would refuse it when the time comes, unless by that time his views have altered again. He might say that so far as novels go he does not mind what views they express, but it is a bad arrangement to take novels to one publisher and non-fiction to another. For example, that Spanish war book, which is about the best I have written, would probably have sold more if published by Gollancz, as by that time I was becoming known to the Gollancz public. With Warburg these difficulties don't arise. He is less interested in propaganda and in any case his views are near enough to mine to prevent serious disagreement. From Gollancz's own point of view I do not imagine I am a good proposition either. Having me on his list simply means that from time to time he will publish a book which neither he nor his friends can disapprove of. It seems to me that if he will agree it would be better to scrap the contract. If he won't agree I will keep to the strict letter, i.e. as regards two more novels, and I have no doubt I can make this all right with Warburg. Perhaps you could approach Gollancz about this. You can quote this paragraph if you wish.[16]

It is worth noting that, as Warburg himself later wrote, *Animal Farm* was published without a signed contract.[17] Orwell received an advance of £88 (though Warburg says £100), and after publication he would get 12% on the first 5,000 copies sold, 15% on the next 10,000, and 17% thereafter.

Even before the publication of the first edition, a second edition was being planned. It was not only the difficulty of finding a publisher willing to take the political risk which had delayed publication: wartime shortages meant that paper was still in very short supply. Anticipating that more paper would soon be available, Warburg planned ahead. On 19 July 1945 Roger Senhouse of Secker & Warburg wrote to Morrison & Gibb, the printers, in Tanfield, Edinburgh:

We have your sample of paper for approval in today – 46 rms. 30x40. 50lb. paper from W. Rolandson marked 'For ANIMAL FARM and CRITICAL ESSAYS.' Today we have heard from the makers that there is a further 10–cwts manufactured, this being the increase in the present quota for the current period, and this too I will have sent up to you for one or other of the same titles. Let us take 20 rms of the 46 now available and use this for a second edition of ANIMAL FARM and we can later decide whether to put the 10 extra cwts into the CRITICAL ESSAYS, or some other title.[18]

Animal Farm was published on 17 August 1945. Advance copies had already gone out, and on 18 August Orwell told Herbert Read, 'I'm glad you liked Animal Farm.' In the same letter he told him that he was about to resume his *Tribune* column, 'I stopped it, of course, while I was in France, and didn't start again because Bevan[19] was terrified there might be a row over Animal Farm, which might have been embarrassing if the book had come out before the election, as it was at first intended to.'[20] Another letter indicates his political and professional optimism immediately after the book was published:

... it is so important that there should be some Labour papers which are not taken in by Russian propaganda. However, I think the intellectual atmosphere is changing a bit. I have been surprised by the friendly reception Animal Farm has had, after lying in type for about a year because the publisher dared not bring it out till the war was over. I don't suppose there will be any more copies yet awhile, as the first edition sold out immediately. Warburg is printing a second edition of 6,000 copies, but I suppose there will be the usual delays before they appear.[21]

In March 1947 Orwell wrote a Preface for the Ukrainian edition of *Animal Farm*. The original text does not survive, although the *Collected Essays, Journalism and Letters* includes a translation back into English from the published Ukrainian translation. Rather than an account of the immediate origins of *Animal Farm*, this Preface is an account of Orwell's early life, his experiences in the Spanish Civil War, his views on Stalinism and the Soviet regime, and his belief in the importance of the Socialist movement. He concludes with an explanation of the genesis of *Animal Farm*:

On my return from Spain I thought of exposing the Soviet myth in a story that could easily be understood by almost anyone and which could be easily translated into other languages. However the actual details of the story did not come to me for some time until one day (I was then living in a small village) I saw a little boy, perhaps ten years old, driving a huge cart-horse along a narrow path, whipping it whenever it tried to turn. It struck me that if only such animals became aware of their strength we should have no power over them, and that men exploit animals in much the same way as the rich exploit the proletariat.

I proceeded to analyse Marx's theory from the animals' point of view. To them it was clear that the concept of a class struggle between humans was pure illusion, since whenever it was necessary to exploit animals, all humans united against them: the true struggle is between animals and humans. From this point of departure, it was not difficult to elaborate the story. I did not write it out till 1943, for I was always engaged in other work which gave me no time; and in the end I included some events, for example the Teheran Conference, which were taking place while I was writing. Thus the main outlines of the story were in my mind over a period of six years before it was actually written.

I do not wish to comment on the work; if it does not speak for itself, it is a failure. But I should like to emphasise two points: first, that although the various episodes are taken from the actual history of the Russian Revolution, they are dealt with schematically and their chronological order is changed; this was necessary for the symmetry of the story. The second point has been missed by most critics, possibly because I did not emphasise it sufficiently. A number of readers may finish the book with the impression that it ends in the complete reconciliation of the pigs and the humans. That was not my intention; on the contrary I meant it to end on a loud note of discord, for I wrote it immediately after the Teheran Conference which everybody thought had established the best possible relations between the USSR and the West. I personally did not believe that such good relations would last long; and, as events have shown, I wasn't far wrong.[22]

Orwell's typescript, marked for the printer, survives, as does a set of marked proofs. Both are in the Orwell Archive. The *Complete Works* edition uses the typescript as its copy text, with references in the notes to the proofs, the first edition and its reissue, and other editions as late as 1977. Orwell's proposed Preface to the first edition, 'The Freedom of the Press', was not in the end included. It was only discovered many years later by Ian Angus and first published in 1972 in the *Times Literary Supplement*.[23] Orwell adapted *Animal Farm* for radio performance in January 1947 [See E.270]. The *Complete Works* edition reprints his script.

A.10a   First Edition, 1945

ANIMAL FARM | *A Fairy Story* | BY | GEORGE ORWELL | LONDON | SECKER & WARBURG | 1945

Collation [A]–F⁸; 48 leaves (18.5 × 12.2); [1–8] 9–91 [92–96]; [A]1 and F8 pasted down as front and back fixed endpapers

Contents [1–2] fixed endpaper [3–4] free endpaper [5] halftitle: ANIMAL FARM [6] blank [7] titlepage [8] imprint: Martin Secker & Warburg Ltd. | 7 John Street, Bloomsbury, London, W.C.1 | *First Published May 1945* | MADE AND PRINTED IN GREAT BRITAIN BY | MORRISON AND GIBB LTD., LONDON AND EDINBURGH 9–[92] text, on [92]: *November 1943–February 1944.* [and at foot] W217 [93–94] free endpaper [95–96] fixed endpaper

Binding Green calico textured cloth on boards. Endpapers as above.

Front and back covers Plain.

Spine Stamped in white laterally: Animal Farm | George Orwell | Secker & Warburg

Paper Cream esparto rolled wove

Notes
Published 17 August 1945
6s 0d
4,500 copies
Publication delayed after the 'May' imprint due to paper shortage.

Contemporary reviews
Hugo Manning *Adelphi* (January–March 1946)
Fenner Brockway *New Leader* (1 September 1945)
R.F. Aickmann *Nineteenth Century* (December 1945)
J.C. Trewin *Observer* (26 August 1945)
W.J. Turner *Spectator* (17 August 1945)
Times Literary Supplement (25 August 1945)
T.R. Fyvel *Tribune* (24 August 1945)

Locations
Cambridge University Library
Orwell Archive

A.10b   Reissue of First Edition, 1945

As A.10a, but with imprint on [8] amended to: *First Published August 1945 | Reprinted August 1945*

Jacket Grey and green.
Front Divided diagonally from bottom left to top right. Left and upper grey, right and bottom green. Picked out in white: ANIMAL | FARM | A FAIRY STORY | by [cursive script] | GEORGE ORWELL
Back Off white, with publisher's advertisement for recent Secker & Warburg books printed in green
Spine Grey. Printed laterally in green: ANIMAL FARM George Orwell Secker & Warburg
Front flap Plot summary | *Second Edition.* | 6s.
Back flap Advertisement for the BBC

Notes
Published late August 1945
10,000 copies
6s 0d

Location
Orwell Archive, with jacket

A.10c   Reissue of First Edition, 1946

Collation and Contents as A.10a, but with imprint on [8] amended to: *First Published August 1945 | Reprinted August 1945 | Reprinted October 1946*

Binding Blue calico textured cloth on boards. Endpapers as A.10a.

Front and back covers Plain.

Spine Stamped in white laterally: Animal Farm | George Orwell | Secker & Warburg

Jacket Blue and white. All print in black.
Front Against a blue background are two white rectangular panels outlined in black. Within the top panel is printed: ANIMAL | FARM [between the panels]: *A Fairy Story* [and in the bottom panel]: GEORGE | ORWELL
Back Against a white background, selections from reviews.
Spine Against a blue background are two white rectangular panels outlined in black. Within the first, laterally is: ANIMAL FARM [swirl device] GEORGE ORWELL [and in the second]: SECKER & WARBURG.
Front flap Plot summary | *3rd large impression* | *For Press opinions see back of jacket* | 6s. NET | *Code No.:* | W.217
Back flap Plain

Notes
Published October 1946
6s 0d
6,000 copies

Locations
Orwell Archive, with jacket

A.10d   First American Edition, 1946

ANIMAL FARM | *George Orwell* | NEW YORK | HARCOURT, BRACE AND COMPANY

Collation There are eight unmarked gatherings of eight leaves each, arranged: [A–H]⁸; 64 leaves (18.6 × 12.5); [i–vi] [1–2] 3–118 [119–122]

Contents [i–ii] blank [iii] halftitle: ANIMAL FARM [iv] blank [v] titlepage [vi] imprint: COPYRIGHT, 1946, BY | HARCOURT, BRACE AND COMPANY, INC. | *All rights reserved, including | the right to reproduce this book | or portions thereof in any form.* | *first American edition* | PRINTED IN THE UNITED STATES OF AMERICA [1] halftitle: ANIMAL FARM [2] blank 3–118 text [119–122] blank

Binding Black calico textured cloth on boards. Cream endpapers.

Front and back covers Plain.

Spine Stamped in gilt laterally: GEORGE ORWELL ANIMAL FARM HARCOURT, BRACE | AND COMPANY

Jacket Black.
Front Against a black background with an irregular pattern of white lines is an irregular white rectangle, in which is printed in alternate red and white letters: ANIMAL | FARM | [and in black] GEORGE ORWELL
At bottom left is the signature: Art Brenner
Back Against a white background: [in red] GEORGE ORWELL [and in black, a brief biographical sketch of Orwell]
Front and back flaps At top of front: $1.75. Both have at top in alternate red and white letters: ANIMAL | FARM | [and in black] GEORGE ORWELL | [plot summary] | [publisher's address at foot of both front and back flap]

Notes
Published 26 August 1946
50,000 copies
$1.75
Payment £100 advance. 10% royalty on the understanding that the edition would not be sold at more than $2.00.
Ian Willison quotes Peter Viereck, 'Bloody-minded Professors', *Confluence* (September 1952): '[Angus] Cameron was among those who after the war prevented Little, Brown from publishing George Orwell's anti-Communist satire, *Animal Farm*. Some 18 to 20 publishers, almost all the leading ones, turned down the best anti-Soviet satire of our time. In view of its wit, its readability, and its democratic outlook, the most likely motive for these rejections is the brilliantly successful infiltration (then, not now) of Stalinoid sympathizers in the book world.' Ian Willison adds that Harcourt, Brace confirmed the account but suggested to him that the number of publishers who 'missed the many merits' of the book was more like eight or ten.
Willison notes that a remainder advertisement by H.E. Briggs appeared in the February 1950 edition of *Partisan Review*, price 50 cents.

Fredric Warburg notes that by 1971 the American edition had sold 150,000 copies.

Contemporary reviews
E. Weeks *Atlantic* (September 1946)
E.F. Boyd *Christian Science Monitor* (15 December 1946)
K.T. Willis *Library Journal* (August 1946)
Edmund Wilson *New Yorker* (7 September 1946)
I. Rosenfeld *The Nation* (7 September 1946)
G. Soule *New Republic* (2 September 1946)
Time (4 February 1947)
O. Prescott *Yale Review* (Winter 1947)

Locations
Orwell Archive, three copies with jackets
English Library, University College, London. Jacket in Orwell Archive

A.10e   First Canadian Edition, 1946

ANIMAL | FARM | by George Orwell | Secker & Warburg . London | Reginald Saunders . Toronto

Collation There are eight unmarked gatherings of eight leaves each, arranged: [A–H]^8; 64 leaves (20.0 × 13.3); [i–vi] [1–2] 3–118 [119–122]

Contents [i–ii] blank [iii] halftitle: ANIMAL FARM [iv] blank [v] titlepage [vi] imprint: COPYRIGHT, 1946, BY | S.J. REGINALD SAUNDERS & COMPANY LIMITED | All rights reserved, including | the right to reproduce this book | or portions thereof in any form. | *first Canadian edition* | Printed in Canada [1] halftitle: ANIMAL FARM [2] blank 3–118 text [119–122] blank

Binding Red calico textured cloth on boards. Off white endpapers.

Front and back covers Plain.

Spine Stamped in gilt laterally: ORWELL ANIMAL FARM SAUNDERS

Jacket Black
Front Against a black background are two irregular white rectangles. The first is outlined on two sides by a white line, and within it is printed in alternate red and white letters: ANIMAL | FARM | [and in black] GEORGE ORWELL
The second is headed: WARNING! | [followed by a brief plot summary]
Back Against a white background: [in red] GEORGE ORWELL [and in black, a brief biographical sketch of Orwell] | [in red] DICKENS, DALI AND OTHERS [and a brief advertisement]
Front and back flaps Both have at top: ANIMAL | FARM | GEORGE ORWELL | [plot summary] | [publisher's address at foot of front flap]

Notes
This is a new reset edition
Published November 1946
2,000 copies
$2.00
Price reduced to 89 cents in August 1947. Out of print September 1947.
Saunders subsequently bought surplus stock from the American Book-of-the-Month Club edition – approximately 1,500 copies.

A.10f   Book-of-the-Month Edition, a reissue of First American Edition, no date [1946]

ANIMAL FARM | *George Orwell* | NEW YORK | HARCOURT, BRACE AND COMPANY

Collation There are four unmarked gatherings of 16 leaves each, arranged: [A–D]^{16}; 64 leaves (18.7 × 12.3); [i–iv] [1–2] 3–118 [119–124]

Contents [i] halftitle: ANIMAL FARM [ii] blank [iii] titlepage [iv] imprint: COPYRIGHT, 1946, BY | HARCOURT, BRACE AND COMPANY, INC. | *All rights reserved, including* | *the right to reproduce this book* | *or portions thereof in any form.* | PRINTED IN THE UNITED STATES OF AMERICA | BY THE HADDEN CRAFTSMEN | SCRANTON, PA. [1] halftitle: ANIMAL FARM [2] blank 3–118 text [119–124] blank

Binding Green calico-textured cloth on boards. Off white endpapers.

Front and back covers Plain.

Spine Stamped in gilt laterally: GEORGE ORWELL ANIMAL FARM HARCOURT, BRACE | AND COMPANY

Jacket
Front Black with grey criss-cross lines. At bottom left is the signature: Art Brenner [Within an irregular white rectangle is printed in alternate red and black letters, starting red]: ANIMAL | [and starting black]: FARM | [and in black] GEORGE ORWELL
Back Biographical sketch of Orwell.
Spine Black and grey, wrapping from front. Laterally in alternate red and white letters, starting red: ANIMAL FARM [and laterally in red] GEORGE ORWELL Harcourt, Brace | and Company
Front flap [In alternate red and black letters, starting red]: ANIMAL | [and starting black]: FARM | [and in black] GEORGE ORWELL | [plot summary] | HARCOURT, BRACE AND COMPANY | 383 Madison Avenue, New York 17
Back flap As front flap with continued summary. In bottom right: PRINTED | IN | U.S.A.

Notes
Although this is similar to the first American Edition, it is a separate issue with different collation, pagination and binding. Ian Willison describes yet another issue with the imprint: Printed and bound in the U.S.A. by Kingsport Press, Inc., Kingsport, Tenn.

400,000 copies
20c per copy
Advance of $75,000 against royalties split evenly between Harcourt, Brace and Orwell. The dollar was then currently at 4.03 to the pound sterling. Tax at 30% withheld. Orwell therefore received approximately £6,500 in royalties at this point, however this amount was then also subject to British tax at the 50% wartime rate, reduced to 45% on 25 October 1945, although he was then also subject to supertax. The $75,000 was an advance against royalties which would in fact be earned when 375,000 copies were sold.

A second printing of 110,000 copies was ordered, some of which were distributed to Canadian Book-of-the-Month Club members. Saunders in Canada also bought the balance of the stock, 1,500 copies.

A.10g   Cheap Edition, 1949

Collation and Contents as A.10a First Edition, but with imprint on [8] amended to: *First Published August 1945 | Reprinted August 1945 | Reprinted October 1946 | First Cheap Edition, June 1949*

Binding Fine calico textured green cloth on boards. Off white endpapers.

Front and back covers Plain.

Spine Stamped in brown laterally: Animal Farm George Orwell Secker & Warburg

Jacket Green. All print in black.
Front Against a green background are two white rectangular panels outlined in black. Within the top panel is printed: ANIMAL | FARM [between the panels]: *Cheap Edition* [and in the bottom panel]: GEORGE | ORWELL
Back Against a white background, selections from reviews.
Spine Against a green background are two white rectangular panels outlined in black. Within the first, laterally is: ANIMAL FARM [swirl device] GEORGE ORWELL [and in the second]: SECKER & WARBURG.
Front flap Plot summary | *Cheap edition | For Press opinions see back of jacket* | 3s. 6d NET | *Code No.:* | W.217
Back flap Publisher's advertisement

Locations
Orwell Archive, with jacket

Reissues
April 1950, 5,000 copies, 3s 6d
May 1950, 5,000 copies, 3s 6d, Orwell Archive, with jacket
November 1950, 5,090 copies, 3s 6d, Orwell Archive, with jacket
April 1951, 5,070 copies, 4s 6d
May 1952, 3,000 copies, 6s 0d
December 1953
March 1955, 6s 0d, Orwell Archive, with jacket. Hereafter there is a list of Orwell's other works on [6], and binding is green paper on boards, embossed to resemble bubble grain cloth
January 1959, Orwell Archive
February 1961

A.10b   First Penguin Edition, 1951

GEORGE ORWELL | ANIMAL FARM | A FAIRY STORY | PENGUIN BOOKS | HARMONDSWORTH . MIDDLESEX

Collation [A]–D¹⁶; 64 leaves (17.9 × 11.0); [1–4] 5–119 [120–128]

Contents [1] halftitle: PENGUIN BOOKS | 838 | ANIMAL FARM | GEORGE ORWELL | [penguin motif in oval frame] [2] blank [3] titlepage [4] imprint: FIRST PUBLISHED AUGUST 1945 | BY SECKER AND WARBURG LTD | PUBLISHED IN PENGUIN BOOKS 1951 | MADE AND PRINTED IN GREAT BRITAIN | FOR PENGUIN BOOKS LTD | BY SPOTTISWOODE, BALLANTYNE AND CO LTD 5–[120] text, on [120]: November 1943–February 1944 [121] penguin motif | publisher's notice [122] blank [123–128] publisher's advertisements

Binding Paper bound in orange and white.

Front cover Broad orange stripe above broad off white stripe above another broad orange stripe. Within the top stripe is a rounded white diamond, outlined in black, within which is printed: PENGUIN | BOOKS [Within the middle stripe is printed]: ANIMAL | FARM | GEORGE | ORWELL [and printed laterally in orange to each side]: FICTION [Within the bottom stripe is printed]: COMPLETE [penguin device in black and off-white] UNABRIDGED | 1|6 [no line break]

Inside front cover Plot summary and extracts from reviews.

Back cover Within an orange border is a black and white photograph of Orwell and a biographical sketch.

Inside back cover Publisher's advertisement

Spine The three broad stripes are wrapped around from the front cover. Printed laterally [in top stripe]: GEORGE ORWELL [in middle stripe]: ANIMAL FARM [and vertically in black and off white in the bottom stripe]: [penguin device] | 838

Notes
published 27 July 1951
60,000 copies
1s 6d

Fredric Warburg notes that by 1973 more than 2 million Penguin copies had been sold, and that it continues to sell about 140,000 a year.

Locations
Cambridge University Library
Orwell Archive, two copies

Reissues
1952, 24 October, 40,000 copies, 2s 0d
1954
1955, 2s 0d, Orwell Archive
1955, another issue
1957
1958
1959, back cover photograph changed, 2s 6d, Orwell Archive
1960, 2s 6d, Orwell Archive
1961, 2s 6d, photograph inside front cover, Orwell Archive
1962
1962, another issue, new cover with drawing of pigs by Paul Hogarth in green, orange, grey and black, 2s 6d, Orwell Archive
1963
1963 Penguin Modern Classics, new cover, Paul Hogarth drawing as above but in orange, grey and black, 2s 6d, Orwell Archive
1964
1965
1966, Penguin Modern Classics, redesigned cover with Paul Hogarth drawing, 2s 6d. Cambridge University Library, Orwell Archive
1967
1968 two issues
1969 three issues
1970 two issues
1971
1972 two issues
1973 three issues
1974 two issues
1975 two issues
1976 two issues
1977 two issues
1978
1979 two issues
1980 three issues
1981, front cover photograph of pig looking over fence by Humphrey Sutton and back cover photograph of Orwell, 85p, Orwell Archive
1981 another issue
1982
1983 two issues
1984 two issues
1985 cover illustration by Christopher Corr, £1.50, Orwell Archive
1989 Penguin Twentieth Century Classics edition, based on the Complete Works Edition, with an Introduction by Malcolm Bradbury. £4.99.

A.10i   The Bridge Series Edition, 1954

ANIMAL FARM | *A Fairy Story* | *by* | GEORGE ORWELL | LONGMAN'S, GREEN AND CO | LONDON . NEW YORK . TORONTO

Collation [A]–D¹⁶; 64 leaves (18.4 × 12.3); [i–vi] vii–viii 1–120

Contents [i–ii] blank [iii] halftitle: *The* | *Bridge* | *Series* | ANIMAL FARM [iv] publisher's list [v] titlepage [vi] imprint vii–viii editor's note 1–97 text, on 97: November 1943–February 1944 98–120 glossary

Binding Paper bound

Front cover Against a blue background is an elaborate grey and white panel with lines and scrolls, in which is printed in blue: THE BRIDGE SERIES | ANIMAL FARM | *A Fairy Story* | *by* | GEORGE | ORWELL | *General Editor* | J.A. BRIGHT

Back cover Within a grey panel bordered with white is a motif of a blue ship and: 1724 | LONGMANS

Spine Laterally in blue: ANIMAL FARM GEORGE ORWELL

Notes
The Bridge Series was specially produced for students of English as a second language. The glossary of notes for their use is by R.H. Durham.

Locations
Cambridge University Library. Acquisition 2 September 1955.

A.10j   *Secker and Warburg Illustrated Edition, 1954*

ANIMAL FARM | *A Fairy Story* | By | GEORGE ORWELL | Illustrated by | JOY BATCHELOR & JOHN HALAS | LONDON | SECKER & WARBURG | 1954

Collation [1]–7⁸; 56 leaves (19.8 × 13.5); [1–6] 7–108 [109–112]

Contents [1] halftitle: ANIMAL FARM [2] against a pink background is printed in red in irregular type: ILLUSTRATED BY | Joy Batchelor & John Halas | [and in black and white is a drawing of a cow, two sheep, a goat, a goose, five ducks and a hen] [3] halftitle: against a pink background is printed in red in irregular type: GEORGE ORWELL | ANIMAL | FARM | [in the background and below is a drawing in black and white of two pigs, a horse, a donkey and a chicken by a bonfire] | [in red in irregular type]: SECKER AND WARBURG [4] blank [5] titlepage [6] imprint: Martin Secker & Warburg Ltd. | 7 John Street, Bloomsbury, London, W.C.1 | *First Published August 1945* | *Ninth Impression 1953* | *Illustrated Edition* | *First Published 1954* | MADE AND PRINTED IN GREAT BRITAIN BY | WILLIAM CLOWES AND SONS, LIMITED, LONDON AND BECCLES 7–[109] text, on 109: *November 1943– February 1944* [110–112] blank
There are 38 black and white drawings interspersed with the text.

Binding Red linen grain cloth on boards. Off white endpapers.

Front cover Stamped in silver gilt: ANIMAL FARM [irregular type] | [drawing of hen]

Back cover Plain.

Spine Stamped in silver gilt laterally in irregular type: ANIMAL FARM ILLUSTRATED | EDITION

Jacket Pink
Front Against a pink background is printed in red in irregular type: GEORGE ORWELL | ANIMAL | FARM | [in the background and below is a drawing in black and white of two pigs, a horse, a donkey and a chicken by a bonfire] | [in red in irregular type]: ILLUSTRATED BY | Joy Batchelor & John Halas
Back Against a pink background in black and white is a drawing of a cow, two sheep, a goat, a goose, five ducks and a hen
Spine Against a pink background is a drawing of a bonfire with laterally in red irregular type: ANIMAL FARM ILLUSTRATED | EDITION
Front flap Summary of illustrations | 10s. 6d. | NET
Back flap Plain.

Notes
The jacket note says that publication of this edition shortly preceded the appearance of the cartoon film of the book, the first full-length cartoon film ever made in England, and produced by the same artists.
10s 6d

Locations
Cambridge University Library
Orwell Archive – two copies, with jackets.

A.10k   *Harcourt, Brace Illustrated Edition, 1954*

GEORGE ORWELL | Animal Farm | [drawing in red of two pigs, a horse, a donkey and a chicken by a bonfire] | HARCOURT, BRACE AND COMPANY | NEW YORK

Collation There are five unmarked gatherings of 16 leaves each, arranged [A–E]¹⁶; 80 leaves (20.2 × 13.4); [i–iv] [1–3] 4–155 [156]

Contents [i] halftitle: ANIMAL FARM [ii] *illustrated by Joy Batchelor and John Halas* | in red is a drawing of a cow, two sheep, a goat, a goose, five ducks and a hen [iii] titlepage [iv] imprint: COPYRIGHT, 1946, BY HARCOURT, BRACE AND COMPANY, INC. | COPYRIGHT, 1954, BY JOY BATCHELOR AND JOHN HALAS | *All rights reserved, including* | *the right to reproduce this book* | *or portions thereof in any form* | LIBRARY OF CONGRESS CATALOG CARD NUMBER: 54–11330 | PRINTED IN THE UNITED STATES OF AMERICA [1] halftitle: ANIMAL FARM [2] blank [3]–155 text [156] illustration There are 36 red and white drawings interspersed with the text.

Binding Cream marbled paper on boards. Off white endpapers.

Front cover In lower half, drawing in red of a countryside scene.

Back cover Plain.

Spine Laterally in pinkish brown: GEORGE ORWELL ANIMAL FARM HARCOURT, BRACE AND COMPANY

Jacket Yellow
Front [in red] GEORGE ORWELL | [in black irregular type] ANIMAL | FARM | [in black] "…A PARABLE THAT MAY | RANK AS ONE OF THE | GREAT POLITICAL SATIRES OF OUR ANXIOUS TIMES." | Christopher Morley | [drawing in red and white of two pigs, a horse, a donkey and a chicken by a bonfire] | ILLUSTRATED BY JOY BATCHELOR and JOHN HALAS
Back Quotation about Orwell | drawing in red and white of a cow, two sheep, a goat, a goose, five ducks and a hen
Spine In red and white is a drawing of a bonfire with laterally [in red] ORWELL | [in black irregular type] ANIMAL FARM | Harcourt, Brace | and Company
Front flap $2.95 | George Orwell | ANIMAL FARM | *Illustrated Edition* | Assessment of book
Back flap Biographical sketch of Orwell | list of books by Orwell | HARCOURT, BRACE AND COMPANY | *383 Madison Avenue, New York 17, N.Y.*

Locations
Orwell Archive, with jacket

A.10l   *Signet Edition, 1956*

Animal Farm | *A Fairy Story* | by GEORGE ORWELL | With an Introduction by | C.M. Woodhouse | oval frame within which is printed: N.A.L | SIGNET | BOOKS | [and beneath] A SIGNET BOOK | Published by THE NEW AMERICAN LIBRARY

Collation 64 leaves in a perfect binding (17.9 × 10.5); [1–14] 15–128

Contents [1] extracts from reviews | [rule] | THIS IS A REPRINT OF THE ORIGINAL HARDCOVER EDITION | PUBLISHED BY HARCOURT, BRACE AND CO. [2]

publisher's advertisements and notice [3] titlepage [4] imprint: COPYRIGHT, 1946, BY HARCOURT, BRACE AND | COMPANY, INC. ©1956 BY THE NEW AMERICAN | LIBRARY OF WORLD LITERATURE, INC. | *All rights reserved, including* | *the right to reproduce this book* | *or portions thereof in any form.* | *Published as a* SIGNET BOOK | *By Arrangement with Harcourt, Brace and Company, Inc.* | FIRST PRINTING, MARCH, 1956 | [within a frame]: SIGNET BOOKS *are published by* | *The New American Library of World Literature, Inc.* | *501 Madison Avenue, New York 22, New York* | [and beneath]: PRINTED IN THE UNITED STATES OF AMERICA [5–14] Introduction 15–128 text

Binding Paper bound in black, yellow, red, green and blue.

Front cover Within a black panel bordered by yellow, red, green and blue rectangles is [in white]: 1289 | *A Provocative Novel* | [black and white oval within which is]: SIGNET | 35c | BOOKS | [in yellow] Animal | Farm | [in white] GEORGE ORWELL | *Author of* 1984 | [in red, drawing of a pig's head] | [in white] A SIGNET BOOK Complete and Unabridged

Back cover Yellow band at top within which is an oval frame in which is printed: N.A.L | SIGNET | BOOKS [and to the right] ...Good Reading for the Millions | [white panel with extracts from reviews in pink and white | photograph of Orwell and assessment of his work] | [in yellow panel] Published by the New American Library

Spine Against a yellow background is printed in black: 1289 [and laterally] ANIMAL FARM . ORWELL

Notes
March 1956
35 cents
Introduction by C.M. Woodhouse was originally published in the *Times Literary Supplement*, 6 August 1954.

Fredric Warburg notes that by 1973 this edition had sold over 5,000,000 copies, and that it continues to sell more than 350,000 a year.

Locations
Orwell Archive

Reissues
Three more Signet Books issues between March 1956 and April 1959 when the fourth was issued.
August 1959, First Signet Classics Edition
December 1959, 'Second Signet Classics Edition'
April 1960, 'Third Signet Classics Edition'
October 1960, 'Fourth Signet Classics Edition', Orwell Archive. Cover with drawing of a donkey and a pig.
Eight more Signet issues between October 1960 and July 1964 when the 'Sixteenth printing' was issued, Orwell Archive

A.10m   Longmans Edition, 1960

[within a zigzag border with dots] ANIMAL FARM | A FAIRY STORY | BY | GEORGE ORWELL | *With an Introduction and Notes by* | LAURENCE BRANDER | LONGMANS

Collation [A]–H⁸ I⁴; 68 leaves (17.1 × 11.5); [i–iv] v–xxiii [xxiv] 1–111 [112]

Contents [i] halftitle: [within a solid black oval frame is a lamp with shade] | *The Heritage of Literature Series* | [short rule] | SECTION B NO. 45 | ANIMAL FARM [ii] series advertisement [iii] titlepage [iv] imprint | v–xxii Introduction xxiii publisher's acknowledgement [xxiv] blank 1–96 text 97–[112] Notes

Binding Orange paper on boards, embossed to resemble bubble grain cloth. Off-white endpapers.

Front cover Blind-stamped lamp and book motif.

Back cover Stamped in gilt in lower right: B45

Spine Stamped in gilt: *Animal* | *Farm* | *George* | *Orwell* | [lamp and book motif] | *Longmans*

Locations
Cambridge University Library
1960, second issue
1961, third issue
1961, fourth issue, Orwell Archive
1962, fifth issue
1963, sixth issue, Orwell Archive

A.10n   Collected Edition, 1965

ANIMAL | FARM | A Fairy Story | BY | GEORGE ORWELL | LONDON | SECKER & WARBURG

Collation [A]–C^{16} D^8; 56 leaves (18.4 × 12.2); [1–4] 5–110 [111–112]

Contents [1] halftitle: ANIMAL FARM [2] list of books by Orwell [3] titlepage [4] imprint: MARTIN SECKER & WARBURG LIMITED | 14 Carlisle Street, Soho Square, London W.1. | ALL RIGHTS RESERVED | [list of Secker & Warburg editions and reissues] | Printed in Great Britain by | Fletcher & Son Ltd, Norwich 5–110 text, on 110: *November 1943–February 1944* [111–112] blank

Binding Green paper on boards, embossed to resemble bubble grain cloth. Off white endpapers.

Front and back covers Plain.

Spine Stamped in gilt: [pyramid of six rules] | ANIMAL | FARM | [ornate leaf device] | GEORGE | ORWELL | [inverted pyramid of six rules] | S&W

Jacket Blue, grey and yellow
Front Against a blue background: Animal farm | [in white] George Orwell | [illustration of two pigs in black, grey and yellow against a background of trees] | [in lower right, vertically] Denis Piper
Back Against a yellow background is a list of the uniform edition of Orwell's works.
Spine Illustration wrapping round from front with trees and a donkey in black and white against a blue and black background. Printed laterally: [in black] Animal Farm [in white] George Orwell [in yellow] Secker & | Warburg
Front flap Plot summary | Jacket design by | DENIS PIPER | 18s. net
Back flap MP|[not line break]L8162

Notes
Published October 1965
18s 0d

Locations
Orwell Archive

A.10o   Time Illustrated Edition, 1965

[across two pages] [in brown] animal farm | [on right-hand page in black] GEORGE ORWELL | illustrated by | JOY BATCHELOR and JOHN HALAS | with a new introduction by | MALCOLM MUGGERIDGE | [at foot of left hand page] [in brown] [publisher's device in rectangular frame]: RTP [and in black] TIME Reading Program Special Edition [on right hand page] TIME INCORPORATED . NEW YORK

Collation 80 leaves in a perfect binding (20.3 × 13.0); [X1–X2] [i–vii] viii–xiii [xiv] xv–xx [xxi–xxii] 1–131 [132–136]. There are 38 brown and white drawings interspersed with the text.

Contents [X1–X2] blank [i] halftitle: animal farm | [drawing in brown of a pig] [ii–iii] titlepage [iv] [in brown and white is a drawing of a cow, two sheep, a goat, a goose, five ducks and a hen] | imprint: [list of *Time* editors and directors] | COVER DESIGN *Joseph Low* | [copyright notices] [v] [drawing in brown and white of two pigs, a horse, a donkey and a chicken by a bonfire] [vi–vii] photograph of Orwell, on [vi] in brown: editors' preface | [in black above photograph] V. Richards | [vii]–xiii preface, on xiii –THE EDITORS OF TIME [xiv] [publisher's device in rectangular frame]: RTP [in brown]: introduction xv–xx introduction, on xx: –MALCOLM MUGGERIDGE [xxi] halftitle: animal farm | [drawing in brown of a pig] [xxii] [illustration of country scene] | chapter I 1–131 text [132–133] publisher's note [134–136] blank

Binding Paperbound in orange, green and black. Wrapping around covers and spine is a print from a linoleum cut of a pig's head in black against a green and orange background.

Front cover As described, and at top: [in pink] Animal Farm | [in black] George Orwell

Back cover As described, and at foot publisher's device in rectangular frame: RTP [and in grey is the signature]: Joseph Low

Spine As described, and laterally: ANIMAL | FARM [to the right]: GEORGE | ORWELL [to the right] Time | Inc.

Notes
The publisher's note says that the text is set in Caledonia Light by V. & M. Typographical Inc, Brooklyn, New York. It was printed by W.R. Bean & Son, Atlanta, Georgia, and bound by J.W. Clement Co, Buffalo, New York. The cover was printed by Livermore and Knight Co., a division of Printing Corporation of America, Providence, Rhode Island. The paper is *Time* Reading Text, from the Mead Corporation, Dayton, Ohio; and the cover stock is from the Plastic Coating Corporation, Holyoke, Massachusetts.
An advertisement in the copy at the Orwell Archive says that Joseph Low prints with linoleum cuts at Norwalk, Connecticut.

Locations
Orwell Archive

A.10p *New Collected Edition, 1971*

GEORGE ORWELL | ANIMAL FARM | *A Fairy Story* | SECKER & WARBURG | LONDON

Collation There are four unmarked gatherings, arranged: [A–B]^{16} [C]^8 [D]^{16} 56 leaves (19.8 × 12.7); [i–iv] [1–4] 5–104 [105–108]. [A]1 and [D]16 pasted down as front and back fixed endpapers.

Contents [i–ii] fixed endpaper [iii–iv] free endpaper [1] halftitle: ANIMAL FARM [2] list of books by Orwell [3] titlepage [4] imprint: Martin Secker & Warburg Limited | 54 Poland Street, London W1V 3DF | ALL RIGHTS RESERVED | list of Secker & Warburg editions and reissues | SBN 436 35000 9 | *Printed and bound in Great Britain by* | *Biddles Ltd, Guildford and King's Lynn* 5–104 text, on 104: *November 1943–February 1944.* [105–106] free endpaper [107–108] fixed endpaper

Binding Black paper on boards, embossed to resemble linen grain cloth. Endpapers as above.

Front and back covers Plain.

Spine Stamped in gilt: [pyramid of six rules] | ANIMAL | FARM | [ornate leaf device] | GEORGE | ORWELL | [inverted pyramid of six rules] | S&W
Jacket Cream
Front GEORGE ORWELL | [rule] | [drawing of four pigs in pink, yellow, brown, grey and black] | ANIMAL FARM | [rule]
Back [mirror image of drawing on front]
Spine [laterally] GEORGE ORWELL ANIMAL FARM [vertically] SECKER & | WARBURG
Front flap [plot summary] | [list of books by Orwell] | Jacket design by David Quay | £3.95 | net
Back flap [photograph of Orwell] | [extracts from reviews] | Photograph of George Orwell, | courtesy of BBC | Secker & Warburg | 0–436–35000–9

Notes
October 1971
£3.95
Reissued February 1984

Locations
Cambridge University Library.
Orwell Archive, with jacket

A.10q   *Heinemann Edition, 1972*

Animal Farm | *by* | *GEORGE ORWELL* | [publisher's device in rectangular frame of windmill and]: H.E.B | HEINEMANN EDUCATIONAL BOOKS | LONDON

Collation There are three unmarked gatherings of 16 leaves each, arranged [A–C]^{16}; 48 leaves (18.6 × 12.1); [i–iv] 1–89 [90–92]

Contents [i] halftitle: THE NEW WINDMILL SERIES | *General Editors:* Anne and Ian Serraillier | 165 | *Animal Farm* | [plot summary] [ii] blank [iii] titlepage [iv] imprint: [publisher's addresses] | ISBN 0 435 12165 0 | First published by Martin Secker and Warburg 1945 | First published in New Windmill Series 1972 | Published by | Heinemann Educational Books Ltd | 48 Charles Street, London W1X 8AH | Printed and bound in Great Britain by | Morrison and Gibb Ltd, London and Edinburgh 1–89 text [90–92] publisher's advertisements

Binding Red paper on boards, embossed to resemble calico grain cloth.

Front cover Against a red background is printed in white a publisher's device in rectangular frame, of a windmill and: H.E.B [to the right in decorative print]: Animal Farm | George Orwell | [coloured drawing in black, red, yellow and white of a giant pig in a minute farmyard scene] | New Windmill Series

Back cover Plain

Spine Laterally in white: Animal Farm GEORGE ORWELL [and vertically at foot, publisher's device in rectangular frame, of a windmill and]: H.E.B

Locations
Cambridge University Library
Orwell Archive

Reissues
1974, 1975, 1976, 1977, 1979, 1981, 1982, 1983
1983 at Orwell Archive; covers have a coloured cartoon of animals.

A.10r   Lythway Large Print Edition, 1975

Animal Farm | *A FAIRY STORY* | *George Orwell* | LP | LYTHWAY PRESS | BATH

Collation There are ten unmarked gatherings of eight leaves each, arranged: [A–K]⁸; 80 leaves (21.5 × 13.7); [i–vi] 1–154

Contents [i] plot summary [ii] blank [iii] titlepage [iv] imprint: copyright notices | ISBN 0 85046 620 2 | © Copyright the Estate of Eric Blair 1945 | Phototypeset by | Woodspring Press Ltd | Printed by Redwood Burn Ltd | Trowbridge & Esher | Bound by Cedric Chivers Ltd Bath [v] halftitle: ANIMAL FARM [vi] blank 1–154 text, on 154: *November 1943–February 1944.*

Binding Blue paper on boards, embossed to resemble bubble grain cloth. Off white endpapers.

Front and back covers Plain.

Spine Stamped in gilt: LARGE | PRINT | [laterally] ANIMAL FARM GEORGE | ORWELL [vertically] LYTHWAY

Locations
Cambridge University Library
Orwell Archive

A.10s   Octopus Edition, 1976

GEORGE | ORWELL | [in red] animal farm | burmese days | a clergyman's daughter | coming up for air | keep the aspidistra flying | nineteen eighty-four | [in black] Secker & Warburg | [not a line break, the slash is on the page] Octopus

Published by Secker & Warburg|Octopus, 1976.
Animal Farm is on pp11–66.
Hard bound with jacket.
Printed by Jarrold & Sons Ltd., Norwich

Locations
Cambridge University Library. Acquisition 7 January 1977.

A.10t   The Penguin Complete Novels of George Orwell Edition, 1983

(Harmondsworth: Penguin, 1983) 925pp

A compendium edition of the following novels:

Animal Farm
Burmese Days
A Clergyman's Daughter
Coming Up for Air
Keep the Aspidistra Flying
Nineteen Eighty-Four

Paper bound
£4.95

Locations
Orwell Archive: two copies

A.10u   Folio Society Edition, 1984

GEORGE ORWELL | *Animal Farm* | *A FAIRY STORY* | [swirl device] | *Drawings by* | QUENTIN BLAKE | LONDON | *The Folio Society* | *1984*

Collation There are seven unmarked gatherings, arranged: [A–D]⁸ [E]⁴ [F–G]⁸; 52 leaves (22.2 × 15.5); [1–4] 5–104 There are 27 drawings interspersed with the text.

Contents [1] halftitle: [swirl] *Animal Farm* [swirl] [2] [drawing of a pig] [3] titlepage [4] imprint and copyright notices | *Photoset in 11 point Plantin spaced two points* | *with Klang for display.* | *Printed by Jolly & Barber Ltd, Rugby* | *on Finewhite Opaque paper.* | *Bound by Hunter & Foulis Ltd, Edinburgh* | *in full cloth printed lithographically* | *with an illustration by the artist.* | *Printed in Great Britain* 5–104 text

Binding Pink and beige linen grain cloth on boards. Beige endpapers.

Front and back covers Across the covers and wrapping around the spine is a drawing of three pigs in beige and brown, against a pink washed background.

Spine Stamped in gilt laterally: *George Orwell . Animal Farm*

Slip case Off white morocco grain paper on boards.

Notes
Illustrations and cover illustration by Quentin Blake.

Locations
Cambridge University Library. Acquisition 18 October 1984.
Orwell Archive

A.10v   *Charnwood Large Print Edition, 1984*

GEORGE ORWELL | [short ornamental rule] | ANIMAL | FARM | *Complete and Unabridged* | [tree motif] | CHARNWOOD | *Leicester*

Collation [1–9]⁸; 72 leaves (21.3 × 13.4); [i–vi] 1–124 [125–138]

Contents [i–ii] publisher's note [iii] plot summary [iv] list of Orwell's books in this series [v] titlepage [vi] imprint: First published in Great Britain 1945 by | Secker & Warburg Ltd. | London | First Charnwood Edition | published July 1984 | by arrangement with | Martin Secker & Warburg Ltd. | London | and | Harcourt Brace Jovanovich, Inc., | New York | © 1945 by George Orwell | All rights reserved | [in a frame is British Library data] | Published by | F.A. Thorpe (Publishing) Ltd. | Anstey, Leicestershire | Printed and bound in Great Britain by | T.J. Press (Padstow) Ltd., Padstow, Cornwall 1–[125] text, on [125]: *November 1943–February 1944.* | THE END [126] blank [127–138] publisher's advertisements

Binding White glossy plastic paper on boards, embossed to resemble calico grain cloth.

Front cover Against a white background is a drawing of two pigs looking over a wall and barbed wire fence, in blue, grey, orange, brown pink and yellow.

Back cover Within an oval frame is a tree motif | *Charnwood* | *Library* | *Series* | [within a blue frame]: Animal | Farm | *George* | *Orwell* | [plot summary] | ISBN 0 7089 8200 X

Spine [within an orange rectangle is picked out in white]: Large | Type | [laterally in black against a white background]: *George Orwell* Animal Farm | [and vertically within an oval frame is a black tree motif] | THORPE

Notes
Published July 1984

Locations
Orwell Archive

A.10w   Nineteen Eighty-Four and Animal Farm Chancellor Press edition, 1984
The two novels in a single volume. London: Chancellor Press, 1984.
An imprint of Octopus Publishing.
Cloth on boards.
Printed at the Pitman Press, Bath.

Nineteen Eighty-Four is on 11–326, and *Animal Farm* on 329–430.

Location
Cambridge University Library

A.10x   The Complete Works Edition, 1987
THE COMPLETE WORKS OF | GEORGE ORWELL | VOLUME EIGHT |
Animal Farm | *A Fairy Story* | SECKER & WARBURG | [short rule] | LONDON

Collation There are seven unmarked gatherings: [A–C]^{16} [D]^{12} [E–G]^{16}; 108 leaves (23.2 ×
15.3); [i–viii] 1–[95] [96] 97–195 [196] 197–203 [204–208]

Contents [i] halftitle: THE COMPLETE WORKS OF | GEORGE ORWELL . EIGHT |
ANIMAL FARM [ii] blank [iii] publisher's note [iv] blank [v] titlepage [vi] imprint:
[selective publishing history of editions and reissues] | [copyright notices] | [British Library
Cataloguing in Publication Data] | ISBN 0–436–35030–0 | Typeset in Monophoto Bembo |
Printed and bound in Great Britain by | Richard Clay Ltd, Bungay, Suffolk [vii]
acknowledgements [viii] blank 1–[95] text, on [95]: *November 1943–February 1944* | THE
END [96] blank 97–195 appendices [196] blank 197–203 textual note [204–208] blank

Binding Blue paper on boards, embossed to resemble calico textured cloth. Black endpapers.

Front and back covers Plain.

Spine Stamped in gilt: [double rule] | GEORGE | ORWELL | [rule] | Animal | Farm [double
rule] | SECKER & | WARBURG

Jacket Smooth dull black. Flaps white.
Front [in white]: GEORGE | ORWELL | [in green and white]: ANIMAL FARM
Back [in white, note on *The Complete Works of George Orwell* and extracts from reviews.
ISBN code and bar strip within a white rectangle.]
Spine laterally [in white]: GEORGE ORWELL | [in green and white]: ANIMAL FARM
[horizontally in white]: Secker & Warburg
Front flap Note on publishing history. At foot: £12.95 | net
Back flap [biographical notes on Orwell and Peter Davison] | Jacket design by David Quay |
Secker & Warburg

Notes
There are three appendices. Appendix I is Orwell's proposed preface to *Animal Farm*,
'The Freedom of the Press' [see C.839]; Appendix II is Orwell's preface to the Ukrainian
edition, published in 1947; and Appendix III is Orwell's radio adaptation of *Animal Farm*.
Reprinted 1996

Locations
Orwell Archive, with jacket
Robarts Library, University of Toronto

A.10y   Everyman Library edition, 1993

GEORGE ORWELL | [within an elaborate grey floral border] *Animal Farm* |
with an Introduction by Julian Symons | [triangle motif with a dog jumping over
a book] | [short rule] | EVERYMAN'S LIBRARY | *150*

Collation There are 5 unmarked gatherings of 16 leaves each arranged [1–5]^{16}; 80 leaves (20.4 × 12.3); [i–viii] ix [x] xi–xliv [xlv–xlvi] 1–[93] [94–96] 97–113 [114]

Contents [i–ii] blank [iii] halftitle: EVERYMAN'S LIBRARY [iv] [against a grey sunburst motif] EVERYMAN, | I WILL GO WITH THEE, | AND BE THY GUIDE, | IN THY MOST NEED | TO GO BY THY SIDE [v] titlepage [vi] imprint [vii] halftitle: ANIMAL FARM | [short rule] [viii] blank ix contents [x] blank xi–xxiii introduction xxiv–xxv select bibliography xxvi–xli chronology xlii–xliv textual note [xlv] halftitle: *Animal Farm* | A FAIRY STORY [xlvi] blank 1–[93] text, on [93] *November 1943–February 1944* | THE END [94] blank [95] halftitle: APPENDICES | [short rule] [96] blank 97–113 appendices [114] publisher's note

Binding Blue cloth on boards. Off-white endpapers with pale yellow triangle motif and dog jumping over book. Fixed blue silk bookmark.

Front and back covers Plain

Spine Stamped in gilt: [broad rule] | [black panel, on which is stamped in gilt]: [rule] | GEORGE | ORWELL | [sunburst motif] | ANIMAL | FARM | [rule] | [and below the black panel, broad rule] | EVERY- | MAN'S | LIBRARY

Jacket
Grey and white with red print.

Locations
Cambridge University Library. Acquisition 29 April 1993.

Imprint: London: David Campbell Publishers Ltd, 1993. Distributed by Random House (UK).

Includes Introduction, Select Bibliography, Chronology, Textual note by Peter Davison. Appendix I is Orwell's proposed preface, 'The Freedom of the Press', first published in the *Times Literary Supplement* 15 September 1972 [see C.839].
Appendix II is Orwell's preface to the Ukrainian edition [A.10.T25].

On acid-free cream wove paper.

A.10z   Compact Books edition, 1993

ANIMAL FARM | *A FAIRY STORY* | George Orwell | [within a small frame] compact | books

Collation 56 leaves in a perfect binding (17.6 × 11.0); [i–iv] 1– [108]

Contents [i] halftitle: ANIMAL FARM [ii] list of books by Orwell [iii] titlepage [iv] imprint 1–[108] text

Binding Green paper lightly embossed to resemble linen grain cloth on boards. Off white endpapers

Front and Back covers Plain

Spine Stamped in white in three framed boxes: GEORGE ORWELL *Animal Farm* compact | books

Jacket Green
Front [within a white frame, printed in white] compact | books [publisher's adhesive price sticker within a white frame, printed in white] compact price | £4.99 | [picture of pig] | [within a white frame, printed in white] GEORGE ORWELL | *Animal Farm*
Back [within a white frame, printed in white] compact price price | £4.99 | [within a white frame] *Animal Farm* | [plot summary] | [ISBN and bar code]
Spine Stamped in white in three framed boxes: GEORGE ORWELL *Animal Farm* compact | books

Notes Follows the *Complete Works* text.

Locations
Cambridge University Library

MISCELLANEOUS

A.10.M1   *Animal Farm Animated cartoon version*, 1955.

By Joy Batchelor and John Halas, 1955. See the 1954 illustrated edition above, A.10k, the publication of which shortly preceded the appearance of the cartoon film. It was the first full-length cartoon film ever made in England. The book illustrations are adapted from the film.
There was also a strip cartoon version, based on the animated cartoon version, run by many regional newspapers in Britain and the United States.

Film Production Company: Louis de Rochemont.
Written and produced by John Halas and Joy Batchelor.
Filmed in Technicolour.
Voices: Maurice Denham
75 minutes

A.10.M2   *Animal Farm: A Fable in Two Acts*, 1964.

Adapted by Nelson Bond.
New York: Samuel French, Inc., 1964.
First presented at the Showtimers Studio Theater, Roanoke, Virginia, 29 September 1961.
Directed and produced by Nelson Bond
Paperbound. $1.25
Includes play text, production notes on staging, lighting, music, costuming.
There is a note on royalties, saying that the play may be given as a stage presentation by amateurs upon payment of $25 for the first performance and $20 for each additional performance, payable one week in advance of the performance, whether the performance is for charity or for gain, and whether or not admission is charged.

A.10.M3   *George Orwell's Animal Farm*, 1985

Musical stage play.
Adapted by Peter Hall with lyrics by Adrian Mitchell and music by Richard Peaslee.

Printed text, London: Methuen, 1985

Location
Cambridge University Library.

TRANSLATIONS

All Orwell Archive unless otherwise noted

AFRIKAANS

A.10.T1   *Die Opstand*, 1963

Johannesburg: Pers
Translated by Taboureux Bruwer

BASQUE

A.10.T2   *Abereen Etxaldea*, 1982

Navarra: Elkar
Translated by Juan Martin Elexpuru
Illustrated by Isabel Alonso
Paper bound

CATALAN

A.10.T3   *La Revolta Dels Animals*, 1984

Barcelona: Destino
Translated by Andreu Teixidor de Ventós and Josep M. Castellet
Paper bound
Published July 1984

DANISH

A.10.T4a   *Kammerat Napoleon*, 1947

Copenhagen: Vilhelm Priors
Translated by Ole Brandstrup
Illustrated by Sys Gauguin
Paper bound

A.10.T4b   *Kammerat Napoleon*, 1963

Copenhagen: Vintens
Translated by Ole Brandstrup
Paper bound
Hft 6.00, Indb 8.50

A.10.T4c   *Kammerat Napoleon*, 1981

Copenhagen: Gyldendals
Translated by Ole Brandstrup
Paper bound

DUTCH

A.10.T5a   *De Boerderij der Dieren*, 1947

Bussum: Phoenix
Translated by Anthony Ross
Illustrated by Van Karel Thole

A.10.T5b   *Animal Farm*, 1961

Dutch edition in English
Amsterdam: J.M. Meulenhoff
Edited and annotated by H. Otto Levenbach
With an unbound supplement of notes on the text in Dutch

A.10.T5c   *De Boerderij der Dieren*, 1979

Amsterdam: Arbeiderspers
Translated by Anthony Ross

FINNISH

A.10.T6a   *Eläinten Vallankumous*, 1969

Helsinki: Söderström
Translated by Panu Pekkanen
Paper bound

Reissued Helsinki: Söderström, 1971, 1973 and 1990
Paper bound

A.10.T6b   *Kammalaat Napoleon, no date*

Nuuk: Atuakkiorfik
Translated by Peter Brandt
Paper bound

FRENCH

A.10.T7a   *Les Animaux Partout*, 1947

Paris: Odile Pathé
Translated by Sophie Dévil
Paper bound
Published 15 October 1947
150 fr

A.10.T7b   *La République des Animaux*, 1964

Paris: Gallimard
translator not named
Paper bound
Published June 1964
8,80 fr

A.10.T7c   *La Ferme des Animaux*, 1981

Paris: Champ Libre
Translated by Jean Queval
Illustrated
Paper bound
Published 20 May 1981
40 fr

A.10.T7d   *La Ferme des Animaux*, 1983

Paris: Gallimard
Translated by Jean Queval
With dust jacket at Orwell Archive
Published October 1983

A.10.T7e   *La Ferme des Animaux*, 1983

Paris: Champ Libre
Translated by Jean Queval
Paper bound
Published 14 December 1983

GERMAN

A.10.T8a   *Farm der Tiere*, 1946

Zurich: Amstutz, Herdeg
Translated by N.O. Scarpi

A.10.T8b   *Farm der Tiere*, 1958

Frankfurt am Main & Hamburg: Fischer Bücherei
Translated by N.O. Scarpi
Paper bound
Published June 1958
DM 2.20

A.10.T8c   *Farm der Tiere*, 1974

Zurich: Diogenes
Translated by N.O. Scarpi
Paper bound

A.10.T8d   *Ferdinand Schöningh Edition*, 1977

Edition in English
Zeichnungen: Heinz Draeger. Paderborn: Ferdinand Schöningh
Edited by Rudolf Höppner, Maria Herold and Dieter Herold

A.10.T8e   *Farm der Tiere*, 1982

Zurich: Diogenes
Illustrated by F.K. Waechter
Translated by Michael Walter

A.10.T8f   *Farm der Tiere*, 1982

Zurich: Diogenes
Translated by Michael Walter
Paper bound
DM 6.80

GREEK

A.10.T9   Αγρυκτημα Ζωικος, 1974

Athens: Orora
Translated by Manole Gialourake
Paperbound with jacket

HUNGARIAN

A.10.T10a   *Állati Gazdaság*, 1984

Budapest: Kiadáa Alapján Készült
Translated by Zúz Tamás
Illustrated
Paper bound

A.10.T10b   *Állati Gazdaság*, 1985

Budapest: Az Irodalmi Újság Sorozata
Translated by Zúz Tamás
Illustrated by Árendás Pál
Paper bound

A.10.T10c   *Állatfarm*, 1989

Budapest: Európa Könyvkiadó
Translated by Szíjgyártó Lászlo Jogutóda
Paper bound
35,– Ft

ICELANDIC
A.10.T11   *Félagi Napóleon*, 1949

Seydisfirdi: Prentsmidja Austurlands
Translator not named
Paper bound

INDONESIAN
A.10.T12   *Negara Binatang*, 1949

Bandung: Penerbitan Sangkreti
Translated by Aus Suriatna
Illustrated
Paper bound

ITALIAN
A.10.T13a   *La Fattoria Degli Animali*, 1947

Verona: Mondadori Medusa
Translated by Bruno Tasso
Paper bound
Published October 1947
Reissued in July 1948, and March 1949

A.10.T13b   *La Fattoria Degli Animali*, 1967

Verona: Oscar Mondadori
Translated by Bruno Tasso
Paper bound
Published May 1967

A.10.T13c   *La Fattoria Degli Animali*, 1970

Milan: Mondadori
Translated by Bruno Tasso
Illustrated by Bruno Morelli
With dust jacket at Orwell Archive
Lire 1600
Reissued September 1984 at Lire 9,000, and March 1986 at Lire 10,000

A.10.T13d   *La Fattoria Degli Animali*, 1970

Verona: Mondadori
Translated by Bruno Tasso
Reissued paper bound in 1972 at Lire 600, 1973 at Lire 650 and 1975 at Lire 950

A.10.T13e   *La Fattoria Degli Animali*, 1972

Milan: Club Degli
Translated by Bruno Tasso

A.10.T13f   *La Fattoria Degli Animali*, 1980

Verona: Edizioni Scolastiche Bruno Mondadori
Translated by Bruno Tasso
Paper bound
Lire 3800

A.10.T13g   *La Fattoria Degli Animali*, 1983

Milan: Mondadori
Translated by Bruno Tasso
Published with *1984* [see A.12.T12b]
Published March 1983

A.10.T13h   *La Fattoria Degli Animali*, 1984

Verona: Mondadori Omnibus
Translated by Bruno Tasso
Published February 1984

A.10.T13i   *La Fattoria Degli Animali*, 1984

Verona: Mondadori Special Edition per Epoca
Translated by Bruno Tasso
Paper bound
Published February 1984

MALTESE

A.10.T14   *Ir-Razzett Tal-Bhejjem*, 1972

Malta: Klabb Kotba Maltin
Translated by Ġorġ Borg
Paper bound

NORWEGIAN

A.10.T15a   *Dictatoren*, 1946

Oslo: Brann
Translated by Sigrid Munthe Mossige
Illustrated
Paper bound

A.10.T15b   *Kamerat Napoleon*, 1964

Oslo: Pax
Translated by Tor Bjerkmann
Paper bound
8,00

A.10.T15c   *Kamerat Napoleon*, 1988

Oslo: Pax
Translated by Tor Bjerkmann

PERSIAN

A.10.T16   1974

Tehran: Farsi
Paper bound

POLISH

A.10.T17a   *Zwierzecy Folwark*, 1947

London: Wydawnictwo Światowego Zwiazku Polaków z Zagranicy.
Printed in England for the League of Poles Abroad
Translated by Teresa Jeleńska
Illustrated
Paper bound

Reissued as: *Folwark Zwierzecy*
London: Odnowa, 1974, 1984.
Copy at Cambridge University Library.

A.10.T17b   *Folwark Zwierzecy*, 1981

Warsaw: Biblioteka Historyczna Literacka
Translated by Teresa Jeleńska
With a 1980s introduction signed: H. Lewis Allways, presumably a joke and one of the
pseudonyms Eric Blair had considered before choosing George Orwell.

PORTUGUESE

A.10.T18a   *O Porco Triunfante*, 1946

Lisbon: Francisco Franco
Translated by Almirante Alberto Aprá
Paper bound

A.10.T18b   *A Revolução Dos Bichos*, 1964

Rio de Janeiro: Editôra Globo
Translated by Heitor Ferreira
Paper bound

A.10.T18c   *O Triunfo dos Porcos*, 1976

Lisbon: Perspectivas & Realidades
Translated by Maria Antunes
Published January 1976
Paper bound

A.10.T18d   *Otriunfo dos Porcos*, 1990

Lisbon: Europa-América
Translated by Madalena Esteves
Paper bound

SERBO-CROATIAN

A.10.T19a   *Životinjska Farma*, 1979

Zagreb: Naprijed
Translated by Vladimir Roksandić

A.10.T19b   *Životinjska Farma*, 1984

Zagreb: August Cesarec
Translated by Vladimir Roksandić

SINHALESE

A.10.T20   1974

Colombo
Translated by Dayaratne Garuinghe
Paper bound

SLOVENIAN

A.10.T21   *Živalska Farma*, 1970

Ljubljana: Tehniška Založba Slovenije
Translated by Boris Grabnar

SPANISH

A.10.T22a   *Rebelion en la Granja*, 1948

Buenos Aires: Guillermo Kraft
Translated by Abraham Scheps
Illustrated by Lino Palacio
Published July 1948

A.10.T22b   *Rebelión en la Granja*, 1973

Barcelona: Destino
Translated by Rafael Abella
Published April 1973

Reissued paper bound November 1977

SWAHILI

A.10.T23   *Shamba la Wanyama*, 1967

Nairobi: East African Publishing House
Translated by Kawegere Fortunatus
Paper bound

SWEDISH

A.10.T24a *Djurfarmen*, 1946

Stockholm: Albert Bonniers
Translated by Nils Holmberg
Paper bound
4.25

A.10.T24b *Djurfarmen*, no date

Bra Klassiker
Translated by Jan Wahlén
Cloth on boards. Jacket design by Jonas Lindström

A.10.T24c *Djurens Gård*, 1983

Stockholm: Atlantis
Translated by Jan Wahlén

A.10.T24d *Djurens Gård*, 1985

Litteraturfrämjandet
Translated by Jan Wahlén
Paper bound
10.–

UKRAINIAN

A.10.T25 *Kolgosp Tvarin*, 1947

Munich: Vidavnitstvi Prometei
Translated by Ivan Chernyatinskii
Contains Orwell's Preface, especially written for this edition
Paper bound

VIETNAMESE

A.10.T26 *Cuôc Cách-mang Trong Trai Súc-Vât*, 1951

Saigon: Imprimerie d'Extreme Orient
Paper bound

A.11 THE ENGLISH PEOPLE

... that silly little *English People* book[1]

Composition and publication

The book was commissioned by W.J. Turner, General Editor at Collins, in September 1943 for the series *Britain in Pictures*. Orwell's contract for the book is dated 20 September 1943. He was commissioned to write approximately 14,000 words, for which he would receive an outright payment of £50 within 14 days of publication. Orwell completed it on 22 May 1944. His payments book shows that he received a £20 advance from the publisher on 14 July 1945. But the book was not eventually published until August 1947. Because of the delay some references were updated by the publisher in 1946. The earlier text is reprinted in *Essays, Journalism and Letters* III 1–38.

There were a few questions in Orwell's mind about its status in terms of his contract with Gollancz, and, indeed, with his new publisher, Fredric Warburg, however, as he told Leonard Moore in July 1945:

> I had a talk with Warburg about the contract position. He is quite satisfied with my assurance that I will bring him all my future work, subject to books of a special nature (e.g. that "Britain in Pictures" book) being allowed to go elsewhere.[2]

In the same letter he told Moore,

> I saw W. J. Turner the other day and asked him about the "Britain in Pictures" book. He said Edmund Blunden is writing the companion volume simultaneously. I said that as they had had the MS a year I thought I ought to have some money. The agreed advance was £50 and I suggested they should give me £25 now. He said there would be no objection to this and I told him you would write to him, which you have perhaps done already.

When the book was eventually published Julian Symons reviewed it in the *Manchester Evening News*. Orwell wrote to him in response in October 1947,

> You gave me much too kind a review of that silly little *English People* book in the M E *News*. The only real excuse for it was that I was almost physically bullied into writing it by Turner. It was written about the beginning of 1944, but this didn't appear from the text, as last year the proof-reader hurriedly went through it shoving in a remark here and there to show the general election had happened in the mean time.[3]

> Fairly typically, Orwell and Symons went on to discuss what Orwell termed 'a point of pedantry' about a boxer, perhaps a welter-weight, perhaps a light-weight, whom Orwell had mentioned in the book and to whom Symons referred in the review.[4]

A.11a   *First Edition, 1947*

THE | ENGLISH PEOPLE | [ornamental short rule] | GEORGE ORWELL | [ornamental short rule] | *WITH* | *8 PLATES IN COLOUR* | *AND* | *17 ILLUSTRATIONS IN* | *BLACK & WHITE* | [publisher's ornamental device of columned building] | COLLINS . 14 ST. JAMES'S PLACE . LONDON | MCMXLVII

Collation There are six unmarked gatherings arranged [A–F]⁴; 24 leaves (22.0 × 16.3); [1–6] 7–47 [48]
There are four additional leaves, with coloured illustrations, bound in between pages 8 and 9, 16 and 17, 32 and 33, and 40 and 41.

Contents [1] halftitle: BRITAIN IN PICTURES | THE BRITISH PEOPLE IN PICTURES | [ornamental short rule] | THE ENGLISH PEOPLE [2] imprint: GENERAL EDITOR | W. J. TURNER | [editor's acknowledgement] [3] titlepage [4] imprint: PRODUCED BY | ADPRINT LIMITED LONDON | PRINTED IN GREAT BRITAIN | BY JARROLD AND SONS LTD NORWICH | ON MELLOTEX BOOK PAPER MADE | BY TULLIS RUSSELL AND CO LTD MARKINCH SCOTLAND [5–6] list of illustrations 7–[48] text

Binding Green paper on boards. Off white endpapers.

Front cover Within an off white frame of three narrow rules and one broad rule is picked out in off white: THE ENGLISH | PEOPLE | [illustration of park scene with soap-box orator addressing a crowd] | GEORGE ORWELL

Back cover Off white frame of three narrow rules and one broad rule.

Spine [in off white, three narrow rules and one broad rule] | [laterally] GEORGE ORWELL . THE ENGLISH PEOPLE | [horizontally, one broad rule and three narrow rules]

Jacket
Front As binding.
Back Publisher's advertisement.
Spine [in off white] [double rule] | 100 | [laterally] GEORGE ORWELL . THE ENGLISH PEOPLE | [horizontally] 100 | [double rule]
Front flap Within a green line frame is a green rectangle, in which is picked out in white: BRITAIN IN PICTURES | [in green] THE ENGLISH | PEOPLE | *by* | George Orwell | [summary] | [publisher's advertisement]
Back flap Publisher's advertisement

Notes
26,000 copies
5s 0d

In his letter to Moore of 23 June 1945 Orwell describes the book as 'a piece of propaganda for the British Council', and says that Collins had wanted him to make changes to the text which he refused to do.

Contemporary reviews
Times Literary Supplement (23 August 1947)

Locations
Cambridge University Library. Acquisition 11 August 1947.
Orwell Archive, three copies, with jackets.
E.J. Pratt Library, Victoria University in the University of Toronto.

A.11b   *The Times Authors Reissue, 1970*

There is a paperback reprint of the covers, titlepage, 16 pages of text and five illustrations in *The Times Authors* folder, published by Times' Education Services, Times Newspapers Limited, in 1970. The folder is No. 2 in the series.

Location
Cambridge University Library. Acquisition 15 September 1970.

A.11c   *Haskell House Reissue, 1974*

There was a photographic reprint produced in New York in 1974 by Haskell House. The illustrations are all black and white.

Location
Kelly Library, St Michael's College, University of Toronto.

TRANSLATIONS

All Orwell Archive unless otherwise noted

DANISH

A.11.T1a   *Det Engelske Folk*, 1948

Copenhagen: Steen Hasselbalchs Forlag
Translated by Paul Monrad
Paper bound
Published February 1948
2,350 copies
7.50

The essay *Det Engelske Folk* is also published in Danish in the same translation in a volume of essays with the same title. [See D.T1b].

A.11.T1b   *Det Engelske Folk og Andre Essays*, 1976

Copenhagen: Det Schonbergske Forlag
Translated by Paul Monrad
Paper bound
pp 13–62

The other essays are:
Shooting an Elephant 63–71
En henrettelse 72–77
Sadan dor de fattige 78–91
Jeg skriver, som det passer mig 92–114 – 6 sections:
en boganmelders bekendelser
gode darlige boger
sportsand
det engelske mords forfald
nogle betragtninger over den almindelige tudse

GERMAN

A.11.T2a   *Die Engländer*, 1948

Braunschweig: Schlösser Verlag
Translated by Arno Dohm
Paper on boards with cloth spine
There are eight pages of black and white illustrations

A.11.T2b   *The English People Die Engländer*, 1958

Munich: Edition, Langewiesche-Brandt
Translated by Walter Falke
English and German parallel texts
Afterword, biographical sketch of Orwell, in German only
Stiff paper bound
No. 59 in the Huebers Fremdsprachllichen Texten series

A.12   NINETEEN EIGHTY-FOUR

> . . . it is in a sense a fantasy, but in the form of a naturalistic novel. That is what makes
> it a difficult job – of course as a book of anticipations it would be comparatively
> simple to write.[1]

Composition and publication

Writing *The English People* in 1943, Orwell discussed the future, the kind of life people
might expect to live, and he envisaged a world dominated by two superstates. They were
ideas which he began to think of using in fiction. In February 1944 he wrote to Gleb Struve
of his 'interest in Zamyatin's *We*, which I had not heard of before. I am interested in that
kind of book, and even keep making notes for one myself that may get written sooner or
later'.[2] Later that year he again expressed ideas, this time in a letter, which he went on to
transfer to his fiction. He told H.J. Willmet,

> if the sort of world I am afraid of arrives, a world of two or three superstates which
> are unable to conquer one another, two and two could become five if the fuehrer
> wished it. That, so far as I can see, is the direction in which we are actually moving,
> though, of course, the process is reversible.[3]

And in an 'As I Please' article early in 1945, anticipating the end of the War, a period of peace and, again, the establishment of superstates, he wrote, 'it is likely that these vast states will be permanently at war with one another'.[4]

Orwell began to write *Nineteen Eighty-Four* in 1945, and at an early stage he was anxious to secure the right publisher, and hence preferably not Gollancz, whom in any case he felt fairly certain would refuse it:

> I doubt whether I could now write anything that Gollancz would approve of. For instance, I recently started a novel. Considering how much work I have to do elsewhere I don't expect to finish it till sometime in 1947, but I am pretty sure Gollancz would refuse it when the time comes unless by that time his views have altered again'.[5]

In 1937 Eileen, acting for him during his absence in Spain, had made a contractual agreement with Victor Gollancz, giving him an option on Orwell's next three novels. Gollancz published *Coming Up for Air* rejected *Animal Farm* on what Orwell termed 'political grounds' – he felt that criticising the Soviet Union was playing into the hands of the Nazis – and he convinced at least one other publisher, Jonathan Cape, that its controversial subject made it too hot to handle. Orwell was, therefore, reluctant to risk Gollancz's accepting the new novel, unlikely though this seemed, given the publisher's unquestioning support for the Soviet Union and its ideals. But, perhaps even worse, he might delay his decision or warn off other publishers. In March 1947 Orwell wrote to Gollancz confirming his wish to be released from the contract, suggesting that it would be to the advantage of both parties. He stated:

> The crucial case was *Animal Farm*. At the time when this book was finished it was very hard indeed to get it published, and I determined then that if possible I would take all my future output to the publisher who would produce it, because I knew that anyone who would risk this book would risk anything ... I recognise, of course, that your political position is not now exactly what it was when you refused *Animal Farm*, and in any case I respect your unwillingness to publish books which go directly counter to your political principles. But it seems to me that this difficulty is likely to arise again in some form or other, and that it would be better if you are willing to bring the whole thing to an end.[6]

Gollancz at first resisted, but eventually, reluctantly, agreed to terminate the contract.

Meanwhile, in 1946, Orwell decided seriously to reduce the amount of journalism he was doing, in order to concentrate on the new novel. He believed he could write the bulk of it if he took six months' break on the island of Jura in the Hebrides, although, once there, it was motor boats and fishing trips, the garden and its rabbits which occupied the bulk of his time, 'With all this you can imagine that I don't do much work – however I have actually begun my new book and hope to have done four or five chapters by the time I come back in October.'[7] By May 1947 he was making progress, and he told his new publisher, Fredric Warburg:

> I have made a fairly good start of the book and I think I must have written nearly a third of the rough draft. I have not got as far as I had hoped to do by this time, because I have really been in the most wretched health ... However I keep pegging away, and I hope that when I leave here in October I shall either have finished the rough draft or at any rate broken its back. Of course the rough draft is always a ghastly mess having very little relation to the finished result, but all the same it is the main part of the job. So if I do finish the rough draft by October I might get the book done fairly early in 1948, barring illness. I don't like talking about books before they are written, but I will tell you now that this is a novel about the future – that is, it is in a sense a fantasy, but in the form of a naturalistic novel. That is what makes it a difficult job – of course as a book of anticipations it would be comparatively simple to write.[8]

In August he was still planning more or less the same schedule, although as he told George Woodcock, 'It always takes me a hell of a time to write a book even if I am doing nothing else'.[9] The effects of almost constant ill-health were taking their toll. As he told Anthony Powell, 'One just seems to have a limited capacity for work nowadays and one has to husband it.'[10] In October he described himself as being on the last lap of the novel, although adding, 'But it's a most dreadful mess and about two-thirds of it will have to be rewritten entirely besides the usual touching up.'[11] In December 1947, with the rough draft finished, he was admitted to hospital where tuberculosis was diagnosed. He had told Anthony Powell that finishing the rough draft was the half-way mark,[12] and he now said, 'I've written half the book, which in my case is much the same as not starting it.'[13] He refused Julian Symons's request to read the draft, 'I can't show you the part-finished novel. I never show them to anybody, because they are just a mess & don't have much relationship to the final draft. I always say a book doesn't exist until it's finished … It is such a ghastly effort ever to finish a book nowadays.'[14] The best he could hope for now was to finish it by the end of 1948. He told Fred Warburg,

> It is just a ghastly mess as it stands, but the idea is so good that I could not possibly abandon it. If anything should happen to me I've instructed Richard Rees, my literary executor, to destroy the MS without showing it to anybody[15]

By May 1948 he was revising it, 'but I only do a very little, perhaps an hour's work each day.'[16] In July, still in hospital in Scotland, he wrote that he hoped to finish 'this blasted novel' by the winter.[17] By late October, back on Jura, he was only days away from completion, and he told Warburg,

> I am rather flinching from the job of typing it, because it is a very awkward thing to do in bed, where I still have to spend half the time. Also there will have to be carbon copies, a thing which always fidgets me, and the book is fearfully long, I should think well over 100,000 words, possibly 125,000. I can't send it away because it is an unbelievably bad MS and no one could make head or tail of it without explanation. On the other hand a skilled typist under my eye could do it easily enough …
>
> I am not pleased with the book but I am not absolutely dissatisfied. I first thought of it in 1943. I think it is a good idea but the execution would have been better if I had not written it under the influence of TB. I haven't definitely fixed on the title but I am hesitating between "Nineteen Eighty-Four" and "The Last Man in Europe".[18]

He told Anthony Powell, 'It's awful to think I've been mucking about with this book since June of 1947, and it's a ghastly mess now, a good idea ruined'.[19]

When Fred Warburg saw the finished book, he liked it, but Orwell wrote to him, 'It isn't a book I would gamble on for a big sale, but I suppose one could be sure of 10,000 anyway.'[20] Discussing the blurb for the book's jacket with Roger Senhouse, a director of Secker & Warburg, Orwell rejected a draft:

> It makes the book sound as though it were a thriller mixed up with a love story, & I didn't intend it to be primarily that. What it is really meant to do is to discuss the implication of dividing the world up into "Zones of influence". I thought of it in 1944 as a result of the Teheran Conference, & in addition to indicate by parodying them the intellectual implications of totalitarianism. It has always seemed to me that people have not faced up to these & that, e.g. the persecution of scientists in Russia, is simply part of a logical process which should have been foreseeable 10–20 years ago.[21]

He went on to suggest that once the proofs were ready they might be sent to 'some eminent person who might be interested, e.g. Bertrand Russell or Lancelot Hogben, to give his opinion abt the book, & (if he consented) use a piece of that as the blurb'. This plan was eventually adopted and Bertrand Russell's comments, which, presumably, did concur with Orwell's intentions, appear on the front flap of the jacket of the first edition. He says,

NINETEEN EIGHTY-FOUR depicts, with very great power, the horrors of a well-established totalitarian régime of whatever type. It is important that the western world should be aware of these dangers, and not only in the somewhat narrow form of fear of Russia.

In January 1949 Orwell was admitted to a sanatorium in Gloucestershire. Fred Warburg visited him and they agreed that the title 'Nineteen Eighty-Four' was better than 'The Last Man in Europe'. Meanwhile Orwell told Richard Rees that there was strong interest in the novel from Harcourt, Brace in the United States:

> The American publishers seem quite excited abt my book, so they are going to go ahead without waiting for the proofs from Warburg. This will mean 2 sets of proofs to correct. I don't suppose it will arise, but *if* I should feel very poorly & unequal to correcting proofs, do you think you could do them for me? As there are a lot of neologisms there are bound to be many printers' errors of a stupid kind, & American compositors are very tiresome to deal with as they always think they know better than the author. I wouldn't trust publishers or agents to do the job. On the other hand you could trust the MS, in which I don't expect there are more than a very few slips. It is most important that there shouldn't be misprints in a book of this kind.[22]

In England it was already scheduled to be the *Evening Standard* book of the month, 'which I believe doesn't mean anything in particular'[23], Orwell told Richard Rees, although it in fact guaranteed it further important publicity. He told Julian Symons, 'My new book is a Utopia in the form of a novel. I ballsed it up rather, partly owing to being so ill while I was writing it, but I think some of the ideas might interest you.'[24]

Leonard Moore negotiated the sale of the American rights to Harcourt, Brace, but they had reservations about 'Nineteen Eighty-Four' as a title. But Orwell told Moore that he did not mind if the American edition had a different title, 'I doubt whether it hurts a book to be published under different names in Britain and the USA ... and I would like Harcourt Brace to follow their own wishes in the matter of the title.'[25] Changing the title was one thing, but in March he rejected Harcourt, Brace's suggestion that the section 'The Theory and Practice of Oligarchical Collectivism' and the Appendix, 'The Principles of Newspeak', be cut as a condition of Book-of-the-Month publication in the United States. Warburg told him that he risked losing at least £40,000 in Book-of-the-Month Club royalties, but Orwell was adamant, as he told Moore:

> I can't possibly agree to the kind of alteration and abbreviation suggested. It would alter the whole colour of the book and leave out a good deal that is essential. I think it would also – though the judges, having read the parts that it is proposed to cut out, may not appreciate this – make the story unintelligible. There would also be something visibly wrong with the structure of the book if about a fifth or a quarter were cut out and the last chapter then tacked on to the abbreviated trunk. A book is built up as a balanced structure and one cannot simply remove large chunks here and there unless one is ready to recast the whole thing. In any case, merely to cut out the suggested chapters and abridge the passages from the "book within the book" would mean a lot of rewriting which I simply do not feel equal to at present.
> The only terms on which I could agree to any such arrangement would be if the book were published definitely as an abridged version and if it were clearly stated that the English edition contained several chapters which had been omitted. But obviously the Book of the Month people couldn't be expected to agree to any such thing. As Robert Giroux [an editor at Harcourt, Brace] says in his letter, they have not promised to select the book in any case, but he evidently hopes they might, and I suppose it will be disappointing to Harcourt Brace if I reject the suggestion. I suppose you, too, stand to lose a good deal of commission. But I really cannot allow my work to be mucked about beyond a certain point, and I doubt whether it even pays in the long run. I should be much obliged if you would make my point of view clear to them.[26]

He was anxious to make clear in his will that, in the event of his death, Richard Rees should have absolute authority on literary matters. He pointed out to Rees:

> It's important that your powers should be made clear, i.e. that you should have the final say when any definitely literary question is involved. For example. The American Book of the Month people, though they didn't actually promise, half promised to select my present book if I could cut out abt a quarter of it. Of course I'm not going to do this, but if I had died the week before, Moore & the American publishers wld have jumped at the [Book-of-the-Month] offer, ruining the book and not even benefitting my estate much'.[27]

His decision to hold out against the cuts proved successful and on 8 April he received a cable from the Book-of-the-Month Club announcing the selection of *Nineteen Eighty-Four* after all,

> in spite of my refusing to make the changes they demanded. So that shows that virtue is its own reward, or honesty is the best policy, I forget which. I don't know whether I shall ultimately end up with a net profit, but at any rate this should pay off my arrears of income tax.[28]

Advance publicity assured good advance sales, although Orwell remained cynical, as he indicated to Warburg:

> I am glad *1984* has done so well before publication. The *World Review*[29] published a most stupid extract, abridged in such a way as to make nonsense of it. I wouldn't have let Moore arrange this if I'd known they meant to hack it abt. However, I suppose it's advertisement.[30]

Nineteen Eighty-Four was published in London by Secker & Warburg on 8 June 1949, and in New York by Harcourt Brace on 13 June. *The Collected Essays, Journalism and Letters* includes an amalgam of excerpts from two letters in reply to questions from Francis Henson of the United Automobile Workers, in which Orwell further explains his aims in writing the novel:

> My recent novel is NOT intended as an attack on Socialism or on the British Labour Party (of which I am a supporter) but as a show-up of the perversions to which a centralised economy is liable and which have already been partly realised in Communism and Fascism. I do not believe that the kind of society I describe necessarily *will* arrive, but I believe (allowing of course for the fact that the book is a satire) that something resembling it *could* arrive. I believe also that totalitarian ideas have taken root in the minds of intellectuals everywhere, and I have tried to draw these ideas out to their logical consequences. The scene of the book is laid in Britain in order to emphasise that the English-speaking races are not innately better than anyone else and that totalitarianism, *if not fought against*, could triumph anywhere.[31]

Within a month there had been more than 60 reviews in the United States, almost all favourable. There were more than enough positive reviews to cheer Orwell, though, as he told Rees, '*1984* has had good reviews in the USA ... but of course also some very shame-making publicity.'[32], and then there was a *Partisan Review* literary award and a cheque for $1,000, as well as a good review there by Philip Rahv. In the *TLS* Julian Symons wrote a very positive review, although criticising the 'schoolboyish sensationalism' and 'crudity' of the rats in Room 101.[33] Orwell wrote to thank Symons for 'a brilliant as well as a generous review', adding, 'You are of course right abt the vulgarity of the "Room 101" business. I was aware of this while I was writing it, but I didn't know another way of getting somewhere near the effect I wanted.'[34] Most contemporary critics understood that Orwell was not writing a prediction but a warning about the future, based on observations of Communist, Nazi and Fascist institutions, although certain publishers chose to interpret *Nineteen Eighty-Four* as merely anti-Communist. An illustrated article in *Life* magazine and a *Readers Digest* abridgement were no doubt excellent publicity for the novel, but they saw only anti-communist aspects, the 'regimented left wing police state'. According to *Life*, Orwell 'saw firsthand [in the Spanish Civil War] what the communists were up to and has since devoted all his talents to warning the world of the fate which awaits it if it confuses liberalism with regimentation.' The implication is that this couldn't happen in America, whereas Orwell's intention was to show that this can happen anywhere. These American abridgements focus on details – details which Orwell uses to build a picture of a possibility which is already present everywhere within existing political structures and within individuals now. The abridgements, on the other hand, distort his meaning by mistaking those details for the whole picture. Contemporary Communist reviews also interpreted the novel as purely anti-Communist. *Pravda* called it 'squalid ... a filthy book ... a real attack against the people of the world [as opposed to] the living forces of peace [which] will assure mankind happiness and prosperity despite the monstrous intrigues of the imperialists, the instigators of war.'[35] But, more worryingly, *The Economist* and *The Wall Street Journal* also saw *Nineteen Eighty-Four* as merely anti-Communist and anti-Socialist. Orwell noted, 'I am afraid some of the US Republican papers have tried to use *1984* as propaganda against the Labour Party, but I have issued a sort of démenti which I hope will be printed.'[36] To counter the misunderstandings Orwell felt obliged to prepare this defence, dictated from his sickbed and polished by Warburg into a press release. Orwell was anxious to emphasise that the novel was not a prediction but an indication of what *could* happen to both Socialist and Liberal capitalist communities not only from war and the atomic bomb, but from the 'acceptance of a totalitarian outlook by intellectuals of all colours.' His conclusion is *'Don't let it happen. It depends on you.'*[37]

A.12a   First Edition, 1949

NINETEEN | EIGHTY-FOUR | *A Novel* | BY | GEORGE ORWELL | LONDON | SECKER & WARBURG | 1949

Collation [A]–I[16] K[12]; 156 leaves (18.4 × 12.5); [1–5] 6–312

Contents [1] halftitle: NINETEEN EIGHTY-FOUR [2] list of books by Orwell [3] titlepage [4] imprint: Martin Secker & Warburg, Ltd. | 7 John Street, Bloomsbury, London, W.C.1 | *First published 1949* | Printed in Great Britain by The Alcuin Press, | Welwyn Garden City, and bound by Key & Whiting, | Ltd., London [5]–312 text

Binding Green calico-textured cloth on boards. Off white endpapers. Purple topped leaves.

Front and back covers Plain.

Spine Stamped in purplish red: [pyramid of 6 lines] | NINETEEN | EIGHTY-FOUR | [small ornate device of half circles and a dot] | GEORGE | ORWELL | [inverted pyramid of 6 lines] | SECKER & | WARBURG

Jacket
Front Against a red background is faintly picked out in pink: 1984 [over this, in white to resemble cursive script]: George Orwell | nineteen | eighty-four | a novel
Back Printed in red against a white background is an advertisement for books by Orwell.
Spine In white against a red background: NINETEEN | EIGHTY-FOUR | GEORGE | ORWELL | SECKER & | WARBURG
Front flap [Bertrand Russell's comments on proofs of *Nineteen Eighty-Four*] | FOR A DESCRIPTION OF THE | BOOK SEE BACK FLAP | *Jacket design by Michael Kennard* | W.469 | 10s. net
Back flap Plot summary.

Notes
Published 8 June 1949
10s 0d
25,575 copies printed
By the end of October 1949, 22,700 copies sold.
There is another state of the first issue with a green jacket.

Contemporary reviews
Henry de Villose *Adelphi* (July–September 1949)
Booklist (1 June 1949)
G.M. Thomson *Evening Standard* (7 June 1949)
Christopher Hollis *Horizon* (September 1949)
Kirkus Review (15 May 1949)
P. Bloomfield *Manchester Guardian* (10 June 1949)
V.S. Pritchett *New Statesman and Nation* (18 June 1949)
Harold Nicolson *The Observer* (12 June 1949)
Bertrand Russell *The Spectator* (17 June 1949)
Julian Symons *Times Literary Supplement* (10 June 1949)

Locations
Orwell Archive, including jacket
Orwell Archive [second copy, with jacket, is Roger Senhouse's, with annotations on front endpapers quoting Orwell's diary and a letter from Orwell to Senhouse on a draft blurb for the novel].
English Library, University College London [jacket in Orwell Archive].
Cambridge University Library. Acquisition 7 November 1949

In all editions and reissues described below the section 'Principles of Newspeak' is assumed to be part of the text.

A.12b   First American Edition, 1949

NINETEEN EIGHTY-FOUR | A NOVEL BY | George Orwell | HARCOURT, BRACE AND COMPANY NEW YORK

Collation There are ten unmarked gatherings of 16 leaves, arranged [A–K]^{16}; 160 leaves (20.3 × 13.6); [i–iv] [1–2] 3–314 [315–316]

Contents [i] halftitle: NINETEEN EIGHTY-FOUR [ii] list of books by Orwell [iii] titlepage [iv] imprint: COPYRIGHT, 1949, BY | HARCOURT, BRACE AND COMPANY, INC. | *All rights reserved, including the right to repro-* | *duce this book or portion thereof in any form.* | *first American edition* | PRINTED IN THE UNITED STATES OF AMERICA [1] halftitle: ONE [2] blank 3–314 text [315–316] blank

Binding Grey calico grain cloth on boards. Off white endpapers.

Front cover Within a black outline with two straight sides and one jagged to resemble torn paper is stamped in red at an angle: NINETEEN EIGHTY-FOUR

Back cover Plain.

Spine George | Orwell | [laterally, outline and title as on front cover] | Harcourt, Brace | and Company

Jacket
Front Against a blue background: [in white cursive script] A Novel | [against a white background of two straight sides and one jagged to resemble torn paper is printed in black at an angle]: NINETEEN EIGHTY-FOUR | [black shadow of jagged edge] | [in white cursive script] by George Orwell | [regular capitals] AUTHOR OF [cursive script] Animal Farm

Back Against a blue background is printed in white: GEORGE ORWELL | [black and white caricature of Orwell and extracts from reviews by Bertrand Russell, V.S. Pritchett, and Alfred Kazin]
Spine Against a blue background is printed in white cursive script: George | Orwell | [laterally, outline and title as on front] | [in white cursive script] Harcourt, Brace | and Company
Front flap $3.00 | [printed in blue] NINETEEN EIGHTY-FOUR | by George Orwell | [in black, plot summary]
Back flap [continuation of plot summary] | *The caricature of George Orwell which appears on the back panel is by George Holland* | [in blue] HARCOURT, BRACE AND COMPANY | *383 Madison Avenue, New York 17, N.Y.*

Notes
Published 13 June 1949.
20,000 copies.
Jacket designed by Gerald Gross.
There were further printings as follows:
1 July 1949, 10,000 copies
7 September 1949, 10,000 copies
3 February 1950, 4,100 copies
June 1950, 5,000 copies

Contemporary reviews
C.J. Rolo *Atlantic Monthly* (July 1949)
Booklist (June 1949)
Bookmark (October 1949)
M.P. Corcoran *Catholic World* (August 1949)
M. Dedmon *Chicago Sun* (13 June 1949)
H.S. Tigner *Christian Century* (7 September 1949)
Cleveland Open Shelf (July 1949)
D. Burnham *Commonweal* (8 July 1949)
K.T. Willis *Library Journal* (1 June 1949)
The Nation (25 June 1949)
R. Hatch *The New Republic* (1 August 1949)
J. Hilton *New York Herald Tribune* (12 June 1949)
Mark Scherer *New York Times* (12 June 1949)
Lionel Trilling *New Yorker* (18 June 1949)
Philip Rahv *Partisan Review* (July 1949)
V. Bourjailly *San Francisco Chronicle* (12 June 1949)
W. Soskin *Saturday Review of Literature* (11 June 1949)
Springfield Republican (10 July 1949)
Time (20 June 1949)
P. Pickrel *Yale Review* (Autumn 1949)
Virginia Kirkus Bookshop Bulletin (15 May 1949)

Location
Orwell Archive, including jacket.

A.12c   Book-of-the-Month Club Reissue of American First Edition, 1949

Titlepage, collation, contents, binding and jacket as American First Edition, with the additional imprint following PRINTED IN THE UNITED STATES OF AMERICA on [iv]: | BY THE HADDON CRAFTSMEN, SCRANTON, PA.

The jacket has two additional lines on the front flap about the Book-of-the-Month Club.

Location
Orwell Archive, including mutilated jacket.

Notes
Offered by the Book-of-the-Month Club in July 1949.
Advertising blurb leaflet is in Orwell Archive copy. See Notes on First Canadian Edition, A.12d.
190,000 copies sold by March 1952.

A.12d   First Canadian Edition, 1949

NINETEEN EIGHTY-FOUR | A NOVEL BY | George Orwell | SECKER & WARBURG LONDON | S.J. REGINALD SAUNDERS & CO. LTD. TORONTO

Collation, contents, binding and jacket as first American edition, with the following exceptions:

[iv] imprint: COPYRIGHT, CANADA, 1949, BY | S.J. REGINALD SAUNDERS AND COMPANY LIMITED | *All rights reserved, including the right to repro-* | *duce this book or portion thereof in any form.* | *first Canadian edition* | PRINTED IN THE UNITED STATES OF AMERICA | BY THE HADDON CRAFTSMEN, SCRANTON, PA.

Spine George | Orwell | [laterally, outline and title as on front cover] | SAUNDERS

Jacket As First American Edition, but against a red background, Saunders instead of Harcourt, Brace and Company on the spine, and publisher's name and address removed from inside back flap.

Notes
Printed using the American First Edition electroplates. Saunders and the American Book-of-the-Month Club shared the cost of the production, printing 15,000 copies in total. It was out of print by June 1950.

Location
Orwell Archive, including jacket.

A.12e   Signet Edition, 1950

1984 | *a novel by* | GEORGE ORWELL | [within an oval frame]: N.A.L. | *SiGNET* [sic] | BOOKS | Published by THE NEW AMERICAN LIBRARY

Collation 120 leaves in a perfect binding (18.2 × 10.7); [1–5] 6–237 [238–240]

Contents [1] plot synopsis [2] publisher's advertisement [3] titlepage [4] imprint: COPYRIGHT, 1949, BY HARCOURT, BRACE AND COMPANY, INC. | *All rights reserved, including the right to repro-* | *duce this book or portions thereof in any form.* | *Published as a SINGET BOOK* | *By Arrangement with Harcourt, Brace and Company, Inc.* | FIRST PRINTING, JULY, 1950 | [within a rectangle]: *SIGNET BOOKS are published by* | *The New American Library of World Literature, Inc.* | *501 Madison Avenue, New York 22, New York* | [beneath rectangle]: PRINTED IN THE UNITED STATES OF AMERICA [5]–237 text [238–240] publisher's advertisements
Binding Paper bound.

Front cover [within red stripe at top]: 798 | [within an oval frame]: N.A.L. | *SiGNET* [sic] | BOOKS [to the right]: A Startling View of Life in 1984 | Forbidden Love .... Fear .... Betrayal | [in the centre of the cover is a coloured picture of a man and woman, back to back on the edge of a crowd in front of pyramid-like buildings, watched by a guard and overlooked by a Big Brother poster] | [within a black stripe at foot is picked out in white]: SIGNET BOOKS | Complete and Unabridged

Back cover [within red stripe at top is an oval frame, within which is printed]: N.A.L. | *SiGNET* [sic] | BOOKS [to the right]: ... Good Reading for the Millions | [within the central white area is an account of life in 1984, beneath which are a photograph and short biographical sketch of Orwell] | [within a black stripe at foot is picked out in white]: Published by the New American Library

Spine [against a red background] 798 | [laterally] NINETEEN EIGHTY-FOUR GEORGE ORWELL | [black stripe]

Locations
Orwell Archive

Notes
35 cents
Ian Willison records a quote from Saunders that by January 1952 this paper bound edition had sold 'over three-quarters of a million copies' [Willison 93].
Fredric Warburg notes that this edition sold 1,200,000 copies between 1950 and 1957; 2,052,000 between 1958 and 1965; and 1965–1969 5,571,000 [Warburg 115].

A.12f   Reissue of First Edition, 1950

Notes
Published March 1950.
5,570 copies printed

A.12g   Second and third reissues of First Edition, 1950

Notes
April 1950: 5,150 copies, of which 3,150 were bound up for the Star Edition [See A.12h].
November 1950: 5,000 copies

A.12h   Star Edition, 1950

NINETEEN | EIGHTY-FOUR | *A Novel* | BY | GEORGE ORWELL | LONDON | SECKER & WARBURG | 1950

Collation and Contents as First Edition, with addition to imprint on [4]: *Reprinted 1950 | Reprinted 1950*

Binding Stiff off white paper boards. Off white endpapers.

Front cover Stamped in purplish red: George Orwell [cursive script] | [elaborate short rule] | NINETEEN | EIGHTY-FOUR | [star motif] | [elaborate short rule] | Star Editions [cursive script] | TO BE SOLD ON THE CONTINENT OF EUROPE ONLY

Back cover Plain.

Spine Stamped in purplish red laterally in cursive script: George | Orwell [diamond motif] NINETEEN EIGHTY-FOUR [diamond motif] | [horizontally, in plain capitals]: STAR | [star motif] | EDITIONS

Jacket
Front Against a maroon background is picked out in white: George Orwell [cursive script] | [elaborate short rule] | NINETEEN | EIGHTY-FOUR | [star motif] | [elaborate short rule] | Star Editions [cursive script] | TO BE SOLD ON THE CONTINENT OF EUROPE ONLY
Back Plain.
Spine Against a maroon background is picked out in white laterally in cursive script: George | Orwell [diamond motif] NINETEEN EIGHTY-FOUR [diamond motif] | [horizontally, in plain capitals] STAR | [star motif] | EDITIONS
Front flap Printed in purplish red is a plot summary.
Back flap Printed in purplish red is a publisher's advertisement for Star Editions.

Notes
Published August 1950.
3150 copies from second 1950 reissue bound for this Star Edition, for sale in Europe.

Locations
Orwell Archive, with jacket.

A.12i   Second Edition, 1950

The second British Edition was printed in December 1950, reset from the first edition. 4,975 copies were printed. Like its July 1951 reissue [See A.12j], it was printed in France by Régie, Le Livre Universel, and bound in London by Key and Whiting.

A.12j   Reissue of Second Edition, 1951

NINETEEN | EIGHTY-FOUR | *A Novel* | BY | GEORGE ORWELL | LONDON | SECKER & WARBURG | 1951

Collation [A]–U⁸; 160 leaves (18.4 × 12.6); [1–5] 6–318 [319–320]

Contents [1] halftitle: NINETEEN EIGHTY-FOUR [2] list of books by Orwell [3] titlepage [4] imprint: Martin Secker & Warburg, Ltd. | 7 John Street, Bloomsbury, London, W.C.1 | *First published 1949* | *Reprinted 1950* | *Reprinted 1950* | *Reset 1950* | *Reprinted 1951* | Printed in France by Régie | LE LIVRE UNIVERSEL, and bound by Key & Whiting | Ltd., London [5]–318 text [319–320] blank

Binding Green calico-textured cloth on boards. Off white endpapers. Purple topped leaves.

Front and back covers Plain.

Spine Stamped in purplish red: [pyramid of 6 lines] | NINETEEN | EIGHTY-FOUR | [small ornate device of half circles and a dot] | GEORGE | ORWELL | [inverted pyramid of 6 lines] | SECKER & | WARBURG

Jacket
Front Against a green background is faintly picked out in light green: 1984 [over this, in white to resemble cursive script]: George Orwell | nineteen | eighty-four | a novel
Back Printed in green against a white background are appreciations of Orwell.
Spine In white against a green background: NINETEEN | EIGHTY-FOUR | GEORGE | ORWELL | SECKER & | WARBURG
Front flap Advertisement for books by Orwell, with extracts from reviews
Back flap Plot summary | *Jacket design by Michael Kennard* | W.469 12s. 6d net | FIFTH IMPRESSION

Notes
4,000 copies³⁸

Location
Orwell Archive, including jacket.

A.12k   First Penguin Edition, 1954

NINETEEN | EIGHTY-FOUR | A NOVEL BY | GEORGE ORWELL | * | PENGUIN BOOKS | IN ASSOCIATION WITH | SECKER AND WARBURG

Collation 128 leaves in a perfect binding, arranged: [A]–H¹⁶ (18.1 × 10.9); [1–4] 5–250 [251–256]

Contents [1] halftitle: PENGUIN BOOKS | 972 | NINETEEN EIGHTY-FOUR | GEORGE ORWELL | [penguin motif] [2] blank [3] titlepage [4] imprint: Penguin Books

Ltd, Harmondsworth, Middlesex | [list of publisher's Commonwealth addresses] | First published 1949 | Published in Penguin Books 1954 | Made and printed in Great Britain | by Richard Clay and Company, Ltd, | Bungay, Suffolk 5–[251] text [252] blank [253–256] publisher's advertisements

Binding Paper bound.

Front cover Within orange stripe at top is a white area within which is printed: PENGUIN | BOOKS | [within white stripe in centre of cover]: NINETEEN | EIGHTY-FOUR | [short orange rule] | GEORGE ORWELL | [within stripe in lower third of cover]: COMPLETE [penguin motif in black and white] UNABRIDGED | 2|– [not line break]

Back cover [within a narrow orange border is a white rectangle in which is printed]: [photograph of Orwell] | [biographical sketch of Orwell] | [at foot, in border]: NOT FOR SALE IN THE U.S.A.

Spine [within orange stripe at top, laterally] GEORGE ORWELL [within white stripe at centre, laterally] NINETEEN EIGHTY-FOUR | [within orange stripe at bottom]: [penguin motif] | 972

Inside front cover Plot summary | publisher's advertisement

Inside back cover publisher's advertisement

Locations
Orwell Archive

Reissues [OA=Orwell Archive]
1955 OA, 1955 price 2|6 OA, 1956 OA, 1958 3|6 OA, 1959 OA, 1960 not seen, 1961 OA – cover has black and white photograph of an eye looking down a well, 1962, 1963 OA, 1964 OA two copies, 1965 OA.

Later Penguin editions and reissues
1981 – second 1981 issue Orwell Archive
128 leaves in a perfect binding.
Front cover has picture in black and red of a man with a megaphone against a blue background.
£1.00
Reissues 1966, 1967, 1968, 1969, 1970 (twice), 1971, 1972 (twice), 1973 (twice), 1974, 1975 (three times), 1976, 1977 (twice) 1978, 1979 (twice), 1980 (twice), 1981 (twice)

1984 Penguin Classics edition
Cambridge University Library
Orwell Archive
136 leaves in a perfect binding.
Front cover has coloured photograph of an eye looking through the O of FOUR
£1.95

1984 – sixth reissue – as 1984 first issue
Front cover has still of Big Brother from the movie made in 1984, with a coloured still of John Hurt superimposed on it.

1989 Twentieth Century Classics edition, with an Introduction by Ben Pimlott. Based on the Complete Works edition.

A.12l   *Signet Classics Edition, 1961*

[across two pages] 1984 | A Novel by *George Orwell* | *With an Afterword by* ERICH FROMM | [publisher's motif] A SIGNET CLASSIC | Published by THE NEW AMERICAN LIBRARY

Collation 136 leaves in a perfect binding (17.9 × 10.6); [1–4] 5–267 [268–272]

Contents [1] [drawing and biographical sketch of Orwell] [2–3] titlepage [4] imprint and copyright notices 5–256 text 257–267 afterword by Erich Fromm [268] blank [269] selected list of works by Orwell [270–272] publisher's advertisements

Binding Paper bound.

Front cover Within a purple border is a white area in which is printed: CP100 [publisher's motif in black and blue] SIGNET | CLASSICS 60c [cent sign with diagonal stroke | in red] GEORGE ORWELL | [in black] 1984 | [painting of face in black and shades of purple] | [motif of runner] A SIGNET CLASSIC

Back cover [runner motif] 1984 | By GEORGE ORWELL | [plot summary] | With an Afterword by Erich Fromm | PUBLISHED BY THE NEW AMERICAN LIBRARY

Spine cp | 100 | [laterally] Nineteen Eighty-four [motif of runner] George Orwell

Notes
Published August 1961

Location
Orwell Archive

Reissues
April 1962, labelled 'Twenty-sixth Printing'. Orwell Archive.
December 1962, labelled 'Twenty-eighth Printing'. Orwell Archive.
Undated reissue, labelled 'FORTY-NINTH PRINTING', with new cover with green border and printing in blue, orange and purple, 75c. Orwell Archive.

A.12m   *Harbrace Sourcebooks Edition, 1963*

ORWELL'S | Nineteen | Eighty- | Four | TEXT, | SOURCES, | CRITICISM | *Irving Howe* STANFORD UNIVERSITY | [publisher's motif] HARCOURT, BRACE & WORLD, INC. | NEW YORK . BURLINGAME

Collation Nine unmarked gatherings arranged: [A–I][16]; 144 leaves (23.4 × 18.5); [i–vi] vii–x [xi–xii] [1] 2–274 [275–276]

Contents [i] halftitle: ORWELL'S | Nineteen | Eighty- | Four | TEXT, | SOURCES, | CRITICISM [ii] imprint: [publisher's motif of four books on a shelf, around which in a half circle is]: HARBRACE SOURCEBOOKS | [to the right] *Under the General Editorship of* | DAVID LEVIN, *Stanford University* [iii] titlepage [iv] imprint: [copyright symbol] 1963 by Harcourt, Brace & World, Inc. | copyright notices and acknowledgements [v] acknowledgements continued [vi] blank vii–viii introduction by Irving Howe, dated December 1962 ix–x contents [xi] halftitle: ORWELL'S | Nineteen | Eighty- | Four | TEXT, | SOURCES, | CRITICISM [xii] blank [1] halftitle: PART ONE. TEXT 2–137 text, on 137: 1949 [138] blank [139]–174 [Part Two: sources] [175] halftitle: PART THREE. CRITICISM 176–270 criticism 271–273 suggestions for writing [274] suggestions for further reading [275–276] blank

Binding Paper bound.

Front cover Printed in red: [thick short rule] | ORWELL'S | [in grey] Nineteen | Eighty- | Four | [in red, thick red short rule] | TEXT, | SOURCES, | CRITICISM

Back cover list of contents | [in red, publisher's motif as on [ii]] HARBRACE SOURCEBOOKS | Harcourt, Brace & World

Spine [laterally, in grey] Howe [in red] Orwell's Nineteen Eighty-Four [in grey] Text, Sources, Criticism | [horizontally in red] publisher's motif

Locations
Orwell Archive, two copies

Notes
In the Sources section are reprints of three of Orwell's essays:
'Why I Write', 'Politics and the English Language', and 'Freedom and Happiness'.

A.12n *Heinemann Edition, 1965*

GEORGE ORWELL | [short ornate rule] | *Nineteen* | *Eighty-Four* | WITH AN INTRODUCTION BY | STEPHEN SPENDER | [publisher's windmill motif] | HEINEMANN | LONDON

Collation [A]–K^{16} L^8; 168 leaves (18.5 × 12.4); [i–iv] v–xxi [xxii] [5] 6–318

Contents [i] halftitle: *The Modern Novel Series* | NINETEEN EIGHTY-FOUR [ii] publisher's advertisement [iii] titlepage [iv] imprint: Heinemann Educational Books Ltd . LONDON MELBOURNE TORONTO | SINGAPORE CAPE TOWN | AUCKLAND IBADAN | HONG KONG | Introduction [copyright symbol] Stephen Spender 1965 | First published by Secker & Warburg Ltd 1949 | First published in this edition 1965 | Published by | Heinemann Educational Books Ltd | 15–16 Queen Street, Mayfair, London W.1 | Printed in Great Britain by | Butler & Tanner Ltd, Frome and London v–vi biographical note vii–xxi introduction by Stephen Spender, on xxi: 1964 [xxii] blank 5–318 text

Binding Green, black and white irregular striped paper on boards, embossed to resemble calico grain cloth.

Front cover Within a regular black stripe is picked out in white: THE MODERN NOVEL SERIES | [within an irregular white rectangle]: GEORGE ORWELL | *Nineteen eighty-four* | introduction by | Stephen Spender

Back cover Plain.

Spine Within a central white rectangle, laterally: GEORGE ORWELL | *Nineteen eighty-four* | [horizontally in white is a publisher's windmill motif]

Locations
Orwell Archive. Two copies.

A.12o *Canadian Educational Edition, 1967*

[broad vertical rule to left] 1984 | George Orwell | Canadian Educational Edition | *Edited by* | JOSEPH BLAKEY | Head of the English Department | *Victoria Park Secondary School* | *Foreword by* | NORTHROP FRYE | *Introduction by* | STEPHEN SPENDER | [to left of vertical rule is a publisher's ornamental device of a house, and to the right] BELLHAVEN HOUSE LIMITED | DON MILLS, ONTARIO

Collation There are 12 unmarked gatherings arranged [A–L]^{16} [M]^8; 184 leaves (19.4 × 12.9); [i–vi] vii–xxix [xxx] [5]–318 [319–320] 321–340 [341–342]

Contents [i] halftitle: 1984 [ii] [photograph] | *Courtesy Columbia Pictures Corporation* | "Always . . . there was a sort of protest, a feel- | ing that you had been cheated of something | that you had a right to." | *(Page 63)* [iii] titlepage [iv] [broad vertical rule to right] imprint: Foreword | [copyright symbol] NORTHROP FRYE | Introduction | [copyright symbol] STEPHEN SPENDER | Other Editorial Material | [copyright symbol] BELLHAVEN HOUSE LIMITED | First published by Secker and Warburg Limited 1949 | First published in this edition 1967 | Published by | BELLHAVEN HOUSE LIMITED | 98 Lesmill Road, Don Mills, Ontario | Printed and bound in Canada by | T.H. BEST PRINTING

COMPANY LIMITED [v] contents [vi] blank vii–xii foreword, on xii: *Northrop Frye* | *Toronto, 1964* xiii–xxvii introduction, on xxvii: *Stephen Spender* | *1964* xxviii–xxix biographical note [xxx] blank [5]–318 text [319–320] blank 321–326 commentary 327–340 questions and film study [341–342] blank

Binding Paper bound in red paper embossed to resemble linen grain cloth. Off white endpapers.

Front cover stamped in silver gilt: [broad vertical rule to left] 1984 | George Orwell | [to left of vertical rule is a publisher's ornamental device of a house, and to the right] Canadian Educational Edition

Back cover stamped in silver gilt is a broad vertical rule to the right and the publisher's ornamental device of a house

Spine stamped in silver gilt laterally: George | Orwell [horizontal rule] 1984 [horizontal rule] Bellhaven House

Notes
Frye wrote a retrospective article on Orwell in 1950, which included a review of *Nineteen Eighty-Four.* He described it as 'a very wonderful novel, one of the greatest the twentieth century has yet produced, and, again, great by reason of its utter simplicity.' *The Canadian Forum* Vol. XXIX, no. 350 (March 1950) 265–66.

Location
Frye Collection, E.J. Pratt Library, Victoria University in the University of Toronto. This copy is annotated by Frye.

A.12p   Heron Books Edition, 1970

GEORGE ORWELL | [in red] NINETEEN | EIGHTY-FOUR | [in black] *With an Introduction* | *and Appreciation* | *by* | JULIAN SYMONS | [publisher's heron motif] | Distributed by | HERON BOOKS

Collation 184 leaves in a perfect binding (20.0 × 12.0); [X1–X2] [I–VIII] IX [X] XI–XIII [XIV–XVI] 1–313 [314–316] 317–343 [344] 345 [346–350]
The last 18 leaves are thick pale yellow paper – watermarked with tramlines into which are interleaved 10 leaves of black and white photographs on the same yellow paper.

Contents [X1–X2] blank [I] blank [II] imprint: [sunburst motif] *A Collection distributed by Heron Books* [III] halftitle: [in red] BOOKS | THAT | HAVE | CHANGED | MAN'S | THINKING | [in black] NINETEEN | EIGHTY-FOUR [IV] photograph of Orwell | *George Orwell at the time of writing* | Nineteen Eighty-Four [V] titlepage [VI] imprint: *Published by arrangement with* | *Martin Secker & Warburg, Ltd., London* | [copyright symbol] 1970, *Editor's Foreword, Introduction and Appreciation,* | *Edito-Service S.A. Geneva* [VII] contents [VIII] blank IX–[X] editor's foreward, on [X]: COURTLANDT CANBY | EDITOR OF THE SERIES XI–XIII introduction, on XIII: JULIAN SYMONS [XIV] blank [XV] halftitle: NINETEEN | EIGHTY-FOUR [XVI] blank 1–[314] text [315] halftitle: APPRECIATION | *by* | JULIAN SYMONS [316] blank 317–[344] appreciation of Orwell 345–[346] list of sources of illustrations [347] imprint: *This book, designed by* | *Werner Schelling* | *is a production of* | *Edito-Service S.A. Geneva* | [sunburst motif] | *Printed in Switzerland* [348–350] blank

Binding Smooth, mottled yellow front and back covers on boards. Green morocco grain leather spine wrapping around to front and back covers. Green endpapers with all-over pattern of gilt motifs. Fixed yellow silk bookmark.

Front cover Decoration of elaborate gilt tooling.

Back cover Plain.

Spine Stamped in gilt: [rectangular panel of elaborate tooling] | [within a rectangular frame] GEORGE | ORWELL | [within a rectangular frame] NINETEEN | EIGHTY-FOUR | [six rectangular panels of elaborate tooling]

Locations
Orwell Archive, two copies

A.12q   *Uniform Edition, 1970*

NINETEEN | EIGHTY-FOUR | *A Novel by* | GEORGE ORWELL | SECKER & WARBURG LONDON

Collation [A]–K^{16}; 160 leaves (19.7 × 13.1); [1–5] 6–318 [319–320]

Contents [1] halftitle: NINETEEN EIGHTY-FOUR [2] list of books by Orwell [3] titlepage [4] imprint: Martin Secker & Warburg Ltd | 14 Carlisle Street, London W1V 6NN | First published 1949 | Reprinted 1950 (twice), Reset 1950 | Reprinted 1951, 1954, 1955 (twice), 1959, 1962, 1970 | 436 35007 6 | Reprinted by photolithography | and bound in Great Britain | by Bookprint Limited, Crawley, Sussex [5]–318 text [319–320] blank

Binding Green paper, embossed to resemble calico textured cloth, on boards. Off white endpapers.

Spine Stamped in gilt: [pyramid of 6 lines] | NINETEEN | EIGHTY-FOUR | [small ornate device of circles and dots] | GEORGE | ORWELL | [inverted pyramid of 6 lines] | S&W

Jacket Dull brown.
Front [Printed in silver] GEORGE | ORWELL | [in dark brown] NINETEEN | EIGHTY-FOUR
Back Plain.
Spine laterally [in silver]: ORWELL [and in dark brown]: NINETEEN | EIGHTY-FOUR | [horizontally in silver]: SECKER & | WARBURG
Front flap [in dark brown, extracts from reviews | [bottom left]: Jacket design by | Format | [bottom right]: 35s net | £1.75 net
Back flap SBN: 436 35007 6

Location
Orwell Archive

A.12r   *Reissue of 1970 Heron Books Edition, with illustrations, 1974*

George Orwell | [in red] NINETEEN | EIGHTY-FOUR | [in black] Original Illustrations by | Siân Cardy | [publisher's motif]

Collation 161 leaves in a perfect binding. There are seven additional leaves with illustrations on the recto, interleaved with the text; (19.9 × 12.0); [i–vi] 1–[313] [314–316]

Contents [i–ii] blank [iii] halftitle in red: NINETEEN EIGHTY-FOUR [iv] [photograph of Orwell] | *George Orwell* [v] titlepage [vi] imprint: *Published by arrangement with* | *Martin Secker & Warburg Ltd., London* | [copyright symbol] *1974, Edito-Service* S.A., Geneva

Binding Brown morocco-grain leather on boards. Grey endpapers with all over pattern of gilt motifs. Fixed yellow silk bookmark.

Front cover Decoration of elaborate gilt tooling.

Back cover Plain.

Spine Stamped in gilt: [rectangular panel of elaborate tooling] | GEORGE | ORWELL | [short rule] | NINETEEN | EIGHTY-FOUR | [rectangular panel of elaborate tooling]

Notes
The novel text is identical to the 1970 Heron Books Edition, but the reissue has illustrations and new prelims and is without the Appreciation by Julian Symons and accompanying photographs.
The illustrations in this reissue are line drawings.

Locations
Orwell Archive

A.12s   *Octopus Edition, 1976*

For titlepage transcription see *Animal Farm* A.10s

Nineteen Eighty-Four is one of six Orwell novels in this compendium volume. The other novels are *Animal Farm*, *Burmese Days*, *A Clergyman's Daughter*, *Coming Up for Air*, and *Keep the Aspidistra Flying*.
Published by Secker & Warburg|Octopus, 1976.
Nineteen Eighty-Four is on pp. 741–925.

Hard bound with jacket.

Locations
Cambridge University Library. Acquisition 7 January 1977.

A.12t   *Observer Edition, 1981*

[within a double frame] THE OBSERVER | CLASSIC OF THE MONTH | LIBRARY | NINETEEN EIGHTY-FOUR | GEORGE ORWELL | THE OBSERVER

Collation There are ten unmarked leaves arranged: (A–F)^{16} (G–H)^8 (I)^4 (K)^8; 124 leaves (21.5 × 13.7); [i–iv] 1–240 [241–244]

Contents [i] halftitle: NINETEEN EIGHTY-FOUR [ii] blank [iii] titlepage [iv] imprint: Published by | THE OBSERVER | 8 St Andrew's Hill, London EC4V 5JA | [summary of publishing history] | Reset, specially designed and produced for | The Observer in 1981 by | Martin Secker & Warburg Limited | 54 Poland Street, London W1V 3DF | Printed and bound in Great Britain by | Morrison & Gibb Ltd, London and Edinburgh

Binding Blue paper on boards. Blue calico grain cloth on spine wrapping around to front and back covers. Blue endpapers with repeat pattern of *The Observer*'s masthead motif.

Front cover Stamped in gilt is *The Observer*'s masthead motif | ESTABLISHED 1791

Back cover Plain.

Spine Stamped in gilt: [rule | broad rule | rule] | NINETEEN | EIGHTY- | FOUR | [broad rule] | GEORGE | ORWELL | [rule | broad rule | rule] | [broad rule] | THE OBSERVER | [rule]

Locations
Orwell Archive

A.12u   *Charnwood Large Print Edition, 1982*

GEORGE ORWELL | [short ornate rule] | NINETEEN | EIGHTY-FOUR | *Complete and Unabridged* | [publisher's tree motif] | CHARNWOOD | *Leicester*

Collation [NEF1]–NEF28^8; 224 leaves (21.4 × 13.6); [i–vi] [1–2] 3–430 [431–442]

Contents [i–ii] publisher's note [iii] halftitle: NINETEEN EIGHTY-FOUR | [plot summary] [iv] blank [v] titlepage [vi] imprint: First published 1949 | First Charnwood

Edition | published February 1982 | by arrangement with | Martin Secker & Warburg Ltd. | London | and | Harcourt Brace Jovanovich, Inc. | New York | [rectangle containing library data] | Published by | F.A. Thorpe (Publishing) Ltd. | Anstey, Leicestershire | Printed and Bound in Great Britain by | T.J. Press (Padstow) Ltd., Padstow, Cornwall [1] halftitle: Part 1 [2] blank 3–[431] text [432] blank [433–442] publisher's advertisements

Binding White laminated cloth on boards. Off white endpapers.

Front cover Nineteen | Eighty-Four | *George Orwell* | [short blue rule] | Charnwood Large Type | [illustration in brown, red, orange, green and blue of a television screen with man's face, surrounded by circuit wires]

Back cover [within an oval frame is a tree motif] | *Charnwood* | *Library* | *Series* | [within a rectangular blue frame with clipped corners] Nineteen Eighty-Four | *George Orwell* | [plot summary] | ISBN 0 7089 8027 9

Spine [within a red stripe at top is picked out in white] Large | Type | [laterally in black] *George Orwell* [and below] Nineteen | Eighty-Four | [horizontally] [tree motif in oval frame] | THORPE

Locations
Orwell Archive. Two copies.

A.12v   *Permanent Penguins Edition, 1983*

GEORGE ORWELL | [double short rule] | *Nineteen* | *Eighty-Four* | [double short rule] | [penguin motif] | PERMANENT | PENGUINS | *in association with* | *Martin Secker & Warburg*

Collation 136 leaves in a perfect binding (19.8 × 12.8); [1–6] 7–267 [268–272]

Contents [1] [plot summary and biographical sketch of Orwell] [2] blank [3] titlepage [4] imprint: [publisher's addresses, summary of publishing history, and copyright notices] | Made and printed in Great Britain by | Richard Clay (The Chaucer Press) Ltd, | Bungay, Suffolk | Filmset in VIP Palatino by | Northumberland Press Ltd, Gateshead | [short rule] | Cover design by Nicholas Thirkell & Partners | Cover illustration by Ian Pollock | [copyright notice] [5] halftitle: PART 1 | [double short rule] [6] blank 7–[268] text [269–272] blank

Binding Green laminated paper binding.

Front cover Within a yellow rectangle, framed in green, is a further frame of black, red, and white rules, within which is printed: *Permanent Penguins* | [penguin motif in orange, black and white] | NINETEEN | EIGHTY-FOUR | [short rule] | GEORGE ORWELL | [line drawing of a leashed dog's head against a background of tower blocks, and a man with a dog]

Back cover Plain.

Spine Laterally, within a yellow rectangle, bordered by black, red and white rules: George Orwell . Nineteen Eight-Four | [in white, laterally, at foot] ISBN 0 14 | 016.008 6 | [horizontally, orange, black and white penguin motif]

Locations
Orwell Archive.

A.12w   *Longman Bridge Series Edition, 1983*

GEORGE ORWELL | NINETEEN | EIGHTY-FOUR | Complete text edition | Longman [galleon motif]

Collation 176 leaves in a perfect binding (18.0 × 11.2); [i–vii] viii–xix [xx] [1] 2–329 [330–332]

Contents [i] halftitle: NINETEEN | EIGHTY-FOUR [ii] blank [iii] titlepage [iv] imprint: Longman Group Limited, | [publisher's address and copyright notice] | First published by Martin Secker and Warburg 1949 | This edition first published 1983 | ISBN 0 582 53658 8 | Printed in West Germany | by Elsnerdruck GmbH, Berlin [v] publisher's note [vi] blank [vii]–xix introduction by Gwyneth Roberts [xx] blank [1]–314 text 315–329 glossary [330–332] pages for notes, each headed: Notes

Binding Paper bound in black shiny paper.

Front cover [in white] NINETEEN [publisher's motif] | EIGHTY-FOUR | George Orwell | [within a patch of white light fading to blues, the figures curving around the enlarged 8]: 1984 | [picture of grey human figures on a blue and white checked floor, facing the light source]

Back cover In white [plot summary] | Cover illustration by Peter Elson | Longman [publisher's motif] THE BRIDGE SERIES | ISBN 0 582 536 58 8

Spine [laterally in white] NINETEEN EIGHTY-FOUR GEORGE ORWELL | [horizontally, publisher's motif]

Notes
Publisher's note says the series is intended for students of English as a second language. The text has been 'moderately simplified but with little change in syntax.' There are line numberings in fives, page by page.

Locations
Cambridge University Library
Orwell Archive

A.12x   *The Penguin Complete Novels of George Orwell Edition, 1983*

(Harmondsworth: Penguin, 1983) 925pp

A compendium edition of the following novels:

Animal Farm
Burmese Days
A Clergyman's Daughter
Coming Up for Air
Keep the Aspidistra Flying
Nineteen Eighty-Four

Paper bound
£4.95

Locations
Orwell Archive: two copies

A.12y   *Nineteen Eighty-Four and Animal Farm Chancellor Press edition, 1984*

The two novels in a single volume. London: Chancellor Press, 1984.
An imprint of Octopus Publishing.
Cloth on boards.
Printed at the Pitman Press, Bath.

Nineteen Eighty-Four is on 11–326, and *Animal Farm* on 329–430.

Location
Cambridge University Library

A.12z   New Windmills Edition, 1990

Oxford: Heinemann New Windmills.
Published by Heinemann Educational Books.
Printed and bound by Richard Clay Ltd., Suffolk

Location
Cambridge University Library. Acquisition 8 March 1990.

A.12aa   New Secker & Warburg Edition, 1984

NINETEEN | EIGHTY-FOUR | *A novel by* | GEORGE ORWELL | SECKER & WARBURG | LONDON

Collation There are eight unmarked gatherings arranged [A–H]¹⁶; 128 leaves (21.6 × 13.7); [i–iv] 1–240 [241–252]

Contents [i] halftitle: NINETEEN EIGHTY-FOUR [ii] list of books by Orwell [iii] titlepage [iv] imprint: First published in England 1949 by | Martin Secker & Warburg Limited | 54 Poland Street, London W1V 3DF | This edition copyright [then copyright symbol] 1984 | by the Estate of the late Sonia Brownell Orwell | 0–436–35019–X | All rights reserved. No part of this publication | may be reproduced or transmitted, in any form or by | any means, without permission. | Printed and bound in Great Britain by | Biddles Ltd, Guildford and King's Lynn 1–[241] text [242–252] blank

Binding Black paper on boards, embossed to resemble linen grain cloth. White endpapers. *Front and back covers* Plain.

Spine Stamped in gilt: [rule] GEORGE | ORWELL | [triple rule] | Nineteen | Eighty- | Four | [rule] | Secker & | Warburg

Jacket Grey shiny paper.
Front [in white] GEORGE ORWELL | [short rule] | [design of figures cut from printed newspaper columns, yellowed and stained, diagonally slashed, and with brownish black speckled shadows]: 1984 | [in white] NINETEEN | EIGHTY-FOUR | [short rule]
Back [newspaper figures as on front]: 1984 | [ISBN numbers and bar code]
Spine [in white, laterally] GEORGE ORWELL [and underlined]: NINETEEN EIGHTY-FOUR | [horizontally] SECKER & WARBURG
Front flap [plot summary] | Jacket design by David Quay | £7.95 | net
Back flap [photograph of Orwell] | [extracts from reviews] | Photograph of George Orwell, courtesy | of BBC | Secker & Warburg | 0–436–35019–X

Locations
Orwell Archive

A.12bb   Clarendon Press Edition, 1984

GEORGE ORWELL | Nineteen | Eighty-Four | With a Critical Introduction | and Annotations by | BERNARD CRICK | CLARENDON PRESS . OXFORD | 1984

Collation There are 15 unmarked gatherings arranged: [A–N]¹⁶ [O]¹² [P]¹⁶; 236 leaves (21.6 × 13.8); [i–v] vi–vii [viii–ix] x–xi [xii] [1]–460

Contents [i] halftitle: NINETEEN EIGHTY-FOUR [ii] blank [iii] titlepage [iv] imprint and copyright notices | *Typeset by Joshua Associates, Oxford* | *Printed in Great Britain* | *at the University Press, Oxford* [v]–vii contents [viii] blank [ix]–xi editor's note [xii] blank [1]–136 introduction [137]–[154] appendices [155] halftitle: NINETEEN | EIGHTY-FOUR | *A Novel* | By | GEORGE ORWELL [156] blank [157]–428 text [429]–449 annotations [450] blank [451]–460 indices

Binding Blue calico grain cloth on boards. Off white endpapers.

Front cover Plain.

Back cover Blindstamped: 202

Spine Stamped in gilt: [rule] | ORWELL | Nineteen | Eighty- | Four | BERNARD | CRICK | [publisher's motif] | OXFORD | [rule]

Jacket Grey shiny paper.
Front [in white outlined in black] GEORGE ORWELL | [in yellow outlined in black] NINETEEN | EIGHTY | FOUR | [in a rectangular frame is a black and white photograph of an urban street of old buildings with, in the background, a futuristic pyramid] | With a Critical Introduction and | Annotations by BERNARD CRICK
Back publisher's advertisement | ISBN 0 19 818521 9
Spine [laterally at top in white outlined in black] GEORGE | ORWELL | [laterally in centre in yellow outlined in black] NINETEEN | EIGHTY-FOUR | [laterally in lower half] With a Critical Introduction | and Annotations by | BERNARD CRICK | [horizontally] [publisher's motif] | OXFORD
Front flap [plot summary] | [biographical sketch of Bernard Crick] | £17.50 net | in UK
Back flap OXFORD UNIVERSITY PRESS

Notes
This text is the one prepared by Peter Davison for the Complete Works edition [see A.12cc below] but made available to Bernard Crick in advance of the publication of the Complete Works.

Locations
Cambridge University Library
Orwell Archive. Two copies.

A.12cc   *The Complete Works Edition, 1987*

THE COMPLETE WORKS OF | GEORGE ORWELL | VOLUME NINE | Nineteen | Eighty-Four| SECKER & WARBURG | [short rule] | LONDON

Collation There are 11 unmarked gatherings arranged [A–L][16]; 176 leaves (23.3 × 15.4) [i–vi] [1–2] 3–[326] 327–[341] [342–346]

Contents [i] halftitle: THE COMPLETE WORKS OF | GEORGE ORWELL . NINE | NINETEEN EIGHTY-FOUR [ii] blank [iii] publisher's note [iv] blank [v] titlepage [vi] imprint: [selective publishing history of editions and reissues] | [copyright notices] | [British Library Cataloguing in Publication Data] | ISBN 0–436–35031–9 | Typeset in Monophoto Bembo by | Northumberland Press Ltd, Gateshead, Tyne and Wear | Printed and bound in Great Britain by | Richard Clay Ltd, Bungay, Suffolk [1] halftitle: PART I [2] blank 3–[326] text 327–[341] textual note [342–346] blank

Binding Blue paper on boards, embossed to resemble calico textured cloth. Black endpapers.

Front and back covers Plain.

Spine Stamped in gilt: [double rule] | GEORGE | ORWELL | [rule] | Nineteen | Eighty- | Four | [double rule] | SECKER & | WARBURG

Jacket Smooth dull black. Flaps white.
Front [in white]: GEORGE | ORWELL | [in brownish-yellow]: NINETEEN EIGHTY-FOUR
Back [in white, note on *The Complete Works of George Orwell* and extracts from original reviews. ISBN code and bar strip within a white rectangle.]

Spine laterally [in white]: GEORGE ORWELL | [in brownish-yellow]: NINETEEN
EIGHTY-FOUR [horizontally in white]: Secker & Warburg
Front flap Note on publishing history. At foot: £12.95 | net
Back flap [biographical notes on Orwell and Peter Davison] | Jacket design by David Quay

Notes
Reprinted 1996
This text was previously published in 1984 by the Clarendon Press.

Locations
Orwell Archive, with jacket

A.12dd   *Compact Books Edition, 1993*

NINETEEN EIGHTY-FOUR | George Orwell | [within a small frame] compact |
books

Notes
Follows the *Complete Works* text.

TRANSLATIONS

All Orwell Archive unless otherwise noted.

CATALAN

A.12.T1   *Mil Nou-Cents Vuitanta-Quatre*, 1965

Barcelona: Editorial Vergara
Translated by Joan Vinyes
Paper bound

Reissued in the series Libres a mà, March 1984, and again in November 1984

CZECH

A.12.T2   *1984*, 1991

Prague: Naše vojsko
Translated by Eva Šimečková
Paper bound
With an epilogue by Milan Šimečka, 1991

DANISH

A.12.T3a   *1984*, 1950

København: Steen Hasselbalchs Forlag, 1950
Translated by Paul Monrad
Paper bound

Published 21 January 1950. 3,000 copies
Reprinted 9 February 1950. 2,000 copies
Reprinted 13 May 1950. 1,700 copies

A.12.T3b   *1984*, 1961

København: Steen Hasselbalchs Forlag
Translated by Paul Monrad
Paper bound

A.12.T3c   *1984*, 1961

København: Gyldendals Tranebøger
Translated by Paul Monrad
Paper bound

A.12.T3d   *1984*, 1973

København: Steen Hasselbalchs Forlag
Translated by Paul Monrad
Paper bound
Kr.4.85

A new edition of A.12.T3c, but in the same binding

Reissued in paper on boards in 1975 in the Gyldendals Bogklub series, and in a larger paperback format by Gyldendals, also in 1975.
Reissued by Gyldendals in paper on boards in 1984, and in the Gyldendals Paperback series, also in 1984.

DUTCH

A.12.T4a   *1984*, 1950

Amsterdam: N.V. De Arbeiderspers
Translated by Halbo C. Kool
Published May 1950

Orwell Archive 2 copies

A.12.T4b   *1984 Negentien Vier En Tachtig*, 1963

Amsterdam: N.V. De Arbeiderspers
Translated by Halbo C. Kool
Paper bound

Reissued in 1971, in a new cover, paperbound, and again in a new paper cover in 1983. Both reissues have *1984* on both titlepage and cover.

FINNISH

A.12.T5   *Vuonna 1984*, 1950

Helsinki: Werner Söderström Osakeyhtiö
Translated by Oiva Talvitie
Paper bound with jacket

Reissued in smaller paperback format in 1967

FRENCH

A.12.T6a   *1984*, 1950

Paris: Gallimard. La Méridienne series
Translated by Amélie Audiberti
Paper bound
390 fr.

Reissued in 1977 in simulated morocco grain leather on boards by Gallimard.

Reissued in 1977 by France Loisirs, Paris, in cloth on boards with a dust jacket.

A.12.T6b   *1984*, 1956

Paris: Club des Libraires de France
Translated by Amélie Audiberti
Cloth on boards

Published 1 November 1956. 5,000 numbered copies printed for members of the Club des Libraires. 150 copies 'exemplaires de collaborateurs', marked: H.C. Orwell Archive has No. 46.

A.12.T6c   *1984*, 1964

Paris: Gallimard
Translated by Amélie Audiberti
Paper bound

Orwell Archive two copies

GERMAN

A.12.T7a   *Neunzehnhundertvierundachtzig*, 1950

Zurich: Diana Verlag
Translated by Kurt Wagenseil
Cloth on boards.
Published May 1950

There is an undated reissue in simulated leather on boards at the Orwell Archive.

A.12.T7b   *Neunzehnhundertvierundachtzig*, 1950

Vienna: Ullstein Verlag
Translated by Kurt Wagenseil
Published March 1950. 48 Schillings
5,100 copies

Reissue, Berlin: Ullstein, 1981

A.12.T7c   *Neunzehnhundertvierundachtzig*, 1963

Stuttgart: Diana Verlag
Translated by Kurt Wagenseil
Paper bound
Afterword by Arthur Koestler

Reissued in paper on boards, 1974

A.12.T7d   *1984*, 1983

Zurich: Diogenes Verlag
Translated by Kurt Wagenseil
Paper bound

GREEK

A.12.T8   *1984*, 1978

Paper bound

Reissued pre-1984. Paperbound

HEBREW

A.12.T9   *1984*, 1983

Tel Aviv: Am Oved Publishers Ltd
Paper bound

HUNGARIAN

A.12.T10   *1984*, 1989

Budapest: Európa Könyvkiadó
Translated by Szíjgyártó László jogutódja
Paper bound
70 Ft

Orwell Archive 2 copies

INDONESIAN

A.12.T11   *Tahun 1984*, 1953

Bandung: Van Hoeve
Translated by Barus Siregar
Illustrated with the Abner Dean cartoons used in the *Life* article [See C.820]
Paper bound

ITALIAN

A.12.T12a   *1984*, 1950

Verona: Arnoldo Mondadori Editore
Translated by Gabriele Baldini
Collezione Medusa, No. 262.
Paper on boards
Published November 1950

Reissued in March 1967
Reissued, paper bound, with an introduction and brief bibliography by Aldo Chiaruttini,
April 1973. Verona: Oscar Mondadori, 1973
Reissued in leather on boards, June 1974

A.12.T12b   *1984*, 1983

Milan: Mondadori
Translated by Bruno Tasso
Published with *Animal Farm* [see A10.T13g *La Fattoria Degli Animali]*
Published March 1983

A.12.T12c   *1984*, 1984

Milan: Arnoldo Mondadori Editore
Translated by Gabriele Baldini
Paper on boards
With an Introduction by Umberto Eco
Published January 1984
Reissued January 1984

A.12.T12d *1984*, 1984

Milan: Euroclub, 1984
Translated by Gabriele Baldini
Paper on boards

A.12.T12e *1984*, 1989

Milan: Arnoldo Mondadori
Translated by Gabriele Baldini
Paper bound
Published September 1989
There is an unsigned introduction and brief bibliography.

JAPANESE

A.12.T13 *1984*, 1950

Tokyo: Bungei Shunju Shinsha
Translated and with a preface by Yoshida, Konichi and Tatsukuchi Noataro.
Paper bound with jacket illustrated with Abner Dean cartoon, originally published in *Life*
[See C.820].
Published 20 April 1950
Y. 230

NORWEGIAN

A.12.T14a *1984*, 1950

Oslo: Gyldendal Norsk Forlag
Translated by Trygve Width
Paper bound

A.12.T14b *1984*, 1983

Oslo: Den Norske Bokklubben
Translated by Trygve Width
Illustrated by Alan Mackenzie-Robinson
With an afterword by Ebba Haslund
Paper on boards, with dust jacket
Published December 1983

A.12.T14c *1984*, 1990

Oslo: Gyldendal Norsk Forlag
Translated by Trygve Width
Paper bound
Gyldendal Pocket edition
29,–
Lists reissues of earlier editions: 1972, 1975, 1979, 1983, 1984 (twice)

PORTUGUESE

A.12.T15a *1984, undated, but pre-1977*

Lisbon: Editores Associades
Translated by Paulo Santa-Rita
Paper bound
Unibolso Duplo book 36

A.12.T15b   *1984*, 1977

São Paulo [Brazil]: Companhia Editora Nacional
Translated by Wilson Velloso
Paper bound
Biblioteca do espírito moderno, Volume 24
'10th edition'

'11th edition', 1978 [Orwell Archive, two copies]
'12th edition', 1979
'13th edition', 1980
'14th edition', 1981
'17th edition', 1984
'18th edition', 1984

A.12.T15c   *Mil Novecentos E Oitenta E Quatro*, 1984

Lisbon: Moraes Editores
Translated by L. Morais
Preface by José Pacheco Pereira
Paper bound
Jacket has same illustration as Longman Bridge Series Edition, 1983 [See A.12w].

SERBO-CROATIAN

A.12.T16a   *1984*, 1968

Beograd: Kentaur
Translated by Vlada Stojiljković
Paper on boards
Introduction by Leo Mates

A.12.T16b   *1984*, 1977

Beograd: Kentaur
Translated by Vlada Stojiljković

Paper bound
Orwell Archive 2 copies

A.12.T16c   *Tisuću Devetsto Osamdeset Četvrta*, 1984

Zagreb: August Cesarec
Translated by Antun Šoljan
Paper on boards

SLOVENIAN

A.12.T17   *1984*, 1967

Ljubljana: Mladinska Knjiga
Translated by Alenka Puhar
Paper bound

SWEDISH

A.12.T18a   *Nittonhundraattiöfyra*, 1950

Stockholm: Albert Bonniers Förlag
Translated by Nils Holmberg
Paper bound.
Published 9 May 1950
3,000 copies
Price 11.0

Reissued 20 June 1950
2,000 copies

Reissued 2 November 1950
1,000 copies

A.12.T18b   *Nittonhundraattiöfyra*, 1963

Stockholm: Bokförlaget Aldus|Bonniers
Translated by Nils Holmberg
Paper bound
A Delfinbok, D80
5.50

Orwell Archive 2 copies

Reissued, Stockholm: Albert Bonniers Förlag, 1980
Paper on boards

MISCELLANEOUS

A.12.M1   *Nineteen Eighty-Four* 1949–1950

Braille edition, 1949–1950
Published by the National Institute for the Blind.
6 volumes.

A.12.M2   *BBC Television Play, Nineteen Eighty-Four*

Broadcast 6 December 1954.
Reportedly, at that time, it attracted the largest ever television audience.

A.12.M3   *Reader's Digest Abridgement*, 1956

[in green] TWENTY | BEST BOOKS | [in black] *A Selection | of | Memorable
Book | Condensations | from | The Reader's Digest* | [spiral motif in green] | [in
black] THE READER'S DIGEST ASSOCIATION | London Sydney Cape Town

Collation There are 18 unmarked gatherings arranged [A–S][16]; 288 leaves (18.3 × 13.5);
[1–10] 11–575 [576]

Contents [1] halftitle: TWENTY | BEST BOOKS [2] blank [3] titlepage [4] imprint:
FIRST EDITION | Published 1956 by | THE READER'S DIGEST ASSOCIATION
LIMITED | [publisher's addresses] | [short rule] | [copyright notices] [5] foreward [6] blank
[7] contents [8] [9]–575 texts [576] imprint: Printed in France | by BRODARD & TAUPIN
– PARIS | No 1616

Binding Green calico grain cloth on boards. Off white endpapers with all over pattern of green spirals, crossed by the yellow initials: RD
Front free endpaper has an ornate green rectangular frame incorporating: EX LIBRIS | [two short rules]
Grey topped leaves.

Front cover Stamped in gilt is an elaborate central motif of swirls and the initials: RD

Back cover Plain.

Spine Stamped in brownish yellow: [five rules] | [rule] | 20 | BEST | BOOKS | THE | READER'S | DIGEST | [within an oval is a flying horse motif] | [seven rules]

Notes
Nineteen Eighty-Four is on pages 347–379.
There is a decorated forward page, and an illustration in green, blue and yellow, showing an urban street, across the top of page 348.

Reissued in *Ten Best Books: A Selection of Memorable Book Condensations from The Reader's Digest* (London: The Reader's Digest, n.d. [but pre-1965]) 133–164.

Fredric Warburg records that these editions sold 596,000 copies in the first 18 months after their publication.

A.12.M4   *1984 Film*, 1956

Associated British Studios
An Associated British-Pathe' Film
Executive Producer: N. Peter Rathvon
Producer: John Croydon
Director: Michael Anderson
Photography: C. Pennington Richards
Art Director: Terence Verity
Editing: Bill Lewthwaite
Screenplay: William P. Templeton and Ralph Bettinson
Music: Malcolm Arnold
With Edmond O'Brien as Winston Smith, Jan Sterling as Julia, and Michael Redgrave, David Kossoff, Mervyn Johns and Donald Pleasence.
91 minutes.
Black and white.

A.12.M5   *Abridged Muse Library Edition*, 1962

MUSE LIBRARY | George Orwell | NINETEEN EIGHTY-FOUR | Edited, with Notes, by | MASANORI NAKANO | [publisher's motif of muse's head] | Apollon-sha | KYOTO

Collation Six unmarked gatherings of eight leaves each, arranged [A–F]^8; 48 leaves (18.2 × 12.8); [X1–X2] i–ii [iii–iv] 1–87 [88–90]

Contents [X1] titlepage [X2] blank i–ii foreward in Japanese [iii] contents [iv] blank 1–76 text 77–87 notes [88] blank [89] imprint [90] blank

Binding Paper bound in yellowish white.

Front cover Across top is a brown strip in which is picked out: MUSE LIBRARY | [in main area of cover] George Orwell | NINETEEN | EIGHTY-FOUR | Edited, with Notes, by | MASANORI NAKANO | [brown stripe depicting classical frieze of muses] APOLLON-SHA

Back cover [narrow and broad brown stripes wrapping from front cover]

Spine [narrow brown stripe] | [laterally] *G. Orwell* NINETEEN EIGHTY-FOUR | [broad horizontal brown stripe] | [laterally] 55

Notes
Abridged version with Japanese foreward and notes. Imprint shows 1962 date and price Y140.

Locations
Orwell Archive

A.12.M6   *Short extract from Nineteen Eighty-Four*, 1974

in Jennifer Curry, *Investigation into the Police* (Glasgow: Blackie and Son, 1974) 37–38.

A.12.M7   *1984 Nostalgia Broadcasting Corporation theatrical adaptation*, 1977.

Published in Cedar Rapids, Iowa, in the series 'Great Moments in Literature'.
Double-sided cassette tape.

A.12.M8   *The Facsimile of the Extant Manuscript*, 1984

GEORGE ORWELL | [blue rule] | NINETEEN | EIGHTY-FOUR | [blue rule] THE FACSIMILE OF THE EXTANT MANUSCRIPT | *Edited by* | *Peter Davison* | *With a preface by Daniel G. Siegal* | SECKER & WARBURG | LONDON | [short blue rule] | M&S PRESS | WESTON, MASSACHUSETTS

Collation There are 26 unmarked gatherings, arranged: [1–25]^8 [26]^2; 202 leaves (34.0 × 24.6); [i–v] vi–vii [viii] ix–xix [xx] [1–2] 3–381 [382–384]
The final gathering is pasted in.

Contents [i] halftitle: GEORGE ORWELL | [short blue rule] | NINETEEN | EIGHTY-FOUR | [short blue rule] [ii] blank [iii] titlepage [iv] imprint [v]–vii preface [viii] blank ix–xix introduction [xx] blank [xxi] halftitle: THE FACSIMILE | AND | TRANSCRIPT [2]–381 text [382–384] blank

Binding Red calico grain cloth on boards. Grey endpapers.

Front and back covers Plain.

Spine Stamped in gilt laterally: GEORGE ORWELL | [short rule] | NINETEEN | EIGHTY-FOUR | [short rule] | THE FACSIMILE | [at foot, horizontally] SECKER & | WARBURG | [rule] | M&S PRESS

Jacket Off white
Front Within a thin red frame: GEORGE ORWELL | [red rule] | NINETEEN | EIGHTY-FOUR | [red rule] | THE FACSIMILE
Back Against an off-white background, photograph of first page of manuscript.
Spine Against an off-white background: GEORGE ORWELL | [short red rule] | NINE-TEEN | EIGHTY-FOUR | [short red rule] | THE FACSIMILE | [at foot, horizontally] SECKER & | WARBURG | [red rule] | M&S PRESS
Front flap [summary] | Jacket design by David Quay | £25.00 | net
Back flap [biographical notes] | Secker & Warburg | [sic, this is not a line break] M&S Press | 0–436–35022–X

Notes
Jacket design by David Quay
£25.00

Locations
Orwell Archive, three copies, one with jacket
Robarts Library, University of Toronto

A.12.M9   *Nineteen Eighty-Four Film*, 1984

Produced by Simon Perry
Writer-director Michael Radford
Winston Smith played by John Hurt, and featuring Richard Burton and Suzanna Hamilton
An Umbrella Rosenblum Films production for Virgin Films.

A.12.M10   *Listen For Pleasure recording*, 1984

Read by Derek Jacobi
2 double-sided cassette tapes of *Nineteen Eighty-Four*
2 hours
Produced by Music For Pleasure, Hayes, Middlesex
Abridged for recording by Sue Dawson
Produced by Graham Goodwin.

A.12.M11   *Other related material*s, 1984–present

Aside from study texts, with notes for students, *Nineteen Eighty-Four* has spawned a huge quantity of paraphernalia. Particularly approaching and in 1984 there were all kinds of direct and indirect references to it in newspapers, cartoon, advertisements and so on. The Orwell Archive has a large collection of such materials, including Christmas cards, bookmarks, and posters, as well as articles about Orwell and about the novel. The series of *Largely Literary* T-shirts, produced in the United States, includes Orwell. The Cragg cartoon drawing of Orwell, dated 1992, represents him against a background of huge staring eyes, clearly meant to suggest Big Brother. As well as movie versions of *Nineteen Eighty-Four*, there have been a number of documentary films and television programmes about Orwell and specifically about *Nineteen Eighty-Four*. These include study documentaries such as those produced in the United States in the series 'Films for the Humanities and Sciences'. Their 15–minute movie, *George Orwell's 1984*, is narrated by Anthony Burgess, and examines the connection between the novel and Orwell's earlier work and concerns, as well as the ways in which human freedom has been and continues to be threatened. They also have a 2–hour documentary, *George Orwell*, which includes film of Orwell as well as analyses of his work, and interviews with people who knew him.

Notes to A.1

1 Letter from Orwell to Leonard Moore, 26 April 1932.
2 From an autobiographical sketch, dated 17 April 1940, prepared by Orwell for Stanley J. Kunitz and Howard Haycraft, the editors of *Twentieth Century Authors* a biographical world dictionary of contemporary writers, published by H.W. Wilson Company, New York, 1942, p 1058.
3 Orwell's Introduction to the French edition of *Down and Out in Paris and London*, *La Vache enragée* (Paris: Gallimard, 1935).
4 Letter from L.I. Bailey, 19 February 1929. Orwell Archive. Reprinted in Crick 117.
5 Letter to Max Plowman, 1 November 1930. *CEJL* I 27–29.
6 Letter to Leonard Moore, 26 April 1932. *CEJL* I 77–78.
7 See letters in Orwell Archive, 30 October 1931 and 4 November 1931.
8 Crick 121.
9 Postcard from Orwell to T.S. Eliot, 17 February 1932. Orwell Archive.
10 Letter from T.S. Eliot to Orwell, 19 February 1932. Orwell Archive.
11 Letter to Leonard Moore, 1 July 1932. *CEJL* I 84.
12 This alteration was sufficient for Gollancz, and Chapter II was published.
13 Letter to Leonard Moore, 6 July 1932. *CEJL* I 84–85.
14 Sheila Hodges, *Gollancz: The Story of a Publishing House 1928–1978* (London: Victor Gollancz, 1978) 106.

15 Letter to Leonard Moore, 15 November 1932. *CEJL* I 104–105.
16 Letter to Eleanor Jaques, 18 November 1932. *CEJL* I 105– 106.
17 Letter to Leonard Moore, 19 November 1932. *CEJL* I 106–107.
18 Letter to Leonard Moore, 23 December 1932. *CEJL* I 109–110.
19 Letter to Leonard Moore, 1 February 1933. *CEJL* I 115.
20 Letter to Eleanor Jaques, 26 February 1933. *CEJL* I 117.
21 Letter to Leonard Moore, 27 January 1934. *CEJL* I 133.
22 Letter to Henry Miller, 27 August 1936. *CEJL* I 227–229.
23 Letter to Jack Common, 26 December 1938. *CEJL* I 367–371.
24 For a discussion of the page proofs see McDonald Emslie and P.G. Scott's article in *The Library* Vol V, No 32 (1977) 372–376.
25 Each volume of the *Complete Works* edition has an extensive textual note by Peter Davison. These introductory essays describe the process of establishing this edition, the resources, editions, proofs etc available to the editor, and problems and editorial decisions. Each essay ends with a list of the most significant textual variants in the various editions. In addition, this volume, *Down and Out in Paris and London*, has a General Introduction to the *Complete Works* in which Peter Davison describes the full project, writes generally on the editing of texts, on in-house censorship, and on the materials used in the Orwell edition.

Notes to A.2

1 'Why I Write', *CEJL* I 3.
2 *Polemic 5.*
3 Letter to Leonard Moore, 26 April 1932. *CEJL* I 78.
4 Letter to Brenda Salkeld [September 1932]. *CEJL* I 100.
5 Letter to Eleanor Jaques [19 October 1932]. *CEJL* I 103.
6 Letter to Leonard Moore, 15 November 1932. *CEJL* I 104–105.
7 Letter to Leonard Moore [19 November 1932]. *CEJL* I 107.
8 Letter to Leonard Moore [23 December 1932]. *CEJL* I 110.
9 Letter to Leonard Moore, 1 February 1933. *CEJL* I 115.
10 Letter to Eleanor Jaques [26 February 1933]. *CEJL* I 117.
11 Letter to Brenda Salkeld [June 1933]. *CEJL* I 120.
12 Letter to Eleanor Jaques [20 July 1933]. *CEJL* I 123.
13 Letter to Leonard Moore [26 November 1933]. *CEJL* I 125.
14 Letter to Brenda Salkeld [10 December 1933]. *CEJL* I 129.
15 Letter to Leonard Moore [27 January 1934]. *CEJL* I 133.
16 Letter to Leonard Moore [8 February 1934]. *CEJL* I 134.
17 Letter to Leonard Moore, 11 April 1934. *CEJL* I 135.
18 Letter to Leonard Moore, 14 November 1934. *CEJL* I 143.
19 Letter to Brenda Salkeld [August 1934]. *CEJL* I 138.
20 Letter to Leonard Moore, 22 January 1935. *CEJL* I 147.
21 Letter to Brenda Salkeld, 16 February 1935. *CEJL* I 147–148.
22 Letter to Leonard Moore, 22 February 1935. Orwell Archive.
23 Letter to Brenda Salkeld, 7 March 1935. *CEJL* I 150.
24 Letter to Henry Miller, 26 August 1936. *CEJL* I 229.
25 From 'As I Please' (10 December 1943). Reprinted in part in the *Complete Works* edition, p 310.
26 Letter to Julian Symons, 20 April 1948. *CEJL* IV 416–417.

Notes to A.3

1 Letter to Henry Miller, 26 August 1936. *CEJL* I 229.
2 Letter to Brenda Salkeld, 10 December 1933. *CEJL* I 129.
3 Letter to Leonard Moore, 28 December 1933. *CEJL* I 129.
4 Letter to Leonard Moore, 11 April 1934. *CEJL* I 136.
5 Letter to Brenda Salkeld, 27 July 1934. *CEJL* I 136.
6 Letter to Brenda Salkeld, late August 1934. *CEJL* I 137,
7 Letter to Brenda Salkeld, early September 1934. *CEJL* I 139.
8 Letter to Brenda Salkeld, early September 1934. *CEJL* I 139.
9 Letter to Leonard Moore, 3 October 1934. *CEJL* I 141.
10 Letter to Leonard Moore, 14 November 1934. *CEJL* I 142–143.
11 Letter to Leonard Moore, 22 January 1935. *CEJL* I 147.

12 Letter to Brenda Salkeld, 7 March 1935. *CEJL* I 150.
13 Letter to Victor Gollancz, 17 December 1934, and *Complete Works* edition of *A Clergyman's Daughter* 303–304.
14 Unpublished letter to Leonard Moore, 27 May 1944. Orwell Archive.
15 *Complete Works* edition 301–302.

Notes to A.4

1 Letter to Brenda Salkeld, 16 February 1935. *CEJL* I 148.
2 Letter to Brenda Salkeld, 16 February 1935. *CEJL* I 148.
3 Letter to Rayner Heppenstall, September 1935. *CEJL* I 152.
4 Letter to Rayner Heppenstall, 5 October 1935. *CEJL* I 154.
5 Letter to Cyril Connolly, 14 February 1935. *CEJL* I 163.
6 Letter to Norman Collins, 18 February 1936. Extract in Shelden 225.
7 Telegram to Victor Gollancz, 11.55am, 19 February 1936.
8 Letter to Victor Gollancz, 24 February 1936.
9 Letter to Richard Rees, 29 February 1936. *CEJL* I 165.
10 Letter to Jack Common, 17 March 1936. *CEJL* I 168. The *Adelphi* review, written by Richard Rees, was published in June 1936.
11 Letter to Jack Common, 3 April 1936. *CEJL* I 215.
12 Letter to Richard Rees, 20 April 1936. *CEJL* I 218. Frank Meade was an official of the Amalgamated Society of Woodworkers in Manchester. He also ran the Manchester office of the *Adelphi* and was business manager of *Labour's Northern Voice*, published by the Independent Socialist Party. Orwell met him on his visit to the north of England to collect material for *The Road to Wigan Pier*.
13 Letter to Anthony Powell, 8 June 1936. *CEJL* I 223.
14 Unpublished letter to Leonard Moore, 27 May 1944. Orwell Archive.
15 Letter to Henry Miller, 26 August 1936. *CEJL* I 229.

Notes to A.5

1 Letter to Jack Common, 5 October 1936. *CEJL* I 233.
2 Letter to Cyril Connolly, 14 February 1936. *CEJL* I 163.
3 See note on Meade in A.4 *Keep the Aspidistra Flying*.
4 Letter to Richard Rees, 29 February 1936. *CEJL* I 164.
5 Letter to Jack Common, 17 March 1936. *CEJL* I 168.
6 The diary is printed in *CEJL* I 170–214.
7 Letter to Jack Common, 3 April 1936. *CEJL* I 215.
8 Letter to Jack Common, 16 April 1936. *CEJL* I 216.
9 Letter to Richard Rees, 16 April 1936. *CEJL* I 218.
10 Letter to Geoffrey Gorer, May 1936. *CEJL* I 222.
11 Letter to Jack Common, 12 October 1938. *CEJL* I 356.
12 Letter to Henry Miller, 26 August 1936. *CEJL* I 229.
13 Letter to Jack Common, 5 October 1936. *CEJL* I 233.
14 Letter to Leonard Moore, 15 December 1936. Berg Collection, New York Public Library. Quoted in Crick 181.
15 See the illustration in Volume I of the *Complete Works* edition, *Down and Out in Paris and London* xxxiii.
16 Letter from Norman Collins to the Rev Gilbert Shaw (22 December 1936). Quoted in the General Introduction to the *Complete Works* edition, in Volume I, *Down and Out in Paris and London*, xxxiv.
17 Postcard to James Hanley (13 February 1937). *CEJL* I 263.
18 For these and other contemporary reviews, see the sections on the two editions below.
19 Letter to Victor Gollancz, 9 May 1937. *CEJL* I 267.
20 Orwell's reply in the BBC radio programme 'Your Questions Answered', broadcast 2 December 1943.

Notes to A.6

1 Letter to Victor Gollancz, 9 May 1937. *CEJL* I 267.
2 *Homage to Catalonia* 3.
3 Letter to Victor Gollancz, 9 May 1937. *CEJL* I 267.
4 Letter to Cyril Connolly, 8 June 1937. *CEJL* I 269.

5 The article was published as 'Spilling the Spanish Beans' in two parts in July and September 1937 in *The New English Weekly*. See C.100 and C.105.
6 Orwell's review of Franz Borkenau's *The Spanish Cockpit* was published in *Time & Tide* in July 1937. See C.101.
7 Letter to Rayner Heppenstall, 31 July 1937. *CEJL* I 279–280.
8 Letter to Geoffrey Gorer, 16 August 1937. *CEJL* I 281.
9 Letter to Geoffrey Gorer, 15 September 1937. *CEJL* I 285.
10 Letter to Jack Common, October 1937. *CEJL* I 289.
11 Letter to Jack Common, 5 February 1938. *CEJL* I 296.
12 Letter to Jack Common, March 1938. *CEJL* I 310.
13 Letter to Stephen Spender, 2 April 1938. *CEJL* I 311.
14 Letter to Stephen Spender, 15 April 1938. *CEJL* I 313.
15 *CEJL* I 316.
16 Letter to Cyril Connolly, 27 April 1938. *CEJL* I 329.
17 Letter to Jack Commmon, May 1938. *CEJL* I 330.
18 Letter to Cyril Connolly, 8 July 1938. *CEJL* I 343.
19 Letter to Jack Common, 12 October 1938. *CEJL* I 356.
20 Letter to Frank Jellinek, 29 December 1938. *CEJL* I 364.
21 Letter to Jack Common, 26 December 1938. *CEJL* I 368.
22 Unpublished letter to Leonard Moore, 27 May 1944. Orwell Archive.
23 'Why I Write', *Such, Such Were the Joys*.
24 Orwell's note, printed in the *Complete Works* edition, p.251.
25 Letter to Frank Jellinek, 20 December 1938. *CEJL* I 366.

Notes to A.7

1 Letter to Cyril Connolly, 8 July 1938. *CEJL* I 344.
2 Letter to Leonard Moore, 6 December 1937. Lilly Library, Indiana University. Quoted in Shelden 292.
3 Letter to Alec Houghton Joyce, 12 February 1938. *CEJL* I 303.
4 Letter to Jack Common, 16 February 1938. *CEJL* I 304.
5 Letter to Cyril Connolly, 14 March 1938. *CEJL* I 309.
6 Letter to Jack Common, March 1938. *CEJL* I 310.
7 Letter to Stephen Spender, 2 April 1938. *CEJL* I 311.
8 Letter to Cyril Connolly, 27 April 1938. *CEJL* I 329.
9 Letter to Jack Common, May 1938. *CEJL* I 330.
10 Letter from Eileen Blair to Leonard Moore, 30 May 1938. Lilly Library, Indiana University. Quoted in Shelden 292.
11 Letter to Cyril Connolly, 8 July 1938. *CEJL* I 344.
12 Letter to Ida Mabel Blair, 8 August 1938. *CEJL* I 348.
13 Letter to Jack Common, 29 September 1938. *CEJL* I 354.
14 Letter to Jack Common, 12 October 1938. *CEJL* I 355–356.
15 John Sceats, 26 October 1938. *CEJL* I 358.
16 Letter to John Sceats, 24 November 1938. *CEJL* I 360.
17 Letter to Jack Common, 16 December 1938. *CEJL* I 368.
18 Letter to Jack Common, 26 December 1938. *CEJL* I 368.
19 Letter to Herbert Read (4 January 1939). *CEJL* I 377.
20 Letter to Geoffrey Gorer, 20 January 1939. *CEJL* I 381.
21 Letter to Geoffrey Gorer, 20 January 1939. *CEJL* I 382.
22 Letter to Jack Common, 9 April 1939. *CEJL* I 394.
23 Letter to Leonard Moore, 25 April 1939. Lilly Library, Indiana University. Quoted in Shelden 309.
24 Letter to Leonard Moore, 4 August 1939.
25 See William B. Todd and Ann Bowden, *Tauchnitz International Editions in English 1841–1955* (New York, 1988) 745–747, 770 and 879–881.
26 Unpublished letter to Leonard Moore, 27 May 1944. Orwell Archive.
27 Letter to Roger Senhouse, 22 October 1947. *CEJL* IV 381–382.
28 Letter to Anthony Powell, 29 November 1947. *CEJL* IV 384.
29 Letter to Julian Symons, 20 April 1948. *CEJL* IV 416–417.
30 Letter to Julian Symons, 21 March 1948. *CEJL* IV 406.
31 Letter to Julian Symons, 10 May 1948. *CEJL* IV 422.

32 Peter Davison, in the Textual Note to the *Complete Works* edition, 250.
33 *Complete Works* edition, 251.
34 See Peter Davison's Textual Note to *Coming Up for Air*, Volume Seven of *The Complete Works of George Orwell* (London: Secker & Warburg, 1986) 249–255.

Notes to A.8

1 Letter to Geoffrey Gorer, 3 April 1940. *CEJL* I 528.
2 Letter to Geoffrey Gorer, 10 January 1940. *CEJL* I 410.
3 Letter to Victor Gollancz, 8 January 1940. *CEJL* I 409–410.
4 Letter to Geoffrey Gorer, 3 April 1940. *CEJL* I 528.
5 Letter to James Laughlin, 16 July 1940. *CEJL* II 33.

Notes to A.9

1 *The Lion and the Unicorn* 7.
2 Autobiographical note, written 17 April 1940, for *Twentieth Century Authors* [See B.16].
3 For Orwell's nine editing contributions, see Section B.
4 Reprinted in *CEJL* II 118.
5 Letter to the Rev. Iorwerth Jones, 8 April 1941. *CEJL* II 109–112.
6 Letter to H.J. Willmett, 18 May 1944. *CEJL* III 149.

Notes to A.10

1 From the Author's Preface to the 1947 Ukrainian Edition of *Animal Farm*, reprinted in *CEJL* III 406.
2 Letter to Jack Common, 26 December 1938. *CEJL* I 368.
3 Letter to Geoffrey Gorer, 20 January 1939. *CEJL* I 382.
4 Letter to Philip Rahv, 9 December 1943. *CEJL* III 53.
5 Letter to Gleb Struve, 17 February 1944. *CEJL* III 95.
6 Letter to Leonard Moore, 5 April 1944. *Ten Animal Farm Letters*.
7 Letter to Leonard Moore, 15 April 1944. *Ten Animal Farm Letters*.
8 Letter to Philip Rahv, 1 May 1944. *CEJL* III 141.
9 There is a carbon copy of the typescript with a few handwritten corrections in the Orwell Archive, 116ff.
10 Letter to T.S. Eliot, 28 June 1944. *CEJL* III 176.
11 Letter from T.S. Eliot to Orwell, 13 July 1944.
12 Letter to Leonard Moore, 18 July 1944. *CEJL* III 187.
13 Letter to Leonard Moore, 15 February 1945. *CEJL* III 358.
14 Letter to Roger Senhouse, 17 March 1945. *CEJL* III, 359.
15 Letter to F.J. Warburg, 13 June 1945. *CEJL* III 386–387.
16 Letter to Leonard Moore, 3 July 1945. *CEJL* III 392–393.
17 Warburg 51.
18 Letter from Roger Senhouse to Morrison & Gibb (Printers), 19 July 1945. Orwell Archive.
19 Aneurin Bevan, MP, Minister of Health and director of *Tribune*.
20 Letter to Herbert Read, 18 August 1945. *CEJL* III 400–401.
21 Letter to Frank Barber, 3 September 1945. *CEJL* III 402.
22 *CEJL* III 405–406.
23 See C.839.

Notes to A.11

1 Letter to Julian Symons, 9 October 1947. *CEJL* IV 380–381.
2 Letter to Leonard Moore, 3 July 1945. *CEJL* III 392.
3 Letter to Julian Symons, 9 October 1947. *CEJL* IV 380–381.
4 See letter to Julian Symons, 25 October 1947. *CEJL* IV 383.

Notes to A.12

1 Letter to F. J. Warburg, 31 May 1947. *CEJL* IV 329–330.
2 Letter to Gleb Struve, 17 February 1944. *CEJL* III 95. Zamyatin's *We* (1923) was a Russian anti-Utopian novel, which Orwell read now in French translation.

3 Letter to H.J. Willmett, 18 May 1944. *CEJL* III 149.
4 'As I Please', *Tribune* (2 February 1945).
5 Letter to Leonard Moore, 3 July 1945. *CEJL* III 392.
6 Letter to Victor Gollancz, 14 March 1947. *CEJL* IV 307–308.
7 Letter to Celia Kirwan, 17 August 1946. *CEJL* IV 199.
8 Letter to F. J. Warburg, 31 May 1947. *CEJL* IV 329–330.
9 Letter to George Woodcock, 9 August 1947. *CEJL* IV 376.
10 Letter to Anthony Powell, 8 September 1947. *CEJL* IV 378.
11 Letter to Roger Senhouse, 22 October 1947. *CEJL* IV 382.
12 Letter to Anthony Powell, 29 November 1947. *CEJL* IV 384.
13 Letter to T.R. Fyvel, 31 December 1947. *CEJL* IV 386.
14 Letter to Julian Symonds, 2 January 1948. *CEJL* IV 393–394.
15 Letter to F.J. Warburg, 4 February 1948. *CEJL* IV 404.
16 Letter to Roger Senhouse, [6? May 1948]. *CEJL* IV 421.
17 Letter to Julian Symonds, 10 July 1948. *CEJL* IV 438.
18 Letter to F.J. Warburg, 22 October 1948. *CEJL* IV 448.
19 Letter to Anthony Powell, 15 November 1948. *CEJL* IV 454.
20 Letter to F.J. Warburg, 21 December 1948. *CEJL* IV 459.
21 Letter to Roger Senhouse, 26 December 1948. *CEJL* IV 460.
22 Letter to Richard Rees, 28 January 1949. *CEJL* IV 472–473.
23 Letter to Richard Rees, 16 March 1949. *CEJL* IV 483.
24 Letter to Julian Symons, 4 February 1949. *CEJL* IV 475.
25 Letter to Leonard Moore, 20 & 22 January 1949. Shelden 429.
26 Letter to Leonard Moore, 17 March 1949. *CEJL* IV 483–484.
27 Letter to Richard Rees, 31 March 1949. *CEJL* IV 487.
28 See letter to Richard Rees, 8 April 1949. *CEJL* IV 487–488.
29 See C.816.
30 Letter to F.J. Warburg, 16 May 1949. *CEJL* IV 500.
31 Letter to Francis A. Henson (amalgam) June–July 1949. *CEJL* IV 502.
32 Letter to Richard Rees, 28 July 1949. *CEJL* IV 505.
33 *Times Literary Supplement*, 10 June 1949, 380.
34 Letter to Julian Symons, 16 June 1949. *CEJL* IV 502–503.
35 Review by I. Anisimov, *Pravda* 12 May 1950.
36 Letter to Vernon Richards, 22 June 1949. *CEJL* IV 504.
37 Reprinted in *Nineteen Eighty-Four* (Oxford: Clarendon Press, 1984) 152–153.
38 Fredric Warburg notes that by 1951, about 49,000 had been printed. In the next 15 years up to 1996, another 21,400 copies were sold in Great Britain. Between 1966 and 1971 hard-cover sales averaged 2,000 a year, or about 81,000 in total [See Warburg 114–115].

B: Contributions to books, books edited by Orwell, and works reprinted in anthologies

B.1 'On a Ruined Farm near the His Master's Voice Gramophone Factory', Thomas Moult ed. *The Best Poems of 1934* (London: Jonathan Cape Limited, 1934) 113–114.

> *Notes*
> Signed: Eric Blair
> Poem
> Originally published in *The Adelphi* Vol. 8, No. 1 (April 1934) 35–36 [C.060].
> British Library acquisition 20 September 1934
> Cloth on boards
> Illustrations and decorations by Merlyn Mann
> *CEJL* I 134–135.
> *Locations*
> Cambridge University Library
> Orwell Archive
> Pratt Library, Victoria University, University of Toronto.
> *Reissue*
> New York: Harcourt Brace and Company, 1935. Paper on boards with cloth spine. The British edition, with new titlepage.
> Orwell Archive.

B.2 'My Country Right or Left', *Folios of New Writing: Autumn 1940* (London: The Hogarth Press, 1940) 36–41.

> *Notes*
> The second volume of *Folios of New Writing*.
> Edited by John Lehmann.
> Reprinted in John Lehmann, ed. *The Pleasures of New Writing: An Anthology from New Writing* (London: John Lehmann, 1952) 71–76.
> *CEJL* I 535–540
> *Locations*
> Cambridge University Library
> Orwell Archive

B.3 'Inside the Whale', in James Laughlin, ed. *New Directions in Prose and Poetry* (Norfolk, Connecticut: New Directions, 1940) 205–246.

> *Notes*
> Reprint of the title essay from *Inside the Whale* [See A.8].
> *CEJL* I 493–527.

B.4 'Shooting an Elephant', *The Penguin New Writing* Vol. 1, Ed. John Lehmann (Harmondsworth: Allen Lane Penguin Books, 1940) 9–15.

> *Notes*
> First published December 1940. Reissued January 1941.
> Paper bound
> See also D.3
> Reprinted in *English Stories From New Writing* Ed. John Lehmann (London: John Lehmann, 1951) 47–54.
> Reissued in *The Penguin New Writing: An Anthology* Ed. John Lehmann (Harmondsworth: Penguin Books, 1985) 217–223.
> *CEJL* I 235–242
> *Locations*
> Cambridge University Library
> Orwell Archive, two copies

B.5 'Fascism and Democracy', and 'Patriots and Revolutionaries', in Victor Gollancz, ed. *The Betrayal of The Left* (London: Gollancz, 1941) Chapter 8, 206–15 and Chapter 10, 234–245.

Notes

'Patriots and Revolutionaries' was first published as 'Our Opportunity' in *Left News* (January 1941) [C.236].

'Fascism and Democracy' was first published in *Left News* (February 1941) [C.246].

Other chapters in the book by Victor Gollancz, John Strachey et al. Preface by H.J. Lasky

Published 3 March 1941 in a Left Book Club Edition of 500 copies, not for sale to the public, and a public Edition of 1,300 copies.

Orwell received payment of 10s 6d.

Locations

Cambridge University Library

University of Toronto Library

Orwell Archive – Left Book Club Edition, and public Edition two copies, one rebound

Reissue

May 1941, 'Second impression'.

With correction slip inserted in vi.

500 copies Left Book Club

200 copies public Edition

Locations

Cambridge University Library

B.6 Editor (with T.R. Fyvel), Sebastian Haffner *Offensive Against Germany* (London: Secker & Warburg, 1941).

Notes

Searchlight Book No. 2.

Cloth on boards.

Made and printed in Great Britain at the Mayflower Press, Plymouth. William Brendon & Son Ltd.

Locations

Cambridge University Library. Acquisition 19 May 1941

Orwell Archive

B.7 Editor (with T.R. Fyvel), Ritchie Calder *The Lesson of London* (London: Secker & Warburg, 1941).

Notes

Searchlight Book No. 3.

Cloth on boards.

Made and printed in Great Britain at the Mayflower Press, Plymouth. William Brendon & Son Ltd.

Locations

Cambridge University Library. Acquisition 19 May 1941.

Orwell Archive

B.8 Editor (with T.R. Fyvel), Cassandra *The English at War* (London: Secker & Warburg, 1941).

Notes

Cassandra was William N. Connor of the *Daily Mirror*.

Searchlight Book No. 4.

First published April 1941. Note says 5,000 copies and type destroyed by enemy action.

Reset and republished May 1941.

Reprinted May 1941, and June 1941.

Locations
Cambridge University Library
Orwell Archive – June 1941 reissue, paper bound, with jacket.

B.9   Editor (with T.R. Fyvel) and Foreword to T.C. Worsley, *The End of the 'Old School Tie'* (London: Secker and Warburg, 1941) 5–6.

Notes
Foreword dated May 1941.
Note says first printed April 1941, and destroyed by enemy action.
Paper bound, with jacket.
Reset in May and published in June 1941.
Searchlight Book No. 5.

Locations
Cambridge University Library
Orwell Archive

B.10   Editor (with T.R. Fyvel) Arturo Barea, *Struggle for the Spanish Soul* (London: Secker and Warburg, 1941).

Notes
Published July 1941.
Searchlight Book No.10.
Paper bound, with jacket.
Foreword by T.R. Fyvel, dated June 1941.
The typescript and first proof were destroyed by enemy action in May 1941.

Locations
Cambridge University Library
Orwell Archive

B.11   Editor (with T.R. Fyvel) and Foreword to Joyce Cary, *The Case For African Freedom* (London: Secker and Warburg, 1941).

Notes
Published July 1941.
Searchlight Book No. 11.
Paper bound, with jacket.
Orwell's Foreword is on 5–6.

Locations
Cambridge University Library. Acquisition 17 December 1941.
Orwell Archive

B.12   Editor (with T.R. Fyvel) Bernard Causton, *The Moral Blitz: War, Propaganda and Christianity* (London: Secker and Warburg, 1942).

Notes
Searchlight Book No. 15.
Paper bound, with jacket.

Locations
Cambridge University Library
Orwell Archive

B.13   Editor (with T.R. Fyvel) Olaf Stapleton, *Beyond the "Isms"* (London: Secker and Warburg, 1942).

Notes
Searchlight Book No. 16.
Paper bound, with jacket.

Locations
Cambridge University Library
Orwell Archive

B.14   Editor (with T.R. Fyvel) Stephen Spender, *Life and the Poet* (London: Secker and Warburg, 1942).

Notes
Published March 1942.

Searchlight Book No. 18.
Paper bound, with jacket.
Locations
Cambridge University Library
Orwell Archive

B.15 'Shooting an Elephant', in A.F. Scott, ed. *Modern Essays* (London: Macmillan & Co. Ltd., 1942) 80–87.
Location
Orwell Archive

B.16 Autobiographical note in Stanley J. Kunitz and Howard Haycraft, eds. *Twentieth Century Authors* (New York: The H.W. Wilson Company, 1942) 1058–1059.
Notes
Written 17 April 1940
CEJL II 23–24.
Locations
Robarts Library, University of Toronto

B.17 'Culture and Democracy', in *Victory or Vested Interest?* (London: George Routledge & Sons, Ltd., 1942) 77–97.
Notes
Published 15 May 1942.
6,311 copies.
Also published by The Labour Book Service, 1942.
A lecture to the Fabian Society, 22 November 1941.
Other chapters in the book are by G.D.H. Cole, Harold J. Laski, Mary Sutherland, and Francis Williams.
Orwell noted '[The text is] transcribed from shorthand notes of a lecture and grossly altered without my knowledge.'
Locations
Cambridge University Library
Orwell Archive – both issues.
Routledge edition at E.J. Pratt Library, Victoria University, University of Toronto.

B.18 Editor and Introduction, E.M. Forster, Ritchie Calder, Cedric Dover, Hsiao Ch'ien and Others *Talking to India* (London: George Allen & Unwin Ltd., 1943).
Notes
Published 18 November 1943.
7s 6d
Orwell received 12 copies on 23 November.
2,017 copies printed. Sold out by 1945. 1,018 copies sold in Britain, 897 overseas, 102 copies given away.
Introduction 7–9.
'The Rediscovery of Europe' 40–51, broadcast in the BBC Eastern Service (10 March 1942) [E.033], and reprinted in *The Listener* (19 March 1942) 370–372 [C.305].
CEJL II 197–207.
Royalty payment 16 October 1945, £16.
Locations
Cambridge University Library
Orwell Archive, with jacket
In December 1942 Orwell told George Woodcock,
I am trying to get some of our b'casts for the Indian section published in book form. If this goes through you may see from the book that our b'casts, though of course much as all radio stuff is, aren't as bad as they might be.[1]
The book was published in November 1943, and in December Orwell told Philip Rahv,

I'll try and send PR [*Partisan Review*] a copy of the book of broadcasts which the Indian Section of the BBC recently published. It might possibly be worth reviewing. In any case it has some interest as a specimen of British propaganda (rather a favourable specimen, however, as the Indian Section were regarded as very unimportant and therefore left a fairly free hand.)[2]

B.19   'T.S. Eliot': review of 'Burnt Norton', 'East Coker', and 'The Dry Salvages', in Denys Val Baker, ed. *Little Reviews Anthology* (London: George Allen & Unwin, 1943) 212–219.

Notes
Originally published in *Poetry (London)* Vol. 2, No. 7 (October–November 1942) 56–59 [C.319]
CEJL II 236–242.
Locations
Cambridge University Library
Orwell Archive
Robarts Library, University of Toronto
Reissued 1944.
Orwell Archive
Reissued London: Allen & Unwin, Readers Union, 1945
Orwell Archive

B.20   'Looking Back on the Spanish War', *New Road: New Directions in European Art and Letters* Eds. Alex Comfort and John Bayliss, (Billericay: The Grey Walls Press, 1943) 149–157.

Notes
Published March 1943.
New Road was an occasional anthology of prose and verse, published between 1943 and 1949. Comfort and Bayliss edited the first two volumes.
In this version three original sections, iv, v, and vi, are omitted. The full version of the essay was first published in *Such, Such Were the Joys*, and reprinted in *England Your England*, *Collected Essays*, and *CEJL* II 249–267.

B.21   'Benefit of Clergy: Some Notes On Salvador Dali', in Leonard Russell, ed. *The Saturday Book* 4 (London: Hutchinson, 1944) 255–260.

Notes
Written June 1944.
Published October 1944.
Orwell wrote in *Tribune* (9 February 1945) 10:
Some time ago I was commissioned to write an essay for an annual scrapbook which shall be nameless. At the very last minute (and when I had had the money, I am glad to say) the publishers decided that my essay must be suppressed. By this time the book was actually in process of being bound. The essay was cut out of every copy, but for technical reasons it was impossible to remove my name from the list of contributors on the title page.
Although Orwell indicates that *The Saturday Book* had been printed when the publishers decided the essay must be suppressed on grounds of obscenity, there is no break in pagination where the essay should appear. Hutchinsons gave Orwell a copy of the full publication. There is a note on 255 that his essay 'has been unavoidably omitted.'
Critical Essays 120–129, *Dickens, Dali & Others* 170–184, *Collected Essays* 225–235, *Decline of the English Murder* 20–31, and *CEJL* III 156–165 [see also C.522].
Locations
Ian Angus has a copy with the article included and he notes that the only other copy known to him was that sent to Orwell by the publishers and which in 1964 was owned by his sister Avril, Mrs William Dunn.

Cambridge University Library and the Orwell Archive have copies of the issue in which Orwell's article was to have appeared, where it is listed in the contents, but the omissions note appears on 255.

B.22 'World Affairs, 1945', *Junior: Articles Stories and Pictures* 1 (London: Children's Digest Publications Ltd., 1945) 79–88.

Notes

Published November 1945.

Completed 24 July 1945.

Payment £13 2s 6d.

Editorial board: Freda Lingstrom, Audrey Harvey, André Deutsch.

Editorial note says, 'This collection of stories, articles and pictures is for the junior members of the family.'

Note by Orwell at beginning says: 'The following essay was written before the world at large learned of the existence of the atomic bomb.'

There is also a biographical note on Orwell, probably written by him:

George Orwell has been a schoolmaster, a civil servant in Burma and fought in the Spanish civil-war. He has written many novels and is a great lover of Dickens. He is a journalist and has visited Europe during and since the War. Is careless about his clothes and rolls his own cigarettes.

Locations

Cambridge University Library

Orwell Archive

B.23 Text of Orwell's radio broadcast on George Bernard Shaw's *Arms and the Man*, *BBC Pamphlets No. 2, Books and Authors* ed. Laurence Brander (Bombay: Oxford University Press, 1946).

Notes

Broadcast 22 January 1943. See E.177.

Surviving typescript.

Reprinted in *The War Broadcasts* 118–121.

Essays in the pamphlet are:

E.M. Forster on Shakespeare's *Julius Caesar*

George Sampson on Milton's Shorter Poems

Edmund Blunden on Thomas Hardy

D. Nichol Smith on William Hazlitt

George Orwell on George Bernard Shaw's *Arms and the Man*

W.J. Turner on the Book of *Job*

Published 29 October 1946

2,500 copies

12 annas

2,103 pulped February 1949

Location

Copy in the collection of Ian Angus.

B.24 Text of Orwell's radio talk on Jack London, *BBC Pamphlets No. 3, Books and Authors* ed. Laurence Brander (Bombay: Oxford University Press, 1946).

Notes

Broadcast in the series 'Landmarks in American Literature', 5 March 1943. See E.187.

Surviving typescript.

Reprinted in *The War Broadcasts* 122–125.

Essays in the pamphlet are:

Herbert Read on Nathaniel Hawthorne

T.S. Eliot on Edgar Allen Poe

Geoffrey Grigson on Herman Melville

V.S. Pritchett on Mark Twain

George Orwell on Jack London

Rayner Heppenstall on The contemporary American short story
Published 29 October 1946
1,500 copies
12 annas
316 sold by February 1949. Remaining stock destroyed by 12 December 1949.
Location
Copy in the collection of Ian Angus

B.25 Introduction to Jack London *Love of Life and Other Stories* (London: Paul Elek, 1946) 7–15.
Notes
Written October/November 1945; published November 1946.
Payment £21 0s 0d.
CEJL IV 23–29.
Locations
Orwell Archive
Cambridge University Library, with jacket. Acquisition 29 November 1946.

B.26 'A Hanging', *The New Savoy* ed. Mara Meulen and Francis Wyndham (London: The New Savoy Press, 1946) 50–56.
Notes
Paper bound.
5s 0d.
Originally published in *The Adelphi* (August 1931).
See C.042.
Reprinted in *Shooting An Elephant* D.3, *The Orwell Reader* D.7, *Collected Essays* D.10, *Decline of the English Murder* D.11, *CEJL* I 44–48.
Locations
Cambridge University Library
Orwell Archive

B.27 'Arthur Koestler', *Focus Two* Ed. B. Rajan and Andrew Pearse (London: Dennis Dobson Limited, 1946) 27–38.
Notes
Written September 1944.
First published in *Critical Essays* 130–141, and in *Dickens, Dali & Others* 185–201.
Collected Essays 236–248, and *CEJL* III 234–244.
Locations
Cambridge University Library
Orwell Archive

B.28 Response to *Horizon* Questionnaire on the cost of letters, reprinted in Ivor Brown, ed. *Current British Thought No. 1* (London: Nicholas Kaye, 1947) 424–426.
Notes
First published in 'Questionnaire The Cost of Letters', *Horizon* (September 1946) 157–159 [C.706].
CEJL IV 200–203.
The volume was reissued in the United States as *British Thought 1947* (New York: The Gresham Press, 1947).

B.29 'Politics and the English Language', in Denys Val Baker, ed. *Modern British Writing* (New York: The Vanguard Press, 1947) 189–206.
Notes
First published in *Horizon* Vol. XIII, No. 76 (April 1946) 252–265.
See C.679.
Location
Orwell Archive

B.30 'Politics and the English Language', in Denys Val Baker, ed. *Little Reviews Anthology 1947–8* (London: Eyre and Spottiswoode, 1948) 92–103.
 Notes
 First published in *Horizon* Vol. XIII, No. 76 (April 1946) 252–265 [C.679].
 Locations
 Cambridge University Library
B.31 Editor (with Reginald Reynolds) and Introduction to *British Pamphleteers* Volume One (London: Allan Wingate, 1948).
 Notes
 Introduction by Orwell alone, written Spring 1947.
 Orwell's Introduction is on pp7–16.
 Published 15 November 1948.
 There was a second volume, Volume Two, published in 1951, after Orwell's death.
 Part of the Introduction has been reprinted in a pamphlet, the *Pendle Hill Bulletin*, No. 135 (April 1957) 1–6.
 See C.836.
 Locations
 Cambridge University Library. Acquisition 15 March 1949.
 Orwell Archive – two copies, with jackets
 Kelly Library, St Michael's College, University of Toronto.
B.32 'Reflections on Gandhi', in William Phillips and Philip Rahv, eds. *The New Partisan Reader 1945–1953* (New York: Harcourt, Brace and Company, 1953) 281–288.
 Locations
 Cambridge University Library
B.33 'Mr Joad's Point of View', in Anthony Lejeune, ed. *Time & Tide Anthology* (London: Andre Deutsch, 1956) 253–254.
 Locations
 Cambridge University Library
B.34 'Literature and the Left', 'You and the Atom Bomb', and 'What I Think of *Tribune*', *Tribune 21* ed. Elizabeth Thomas (London: MacGibbon & Kee, 1958) 91–93, 121–123, 138–141.
 Notes
 The three Orwell essays were originally published as follows:
 'Literature and the Left', originally published in *Tribune* (4 June 1943) [C.346].
 'You and the Atom Bomb', originally published in *Tribune* (19 October 1945) [C.587].
 'What I think of *Tribune*', originally published as 'As I Pleased' in *Tribune* (31 January 1947) [C.737].
B.35 'The Prevention of Literature', in Robert B. Downs, ed. *The First Freedom: Liberty and Justice in the World of Books and Reading* (Chicago: American Library Association, 1960) 411–417.
 Notes
 Abridged version of article originally published in *Polemic* No. 2 (January 1946) 4–14.
 See C.624.
 Abridged version originally published in *The Atlantic Monthly* Vol. 179, No. 3 (March 1947) 115–119.
 See C.751.
B.36 Extract from *Nineteen Eighty-Four* in Eugen Weber, ed. *Paths to the Present: Aspects of European Thought from Romanticism to Existentialism* (New York: Dodd, Mead and Co., 1960) 386–393.
B.37 'Reflections on Ghandi', in William Phillips and Philip Rahv, eds. *The Partisan Review Anthology* (London: Macmillan and Co. Ltd., 1962) 60–65.

Notes

Another edition published in the United States and Canada by Holt, Rinehart and Winston, 1962.

B.38   'Common Lodging Houses', in Edward Hyams, ed. *New Statesmanship: An Anthology* (London: Longmans, 1963) 86–93.

Notes

Under the name of Eric Blair.

Dated 10 September 1932.

B.39   'Rudyard Kipling' in Andrew Rutherford, ed. *Kipling's Mind and Art* (Edinburgh and London: Oliver & Boyd, 1964) 70–84.

Notes

First published in *Horizon* (February 1942) [C.302]. Note in this book says the essay was revised in 1945 and is here printed from *Critical Essays* (1946).

Other essays in this collection by W.L. Renwick, Edmund Wilson, Lionel Trilling, Noel Annan, George Shepperson, Alan Sandison, Andrew Rutherford, Mark Kinkead-Weekes, J.H. Fenwick, and W.W. Robson.

Location

Cambridge University Library [rebound]. Acquisition 30 April 1964.

B.40   'A Queer Tale' in Rudolf Flesch, ed. *The Book of Surprises: An Anthology of the Unusual* (New York: Harper & Row, 1965) 335–339.

Notes

From *Down and Out in Paris and London.*

B.41   'T.S. Eliot', in Bernard Bergonzi, ed. *T.S. Eliot. Four Quartets. A Casebook* (London: Macmillan, 1969) 81–87.

Notes

Reprint of 'Points of View': review of T.S. Eliot 'Burnt Norton', 'East Coker', and 'The Dry Salvages', originally published in *Poetry (London)* (October–November 1942) 56–59 [C.319].

B.42   *George Orwell: The Times Authors*

Number 2.

London: Times Education Services, Times Newspapers Limited, 1970.

Edited by Michael Morland

A loose-leaf folder of items described as 'the raw material for research into the author'.

Contents

[NB the items are in no particular order in the folder]

Selection of contemporary reviews and retrospective surveys.

Samples of Orwell's writings from *Tribune*, *The Observer* etc.

Fold-out sheet of 10 still shots from the animated cartoon version of *Animal Farm*. Poster.

The complete strip cartoon serial of *Animal Farm.*

Long extract from *The English People*, reproduced covers, 16 pages of text, and 5 illustrations.

Daily Mirror article, published 7 December 1954 on BBC television play of *Nineteen Eighty-Four*, said at that time to have attracted the largest-ever television audience in Britain. Stills from the production.

'World background' – notes by various historians on the Spanish Civil War and the Russian Revolution, the Russian peasants, and Britain and India.

Bibliography of sources and references.

Location

Cambridge University Library. Acquisition 15 September 1970.

B.43   'The Lower Classes Smell', in Thomas Ford Hoult, ed. *Sociology Readings for a New Day* (New York: Random House, 1974) 145–152.

Notes
From *The Road to Wigan Pier*.
Reissue (at Orwell Archive) 1979.

B.44 Review of Arthur Koestler *Spanish Testament*, and 'Arthur Koestler', in Murray A. Sperber, ed. *Arthur Koestler: A Collection of Critical Essays* (Englewood Cliffs, N.J.: Prentice Hall, Inc., 1977) 11–12 and 13–24.
Notes
The review of *Spanish Testament* was first published in *Time & Tide* (5 February 1938) 177 [C.119].
'Arthur Koestler' was first published in *Focus* No. 2 (1946) 27–38 [C.621].

B.45 'Escape from the Consciousness of Futility', in B.C. Southam, ed. *T.S. Eliot: 'Prufrock', 'Gerontion', Ash Wednesday and Other Shorter Poems. A Casebook* (London: Macmillan, 1978) 92–96.
Notes
Extract from 'Points of View': review of T.S. Eliot 'Burnt Norton', 'East Coker', and 'The Dry Salvages', *Poetry (London)* (October–November 1942) 56–59 [C.319] *Poetry* (2 July 1942) 81–85.

B.46 'Bozo, the Screever', in Robert E. Beck, ed. *Experiencing Biography* (Rochelle Park, N.J.: Hadden Book Company Inc., 1978) 113–116.
Notes
From *Down and Out in Paris and London*.
With questions and exercises for students on pp. 116–119.
Location
Orwell Archive

B.47 'Points of View': T.S. Eliot', in Michael Grant, ed. *T.S. Eliot: The Critical Heritage* (London: Routledge & Kegan Paul, 1982) Vol. 2 483–488.
Notes
Review of T.S. Eliot 'Burnt Norton', 'East Coker', and 'The Dry Salvages', originally published in *Poetry (London)* (October–November 1942) 56–59 [C.319] [see also B.19].

B.48 'The Sanctified Sinner' in Nobuo Tsuru, ed. *Graham Greene* (Kyoto: Yamaguchi Shoten, 1982) 217–221.
Notes
In the series *Seminars on Modern English and American Literature* No. 20.
First published in *The New Yorker* (17 July 1948) 66, 69–71 See C.786.

B.49 'Shooting an Elephant', in John Lehmann, ed. *The Penguin New Writing: An Anthology* (Harmondsworth: Penguin Books, 1985) 217–223.

B.50 'Awake! Young Men of England', and 'Kitchener', in Neville Braybrooke, ed. *Seeds in the Wind: Juvenilia from W.B. Yeats to Ted Hughes* (London: Hutchinson, 1989) 124–125.
Notes
See C.001 and C.002.
Locations
Cambridge University Library
Orwell Archive
University of Toronto Library

Notes to B
1 Letter to George Woodcock, 2 December 1942. *CEJL* II 268.
2 Letter to Philip Rahv, 9 December 1943. *CEJL* III 53–53.

C: Contributions to periodicals

... there has literally been not one day in which I did not feel that I was idling, that I was behind with the current job, and that my total output was miserably small. Even at periods when I was working ten hours a day on a book, or turning out four or five articles a week, I have never been able to get away from this neurotic feeling, that I was wasting time![1]

C.001   'Awake! Young Men of England', *The Henley and South Oxfordshire Standard* Vol. XXV, No. 1455 (2 October 1914) 8.
   Notes
   Signed: Eric Blair
   Poem.
   Note at head: 'The following verses were composed and written by Master Eric Blair, the eleven-year-old son of Mr R.W. Blair, of Rose Lawn, Shiplake.' Reprinted in Neville Braybrooke, ed. *Seeds in the Wind: Juvenilia from W.B. Yeats to Ted Hughes* (London: Hutchinson, 1989) 124.

C.002   'Kitchener', *The Henley and South Oxfordshire Standard* Vol. XXVI, No. 1549 (21 July 1916) 3.
   Notes
   Signed: E.A. Blair
   Poem.
   Reprinted in Neville Braybrooke, ed. *Seeds in the Wind: Juvenilia from W.B. Yeats to Ted Hughes* (London: Hutchinson, 1989) 125.

C.003   'A Peep into the Future' *The Election Times* No. 4 (3 June 1918) 15–24.
   Notes
   Unsigned.
   Handwritten by Eric Blair.
   The Election Times was produced by Eton scholars. Blair is listed as its Business Manager; Roger Mynors, Editor; Denys King-Farlow, Art Manager. The attribution of authorship is complicated because the producers sometimes wrote out contributions other than their own.
   MS in Orwell Archive.

C.004   'Free Will', *The Election Times* No. 4 (3 June 1918) 25–27.
   Notes
   Unsigned.
   Handwritten by Eric Blair.
   One-act play.
   Reprinted in *College Days* No. 5 (9 July 1920) 129 [See C.019]. Unsigned.

C.005   'The Slack-bob', *The Election Times* No. 4 (3 June 1918) 29–32.
   Notes
   Unsigned.
   Handwritten by Eric Blair.
   Revised and reprinted in *College Days* No. 5 (9 July 1920) 146 [See C.023]. Unsigned.

C.006   'The Adventures of the Lost Meat-card', *The Election Times* No. 4 (3 June 1918) 43–46.
   Notes
   Unsigned.
   Handwritten by Eric Blair.

C.007 'The Wounded Cricketer (Not by Walt Whitman)', *The Election Times* No. 4 (3 June 1918) 61.
       Notes
       Unsigned.
       Handwritten by Eric Blair.
       Poem.
       Reprinted in *College Days* No. 5 (9 July 1920) 136. Unsigned.
       MS in Orwell Archive, 1f.
C.008 Two stanzas of 'The Youthful Mariner', *The Election Times* No. 4 (3 June 1918) 62.
       Notes
       Unsigned.
       Handwritten by Eric Blair.
       Poem.
       Reprinted in *College Days* No. 5 (9 July 1920) 156, 158. Unsigned.
       MS in Orwell Archive, 1f.
C.009 'To A.R.H.B.', *College Days* No. 2 (27 June 1919) 42.
       Notes
       Unsigned.
       Poem.
       College Days was a printed publication produced by Eton scholars.
       A.R.H.B. was A. Roland Hanbury Bateman, an Eton scholar.
C.010 'Things We Do Not Want to Know', *College Days* No. 3 (29 November 1919) 78.
       Notes
       Unsigned.
C.011 'Wall Game', *College Days* No. 3 (29 November 1919) 78.
       Notes
       Unsigned.
       Poem.
C.012 'Eton Masters' Strike', *College Days* No. 3 (29 November 1919) 90.
       Notes
       Unsigned.
C.013 'The White Man's Burden', *College Days* No. 3 (29 November 1919) 93–95.
       Notes
       Unsigned.
C.014 'A.R.D. – After rooms – JANNEY', *College Days* No. 4 (1 April 1920) 103.
       Notes
       Unsigned.
       Mock advertisement in personal column, referring to a boy and a master.
C.015 'After Twelve', *College Days* No. 4 (1 April 1919) 104.
       Notes
       Unsigned.
       Poem.
C.016 'Ode to Field Days', *College Days* No. 4 (1 April 1919) 114.
       Notes
       Unsigned.
       Poem.
       Galley proof in Orwell Archive, 1f.
C.017 'A Summer Idyll', *College Days* No. 4 (1 April 1919) 116, 118.
       Notes
       Unsigned.
C.018 'Mr Simpson and the Supernatural', *Bubble and Squeak*, No. 2 (4 June 1920) 40–42.
       Notes
       Unsigned.
       Bubble and Squeak was a printed publication produced by Eton scholars.

C.019   'Free Will', *College Days* No. 5 (9 July 1920) 129.
        Notes
        Unsigned.
        One-act play.
        First published in *The Election Times* No. 4 (3 June 1918) 25–27 [See C.004].
        Ms in Orwell Archive, 4ff.

C.020   'The Photographer', *College Days* No. 5 (9 July 1920) 130.
        Notes
        Unsigned.
        Poem.
        MS in Orwell Archive, 1f.

C.021   'The Wounded Cricketer (Not by Walt Whitman)', *College Days* No. 5 (9 July 1920) 136.
        Notes
        Unsigned.
        Poem.
        First published in *The Election Times* No. 4 (3 June 1918) 61 [See C.007].

C.022   'Is There Any Truth in Spiritualism?', *College Days* No. 5 (9 July 1920) 140.
        Notes
        Signed: The Bishop of Borstall.

C.023   'The Slack-bob', *College Days* No. 5 (9 July 1920) 146.
        Notes
        Unsigned.
        First published in *The Election Times* No. 4 (3 June 1918) 29–32 [See C.005].

C.024   'The Cricket Enthusiast', *College Days* No. 5 (9 July 1920) 150.
        Notes
        Unsigned.

C.025   'The Millionaire's Pearl', *College Days* No. 5 (9 July 1920) 152, 154, 156.
        Notes
        Unsigned.
        MS of last folio, Orwell Archive.

C.026   'The Youthful Mariner', *College Days* No. 5 (9 July 1920) 156, 158.
        Notes
        Unsigned.
        Poem.
        Two stanzas first published in *The Election Times* No. 4 (3 June 1918) 62 [See C.008].

C.027   'La censure en Angleterre' *Monde* (6 October 1928) 5.
        Notes
        Signed: E.A. Blair
        Translated from English by H.J. Salemson.

C.028   'La grande misère de l'ouvrier britannique – I. Le chomage', *Le Progrès Civique* No. 489 (29 December 1928) 1726–1728.
        Notes
        Signed: E.A. Blair
        At head of title: Une enquête du "Progrès Civique" en Angleterre: La grande misère de l'ouvrier britannique.
        Translated from English by Raoul Nicole.
        Payment: 225 francs.

C.029   'A Farthing Newspaper', *G.K.'s Weekly* Vol. VIII, No. 198 (29 December 1928) 248.
        Notes
        Signed: E.A. Blair
        The farthing newspaper was the Paris *Ami du Peuple*.
        CEJL I 12–15.

C.030 'La grande misère de l'ouvrier britannique – II. La journée d'un "tramp"',
Le Progrès Civique No. 490 (5 January 1929) 13–15.
Notes
Signed: E.A. Blair
At head of title: Une enquête du "Progrès Civique" en Angleterre.
Translated from English by Raoul Nicole.
Payment: 225 francs.
C.031 'La grande misère de l'ouvrier britannique – III. Les mendiants de Londres',
Le Progrès Civique No. 491 (12 January 1929) 42–44.
Notes
Signed: E.A. Blair
At head of title: Une enquête du "Progrès Civique" en Angleterre.
Translated from English by Raoul Nicole.
Payment: 225 francs.
C.032 'John Galsworthy', *Monde* (23 March 1929) 5.
Notes
Signed: E.A. Blair.
At head of title: Notre Galerie.
An article in the section 'Les Lettres'.
C.033 'Comment on Exploite un Peuple: L'Empire Britannique en Birmanie', *Le Progrès
Civique* No. 507 (4 May 1929) 562–564.
Notes
Signed: E.A. Blair
Payment: 225 francs.
C.034 'Herman Melville': review of Lewis Mumford *Herman Melville*, *The New
Adelphi* Vol. III, No. 3 (March–May 1930) 206–208.
Notes
Signed: E.A. Blair
CEJL I 19–21.
Originally *The Adelphi*, the magazine was published as *The New Adelphi*
from September 1927–June/August 1930, and then as *The Adelphi (new series)*
from October 1930.
C.035 Review of Edith Sitwell *Alexander Pope*, and Sherard Vines *The Course of
English Classicism*, *The New Adelphi* Vol. III, No. 4 (June–August 1930)
338–340.
Notes
Signed: E.A. Blair
CEJL I 22–24.
C.036 'A Good "Middle"': review of J.B. Priestley *Angel Pavement*, *The Adelphi* Vol. 1,
No. 1 (October 1930) 71–74.
Notes
Signed: E.A. Blair
CEJL I 25–27.
C.037 Review of Karl Bartz *The Horrors of Cayenne* translated by Beatrice Marshall,
The Adelphi Vol. 1, No. 3 (December 1930) Review Supplement xxxi–xxxii.
Notes
Signed: E.A.B.
On 12 January 1931, Orwell wrote to Max Plowman about this review, 'I can-
not of course let you pay for it. It was a poor piece of work, and that should
be an end of it.'
C.038 'Carlyle': review of Osbert Burdett *The Two Carlyles*, *The Adelphi* Vol. 1, No. 6
(March 1931) 534–536.
Notes
Signed: Eric Blair
CEJL I 33–36.

C.039   'The Spike', *The Adelphi* Vol. 2, No. 1 (April 1931) 24–33.
    Notes
    Signed: Eric Blair
    Article revised for *Down and Out in Paris and London* Chapters 27 and 35
    [See A.1].
    CEJL I 36–43.
    In September 1929, Orwell wrote to May Plowman at *The Adelphi*:
    During August I sent you an article describing a day in a casual ward. As
    a month has now gone by, I should be glad to hear from you about it. I have
    no other copy of the article, & I want to submit it elsewhere if it is no use to
    you.[2]
    The article was an early version of 'The Spike'. A year later, Orwell was still
    trying to get it published. In October 1930 he wrote to Max Plowman,
    You said something about wanting that other article which you have of mine
    made shorter. If you want that done, perhaps you will send it to me and I will
    attend to it.
    Then in November 1930 he told him, 'I enclose the other article reduced to
    3500 words',[3] and in this form it was published in April 1931.

C.040   'Poverty – Plain and Coloured': review of Lionel Britton *Hunger and Love*, and
    F.O. Mann *Albert Grope*, *The Adelphi* Vol. 2, No. 1 (April 1931) 80–82.
    Notes
    Signed: Eric Blair

C.041   Review of Pearl S. Buck *The Good Earth*, *The Adelphi* Vol. 2, No. 3 (June 1931)
    269–270.
    Notes
    Signed: E.A.B.

C.042   'A Hanging', *The Adelphi* Vol. 2, No. 5 (August 1931) 417–422.
    Notes
    Signed: Eric A. Blair
    Also published in *The New Savoy*.
    See B.26.
    Shooting An Elephant 11–17, *The Orwell Reader* 9–13, *Collected Essays* 9–14,
    Decline of the English Murder 14–19, and *CEJL* I 44–48.

C.043   'Hop-Picking', *The New Statesman and Nation* Vol. II, No. 34 [new series] (17
    October 1931) 477.
    Notes
    Signed: Eric Blair
    CEJL I 52–71.
    Early in October 1931, Orwell sent a copy of the article about to be published
    to Dennis Collings:
    Herewith the narrative of my adventures. Much of it repeats what I have told
    you before, but I wanted a full account for my own future reference. Keep it
    for me, will you? You will excuse carbon copy & bad typing.[4]
    A 1970 version, published as *George Orwell in Kent*, omits the final section,
    describing Orwell's return to London and his time in common lodging houses
    there from 19 September to 8 October 1931. It also omits his glossary of "New
    Words (i.e. words new to me) discovered this time." [See D.13].

C.044   Letter to the Editor, *The New English Weekly* Vol. I, No. 3 (5 May 1932) 75.
    Notes
    Signed: Eric A. Blair
    On remarks about Ivar Kreuger made by Sir Arthur Salter in 'Referee or Super
    State?', a radio lecture, an abridged version of which was published in *The
    Listener* (23 March 1932) 436–437.

C.045   Review of Ernst Robert Curtius *The Civilization of France* translated by Olive
    Wyon, *The Adelphi* Vol. 4, No. 2 (May 1932) 553–555.

Notes
Signed: Eric Blair

C.046 Review of Karl Adam *The Spirit of Catholicism* translated by Dom Justin McCann, *The New English Weekly* Vol. I, No. 8 (9 June 1932) 192.
Notes
Unsigned.
CEJL I 79–81.
See C.047.

C.047 '"The Spirit of Catholicism"', *The New English Weekly* Vol. I, No. 11 (30 June 1932) 267.
Notes
Letter to the Editor.
Signed: Eric A. Blair.
In reply to G.C. Martindale's letter, *The New English Weekly* (23 June 1932) 243–244 on Blair's unsigned review.
See C.046.

C.048 'Common Lodging Houses', *The New Statesman and Nation* Vol. IV (3 September 1932) 256–257.
Notes
Signed: Eric Blair
CEJL I 97–100.

C.049 Review of Ruth Pitter *Persephone in Hades*, *The Adelphi* Vol. 4, No. 6 (September 1932) 870–871.
Notes
Signed: Eric Blair

C.050 Review of Charles du Bos *Byron and the Need of Fatality* translated by Ethel Colburn Mayne, *The Adelphi* Vol. 4, No. 6 (September 1932) 873–875.
Notes
Signed: Eric Blair
CEJL I 95–97.

C.051 Review of Harry Reichenbach *Phantom Fame*, *The Adelphi* Vol. 5, No. 1 (October 1932) 76.
Notes
Signed: E.B.

C.052 'Hotel Kitchens', *The Times* (11 February 1933) 6.
Notes
Signed: George Orwell
Letter to the Editor in reply to Humbert Possenti's letter, 'Hotel Kitchens', *The Times* (31 January 1933) 6.
CEJL I 115–116.
First periodical contribution to be signed 'George Orwell'.
Hereafter, unless otherwise noted, all contributions are signed 'George Orwell'.

C.053 'Sometimes in the middle autumn days', *The Adelphi* Vol. 5, No 6 (March 1933) 410.
Notes
Signed: Eric Blair
Poem.
CEJL I 118.

C.054 Review of Boris de Schloezer *Gogol*, *The Adelphi* Vol. 6, No. 1 (April 1933) 74–75.
Notes
Signed: Eric Blair

C.055 'Summer-like for an instant the autumn sun bursts out', *The Adelphi* Vol. 6, No. 2 (May 1933) 102.

> *Notes*
> Signed: Eric Blair
> Poem.

C.056   Review of Enid Starkie *Baudelaire*, *The Adelphi* Vol. 6, No. 5 (August 1933) 382–383.
> *Notes*
> Signed: Eric Blair

C.057   'A dressed man and a naked man', *The Adelphi* Vol. 7, No. 1 (October 1933) 47–48.
> *Notes*
> Signed: Eric Blair
> Poem.
> *CEJL* I 123–125.

C.058   Review of G.K. Chesterton *Criticisms and Opinions of the Works of Charles Dickens*, *The Adelphi* Vol. 7, No. 3 (December 1933) 224–225.
> *Notes*
> Signed: Eric Blair

C.059   Review of Michael Roberts *Critique of Poetry*, *The Adelphi* Vol. 7, No. 6 (March 1934) 468.
> *Notes*
> Signed: E.A.B.

C.060   'On a Ruined Farm near the His Master's Voice Gramophone Factory', *The Adelphi* Vol. 8, No. 1 (April 1934) 35–36.
> *Notes*
> Signed: Eric Blair
> Poem.
> Thomas Moult, ed. *The Best Poems of 1934* 113–114 [B.1].
> *CEJL* I 134–135.

C.061   Review of A.T. Bartholomew, ed. *Further Extracts from the Notebooks of Samuel Butler*, *The Adelphi* Vol. 8, No. 1 (April 1934) 72–73.
> *Notes*
> Signed: Eric Blair

C.062   Review of Hasye Cooperman *The Aesthetic of Stephane Mallarmé*, and G.T. Clapton *Baudelaire, the Tragic Sophist*, *The Adelphi* Vol. 8, No. 4 (July 1934) 291–293.
> *Notes*
> Signed: Eric Blair

C.063   Review of *Poems of Rainer Maria Rilke* translated by J.B. Leishman, *The Adelphi* Vol. 8, No. 5 (August 1934) 356–357.
> *Notes*
> Signed: Eric Blair

C.064   Review of Christopher Dawson *Mediaeval Religion*, *The Adelphi* Vol. 9, No. 2 (November 1934) 126–127.
> *Notes*
> Signed: Eric Blair

C.065   Review of Kenneth Saunders *The Ideals of East and West*, *The Adelphi* Vol. 9, No. 3 (December 1934) 190–191.
> *Notes*
> Signed: E.B.

C.066   Review of Jack Hilton *Caliban Shrieks*, *The Adelphi* Vol. 9, No. 6 (March 1935) 379–380.
> *Notes*
> Unsigned. From this point, his contributions to *The Adelphi* were signed 'George Orwell'.
> *CEJL* I 148–150.

C.067 'Some Recent Novels': review of Patrick Hamilton *Twenty Thousand Streets under the Sky*, Katharine M. Williams *The Proceedings of the Society*, and Robert Godfrey Goodyear *I Lie Alone*, *The New English Weekly* Vol. VII, No. 16 (1 August 1935) 317–318.

C.068 Review of V.F. Calverton *The Passing of the Gods*, and Amy Cruse *The Victorians and Their Books*, *The Adelphi* Vol. 10, No. 5 (August 1935) 314–316.

C.069 'Some Recent Novels': review of Roger Vercel *Captain Conan* translated by Warre Bradley Wells, William Francis Casey *Private Life of a Successful Man*, T. Thompson *Song o' Sixpence*, Don Tracy *Criss-Cross*, and Richard Hull *Keep it Quiet*, *The New English Weekly* Vol. VII, No. 20 (26 September 1935) 393–394.

C.070 Review of Edith J. Morley *The Life and Times of Henry Crabb Robinson*, *The Adelphi* Vol. 11, No. 1 (October 1935) 61.

C.071 'St Andrew's Day, 1935', *The Adelphi* Vol. 11, No. 2 (November 1935) 86.
Notes
Poem.
Also published, without title and with six minor changes, in *Keep the Aspidistra Flying*, Chapter 7.

C.072 'Some Recent Novels': review of Henry Miller *Tropic of Cancer*, and Robert Francis *The Wolf at the Door* translated by Françoise Delisle, *The New English Weekly* Vol. VIII, No. 5 (14 November 1935) 96–97.
Notes
Section on *Tropic of Cancer* in *CEJL* I 154–156.

C.073 'Rudyard Kipling', *The New English Weekly* Vol. VIII, No. 15 (23 January 1936) 289.
Notes
Obituary on Rudyard Kipling.
CEJL I 159–160.

C.074 'Some Recent Novels': review of Thomas Burke *Night Pieces*, Mary Dunstan *Jagged Skyline*, Hilda Lewis *Full Circle*, Kenneth Roberts *The Lively Lady*, F.V. Morley *War Paint*, Lady Sanderson *Long Shadows*, Richard Curle *Who Goes Home?*, Dorothy Sayers *Gaudy Night*, Thomas Coulson *The Queen of Spies*, and Monica Salmond *Bright Armour*, *The New English Weekly* Vol. VIII, No. 15 (23 January 1936) 295–296.
Notes
Signed: G.O.
Section on *The Lively Lady*, *War Paint*, *Long Shadows*, *Who Goes Home?*, and *Gaudy Night* in *CEJL* I 160–162.

C.075 'Some Recent Novels': review of George Moore *Esther Waters*, Sinclair Lewis *Our Mr Wrenn*, Helen Ashton *Dr Serocold*, Crosbie Garstin *The Owls' House*, Donn Byrne *Hangman's House*, W.W. Jacobs *Odd Craft*, Bartimeus *Naval Occasions*, P.G. Wodehouse *My Man Jeeves*, and Margot Asquith *Autobiography* Vols. I & II, *The New English Weekly* Vol. VIII, No. 21 (5 March 1936) 414–415.
Notes
CEJL I 165–167.
Extracts reprinted in 'Penguin Celebrates with Orwell', *The Bookseller* (26 July 1975).
See C.841

C.076 'Some Recent Novels': review of Michael Fraenkel *Bastard Death*, Paul Cain *Fast One*, Joseph Shearing *The Golden Violet*, Muriel Hine *A Different Woman*, and Ngaio Marsh and H. Jellett *The Nursing Home Murder*, *The New English Weekly* Vol. IX, No. 2 (23 April 1936) 35–36.
Notes
Section on *Bastard Death* and *Fast One* in *CEJL* I 219–220.

C.077 Review of Alec Brown *The Fate of the Middle Classes*, *The New English Weekly* Vol. IX, No. 3 (30 April 1936) 58.

> *Notes*
> Unsigned.

C.078 Review of Alec Brown *The Fate of the Middle Classes*, *The Adelphi* Vol. 12, No. 2 (May 1936) 127–128.

C.079 'New Novels': review of Vardis Fisher *We Are Betrayed*, George Blake *David and Joanna*, Nicolai Gubsky *Surprise Item*, and Elizabeth Jenkins *The Phoenix' Nest*, *Time & Tide* Vol. XVII, No. 21 (23 May 1936) 764–765.

C.080 'Treasure and Travel': review of James Stead *Treasure Trek*, S.E.G. Ponder *Sun on Summer Seas*, and Walter Starkie *Don Gypsy*, *Time & Tide* Vol. XVII, No. 28 (11 July 1936) 1008–1009.

C.081 Review of Mark Channing *Indian Mosaic*, *The Listener* Vol. 16, No. 392 (15 July 1936) 138.

> *Notes*
> Unsigned.
> Payment £1 11s 6d.

C.082 'Real Adventure': review of Rosa E. King *Tempest over Mexico*, and Fred Bower *Rolling Stonemason*, *Time & Tide* Vol. XVII, No. 29 (18 July 1936) 1041–1042.

C.083 'Recent Novels': review of Cyril Connolly *The Rock Pool*, Joseph Conrad *Almayer's Folly*, Ernest Bramah *The Wallet of Kai Lung*, Arnold Bennett *Anna of the Five Towns*, H.C. Bailey *Mr Fortune, Please*, and George R. Preedy *The Rocklitz*, *The New English Weekly* Vol. IX, No. 15 (23 July 1936) 294–295.

> *Notes*
> Section on *The Rock Pool* and *Almayer's Folly* in *CEJL* I 225–227.
> In a letter to Henry Miller, Orwell reported that he had reviewed Connolly's book, 'but though it amused me I didn't think a lot of it.' *CEJL* I 229.

C.084 'From Tartary to Egypt': review of Peter Fleming *News from Tartary*, General Virgin *The Abyssinia I Knew*, and R. Raven-Hart *Canoe Errant on the Nile*, *Time & Tide* Vol. XVII, No. 33 (15 August 1936) 1158.

C.085 'Five Travellers': review of Carl R. Raswan *The Black Tents of Arabia*, Lawrence Green *Secret Africa*, P.B. Williams *In Lightest Africa and Darkest Europe*, Eric Muspratt *Going Native*, and E. Alexander Powell *Aerial Odyssey*, *Time & Tide* Vol. XVII, No. 37 (12 September 1936) 1252, 1254.

C.086 'Some Recent Novels': review of Henry Miller *Tropic of Cancer* and *Black Spring*, E.M. Forster *A Passage to India*, Richard Aldington *Death of a Hero*, Upton Sinclair *The Jungle*, C.E. Montague *A Hind Let Loose*, and Ian Hay *A Safety Match*, *The New English Weekly* Vol. IX, No. 24 (24 September 1936) 396–397.

> *Notes*
> *CEJL* I 230–232.

C.087 'Shooting an Elephant', *New Writing* No. 2 (Autumn 1936) 1–7.

> *Notes*
> Also published in *Penguin New Writing* No. 1 ([November] 1940) 9–15.
> Broadcast in the BBC Home Service (12 October 1948) 3.40–4.00pm. Read by Arthur Bush.
> *Shooting an Elephant* 1–10, *A Collection of Essays* 148–156, *The Orwell Reader* 3–9, *Selected Essays* 91–99, *Selected Writings* 25–33, *Collected Essays* 15–23, and *CEJL* I 235–242.
> Reprinted in *Modern Essays* ed. A.F. Scott (London: Macmillan, 1942).
> Reprinted in the *Scholar's Library Series* (1944).
> Reprinted many times in anthologies, English as a second language texts, study guides etc.
> In May 1936, Orwell wrote to John Lehmann,
> . . . the only other thing I have in mind is a sketch, (it would be abt 2000–3000 words), describing the shooting of an elephant. It all came back to me very vividly the other day & I would like to write it, but it may be that it is quite out of your line. I mean it might be a bit too low brow for your paper &

I doubt whether there is anything anti-Fascist in the shooting of an elephant! Of course you can't say in advance that you would like it, but perhaps you could say tentatively whether it is at all likely to be in your line or not. If not, then I won't write it; if you think it might interest you I will do it & send it along for you to consider. I am sorry to be so vague but without seeing a copy of *New Writing* I can't tell what sort of stuff it uses.[5]

In 1940, John Lehmann was planning a new volume, *Penguin New Writing*. He asked Orwell's permission to reprint the essay, and Orwell replied, 'Of course you can use the elephant sketch again if you like. Two guineas would be very handsome.'[6]

C.088 'Travel Round and Down': review of Johann Wöller *Zest for Life* translated by Claude Napier, and Hugh Massingham *I Took Off My Tie*, *Time & Tide* Vol. XVII, No. 42 (17 October 1936) 1453.
  Notes
  Section on *Zest for Life* in *CEJL* I 234–235.

C.089 Review of W.F.R. Macartney *Walls Have Mouths*, *The Adelphi* Vol. 13, No. 2 (November 1936) 121–122.

C.090 'Bookshop Memories', *The Fortnightly* Vol. CXL (CXLVI old series) (November 1936) 600–604.
  Notes
  CEJL I 242–246.
  Extracts reprinted in *The Bookseller* (26 July 1975) as 'Penguin Celebrates with Orwell'.
  See C.841.
  Reprinted in a bound volume, *Bookshop Memories* (Baarn, Netherlands: Arethusa Pers Herber Blokland, 1987), with a foreword by W.E. Butler and a wood engraving by Hilary Paynter. Edition of 150 copies.
  Copy at Orwell Archive.

C.091 'In Defence of the Novel. I', *The New English Weekly* Vol. X, No. 5 (12 November 1936) 91–92.
  Notes
  In the section 'Views and Reviews'.
  Reprinted with 'In Defence of the Novel. II' [C.093] in *CEJL* I 249–255.

C.092 'Some Recent Novels': review of Scholem Asch *The Calf of Paper*, and Julian Green *Midnight* translated by Vyvyan Holland, *The New English Weekly* Vol. X, No. 5 (12 November 1936) 93–94.
  Notes
  Signed: G.O.
  CEJL I 247–249.

C.093 'In Defence of the Novel. II', *The New English Weekly* Vol. X, No. 6 (19 November 1936) 111–112.
  Notes
  In the section 'Views and Reviews'.
  Reprinted with 'In Defence of the Novel. I' [C.091] in *CEJL* I 249–255.

C.094 'Desert and Islands': review of Knud Holmboe *Desert Encounter* translated by Helga Holbek, and J.A.F. Ozanne *Coconuts and Creoles*, *Time & Tide* Vol. XVII, No. 47 (21 November 1936) 1643–1644.

C.095 'A happy vicar I might have been', *The Adelphi* Vol. 13, No. 3 (December 1936) 173.
  Notes
  Poem.
  The last three stanzas were reprinted in *Gangrel* No. 4 (Summer 1946) 5–10, as part of 'Why I Write' [See C.701].

C.096 Review of Adrian Bell *The Open Air*, *The Listener* Vol. 16, No. 412 (2 December 1936) 1033.

        Notes
        Unsigned.
        Payment £1 1s 0d.

C.097 'Propagandist Critics': review of Philip Henderson *The Novel To-Day*, *The New English Weekly* Vol. X, No. 12 (31 December 1936) 229–230.
        Notes
        CEJL I 256–259.

C.098 'Night Attack on the Aragon Front', ed. John McNair *The New Leader* [New York] (30 April 1937) 3.
        Notes
        Note at head of story: 'The whole of this story is in the words of the men who took part in it. It consists entirely of extracts from letters to John McNair from Bob Smillie, Eric Blair, Albert Gross and Paddy Donovan.'

C.099 'Presenting the Future', *News Chronicle* (10 June 1937) 6.
        Notes
        A short extract from *The Road to Wigan Pier*, the fourth of a five-part series illustrating the work of 'young writers already famous among critics, less well-known by the public.'

C.100 'Spilling the Spanish Beans. I', *The New English Weekly* Vol. XI, Nos. 16–20 (29 July 1937) 307–308.
        Notes
        Reprinted with 'Spilling the Spanish Beans. II' [C.105] in *CEJL* I 269–276.

C.101 'Spanish Nightmare': review of Franz Borkenau *The Spanish Cockpit*, and John Sommerfield *Volunteer in Spain*, *Time & Tide* Vol. XVIII, No. 31 (31 July 1937) 1047–1048.
        Notes
        CEJL I 276–278.

C.102 'Eye-Witness in Barcelona', *Controversy: The Socialist Forum*, Vol. I, No. 11 (August 1937) 85–88.

C.103 'Experientia Docet': review of F.P. Crozier *The Men I Killed*, *The New Statesman and Nation* Vol. XIV (28 August 1937) 314.
        Notes
        CEJL I 282–283.

C.104 'J'ai été té á Barcelone', *La Révolution Prolétarienne: revue bimensuelle syndicaliste révolutionnaire* Vol. 13, No. 255 (25 September 1937) 1(709)–3(711).
        Notes
        French translation by Yvonne Davet of 'Eye-Witness in Barcelona', *Controversy: The Socialist Forum* (August 1937) [C.102].

C.105 'Spilling the Spanish Beans. II', *The New English Weekly* Vol. XI, No. 21 (2 September 1937) 328–329.
        Notes
        Reprinted with 'Spilling the Spanish Beans. I' [C.100] in *CEJL* I 269–276.

C.106 Letter to the Editor, *New Statesman and Nation* (4 September 1937).

C.107 'More News From Tartary': review of Ella K. Maillart *Forbidden Journey* translated by Thomas McGreevy, *Time & Tide* Vol. XVIII, No. 36 (4 September 1937) 1175.

C.108 'That Mysterious Cart', *New Leader* (24 September 1937) 3.
        Notes
        Reply to F.A. Frankfort's statements about the P.O.U.M. in *The Daily Worker* (14 September 1937) 2, and (16 September 1937) 6.

C.109 'Background to Travel': review of Eric Teichman *Journey to Turkistan*, *Time & Tide* Vol. XVIII, No. 39 (25 September 1937) 1269.
        Notes
        CEJL I 286.

C.110 'Spain: Today and Yesterday': review of Mary Low and Juan Brea *Red Spanish Notebook*, R. Timmermans *Heroes of the Alcazar*, and Martin Armstrong *Spanish Circus*, *Time & Tide* Vol. XVIII, No. 41 (9 October 1937) 1334–1335.
Notes
Section on *Red Spanish Notebook* and *Heroes of the Alcazar* in CEJL I 287–288.

C.111 'Back to the Twenties': review of the September 1937 issue of *The Booster*, *The New English Weekly* Vol. XII, No. 2 (21 October 1937) 30–31.
Notes
The Booster was a new literary magazine edited by Alfred Perlès, Lawrence Durrell, Henry Miller, and others.

C.112 'Excursions in Autobiography': review of James Hanley *Broken Water*, and Beirne Lay *I Wanted Wings*, *Time & Tide* Vol. XVIII, No. 45 (6 November 1937) 1475.

C.113 'The Booster', *The New English Weekly* Vol. XII, No. 5 (11 November 1937) 100.
Notes
Letter to the Editor in reply to letter from 'The Booster', *The New English Weekly* (4 November 1937) 78–79.

C.114 'Our Own Have-Nots': review of Wal Hannington *The Problem of the Distressed Areas*, James Hanley *Grey Children*, and Neil Stewart *The Fight for the Charter*, *Time & Tide* Vol. XVIII, No. 48 (27 November 1937) 1588.

C.115 'Spanish Quintet': review of Mairin Mitchell *Storm Over Spain*, Arnold Lunn *Spanish Rehearsal*, E. Allison Peers *Catalonia Infelix*, José Castillejo *Wars of Ideas in Spain*, and José Ortega y Gasset *Invertebrate Spain*, *Time & Tide* Vol. XVIII, No. 50 (11 December 1937) 1708–1709.
Notes
Section on *Storm Over Spain*, *Spanish Rehearsal*, and *Catalonia Infelix* in CEJL I 290–291.

C.116 'The Lure of Profundity': review of José Ortega y Gasset *Invertebrate Spain*, *The New English Weekly* Vol. XII, No. 12 (30 December 1937) 235–236.

C.117 Review of C.V. Warren *Burmese Interlude*, *The Listener* (12 January 1938) 101.
Notes
Unsigned.
Payment £1 1s 0d.

C.118 '"Trotskyist" Publications', *Time & Tide* Vol. XIX, No. 6 (5 February 1938) 164–165.
Notes
Letter to the Editor in response to remarks made by Ellen Wilkinson in 'France in Crisis', and by Sirocco in 'Time-Tide Diary', both in *Time & Tide* (22 January 1938) 93–94 and 98.
CEJL I 297–298.

C.119 'Terror in Spain': review of G.L. Steer *The Tree of Gernika*, and Arthur Koestler *Spanish Testament*, *Time & Tide* Vol. XIX, No. 6 (5 February 1938) 177.
Notes
Section on *Spanish Testament* in CEJL I 295–296.

C.120 'Eyes Left, Dress!': review of Fenner Brockway *Workers' Front*, *The New English Weekly* Vol. XII, No. 19 (17 February 1938) 368.
Notes
CEJL I 304–306.

C.121 Review of Maurice Collis *Trials in Burma*, *The Listener* (9 March 1938) 534.
Notes
Unsigned.
Payment £1 11s 6d.
CEJL I 306–307.

C.122 Review of John Galsworthy *Glimpses and Reflections*, *The New Statesman and Nation* Vol. XV (12 March 1938) 428.

> *Notes*
> *CEJL* I 307–308.

C.123 'Homage to Catalonia', *Times Literary Supplement* (14 May 1938) 336.
> *Notes*
> Letter to the Editor in response to review of *Homage to Catalonia*, *Times Literary Supplement* (30 April 1938) 286.
> See also C.125.

C.124 'Ends and Means', *The New English Weekly* Vol. XIII, No. 7 (26 May 1938) 139.
> *Notes*
> Letter to the Editor in reply to A. Romney Green's letter, 'Delinquent Stars', *The New English Weekly* (12 May 1938) 39.
> *CEJL* I 330–332.

C.125 'Homage to Catalonia', *Times Literary Supplement* (28 May 1938) 370.
> *Notes*
> Continuing correspondence on *Homage to Catalonia*. See C.123.

C.126 'Impenetrable Mystery': review of Eugene Lyons *Assignment in Utopia*, *The New English Weekly* Vol. XIII, No. 9 (9 June 1938) 169–170.
> *Notes*
> *CEJL* I 332–334.

C.127 'Authentic Socialism': review of Jack Common *The Freedom of the Streets*, *The New English Weekly* Vol. XIII, No. 10 (16 June 1938) 192.
> *Notes*
> *CEJL* I 335–336.

C.128 'Review of *Homage to Catalonia*', *The Listener* (16 June 1938) 1295.
> *Notes*
> Letter to the Editor in response to review of *Homage to Catalonia*, *The Listener* (25 May 1938) 1140, 1142.

C.129 'The Lure of Atrocity': review of Robert Sencourt *Spanish Ordeal*, and the anonymous *Franco's Rule*, *The New English Weekly* Vol. XIII, No. 11 (23 June 1938) 210.

C.130 'Why I Joined the I.L.P.' *The New Leader* (24 June 1938) 4.
> *Notes*
> *CEJL* I 336–338.

C.131 'Spain: The True and the False': review of Frank Jellinek *The Civil War in Spain*, *The New Leader* (8 July 1938) 7.
> *Notes*
> *CEJL* I 340–343.

C.132 'The Spanish Tragedy': review of the Duchess of Atholl *Searchlight on Spain*, Frank Jellinek *The Civil War in Spain*, and Robert Sencourt *Spain's Ordeal*, *Time & Tide* Vol. XIX, No. 29 (16 July 1938) 1030–1031.
> *Notes*
> Brief excerpt from section on *Searchlight on Spain* in *CEJL* I 346–347.

C.133 'Stalinism and Aristocracy': review of the Duchess of Atholl *Searchlight on Spain*, *The New English Weekly* Vol. XIII, No. 15 (21 July 1938) 275–276.
> *Notes*
> Section on *Searchlight on Spain* in *CEJL* I 344–346.

C.134 'Pressure from Outside', *Manchester Guardian* (5 August 1938) 18.
> *Notes*
> Letter to the Editor on espionage trial in Spain.

C.135 'Franz Borkenau on the Communist International': review of Franz Borkenau *The Communist International*, *The New English Weekly* Vol. XIII, No 24 (22 September 1938) 357–358.
> *Notes*
> In the section 'Views and Reviews'.
> *CEJL* I 348–351.

C.136   'If War Comes, We Shall Resist', *The New Leader* (30 September 1938) 4–5.
         Notes
         Manifesto, signed by 149 people, 48 of whose names, including Orwell's, were
         printed.

C.137   'We, The Undersigned', *Controversy* No. 25 (October 1938) 251.
         Notes
         Letter to the editor from Orwell and 44 others, supporting the editorial appeal
         for funds to keep *Controversy* alive.

C.138   'Two Franco Apologists': review of E. Allison Peers *The Church in Spain*, and
         Eoin O'Duffy *Crusade in Spain*, *The New English Weekly* Vol. XIV, No. 7
         (24 November 1938) 105–106.
         Notes
         In the section 'Views and Reviews'.

C.139   'Political Reflections on the Crisis', *The Adelphi* Vol. 15, No. 3 (December 1938)
         108–112.

C.140   'Will Gypsies Survive?': review of Martin Block *Gypsies* translated by Barbara
         Kuczynski and Duncan Taylor, *The Adelphi* Vol. 15, No. 3 (December 1938)
         137–138.

C.141   'Spanish Clericalism', *The New English Weekly* Vol. XIV, No. 11 (22 December
         1938) 180.
         Notes
         Letter to the Editor in reply to E. Allison Peers's letter, 'The Church in Spain',
         The New English Weekly (8 December 1938) 144.

C.142   'The Taming of Power': review of Bertrand Russell *Power: A New Social Analysis*,
         The Adelphi Vol. 15, No. 4 (January 1939) 205–206.
         Notes
         CEJL I 375–376.

C.143   'The Russian Régime': review of N. De Basily *Russia Under Soviet Rule*, *The New
         English Weekly* Vol. XIV, No. 14 (12 January 1939) 202–203.
         Notes
         CEJL I 378–381.

C.144   'A Mistake Corrected', *The New Leader* (13 January 1939) 7.
         Notes
         Explanation of an error in review of Frank Jellinek's *The Civil War in Spain*
         [C.132].

C.145   'A Catholic Confronts Communism': review of F.J. Sheed *Communism and Man*,
         Peace News (27 January 1939) 8.
         Notes
         CEJL I 383–385.

C.146   Contribution to a symposium on John Macmurray *The Clue to History*, *The
         Adelphi* Vol. 15, No. 5 (February 1939) 225–227.

C.147   'Caesarean Section in Spain', *The Highway: A Review of Adult Education and
         the Journal of the Workers' Educational Association* Vol. 31 (March 1939)
         145–147.

C.148   'Outside and Inside Views': review of Wyndham Lewis *The Mysterious Mr Bull*,
         and Ignazio Silone *The School for Dictators*, *The New English Weekly* Vol. XV
         (8 June 1939) 128–129.

C.149   'Not Counting Niggers': review of Clarence K. Streit *Union Now*, *The Adelphi*
         Vol. 15, No. 10 (July 1939) 469–473.
         Notes
         CEJL I 394–398.

C.150   Review of F.C. Green *Stendhal*, *The New English Weekly* Vol. XV, No. 15 (27 July
         1939) 237–238.
         Notes
         CEJL I 398–401.

C.151   'About it and About': review of twelve British Journalists *Foreign Correspondent*, L.B. Namier *In the Margin of History*, and Ferdinand Czernin *Europe Going, Going, Gone!*, *Time & Tide* Vol. 20, No. 32 (12 August 1939) 1096–1097.
    Notes
    After Volume XIX, *Time & Tide* volumes had Arabic numerals.

C.152   'The Book Racket': review of George Stevens and Stanley Unwin *Best-Sellers*, *The Adelphi* Vol. 15, No. 12 (September 1939) 605–606.

C.153   'Democracy in the British Army', *The Left Forum* No. 36 (September 1939) 235–238.
    Notes
    Left Forum was formerly *Controversy*.
    CEJL I 401–405.

C.154   'Looking Before and After': review of Maurice Hindus *Green Worlds*, and William Holt *I Haven't Unpacked*, *Time & Tide* Vol. 20, No. 42 (21 October 1939) 1372.

C.155   'Marrakech', *New Writing*, No. 3 (New Series) (Christmas 1939) 272–277.
    Notes
    Written Spring 1939.
    Such, Such Were The Joys 121–128, *England Your England*, *A Collection of Essays* 180–187, *Selected Writings* 61–67, *Collected Essays* 24–30, and *CEJL* I 387–393.

C.156   Review of Crichton Porteus *Teamsman*, *The Listener* (23 November 1939) 1034.
    Notes
    Unsigned.
    Payment £1 11s 6d.

C.157   'The Spanish War': review of Nancy Johnstone *Hotel in Flight*, *The Adelphi* Vol. XVI, No. 3 (December 1939) 125–126.

C.158   'Good Travellers': review of Bernard Newman *Baltic Roundabout*, John Gibbons *I Gathered No Moss*, and Max Relton *A Man in the East*, *Time & Tide* Vol. 20, No. 48 (2 December 1939) 1534.

C.159   'Moscow and Madrid': review of S. Casado *The Last Days of Madrid* translated by Rupert Croft-Cooke, and T.C. Worsley *Behind the Battle*, *Time & Tide* Vol. 21, No. 3 (20 January 1940) 62.
    Notes
    CEJL I 411–412.

C.160   Review of Ruth Pitter *The Spirit Watches*, *The Adelphi* Vol. XVI, No. 5 (February 1940) 221–222.

C.161   'The Lessons of War': review of Ludwig Renn *Warfare*, and E.L. Spears *Prelude to Victory*, *Horizon* Vol. I, No. 2 (February 1940) 133–137.

C.162   'Democrat and Dictators': review of Godfrey Lias *Benes of Czechoslovakia*, and Frank Owen *The Three Dictators*, *Time & Tide* Vol. 21, No. 7 (17 February 1940) 174–175.

C.163   'Boys' Weeklies', *Horizon* Vol. 1, No. 3 (March 1940) 174–200.
    Notes
    Inside the Whale, *Critical Essays* 57–82, *Dickens, Dali & Others* 76–114, *A Collection of Essays* 279–309, *Selected Essays* 175–203, *Selected Writings* 116–144, *Collected Essays* 88–117, and *CEJL* I 460–484.

C.164   'We Are Observed!': review of Tom Harrisson and Charles Madge, eds. *War Begins at Home*, *Time & Tide* Vol. 21, No. 9 (2 March 1940) 225–226.

C.165   'Hitler': review of Adolf Hitler *Mein Kampf*, *The New English Weekly* Vol. XVI, No. 22 (21 March 1940) 321–322.
    Notes
    Unabridged translation published by Hurst & Blackett.
    CEJL II 12–14.
    Reprinted in *Worldview* 18, No. 7–8, (1975) 27.

C.166   'Napoleon's Retreat from Moscow: An N.C.O.'s Story': review of the *Memoirs of Sergeant Bourgogne*, *The Tribune* No. 170 (29 March 1940) 16–17.
Notes
Towards the end of his time as a *Tribune* writer, in 1947, Orwell looked back on his association with the paper. He wrote,
One's relations with a newspaper or a magazine are more variable and inter-mittent than they can be with a human being ... a periodical will go through a whole series of different existences under the same name. *Tribune* in its short life has been two distinct papers, if not three, and my own contacts with it have varied sharply, starting off, if I remember rightly, with a rap on the knuckles ... I never had what is called a "good" review in *Tribune* until after I became a member of the staff ...Somewhat later, in the cold winter of 1939, I started writing for *Tribune*, though at first, curiously enough, without seeing it regularly or getting a clear idea of what kind of paper it was.
Raymond Postgate, who was then editor, had asked me to do the novel reviews from time to time. I was not paid ... *Tribune* ... was at that time in difficulties. It was still a threepenny paper aimed primarily at the industrial workers and following more or less the Popular Front line which had been associated with the Left Book Club and the Socialist League. With the outbreak of war its circulation had taken a severe knock, because the Communists and near-Communists who had been among its warmest supporters now refused to help in distributing it ... After that *Tribune* passed out of my consciousness for nearly two years.[7]

C.167   'Notes on the Way', *Time & Tide* Vol. 21, No. 13 (30 March 1940) 336–337.
Notes
First part of two-part article. Reprinted with 'Notes on the Way', *Time & Tide* (6 April 1940) [C.169], in *CEJL* II 15–18.

C.168   Review of J.O. Hannula *Finland's War of Independence*, and George Aston *Secret Service*, *Horizon* Vol. I, No. 4 (April 1940) 302–303.

C.169   'Notes on the Way', *Time & Tide* Vol. 21, No. 14 (6 April 1940) 358–359.
Notes
Concluding part of two-part article. Reprinted with 'Notes on the Way', *Time & Tide* (30 March 1940) [C.167], in *CEJL* II 15–18.

C.170   'From Bloomsbury to the Bowery': review of L.A.G. Strong *Sun on the Water*, Kay Boyle *The Crazy Hunter*, Stephen Longstreet *Decade*, James McConnaughey *Stephen Ayers*, and Francis Griswold *A Sea Island Lady*, *The Tribune* No. 172 (12 April 1940) 20–21.

C.171   'Entre Chien et Loup': review of Julian Green *Personal Record 1928–1939* translated by Jocelyn Godefroi, *Time & Tide* Vol. 21, No. 15 (13 April 1940) 404–405.
Notes
CEJL II 19–21.

C.172   Review of Edward Shanks *Rudyard Kipling*, *The Listener* Vol. 23, No. 589 (25 April 1940) 850.
Notes
Unsigned.
Payment £1 11s 6d.

C.173   'The Limit to Pessimism': review of Malcolm Muggeridge *The Thirties*, *The New English Weekly* Vol. XVII, No. 1 (25 April 1940) 5–6.
Notes
CEJL I 533–535.

C.174   'Black Man's Burden': review of Richard Wright *Native Son*, B. Traven *The Bridge in the Jungle* and *The Death Ship*, Fred Urquhart *I Fell for a Sailor*, Philip Ordan *Say That She Was Gone*, Leon Freuchtwanger *Paris Gazette*, and Geoffrey Trease *Only Natural*, *The Tribune* No. 174 (26 April 1940) 16–17.

C.175   Review of Havelock Ellis *My Life: The Autobiography of Havelock Ellis*, *The Adelphi* Vol. XVI, No. 8 (May 1940) 362–363.

C.176   'Red, White and Brown': review of F. Borkenau *The Totalitarian Enemy*, *Time & Tide* Vol. 21, No. 18 (4 May 1940) 484.
    Notes
    CEJL II 24–26.

C.177   Review of *Folios of New Writing (Spring, 1940)*, *The Listener* Vol. 23, No. 592 (16 May 1940) 983–984.
    Notes
    Unsigned.
    Payment £1 11s 6d.

C.178   Theatre review of George Bernard Shaw *In Good King Charles's Golden Days*, *Time & Tide* Vol. 21, No. 20 (18 May 1940) 534.

C.179   'Unwillingly to School': review of Stephen Spender *The Background Son*, Thomas Mann *Royal Highness*, Hans Fallada *Iron Gustav*, Maurice Hindus *Sons and Fathers*, Arthur Calder Marshall *The Way to Santiago*, Ben Hecht *A Book of Miracles*, and Sinclair Lewis *Bethel Merriday*, *The Tribune* No. 178 (24 May 1940) 14–15.

C.180   Theatre review of Jean Cocteau *Les Parents Terribles*, and of *Garrison Theatre* a variety show, *Time & Tide* Vol. 21, No. 21 (25 May 1940) 558.

C.181   'The Dark Horse of the Apocalypse': review of *The New Apocalypse: An Anthology of Criticism, Poems and Stories* and Henry Treece *Thirty-Eight Poems*, *Life and Letters* Vol. 25, No. 34 (June 1940) 315–318.

C.182   Review of Jim Phelan *Jail Journey*, *Horizon* Vol. 1, No. 6 (June 1940) 458–460.

C.183   Theatre review of the revue *Swinging the Gate*, *Time & Tide* Vol. 21, No. 22 (1 June 1940) 585–586.

C.184   Review of *Indian Writing Vol. I*, *The Listener* Vol. 23, No. 595 (6 June 1940) 1103.
    Notes
    Unsigned.
    Payment £1 1s 0d.

C.185   Theatre review of William Shakespeare *The Tempest*, Denis Ogden *The Peaceful Inn*, and Audrey Lucas *Portrait of Helen*, *Time & Tide* Vol. 21, No. 23 (8 June 1940) 610–611.

C.186   'Mr Joad's Point of View': review of C.E.M. Joad *Journey Through the War Mind*, Anthony Weymouth *A Psychologist's Wartime Diary*, and Hector Bolitho *America Expects*, *Time & Tide* Vol. 21, No. 23 (8 June 1940) 613.

C.187   Theatre review of Noel Coward *I'll Leave it to You*, *Time & Tide* Vol. 21, No. 24 (15 June 1940) 642.

C.188   'The Male Byronic': review of Mikhail Yurevich Lermontoff *A Hero of Our Times*, E.L. Grant Watson *Priest Island*, and H.G. Wells *Film Stories*, *The Tribune* No. 182 (21 June 1940) 20–21.

C.189   'Against Invasion', *Time & Tide* Vol. 21, No. 25 (22 June 1940) 662.
    Notes
    Letter to the Editor.
    CEJL II 27–28.

C.190   Theatre review of Reginald Beckwith *Boys in Brown*, *Time & Tide* Vol. 21, No. 25 (22 June 1940) 665.

C.191   Theatre review of Robert Ardrey *Thunder Rock*, *Time & Tide* Vol. 21, No. 26 (29 June 1940) 691.

C.192   'England With the Knobs Off': review of Jack Hilton *English Ways*, *The Adelphi* Vol. XVI, No. 10 (July 1940) 430–431.

C.193   Review of A.J. Jenkinson *What Do Boys and Girls Read?*, *Life and Letters Today* Vol. 26, No. 35 (July 1940).

C.194   Review of Douglas Goldring *Facing the Odds*, *The Tribune* (5 July 1940) 17.

C.195   'Prophecies of Fascism': review of Jack London *The Iron Heel*, H.G. Wells *The Sleeper Wakes*, Aldous Huxley *Brave New World*, and Ernest Bramah *The Secret of the League*, *The Tribune* No. 185 (12 July 1940) 16–17.
        Notes
        CEJL II 30–33.
        See also C.203.

C.196   'On the Brink': review of Princess Paul Sapieha *Polish Profile*, *The New Statesman and Nation* (13 July 1940) 45–46.

C.197   Theatre review of Oscar Asche *Chu Chin Chow*, and Margaret Branford *Wages For Wives*, *Time & Tide* Vol. 21, No. 28 (13 July 1940) 735–736.

C.198   Theatre review of Vernon Sylviane *Women Aren't Angels*, *Time & Tide* Vol. 21, No. 30 (27 July 1940) 789.

C.199   Theatre review of George Bernard Shaw *The Devil's Disciple*, *Time & Tide* Vol. 21, No. 31 (3 August 1940) 808–809.

C.200   Review of A.J. Jenkinson *What Do Boys and Girls Read?*, *The Listener* Vol. 24, No. 604 (8 August 1940) 210–211.
        Notes
        Unsigned.
        Payment £2 12s 6d.

C.201   'A Soviet Farce With a Socialist Moral': review of Ilya Ilf and Eugene Petrov *Diamonds To Sit On* translated by E. Hill and D. Mudoe, Louis Branfield Cassell *Night in Bombay*, Eric Knight *Now Pray We For Our Country*, Ethel Mannin *Rolling In The Dew*, A.G. Street *A Crook in the Furrow*, and C.J. Cotliffe Heyne *The Adventures of Captain Kettle*, *The Little Red Captain*, *Captain Kettle, K.C.B.*, and *Further Adventures of Captain Kettle*, *The Tribune* No. 189 (9 August 1940) 16–17.

C.202   Theatre review of Clare Boothe *Margin for Error*, *Time & Tide* Vol. 21, No. 32 (10 August 1940) 829.

C.203   Reply to a letter to the Editor, *The Tribune* (16 August 1940) 22.
        Notes
        Reply to letter from E.W. Robson and M.M. Robson on Orwell's article 'Prophecies of Fascism'.
        See C.195.

C.204   'Books in General', *The New Statesman and Nation* (17 August 1940) 162.
        Notes
        Article on Charles Reade.
        Abridged version, 'A Desert Island You Mustn't Miss', *English Digest* 1 (March 1941).
        See C.253
        CEJL II 34–37.

C.205   Theatre review of Clifford Odets *Till the Day I Die*, *Time & Tide* Vol. 21, No. 33 (17 August 1940) 847–848.

C.206   'Life in London's Underworld': review of Mark Benney *The Big Wheel*, Erika Mann *The Lights Go Down*, and George and Weedon Grossmith *The Diary of a Nobody*, *The Tribune* No. 191 (23 August 1940) 18–19.

C.207   'The English Civil War': review of Christopher Hill *The English Revolution: 1640*, *The New Statesman and Nation* (24 August 1940) 193.

C.208   Theatre review of Winifred Holtby *Take Back Your Freedom*, and Frank Launder and Sidney Gilliat *The Body was Well Nourished*, *Time & Tide* Vol. 21, No. 34 (24 August 1940) 866.

C.209   Review of Francis Williams *War by Revolution*, *The Labour Book Service Bulletin* No. 8 (September 1940) 6.

C.210   Review of Sacheverell Sitwell *Poltergeists*, *Horizon* Vol. II, No. 9 (September 1940) 139–141.

C.211   Theatre review of J.B. Priestly *Cornelius*, the variety show *Applesauce*, and

Sutton Vane *Outward Bound*, *Time & Tide* Vol. 21, No. 36 (7 September 1940) 907–908.

C.212   'Propaganda in Novels': review of Upton Sinclair *World's End*, Phyllis Bottome *Masks and Faces*, and Paul Dukes *An Epic of the Gestapo*, *The Tribune* No. 194 (13 September 1940) 14–15.

C.213   'Holding Out': review of Emanuel Miller, ed. *The Neuroses in War*, and Edward Glover *Fear and Courage*, *The New Statesman and Nation* (14 September 1940) 269–270.

C.214   'Public Schoolboys': review of T.C. Worsley *Barbarians and Philistines: Democracy and the Public Schools*, *Time & Tide* Vol. 21, No. 37 (14 September 1940) 927–928.

C.215   'History Books': review of Robert Graves *Sergeant Lamb of the Ninth*, Constance W. Dodge *The Luck of Maclean*, C.S. Forester *The Earthly Paradise*, and Maurice Bethell Jones *The Wake of the Conquered*, *The New Statesman and Nation* Vol. XX (21 September 1940) 290–291.

C.216   Film review of *The Doctor Takes a Wife*, *Time & Tide* Vol. 21, No. 40 (5 October 1940) 986.

C.217   'Wishful Thinking and the Light Novel': review of P.G. Wodehouse *Quick Service*, Angela Thirkell *Cheerfulness Breaks In*, Olga L. Rosmanith *Passenger List*, Frank Baker *Miss Hargreaves*, and Damaris Arklow *Just As I Feared*, *The New Statesman and Nation* (19 October 1940) 384.

C.218   'Mis-Observation': review of Hadley Cantril *The Invasion From Mars*, *The New Statesman and Nation* (26 October 1940) 422, 424.

C.219   'My Country Right Or Left', *Folios of New Writing* No. 2 (Autumn 1940) 36–41.
   Notes
   Abridged version in *English Digest* Vol. 6, No. 3 (May 1941) 22–24.
   Full version in John Lehmann, ed. *The Pleasures of New Writing* (1952) [See B.2].
   CEJL I 535–540.

C.220   'Fiction and Life': review of John Masefield *Basilissa*, Basil Woon *Eyes West*, and William Faulkner *The Hamlet*, *Time & Tide* Vol. 21, No. 45 (9 November 1940) 1097.

C.221   'By-Words': review of Ernest Raymond *A Song of the Tide*, A.S.M. Hutchinson *He Looked for a City*, Mary Lutyens *Family Colouring*, and Susan Gillespie *They Went to Karathia*, *The New Statesman and Nation* (16 November 1940) 498–500.

C.222   Film review of *Waterloo Bridge*, *Time & Tide* Vol. 21, No. 47 (23 November 1940) 1139.

C.223   Film review of *The Lady in Question*, *Time & Tide* Vol. 21, No. 48 (30 November 1940) 1160.

C.224   'The Ruling Class', *Horizon* Vol. 2, No. 12 (December 1940) 318–323.
   Notes
   Reprinted as part of 'England Your England' in *Such, Such Were The Joys* 217–222, *England Your England*, *The Lion and the Unicorn*, *The Orwell Reader*, and *CEJL* II 67–73.

C.225   Review of Archibald Wavell *Allenby, a Study in Greatness*, *Horizon* Vol. 2, No. 12 (December 1940) 348, 350.

C.226   'New Novels': review of Nevil Shute *Landfall*, Albert Cohen *Nailcruncher* translated by Vyvyan Holland, and Peter Conway *A Dark Side Also*, *The New Statesman and Nation* (7 December 1940) 574.
   Notes
   Section on *Landfall* and *Nailcruncher* in *CEJL* II 44–46.

C.227   Film review of *The Gay Mrs Trexel*, *Time & Tide* Vol. 21, No. 49 (7 December 1940) 1184.

C.228   'At School and On Holiday': review of L.A.G. Strong *Wrong Foot Foremost*, Gunby Hadath *From Pillar to Post*, Michael Patrick *Tommy Hawke at School*,

M.E. Atkinson *Going Gangster*, Doris Twinn *The New Carthaginians*, A.R. Channel *Phantom Patrol*, Aubrey de Selincourt *Family Afloat*, and E.H. Young *Caravan Island*, *Time & Tide* Vol. 21, No. 49 (7 December 1940) Children's Christmas Supplement ii.

C.229 'Guerillas': review of Tom Wintringham *Armies of Freemen*, *The New Statesman and Nation* (14 December 1940) 632, 634.

C.230 Film review of *I Love You Again!*, and *The Great Dictator*, *Time & Tide* Vol. 21, No. 50 (14 December 1940) 1232.

> *Notes*
> A short review of *The Great Dictator* is printed here, with a note about a fuller review the next week.
> See C.233.

C.231 'The Proletarian Writer', *The Listener* Vol. 24, No. 623 (19 December 1940) 878–879.

> *Notes*
> A printed version of the discussion between George Orwell and Desmond Hawkins in the series 'The Writer in the Witness-Box', No. 10, broadcast in the BBC Home Service (6 December 1940, 7.40pm) [E.001].
> *CEJL* II 38–44.

C.232 'The Home Guard and You', *The Tribune* No. 208 (20 December 1940) 8–9.

C.233 Film review of *The Great Dictator*, *Time & Tide* Vol. 21, No. 51 (21 December 1940) 1250.

> *Notes*
> A fuller review than that of 14 December 1940.
> See C.230.

C.234 'Franco Spain': review of E. Allison Peers *The Spanish Dilemma*, and Charles Duff *A Key To Victory: Spain*, *Time & Tide* Vol. 21, No. 51 (21 December 1940) 1260–1261.

C.235 Film review of *A Date with Destiny*, *Time & Tide* Vol. 21, No. 52 (28 December 1940) 1272.

C.236 'Our Opportunity', *The Left News* No. 55 (January 1941) 1608–1612.

> *Notes*
> Reprinted as 'Patriots and Revolutionaries' in *The Betrayal of the Left* [B.5].

C.237 'New Novels': review of Arthur Koestler *Darkness At Noon*, John Mair *Never Come Back*, and W.A. Darlington *Alf's New Button*, *The New Statesman and Nation* (4 January 1941) 15–16.

C.238 Theatre review of William Shakespeare *The Merry Wives of Windsor*, and John L. Balderston and J.C. Squire *Berkeley Square*, *Time & Tide* Vol. 22, No. 1 (4 January 1941) 10–11.

C.239 'Don't Let Colonel Blimp Ruin the Home Guard', *Evening Standard* (8 January 1941) 5.

C.240 Theatre review of Herbert Farjeon's rearrangement of the revue *Diversion 2*, *Time & Tide* Vol. 22, No. 2 (11 January 1941) 30.

C.241 Film review of *They Knew What they Wanted*, *Spring Parade*, and *Gold Rush Maisie*, *Time & Tide* Vol. 22, No. 2 (11 January 1941) 30.

C.242 'Two Glimpses of the Moon': review of Kenneth Allott *Jules Verne: A Biography*, *The New Statesman and Nation* (18 January 1941) 64.

C.243 Film review of *Brigham Young*, and *Spellbound*, *Time & Tide* Vol. 22, No. 3 (18 January 1941) 49.

C.244 'New Novels': review of H.E. Bates *The Beauty of the Dead*, Glyn Jones, ed. *Welsh Short Stories*, T.O. Beachcroft *The Parents Left Alone*, and Kylie Tennant *The Battlers*, *The New Statesman and Nation* (25 January 1941) 89–90.

C.245 Film review of *Escape*, *Time & Tide* Vol. 22, No. 4 (25 January 1941) 66–67.

C.246 'Fascism and Democracy', *The Left News* (February 1941) 1637–1639.

Notes

Reprinted as 'Patriots and Revolutionaries', Chapter 8 of Victor Gollancz, ed. *The Betrayal of the Left* (1941) [B.5].

C.247   Theatre review of Peter Blackmore *The Blue Goose*, and J.M. Barrie *Dear Brutus*, *Time & Tide* Vol. 22, No. 5 (1 February 1941) 91–92.

C.248   Film review of *Quiet Wedding*, *Time & Tide* Vol. 22, No. 6 (8 February 1941) 108.

C.249   'The People's Army': review of Hugh Slater *Home Guard For Victory!*, *The New Statesman and Nation* (15 February 1941) 168.

C.250   Film review of *Dulcy*, *Eyes of the Navy*, *The Heart of Britain*, and *Unholy War*, *Time & Tide* Vol. 22, No. 7 (15 February 1941) 131–132.

C.251   'New Novels': review of John Llewelyn Rhys *England is My Village*, Nina Fedorova *The Family*, Dan Wickenden *Walk Like a Mortal*, and Bruce Marshall *Delilah Upside Down*, *The New Statesman and Nation* (22 February 1941) 190–192.

C.252   Film review of *Arise, My Love*, and *Third Finger, Left Hand*, *Time & Tide* Vol. 22, No. 8 (22 February 1941) 150, 152.

C.253   'A Desert Island You Mustn't Miss', *English Digest* Vol. 6, No. 1 (March 1941) 58–60.

Notes

Abridged version of 'Books in General', *The New Statesman and Nation* (17 August 1940).
See C.204.

C.254   Review of Hugh Slater *Home Guard For Victory!*, *Horizon* Vol. 3, No. 15 (March 1941) 219–221.

C.255   'London Letter', *Partisan Review* Vol. VIII, No. 2 (March–April 1941) 108–113.

Notes

On the backlash of a mood for social change; wartime morale; British Fascism; wartime intellectual life; air raids.
Dated 3 January 1941 by Orwell.
CEJL II 49–55.
From March 1941 until January 1949 Orwell wrote a regular column for *Partisan Review*, 'London Letter'. He was paid $2.00 per printed page, about $11.00 per letter.

C.256   'New Novels': review of Franz Hoellering *The Defenders* translated by L. Lewisohn, and Alfred Neumann *The Friends of the People* translated by Nora Wydenbruck, *The New Statesman and Nation* (15 March 1941) 278–280.

C.257   'A Roadman's Day', *Picture Post* (15 March 1941) 27–30.

C.258   'The Bayonet in War', *The Spectator* No. 5882 (21 March 1941) 309.

Notes

Letter to the Editor in reply to Janus's remarks on Orwell, *The Spectator* (21 February 1941) 193, and to A.C. Taylor's letter, *The Spectator* (7 March 1941) 253.

C.259   'Will Freedom Die With Capitalism?', *The Left News* (April 1941) 1682–1685.

C.260   'My Country Right Or Left', *English Digest* Vol. 6, No. 3 (May 1941) 22–24.

Notes

Abridged version of original publication in *Folios of New Writing* (Autumn 1940) [C.219].

C.261   Film review of *So Ends Our Night*, *Time & Tide* Vol. 22, No. 17 (26 April 1941) 345–346.

C.262   Theatre review of the revue *Black Vanities*, and Kim Peacock *Under One Roof*, *Time & Tide* Vol. 22, No. 18 (3 May 1941) 364.

C.263   Film review of *Little Men*, *Kitty Foyle*, and *Back Street*, *Time & Tide* Vol. 22, No. 19 (10 May 1941) 381.

C.264   Theatre review of Geoffrey Kerr *Cottage To Let*, *Time & Tide* Vol. 22, No. 20 (17 May 1941) 402.

C.265 Film review of H.G. Wells *Kipps*, *Time & Tide* Vol. 22, No. 20 (17 May 1941) 402.

C.266 Film review of *The Lady Eve*, *Honeymoon For Three*, and *Tugboat Annie Sails Again*, *Time & Tide* Vol. 22, No. 21 (24 May 1941) 441–442.

C.267 'The Frontiers of Art and Propaganda', *The Listener* Vol. 25, No. 646 (29 May 1941) 768–769.
Notes
The first of four talks on literary criticism, broadcast in the BBC Overseas Service (30 April 1941).
CEJL II 123–127 [E.003].

C.268 Film review of *This England*, and *I Married Adventure*, *Time & Tide* Vol. 22, No. 22 (31 May 1941) 463.

C.269 'Literary Criticism – II: Tolstoy and Shakespeare', *The Listener* Vol. 25, No. 647 (5 June 1941) 809–810.
Notes
The second of four talks on literary criticism, broadcast in the BBC Overseas Service (7 May 1941).
CEJL II 127–130 [E.004].

C.270 Film review of *Escape to Glory*, *Time & Tide* Vol. 22, No. 23 (7 June 1941) 481.

C.271 'Literary Criticism – III: The Meaning of a Poem', *The Listener* Vol. 25, No. 648 (12 June 1941) 841.
Notes
The third of four talks on literary criticism, broadcast in the BBC Overseas Service (14 May 1941) [E.005].
CEJL II 131–134.

C.272 Theatre review of Emlyn Williams *The Light of Heart*, *Time & Tide* Vol. 22, No. 24 (14 June 1941) 503.

C.273 Film review of *Bitter Sweet*, *Time & Tide* Vol. 22, No. 24 (14 June 1941) 503.

C.274 'Literary Criticism IV: Literature and Totalitarianism', *The Listener* Vol. 25, No. 649 (19 June 1941) 882.
Notes
The last of four talks on literary criticism, broadcast in the BBC Overseas Service (21 May 1941) [E.006].
Orwell delivered a version of this talk to the Oxford University Democratic Social Club on 23 May 1941.
This is the only one of these four BBC broadcasts for which a script survives. It is a carbon typescript, about twenty per cent longer than the version published in *The Listener*.
CEJL II 134–137.

C.275 Film review of *Nice Girl?*, *That Uncertain Feeling*, and *Cheers For Miss Bishop*, *Time & Tide* Vol. 22, No. 25 (21 June 1941) 523.

C.276 Theatre review of *Hommage aux Alliés*, *Time & Tide* Vol. 22, No. 26 (28 June 1941) 543.

C.277 Film review of *Atlantic Ferry*, *Time & Tide* Vol. 22, No. 26 (28 June 1941) 543.

C.278 'Spaniard In Spain': review of Arturo Barea *The Forge*, *Time & Tide* Vol. 22, No. 26 (28 June 1941) 544.

C.279 Film review of *Western Union*, and *Moon Over Burma*, *Time & Tide* Vol. 22, No. 27 (5 July 1941) 564.

C.280 Theatre review of Noel Coward *Blithe Spirit*, and William Shakespeare *The Taming of the Shrew*, *Time & Tide* Vol. 22, No. 28 (12 July 1941) 582.

C.281 'English Writing in Total War', *The New Republic* Vol. 105 (14 July 1941) 57–58.
Notes
Reprinted in *The New Republic* Vol. 131 (22 November 1954) 56–58.
See C.835.

C.282   Theatre review of William Shakespeare *King John*, *Time & Tide* Vol. 22, No. 29 (19 July 1941) 602.

C.283   Film review of *The Devil and Miss Jones*, and *The Flame of New Orleans*, *Time & Tide* Vol. 22, No. 29 (19 July 1941) 602.

C.284   'Dear Doktor Goebbels – Your British Friends are Feeding Fine!', *Daily Express* No. 12,842 (23 July 1941) 3.

   Notes

   Not in all editions. Orwell's article was definitely in the first edition, released at approximately 10.00pm on 22 July, and probably in the second edition and in all Scottish editions, but not in the third edition, where the latest war news about attacks on Russia required more space.

C.285   Review of Firozkhan Noon *India*, *The Listener* Vol. 26, No. 654 (24 July 1941) 136.

   Notes

   Unsigned.

   Payment £1 1s 0d.

C.286   'London Letter', *Partisan Review* Vol. VIII, No. 4 (July–August 1941) 315–323.

   Notes

   On late wartime London; the mining industry; pro-Russian feeling.

   Dated 15 April 1944 by Orwell, with a postscript dated 15 May 1941.

   CEJL II 112–123.

C.287   'Wells, Hitler and the World State', *Horizon* Vol. 4, No. 20 (August 1941) 133–139.

   Notes

   Critical Essays 83–88, *Dickens, Dali & Others* 115–123, *Collected Essays* 160–166, and *CEJL* II 139–145.

C.288   Theatre review of The Old Vic on tour, the musical comedy *Lady Behave*, *New Ambassadors Revue*, and *This Sceptred Isle*, *Time & Tide* Vol. 22, No. 31 (2 August 1941) 645.

C.289   Theatre review of W.O. Somin *Close Quarters*, *Time & Tide* Vol. 22, No. 32 (9 August 1941) 666.

C.290   Film review of *High Sierra*, *Time & Tide* Vol. 22, No. 32 (9 August 1941) 666.

C.291   Film review of *One Night in Lisbon*, and *Jeannie*, *Time & Tide* Vol. 22, No. 33 (16 August 1941) 687.

C.292   Film review of *South of Suez*, *Time & Tide* Vol. 22, No. 34 (23 August 1941) 708.

C.293   'The Art of Donald McGill', *Horizon* Vol. 4, No. 21 (September 1941) 153–163.

   Notes

   A shortened version also published in *The Strand Magazine* (August 1943) as 'Those Seaside Postcards'.

   See C.349.

   Critical Essays 89–99, *Dickens, Dali & Others* 124–139, *A Collection of Essays* 104–116, *Collected Essays* 167–178, *Decline of the English Murder* 142–154, and *CEJL* II 155–165.

C.294   Review of Arturo Barea *The Forge* translated by Peter Chalmers Mitchell, *Horizon* Vol. 4, No. 21 (September 1941) 214–217.

C.295   'No, Not One': review of Alex Comfort *No Such Liberty*, *The Adelphi* Vol. 18, No. 1 (October 1941) 4–8.

   Notes

   CEJL II 165–171.

C.296   'Why Not War Writers? A Manifesto', *Horizon* Vol. 4, No. 22 (October 1941) 236–239.

   Notes

   Signed by Arthur Calder-Marshall, Cyril Connolly, Bonamy Dobrée, Tom Harrisson, Arthur Koestler, Alun Lewis, George Orwell, and Stephen Spender. See C.299.

C.297 'Questionnaire: Socialists Answer Our Questions on the War', *Left* No. 61 (November 1941) 241–246.
   Notes
   Orwell's responses to thirty-five questions are laid out in tabular form.
   Left was formerly *Left Forum*, and before that *Controversy*.

C.298 'London Letter', *Partisan Review* Vol. VIII, No. 6 (November–December 1941) 491–498.
   Notes
   On the Anglo-Soviet alliance; the Home Guard.
   Dated 17 August 1941 by Orwell.
   CEJL II 145–154.

C.299 'Why Not War Writers?', *Horizon* Vol. IV, No. 24 (December 1941) 437–438.
   Notes
   Letter to the Editor.
   See C.296.
   Signed: 'Combatant'

C.300 'Men and Politics': review of Louis Fischer *Men and Politics*, *Now and Then* No. 70, War-time issue No. 7 (Christmas 1941) 2.

C.301 'Nicholas Moore vs. George Orwell', *Partisan Review* Vol. IX, No. 1 (January–February 1942) 74–75.
   Notes
   Letter, dated 23 September 1941, in reply to Moore's attack on Orwell's 'London Letter', *Partisan Review* (July–August 1941) 315–323.

C.302 'Rudyard Kipling', *Horizon* Vol. 5, No. 26 (February 1942) 111–125.
   Notes
   Critical Essays 100–113, *Dickens, Dali & Others* 140–160, *A Collection of Essays* 116–132, *The Orwell Reader* 271–283, *Collected Essays* 179–194, *Decline of the English Murder* 45–62, and *CEJL* II 184–197.
   In his 1942 Diary, Orwell noted, *Horizon* was nearly stopped from getting its extra paper to print copies for export on the strength of my article on Kipling.'[8]

C.303 'India Next', *The Observer* (22 February 1942) 4.
   Notes
   Unsigned.
   Orwell began writing regularly for *The Observer*, although not always happily. In 1946, describing the editorial practices of the *Evening Standard*, Orwell added, '*The Observer* . . . habitually cuts my articles without consulting me if there is a last-minute shortage of space.'[9]

C.304 'Mood of the Moment', *The Observer* (8 March 1942) 6.
   Notes
   Unsigned.

C.305 'The Rediscovery of Europe', *The Listener* Vol. XXVII, No. 688 (19 March 1942) 370–372.
   Notes
   A talk broadcast in the BBC Eastern Service (10 March 1942) [E033].
   Reprinted in *Talking to India* 41–50 [B.18].
   CEJL II 197–207.

C.306 'London Letter', *Partisan Review* Vol. IX, No. 2 (March–April 1942) 153–159.
   Notes
   On identifying the enemy; the Allies; defeatism and German propaganda; the quiet literary scene; wartime privations.
   Dated 1 January 1942 by Orwell.
   CEJL II 175–183.
   See also C.317 and C.318.

C.307   'The Rediscovery of Europe', *The Listener* Vol. 27, No. 691 (9 April 1942) 469.
        Notes
        Letter to the Editor in reply to Robert Nichols's letter, *The Listener* (26 March
        1942) 407.
C.308   'Mood of the Moment', *The Observer* (19 April 1942) 7.
        Notes
        Unsigned.
C.309   'An American Critic': review of Edmund Wilson *The Wound and the Bow*, *The
        Observer* No. 7876 (10 May 1942) 3.
C.310   'The Sword and the Sickle', *Times Literary Supplement* (23 May 1942) 259.
        Notes
        Letter to the Editor on the review of Mulk Raj Anand *The Sword and the
        Sickle*, *Times Literary Supplement* (2 May 1942) 221.
C.311   Review of Mulk Raj Anand *The Sword and the Sickle*, *Horizon* Vol. 6, No. 31
        (July 1942) 70–72.
        Notes
        CEJL II 216–219.
C.312   'The British Crisis: A Letter From London', *Partisan Review* Vol. IX, No. 4
        (July–August 1942) 274–280.
        Notes
        On social equality; political leadership; the Russian alliance; the need for
        social and economic change.
        Dated 8 May 1942 by Orwell.
        CEJL II 207–216.
C.313   'What They Say About Bartlett and Priestley', *Picture Post* (11 July 1942) 2.
        Notes
        Letter in response to J.B. Priestley's article, 'Britain's Silent Revolution'
        (27 June 1942).
C.314   'Portrait of the General': review of Philippe Barrès *Charles de Gaulle*, *The
        Observer* No. 7888 (2 August 1942) 3.
C.315   'Portrait of an Addict': review of H.R. Robinson *A Modern de Quincey*, *The
        Observer* No. 7894 (13 September 1942) 3.
C.316   'Thomas Hardy Looks at War', *Tribune* No. 299 (18 September 1942) 13.
        Notes
        From 9 January 1942 *The Tribune* became *Tribune*.
        Article on *The Dynasts*.
        There had been almost a two year gap since Orwell last wrote for *Tribune*, in
        December 1940. Orwell later wrote,
        I became aware of *Tribune* again when I was working in the Eastern Service of
        the BBC. It was now an almost completely different paper. It had a different
        make-up, cost sixpence, was orientated chiefly towards foreign policy, and was
        rapidly acquiring a new public which mostly belonged, I should say, to the out-
        at-elbow middle class. Its prestige among the BBC personnel was very strik-
        ing. In the libraries where commentators went to prime themselves it was one
        of the most sought-after periodicals, not only because it was largely written
        by people who knew something at first hand about Europe, but because it was
        then the only paper of any standing which criticised the Government.[10]
C.317   'Pacifism and the War: A Controversy', *Partisan Review* Vol. IX, No. 5 (September–
        October 1942) 419–21.
        Notes
        Letter, dated 12 July 1942 by Orwell, in reply to D.S. Savage, George Woodcock,
        and Alex Comfort, on remarks in Orwell's 'London Letter', *Partisan Review*
        Vol. IX (March–April 1942) 153–159.
        See C.306.
        The complete correspondence is reprinted in *CEJL* II 220–230.

C.318 'Social Credit and Fascism', *Partisan Review* Vol. IX, No. 5 (September–October 1942) 446.
Notes
Reply to a letter to the Editor from Gorham Munson on Orwell's comments in 'London Letter', *Partisan Review* Vol. IX (March–April 1942) 153–159.
See C.306 and C.317.

C.319 'Points of View': review of T.S. Eliot 'Burnt Norton', 'East Coker', and 'The Dry Salvages', *Poetry* (London) Vol. 2, No. 7 (October–November 1942) 56–59.
Notes
Reprinted in *Little Reviews Anthology* (1943) 212–219 [B.19].
CEJL II 236–242.

C.320 'Background of French Morocco', *Tribune* No. 308 (20 November 1942) 10–11.
Notes
Abridged version, 'Morocco is Poor But Happy', *World Digest* (February 1943) 19–20.
See C.331.

C.321 'Perfide Albion': review of B.H. Liddell Hart *The British Way in Warfare*, *The New Statesman and Nation* (21 November 1942) 342–343.
Notes
CEJL II 246–249.

C.322 'Too Hard on Humanity', *The Listener* Vol. 28 (26 November 1942) 692–693.
Notes
An imaginary interview between George Orwell and Jonathan Swift, broadcast in the BBC Overseas Service 6 November 1942.
See E.132.
Reprinted as 'Jonathan Swift, an Imaginary Interview' in *The War Broadcasts* 112–116.

C.323 'In the Darlan Country', *The Observer* No. 7905 (29 November 1942) 4.

C.324 'London Letter', *Partisan Review* Vol. IX, No. 6 (November–December 1942) 494–498.
Notes
On the state of frozen crisis; left wing politics; minor social changes; wartime food, clothes, publications, American soldiers.
Dated 29 August 1942 by Orwell.
CEJL II 230–236.

C.325 'The End of Henry Miller': review of Henry Miller *The Colossus of Maroussi*, *Tribune* No. 310 (4 December 1942) 18–19.
Notes
See C.326.

C.326 Reply to a letter to the Editor, *Tribune* No. 312 (18 December 1942) 12–13.
Notes
Response to Nicholas Moore's letter to the Editor, published in this issue, on Orwell's review 'The End of Henry Miller', *Tribune* (4 December 1942) 18–19.
See C.325.

C.327 Review of Herbert Lewis Samuel *An Unknown Land*, *The Listener* (24 December 1942) 826.
Notes
Unsigned.
Payment £2 2s 0d.

C.328 Review of V.K. Narayana Menon *The Development of William Butler Yeats*, *Horizon* Vol. 7, No. 37 (January 1943) 67–71.
Notes
Critical Essays 114–119, *Dickens, Dali & Others* 161–169, *Collected Essays* 195–201, and *CEJL* II 271–276.

C.329   'Pamphlet Literature': review of fifteen current pamphlets, *The New Statesman and Nation* (9 January 1943) 23–24.
　　　　Notes
　　　　CEJL II 283–285.

C.330   Review of Mass Observation *The Pub and the People*, *The Listener* (21 January 1943) 89.
　　　　Notes
　　　　Unsigned.
　　　　Payment £2 2s 0d.
　　　　CEJL III 43–44.

C.331   'Morocco is Poor But Happy', *World Digest* (February 1943) 19–20.
　　　　Notes
　　　　Abridged version of 'Background of French Morocco', *Tribune* (20 November 1942) 10–11.
　　　　See C.320.

C.332   'The Truth about "Truth"', *Picture Post* (27 February 1943) 3.
　　　　Notes
　　　　Letter to the Editor.

C.333   'Poetry and Prejudice', *Times Literary Supplement* (6 March 1943) 115.
　　　　Notes
　　　　Letter to the Editor on the review of *Le Crève Coeur*, *Times Literary Supplement* (20 February 1943) 87.

C.334   'Letter To An Indian': review of Mulk Raj Anand *Letters From India*, *Tribune* (19 March 1943) 15.

C.335   'Poetry and Prejudice', *Times Literary Supplement* (27 March 1943) 151.
　　　　Notes
　　　　Letter to the Editor in reply to David Cecil's letter, *Times Literary Supplement* (20 March 1943) 139.

C.336   'A Letter From England', *Partisan Review* Vol. X, No. 2 (March–April 1943) 178–183.
　　　　Notes
　　　　On the political move to the right; Anglo-American relations and anti-American feeling; political factions within the churches.
　　　　Dated 3 January 1943 by Orwell.
　　　　CEJL II 276–283.

C.337   Background note to Robert Duval's article, 'Whitehall's Road To Mandalay', *Tribune* (2 April 1943) 12.

C.338   'Not Enough Money', *Tribune* (2 April 1943) 15.
　　　　Notes
　　　　On George Gissing.

C.339   'The Way of a Poet': review of V.K. Narayana Menon *The Development of William Butler Yeats*, *Time & Tide* (17 April 1943) 325–326.

C.340   'Burma', *Tribune* (23 April 1943) 13.
　　　　Notes
　　　　Reply to two letters headed 'Burma's Status', *Tribune* (16 April 1943) 13.

C.341   'Speaking to Europe': review of Tangye Lean *Voices in the Darkness*, *Tribune* (30 April 1943) 11.

C.342   'Three Years of Home Guard. Unique Symbol of Stability', *The Observer* No. 7928 (9 May 1943) 3.

C.343   'Nationalism', *Tribune* (14 May 1943) 14.
　　　　Notes
　　　　Letter to the Editor in reply to Keidrych Rhys's letter, 'Nationalism', *Tribune* (7 May 1943) 14.

C.344   'Profile: Sir Richard Acland', *The Observer* No. 7930 (23 May 1943) 3.

Notes
Unsigned.

C.345   Review of D.W. Brogan *The English People*, *The Listener* (27 May 1943) 637.
Notes
Unsigned.
Payment £2 12s 6d.

C.346   'Literature and The Left', *Tribune* (4 June 1943) 19.
Notes
Reprinted in Elizabeth Thomas, ed. *Tribune* 21 (1958) 91–93.
CEJL II 292–294.

C.347   'As One Non-Combatant To Another: A Letter to "Obadiah Hornbooke"', *Tribune* (18 June 1943) 18–19.
Notes
Poem in reply to Alex Comfort's poem, 'Letter to an American Visitor', *Tribune* (4 June 1943) 18–19.
Both poems are reprinted in *CEJL* II 294–303.
See C.437.

C.348   'Young Writers': review of John Lehmann, ed. *New Writing and Daylight*, *The Spectator* (30 July 1943) 110.
Notes
Completed 12 July 1943.
Payment £2 12s 6d.

C.349   'Those Seaside Postcards', *The Strand Magazine* Vol. 105 (August 1943) 48–52.
Notes
Payment £8 8s 0d.
A shortened version of 'The Art of Donald McGill', *Horizon* (September 1941) 153–163.
See C.293.

C.350   'London Letter', *Partisan Review* Vol. X, No. 4 (July–August 1943) 345–349.
Notes
Completed 23 May 1943.
Payment £2 10s 0d.
On British Communism; the growth of British Socialism; anti-semitism; wartime hardships.
CEJL II 286–292.

C.351   'War In Burma': review of George Rodger *Red Moon Rising*, and Alfred Wagg *A Million Died!*, *The New Statesman and Nation* (14 August 1943) 109–110.
Notes
Completed 5 August 1943.
Payment £3 14s 0d.

C.352   'Where To Go – But How?': review of Edward Hulton *The New Age*, *The Observer* No. 7942 (15 August 1943) 3.
Notes
Completed 9 August 1943.
Payment £5 5s 0d.

C.353   'Gandhi in Mayfair': review of Lionel Fielden *Beggar My Neighbour*, *Horizon* Vol. 8, No. 45 (September 1943) 210–216.
Notes
Completed 15 July 1943. Payment £6 6s 0d.
Reprinted in *Partisan Review* (Winter 1944) 106–114.
See C.373.
CEJL II 306–315.

C.354   'The Faith of Thomas Mann': review of Thomas Mann *Order of the Day*, *Tribune* (10 September 1943) 13.

Notes
Completed 16 August 1943.
Payment £2 2s 0d.

C.355   'Paris Is Not France': review of Louis Lévy *France Is A Democracy*, *The Observer* No. 7946 (12 September 1943) 3.
Notes
Completed 30 August 1943.
Payment £6 6s 0d.

C.356   'Revolt In The Urban Desert': review of Harold J. Laski *Reflections On The Revolution Of Our Time*, *The Observer* No. 7950 (10 October 1943) 3.
Notes
Completed 4 October 1943.
Payment £6 6s 0d.

C.357   Review of C.E.M. Joad *The Adventures of a Young Soldier in Search of a Better World*, *The Listener* (21 October 1943).
Notes
Payment £2 2s 0d.

C.358   'Who Are the War Criminals?': review of Cassius *The Trial Of Mussolini*, *Tribune* (22 October 1943) 6–7.
Notes
Completed 18 October 1943.
Payment £5 5s 0d.
CEJL II 319–325.

C.359   'Out Of Step': review of Douglas Reed *Lest We Forget*, and Sidney Dark *I Sit and I Think and I Wonder*, *The Observer* No. 7954 (7 November 1943) 3.
Notes
Completed 5 November 1943.
Payment £5 5s 0d.

C.360   'Brailsford on India': review of Henry Noel Brailsford *Subject India*, *The Nation* [New York] Vol. 157, No. 21 (20 November 1943) 588–589.
Notes
Completed 27 October 1943.
Payment £4 4s 0d.

C.361   'Mark Twain – The Licensed Jester', *Tribune* (26 November 1943) 14–15.
Notes
Completed 22 November 1943.
Payment £2 2s 0d.
CEJL II 325–329.
Orwell resigned from the BBC on 24 November 1943 and by the end of the month had taken up his new job as literary editor of *Tribune*. He later wrote, I went on being literary editor, as well as writing the "As I Please" column, until the beginning of 1945. It was interesting, but it is not a period that I look back on with pride. The fact is that I am no good at editing. I hate planning ahead, and I have a psychical or even physical inability to answer letters. My most essential memory of that time is of pulling out a drawer here and a drawer there, finding it in each case to be stuffed with letters and manuscripts which ought to have been dealt with weeks earlier, and hurriedly shutting it up again. Also I have a fatal tendency to accept manuscripts which I know very well are too bad to be printed. It is questionable whether anyone who has had long experience as a free-lance journalist ought to become an editor. It is too like taking a convict out of his cell and making him governor of the prison.[11]

C.362   'Hidden Spain': review of E. Allison Peers *Spain in Eclipse*, and Lawrence Dundas *Behind The Spanish Mask*, *The Observer* No. 7957 (28 November 1943) 3.

Notes

Completed 10 November 1943.

Payment £5 5s 0d.

C.363 'As I Please', *Tribune* No. 362 (3 December 1943) 10.

Notes

On anti-American feeling; Fascism; Mark Rutherford.

CEJL III 54–57.

From December 1943 until February 1945 Orwell was literary editor of *Tribune*, and wrote a regular weekly article, 'As I Please'. These articles are not always reprinted in full in *CEJL*.

C.364 'Freud or Marx?': review of Arthur Koestler *Arrival and Departure*, and Philip Jordan *Jordan's Tunis Diary*, *Manchester Evening News* (9 December 1943) 2.

Notes

The two reviews were completed on 27 November 1943 and 8 December 1943 respectively.

Payment £8 8s 0d.

Orwell's fortnightly book review appeared in the *Manchester Evening News* from December 1943 until November 1946, usually under the title 'Life, People and Books'.

C.365 'As I Please', *Tribune* (10 December 1943) 12.

Notes

On negroes in the USA; exploitation of Asian and African workers; standards of living; insulting racial nicknames.

C.366 'As I Please', *Tribune* No. 364 (17 December 1943) 11.

Notes

On anti-American and anti-British feeling; political predictions; Lamprière's *Classical Dictionary*.

CEJL III 58–60.

See C.372.

C.367 'Wandering Star': review of W.H. Davies *Collected Poems*, *The Observer* No. 7960 (19 December 1943) 3.

Notes

Completed 13 December 1943.

Payment £7 7s 0d.

CEJL III 61–62.

C.368 'Interglossa – Make Do and Talk With 750 Words': review of Lancelot Hogben *Interglossa*, and Compton Mackenzie *Mr Roosevelt*, *Manchester Evening News* (23 December 1943) 2.

Notes

Completed 20 December 1943.

Payment £8 8s 0d.

C.369 'As I Please', *Tribune* (24 December 1943) 11–12.

Notes

On neo-pessimist writers; exterminating the Germans; 'My country, right or wrong'.

CEJL III 63–65.

C.370 'Can Socialists Be Happy?', *Tribune* No. 365 (24 December 1943) 6–7.

Notes

Signed: John Freeman.

C.371 'As I Please', *Tribune* No. 366 (31 December 1943) 11–12.

Notes

On war guilt; ugly architecture; Shaw and the National Anthem; *Old Moore's Almanac*; the creation of the world.

CEJL III 65–68.

C.372 'People's Convention' *Tribune* (31 December 1943) 13.

Notes

Letter to the Editor in reply to another from D.N. Pritt criticising Orwell's 'As I Please', *Tribune* (17 December 1943) 11.

See C.366.

C.373 'Gandhi in Mayfair': review of Lionel Fielden *Beggar My Neighbour*, *Partisan Review* Vol. XI, No. 1 (Winter 1944) 106–114.

Notes

Previously published in *Horizon* (September 1943) 210–216.

See C.353.

C.374 'In the Firing Line': review of K.C. Chorley *Armies and the Art of Revolution*, *The Observer* No. 7962 (2 January 1944) 3.

Notes

Completed 27 December 1943.

Payment £7 7s 0d.

C.375 'Wise Ruler and Great Fighter': review of Field Marshall Viscount Wavell *Allenby in Egypt*, *Manchester Evening News* No. 23,288 (6 January 1944) 2.

Notes

Completed 4 January 1944.

Payment £8 8s 0d.

C.376 'As I Please', *Tribune* No. 367 (7 January 1944) 11–12.

Notes

On the New Year's Honours List; surface shelters; the short story.

CEJL III 71–73.

C.377 'As I Please', *Tribune* No. 368 (14 January 1944) 11.

Notes

On binding magazines; James Burnham's *Managerial Revolution*.

CEJL III 73–74.

See C.401.

C.378 'Tapping the Wheels': review of C.K. Allen *Democracy and the Individual*, and R. George Stapledon *Disraeli and the New Age*, *The Observer* (16 January 1944) 3.

Notes

Completed 14 January 1944.

Payment £7 7s 0d.

C.379 'Why Machiavellis of To-day Fall Down': review of James Burnham *The Machiavellians*, *Manchester Evening News* No. 23,300 (20 January 1944) 2.

Notes

Completed 19 January 1944.

Payment £8 8s 0d.

C.380 'As I Please', *Tribune* No. 369 (21 January 1944) 10.

Notes

On the BBC; Woolworth's roses.

CEJL III 82–83.

See C.386.

C.381 'Memories of the Blitz', *Tribune* (21 January 1944) 18.

Notes

Poem.

Completed 17 January 1944.

Payment 10s 6d.

C.382 'As I Please', *Tribune* No. 370 (28 January 1944) 10.

Notes

Indians and military service; Ezra Pound; old wives' tales; an international language.

CEJL III 83–86.

C.383 'Chosen People': review of Joshua Trachtenberg *The Devil and the Jews*, and Edmond Fleg *Why I Am A Jew* translated by Victor Gollancz, *The Observer* No. 7966 (30 January 1944) 3.

    Notes

    Completed 26 January 1944.

    Payment £7 7s 0d.

C.384 'All That is Best in Mark Twain': review of Mark Twain *The Adventures of Tom Sawyer* and *The Adventures of Huckleberry Finn*, and The Countess of Oxford and Asquith *Off The Record*, *Manchester Evening News* No. 23,312 (3 February 1944) 2.

    Notes

    Completed 2 February 1944.

    Payment £8 8s 0d.

C.385 'As I Please', *Tribune* (4 February 1944) 11–12.

    Notes

    On writing history; clothes snobbery; comic draughtsmanship.

    CEJL III 87–89.

C.386 Reply to a letter to the editor, *Tribune* No. 371 (4 February 1944) 14.

    Notes

    Reply to response to his comments on Woolworth's roses, *Tribune* (21 January 1944) 10.

    See C.380.

C.387 'As I Please', *Tribune* No. 372 (11 February 1944) 10–11.

    Notes

    On anti-Semitism; Anthony Trollope's *Autobiography*; maps.

    CEJL III 89–93.

C.388 'A Hundred Up', *The Observer* No. 7968 (13 February 1944) 3.

    Notes

    Completed 9 February 1944.

    Payment £7 7s 0d.

    On the centenary of Charles Dickens's *Martin Chuzzlewit*.

    CEJL III 93–95.

C.389 'Elisabet Ney – Feminist and Mad King's Sculptress': review of Jan Fortune and Jean Burton *Elisabet Ney*, *Manchester Evening News* No. 23,324 (17 February 1944) 2.

    Notes

    Completed 4 January 1944.

    Payment £8 8s 0d.

C.390 'As I Please', *Tribune* (18 February 1944) 11–12.

    Notes

    On post-war housing; clothes rationing; *Punch*.

C.391 'As I Please', *Tribune* No. 374 (25 February 1944) 10–11.

    Notes

    On commercial fiction; new ideas.

    CEJL III 96–98.

    See C.396.

C.392 'Utmost Edge': review of Alfred Noyes *The Edge of the Abyss*, *The Observer* No. 7970 (27 February 1944) 3.

    Notes

    Completed 21 February 1944.

    Payment £7 7s 0d.

    CEJL III 99–101.

C.393 'Elephantine Crossword or Masterpiece?': review of Harry Levin *James Joyce*, *Manchester Evening News* No. 23,336 (2 March 1944) 2.

Notes
Completed 28 February 1944.
Payment £8 8s 0d.

C.394 'As I Please', *Tribune* No. 375 (3 March 1944) 10–11.
Notes
On life after death; *The Cornhill Magazine*.
CEJL III 101–104.

C.395 'As I Please', *Tribune* No. 376 (10 March 1944) 10.
Notes
On Derrick Leon *Life of Tolstoy*; Gladys Storey *Dickens and Daughter*; Harry Levin *James Joyce*; unpublished autobiography of Salvador Dali.
CEJL III 105–108.

C.396 Reply to a letter to the Editor, *Tribune* No. 376 (10 March 1944) 14.
Notes
On Orwell's comments on commercial fiction, *Tribune* (25 February 1944) 10.
See C.391.

C.397 'Wavell on Helicon': review of A.P. Wavell, ed. *Other Men's Flowers*, *The Observer* No. 7972 (12 March 1944) 3.
Notes
Completed 9 March 1944.
Payment £5 5s 0d.

C.398 'As I Please', *Tribune* No. 377 (17 March 1944) 11–12.
Notes
On Marxist English.
CEJL III 108–111.

C.399 'Countryman's World': review of William Beach Thomas *The Way of a Countryman*, *Manchester Evening News* No. 23,354 (23 March 1944) 2.
Notes
Completed 22 March 1944.
Payment £8 8s 0d.

C.400 'As I Please', *Tribune* No. 378 (24 March 1944) 2.
Notes
On Fascism.
CEJL III 111–114.

C.401 Reply to a letter to the Editor, *Tribune* No. 378 (24 March 1944) 14.
Notes
On Orwell's comments on *The Managerial Revolution*, *Tribune* (14 January 1944) 11.
See C.377.

C.402 'Old Master': review of Derrick Leon *Tolstoy: His Life and Work*, *The Observer* No. 7974 (26 March 1944) 3.
Notes
Completed 20 March 1944.
Payment £5 5s 0d.

C.403 'As I Please', *Tribune* No. 379 (31 March 1944) 11–12.
Notes
On war criminals.
CEJL III 114–117.

C.404 'London Letter', *Partisan Review* Vol. XI, No. 2 (Spring 1944) 138–144.
Notes
Completed 15 January 1944.
Payment £3 10s 0d.
On Parliament and the monarchy.
CEJL III 74–82.

C.405 'Beneath Friendly Skies': review of Maurice Collis *She Was a Queen*, and Margaret Mead *Coming of Age in Samoa*, *Manchester Evening News* No. 23,366 (6 April 1944) 2.
  Notes
  Completed 5 April 1944.
  Payment £8 8s 0d.

C.406 'As I Please', *Tribune* No. 380 (7 April 1944) 10.
  Notes
  On wartime newspapers and the radio.

C.407 'Grounds For Dismay': review of F.A. Hayek *The Road To Serfdom*, and K. Zilliacus *The Mirror of the Past*, *The Observer* No. 7976 (9 April 1944) 3.
  Notes
  Completed 3 April 1944.
  Payment £7 7s 0d.
  Notes
  CEJL III 117–119.

C.408 'As I Please', *Tribune* No. 381 (14 April 1944) 11–12.
  Notes
  On population changes; a cricket incident; life after death.
  CEJL III 119–122.
  See C.424.

C.409 'The English Ritual': review of Edmund Blunden *Cricket Country*, *Manchester Evening News* No. 23,377 (20 April 1944) 2.
  Notes
  Completed 19 April 1944.
  Payment £8 8s 0d.
  CEJL III 47–50.

C.410 'As I Please', *Tribune* No. 382 (21 April 1944) 12.
  Notes
  On radio and newspapers; foreign words used in English.
  CEJL III 128–131.

C.411 'Power House': review of Hugh Kingsmill *The Poisoned Crown*, *The Observer* No. 7978 (23 April 1944) 3.
  Notes
  Completed 17 April 1944.
  Payment £7 7s 0d.

C.412 'As I Please', *Tribune* No. 383 (28 April 1944) 10.
  Notes
  On dictatorial government; women's cosmetics.
  CEJL III 131–134.

C.413 'Population Statistics': letter to the Editor, *Tribune* No. 383 (28 April 1944) 11–12.
  Notes
  Reply to letters from 'Statistician' and G.W. Gower.

C.414 'General de Gaulle': review of Alfred Hessenstein *A Giant in the Age of Steel: The Story of General de Gaulle*, *Manchester Evening News* No. 23,390 (5 May 1944) 2.
  Notes
  Completed 3 May 1944.
  Payment £8 8s 0d.

C.415 'As I Please', *Tribune* No. 384 (5 May 1944) 10.
  Notes
  On I.A. Richards *Practical Criticism*; pheasant protection; short story competition.
  CEJL III 143–145.

C.416 'All Change Here': review of J.R.M. Brumwell, ed. *This Changing World*, Julian Huxley *On Living In A Revolution*, and various authors *Reshaping Man's Heritage*, *The Observer* No. 7982 (7 May 1944) 3.

Notes
Completed 2 May 1944.
Payment £7 7s 0d.

C.417   'As I Please', *Tribune* No. 385 (12 May 1944) 10–11.
Notes
On effects of modern inventions; price increases; realism in politics.
CEJL III 145–148.
See C.421.

C.418   'Empire and India': review of Louis Fischer *Empire*, *The Nation* Vol. 158, No. 20 (13 May 1944) 572–573.
Notes
Completed 15 April 1944.
Payment £2 10s 0d.

C.419   'An Irish Tragedy': review of St John Ervine *Parnell*, *Manchester Evening News* No. 23,401 (18 May 1944) 2.
Notes
Completed 17 May 1944.
Payment £8 8s 0d.

C.420   'As I Please', *Tribune* No. 386 (19 May 1944) 11.
Notes
On limiting war; prejudices.
CEJL III 150–153.
See C.433.

C.421   'Inventions and Progress': reply to a letter to the Editor, *Tribune* No. 386 (19 May 1944) 14–15.
Notes
Reply to J.F. Horrabin's letter on Orwell's article on the misuse of modern inventions in *Tribune* (12 May 1944) 10–11.
See C.417.

C.422   'Vessel Of Wrath': review of H.G. Wells *'42 to '44: A Contemporary Memoir upon Human Behaviour During the Crisis of the World Revolution*, *The Observer* No. 7982 (21 May 1944) 3.
Notes
Completed 16 May 1944.
Payment £7 7s 0d.

C.423   'As I Please', *Tribune* No. 387 (26 May 1944) 12.
Notes
On anti-British feeling; loneliness of town life.
CEJL III 153–156.

C.424   Reply to a letter to the Editor, *Tribune* (26 May 1944) 14.
Notes
Reply to A.M. Currie's letter on Orwell's mis-attribution of some verses of G.K. Chesterton, *Tribune* (14 April 1944) 11–12.
See C.408.

C.425   'Are Books Too Dear?', *Manchester Evening News* No. 23,413 (1 June 1944) 2.
Notes
Completed 30 May 1944.
Payment £8 8s 0d.
Reprinted in *The News & Book Trade Review and Stationers' Gazette* (16 September 1944).
See C.463.
Abridged version in *Synopsis* (Autumn 1944).
See C.469.

C.426   'As I Please', *Tribune* No. 388 (2 June 1944) 12.
        Notes
        On propaganda; names; short stories; Babylonian marriage customs.
        CEJL III 165–168.

C.427   'Survey of "Civvy Street"': review of Mass Observation *The Journey Home*, *The
        Observer* No. 7984 (4 June 1944) 4.
        Notes
        Completed 30 May 1944.
        Payment £7 7s 0d.

C.428   'As I Please', *Tribune* No. 389 (9 June 1944) 13.
        Notes
        On book reviewing; keeping quiet.
        CEJL III 168–170.

C.429   'Behind the Ranges': review of Gordon S. Seagrave *Burma Surgeon*, and Horace
        Alexander *India Since Cripps*, *The Observer* No. 7985 (11 June 1944) 3.
        Notes
        Completed 7 June 1944.
        Payment £7 7s 0d.

C.430   'Colour Bar Candour': review of William Russell *Robert Cain*, *Manchester
        Evening News* No. 23,425 (15 June 1944) 2.
        Notes
        Completed 13 June 1944.
        Payment £8 8s 0d.

C.431   'As I Please', *Tribune* No. 390 (16 June 1944) 10–11.
        Notes
        On the 'Brains Trust'; *Your MP*; American magazines.
        CEJL III 170–172.

C.432   'As I Please', *Tribune* No. 391 (23 June 1944) 11–12.
        Notes
        Anatole France; Catholic propaganda.
        CEJL III 172–174.

C.433   Reply to a letter to the Editor, *Tribune* No. 391 (23 June 1944) 13–14.
        Notes
        Response to Vera Brittain's letter on Orwell's article on humanising war,
        Tribune (19 May 1944) 11.
        See C.420.

C.434   'Temperature Chart': review of L.L. Schucking *The Sociology of Literary Taste*,
        The Observer No. 7987 (25 June 1944) 3.
        Notes
        Completed 22 June 1944.
        Payment £7 7s 0d.

C.435   'Sweated Woman Labour': review of Hilda Martindale *From One Generation to
        Another*, *Manchester Evening News* No. 23,437 (29 June 1944) 2.
        Notes
        Completed 28 June 1944.
        Payment £8 8s 0d.

C.436   'As I Please', *Tribune* No. 392 (30 June 1944) 10.
        Notes
        On new weapons; romantic nationalism; American jargon; Jack London.
        CEJL III 176–178.

C.437   'The Little Apocalypse of Obadiah Hornbrook' *Tribune* (30 June 1944) 19.
        Notes
        Poem.
        See C.347.

C.438 'London Letter', *Partisan Review* Vol. XI, No. 3 (Summer 1944) 278–282.
Notes
Completed 17 April 1944.
Payment £2 10s 0d.
Extract in *War Commentary – For Anarchism* (October 1944).
See C.471.
CEJL III 123–128.

C.439 'Propaganda and Demotic Speech', *Persuasion* Vol. 2, No. 2 (Summer 1944) 14–18; 41.
Notes
Completed 28 April 1944.
Payment £15 15s 0d.
CEJL III 135–141.

C.440 'As I Please', *Tribune* No. 393 (7 July 1944) 10–11.
Notes
On eighteenth-century classics; an air raid; voluntary censorship; a riddle.
CEJL III 178–181.

C.441 'Return Journey': review of Eric Gill *In A Strange Land*, *The Observer* No. 7989 (9 July 1944) 3.
Notes
Completed 7 July 1944.
Payment £7 7s 0d.

C.442 'Art and the Sciences': review of Martin Johnson *Art and Scientific Thought*, *Manchester Evening News* No. 23,449 (13 July 1944) 2.
Notes
Completed 12 July 1944.
Payment £8 8s 0d.

C.443 'As I Please', *Tribune* No. 394 (14 July 1944) 12.
Notes
On bombing civilians; commercial advertisements.
CEJL III 181–184.

C.444 'The Eight Years of War: Spanish Memories', *The Observer* No. 7990 (16 July 1944) 3.
Notes
Completed 15 July 1944.
Payment £7 7s 0d.

C.445 'As I Please', *Tribune* No. 395 (21 July 1944) 10.
Notes
On Samuel Butler; human nature; a riddle.
CEJL III 187–190.

C.446 'The Romantic Case': review of Jacques Barzun *Romanticism and the Modern Ego*, *The Observer* No. 7991 (23 July 1944) 3.
Notes
Completed 20 July 1944.
Payment £7 7s 0d.

C.447 'The Lost Art of Keeping Diaries': review of James Aitken, ed. *English Diaries of the Nineteenth Century*, *Manchester Evening News* No. 23,462 (28 July 1944) 2.
Notes
Completed 27 July 1944.
Payment £8 8s 0d.

C.448 'As I Please', *Tribune* No. 396 (28 July 1944) 12–13.
Notes
On the supposed moral superiority of the poor; Arthur Koestler's *The Gladiators*; defence of *Tribune*'s policies.
CEJL III 196–199.

C.449   'As I Please', *Tribune* No. 397 (4 August 1944) 11.
        Notes
        On the damages of war; park railings; evacuation; out-of-date people.
        CEJL III 199–202.
C.450   'Chinese Miracles': review of Hsiao Ch'ien *The Dragon Beards versus the Blue Prints*, *The Observer* No. 7993 (6 August 1944) 3.
        Notes
        Completed 2 August 1944.
        Payment £10 0s 0d.
C.451   'English Fiction is at a Low Ebb': review of Richard Church *The Porch and The Stronghold*, *Manchester Evening News* No. 23,473 (10 August 1944) 2.
        Notes
        Completed 9 August 1944.
        Payment £8 8s 0d.
C.452   'As I Please', *Tribune* No. 398 (11 August 1944) 12.
        Notes
        On colour bar; pacifist beliefs.
        CEJL III 204–206.
C.453   'The Children Who Cannot Be Billeted': review of Marie Paneth *Branch Street*, *The Observer* No. 7994 (13 August 1944) 3.
        Notes
        Completed 11 August 1944.
        Payment £8 8s 0d.
C.454   'As I Please', *Tribune* No. 399 (18 August 1944) 11.
        Notes
        On park railings; licensing laws; archaic language.
        CEJL III 207–210.
C.455   'Puritan Poet': review of Denis Saurat *Milton: Man and Thinker*, *The Observer* No. 7995 (20 August 1944) 3.
        Notes
        Completed 17 August 1944.
        Payment £10 0s 0d.
C.456   'The Wretched Kaffirs': review of Selwyn James *South of the Congo*, *Manchester Evening News* No. 23,485 (24 August 1944) 2.
        Notes
        Completed 23 August 1944.
        Payment £8 8s 0d.
C.457   'As I Please', *Tribune* No. 400 (25 August 1944) 11.
        Notes
        On the 1942 Burma campaign; Leonard Merrick; willowherb.
        CEJL III 210–212.
C.458   'As I Please', *Tribune* No. 401 (1 September 1944) 12.
        Notes
        On the Warsaw rising; Russomania.
        CEJL III 224–228.
C.459   'Back to the Land': review of Leonard Hamilton, ed. *Selections from the Works of Gerrard Winstanley*, *The Observer* No. 7997 (3 September 1944) 3.
        Notes
        Completed 31 August 1944.
        Payment £10 0s 0d.
C.460   'How Long is a Short Story?', *Manchester Evening News* No. 23,497 (7 September 1944) 2.
        Notes
        Completed 6 September 1944.
        Payment £8 8s 0d.

Abridged version in *Synopsis* (Winter 1944).
See C.506.

C.461 'As I Please', *Tribune* No. 402 (8 September 1944) 11–12.
Notes
On Osbert Sitwell's *A Letter To My Son*; humiliating prisoners; willowherb.
CEJL III 228–231.

C.462 'As I Please', *Tribune* No. 403 (15 September 1944) 11.
Notes
On French revolutionary feeling in 1936; the doodlebug.
CEJL III 231–234.

C.463 'Are Books Too Dear?', *The News & Book Trade Review and Stationers' Gazette* Vol. 107, No. 38 (16 September 1944) 1.
Notes
First published in *Manchester Evening News* (1 June 1944).
See C.425.

C.464 'New World': review of D.W. Brogan *The American Problem*, *The Observer* No. 7999 (17 September 1944) 3.
Notes
Completed 15 September 1944.
Payment £10 0s 0d.

C.465 'As I Please', *Tribune* No. 403 (15 September 1944) 11.
Notes
On French revolutionary feeling in 1936; the doodlebug.
CEJL III 231–234.

C.466 'Tobias Smollett: Scotland's Best Novelist', *Tribune* No. 404 (22 September 1944) 15–16.
Notes
CEJL III 244–248.

C.467 'London Letter', *Partisan Review* Vol. XI, No. 4 (Fall 1944) 408–411.
Notes
Completed 24 July 1944.
Payment £2 2s 0d.
Party politics in Britain and election fever; the housing crisis; the late wartime literary scene.
Written 24 July 1944.
CEJL III 191–196.

C.468 'Direct Rule May Return To Burma', *New Vision* No. 19 (Autumn 1944) 6–9.
Notes
An interview with George Orwell by G.B. Pittock-Buss.

C.469 'Are Books Too Dear?', *Synopsis* Vol. 5 No. 2 (Autumn 1944) 12–14.
Notes
Abridged version of article originally published in *Manchester Evening News* (1 June 1944).
See C.425.

C.470 'Raffles and Miss Blandish', *Horizon* Vol. 10, No. 58 (October 1944) 232–244.
Notes
Completed 28 August 1944.
Payment £13 0s 0d.
Also published as 'The Ethics of the Detective Story – from Raffles to Miss Blandish' in *Politics* [New York] Vol. I (November 1944) 310–315.
See C.481. See also C.795.
Critical Essays 142–155, *Dickens, Dali & Others* 202–221, *A Collection of Essays* 132–147, *Collected Essays* 249–263, *Decline of the English Murder* 63–79, and *CEJL* III 212–224.

C.471   'Unexpected Effects of Propaganda', *War Commentary – For Anarchism* Vol. 3, No. 23 (October 1944) 9.
Notes
Extract from 'London Letter', *Partisan Review* (Summer 1944).
See C.438.

C.472   'Burma Roads': review of V.R. Pearn *Burma Background*, O.H.K. Spate *Burma Setting*, G. Appleton *Buddhism in Burma*, Ma Mya Sein *Burma*, Kenneth Hemingway *Wings Over Burma*, and Charles J. Rolo *Wingate's Raiders*, *The Observer* No. 8001 (1 October 1944) 3.
Notes
Completed 29 September 1944.
Payment £10 0s 0d.
The first three titles were published as *Burma Pamphlets*.

C.473   'The Changing Magic of T.S. Eliot': review of T.S. Eliot *Four Quartets*, *Manchester Evening News* (5 October 1944) 2.
Notes
Completed 4 October 1944.
Payment £8 8s 0d.

C.474   'As I Please', *Tribune* (6 October 1944) 10.
Notes
On journalism courses; the discomfort and expense of travel.
CEJL III 248–252.

C.475   'As I Please', *Tribune* No. 407 (13 October 1944) 11.
Notes
On Tibetans in the German army; an Indian interview with George Bernard Shaw; artistic patronage.
CEJL III 252–255.

C.476   'Home Guard Lessons For the Future', *The Observer* (15 October 1944) 5.
Notes
Completed 13 October 1944.
Payment £10 0s 0d.

C.477   'How Can Civilisation Be Saved?': review of John Middleton Murry *Adam and Eve*, *Manchester Evening News* (19 October 1944) 2.
Notes
Completed 18 October 1944.
Payment £8 8s 0d.

C.478   'As I Please', *Tribune* No. 408 (20 October 1944) 10.
Notes
On pith helmets; paper consumption.
CEJL III 260–263.

C.479   'As I Please', *Tribune* No. 409 (27 October 1944) 11.
Notes
On C.S. Lewis; Mosley's release.
CEJL III 263–266.

C.480   'Indian Ink': review of Beverley Nichols *Verdict on India*, *The Observer* No. 8005 (29 October 1944) 3.
Notes
Completed 26 October 1944.
Payment £10 0s 0d.

C.481   'The Ethics of the Detective Story – from Raffles to Miss Blandish', *Politics* [New York] Vol. I (November 1944) 310–315.
Notes
Previously published in *Horizon* (October 1944) 232–244.
See C.470.

C.482   Quotations from a letter to the Editor, *Politics* (November 1944) 295.
    Notes
    Letter from Orwell to Dwight Macdonald about Orwell's review of Harold
    Laski's *Faith, Reason and Civilisation*, which was written for *Manchester
    Evening News*, but rejected. It should have appeared on 16 March 1944.
    There is a footnote on the rejection, with quotations from the letter, in *CEJL*
    III 141–142.
    Orwell wrote, 'A few weeks back a newspaper I regularly write for refused to
    print a book review of mine because it was anti-Stalinist in tone.'[12]
C.483   'Trollope of Barchester': discussion of Anthony Trollope *The Warden*, George
    Eliot *Silas Marner*, Harold Nicolson *Public Faces*, V. Sackville-West *Seducers in
    Ecuador*, Anatole France *Les Dieux ont Soif*, and Edmond Vermeil *Hitler et le
    Christianisme*, *Manchester Evening News* (2 November 1944) 2.
C.484   'As I Please', *Tribune* No. 410 (3 November 1944) 11–12.
    Notes
    On writings about executions; melon growing; reviewing policy.
    CEJL III 266–268.
C.485   'What Really Happened at Singapore': review of Giles Playfair *Singapore Goes
    Off the Air* and Richard Winstedt *Britain and Malaya*, *Manchester Evening News*
    (8 November 1944) 2.
C.486   'Books and the People: Money and Virtue': review of Oliver Goldsmith *The Vicar
    of Wakefield*, *Tribune* No. 411 (10 November 1944) 15–16.
    Notes
    CEJL III 268–273.
C.487   'Poet and Priest': review of W.H. Gardner *Gerard Manley Hopkins*, *The Observer*
    No. 8007 (12 November 1944) 3.
    Notes
    Completed 10 November 1944.
    Payment £10 0s 0d.
C.488   'A Pat On The Back': review of A.L. Rowse *The English Spirit*, and Cassius
    Brendan and Beverley, *Manchester Evening News* (16 November 1944) 2.
    Notes
    Completed 14 November 1944.
    Payment £8 8s 0d.
    Cassius was Michael Foot.
C.489   'As I Please', *Tribune* (17 November 1944) 10.
    Notes
    On schools of journalism; falsifying history; Signpost Booklets.
    CEJL III 273–276.
C.490   'Literary Propaganda': letter to the Editor, *Tribune* (17 November 1944) 14.
    Notes
    Signed: Francophil
C.491   'A Champion of Freedom': review of J.A. Spender *Last Essays*, Walter Clay
    Lowdermilk *Palestine, Land of Promise*, and Reginald Moore *Selected Writing*,
    Manchester Evening News (23 November 1944) 2.
    Notes
    Completed 21 November 1944.
    Payment £8 8s 0d.
C.492   'As I Please', *Tribune* No. 413 (24 November 1944) 11.
    Notes
    On the rudeness of shopkeepers; answering advertisements; *Memoirs of a
    Surrey Labourer* and *The Follies and Frauds of Spiritualism*.
    CEJL III 276–279.
C.493   'Communists Whitewashed', *War Commentary – For Anarchism* Vol. 6, No. 3
    (25 November 1944) 3.

Notes
Extract from 'As I Please', *Tribune* (17 November 1944) [C.489].

C.494   'Singing Men': review of Herbert J.C. Grierson and J.C. Smith *A Critical History of English Poetry*, *The Observer* No. 8009 (26 November 1944) 3.
Notes
Completed 24 November 1944.
Payment £10 0s 0d.

C.495   'No Vacuum For The Artist': review of James Agate *Noblesse Oblige – Another Letter To Another Son*, and Jack Lindsay *Perspective for Poetry*, *Manchester Evening News* (30 November 1944) 2.
Notes
Completed 28 November 1944.
Payment £8 8s 0d.
The Agate review, together with the ensuing published correspondence between Agate and Orwell, is reprinted in *CEJL* III 255–260
See C.500.

C.496   'Points of View': review of T.S. Eliot *The Classics and the Man of Letters*, and Francis Scarfe *The Music of Poetry*, *Poetry* (London) (December 1944) 239–242.

C.497   'As I Please', *Tribune* No. 414 (1 December 1944) 11–12
Notes
On rocket bombs; *The Diary of a Nobody*; mudlarks; Trotsky's *Life of Stalin*; a riddle.
CEJL III 279–283.

C.498   'The Fighting Pacifist': review of *Bridge into the Future: The Letters of Max Plowman*, *Manchester Evening News* (7 December 1944) 2.
Notes
Completed 6 December 1944.
Payment £8 8s 0d.

C.499   'As I Please', *Tribune* No. 415 (8 December 1944) 10.
Notes
On political controversy; a pro-Irish leaflet; schools of journalism; riddle answer.
CEJL III 288–291.

C.500   Reply to James Agate's response to Orwell's review of Agate's *Noblesse Oblige – Another Letter To Another Son*, *Manchester Evening News* (21 December 1944) 2.
Notes
See C.495.

C.501   'Oysters and Brown Stout', *Tribune* No. 417 (22 December 1944) 11–12.
Notes
CEJL III 299–302.

C.502   'Spanish Prison': review of Charles d'Ydewalle *An Interlude in Spain* translated by Eric Sutton, *The Observer* No. 8013 (24 December 1944) 3.
Notes
Completed 22 December 1944.
Payment £10 0s 0d.

C.503   'The Valley of the Fairies': review of Robert Gibbings *Lovely is the Lee*, and Vera T. Mirsky *The Cup of Astonishment*, *Manchester Evening News* (28 December 1944) 2.

C.504   'As I Please', *Tribune* No. 418 (29 December 1944) 10–11.
Notes
On battle schools; battle poems; Indian troops in Greece.
CEJL III 302–306.

C.505   'Poet in Darkness': review of Edwin Morgan *Flower of Evil: A Life of Charles Baudelaire*, *The Observer* No. 8014 (31 December 1944) 3.

Notes
Completed 29 December 1944.
Payment £10 0s 0d.

C.506   'How Long is a Short Story', *Synopsis* Vol. 5, No. 3 (Winter 1944) 15–17.
Notes
Abridged version of article originally published in *Manchester Evening News* (7 September 1944).
See C.460.

C.507   'London Letter', *Partisan Review* Vol. XII, No. 1 (Winter 1945) 77–82.
Notes
On Orwell's own comments made during the war, his accuracy on facts but misreading of the relative importance of trends.
Written October 1944.
CEJL III 293–299.

C.508   'Discovering Adolph Hitler': review of Conrad Heiden *Der Führer*, *Manchester Evening News* (4 January 1945) 2.
Notes
Payment £8 8s 0d.

C.509   'As I Please', *Tribune* No. 419 (5 January 1945) 10–11.
Notes
On *The Quarterly Review* 1810; Burmese place names; Mrs Sherwood's *The Fairchild Family*.
CEJL III 313–316.

C.510   'Books and the People: A New Year Message', *Tribune* No. 419 (5 January 1945) 15–16.
Notes
CEJL III 309–313.

C.511   'The Art of Authorship': review of L.A.G. Strong *Authorship*, *Manchester Evening News* (11 January 1945) 2.
Notes
Completed 10 January 1945.
Payment £8 8s 0d.
Abridged version in *Synopsis* (Spring 1945).
See C.533.

C.512   'As I Please', *Tribune* No. 420 (12 January 1945) 11–12.
Notes
On Nazi atrocities; the defamation of Mihailovich; newspapers.
CEJL III 316–318.

C.513   'Going Down': review of Palinurus *Unquiet Grave: A Word Cycle*, *The Observer* No. 8016 (14 January 1945) 3.
Notes
Completed 11 January 1945.
Payment £10 0s 0d.
Palinurus was Cyril Connolly.
CEJL III 318–320.

C.514   'As I Please', *Tribune* No. 421 (19 January 1945) 10.
Notes
On Henri Béraud; wartime reviews of German scientific books; incredulity; Edgar Wallace.
CEJL III 320–323.
See C.520

C.515   'Conquer Nature or Care For It?': review of H.J. Massingham, ed. *The Natural Order: Essays on the Return to Husbandry*, *Manchester Evening News* (25 January 1945) 2.

Notes
Completed 24 January 1945.
Payment £8 8s 0d.

C.516   'As I Please', *Tribune* No. 422 (26 January 1945) 10.
Notes
On political liberty; plaque to William Blake; corruption of language.
CEJL III 323–326.

C.517   'Pen and Sword': review of H.W. Nevinson *Visions and Memories, The Observer* (28 January 1945) 3.
Notes
Completed 25 January 1945.
Payment £10 0s 0d.

C.518   'China Saved the World': review of Rhodes Farmer *Shanghai Harvest*, and Norman Douglas *Fountains in the Sand, Manchester Evening News* (2 February 1945) 2.
Notes
Completed 31 January 1945.
Payment £8 8s 0d.

C.519   'As I Please', *Tribune* No. 423 (2 February 1945) 11–12.
Notes
On offensive names; population transfers; pessimistic thoughts.
CEJL III 326–329.

C.520   Reply to a letter to the Editor, *Tribune* No. 423 (2 February 1945) 14.
Notes
Response to a letter from Quintin Hogg on Orwell's 'As I Please', *Tribune* (19 January 1945) 10.
See C.514.

C.521   'A World of Sheep': review of Halldor Laxness *Independent People, Manchester Evening News* (8 February 1945) 2.
Notes
Completed 7 February 1945.
Payment £8 8s 0d.

C.522   'As I Please', *Tribune* No. 424 (9 February 1945) 10.
Notes
On dishwashing; book reviewing; worn-out metaphors; Bret Harte.
See B.21 for the suppressed Orwell article in *The Saturday Book* mentioned in the section on book reviewing.
CEJL III 329–332.

C.523   'As I Please', *Tribune* No. 425 (16 February 1945) 10.
Notes
On Burma; grey seals; Beachcomber.
CEJL III 355–357.

C.524   'Inside the Pages in Paris', *Manchester Evening News* (28 February 1945) 2.
Notes
Report 'By George Orwell, the "Manchester Evening News" Correspondent in Paris.'

C.525   'Poetry and the Microphone', *New Saxon Pamphlets* No. 3 (March 1945) 33–39.
Notes
Such, Such Were the Joys 110–120, *England Your England, Selected Writings* 106–115, *Collected Essays* 315–324, and *CEJL* II 329–336.
Written Autumn 1943.

C.526   'Occupation's Effect on French Outlook. Different Political Thinking', *The Observer* No. 8023 (4 March 1945) 5.

C.527   'The Political Aims of French Resistance', *Manchester Evening News* (7 March 1945) 2.

Notes

Report from Paris.

C.528 'Clerical Party May Re-emerge in France. Educational Controversy', *The Observer* No. 8024 (11 March 1945) 5.

Notes

Report from Paris, dated 10 March.

C.529 'De Gaulle Intends to Keep Indo-China, but French Apathetic on Empire', *The Observer* No. 8025 (18 March 1945) 5.

Notes

Report from Paris, dated 17 March.

C.530 'The French Believe We Have Had a Revolution', *Manchester Evening News* (20 March 1945) 2.

Notes

Report from Paris.

C.531 'Creating Order Out Of Cologne Chaos. Water Supplied From Carts', *The Observer* No. 8026 (25 March 1945) 5.

Notes

Report from Cologne, dated 24 March.

C.532 'Grandeur et décadence du roman policier anglais', *Fontaine* Numéro spécial 37–40 ([Spring] 1945) 69–75.

Notes

Translated by Fernand Auberjonois.

Orwell's original English version is not known to exist.

Payment £3 3s 0d.

Reprinted in *Aspects de la littérature anglais (1918–1945)* (Paris: Fontaine, 1946) 62–67.

C.533 'The Art of Authorship', *Synopsis* Vol. 6, No. 1 (Spring 1945) 40–42.

Notes

Abridged version of article first published in *Manchester Evening News* (11 January 1945).

See C.511.

C.534 'Anti-Semitism in Britain', *The Contemporary Jewish Record* Vol. VIII (April 1945) 163–171.

Notes

Completed 26 February 1945.

Payment £30 0s 0d.

Such, Such Were the Joys 98–109, *England Your England*, *Collected Essays* 304–314, and *CEJL* III 332–341.

C.535 'Future of A Ruined Germany. Rural Slum Cannot Help Europe', *The Observer* No. 8028 (8 April 1945) 5.

Notes

Extract, 'Europe's Homeless Millions', *Forward* (21 April 1945).

See C.538.

C.536 'Allies Facing Food Crisis in Germany. Problem of Freed Workers', *The Observer* No. 8029 (15 April 1945) 5.

Notes

Report from Paris, dated 14 April.

C.537 'The French election will be influenced by the fact that women will have first vote', *Manchester Evening News* (16 April 1945) 2.

C.538 'Europe's Homeless Millions', *Forward* (21 April 1945) 1.

Notes

Extract from Orwell's article in *The Observer* (8 April 1945).

See C.535.

C.539 'Bavarian Peasants Ignore the War. Germans Know They Are Beaten', *The Observer* No. 8030 (22 April 1945) 5.

Notes
Report from Nuremberg, dated 21 April.

C.540 'The Germans Still Doubt Our Unity. The Flags Do Not Help', *The Observer* No. 8031 (29 April 1945) 5.
Notes
Report from Stuttgart, 'With the U.S. Third Army', dated 28 April.

C.541 'Now Germany Faces Hunger', *Manchester Evening News* (4 May 1945) 2.
Notes
Report from Germany.

C.542 'Anarchist Trial': letter to the Editor, *Tribune* No. 436 (4 May 1945) 12.
Notes
Signed by Lazarus Aarenson, Yankel Adler, George Baker, Alex Comfort, Nicholas Moore, George Orwell, Dylan Thomas, R.E. Waterfield, and Paul Potts. On the nine months' prison sentence imposed on three members of the *War Commentary* editorial board.

C.543 'France's Interest in the War Dwindles. Back To Normal Is The Aim', *The Observer* No. 8032 (6 May 1945) 5.
Notes
Report from Paris, dated 5 May.

C.544 'Freed Politicians Return To Paris. T.U. Leader Sees De Gaulle', *The Observer* No. 8033 (13 May 1945) 5.
Notes
Report from Paris, dated 12 May.

C.545 'Danger of Separate Occupation Zones. Delaying Austria's Recovery', *The Observer* No. 8034 (20 May 1945) 5.
Notes
Report from Austria, dated 19 May.

C.546 'Obstacles to Joint Rule In Germany, *The Observer* No. 8035 (27 May 1945) 1.
Notes
Completed 25 May 1945.
Payment £10 3s 4d net. Income tax deducted at source.

C.547 'Test of the Historical Novel': review of W.P. Crozier *The Fates Are Laughing*, and George Baker *Cry Hylas on the Hills*, *Manchester Evening News* (7 June 1945) 2.
Notes
Completed 6 June 1945.
Payment £8 8s 0d.

C.548 'Uncertain Fate of Displaced Persons', *The Observer* No. 8037 (10 June 1945) 1.
Notes
Completed 8 June 1945.
Payment £10 3s 4d net. Income tax deducted at source.

C.549 'A Muffled Voice': review of Jacques Maritain *Christianity and Democracy*, *The Observer* No. 8037 (10 June 1945) 3.
Notes
Completed 1 June 1945.
Payment £10 3s 4d net. Income tax deducted at source.

C.550 'The Hunter Home To Peace': review of George Sava *Land Fit For Heroes*, and Leonid Grossman *Death of a Poet*, *Manchester Evening News* (14 June 1945) 2.
Notes
Completed 13 June 1945.
Payment £8 8s 0d.

C.551 'Quality As A War Casualty': review of Kenneth Reddin *Another Shore*, and Vicky Baum *The Weeping Wood*, *Manchester Evening News* (21 June 1945) 2.
Notes
Completed 20 June 1945.
Payment £8 8s 0d.

C.552   'Man From The Sea': review of Joseph Conrad *The Nigger of the Narcissus, Typhoon, The Shadow Line*, and *Within the Tides*, *The Observer* No. 8039 (24 June 1945) 3.
Notes
Completed 22 June 1945.
Payment £10 3s 4d net. Income tax deducted at source.

C.553   'Morrison and Bracken Face Stiff Fights: Heavy Poll Expected', *The Observer* No. 8039 (24 June 1945) 5.
Notes
Completed 23 June 1945.
Payment £10 3s 4d net. Income tax deducted at source.
CEJL III 387–389.

C.554   'The Tales of Joseph Conrad': review of Joseph Conrad *The Nigger of the Narcissus, Typhoon*, and *The Shadow Line*, and Richard Church and M.M. Bozman, eds. *Poems of Our Time 1900–1942*, *Manchester Evening News* (28 June 1945) 2.
Notes
Completed 27 June 1945.
Payment £8 8s 0d.

C.555   'London Letter', *Partisan Review* Vol. XII, No. 3 (Summer 1945) 322–326.
Notes
Completed 5 June 1945.
Payment £2 10 0d.
On the forthcoming General Election; the cooling of pro-Russian feeling; wartime privations now accepted as part of life; common British lack of reaction to the war.
CEJL III 380–386.

C.556   'In Defence of P.G. Wodehouse', *The Windmill* Vol. I, No. 2 ([July 1945]) 10–19.
Notes
Completed 20 February 1945.
Payment £10 0s 0d.
The Windmill was reissued by Kraus Reprint Corporation, New York, in 1967. This article is in Vol. 1, which covers the issues 1944–1946.
Critical Essays 156–169, *Dickens, Dali & Others* 222–243, *The Orwell Reader* 315–328, *Collected Essays* 264–280, and *CEJL* III 341–355.
Published in July 1945, written February 1945.

C.557   'Liberal Intervention Aids Labour. "Puzzle" Block of Voters', *The Observer* No. 8040 (1 July 1945) 5.
Notes
Completed 30 June 1945.
Payment £10 3s 4d net. Income tax deducted at source.

C.558   'Authors Deserve a New Deal', *Manchester Evening News* (5 July 1945) 2, 3.
Notes
Completed 4 July 1945.
Payment £8 8s 0d.

C.559   'French Farce': review of Honoré de Balzac *Nine Tales From Les Contes Drôlatiques*, *The Observer* No. 8041 (8 July 1945) 3.
Notes
Completed 6 July 1945.
Payment £10 0s 0d.

C.560   'Noisy, Dark Haired Foreigners': review of Pierre Maillaud *The English Way*, John L. Keenan *A Steel Man In India*, and Thomas Mann *Joseph The Provider*, *Manchester Evening News* (12 July 1945) 2.
Notes
Completed 11 July 1945.
Payment £8 8s 0d.

C.561   'A Basque in Hitler's Germany': review of Jose Antonio de Aguirre *Freedom Was Flesh and Blood*, and Robin Feddin et al *Personal Landscape. An Anthology of Exile*, *Manchester Evening News* (19 July 1945) 2.
   Notes
   Completed 18 July 1945.
   Payment £8 8s 0d.

C.562   'On Scientifiction', *Leader Magazine* (21 July 1945) 11.
   Notes
   Completed 9 July 1945.
   Payment £15 0s 0d.

C.563   'So Runs The World': review of Erich Kahler *Man the Measure*, *The Observer* No. 8043 (22 July 1945) 3.
   Notes
   Completed 19 July 1945.
   Payment £10 0s 0d.

C.564   Letter to the Editor, *Tribune* No. 448 (27 July 1945) 11.
   Notes
   Response to J.E. Miller's letter, 'Orwell and the Stinkers', *Tribune* (20 July 1945) 11.

C.565   'Funny, But Not Vulgar', *Leader Magazine* (28 July 1945) 15–16.
   Notes
   Completed 1 December 1944.
   Payment £15 0s 0d.
   CEJL III 283–288.
   Written December 1944.

C.566   'Front Seat View of Politics': review of Viscount Samuel *Memoirs*, Christopher Isherwood *Good-bye To Berlin*, Virginia Woolf *A Room of One's Own*, and Chapman Cohen *Thomas Paine*, *Manchester Evening News* (2 August 1945) 2.
   Notes
   Completed 1 August 1945.
   Payment £8 8s 0d.

C.567   'In Fields of Air': review of Edward Sackville-West *The Rescue*, *The Observer* (5 August 1945) 3.
   Notes
   Completed 2 August 1945.
   Payment £10 0s 0d.

C.568   'They Throw New Light On India': review of Mulk Raj Anand *Coolie*, *Manchester Evening News* (9 August 1945) 2.
   Notes
   Completed 8 August 1945.
   Payment £8 8s 0d.

C.569   'The Scientist Takes Over': review of C.S. Lewis *That Hideous Strength*, and Nerina Shute *We Mixed Our Drinks*, *Manchester Evening News* (16 August 1945) 2.
   Notes
   Completed 15 August 1945.
   Payment £8 8s 0d.

C.570   'Tale of a "Head"': review of Lionel James *A Forgotten Genius: Sewell of St Columba's and Radley*, *The Observer* No. 8047 (19 August 1945) 3.
   Notes
   Completed 16 August 1945.
   Payment £10 0s 0d.

C.571   'Personality Behind the Pen': review of Kornei Chukovsky *Chekov the Man*, *Manchester Evening News* (23 August 1945) 2.

Notes

Completed 22 August 1945.

Payment £8 8s 0d.

C.572 'The Errors Leading Up To Hitler': review of Evelyn Anderson *Hammer or Anvil: The Story of the German Working-Class Movement*, and Julius Braunthal *In Search of the Millennium*, *Manchester Evening News* (30 August 1945) 2.

Notes

Completed 29 August 1945.

Payment £8 8s 0d.

C.573 'Charles the Great': review of Una Pope-Hennessy *Charles Dickens*, *The Observer* No. 8049 (2 September 1945) 3.

Notes

Completed 30 August 1945.

Payment £10 0s 0d.

C.574 'Why Families Are Smaller': review of Mass Observation *Britain and Her Birth-Rate*, *Manchester Evening News* (6 September 1945) 2.

Notes

Completed 5 September 1945.

Payment £8 8s 0d.

C.575 'Satirical Bullseyes': review of Sagittarius *Quiver's Choice*, *Tribune* No. 454 (7 September 1945) 14.

Notes

Completed 3 September 1945.

Payment £1 1s 0d.

C.576 'The French Cooks' Syndicate': review of W. McCartney *The French Cooks' Syndicate*, *Freedom Through Anarchism* Vol. 3, No. 46a (8 September 1945) 4.

Notes

3d pamphlet.

Completed 22 August 1945.

Unpaid.

Freedom Through Anarchism was previously *War Commentary*, and later *Freedom*.

C.577 Untraced article for *The Observer*, completed 7 September 1945.

Notes

Orwell records a payment of £10 0s 0d for an 800-word article completed on this date.

C.578 'Poet From The Wild Hills': review of Bryan Merryman *The Midnight Court* translated by Frank O'Connor. *Manchester Evening News* (27 September 1945) 2.

Notes

Completed 9 September 1945.

Payment £8 8s 0d.

C.579 'London Letter', *Partisan Review* Vol. XII, No. 4 (Fall 1945) 467–472.

Notes

Completed 11 August 1945.

Payment £2 10s 0d.

The new Labour Government; European devastation and confusion; reconstruction of post-war Britain; foreign policy.

CEJL III 393–400.

C.580 '*Notes* on Nationalism', *Polemic* No. 1 (October 1945) 32–47.

Notes

Completed 15 May 1945.

Payment £25 0s 0d.

Such, Such Were the Joys 73–97, *Collected Essays* 281–303, *Decline of the English Murder* 155–179, and *CEJL* III 361–380.

C.581 'What is a Novel?': review of Crichton Porteous *The Earth Remains*, and Leo Kiacheli *Gvadi Bigva*, *Manchester Evening News* (4 October 1945) 2.
 Notes
 Completed 3 October 1945.
 Payment £8 8s 0d.

C.582 'Pity and Terror': review of Fyodor Dostoevsky *The Brothers Karamazov* and *Crime and Punishment* translated by Constance Garnett, *The Observer* No. 8054 (7 October 1945) 3.
 Notes
 Completed 4 October 1945.
 Payment £10 0s 0d.

C.583 'Talent Gone to Waste': review of C.E. Vuillamy *Edwin and Eleanor*, Elizabeth Taylor *At Mrs Lippincote's*, and Inez Holden *To the Boating*, *Manchester Evening News* (11 October 1945) 2.
 Notes
 Completed 10 October 1945.
 Payment £8 8s 0d.

C.584 'Milton in Striped Trousers': review of Hermon Ould, ed. *Freedom From Expression*, *Tribune* No. 459 (12 October 1945) 12.
 Notes
 Completed 5 October 1945.
 Payment £5 5s 0d.

C.585 'Profile – Aneurin Bevan', *The Observer* (14 October 1945) 6.
 Notes
 Unsigned.
 Most of this profile was written by Orwell.
 Completed 7 September 1945.
 Payment £10 0s 0d.
 Abridged version, 'Aneurin Bevan', *English Digest* Vol. 20, No. 3 (January 1946).
 See C.622.

C.586 'The Modern Short Story': review of Rhys Davies *Selected Stories*, *Manchester Evening News* (18 October 1945) 2.
 Notes
 Completed 17 October 1945.
 Payment £8 8s 0d.

C.587 'You And The Atom Bomb', *Tribune* No. 460 (19 October 1945) 7–8.
 Notes
 Completed 11 October 1945.
 Payment £3 3s 0d.
 CEJL IV 6–10.

C.588 'The Modern Stoics': review of Kenneth Mellanby *Human Guinea Pigs*, *Manchester Evening News* (25 October 1945) 2.
 Notes
 Completed 24 October 1945.
 Payment £8 8s 0d.

C.589 'What is Science?', *Tribune* No. 461 (26 October 1945) 8–9.
 Notes
 Completed 18 October 1945.
 Payment £3 3s 0d.
 CEJL IV 10–13.

C.590 'The Green Flag': review of Sean O'Casey *Drums Under The Windows*, *The Observer* No. 8057 (28 October 1945) 3.
 Notes
 CEJL IV 13–15.

C.591   'Catastrophic Gradualism': review of Arthur Koestler's essay 'The Yogi and the Commissar', *C.W. Review* (November 1945) 12, 14.

> *Notes*
> Completed 21 October 1945.
> Payment £2 12s 6d.
> *C.W. Review* was the Common Wealth Review.
> Also published in *Politics* (September 1946) 268–270.
> See C.707.
> *CEJL* IV 15–19.

C.592   'The British General Election', *Commentary* [New York] (November 1945) 65–70.

> *Notes*
> *Commentary* was formerly *The Contemporary Jewish Record*.

C.593   'The Captain and the Prophet': review of Howard Clewes *Dead Ground*, N. Gangulee, ed. *Giuseppe Mazzini – Selected Writings*, and C.E. Bechhofer Roberts, ed. *The Trial of Jones and Hulten*, *Manchester Evening News* (1 November 1945) 2.

> *Notes*
> Completed 31 October 1945.
> Payment £8 8s 0d.

C.594   'Good Bad Books', *Tribune* No. 462 (2 November 1945) 15.

> *Notes*
> Completed 26 October 1945.
> Payment £3 3s 0d.
> Abridged version in *World Digest*, February 1946.
> See C.651.
> *Shooting an Elephant* 174–178, and *CEJL* IV 19–22.

C.595   'Are We Really Done For?': review of H.G. Wells *Mind at the End of its Tether*, *Manchester Evening News* (8 November 1945) 2.

> *Notes*
> Completed 7 November 1945.
> Payment £8 8s 0d.

C.596   'Revenge is Sour', *Tribune* No. 463 (9 November 1945) 10–11.

> *Notes*
> Completed 2 November 1945.
> Payment £3 3s 0d.
> *CEJL* IV 3–6.

C.597   'Cycle of Cathay': review of Hsiao Ch'ien, ed. *A Harp with a Thousand Strings*, *The Observer* No. 8059 (11 November 1945) 3.

> *Notes*
> Completed 8 November 1945.
> Payment £10 0s 0d.

C.598   '"My Dear Watson"': review of Adrian Conan Doyle *The True Conan Doyle*, *Manchester Evening News* (15 November 1945) 2.

> *Notes*
> Completed 14 November 1945.
> Payment £8 8s 0d.

C.599   'D.H. Lawrence's Short Stories': review of D.H. Lawrence *The Prussian Officer*, *Tribune* No. 464 (16 November 1945) 15–16.

> *Notes*
> Completed 9 November 1945.
> Payment £3 3s 0d.
> *CEJL* IV 30–33.

C.600   'Teller of Tales': review of Robert Louis Stevenson *Novels and Stories*, *The Observer* No. 8060 (18 November 1945) 3.

Notes
Completed 15 November 1945.
Payment £10 0s 0d.

C.601   'The Fascination of Escape': review of James Hargest *Farewell Campo 12*, Evelyn Wrench *Immortal Years*, and A.L. Lloyd, ed. *Corn on the Cob: Popular and Traditional Poetry of the U.S.A.*, *Manchester Evening News* (22 November 1945) 2.
Notes
Completed 21 November 1945.
Payment £8 8s 0d.

C.602   'Through A Glass, Rosily', *Tribune* No. 465 (23 November 1945) 8.
Notes
Completed 16 November 1945.
Payment £3 3s 0d.
CEJL IV 34–37.

C.603   'What Is Science?': letter to the Editor, *Tribune* No. 465 (23 November 1945) 11.
Notes
Reply to a letter from Edward R. Ward, *Tribune* (9 November 1945) 13.

C.604   'Five Sets of Lodgers': review of Norman Collins *London Belongs to Me*, *Manchester Evening News* (29 November 1945) 2.
Notes
Completed 28 November 1945.
Payment £8 8s 0d.

C.605   'Escape or Escapism?': review of Jean-Paul Sartre *Huis Clos*, Peter Ustinov *The Banbury Nose*, and Arthur Koestler *Twilight Bar*, *Tribune* No. 466 (30 November 1945) 15–16.
Notes
Completed 23 November 1945.
Payment £3 3s 0d.

C.606   'The Song of the Beasts', *Compass: Current Reading* (December 1945) 45.
Notes
The song, 'Beasts of England', from *Animal Farm*.

C.607   'Bare Christmas for the Children', *Evening Standard* (1 December 1945) 6.
Notes
Completed 30 November 1945.
Payment £20 0s 0d.
In January 1946 Orwell wrote to Geoffrey Gorer:
I forget if I'd started doing weekly articles for the *Evening Standard* before you left. In spite of – by my standards – enormous fees it doesn't do me much good financially, because one extra article a week just turns the scale and makes it necessary for me to have a secretary. However, even with the extra article she takes a certain amount of drudgery off me ... I have definitely arranged I am going to stop doing the *Evening Standard* stuff and most other journalism in May.[13]
Later in 1946 he gave interesting insight into the paper's editorial policy:
In writing for papers like the *Evening Standard*, I have had things not merely cut but actually altered, and of course even a cut always modifies the sense of an article to some extent.

C.608   'A Nipping Air': review of Cyril Connolly *The Condemned Playground*, *The Observer* No. 8062 (2 December 1945) 3.
Notes
Completed 29 November 1945.
Payment £10 10s 0d.

C.609   'Bunter's Creator': review of Leonard Russell, ed. *The Saturday Book* No. 5, *Manchester Evening News* (6 December 1945) 2.

Notes
Completed 5 December 1945.
Payment £8 8s 0d.

C.610 'Freedom of the Park', *Tribune* (7 December 1945) 9-10.
Notes
Completed 3 December 1945.
Payment £3 3s 0d.
Reprinted in *Freedom Defence Committee Bulletin*, February–March 1946.
See C.664.
CEJL IV 37–40.

C.611 'The Case for the Open Fire', *Evening Standard* (8 December 1945) 6.
Notes
Completed 6 December 1945.
Payment £20 0s 0d.
Reprinted as 'Open Fire' in *SEAC* (2 January 1946).
See C.625.

C.612 'Diary of Disintegration': review of F.C. Weiskopf *The Firing Squad*, and Lord Dunsany *The Siren's Wake*, *Manchester Evening News* (13 December 1945) 2.
Notes
Completed 12 December 1945.
Payment £8 8s 0d.

C.613 'The Sporting Spirit', *Tribune* No. 468 (14 December 1945) 10–11.
Notes
Completed 7 December 1945.
Payment £3 3s 0d.
Shooting an Elephant 192–196, *Selected Writings* 159–162, and *CEJL* IV 40–44.

C.614 'In Defence of English Cooking', *Evening Standard* (15 December 1945) 6.
Notes
Completed 13 December 1945.
Payment £20 0s 0d.
Reprinted as 'Bird's Nest Soup?', *SEAC* (9 March 1946).
See C.668.
CEJL III 38–40.

C.615 'Battle Ground': review of William Bowyer Honey *Science and the Creative Arts*, *The Observer* No. 8064 (16 December 1945) 3.
Notes
Completed 13 December 1945.
Payment £10 0s 0d.

C.616 'Gaolbreaker's Shelter': review of William Russell *Cellar: A Play in Three Acts*, *Manchester Evening News* (20 December 1945) 2.
Notes
Completed 19 December 1945.
Payment £8 8s 0d.

C.617 'Nonsense Poetry': review of R.L. Megroz, ed. *The Lear Omnibus*, *Tribune* No. 469 (21 December 1945) 13.
Notes
Completed 14 December 1945.
Payment £3 3s 0d.
Abridged version in *The Literary Digest* (Autumn 1948).
See C.794.
Shooting an Elephant 179–184, and *CEJL* IV 44–48.

C.618 'Banish This Uniform', *Evening Standard* (22 December 1945) 6.
Notes
Completed 20 December 1945.
Payment £20 0s 0d.

C.619 'Old George's Almanac', *Tribune* No. 470 (28 December 1945) 9.
  Notes
  Completed 20 December 1945.
  Payment £3 3s 0d.
  Signed: Crystal-Gazer Orwell

C.620 Review of Herbert Read *A Coat of Many Colours: Occasional Essays*, *Poetry Quarterly* Vol. 7, No. 4 (Winter 1945) 147–150.
  Notes
  Completed 30 November 1945.
  Payment £3 3s 0d.
  CEJL IV 48–52.

C.621 'Arthur Koestler', *Focus* No. 2 (1946) 27–38.
  Notes
  Completed 11 September 1944.
  The essay was written for *Focus*, although Orwell noted in *Critical Essays* that it 'will probably not have appeared before this book is published', p6.

C.622 'Aneurin Bevan', *English Digest* Vol. 20, No. 3 (January 1946) 16–18.
  Notes
  Unsigned.
  Originally published as 'Profile – Aneurin Bevan', *The Observer* (14 October 1945).
  See C.585.

C.623 Abridged version of *Animal Farm*, *World Digest* (January 1946) 83–94.
  Notes
  Not abridged by Orwell.
  Payment £14 15s 5d.

C.624 'The Prevention of Literature', *Polemic* No. 2 (January 1946) 4–14.
  Notes
  Completed 12 November 1945.
  Payment £26 5s 0d.
  Abridged version published in *The Atlantic Monthly* (March 1947) 115–119.
  See C.751. See also C.712, C.779 and C.833.
  Shooting an Elephant 114–133, *The Orwell Reader* 367–379, *Selected Essays* 159–174, *Collected Essays* 325–340, and *CEJL* IV 59–72.
  Abridged version reprinted in R.B. Downs, ed. *The First Freedom* (Chicago: American Library Association, 1960) 411–417.
  See B.35.

C.625 'Open Fire', *SEAC* (2 January 1946) 2.
  Notes
  First published as 'The Case for the Open Fire' in *Evening Standard* (8 December 1945).
  See C.611.

C.626 '£3 13s Worth of Pleasure', *Manchester Evening News* (3 January 1946) 2.

C.627 'Freedom and Happiness': review of Evgenii I. Zamyatin *We*, *Tribune* No. 471 (4 January 1946) 15–16.
  Notes
  Completed 31 December 1945.
  Payment £3 3s 0d.
  CEJL IV 72–75.

C.628 'Just Junk – But Who Could Resist It?', *Evening Standard* (5 January 1946) 6.

C.629 'Far Away, Long Ago': review of Douglas Goldring *The Nineteen-Twenties*, *The Observer* No. 8067 (6 January 1946) 3.
  Notes
  Completed 25 December 1945.
  Payment £10 0s 0d.

C.630   'Return of the Past': review of Stephen Bagnall *The Crater's Edge*, and Malcolm James *Born of the Desert*, *Manchester Evening News* (10 January 1946) 2.

C.631   'Pleasure Spots', *Tribune* (11 January 1946) 10–11.
Notes
CEJL IV 78–81.

C.632   'A Nice Cup of Tea', *Evening Standard* (12 January 1946) 6.
Notes
Reprinted in *SEAC* (14 February 1946).
See C.634.
CEJL III 40–43.

C.633   'Sensitive Plant': review of Katherine Mansfield *The Collected Stories of Katherine Mansfield*, *The Observer* No. 8068 (13 January 1946) 3.

C.634   'Ten Steps to a Good Cup of Char', *SEAC* (14 February 1946) 2.
Notes
First published as 'A Nice Cup of Tea', *Evening Standard* (12 January 1946).
See C.632.

C.635   'The Edwardian Revolution': review of Mark Abrams *The Condition of the British People, 1911–1945*, *Manchester Evening News* (17 January 1946) 2.

C.636   'The Politics of Starvation', *Tribune* No. 473 (18 January 1946) 9–10.
Notes
CEJL IV 82–85.

C.637   'Songs We Used to Sing', *Evening Standard* (19 January 1946) 6.
Notes
Reprinted in *SEAC* (25 March 1946).
See C.676.

C.638   '"Cat and Mouse" Case', *Manchester Guardian* (18 January 1946) 4.
Notes
Letter to the Editor, protesting against the arrest of Philip Sansom, signed by Orwell and 24 others.
See C.639, C.640, C.641, C.645, C.646 and C.663.

C.639   Letter to the Editor, *Tribune* No. 473 (18 January 1946) 13.
Notes
On Sansom's arrest.
See C.638, C.640, C.641, C.645, C.646 and C.663.

C.640   Letter to the Editor, *Peace News* (18 January 1946) 4.
Notes
On Sansom's arrest.
See C.638, C.639, C.641, C.645, C.646 and C.663.

C.641   'The Sansom Case': letter to the Editor, *The Daily Herald* (21 January 1946) 2.
Notes
See C.638, C.639, C.640, C.645, C.646 and C.663.

C.642   'The Intellectual Revolt 1', *Manchester Evening News* (24 January 1946) 2.
Notes
First part of four-part series.
See C.648, C.653 and C.657.

C.643   'On Housing': review of Lawrence Wolfe *The Reilly Plan*, *Tribune* No. 474 (25 January 1946) 15–16.
Notes
CEJL IV 88–92.

C.644   'But Are We Really Ruder? No.', *Evening Standard* (26 January 1946) 6.
Notes
Reprinted as 'Are We Really Ruder? No.', *SEAC* (13 April 1946).
See C.685.

C.645   Letter to the Editor, *New Leader* (26 January 1946) 7.

Notes
With additional signature of Fenner Brockway.
See C.638, C.639, C.640, C.641, C.646 and C.663.
C.646   Letter to the Editor, *Freedom – Through Anarchism* (26 January 1946) 1.
Notes
See C.638, C.639, C.640, C.641, C.645 and C.663.
C.647   'How to Escape': review of George Millar *Horned Pigeon*, *The Observer* No. 8070 (27 January 1946) 3.
C.648   'The Intellectual Revolt – 2: What is Socialism?', *Manchester Evening News* (31 January 1946) 2.
Notes
Second part of four-part series.
See C.642, C.653 and C.657.
C.649   'Indian Passengers', *Manchester Guardian* (31 January 1946) 4.
Notes
Letter to the Editor.
C.650   'The Cost of Radio Programmes', *Tribune* No. 475 (1 February 1946) 8.
C.651   Abridged version of 'Good Bad Books', *World Digest* (February 1946) 79–80.
Notes
Published in full in *Tribune* (2 November 1945).
See C.594.
C.652   '"Bad" Climates are Best', *Evening Standard* (2 February 1946) 6.
Notes
Reprinted as 'I Don't Mind What the Weatherman Says', *SEAC* (23 February 1946).
See C.660.
C.653   'The Intellectual Revolt – 3: The Christian Reformers', *Manchester Evening News* (7 February 1946) 2.
Notes
Third part of four-part series.
See C.642, C.648 and C.657.
C.654   'Books v. Cigarettes', *Tribune* No. 476 (8 February 1946) 15.
Notes
Abridged version, 'You Too Can Own a Library', *English Digest* 3 (May 1946).
See C.693.
Full version in *Shooting an Elephant* 168–174, and *CEJL* IV 92–96.
C.655   '"The Moon Under Water"', *Evening Standard* (9 February 1946) 6.
Notes
Reprinted in *SEAC* (20 April 1946).
See C.687
CEJL III 44–47.
C.656   'As I Was Saying': review of Colm Brogan *The Democrat at the Supper Table*, *The Observer* No. 8072 (10 February 1946) 3.
Notes
CEJL IV 96–98.
C.657   'The Intellectual Revolt – 4: Pacifism and Progress', *Manchester Evening News* (14 February 1946) 2.
Notes
Final part of four-part series.
See C.642, C.648 and C.653.
C.658   'Decline of the English Murder', *Tribune* No. 477 (15 February 1946) 10–11.
Notes
Shooting an Elephant 197–202, *The Orwell Reader* 379–383, *Decline of the English Murder* 9–13, and *CEJL* IV 98–101.

C.659   'Words and Henry Miller': review of Henry Miller *The Cosmological Eye*, *Tribune* No. 478 (22 February 1946) 15.

       Notes
       CEJL IV 106–109.

C.660   'I Don't Mind What the Weatherman Says', *SEAC* (23 February 1946) 2.

       Notes
       First published as '"Bad" Climates are Best', *Evening Standard* (2 February 1946).
       See C.652.

C.661   'Burmese Days': review of F. Tennyson Jesse *The Story of Burma*, C.J. Richards *The Burman: An Appreciation*, and Harry I. Marshall *The Karens of Burma*, *The Observer* No. 8074 (24 February 1946) 3.

       Notes
       The last two titles were published as *Burma Pamphlets*, Nos. 7 and 8.
       Section on *The Story of Burma* in *CEJL* IV 111–113.

C.662   'Childhood in the South': review of Richard Wright *Black Boy*, James Aldridge *Of Many Men*, and Albert Maltz *The Cross and the Arrow*, *Manchester Evening News* (28 February 1946) 2.

C.663   'Cat and Mouse Treatment', *Freedom Defence Committee Bulletin* No. 2 (February–March 1946) 2.

       Notes
       Letter to the Editor on the arrest of Philip Sansom, signed by Orwell and 24 others.
       See C.638, C.639, C.640, C.641, C.645 and C.646.
       The first issue of the *Bulletin* was published in July 1945. Orwell was Vice-Chairman of the Freedom Defence Committee, but this was his first contribution.

C.664   'Freedom of the Park', *Freedom Defence Committee Bulletin* No. 2 (February–March 1946) 6.

       Notes
       First published in *Tribune*, 7 December 1945.
       See C.610.

C.665   'Nuremberg Prosecution Asked 1. To Give Representation to Natalia Trotsky 2. To Produce Evidence of Moscow Trials', *Socialist Appeal* (March 1946) 3.

       Notes
       Letter to the Editor signed by Orwell and 14 others.
       Also issued by *Social Appeal* as a handbill.
       Abridged version published in *Forward* (16 March 1946) [C.672].

C.666   'That Thing Called "Culture"': review of Jacques Barzun *We Who Teach*, *Manchester Evening News* (7 March 1946) 2.

C.667   'Do Our Colonies Pay?', *Tribune* No. 480 (8 March 1946) 10–11.

C.668   'Bird's Nest Soup?', *SEAC* (9 March 1946) 2.

       Notes
       First published as 'In Defence of English Cooking', *Evening Standard* (15 December 1945).
       See C.614.
       CEJL III 38–40.

C.669   'Black Country': review of Mark Benney *Charity Main*, *The Observer* No. 8076 (10 March 1946) 3.

C.670   'Words and Henry Miller': letter to the Editor, *Tribune* No. 481 (15 March 1946) 13.

       Notes
       Reply to Herman Schrijver's letter, 'Words and Mr Orwell', *Tribune* (1 March 1946) 12.

C.671   Review of Windwood Reade *The Martyrdom of Man*, *Tribune* No. 481 (15 March 1946) 18.

Notes
   CEJL IV 116–120.
C.672 'Nuremberg and the Moscow Trials': letter to the Editor, *Forward* (16 March 1946) 7.
   Notes
   Signed by George Orwell and 12 others. Dated 25 February 1946.
   This is an abridged version of the letter in *Socialist Appeal* (March 1946) [C.665].
   CEJL IV 115–116.
C.673 'The Voyage of the "Beagle"', *Radio Times* (22 March 1946) 4.
   Notes
   On the BBC Home Service programme for which Orwell had written the script [E.268].
C.674 'In Front of Your Nose', *Tribune* No. 482 (22 March 1946) 9–10.
   Notes
   CEJL IV 122–125.
C.675 'Voice of Madrid': review of Arturo Barea *The Clash*, *The Observer* No. 8078 (24 March 1946) 3.
C.676 'Songs We Used to Sing', *SEAC* (25 March 1946).
   Notes
   First published in *Evening Standard* (19 January 1946).
   See C.637.
C.677 'In Search of the Good Companions': review of J.B. Priestley *The Secret Dream*, Norah Hoult *Selected Stories*, Fred Urquhart *Selected Stories*, and John Brophy *Selected Stories*, *Manchester Evening News* (28 March 1946) 2.
C.678 'In Pursuit of Lord Acton': review of David Mathew *Acton: The Formative Years*, *Tribune* No. 483 (29 March 1946) 19.
C.679 'Politics and the English Language', *Horizon* Vol. 13, No. 76 (April 1946) 252–265.
   Notes
   Completed 11 December 1945.
   Reprinted privately by *The Observer* Foreign News Service as 'What Do You Mean?'
   Privately printed by the *News of the World* as an undated pamphlet for staff [British Library acquisition 28 February 1955].
   Abridged version in *The New Republic*, 17 and 24 June 1946.
   See C.698 and C.699.
   This pamphlet version was reproduced as three Christmas Keepsakes (Evansville, Indiana, 1947); one was for the friends of Paul A. Bennett of Brooklyn, New York, with the permission of *The New Republic*, and a note that 'The author has obliged with his consent from Scotland.' With illustrations by Merrill Snethen of Evansville, Printed by Herbert W. Simpson Inc, Evansville, Indiana. 100 copies printed for Herbert W. Simpson [copy in the Orwell Archive], 320 copies for Typophiles, 50 copies for the Friends of Paul Bennett.
   Shortened version in *World Digest*, August 1946.
   See C.704.
   Reprinted many times in anthologies. In Orwell's lifetime see, for example, Denys Val Baker, ed. *Modern British Writing* (New York: The Vanguard Press, 1947) 189–206, and Denys Val Baker, ed. *Little Reviews Anthology 1947–8* (London: Eyre and Spottiswoode, 1948) 92–103.
   See B.29 and B.30.
   Shooting an Elephant 84–101, *A Collection of Essays* 156–171, *The Orwell Reader* 355–366, *Selected Essays* 143–157, *Selected Writings* 75–89, *Collected Essays* 353–367, and *CEJL* IV 127–140.

C.680   'The Changing Face of War': review of B.H. Liddell Hart *The Revolution in Warfare, Manchester Evening News* (4 April 1946) 2.

C.681   'Foreign Policies': review of Grigore Gafencu *Prelude to the Russian Campaign, Tribune* No. 484 (5 April 1946) 19.

C.682   'Willow Pattern': review of G. Lowes Dickinson *Letters From John Chinaman and Other Essays,* and W.J. Turner, ed. *The Englishman's Country, The Observer* No. 8080 (7 April 1946) 3.

C.683   'The Rhymes of an Antiquarian', *Manchester Evening News* (11 April 1946) 2.

C.684   'Some Thoughts on the Common Toad', *Tribune* No. 485 (12 April 1946) 9–10.
　　　　Notes
　　　　Also published in *The New Republic* (20 May 1946) 734–735.
　　　　See C.697 and C.752.
　　　　Shooting an Elephant 202–207, *The Orwell Reader* 383–386, and *CEJL* IV 141–145.

C.685   'Are We Really Ruder? No.', *SEAC* (13 April 1946) 2.
　　　　Notes
　　　　First published as 'But Are We Really Ruder? No', *Evening Standard* (26 January 1946).
　　　　See C.644.

C.686   'Mr Lewis Changes His Mind': review of Sinclair Lewis *Cass Tamberlane, Manchester Evening News* (18 April 1946) 2.

C.687   '"The Moon Under Water"', *SEAC* (20 April 1946) 2. *Evening Standard* (9 February 1946) 6.
　　　　Notes
　　　　First published in *Evening Standard* (9 February 1946).
　　　　See C.655.
　　　　CEJL III 44–47.

C.688   'Why France Fell': review of Georges Bernanos *Plea for Liberty, The Observer* No. 8082 (21 April 1946) 3.

C.689   'Legacy from a House Painter': review of Robert Tressall *The Ragged Trousered Philanthropists, Manchester Evening News* (25 April 1946) 2.

C.690   'A Good Word For the Vicar Of Bray', *Tribune* No. 487 (26 April 1946) 7–8.
　　　　Notes
　　　　Shooting an Elephant 207–212, *The Orwell Reader* 386–389, and *CEJL* IV 149–153.

C.691   'Writers Support U.S. C.Os. Amnesty Campaign', *Freedom – Through Anarchism* (18 May 1946) 1.
　　　　Notes
　　　　Letter to President Truman signed by Orwell and 21 others.

C.692   Editorial, *Polemic* No. 3 (May 1946) 2–8.
　　　　Notes
　　　　Unsigned.
　　　　Reply to an attack on *Polemic* in an editorial in *Modern Quarterly* (December 1945) 1–5.
　　　　CEJL IV 153–160.

C.693   'You Too Can Own a Library', *English Digest* Vol. 21, No. 3 (May 1946) 83–85.
　　　　Notes
　　　　Abridged version of 'Books v. Cigarettes', *Tribune* (8 February 1946).
　　　　See C.654.

C.694   'Second Thoughts on James Burnham', *Polemic* No. 3 (May 1946) 13–33.
　　　　Notes
　　　　Payment £26 5s.
　　　　Reprinted as 'James Burnham', *University Observer* [Chicago] Vol. 1, No. 2 (Summer 1947) 63–74 [C.762], and as a pamphlet, *James Burnham and the Managerial Revolution*, published by the Socialist Book Centre, 1946 [D.2].

'Second Thoughts on James Burnham', *Shooting an Elephant* 134–163, *The Orwell Reader* 335–354, and *Collected Essays* 368–392; 'James Burnham and the Managerial Revolution', *CEJL* IV 160–181.

C.695   'Confessions of a Book Reviewer', *Tribune* No. 488 (3 May 1946) 18.
Notes
Also published in *The New Republic* Vol. 115 (5 August 1946) 144–145. See C.705.
Shooting an Elephant 164–168, and *CEJL* IV 181–184.

C.696   'Go to the Ant': review of Caryl P. Haskins *Of Ants and Men*, *The Observer* No. 8084 (5 May 1946) 3.

C.697   'Thoughts on the Common Toad', *The New Republic* Vol. 114 (20 May 1946) 734–735.
Notes
First published in *Tribune* (12 April 1946) 9–10. See C.684 and C.752.

C.698   'Politics and the English Language', *The New Republic* Vol. 114 (17 June 1946) 872–874.
Notes
First part of a reprint of the article first published in *Horizon* (April 1946). See C.679. See also C.699.

C.699   'Politics and the English Language', *The New Republic* Vol. 114 (24 June 1946) 903–904.
Notes
Second part of a reprint of the article first published in *Horizon* (April 1946).
See C.679. See also C.698.

C.700   Letter to the Editor, *The New Republic* 15 July 1946.

C.701   'Why I Write', *Gangrel* No. 4 (Summer 1946) 5–10.
Notes
Abridged version in *World Digest* (January 1947). See C.731.
Such, Such Were the Joys 3–11, *England Your England*, *A Collection of Essays* 309–316, *The Orwell Reader* 390–396, *Selected Writings* 99–105, *Collected Essays* 435–442, *Decline of the English Murder* 180–188, and *CEJL* I 1–7.

C.702   'London Letter', *Partisan Review* Vol. XIII, No. 3 (Summer 1946) 320–325.
Notes
On post-war privations and discontent; Communism in Britain; the post-war press and broadcasting.
Written early May 1946.
CEJL IV 184–190.

C.703   'Der Aufstand der Intellektuellen', *Neue Auslese aus dem Schrifttum der Gegenwart* No. 8 (August 1946) 86–99.
Notes
Abridged German translation of 'The Intellectual Revolt', first published in four parts in the *Manchester Evening News* in January and February 1946. Published here as a single essay with an added Afterword written by Orwell and translated into German. The original English version of the Afterword has not survived.

C.704   'Do You Use Prefabricated Phrases?', *World Digest* (August 1946) 78–80.
Notes
Abridged version of 'Politics and the English Language', first published in *Horizon* (April 1946).
See C.679.

C.705   'Confessions of a Book Reviewer', *The New Republic* Vol. 115 (5 August 1946) 144–145.

Notes

First published in *Tribune* (3 May 1946) 18.

See C.695.

C.706   'Questionnaire The Cost of Letters', *Horizon* (September 1946) 157–159.

Notes

Orwell's answers to a questionnaire.

Also published in *Current British Thought No. 1* (1947) 424–426.

See C.732.

CEJL IV 200–203.

C.707   'Catastrophic Gradualism': review of Arthur Koestler's essay 'The Yogi and the Commissar', *Politics* Vol. III (September 1946) 268–270.

Notes

Previously published in *C.W. Review* (November 1945) 12, 14.

See C.591.

C.708   'Remarques sur le Chauvinisme', *Echo. Revue Internationale. Ecrits, Faits et Idées de Tous Pays* Vol. I, No. 1 (August 1946) 66–74.

Notes

French version of '*Notes* on Nationalism' first published in *Polemic* (October 1945) [C.580].

Payment £10 10s.

C.709   'Het Nieuwe Chauvinisme', *Internationale Echo: Van Ideen en Gebeurtenissen uit Alle Landen* No. 1 (August 1946) 96–105.

Notes

Dutch version of '*Notes* on Nationalism' first published in *Polemic* (October 1945) [C.580].

Payment £10 10s.

C.710   'Politics vs. Literature: An Examination of *Gulliver's Travels*', *Polemic* No. 5 (September–October 1946) 5–21.

Notes

Payment £26 5s.

Shooting an Elephant 57–83, *The Orwell Reader* 283–300, *Selected Essays* 121–142, *Collected Essays* 393–414, and *CEJL* IV 205–223.

C.711   'Il Nuovo Sciovinismo', *Eco del Mondo: Opere, Fatti, Idee d'Ogni Paese*, Vol. 1, No. 1 (September 1946) 75–82.

Notes

Italian version of '*Notes* on Nationalism' first published in *Polemic* (October 1945) [C.580].

Payment £10 10s.

C.712   'The Right to Free Expression', *Polemic* No. 5 (September–October 1946) 45–53.

Notes

Article by Randall Swingler, annotated by George Orwell, on Orwell's article 'The Prevention of Literature', *Polemic* No. 2 (January 1946) 4–14

See C.624.

C.713   'Chauvinismin Varjo', *Parhaat* No. 1 (October–November 1946) 4–14.

Notes

Finnish version of '*Notes* on Nationalism' first published in *Polemic* (October 1945) [C.580].

Payment £10 10s.

C.714   'How the Poor Die', *Now* Vol. 6 (November 1946) 1–8.

Notes

Shooting an Elephant 18–32, *The Orwell Reader* 86–95, *Collected Essays* 341–352, *Decline of the English Murder* 32–44, and *CEJL* IV 223–233.

C.715 'As I Please', *Tribune* No. 515 (8 November 1946) 12.
  Notes
  On an American magazine; road safety; bread rationing; jury selection.
  CEJL IV 234–237.

C.716 'How Long Have We Been Here?': review of Francis Askham *A Foolish Wind*, Francis Ashton *The Breaking of the Seals*, and Sven Auren *The Tricolour Flies Again*, *Manchester Evening News* (7 November 1946) 2.

C.717 'Troubled Land': review of A. Ramos Oliveira *Politics, Economics and Men of Modern Spain, 1808–1946*, *The Observer* No. 8111 (10 November 1946) 3.

C.718 'Doctor in a Dilemma': review of Erich Maria Remarque *Arch of Triumph*, Derek Gilpin Barnes, ed. *Lords of Life: An Anthology of Animal Poetry*, and Donald Brook *Five Great French Composers*, *Manchester Evening News* (14 November 1946) 2.

C.719 'As I Please', *Tribune* No. 516 (15 November 1946) 12.
  Notes
  On Government's failure to publicise policies; xenophobia; war criminals; a Chekhov quotation.
  CEJL IV 237–240.

C.720 'Would Nelson Have Turned His Blind Eye?': review of Hannen Swaffer *What Would Nelson Do?*, Reginald Pound *Running Commentary*, and Howard Spring *Dunkerley's*, *Manchester Evening News* (21 November 1946) 2.

C.721 'As I Please', *Tribune* No. 517 (22 November 1946) 12.
  Notes
  On jury selection; peat; newspapers.
  Extract, 'Dullness is Truth', *English Digest* (February 1947).
  See C.739.
  Full version in *CEJL* IV 240–242.

C.722 'Riding Down From Bangor': review of John Habberton *Helen's Babies*, *Tribune* (22 November 1946) 20–21.
  Notes
  Abridged version published as 'The World of "Helen's Babies"', *The Literary Digest* (April 1947).
  See C.759.
  Shooting an Elephant 184–192, and *CEJL* IV 242–247.

C.723 'As I Please', *Tribune* No. 518 (29 November 1946) 12.
  Notes
  On the survival of civilisation; the price of clocks; the return of Jews to Palestine.
  CEJL IV 247–251.

C.724 'It Looks Different from Abroad', *The New Republic* (2 December 1946) 726.

C.725 'As I Please', *Tribune* No. 519 (6 December 1946) 13.
  Notes
  On George du Maurier's *Trilby*; the 'falling-off' of imaginative writers; unprintable words.
  Extract in *The Literary Digest* (Winter 1947).
  See C.730.
  CEJL IV 251–254.

C.726 'As I Please', *Tribune* No. 520 (13 December 1946) 12.
  Notes
  On nationalising laundries; book buying; conferences.
  CEJL IV 254–255.
  Extract, 'Let's Play Uno', *World Review* (February 1947).
  See C.740.

C.727 'Those Newspapers': letter to the Editor, *Tribune* No. 520 (13 December 1946) 13.

Notes
Reply to P.R. Lawton's letter, *Tribune* (6 December 1946) 14.

C.728 'As I Please', *Tribune* No. 521 (20 December 1946) 12.
Notes
On over-eating at Christmas.
CEJL IV 256–259.

C.729 'As I Please', *Tribune* No. 522 (27 December 1946) 9.
Notes
On modern credulity; the libel trade; American comics.
CEJL IV 259–262.

C.730 Extract from 'As I Please', *The Literary Digest* Vol. 2, No. 4 (Winter 1947) 5.
Notes
First published in *Tribune* (6 December 1946).
See C.725.

C.731 Abridged version of 'Why I Write', *World Digest* (January 1947) 75–77.
Notes
First published in *Gangrel* (Summer 1946).
See C.701.

C.732 'Questionnaire: The Cost of Letters', *Current British Thought* No. 1 (1947).
Notes
First published in *Horizon* (September 1946) 157–159.
See C.706.

C.733 'As I Please', *Tribune* No. 523 (3 January 1947) 12.
Notes
On function and reward; literary purges; getting up.
CEJL IV 265–268.
See C.830.

C.734 'Communists and Democrats': reply to a letter to the Editor, *Tribune* No. 525 (17 January 1947) 11.
Notes
Reply to Konni Zilliacus's letter protesting against Orwell's article in *Partisan Review* Vol. XIII (Summer 1946).
CEJL IV 192–194.
Zilliacus's letter is published in *CEJL* IV 191–192.

C.735 'As I Please', *Tribune* No. 525 (17 January 1947) 10.
Notes
On Indian broadcasts in wartime Germany; Victor Gollancz's *In Darkest Germany*; a dog diet; superfluous words.
CEJL IV 268–272.

C.736 'As I Please', *Tribune* (24 January 1947) 12.
Notes
On Polish immigrants; public occasions remembered; correction.
CEJL IV 272–275.

C.737 'As I Pleased', *Tribune* No. 527 (31 January 1947) 8–9.
Notes
Recollections, on the tenth anniversary of *Tribune*.
CEJL IV 276–280.

C.738 'Cryptos': letter to the Editor, *Tribune* No. 527 (31 January 1947) 16.
Notes
Reply to K. Zilliacus's letter.

C.739 'Dullness is Truth', *English Digest* Vol. 23, No. 4 (February 1947) 20.
Notes
Extract from 'As I Please', *Tribune* (22 November 1946).
See C.721.

C.740 'Let's Play Uno', *World Review* (February 1947) 91.
  Notes
  Extract from 'As I Please', *Tribune* (13 December 1946).
  See C.726.

C.741 'Freedom Defence Committee', *Freedom* (1 February 1947) 7.
  Notes
  Letter to the Editor signed by the Committee: Herbert Read, George Orwell, George Woodcock, and H.B. Gibson.
  Orwell was Vice-Chairman.
  See C.742 and C.744.

C.742 Letter to the Editor, *Peace News* (7 February 1947) 6.
  Notes
  Appeal for funds for the Freedom Defence Committee. Also published in *Freedom* (1 February 1947) and *Tribune* (7 February 1947).
  See C.741 and C.744.

C.743 'As I Please', *Tribune* No. 528 (7 February 1947) 12.
  Notes
  On household repairs; snow; minorities; H.G. Wells.
  CEJL IV 280–283.

C.744 Letter to the Editor, *Tribune* No. 528 (7 February 1947) 14.
  Notes
  Appeal for funds for the Freedom Defence Committee. Also published in *Freedom* (1 February 1947) and *Peace News* (7 February 1947).
  See C.741 and C.742.

C.745 'Guess or Prediction': letter to the Editor *Tribune* No. 528 (7 February 1947) 14.
  Notes
  Reply to Geoffrey Ashe's letter.

C.746 'As I Please', *Tribune* No. 529 (14 February 1947) 12.
  Notes
  On Scottish Nationalists; warmly-held opinions; light-hearted views of death.
  Extract, 'Britain's Occupied Territory', *English Digest* 1 (July 1947).
  See C.764.
  Full version in *CEJL* IV 283–287.

C.747 'Freedom Defence Committee', *Forward* (15 February 1947) 6.
  Notes
  Letter to the Editor signed by Herbert Read, George Orwell, and George Woodcock.

C.748 Extract from 'As I Please', *Manchester Evening News* (21 February 1947) 2.
  Notes
  Tribune had to suspend publication because of power cuts.
  See C.749 and C.750.

C.749 'As I Please', *The Daily Herald* (27 February 1947) 2.
  Notes
  See C.748 and C.750.

C.750 'As I Please', *Manchester Evening News* (28 February 1947) 2.
  Notes
  See C.748 and C.749.

C.751 'The Prevention of Literature', *The Atlantic Monthly* Vol. 179, No. 3 (March 1947) 115–119.
  Notes
  Abridged version of article originally published in *Polemic* (January 1946) 4–14.
  See C.624.
  Orwell noted that this abridgement was 'inadequate'.
  Reprinted in R.B. Downs, ed. *The First Freedom* (Chicago, 1960).
  See B.35.

C.752   'The Humble Toad', *World Digest* (March 1947) 11–13.
        Notes
        Abridged version of 'Some Thoughts on the Common Toad', first published
        in *Tribune* (12 April 1946).
        See C.684 and C.697.

C.753   'Lear, Tolstoy and the Fool', *Polemic* No. 7 (March 1947) 2–17.
        Notes
        Payment £26 5s.
        Shooting an Elephant 33–56, *The Orwell Reader* 300–315, *Selected Essays*
        101–119, *Collected Essays* 415–434, and *CEJL* IV 287–302.

C.754   'As I Please', *Tribune* No. 530 (7 March 1947) 11.
        Notes
        On Government's failure to publicise itself; the broadcasting art; *The Oxford
        Book of English Verse*.
        CEJL IV 303–304.

C.755   'As I Please', *Tribune* No. 531 (14 March 1947) 10.
        Notes
        On rationalised spelling and the metric system; peat; a customs incident;
        teaching history in private schools.
        CEJL IV 304–307.

C.756   'As I Please', *Tribune* No. 532 (21 March 1947) 13.
        Notes
        On declining birthrate; law and the layman; suspension of weeklies.

C.757   'As I Please', *Tribune* No. 533 (28 March 1947) 12.
        Notes
        On Mass Observation; government publicity; venereal disease; spring; the
        woodwele.
        CEJL IV 309–313.

C.758   'Burnham's View of the Contemporary World Struggle': review of James Burnham
        The Struggle for the World, *The New Leader* [New York] (29 March 1947) 12–14.
        Notes
        CEJL IV 313–326.

C.759   'The World of Helen's Babies', *The Literary Digest* Vol. 2, No. 1 (April 1947) 1–4.
        Notes
        Abridged version of 'Riding Down From Bangor' *Tribune* (22 November
        1946).
        See C.722.

C.760   'As I Please', *Tribune* No. 534 (4 April 1947) 11.
        Notes
        On nationalising the press; tobacco growing in England; pidgin English.

C.761   'The Final Years of Lady Gregory': review of Lennox Robinson, ed. *Lady
        Gregory's Journals*, *The New Yorker* (19 April 1947) 107–108, 110.
        Notes
        Writing to Leonard Moore about his forthcoming *New Yorker* work and
        reprints, and about editorial cuts generally, Orwell said,
        I have read through the *New Yorker*'s proposals carefully, and I do not think
        there is anything to object to. Only two doubtful points arise, i.e. the point
        referred to by them as (c), reprinting of articles of mine in books issued by the
        New Yorker, and the question of "editing" my reviews. I am not much con-
        cerned about reprints of this type of article because they would be strictly
        book reviews and would not be much more than 1,500 words, if that. I would
        never reprint in book form anything of less than 2,000 words, so I don't par-
        ticularly mind if they choose to include things of mine in collections of snip-
        pets. When one has anything included in a book of this type, as one does from
        time to time, one never seems to get more than a few pounds out of it, and I

don't see how anything else can be expected, since the royalties obviously have
to be split up among the various contributors. I don't think it is worth asking
the *New Yorker* to depart from its usual practice in this matter. The question
of "editing" might be more difficult . . .
What really matters here is whether or not one is dealing with a civilised and
intelligent paper. The *New Yorker* would be bound to make cuts occasionally,
and would not as a rule have time to consult me, but I don't fancy they would
alter my articles in any way I strongly objected to. So all in all I think we can
accept their proposition as it stands.[14]

C.762   'Political Writers: 1 James Burnham', *University Observer* [Chicago] Vol. 1,
        No. 2 (Summer 1947) 63–74.
        Notes
        First published as 'Second Thoughts on James Burnham', *Polemic* No. 3 (May
        1946) 13–33.
        See C.694.

C.763   'Hanging To-day', *The Plebs* (June 1947) 85.
        Notes
        Extract from *Tribune*.

C.764   'Britain's Occupied Territory', *English Digest* Vol. 25, No. 1 (July 1947) 11.
        Notes
        Extract from 'As I Please', *Tribune* (14 February 1947).
        See C.746.

C.765   'The Future of Socialism: IV. Toward European Unity', *Partisan Review* Vol. 14,
        No. 4 (July–August 1947) 346–351.
        Notes
        Orwell contributed the fourth of a five-part series, published in *Partisan
        Review* throughout 1947.
        CEJL IV 370–375.
        See C.766.

C.766   'Ein sozialistisches Europa', *Stuttgarter Rundschau* No. 2 (1947) 8–10.
        Notes
        German translation of 'The Future of Socialism', first published as 'The
        Future of Socialism: IV. Toward European Unity', *Partisan Review* (July–
        August 1947).
        See C.765.

C.767   'What is the English Character?', *World Digest* (October 1947) 31–32.
        Notes
        Abridged from the first section, 'English at First Glance', and from the final
        section, 'The Future of the English People', of *The English People* [A.11].

C.768   'L'avenir du socialisme', *Echo* Vol. 3, No. 15 (November 1947) 323–328.
        Notes
        French translation of 'Towards European Unity', the fourth article in the series
        'The Future of Socialism', *Partisan Review* (July–August 1947) [C.765].

C.769   'L'avenir del socialismo', *Eco del Mondo* Vol. 3, No. 15 (November 1947)
        324–328.
        Notes
        Italian translation of fourth article from *Partisan Review* [C.765].

C.770   'Profile. Krishna Menon', *The Observer* (30 November 1947) 3.
        Notes
        Written with David Astor.

C.771   'De toekomst van het socialisme', *Internationale Echo* Vol. 3, No. 15 (November–
        December 1947) 331–336.
        Notes
        Dutch translation of 'Towards European Unity', the fourth article in the series
        'The Future of Socialism', *Partisan Review* (July–August 1947) [C.765].

C.772 'The Three Best Books of 1947', *Horizon* Vol. XVI (December 1947) 368.
Notes
Orwell's answers to a questionnaire.

C.773 'A Lost World': review of Lord Beveridge *India Called Them*, *The Observer* No. 8175 (1 February 1948) 3.
Notes
Believing that he was recovering in East Kilbride Hospital in December 1947, Orwell wrote,
I might be able to get back to some serious work some time in 1948. I am going shortly to start a little book reviewing for the *Observer*. I might as well earn a bit of money while I'm on my back.[15]

C.774 'Marx and Russia': review of John Plamenatz *What is Communism?*, *The Observer* No. 8177 (15 February 1948) 4.

C.775 'Men of the Isles': review of Kenneth Williamson *The Atlantic Islands*, *The Observer* No. 8179 (29 February 1948) 3.

C.776 'Down Under': review of Norbert Casteret *My Caves*, *The Observer* No. 8181 (14 March 1948) 3.

C.777 'Lew i nosorożec: Anglia, Twoja Anglia', *Kultura* [Paris], No. 4 (April 1948) 41–62.
Notes
Polish version of 'England, Your England', from *The Lion and the Unicorn* [A.9].

C.778 'American New Writing: review of James Laughlin, ed. *Spearhead. Ten Years' Experimental Writing in America*, *Times Literary Supplement* (17 April 1948) 218.
Notes
Unsigned.

C.779 'Środki zapobiegawcze w literaturze', *Kultura* [Paris] No. 5 (May 1948) 3–14.
Notes
Polish version of 'The Prevention of Literature', first published in *Polemic* (January 1946).
See C.624.

C.780 'Wilde's Utopia': review of Oscar Wilde *The Soul of Man Under Socialism*, *The Observer* No. 8189 (9 May 1948) 4.
Notes
CEJL IV 426–428.

C.781 'Britain's Left-Wing Press', *Progressive* [Madison, Wisconsin] (June 1948) 17–19.

C.782 '"Mr. Sludge"': review of Jean Burton *Heyday of a Wizard*, *The Observer* No. 8193 (6 June 1948) 3.

C.783 'Writers and Leviathan', *Politics and Letters* No. 4 (Summer 1948) 36–40.
Notes
Published concurrently in *The New Leader* (19 June 1948) 10–11.
See C.784.
Such, Such Were the Joys 64–72, *England Your England*, *Selected Writings* 90–98, *Collected Essays* 443–450, and *CEJL* IV 407–414.

C.784 'Writers and Leviathan', *The New Leader* (19 June 1948) 10–11.
Notes
Published concurrently in *Politics and Letters* (Summer 1948).
See C.783.

C.785 'Prime Minister': review of Roy Jenkins *Mr Atlee: An Interim Biography*, *The Observer* No. 8197 (4 July 1948) 3.

C.786 'The Sanctified Sinner': review of Graham Greene *The Heart of the Matter*, *The New Yorker* (17 July 1948) 66, 69–71.
Notes
CEJL IV 439–443.

C.787 'A Questionable Shape': review of Hugh Kingsmill *The Dawn's Delay*, *The Observer* No. 8199 (18 July 1948) 3.

C.788 'For Ever Eton': review of B.J.W. Hill *Eton Medley*, *The Observer* No. 8201 (1 August 1948) 3.

C.789 'Mainly About the Novel': review of B. Rajan *The Novelist as Thinker*, *Times Literary Supplement* (7 August 1948) 444.
 Notes
 Unsigned.

C.790 'Civil Service Purge', *The Socialist Leader* (21 August 1948) 2.
 Notes
 Statement by the Freedom Defence Committee, signed by Orwell and 23 others.

C.791 'The Writer's Dilemma': review of George Woodcock *The Writer and Politics*, *The Observer* No. 8204 (22 August 1948) 3.

C.792 'The Purge. FDC Outlines its Attitude', *Peace News* (27 August 1948) 6.
 Notes
 Statement by the Freedom Defence Committee, signed by Orwell and 23 others.
 Also published in *Tribune* (17 September 1948).
 See C.796.
 Abridged version published in *The Socialist Leader* (21 August 1948).
 See C.799.
 See also C.797, C.799 and C.800.

C.793 Review of Osbert Sitwell *Great Morning*, *The Adelphi* Vol. 24, No. 4 (July–September 1948) 248–250.
 Notes
 CEJL IV 443–446.

C.794 'Lear and Nonsense Poetry', *The Literary Digest* Vol. 3, No. 3 (Autumn 1948) 33–35.
 Notes
 Abridged version of 'Nonsense Poetry', *Tribune* (21 December 1945).
 See C.617.

C.795 'Raffles i panna Blandish', *Kultura* [Paris] No. 9–10 (September–October 1948) 48–58.
 Notes
 Polish version of 'Raffles and Miss Blandish', first published in *Horizon* (October 1944).
 See C.470.

C.796 'The Freedom Defence Committee', *Tribune* No. 610 (17 September 1948) 15.
 Notes
 Letter to the Editor.
 Signed by Benjamin Britten, E.M. Forster, Augustus John, George Orwell, Herbert Read and Osbert Sitwell.
 Also published in *The Northern Echo* (17 September 1945) [C.797], *The Socialist Leader* (18 September 1945) [C.799], *Freedom Defence Committee Bulletin* (Autumn 1948) [C.800], and in an abridged form in *Peace News* (17 September 1948) [C.798].
 See also C.792.
 CEJL IV 446–447.

C.797 'For Freedom's Defence', *The Northern Echo* (16 September 1948) 2.
 Notes
 Letter to the Editor.
 See C.796.

C.798 'For Freedom', *Peace News* (17 September 1948) 2.
 Notes
 Letter to the Editor.
 See C.796.

C.799 'Freedom Defence Committee', *The Socialist Leader* (18 September 1948) 10.
        Notes
        Letter to the Editor.
        See C.796.

C.800 Letter to the Editor, *Freedom Defence Committee Bulletin* No. 7 (Autumn 1948) 1.
        Notes
        See C.796.

C.801 'F.D.C. Statement on Civil Service Purge', *Freedom Defence Committee Bulletin* No. 7 (Autumn 1948) 2.
        Notes
        Signed by Orwell and 23 others, on fascists and communists in the Civil Service.

C.802 'Britain's Struggle for Survival: The Labour Government After Three Years', *Commentary* (October 1948) 343–349.

C.803 'Contemporary Novelists': review of Edwin Berry Burgum *The Novel and the World's Dilemma*, *Times Literary Supplement* (2 October 1948) 556.
        Notes
        Unsigned.
        See C.807.

C.804 'The Defence of Freedom': review of Louis Fischer *Gandhi and Stalin*, *The Observer* No. 8211 (10 October 1948) 3.

C.805 'Problem Picture': review of Jean-Paul Sartre *Portrait of the Anti-Semite* translated by Erik de Mauny, *The Observer* No. 8215 (7 November 1948) 3.
        Notes
        CEJL IV 452–453.

C.806 'Culture and the Classes': review of T.S. Eliot *Notes Towards the Definition of Culture*, *The Observer* No. 8218 (28 November 1948) 4.
        Notes
        CEJL IV 455–457.

C.807 'Armut und Hoffnung des Grossbritanniens: Bericht aus London', *Der Monat* No. 3 (December 1948) 77–85.
        Notes
        German version of 'Britain's Struggle for Survival', first published as 'Britain's Struggle for Survival: The Labor Government After Three Years', in *Commentary* (October 1948).
        See C.803.

C.808 'Reflections on Gandhi': review of M.K. Gandhi *The Story of My Experiments with Truth* translated by Mahadex Desai, *Partisan Review* Vol. XVI, No. 1 (January 1949) 85–92.
        Notes
        Extract, 'Gandhi: A Critical Study', *Mirror: Monthly International Review*, No. 16 (October 1949).
        See C.825.
        Reprinted in full in *Shooting an Elephant* 102–113, *A Collection of Essays* 171–180, *The Orwell Reader* 328–335, *Collected Essays* 451–460, and *CEJL* IV 463–470.

C.809 'Our Native Humour': review of Leonard Russell and Nicolas Bentley, eds. *The English Comic Album*, *The Observer* No. 8222 (2 January 1949) 3.

C.810 'Exclusive Club': review of F.R. Leavis *The Great Tradition*, *The Observer* No. 8227 (6 February 1949) 3.

C.811 'Mr Waugh Pays a Visit to Perilous Neutralia': review of Evelyn Waugh *Scott-King's Modern Europe*, *The New York Times Book Review* (20 February 1949) 1, 25.

C.812 'I Appeal', *The News Chronicle* (3 March 1949) 5.
  Notes
  Letter to the Editor.
  CEJL IV 477–478.

C.813 'Der Hofstaat der Tiere: *Animal Farm*', *Der Monat* No. 7 (April 1949) 34–43.
  Notes
  German translation of Chapters 9 and 10 of *Animal Farm*.

C.814 'Conrad's Place and Rank in English Letters', *Wiadomości* [London] Vol. 4, No. 15 (158) (Kwietnia) (10 April 1949) 1.
  Notes
  Orwell's answers to a questionnaire.
  CEJL IV 488–490.

C.815 'The Question of the Pound Award', *Partisan Review* Vol. XVI, No. 5 (May 1949) 517–518.
  Notes
  Response to William Barrett's editorial, 'A Prize for Ezra Pound', *Partisan Review* (April 1949) 344–347, on the award to Pound by the Bollingen Foundation.
  CEJL IV 490–491.

C.816 'A Look into the Future: 1984 and Newspeak', *World Review* No. 3 (May 1949) 51–54.
  Notes
  An abridged version of the Appendix to *Nineteen Eighty-Four*, 'The Principles of Newspeak'.

C.817 'Mr. Dickens Sits for His Portrait': review of Hesketh Pearson *Dickens: His Character, Comedy and Career*, *The New York Times Book Review* (15 May 1949) 1, 17.

C.818 'Orwell on Churchill: A Critic Views a Statesman': review of Winston S. Churchill *Their Finest Hour*, *The New Leader* [New York] (14 May 1949) 10.
  Notes
  Written by 9 April 1949.
  CEJL IV 491–495.

C.819 Brief note of condolence on the death of Marie Louise Berneri, *Freedom* Vol. 10, No. 11 (18 May 1949) 3.

C.820 'The Strange World of 1984', *Life* Vol. 27, No. 1 (4 July 1949) 78–85.
  Notes
  Illustrated article on *Nineteen Eighty-Four* with synopsis of the plot and chief ideas of the novel, with quoted extracts. Drawings by Abner Dean.

C.821 Quotation by the Editor from 'a recent letter' by Orwell, *Life* Vol. 27, No. 4 (25 July 1949) 4, 6.
  Notes
  Quotes from a letter by Orwell to Francis A. Henson.

C.822 'Score Sheet', *The New York Times Book Review* (31 July 1949) 8.
  Notes
  Quotes from Orwell's letter to Francis A. Henson.

C.823 'For Freedom in Spain', *Tribune* (2 September 1949) 15.
  Notes
  Letter signed by Orwell and 17 others.

C.824 Excerpts from *Nineteen Eighty-Four*, *Reader's Digest* (October 1949) 74–95.
  Notes
  The first section of the book only.
  Ian Willison estimates the circulation at 6,000,000 worldwide.

C.825 'Gandhi: A Critical Study', *Mirror: Monthly International Review*, No. 16 (October 1949) 22–25.

Notes
Extract from 'Reflections on Gandhi', *Partisan Review* (January 1949).
See C.808.

C.826 'Franco contre les "sévices corporels"', *Le Populaire de Paris* No. 7962 (27 October 1949) 2.
Notes
Letter to the Editor signed by Orwell and 26 others.

C.827 '*1984: Ein Utopischer Roman*', *Der Monat* No. 14 (November 1949) 115–137.
Notes
First extract of German translation of *Nineteen Eighty-Four*. Translated by Kurt Wagenseil.

C.828 '*1984: Ein Utopischer Roman*', *Der Monat* No. 15 (December 1949) 239–277.
Notes
Second extract of German translation of *Nineteen Eighty-Four*, as far as the end of Part 1.

C.829 'Twóczość Donalda Mac Gilla', *Kultura* [Paris] No. 1 (January 1950) 75–84.
Notes
Polish version of 'The Art of Donald McGill', first published in *Horizon* (September 1941) [C.293].

C.830 '. . . by George Orwell', *Tribune* (27 January 1950) 7.
Notes
Reprint of 'As I Please', *Tribune* (3 January 1947) 12.
See C.733.

C.831 '*1984: Ein Utopischer Roman*', *Der Monat* No. 18 (March 1950) 570–602.
Notes
Final extract of German translation of *Nineteen Eighty-Four*, from the middle of Part 2 to the end of the novel, but without the Appendix.

C.832 'From the Notebooks of George Orwell', *World Review* No. 16 (June 1950) 21–44.

C.833 'La littérature encagée', *Preuves* (June 1952).
Notes
French version of 'The Prevention of Literature', first published in *Polemic* (January 1946).
See C.624.

C.834 'Such, Such Were the Joys', *Partisan Review* Vol. XIX, No. 5 (September–October 1952) 505–545.
Notes
Written before May 1947.
Such, Such Were the Joys 12–63, *A Collection of Essays* 1–47, *The Orwell Reader* 419–456, and *CEJL* IV 330–369.

C.835 'English Writing in Total War', *The New Republic* Vol. 131 (22 November 1954) 56–58.
Notes
First published in *The New Republic* Vol. 105 (14 July 1941) 57–58.
See C.281.

C.836 'What is a Pamphlet?', *Pendle Hill Bulletin* No. 135 (April 1957) 1–6.
Notes
Extracts from Orwell's Introduction to *British Pamphleteers* Vol. I.
See B.31.
Published in Wallingford, Pennsylvania.

C.837 'George Gissing', *The London Magazine* (June 1960) 36–43.
Notes
Written May–June 1948.
Originally commissioned for *Politics and Letters*, which ceased publication before the article appeared.

CEJL IV 428–436.

In April 1948 Orwell wrote to Julian Symons,

I am a great fan of [Gissing] . . . & was just in the act of rereading two reprints, which I promised to review for *Politics and Letters*. I think I shall do a long article on him, for them or someone else.[16]

C.838   'Some Letters of George Orwell', *Encounter* Vol. 18, No. 1 (January 1962) 55–65.

Notes

22 letters to Cyril Connolly, T.R. Fyvel, Dennis King-Farlow, Richard Rees, Margaret Catherine Rees, and Stephen Spender, written between February 1936 and July 1949.

C.839   'The Freedom of the Press', *The Times Literary Supplement* No. 3680 (15 September 1972) 1037–1039.

Notes

First publication of a proposed introduction to the first edition of *Animal Farm*.

Reprinted in *The New York Times Magazine* (8 October 1972) 12–13, 72, 74, 76; in *Quest* (November–December 1972) [C.840]; and in *Animal Farm*, *Complete Works* and Penguin, 1989 [A10].

C.840   'The Freedom of the Press', *Quest* [Bombay] No. 79 (November–December 1972) 9–14.

Notes

First published in *The Times Literary Supplement* (15 September 1972).

See C.839.

C.841   'Penguin Celebrates with Orwell', *The Bookseller* (26 July 1975).

Notes

Extracts from 'Bookshop Memories', first published in *The Fortnightly* Vol. CXLVI (November 1936) 600–604, and from 'Some Recent Novels', reviews of Penguin books, first published in *The New English Weekly* Vol. VIII, No. 21 (5 March 1936) 414–415.

See C.075 and C.090.

C.842   'Orwell and His Publishers: New Letters', *The Times Literary Supplement* No. 4214 (6 January 1984) 15–16.

Notes

Seven letters from Orwell to Leonard Moore, written between February 1936 and August 1944.

Notes to C

1 Extract from manuscript notebook written in 1949. *CEJL* IV 510–11.
2 Letter to May Plowman, 22 September 1929. *CEJL* I 15.
3 Letter to May Plowman, 1 November 1930. *CEJL* I 29.
4 Letter to Dennis Collings [c. 12 October 1931]. *CEJL* I 51.
5 Letter to John Lehmann, 27 May 1936. *CEJL* I 221.
6 Letter to John Lehmann, 6 July 1940. *CEJL* II 29.
7 'As I Pleased' *Tribune* (31 January 1947) 8–9. [See C.737].
8 War-time diary, 22 March 1942. *CEJL* II 412.
9 Letter to Leonard Moore, 2 November 1946. *CEJL* IV 234.
10 'As I Pleased', *Tribune* (31 January 1947) 8–9. [See C.737].
11 'As I Pleased', *Tribune* (31 January 1947) 8–9. [See C.737].
12 Letter to Philip Rahv, 1 May 1944. *CEJL* III 141.
13 Letter to Geoffrey Gorer, 22 January 1946. *CEJL* IV 87.
14 Letter to Leonard Moore, 2 November 1946. *CEJL* IV 234.
15 Letter to T.R. Fyvel, 31 December 1947. *CEJL* IV 386–387.
16 Letter to Julian Symons, 20 April 1948. *CEJL* IV 416.

D: Essay collections

... this autumn I intend to publish a book of reprinted literary essays. I would have done it before, but there are several more I want to write before issuing the book, and I haven't been able to do so because of being smothered under other work.[1]

D.1 CRITICAL ESSAYS

D.1a First Edition, 1946

CRITICAL ESSAYS | BY | GEORGE ORWELL | LONDON | SECKER AND WARBURG | 1946

Collation [1]–10⁸ 11⁶; 86 leaves (18.3 × 12.2); [1–4] 5–169 [170–172]

Contents [1] halftitle: CRITICAL ESSAYS [2] blank [3] titlepage [4] imprint: *First Published 1946* | THIS BOOK IS PRODUCED IN | COMPLETE CONFORMITY WITH THE | AUTHORIZED ECONOMY STANDARDS | MADE AND PRINTED IN GREAT BRITAIN BY | MORRISON AND GIBB LTD., LONDON AND EDINBURGH 5 contents 6 author's note 7–169 text [170] imprint: PRINTED IN GREAT BRITAIN BY | MORRISON AND GIBB LTD., | LONDON AND EDINBURGH [171] publisher's advertisement [172] blank

Binding Red linen grain cloth on boards. Off white endpapers.

Front cover Stamped in gilt: *George Orwell's* | [rule] | CRITICAL ESSAYS

Back cover Plain

Spine Stamped in gilt: GEORGE | ORWELL | CRITICAL | ESSAYS | SECKER & | WARBURG

Paper Esparto antique wove

Jacket Off white
Front Large capitals printed in red across full front cover and partly shaded in red: GEORGE ORWELL
Across them is printed diagonally in black: [star] | CRITICAL | ESSAYS
Back [in red] GEORGE ORWELL | [biographical summary and list of books by Orwell] | MARTIN [in red] SECKER & WARBURG [in black] LIMITED | 7 JOHN STREET, BLOOMSBURY, LONDON, W.C.1
Spine [[laterally] [in red] GEORGE ORWELL [across the centre in black] CRITICAL ESSAYS [and horizontally at foot] Secker & | Warburg
Front flap [summary] | 8s.6d. net
Back flap Plain.

Notes
In July 1944 Orwell began planning the content of the collection. He had finished it by 22 January 1945, when he sent the manuscript to Leonard Moore, except for the essay, 'In Defence of P.G. Wodehouse', which he completed and sent off by early February.
Published on 14 February 1946.
8s 6d
3,028 copies

Contemporary reviews
V.S. Pritchett *New Statesman and Nation* (16 February 1946)
Daniel George *The Observer* (17 February 1946)
John Middleton Murry *Adelphi* (July–September 1946)
Stuart Hampshire *The Spectator* (8 March 1946)
Paul Potts *Socialist Leader* (20 July 1946)
Times Literary Supplement (23 February 1946)

Locations
Cambridge University Library.
Orwell Archive, two copies, with jackets.
Robarts Library, University of Toronto.

Proofs of *Critical Essays* 1945
169pp unbound
Note on box contents says uncorrected, but there are five notes on the back endpaper of page numbers, some of which correspond to marked passages in the text.

Corrected proofs of *Critical Essays* 1945
Corrected by Orwell
11 marked unbound gatherings [1]–11
The final gathering is clearly not contemporary with the rest of this corrected proof. The paper is not as faded and the gathering is uncorrected – the only uncorrected gathering.

Corrected final gathering of *Critical Essays* 1945
Corrected by Orwell
Last blank page is filled with pencil notes by Roger Senhouse, a partner in the publishing firm

Location
Orwell Archive. Box 5.

Reissues
May 1946 with corrections, new imprint, and on jacket pink print instead of red. Orwell Archive, with jacket.
5,632 copies

'Reset Edition', January 1951, as part of the Uniform Edition.
3,000 copies
10s 6d
Reissued 1954 – Orwell Archive

There was a Braille edition, published by the National Institute for the Blind, in December 1949.

List of contents
Charles Dickens
Boys' Weeklies
Wells, Hitler and the World State
The Art of Donald McGill
Rudyard Kipling
W.B. Yeats
Benefit of Clergy: Some Notes on Salvador Dali
Arthur Koestler
Raffles and Miss Blandish
In Defence of P.G. Wodehouse

Locations
Cambridge University Library

D.1b   First American Edition, 1946

GEORGE ORWELL | DICKENS, | DALI | & OTHERS | STUDIES | IN POPULAR CULTURE | REYNAL & HITCHCOCK | NEW YORK

Collation There are eight unmarked gatherings of 16 leaves arranged [1–8]^{16}; 128 leaves (18.8 × 13.0); [i–x] 1–243 [244–246]

Contents [i] halftitle: DICKENS | DALI | & OTHERS [ii] list of books by Orwell [iii] titlepage [iv] imprint: COPYRIGHT, 1946, BY GEORGE ORWELL | All rights reserved, | including the right to reproduce | this book or portions thereof in any form. | [note on quotations from W.B. Yeats] | PRINTED IN THE UNITED STATES OF AMERICA | [publisher's logo] I | BY THE CORNWALL PRESS, INC., CORNWALL, N.Y. [v–vi] author's note [vii] contents [viii] blank [ix] halftitle: DICKENS | DALI | & OTHERS [x] blank 1–243 text [244–246] blank

Binding Off white cloth on boards. Off white endpapers.

Front cover Stamped in grey: DICKENS, | DALI | & OTHERS

Back cover Plain.
Spine Stamped in grey: GEORGE | ORWELL [and vertically]: DICKENS, DALI & OTHERS | [and horizontally]: REYNAL & | HITCHCOCK

Jacket Grey
Front [in white] DICKENS | [in yellow] DALI | [in white] & OTHERS | [in yellow] STUDIES | [and laterally] IN POPULAR CULTURE [beside this horizontally in white] Rudyard Kipling | P.G. Wodehouse | W.B. Yeats | Picture Postcards | Salvador Dali | Boys' Magazines | Charles Dickens | Detective Stories | Arthur Koestler | H.G. Wells | [in yellow] BY GEORGE ORWELL
Back Publisher's advertisements
Spine [in yellow] GEORGE | ORWELL | [laterally] [in white] DICKENS, [in yellow] DALI [in white] & OTHERS | [and horizontally in yellow] REYNAL & | HITCHCOCK
Front flap $2.50 | DICKENS, DALI | AND OTHERS | *Studies In Popular Culture* | BY GEORGE ORWELL | [notes on the essays]
Back flap Biographical sketch of Orwell

Notes
Published 29 April 1946.
$2.50
5,000 copies
Price increased to $2.75 1 January 1952

Locations
Cambridge University Library
Orwell Archive, two copies with jackets
Pratt Library, Victoria University, University of Toronto.

Reissue
There was a Canadian Edition of *Dickens, Dali and Others*, published by Saunders in 1946. Price $3.00 [from advertisement on jacket of Canadian Animal Farm, 1946].
New York: Harcourt, Brace & World
San Diego: Harcourt Brace Jovanovich, 1973 A Harvest|HBJ Book. Paperbound.

List of contents
Charles Dickens
Boys' Weeklies
Wells, Hitler and the World State
The Art of Donald McGill
Rudyard Kipling

W.B. Yeats
Benefit of Clergy: Some Notes on Salvador Dali
Arthur Koestler
Raffles and Miss Blandish
In Defence of P.G. Wodehouse

D.2   JAMES BURNHAM AND THE MANAGERIAL REVOLUTION

D.2a   First Edition, 1946

[No separate titlepage. Title on first page of text.]
JAMES BURNHAM and the | MANAGERIAL REVOLUTION | *GEORGE ORWELL*

Collation Single unmarked gathering of eight leaves. Covers are included in pagination, and text extends to inside back cover; (21.7 × 14.0); [1–2] 3–19 [20]

Contents [1] front cover [2] imprint: This essay was first published in | POLEMIC 3 | under the title | *Second Thoughts on James Burnham.* | It is published in the present form by | the Socialist Book Centre, 158, Strand, | London, July, 1946. | *ONE SHILLING* 3–19 text [20] publisher's advertisements

Binding Paper covers stapled to text leaves.

Front cover Overall pattern of white dots on an orange background on which is printed in black: JAMES | BURNHAM | and the | *Managerial* | *Revolution* | GEORGE ORWELL | *ONE SHILLING NET*

Back cover [within a black frame is an advertisement for Orwell's books published by Secker & Warburg] | [rule] | Speedee Press Services Ltd. (T.U. all Depts.), 206 Union Street, S.E.1.

Notes
3,000 copies
1s 0d
First published in *Polemic* as 'Second Thoughts on James Burnham' [See C.694]

Locations
Cambridge University Library. Acquisition 2 October 1946.
Orwell Archive, 3 copies

D.3   SHOOTING AN ELEPHANT AND OTHER ESSAYS

D.3a   First Edition, 1950

SHOOTING AN | ELEPHANT | *and Other Essays* | BY | GEORGE ORWELL | LONDON | SECKER AND WARBURG | 1950

Collation [A]–N⁸ O⁶; 110 leaves (18.3 × 12.2); [i–viii] [1]–212

Contents [i] halftitle: SHOOTING AN ELEPHANT [ii] list of books by Orwell [iii] titlepage [iv] imprint: Martin Secker & Warburg Ltd. | 7 John Street, Bloomsbury, London, W.C.1. | *First Published 1950* | Made and Printed in Great Britain by The Alcuin Press, | Welwyn Garden City, and Bound by Key & Whiting Ltd., | Harecourt Bookbinding Works, London, N.1 [v] acknowledgements and Editor's note [vi] blank [vii] contents [viii] blank [1]–212 text

Binding Green calico grain cloth on boards. Off white endpapers. Purple topped leaves.

Front and back covers Plain.

Spine Stamped in purplish red: [pyramid of six lines] | SHOOTING | AN | ELEPHANT |

[small ornate leaf device] | GEORGE | ORWELL | [inverted pyramid of six lines] | SECKER & | WARBURG

Jacket Grey.
Front Against a grey background is an irregular red block. Across the grey and red areas is picked out in white: Shooting | an Elephant | and other essays | by | George Orwell
Back Publisher's advertisement printed in red on an off-white background.
Spine Grey with irregular vertical red streak. Picked out in white: Shooting | an | Elephant | by | George | Orwell | Secker & | Warburg
Front flap [summary] | *Jacket design by Michael Kennard* | W808 10|- net | RECOM-MENDED BY | THE BOOK SOCIETY
Back flap Publisher's advertisement

Notes
Published 5 October 1950, 10s 0d.
7,530 copies
Reprinted February 1951, 10s 6d.
2,100 copies

Contemporary reviews
Kirkus Review (15 October 1950)
V.S. Pritchett *New Statesman and Nation* (28 October 1950)
R.D. Charques *The Spectator* (15 December 1950)
T.R. Fyvel *Tribune* (27 October 1950)
Times Literary Supplement (20 October 1950)

Locations
Cambridge University Library
Orwell Archive, with jacket
1950 reprint at Kelly Library, St Michael's College, University of Toronto.

List of contents
Shooting an Elephant
A Hanging
How the Poor Die
Lear, Tolstoy and the Fool
Politics vs. Literature: An Examination of *Gulliver's Travels*
Politics and the English Language
Reflections on Gandhi
The Prevention of Literature
Second Thoughts on James Burnham
Confessions of A Book Reviewer
Books v. Cigarettes
Good Bad Books
Nonsense Poetry
Riding Down From Bangor
The Sporting Spirit
Decline of the English Murder
Some Thoughts on the Common Toad
A Good Word For the Vicar of Bray

D.3b   First American Edition, 1950

Shooting an Elephant | AND OTHER ESSAYS | *by George Orwell* | *New York* | HARCOURT, BRACE & WORLD, INC.

Collation There are seven unmarked gatherings, arranged [1–5]¹⁶ [6]⁸ [7]¹⁶; 104 leaves (20.2 × 13.6); [i–viii] [1–2] [3]–200

Contents [i] halftitle: *Shooting an Elephant* [ii] list of books by Orwell [iii] titlepage [iv] imprint [v] editor's note [vi] blank [vii–viii] contents [1] halftitle: *Shooting an Elephant* [2] blank [3]–200 text

Binding Grey linen grain cloth on boards. Off white endpapers.

Front and back covers Plain.

Spine Stamped in silver gilt laterally: GEORGE | ORWELL [within a rectangular frame]: SHOOTING AN ELEPHANT [and to the right]: HARCOURT, BRACE | & WORLD

Jacket Blue, black and white.
Front Against a background of white dots on black are three irregular rectangles. In the first, picked out in white on a blue background: SHOOTING AN | ELEPHANT [in the second, in blue on a white background]: AND OTHER ESSAYS [in the third, against a blue background is picked out in white]: GEORGE ORWELL [and printed in black] | AUTHOR OF NINETEEN EIGHTY-FOUR
Back publisher's advertisement for *Nineteen Eighty-Four*, with extracts from reviews and a list of other books by Orwell.
Spine Against the black and white background wrapped around from front is printed in blue: GEORGE | ORWELL | [and laterally against a blue background is picked out in white] SHOOTING AN ELEPHANT | [and at foot, horizontally, within a white rectangle is printed in blue] HARCOURT, | BRACE | & WORLD
Front flap $3.75 | [summary]
Back flap [biographical summary and extracts from obituary notices]

List of contents
The essays are as in the British first edition, but in a different order:

Shooting an Elephant
A Hanging
How the Poor Die
Lear, Tolstoy and the Fool
Politics vs. Literature: An Examination of *Gulliver's Travels*
Politics and the English Language
Reflections on Gandhi
The Prevention of Literature
Second Thoughts on James Burnham
The Sporting Spirit
Decline of the English Murder
Some Thoughts on the Common Toad
A Good Word For the Vicar of Bray
Confessions of A Book Reviewer
Books v. Cigarettes
Good Bad Books
Nonsense Poetry
Riding Down From Bangor

Notes
Published 26 October 1950.
4,000 copies
$3.75

Contemporary reviews
Booklist (1 December 1950)
J.A. Clark *Chicago Sunday Tribune* (10 December 1950)
R.M. Weaver *Commonweal* (22 December 1950)
Library Journal (1 November 1950)
C. Sykes *New Republic* (4 December 1950)

J. Hilton *New York Herald Tribune* (3 December 1950)
Stephen Spender *New York Times* (29 October 1950)
Time (13 November 1950)
Virginia Kirkus Bookshop Bulletin (15 October)
New Yorker (January 1951)

There was no separate Canadian edition. Saunders and the British Book Service distributed bound copies of the English edition.

There was a Braille edition, published by the National Institute for the Blind, in January 1953.

D.4   SUCH, SUCH WERE THE JOYS

D.4a   First Edition, 1953

Such, Such | Were the Joys | *by George Orwell* | *New York* | HARCOURT, BRACE AND COMPANY

Collation There are eight unmarked gatherings arranged [1–6]¹⁶ [7]⁸ [8]¹⁶; 120 leaves (20.1 × 13.4); [i–vi] [1–3] 4–230 [231–234]

Contents [i] halftitle: *Such, Such Were the Joys* [ii] list of books by Orwell [iii] titlepage [iv] imprint: COPYRIGHT, 1945, 1952, 1953, BY | SONIA BROWNELL ORWELL | *All rights reserved, including* | *the right to reproduce this book* | *or portions thereof in any form.* | *first American edition* | The manuscript of the title essay was found among George | Orwell's papers after his death in 1950, and had its first | publication in *Partisan Review* in 1952. The remaining essays | appeared in periodicals and elsewhere during the author's | lifetime, and the date of their original publication is indi- | cated at the end of each. | Library of Congress Catalog Card Number: 52-13768 | PRINTED IN THE UNITED STATES OF AMERICA [v] contents [vi] blank [1] halftitle: *Such, Such Were the Joys* [2] blank [3]–230 text [231–234] blank

Binding Green calico grain cloth on boards. Off white endpapers.

Front and back covers Plain.

Spine Stamped in gilt, vertically: GEORGE | ORWELL [within a frame]: SUCH, SUCH WERE THE JOYS [and to the right of frame]: HARCOURT, BRACE | AND COMPANY

Jacket Red, yellow and grey.
Front Against a red background and within an irregular yellow halo is printed in grey: GEORGE | ORWELL | [within a grey rectangle is picked out in white]: SUCH, SUCH WERE | THE JOYS | [and against a red background and with an irregular white halo is printed in yellow]: AUTHOR OF | NINETEEN EIGHTY-FOUR
Back On an off-white background is a publisher's advertisement.
Spine Against a red background and within an irregular yellow halo is printed laterally in grey: Orwell | [within a grey rectangle is picked out in white horizontally]: SUCH, | SUCH | WERE | THE | JOYS | [and against a red background is printed laterally in grey]: HARCOURT, | BRACE AND | COMPANY
Front flap $3.50 | [summary]
Back flap [biographical summary and extracts from obituary notices]

Notes
Published 26 February 1953.
$3.50

Locations
Orwell Archive, with jacket
Kelly Library, St Michael's College, University of Toronto.

List of contents
Why I Write
Such, Such Were the Joys
Writers and Leviathan
Notes on Nationalism
Anti-semitism in Britain
Poetry and the Microphone
Marrakech
Looking Back on the Spanish War
Inside the Whale
England Your England

D.5 ENGLAND YOUR ENGLAND

D.5a   First Edition, 1953

ENGLAND YOUR | ENGLAND | *and Other Essays* | BY | GEORGE ORWELL | *LONDON* | SECKER & WARBURG | 1953

Collation [A]–O⁸; 112 leaves (18.3 × 12.3); [1–7] 8–224

Contents [1] halftitle: ENGLAND YOUR ENGLAND [2] list of books by Orwell [3] titlepage [4] imprint: Martin Secker & Warburg Ltd., | 7 John Street, London, W.C.1 | *First published 1953* | *Printed in Great Britain by* | *The Camelot Press Ltd., London and Southampton* [5] contents [6] blank [7]–224 text

Binding Green linen grain cloth on boards. Off white endpapers. Purple topped leaves.

Front and back covers Plain

Spine Stamped in purple: [pyramid of six rules] | ENGLAND | YOUR | ENGLAND | [leaf motif] | GEORGE | ORWELL | [inverted pyramid of six rules] | SECKER & | WARBURG

Jacket Green
Front In white, shaded with dark green | ENGLAND | YOUR | ENGLAND | [in green] AND OTHER ESSAYS | [and in white, shaded with dark green] GEORGE | ORWELL
Back Publisher's advertisement for books by Orwell
Front flap George Orwell | *ENGLAND YOUR ENGLAND* | *AND OTHER ESSAYS* | [note on Orwell and his essays] | 12s 6d. | net.
Back flap Plain

Notes
Published 12 November 1953.
12s 6d

Reissues
1954

Locations
Cambridge University Library. Rebound. Acquisition 6 November 1953.
Orwell Archive, 1953 with jacket, 1954

List of contents
Why I Write
Writers and Leviathan
North and South
Notes on Nationalism
Anti-Semitism in Britain
Poetry and the Microphone
Inside the Whale
Marrakech

Looking Back on the Spanish War
Down the Mine
England Your England

D.6   A COLLECTION OF ESSAYS

D.6a   First Edition, 1954

George Orwell | A COLLECTION | OF ESSAYS | *Doubleday Anchor Books* | DOUBLEDAY & COMPANY, INC. | GARDEN CITY, NEW YORK

Collation There are 160 leaves in a perfect binding (18.1 × 10.5); [1–9] 10–320

Contents [1] halftitle: A COLLECTION OF ESSAYS [2] blank [3–4] biographical sketch of Orwell [5] titlepage [6] imprint: LIBRARY OF CONGRESS CATALOG CARD NUMBER 54-7594 | This volume is published by arrangement | with Harcourt, Brace and Company, Inc. | Copyright, 1954, by Doubleday & Company, Inc. | Copyright, 1946 by George Orwell | Copyright, 1945, 1946, 1949, 1950, 1952, 1953, | by Sonia Brownell Orwell | All Rights Reserved. Printed in the United States of America [7] contents [8] blank [9]–320 text

Binding Paper bound in green.

Front cover Against a green background: A29 [black vertical frame with four orange triangles] [in orange]: 95c | [in orange] a collection | of [in white] ESSAYS [in black] by | [in white] GEORGE | ORWELL | [in black] Author of [in orange] 1984 | [in white is a list of some of the essays] | [in black] [anchor motif] | A DOUBLEDAY ANCHOR BOOK

Back cover Against an orange background: A COLLECTION OF ESSAYS | BY GEORGE ORWELL | [note on the essays and list of some of the titles] | [anchor motif] A DOUBLEDAY ANCHOR BOOK

Spine Printed laterally: [in orange] a collection of [in white] ESSAYS [in black] by [in white] GEORGE ORWELL [in black] Anchor Book | [and horizontally in white] A29

Notes
95c

Location
Orwell Archive

Reissue
New York: Harcourt, Brace, Jovanovich, Inc. 1954 paperback. Harbrace Paperbound Library. New York: A Harvest|HBJ Book. Paper bound.

Locations
Robarts Library, University of Toronto.

List of contents
Such, Such Were the Joys
Charles Dickens
The Art of Donald McGill
Rudyard Kipling
Raffles and Miss Blandish
Shooting an Elephant
Politics and the English Language
Reflections on Gandhi
Marrakech
Looking Back on the Spanish War
Inside the Whale
England Your England
Boys' Weeklies
Why I Write

D.7   THE ORWELL READER

D.7a   First Edition, 1956

The | Orwell | Reader | FICTION, ESSAYS, AND REPORTAGE BY | George Orwell | [triangle] | WITH AN INTRODUCTION BY RICHARD H. ROVERE | HARCOURT, BRACE AND COMPANY . NEW YORK

Collation There are fifteen unmarked gatherings of sixteen leaves each, arranged: [1–15]¹⁶; 240 leaves (21.2 × 14.2); [X1–X2] [i–vi] vii–xxi [xxii] [1–2] 3–456

Contents [X1–X2] blank [i] halftitle: THE ORWELL READER [ii] blank [iii] titlepage [iv] imprint: [copyright dates and notices] | *first edition* | LIBRARY OF CONGRESS CATALOG CARD NUMBER: 56-9137 | PRINTED IN THE UNITED STATES OF AMERICA [v] note on previous publication of essays [vi] blank vii–viii contents ix–xxi introduction [xxii] blank [1] halftitle: Prologue in Burma [2] blank 3–456 text

Binding Bluish green calico textured cloth on boards. Off white endpapers.

Front and back covers Plain.

Spine Stamped in silver gilt laterally: THE [within a silver frame and with alternate letters green on a silver background and silver on a green background in a checkered formation]: ORWELL | READER [and to the right]: HARCOURT, BRACE AND COMPANY

Jacket Yellowish brown and white.
Front On twelve rectangles of alternating yellowish brown and white are printed laterally in white and yellowish brown the titles of some of Orwell's books and essays included in this selection. Across the centre is printed in blue: *A treasury of the best of George Orwell* | *Fiction, essays, reportage* | THE | ORWELL | [and in red] READER | *With an Introduction by Richard H. Rovere*
Back Extracts from the Introduction.
Spine On quarters of yellowish brown and white is printed laterally in grey: THE | ORWELL | [and in red] READER | [in grey] *George Orwell* [in red] *Harcourt, Brace and Company*
Front flap Summary
Back flap List of books by Orwell

Notes
Jacket design by Janet Halverson.

Locations
Cambridge University Library
Orwell Archive, two copies, one with jacket.

List of contents
Shooting an Elephant
A Hanging
From *Burmese Days*
From *Down and Out in Paris and London*
How the Poor Die
From *A Clergyman's Daughter*
From *Keep the Aspidistra Flying*
From *The Road to Wigan Pier*
From *Homage to Catalonia*
From *Coming Up for Air*
England Your England
Rudyard Kipling
Politics vs. Literature: An Examination of *Gulliver's Travels*
Lear, Tolstoy and the Fool

In Defense of P.G. Wodehouse
Reflections on Gandhi
Second Thoughts on James Burnham
Politics and the English Language
The Prevention of Literature
Decline of the English Murder
Some Thoughts on the Common Toad
A Good Word for the Vicar of Bray
Why I Write
From *Nineteen Eighty-Four*
Such, Such Were the Joys

Reissued paper bound in 1956 as A Harvest Book.

Locations
Orwell Archive
Kelly Library, St Michael's College, University of Toronto

D.8   SELECTED ESSAYS

D.8a   First Edition, 1957

GEORGE ORWELL | [rule] | Selected Essays | PENGUIN BOOKS | IN ASSOCIATION WITH | SECKER & WARBURG

Collation [A]–G^{16}; 104 leaves (17.9 × 10.8); [1–8] 9–202 [203–208]

Contents [1] halftitle: PENGUIN BOOKS | 1185 | SELECTED ESSAYS | GEORGE ORWELL | [penguin motif] [2] blank [3] titlepage [4] imprint: Penguin Books Ltd, Harmondsworth, Middlesex | CANADA: Penguin Books (Canada) Ltd, 178 Norseman Street | Toronto 18, Ontario | AUSTRALIA: Penguin Books Pty Ltd, 762 Whitehorse Road, | Mitcham, Victoria | SOUTH AFRICA: Penguin Books (S.A.) Pty Ltd, Gibraltar House, | Regent Road, Sea Point, Cape Town | [short rule] | This selection first published in Penguin Books 1957 | Made and printed in Great Britain | by The Whitefriars Press Ltd | London and Tonbridge [5] contents [6] blank [7] bibliographical note [8] blank 9–[203] text [204] blank [205] [penguin motif] | Some other Penguin books | are described on the | remaining pages [206] blank [207–208] publisher's advertisements

Binding Paper bound.

Front cover Orange stripe at right margin with central black and white penguin motif. To the left against an off white background is printed [in orange]: PENGUIN BOOKS | [black rule] | [in black]: GEORGE ORWELL | [orange rule] | [in black]: Selected | Essays | [orange rule] | [in black]: including | THE PREVENTION OF LITERATURE | ENGLAND YOUR ENGLAND | INSIDE THE WHALE | DOWN THE MINE | BOYS' WEEKLIES | SHOOTING AN ELEPHANT | and others | [black rule] | [in orange]: 2|6 [here the slash does not mark a line break]

Back cover Orange stripe at left margin with central black and white penguin motif. To the right against an off white background is printed [in orange]: PENGUIN BOOKS | [black rule] | [photograph of Orwell] | Vernon Richards | [biographical sketch of Orwell] | [black rule] | NOT FOR SALE IN THE U.S.A.

Spine [orange stripe] | [rule] | [laterally] George Orwell [horizontally is a penguin motif in orange and white] [laterally] Selected Essays [horizontally] 1185 | [rule] | [orange stripe]

List of contents
Inside the Whale
Down the Mine
England Your England

Shooting an Elephant
Lear, Tolstoy and the Fool
Politics vs. Literature: An Examination of *Gulliver's Travels*
Politics and the English Language
The Prevention of Literature
Boys' Weeklies

Locations
Cambridge University Library
Robarts Library, University of Toronto.
1960 reissue Orwell Archive

After 1962, this selection of essays was published by Penguin as *Inside the Whale and Other Essays*, although still in the same edition, with further reissues in 1964, 1966, 1967, 1968, 1969, 1970, 1971, 1972, 1974, 1975, 1976 (twice), 1977, 1978, 1979, 1980, 1981, 1984.

1989 Twentieth Century Classics edition.

D.9   SELECTED WRITINGS

D.9a   *First Edition, 1958*

GEORGE ORWELL | [ornamental short rule] | *Selected Writings* | EDITED BY | GEORGE BOTT | [publisher's ornate device of windmill and initials: HEB] | HEINEMANN EDUCATIONAL BOOKS | LONDON

Collation [1]–12⁸; 96 leaves (18.3 × 12.2); [i–iv] v [vi] vii [viii] 1 [2] 3–23 [24] 25–173 [174] 175–183 [184]

Contents [i] halftitle: *GEORGE ORWELL | SELECTED WRITINGS* [ii] list of books in series [iii] titlepage [iv] imprint: INTRODUCTION AND *Notes* © GEORGE BOTT 1958 | FIRST PUBLISHED 1958 | PUBLISHED BY | WILLIAM HEINEMANN LTD | 15–16 QUEEN STREET, LONDON, W.1 | PRINTED IN GREAT BRITAIN BY MORRISON AND GIBB LTD | LONDON AND EDINBURGH v contents [vi] blank vii preface [viii] blank [1] poem by Robert Conquest [2] blank 3–23 introduction [24] blank 25–173 text [174] blank 175–181 notes 182–183 bibliography [184] blank

Binding Blue paper on boards, embossed to resemble linen grain cloth.

Front cover Stamped in silver gilt: *George | Orwell | Selected | Writings | EDITED BY GEORGE BOTT*

Back cover Plain

Spine Stamped in silver gilt laterally: *GEORGE ORWELL Selected Writings* | [and horizontally is a publisher's windmill motif]

List of contents
Shooting an Elephant
Down the Mine
Skirmish in Spain (from *Homage to Catalonia*)
Marrakech
The English Class System
Politics and the English Language
Writers and Leviathan
Why I Write
Poetry and the Microphone
Boys' Weeklies
Charles Dickens

The Sporting Spirit
The Re-writing of History (from *Nineteen Eighty-Four*)

Reissued in 1960 and 1984.

Locations
Cambridge University Library
Orwell Archive

D.10   COLLECTED ESSAYS

D.10a   First Edition, 1961

COLLECTED | ESSAYS | George Orwell | SECKER & WARBURG | LONDON

Collation [1]⁸ 2–13¹⁶ 14¹⁸; 218 leaves (19.5 × 13.0); [1–8] 9–434 [435–436]

Contents [1] halftitle: COLLECTED ESSAYS [2] list of Orwell's books in the Uniform Edition [3] titlepage [4] imprint: *Originally published in separate volumes* | CRITICAL ESSAYS 1946 | SHOOTING AN ELEPHANT 1950 | ENGLAND YOUR ENGLAND 1953 | *by* | MARTIN SECKER AND WARBURG LTD | 7, JOHN STREET, LONDON, W.C.1 | *First published in this edition* | 1961 | *Printed in Great Britain by* | *Charles Birchall & Sons Ltd.* | *London and Liverpool* [5–6] contents [7] publisher's note [8] blank 9–434 text [435–436] blank

Binding Green calico grain cloth on boards. Grey fibre-flecked endpapers. Red topped leaves.

Front and back covers Plain.

Spine [framed in gilt is an orange oval, on which is stamped in gilt]: GEORGE | ORWELL | [framed in gilt is an irregular orange block, on which is stamped in gilt]: *Collected* | *Essays* | [framed in gilt is an orange rectangle, on which is stamped in gilt]: SECKER & | WARBURG

List of contents
A Hanging
Shooting an Elephant
Marrakech
Charles Dickens
Boys' Weeklies
Inside the Whale
Wells, Hitler and the World State
The Art of Donald McGill
W.B. Yeats
Looking Back on the Spanish War
Benefit of Clergy
Arthur Koestler
Raffles and Miss Blandish
In Defence of P.G. Wodehouse
Notes on Nationalism
Anti-Semitism in Britain
Poetry and the Microphone
The Prevention of Literature
How the Poor Die
Politics and the English Language
Second Thoughts on James Burnham
Politics vs. Literature
Lear, Tolstoy and the Fool

Why I Write
Writers and Leviathan

Locations
Cambridge University Library
Orwell Archive

Reissue
London: Heinemann, 1961.
New titlepage and imprint, but collation and contents as first edition.
General editor Alan Hill
Paper bound
12s 6d.
Mercury Books, No. 17.

Locations
Cambridge University Library
Orwell Archive

D.10b   Second Edition, 1961

COLLECTED ESSAYS | George Orwell | SECKER & WARBURG | LONDON

Collation [1]–14¹⁶ 15⁸; 232 leaves (19.5 × 12.6); [1–8] 9–460 [461–464]

Contents [1] halftitle: COLLECTED ESSAYS [2] list of Orwell's books in the Uniform Edition [3] titlepage [4] imprint: *Originally published in separate volumes* | CRITICAL ESSAYS 1946 | SHOOTING AN ELEPHANT 1950 | ENGLAND YOUR ENGLAND 1953 | *by* | MARTIN SECKER AND WARBURG LTD | *First published in this edition* | 1961 | *Printed in Great Britain by* | *Charles Birchall & Sons Ltd.* | *London and Liverpool* [5–6] contents [7] publisher's note [8] blank 9–460 text [461–464] blank

Binding Green calico grain cloth on boards. Grey fibre-flecked endpapers.

Front and back covers Plain.

Spine [framed in gilt is an orange oval, on which is stamped in gilt]: GEORGE | ORWELL | [framed in gilt is an irregular orange block, on which is stamped in gilt]: *Collected* | *Essays* | [framed in gilt is an orange rectangle, on which is stamped in gilt]: SECKER & | WARBURG

Locations
Orwell Archive, two copies
Pratt Library, Victoria University in the University of Toronto.

Notes
Published in September 1961. Reprinted in 1968 – Orwell Archive copy.
The essays are as in the first edition, with the addition of 'Rudyard Kipling' and 'Reflections on Ghandi'.

List of contents
A Hanging
Shooting an Elephant
Marrakech
Charles Dickens
Boys' Weeklies
Inside the Whale
Wells, Hitler and the World State
The Art of Donald McGill
Rudyard Kipling

W.B. Yeats
Looking Back on the Spanish War
Benefit of Clergy
Arthur Koestler
Raffles and Miss Blandish
In Defence of P.G. Wodehouse
Notes on Nationalism
Anti-Semitism in Britain
Poetry and the Microphone
The Prevention of Literature
How the Poor Die
Politics and the English Language
Second Thoughts on James Burnham
Politics vs. Literature
Lear, Tolstoy and the Fool
Why I Write
Writers and Leviathan
Reflections on Gandhi

D.11   DECLINE OF THE ENGLISH MURDER AND OTHER ESSAYS

D.11a   First Edition, 1965

Decline of the | English Murder | and other essays | George Orwell | [penguin motif] Penguin Books | in association with Secker & Warburg

Collation 81 leaves in a perfect binding (18.0 × 11.0); [1–8] 9–[188] [189–192]

Contents [1] halftitle: Penguin Book 2297 | Decline of the English Murder | and Other essays | [biographical note on Orwell] [2] blank [3] titlepage [4] imprint and copyright notices [5] contents [6] blank [7] bibliographical note [8] blank 9–[188] text [189] publisher's advertisement [200] blank [201–202] publisher's advertisements

Binding Paper bound.

Front cover Against a blue background is a portrait of Orwell in browns and black. Picked out in white at the top: [penguin motif] a Penguin Book 3'6 | DECLINE OF THE | ENGLISH MURDER | and Other Essays | George Orwell | [black rule]

Back cover Against an orange background is printed in black: a Penguin Book [white Penguin motif] | [black rule] | DECLINE OF THE | ENGLISH MURDER | [in black: summary]

Spine Against an orange background, in white [penguin motif] | [laterally] George Orwell [in black] Decline of the English Murder | [horizontally] 2297

List of contents
Decline of the English Murder
A Hanging
Benefit of Clergy
How the Poor Die
Rudyard Kipling
Raffles and Miss Blandish
Charles Dickens
The Art of Donald McGill
Notes on Nationalism
Why I Write

Notes
3s 6d
The cover portrait is by Peter Blake.

Reissues
1968, 1970, 1972, 1975 (twice), 1977, 1978, 1979, 1980, 1986, 1991
The 1980 reissue has a new jacket with a photograph of a young man behind a pint of beer and a copy of the *News of the World*, and on the back a photograph of Orwell.
1975 price 50p
1980 price £1.25
1992 Twentieth Century Classics edition.

Locations
Cambridge University Library. Acquisition 5 August 1965
Orwell Archive 1965, 1975, 1980

D.12   THE COLLECTED ESSAYS, JOURNALISM AND LETTERS

In four volumes.

D.12a   First Edition, 1968

THE COLLECTED | ESSAYS, JOURNALISM | AND LETTERS OF | GEORGE | ORWELL | Volume I | An Age Like This | 1920–1940 | Edited by | SONIA ORWELL AND IAN ANGUS | LONDON . SECKER & WARBURG

Collation [1–2]¹⁶ 3–18¹⁶ 19¹²; 300 leaves (21.2 × 13.9) [i–v] vi–x [xi] xii–xiii [xiv–xv] xvi–xx [xxi] xxii–xxiii [xxiv] 1–574 [575–576]. There is a glossy leaf of illustrations pasted between [ii] and [iii].

Contents [i] halftitle: THE COLLECTED | ESSAYS, JOURNALISM | AND LETTERS OF | GEORGE ORWELL | Volume I | An Age Like This | 1920–1940 [ii] blank [iii] titlepage [iv] imprint: Copyright © 1968 by Sonia Brownell Orwell | Copyright 1945, 1952, 1953 by Sonia Brownell Orwell | First published in England 1968 by | Martin Secker & Warburg Limited | 14 Carlisle Street, London, W.1 | SBN: 436 35018 1 | Made and printed in Great Britain by | William Clowes and Sons, Limited, London and Beccles [v]–x contents [xi]–xiii acknowledgements [xiv] blank [xv]–xx introduction [xxi]–xxiii editors' note [xxiv] blank 1–540 text [541] appendix [542] blank [543]–551 appendix [552] blank [553]–574 index [575–576] blank

Binding Blue calico grain cloth on boards. Greyish blue fibre flecked endpapers.

Front and back covers Plain.

Spine Stamped in gilt: [motif] | THE | COLLECTED | ESSAYS, | JOURNALISM | & LETTERS | of | George | Orwell | [motif] | [single star motif] | AN AGE LIKE | THIS | 1920–1940 | S&W

Volume I *An Age Like This* 1920–1940.

List of contents

1. Articles, essays, introductions and reviews

> Why I Write
> A Farthing Newspaper
> Review of *Herman Melville* by Lewis Mumford
> Review of *Alexander Pope* by Edith Sitwell etc
> Review of *Angel Pavement* by J.B. Priestley

Review of *The Two Carlyles* by Osbery Burdett
The Spike
A Hanging
Hop-Picking
Review of *The Spirit of Catholicism* by Karl Adam
Clink[2]
Review of *Byron and the Need of Fatality* by Charles du Bos
Common Lodging Houses
Introduction to the French edition of *Down and Out in Paris and London*
Poem: ['Sometimes in the middle autumn days']
Poem: ['A dressed man and a naked man']
Poem: 'On a Ruined Farm near the His Master's Voice Gramophone Factory'
My Epitaph by John Flory[3]
Review of *Caliban Shrieks* by Jack Hilton
Review of *Tropic of Cancer* by Henry Miller
[On Kipling's Death]
Review of *The Lively Lady* by Kenneth Roberts etc
Review of Penguin Books
The Road to Wigan Pier Diary
Review of *Bastard Death* by Michael Fraenkel etc
Review of *The Rock Pool* by Cyril Connolly etc
Review of *Black Spring* by Henry Miller etc
Review of *Zest of Life* by Johann Wöller
Shooting an Elephant
Bookshop Memories
Review of *The Calf of Paper* by Scholem Asch etc
In Defence of the Novel
Review of *The Novel Today* by Philip Henderson
Your Questions Answered
Spilling the Spanish Beans
Review of *The Spanish Cockpit* by Franz Borkenau etc
Review of *The Men I Killed* by F.P. Crozier
Review of *Journey to Turkistan* by Eric Teichman
Review of *Red Spanish Notebook* by Mary Low, Juan Brea etc
Review of *Storm over Spain* by Marian Mitchell etc
Review of *Spanish Testament* by Arthur Koestler
Review of *Workers' Front* by Fenner Brockway
Review of *Trials in Burma* by Maurice Collis
Review of *Glimpses and Reflections* by John Galsworthy
Notes on the Spanish Militias
Review of *Assignment in Utopia* by Eugene Lyons
Review of *The Freedom of the Streets* by Jack Common
Why I Joined the Labour Party
Review of *The Civil War in Spain* by Frank Jellinek
Review of *Searchlight on Spain* by the Duchess of Atholl
Review of *The Communist International* by Franz Borkenau
Review of *Power: A New Social Analysis* by Bertrand Russell
Review of *Russia Under Soviet Rule* by N. de Basily
Review of *Communism and Man* by F.J. Sheed
Marrakech
Not Counting Niggers
Review of *Stendhal* by F.C. Green
Democracy in the British Army
Review of *The Last Days of Madrid* by S. Casado
Charles Dickens

Boys' Weeklies and Frank Richards's Reply
Inside the Whale
The Limit to Pessimism
My Country Right or Left

2. Letters to:

Eileen Blair
Ida Mabel Blair
Dennis Collings [2]
Jack Common [16]
Cyril Connolly [7]
T.S. Eliot [2]
Victor Gollancz [2]
Geoffrey Gorer [7]
James Hanley
Rayner Heppenstall [3]
Humphry House
Eleanor Jaques [12]
Frank Jellinek
Alec Houghton Joyce
Denys King-Farlow
John Lehmann
Henry Miller
Leonard Moore [15]
Raymond Mortimer
Editor of *New English Weekly*
Max Plowman [3]
Anthony Powell
Herbert Read [2]
Richard Rees [2]
Steven Runciman
Brenda Salkeld [9]
John Sceats [2]
Stephen Spender [2]
Mr Thompson
David S. Thomson
Editor of *Time and Tide*
Editor of *The Times*

Volume II *My Country Right or Left* 1940–1943.

List of contents

1. Articles, essays, introductions and reviews

New Words
Review of *Mein Kampf* by Adolf Hitler
Notes on the Way
Review of *Personal Record* by Julian Green
[Autobiographical Note]
Review of *The Totalitarian Enemy* by Franz Borkenau
Prophecies of Fascism
The Proletarian Writer
Review of *Landfall* by Nevil Shute etc
London Letter to *The Partisan Review* – 8 entries
The Lion and the Unicorn
The Frontiers of Art and Propaganda

Tolstoy and Shakespeare
The Meaning of a Poem
Literature and Totalitarianism
Wells, Hitler and the World State
The Art of Donald McGill
No, Not One
Rudyard Kipling
The Rediscovery of Europe
Review of *The Sword and the Sickle* by Mulk Raj Anand
Pacifism and the War
Review of 'Burnt Norton', 'East Coker', 'The Dry Salvages' by T.S. Eliot
BBC Internal Memorandum
Review of *The British Way in Warfare* by B.H. Liddell Hart
Looking Back on the Spanish War
W.B. Yeats
Pamphlet Literature
Literature and the Left
Poem: 'As One Non-Combatant to Another'
Review of *Beggar My Neighbour* by Lionel Fielden
Who Are the War Criminals
Mark Twain – The Licensed Jester
Poetry and the Microphone
War-time Diary: 28 May 1940–28 August 1941
War-time Diary: 14 March 1942–15 November 1942

2. Letters to:

Alex Comfort
T.S. Eliot
Rayner Heppenstall [3]
Iorwerth Jones
James Laughlin
John Lehmann
Dorothy Plowman
Charles Reade
Philip Rahv
L.F. Rushbrook-Williams
Editor of *Time and Tide*
Editor of *The Times*
George Woodcock

Volume III *As I Please* 1943–1945.

List of contents

1. Articles, essays, introductions and reviews

The English People
In Defence of English Cooking
A Nice Cup of Tea
Review of *The Pub and the People* by Mass Observation
'The Moon Under Water'
Review of *Cricket Country* by Edmund Blunden
As I Please – 56 entries
Review of *Collected Poems* by W.H. Davies
London Letter to *The Partisan Review* – 6 entries
A Hundred Up
Review of *The Edge of the Abyss* by Alfred Noyse

Review of *The Road to Serfdom* by F.A. Hayek etc
Propaganda and Domestic Speech
Benefit of Clergy: Some Notes on Salvador Dali
Raffles and Miss Blandish
Arthur Koestler
Tobias Smollett
A Controversy. Orwell: Agate
Review of *The Vicar of Wakefield* by Oliver Goldsmith
Funny, But Not Vulgar
Oysters and Brown Stout
A New Year Message
Review of *The Unquiet Grave* by 'Palinurus'
Anti-semitism in Britain
In Defence of P.G. Wodehouse
Notes on Nationalism
Review of *The Nigger of the Narcissus* etc by Joseph Conrad
Preface to the Ukrainian Edition of *Animal Farm*

2. Letters

Frank Barber [2]
T.S. Eliot
Roy Fuller
Rayner Heppenstall
Lydia Jackson
Leonard Moore [3]
John Middleton Murry [4]
Anthony Powell
Philip Rahv [2]
Herbert Read
Roger Senhouse
Gleb Struv
Editor of *The Tribune* (unpublished)
F.J. Warburg
H.J. Willmett

Volume IV *In Front of Your Nose* 1945–1950.

List of contents

1. Articles, essays, introductions and reviews

Revenge is Sour
You and the Atom Bomb
What is Science?
Review of *Drums Under the Windows* by Sean O'Casey
Catastrophic Gradualism
Good Bad Books
Introduction to *Love of Life and Other Stories* by Jack London
Review of *The Prussian Officer and Other Stories* by D.H. Lawrence
Through a Glass, Rosily
Freedom of the Park
The Sporting Spirit
Nonsense Poetry
Review of *A Coat of Many Colours: Occasional Essays* by Herbert Read
Introduction to *The Position of Peggy Harper* by Leonard Merrick[4]
The Prevention of Literature
Review of *We* by E.I. Zamyatin

Pleasure Spots
The Politics of Starvation
Review of *The Reilly Plan* by Lawrence Wolfe
Books v. Cigarettes
Review of *The Democrat at the Supper Table* by Colm Brogan
Decline of the English Murder
Review of *The Cosmological Eye* by Henry Miller
Review of *The Story of Burma* by F. Tennyson Jesse
Review of *The Martyrdom of Man* by Winwood Reade
In Front of Your Nose
Politics and the English Language
Some Thoughts on the Common Toad
A Good Word for the Vicar of Bray
Editorial to *Polemic*
James Burnham and the Managerial Revolution
Confessions of a Book Reviewer
London Letter to *The Partisan Review*
The Cost of Letters
Politics vs. Literature: An Examination of *Gulliver's Travels*
How the Poor Die
As I Please – 16 entries
Riding Down From Bangor
As I Pleased
Lear, Tolstoy and the Fool
Burnham's View of the Contemporary World Struggle
Such, Such Were the Joys
Toward European Unity
In Defence of Comrade Zilliacus[5]
Writers and Leviathan
Review of *The Soul of Man Under Socialism* by Oscar Wilde
George Gissing
Review of *The Heart of the Matter* by Graham Greene
Review of *Great Morning* by Osbert Sitwell
The Freedom Defence Committee
Review of *Portrait of the Antisemite* by Jean-Paul Sartre
Review of *Notes Towards the Definition of Culture* by T.S. Eliot
Reflections on Gandhi
Conrad's Place and Rank in English Letters
The Question of the Pound Award
Review of *Their Finest Hour* by Winston S. Churchill
Extracts from a Manuscript Notebook

2. Letters to:

The Duchess of Atholl
Sonia Brownell
Stafford Cottman
Editor of *Forward*
T.R. Fyvel [3]
Robert Giroux
Victor Gollancz [3]
Geoffrey Gorer
A.S.F. Gow
Francis A. Henson
Rayner Heppenstall

F. Tennyson Jesse [2]
Celia Kirwan [4]
Arthur Koestler [5]
Michael Meyer [2]
Leonard Moore [4]
John Middleton Murry
Editor of *News Chronicle*
Gwen O'Shaughnessy [2]
Dorothy Plowman
Anthony Powell [8]
Philip Rahv [2]
Richard Rees [9]
Reginald Reynolds
Vernon Richards [2]
Herbert Rogers
Roger Senhouse [4]
Gleb Struve
Julian Symons [13]
Editor of *The Tribune*
F.J. Warburg [8]
George Woodcock [8]

Notes
Volume numbers are denoted by star motifs on spines.
Second impression 1969.
Volumes I, II, III and IV were reprinted 1996 in 'Complete Works of George Orwell' vs. 10, 11, 12 and 13.

Locations
Cambridge University Library
Orwell Archive – 2 copies

Locations
Orwell Archive
Pratt Library, Victoria University in the University of Toronto

D.12b   *American Reissue, 1968*

The Collected Essays, Journalism | and Letters of George Orwell | [short rule] | AN AGE LIKE THIS | 1920–1940 | I | Edited by | Sonia Orwell | and | Ian Angus | [publisher's motif] | Harcourt, Brace & World, Inc. | New York

Four volumes. New titlepage and imprint, but collation and contents as first edition. Printed in Great Britain.

Binding As British first edition, but with slightly finer grain cloth. Off white endpapers.

Front cover Stamped in gilt are the signatures: Eric Blair | ("George Orwell") | [Orwell's freehand rule]

Back cover Plain.

Spine Stamped in gilt: The | Collected | Essays, | Journalism | and | Letters of | GEORGE | ORWELL | I | An Age | Like This | 1920–1940 | Edited by | Sonia Orwell | and | Ian Angus | [publisher's motif] | Harcourt, Brace | & World

Volume numbers are denoted by Roman numerals on titlepages and spines.

Locations
Orwell Archive

Reissued in paperback in a boxed set as A Harvest Book, published by Harcourt Brace Jovanovich in New York. Four volumes, 1968.

D.12c   *First Penguin Edition, 1970*

THE COLLECTED ESSAYS, | JOURNALISM AND LETTERS OF | George Orwell | VOLUME I | *An Age Like This 1920–1940* | EDITED BY | SONIA ORWELL AND | IAN ANGUS | [penguin motif in oval frame] | PENGUIN BOOKS | *in association with Secker & Warburg*

Collation [A]–I¹⁶ K–M⁸ N–X¹⁶; 312 leaves in a perfect binding (18.0 × 11.0); [1–5] 6–10 [11] 12 [13] 14–18 [19] 20–21 [22–23] 24–592 [593–594] 595–601 [602] 603–624

Contents [1] halftitle: PENGUIN BOOKS | THE COLLECTED ESSAYS, JOURNALISM | AND LETTERS OF GEORGE ORWELL | *Volume 1. An Age Like This 1920–1940* | [biographical sketch of Orwell] [2] blank [3] titlepage [4] imprint: [list of publisher's addresses] | [short rule] First published in England by Secker & Warburg 1968 | Published in Penguin Books 1970 | [short rule] | Copyright © Sonia Brownell Orwell, 1945, 1952, 1953, 1968 | [short rule] | Made and printed in Great Britain | by Cox & Wyman Ltd, | London, Reading and Fakenham | Set in Linotype Times | [copyright notice] [5]–10 contents [11]–12 acknowledgements [13]–18 introduction [19]–21 editors' note [22] blank [23]–592 text [593]–601 appendices [602]–624 index

Binding Paper bound.

Front cover The covers of the four volumes all have on the front: The Collected Essays, | Journalism and Letters of | George Orwell Volume [number in arabic numerals] | [Volume title] | [volume dates] | [photographs of Orwell] | ORWELL

The volume titles, dates and cover colours are:
1 An Age Like This 1920–1940. Brown
2 My Country Right or Left 1940–1943. Maroon
3 As I Please 1943–1945. Blue
4 In Front of Your Nose 1945–1950. Purple

Back cover [Quote by Cyril Connolly] | [brief description of series and volumes] | Cover design by Idea | [details of cover photographs] | [copyright notice] | [international prices]

Spine [Against an orange background, laterally]: George Orwell [in white] Collected Essays, Journalism and Letters [volume number] | [horizontally, penguin motif in an oval frame]

Notes
Price in England, 10s 0d per volume.

Locations
Cambridge University Library
Orwell Archive

D.13   GEORGE ORWELL IN KENT

> Down and out people seem to read exclusively books of the Buffalo Bill type. Every tramp carries one of these, and they have a kind of circulating library, all swapping books when they get to the spike.⁶

In October 1931 George Orwell wrote an account of his time on the street in London and picking hops in Kent in the summer that year. It was published as 'Hop-Picking' in *The New Statesman and Nation* on 17 October 1931 [See C.043]. *George Orwell in Kent* omits the final section, describing Orwell's return to London and his time in common lodging houses there from 19 September to 8 October 1931. It also omits his glossary of "New Words (i.e. words new to me) discovered at this time."

D.13a   First Edition, 1970

George Orwell in Kent | HOP-PICKING | With a critical introduction by | MEDWAY FITZMORAN | and Postscript by | JOHN BLEST | OF HOME FARM, WATERINGBURY | [publisher's device of two interwoven Bs] | BRIDGE BOOKS | KENT EDITIONS

Collation There are six unmarked gatherings arranged [A–F]⁴; 24 leaves (18.4 × 12.5); [1–4] 5–45 [46–48]

Contents [1] halftitle: GEORGE ORWELL IN KENT [2] blank [3] titlepage [4] imprint: The extract "Hop-Picking" from the | Collected Essays, Journalism and | Letters of George Orwell is reprinted | by permission of Miss Sonia Brownell | and Secker & Warburg Ltd | Introduction and postscript copyright | BRIDGE BOOKS | First published by Bridge Books, | Wateringbury, Kent, 1970, in an | edition of 300 copies of which this is copy No. [space] | Printed in Great Britain by | W. & J. Mackay & Co Ltd, Chatham, Kent 5–13 introduction 14–41 text 42–45 postscript 46–48 blank

Binding Brown marbled paper on boards. White endpapers.

Front and back covers Plain.

Spine Stamped in gilt laterally: GEORGE ORWELL IN KENT | [and vertically, publisher's device of two interwoven Bs]

Notes
300 copies printed.
Also in *CEJL* I 52–71

Locations
Cambridge University Library. Acquisition 9 November 1970. Copy No. 70.
Orwell Archive, 2 copies, Nos. 29 and 99.

D.14   UNWELCOME GUERILLA: GEORGE ORWELL AND THE NEW STATESMAN – AN ANTHOLOGY

D.14a   First Edition, 1984

Edited by Bernard Crick (London: New Statesman, 1984).

Notes
A Collection of 23 articles and reviews by Orwell published in *The New Statesman* 1932–1943.

Orwell's contributions:

Hop Picking 17 October 1931
Common Lodging Houses 3 September 1932
Experientia Docet 28 August 1937
Glimpses and Reflections 12 March 1938
On the Brink 13 July 1940
Charles Reade 17 August 1940
The English Civil War 24 August 1940
Holding Out 14 September 1940
History Books 21 September 1940
Wishful Thinking and the Light Novel 19 October 1940
Mis-Observation 26 October 1940
By-Words 16 November 1940
Landfall 7 December 1940
Guerillas 14 December 1940

Darkness at Noon 4 January 1941
Two Glimpses of the Moon 18 January 1941
The Beauty of the Dead 25 January 1941
The People's Army 15 February 1941
England is My Village 22 February 1941
The Defenders 15 March 1941
Perfide Albion 21 November 1942
Pamphlet Literature 9 January 1943
War in Burma 14 August 1943

D.15   THE PENGUIN ESSAYS OF GEORGE ORWELL

Harmondsworth: Penguin, 1984

The 41 essays in this volume appeared in *The Collected Essays, Journalism and Letters of George Orwell* I–IV

Paper bound
£4.95

List of contents
Why I Write
The Spike
A Hanging
Shooting an Elephant
Bookshop Memories
Marrakech
Charles Dickens
Boys' Weeklies
Inside the Whale
My Country Right or Left
The Lion and the Unicorn
Wells, Hitler and the World State
The Art of Donald McGill
Rudyard Kipling
Looking Back on the Spanish War
W.B. Yeats
Poetry and the Microphone
In Defence of English Cooking
Benefit of Clergy: Some Notes on Salvador Dali
Raffles and Miss Blandish
Arthur Koestler
Anti-semitism in Britain
In Defence of P.G. Wodehouse
Notes on Nationalism
Good Bad Books
The Sporting Spirit
Nonsense Poetry
The Prevention of Literature
Books v. Cigarettes
Decline of the English Murder
Politics and the English Language
Some Thoughts on the Common Toad
A Good Word for the Vicar of Bray
Confessions of a Book Reviewer
Politics vs. Literature: An Examination of *Gulliver's Travels*

How the Poor Die
Riding Down from Bangor
Lear, Tolstoy and the Fool
Such, Such Were the Joys
Writers and Leviathan
Reflections on Gandhi

D.16   GEORGE ORWELL: TEN "ANIMAL FARM" LETTERS TO HIS AGENT, LEONARD MOORE, 1984

Edited by Michael Shelden.
Bloomington, Indiana: Private Press of Frederic Brewer, 1984. Printed for the Friends of the Lilly Library.

These letters are from the extensive collection of Orwell's letters to Moore at the Lilly Library, Indiana University. The collection consists of over 100 letters to Moore, written between 1935 and 1945. The ten published here are dated between January and August 1944. See Section G Letters for details.

D.17   ORWELL: THE WAR BROADCASTS

D.17a   First Edition, 1985

ORWELL | THE WAR | BROADCASTS | Edited with an Introduction by | W.J. West | [duck motif] | Duckworth| [preceding slash is on the page and does not denote a line break] | British Broadcasting Corporation

Collation There are thirteen unmarked gatherings arranged: [A–N]¹²; this gives a total of 156 leaves (23.2 × 15.2) however the first two and last two leaves form the front and back endpapers, the first and last being pasted to the boards; [discounting the pasted and free endpapers] [1–6] 7–304. There are eight glossy leaves with photographs, sewn in between pages 188 and 189.

Contents [1] halftitle: ORWELL: THE WAR BROADCASTS [2] blank [3] titlepage [4] imprint: First published in 1985 by | Gerald Duckworth & Co Ltd | The Old Piano Factory | 43 Gloucester Crescent, London NW1 | and the British Broadcasting Corporation | 35 Marylebone High Street, London W1M 4AA | [copyright notices, ISBN numbers and British Library Cataloguing in Publication Data] | Photoset in North Wales by | Derek Doyle & Associates, Mold, Clwyd | Printed and bound in Great Britain by | Billing & Sons Limited, Guildford, London, and Worcester [5] contents [6] dedication: For Tom and Richard West 7–9 preface [10] blank 11–12 list of illustrations 13–68 introduction [69] halftitle: Part One [70] blank 71–171 text [172] blank [173] halftitle: Part Two [174] blank 175–277 letters [278] blank 279–299 appendices [300]–304 index

Binding Black paper embossed to resemble linen grain cloth on boards. Off white endpapers.

Front and back covers Plain.
Spine Stamped in gilt: W.J. | West | [vertically]: ORWELL: THE WAR BROADCASTS | [horizontally]: [duck motif] | BBC

Jacket Shiny green and beige mottled paper.
Front [in red] ORWELL | [in black] THE WAR BROADCASTS | Edited by W.J. West | [photograph of Orwell seated at BBC microphone]
Back Plain.
Spine W.J. | West | [laterally] ORWELL: THE WAR BROADCASTS | [horizontally] [duck motif] | BBC
Front flap [summary] | [publishers' addresses] | IN UK ONLY £12.95 NET

Back flap [summary continued] | [biographical note on editor] | *Jacket illustration* Colour interpretation of BBC copyright photograph by Nexus

Notes
The imprint shows two different ISBN numbers: one for Duckworth and one for the BBC.

Locations
Orwell Archive

D.17b   First American Edition, 1985

ORWELL | *The* | *Lost Writings* | GEORGE ORWELL | EDITED WITH AN INTRODUCTION BY | W.J WEST | [publisher's leaf motif] ARBOR HOUSE | NEW YORK

Collation 152 leaves in a perfect binding (22.7 × 15.2); [1–6] 7–304. There are eight glossy leaves with photographs between pages 192 and 193.

Contents [1] halftitle: ORWELL | *The* | *Lost Writings* [2] blank [3] titlepage [4] dedication: *For Tom and Richard West* | First published in Great Britain in 1985 under the title *Orwell: The War Broadcasts* | [copyright notices, ISBN numbers and Library of Congress Cataloging in Publication Data] [5] contents [6] blank 7–9 preface [10] blank 11–12 list of illustrations 13–68 introduction [69] halftitle: Part One [70] blank 71–171 text [172] blank [173] halftitle: Part Two [174] blank 175–277 letters [278] blank 279–299 appendices [300]–304 index

Binding Red paper embossed to resemble linen grain cloth on boards, spine bound in black linen grain cloth wrapping around front and back covers. Grey endpapers.

Front cover Blindstamped: [short rule] | THE LOST | [short rule] | WRITINGS | [short rule]

Back cover Blindstamped publisher's leaf motif.

Spine Stamped in red gilt: GEORGE | ORWELL | [stamped in silver gilt vertically]: [short rule] | THE LOST | [short rule] | WRITINGS | [short rule] | [stamped in red gilt horizontally]: [publisher's leaf motif] | ARBOR | HOUSE

D.18   ORWELL: THE WAR COMMENTARIES

D.18a   First Edition, 1985

ORWELL | THE WAR | COMMENTARIES | Edited with an Introduction by | W.J. West | [duck motif] | Duckworth| [preceding slash is on the page and does not denote a line break] | British Broadcasting Corporation

Collation There are eleven unmarked gatherings arranged: [A–I]^{12} [K]^8 [L]^{12}; 128 leaves (23.2 × 15.2); this gives a total of 128 leaves, however the first two and last two leaves form the front and back endpapers, the first and last being pasted to the boards; [discounting the pasted and free endpapers] [1–10] 11–239 [240–244] 245–248

Contents [1] halftitle: ORWELL: THE WAR COMMENTARIES [2] blank [3] titlepage [4] imprint: First published in 1985 by | Gerald Duckworth & Co Ltd | The Old Piano Factory | 43 Gloucester Crescent, London NW1 | and the British Broadcasting Corporation | 35 Marylebone High Street, London W1M 4AA | [copyright notices, ISBN numbers and British Library Cataloguing in Publication Data] | Photoset in North Wales by | Derek Doyle & Associates, Mold, Clwyd | Printed and bound in Great Britain by | Billing & Sons Limited, London and Worcester [5] dedication: For R.F. and R.S. [6] blank [7] contents [8] list of maps [9] preface [10] blank 11–23 introduction [24] blank 25–219 text 220–239 appendix [240–243] maps [244–248] index

Binding Black paper embossed to resemble linen grain cloth on boards. Front endpapers have a map of the world at war in 1942, back endpapers map of the world at war in 1943.

Front and back covers Plain.

Spine Stamped in gilt: W.J. | West | [vertically]: ORWELL: THE WAR COMMENTARIES | [horizontally]: [duck motif] | BBC

Jacket Shiny white paper.
Front Black and white photograph of Indian troops in Egypt. Printed in orange across top: ORWELL | [and in black]: THE WAR COMMENTARIES | Edited by W.J. West | [diagonally in orange, frame within which is printed]: CENSORED
Spine Printed in black: W.J. | West | [vertically]: ORWELL: THE WAR COMMEN-TARIES | [horizontally]: [duck motif] | BBC
Back ORWELL: THE WAR BROADCASTS | Edited by W.J. West | [extracts from reviews] | [ISBN data and bar code]
Front flap [Notes about the book] | [cover photograph credits]

Notes
The imprint shows two different ISBN numbers: one for Duckworth and one for the BBC.

D.18b   First American Edition, 1985

Through Eastern Eyes: Orwell's War Commentaries
Edited by W.J. West
New York: Pantheon Books, 1986.

TRANSLATIONS AND FOREIGN EDITIONS

All Orwell Archive unless otherwise noted

DANISH

D.T1a   *Elefanten og Andre Essays*, 1952

Translated by Paul Monrad
København: Steen Hasselbalchs Forlag
Decorative paper on boards. 65pp

   List of contents
   Elefanten
   En Henrettelse
   Saadan dor de fattige
   Jeg skriver, hvad jeg har Lyst til
   En Boganmelders Bekendelser
   Gode daarlige Boger
   Sportsaand
   Det engelske Mords Forfald
   Nogle Betragtninger over den almindelige Tudse

D.T1b   *Det Engelske Folk og Anre Essays*, 1976

Translated by Paul Monrad
København: Det Schonbergske Forlag
114 pp. Paper bound.

   List of contents
   Det Engelske Folk
   Elefanten

En Henrettelse
Saadan dor de fattige
Jeg skriver, hvad jeg har Lyst til
En Boganmelders Bekendelser
Gode daarlige Boger
Sportsaand
Det engelske Mords Forfald
Nogle Betragtninger over den almindelige Tudse

I hvalfiskens bug og Andre Essays, 1984
Translated by Johannes Riis. (Denmark: Gyldendal, 1984) 304pp. Paperbound.
Selections from *The Collected Essays, Letters and Journalism of George Orwell*.

DUTCH

D.T2a   *Een Olifant Omleggen*, 1973

Translated by Martin Schouten
Amsterdam: Uitgeverij de Arbeiderspers
253pp. Paperbound

> *List of contents*
> Why I Write
> The Spike
> A Hanging
> Shooting an Elephant
> Inside the Whale
> Review of *Mein Kampf*
> England Your England
> The Art of Donald McGill
> Notes on Nationalism
> Revenge is Sour
> What is Science
> Some Thoughts on the Common Toad
> Such, Such were the Joys
> Writers and Leviathan

D.T2b   *Bookshop Memories*, 1987

Foreward by W.E. Butler
Baarn: Arethusa Pers Herber Blokland
The publisher's note says that this is the 77th publication of the Arethusa Pers Herber Blokland. It was designed and printed by Sebastian Carter at the Rampant Lions Press, Cambridge, on Zerkall mould-made paper. The engraving was printed from the wood. The setting is Monotype Baskerville, printed by the Stellar Press. The book was bound by Woolnough of Wellingborough. One hundred and fifty copies were produced.

Orwell Archive, copy number: II | X H.C.

FRENCH

D.T3   *Essais Choisis*, 1960

Translated and with a Preface by Philip Thody
Paris: Gallimard
304pp.

Apart from the main issue, 35 special numbered copies formed part of the edition. The Orwell Archive has number 28, as well as an unnumbered copy. 950fr.

List of contents
Shooting an Elephant
A Hanging
How the Poor Die
Lear, Tolstoy and the Fool
Politics vs. Literature
Benefit of Clergy: Some Notes on Salvador Dali
Why I Write
Reflections on Ghandi
Second Thoughts on James Burnham
The Prevention of Literature
Looking Back on the Spanish War
England Your England

GERMAN

D.T4a   *Im Innern des Wals: Ausgewählte Essays I*, 1975

Translated by Felix Gasbarra
Zurich: Diogenes
185pp. Paperbound. 7.80DM

List of contents
Why I Write
A Hanging
Shooting an Elephant
Hop-Picking
from *The Road to Wigan Pier*
Marrakech
Inside the Whale
Mark Twain – The Licensed Jester
Rudyard Kipling
Wells, Hitler and the World State

D.T4b   *Rache ist Sauer: Ausgewählte Essays II*, 1975

Translated by Felix Gasbarra
Zurich: Diogenes, 1975
181pp. Paperbound. 7.80DM

List of contents
Looking Back on the Spanish War
Benefit of Clergy: Some Notes on Salvador Dali
Raffles and Miss Blandish
Revenge is Sour
The Prevention of Literature
Some Thoughts on the Common Toad
Confessions of a Book Reviewer
Politics vs. Literature
Lear, Tolstoy and the Fool
Reflections on Ghandi
Writers and Leviathan

Reissued as *Rache ist Sauer: Erzählungen und Essays* in 1983. 8.80DM

Reissued as *Rache ist Sauer: Erzählungen und Essays*, 1983.
8.80DM

D.T4c   *Charles Dickens: Ein Essay*, 1986

Translated and with notes by Manfred Papst
Zurich: Diogenes
102pp. Paper bound. DM9.80

D.T4d   *Das George Orwell Lesebuch*, 1981

Zurich: Diogenes
342pp. Paper bound. 8.80DM
Reissued in 1983. 9.80DM

D.T4e   *Such, Such Were the Joys: Die Freuden der Kindheit*, 1989

Parallel text edition, German and English
Munich: Deutscher Taschenbuch Verlag
120pp. Paperbound
9.80DM

INDIAN

D.T5   *Selections from George Orwell*, 1971

Indian Edition in English
Edited by R. Sundararaju
Madras: Orien Longman
160pp. Paper bound. Rs 3.00

> *List of contents*
> Why I Write
> What is Science?
> The Sporting Spirit
> In Defence of the Novel
> Tramps
> Tolstoy and Shakespeare
> Charles Dickens
> Literature and Totalitarianism
> Poetry and the Microphone
> Notes on Nationalism
> Politics and the English Language
> The Prevention of Literature
> Reflections on Gandhi
> Writers and Leviathan

ISRAELI

D.T6   *Shooting an Elephant*, 1969

Edition in English
A Worktext for High Schools with text, exercises and notes.
Yahud: Yahud Comprehensive High School
35pp. Paper bound

ITALIAN

D.T7a *'Inside the Whale'*, 1948

The essay was translated into Italian by Giorgio Monicelli for the December 1948 edition of Henry Miller's *Domenica dopo la Guerra* (Verona: Arnoldo Mondadori), where it appears as the Introduction, pp7–57. 400 lire

D.T7b   *Tra Sdegno e Passione*, 1977

Selections from *The Collected Essays, Journalism and Letters of George Orwell*, translated into Italian by Enzo Giachino
Milan: Rizzoli
445pp.

JAPANESE

D.T8a   *England Your England undated* [1956?]

Japanese edition in English of five of the *England Your England* essays, published in Tokyo by Kinseido Ltd, edited and annotated by Natsua Shumata, in the *Modern English Series*. Paper bound.

> *List of contents*
> Why I Write
> Writers and Leviathan
> Looking Back on the Spanish War
> Down the Mine
> England Your England

D.T8b   *Politics vs. Literature: An Examination of Gulliver's Travels*, 1962

Japanese edition in English
Edited with notes in Japanese by K. Ikejima and T. Takatani
Tokyo: Kobunsha
81pp. Paperbound

D.T8c   *Boys' Weeklies Benefit of Clergy*, 1966

An English-language edition with notes in Japanese edited by Fumiaki Ujiiye
Tokyo: Shimizu Shoin
82pp. Paper bound with jacket and fixed silk bookmark. Illustrated

D.T8d   *In Front of Your Nose*, 1969

Edition in English
Edited and with notes in Japanese by H. Funato and A. Sugie Tokyo: Kobunsha
111pp. Paper bound

D.T8e   *As I Please*, 1972

Edition in English
Tokyo: Kirihara Shoten
A collection of essays edited with notes Tetsuro Honda
Paperbound

List of contents
A Hanging
As I Please
Revenge is Sour
Books vs. Cigarettes
Looking Back on the Spanish War

D.T8f *A Nice Cup of Tea*, 1973

Edition in English
Edited and with notes in Japanese by Takeshi Onodera
Tokyo: Tsurumi Shoten
65pp. Paper bound

List of contents
A Nice Cup of Tea
Propaganda and Demotic Speech
Raffles and Miss Blandish

D.T8g *Eight Humorous Essays from George Orwell*, 1973

Edition in English
Edited and with notes in Japanese by Seitaro Takayama and Hiroshi Ikari
Tokyo: Bunri
81pp plus 31pp of notes in a loose pamphlet at the back. Paper bound

List of contents
The Spike
Clink
Bookshop Memories
The Moon Under Water
The Sporting Spirit
Pleasure Spots
Some Thoughts on the Common Toad
Confessions of a Book Reviewer

D.T8h *Looking Back on the Spanish War*, 1973

Edition in English
Edited and with notes by Hiroshi Kawanari
Tokyo: Taibundo
59pp. Paper bound

D.T8i *Some Thoughts on the Common Toad and Other Essays*, 1983

Edition in English
Edited with Notes by Seitaro Takayama and Hiroshi Ikari
Tokyo: Takemura Shuppan
81pp plus 31pp Japanese notes, pasted in between pages 78 and 79. Paper bound. Y950.

List of contents
The Spike
Clink
Bookshop Memories
The Moon Under Water
The Sporting Spirit
Pleasure Spots

Some Thoughts on the Common Toad
Confessions of a Book Reviewer

D.T8j *The English People*, 1981

Extract in a selection of Japanese translations of English literature. Others include Arnold Joseph Toynbee *Civilization on Trial*, C.P. Snow 'The Changing Nature of Love', and Bertrand Russell *The Conquest of Happiness*. 190pp. Paper on boards.

D.T8k *George Orwell: Selections*, 1982

Edition in English.
Tokyo: Iwanami Shoten
376pp. Paper bound with cellophane wrapper

> *List of contents*
> Why I Write
> A Hanging
> Shooting an Elephant
> Charles Dickens
> Inside the Whale
> Review of Mein Kampf
> As I Please
> Raffles and Miss Blandish
> Anti-semitism in Britain
> In Defense of P.G. Wodehouse
> Notes on Nationalism
> The Freedom of the Press

D.T8l *George Orwell*, 1985

Edition in English
Edited with an Introduction and Notes by Koji Watanabe
Kyoto: Yamaguchi Shoten
273pp. Cloth on boards

> *List of contents*
> *Coming Up for Air*
> Politics v Literature
> Why I Write

D.T8m *Boy's Weeklies | Benefit of Clergy*, undated

Edition in English
Edited with notes by Fumiaki Ujiiye.
Tokyo: Shimizu Shoin
Paper bound

SERBO-CROATIAN

D.T9 *Zasto Pisem i drugi eseji*, 1977

Extracts from *The Collected Essays, Journalism and Letters of George Orwell*. Translated and edited by Mirijan Krmpotic and Vladimir Roksandik
Zagreb: Naprijed
244pp. Cloth on boards, with jacket

SPANISH

D.T10a   *A Mi Manera*, 1976

Selection from *The Collected Essays, Journalism and Letters of George Orwell*
Translated by Ragael Vazquez Zamora Barcelona: Ediciones Destino
438pp. Cloth on boards

D.T10b   *Mi Guerra Civil Española*, 1978

Barcelona: Ediciones Destino
178pp. Paper bound
From *The Collected Essays, Journalism and Letters of George Orwell*
Translated by Rafael Vazquez Zamora and Josep C. Verges.

SWEDISH

D.T11a   *Essaer*, 1963

Translated by Goran Bengtson with an Introduction by Olof Lagercrantz
Malmo: Cavefors Prisma
264pp. Paper bound. 12.50

> *List of contents*
> A Hanging
> Shooting an Elephant
> How the Poor Die
> Charles Dickens
> Boys' Weeklies
> Rudyard Kipling
> Inside the Whale
> Looking Back on the Spanish War
> The Prevention of Literature
> Gandhi
> Why I Write
> Writers and Leviathan

D.T11b   *Mit framför Näsan*, 1975

Two volumes of extracts from *The Collected Essays, Journalism and Letters of George Orwell*
Uddevalla: Raben & Sjogren
230 & 223pp
Paper bound
Vol. 1 1932–1942
Vol. 2 1943–1950

Notes to D
1 Letter to Philip Rahv, 1 May 1944. *CEJL* III 143.
2 Written August 1932. First publication *CEJL* I.
3 Excerpt from an unpublished draft of *Burmese Days*. First publication *CEJL* I.
4 Written in late 1945 for Eyre and Spottiswoode who wanted to publish a reprint of *The Position of Peggy Harper* with this as the Introduction. The book was, however, never published. This piece was finally published in *CEJL* IV.
5 Written between October 1947 and January 1948. First publication *CEJL* IV.
6 'Hop-Picking in Kent', *CEJL* I 54.

E: Radio broadcasts

I wrote enough rubbish (news commentaries and so on) to fill a shelf of books. (Letter to A.S.F. Gow, 13 April 1946. *CEJL* IV 146.)

The following list includes Orwell's own radio broadcasts, as well as talks written by Orwell but broadcast by others. The distinction is noted.

E.001   'Proletarian Literature': a discussion with Desmond Hawkins. No. 10 in the series 'The Writer in the Witness Box', broadcast in the BBC Home Service, 6 December 1940, 7.40pm. Printed as 'The Proletarian Writer' in *The Listener* (19 December 1940) 878–879 [C.231].

E.002   'What's Wrong with the Modern Short Story': a discussion between Orwell, Desmond Hawkins and V.S. Pritchett. Empire Service, Indian Section [after 19 December 1940].

E.003   'The Frontiers of Art and Propaganda': the first of four talks on literary criticism, broadcast in the BBC Overseas Service, Empire Service, Indian Section, 30 April 1941. Printed in *The Listener* (29 May 1941) 768–769 [C.267].

E.004   'Tolstoy and Shakespeare': the second of four talks on literary criticism, broadcast in the BBC Overseas Service, Empire Service, Indian Section, 7 May 1941. Printed in *The Listener* (5 June 1941) 809–810 [C.269].

E.005   'The Meaning of a Poem': the third of four talks on literary criticism, broadcast in the BBC Overseas Service, Empire Service, Indian Section, 14 May 1941. Printed in *The Listener* (12 June 1941) 841 [C.271].

E.006   'Literature and Totalitarianism': the last of four talks on literary criticism, broadcast in the BBC Overseas Service, Empire Service, Indian Section, 21 May 1941. Printed in *The Listener* (19 June 1941) 882 [C.274].
        Notes
        Surviving carbon typescript.
Orwell was appointed a talks assistant in the BBC Overseas Service on 18 August 1941 at a salary of £640 a year. After a two-week training course he began work on 1 September 1942. He organised talks designed for Indian university students, wrote weekly news reviews and commentaries, referred to by the BBC as 'News Reviews', 'Weekly News Reviews', 'Newsletters', and 'Commentaries', and prepared scripts in English for translation and broadcast in Gujarati, Marathi, Bengali, Tamil and Hindustani.

E.007   'Through Eastern Eyes: From Colliery to Kitchen', 21 October 1941. Written by Orwell, read by Z.A. Bokhari. 14 minutes 45 seconds.
        Notes
        No surviving script.

E.008   News review, broadcast 15 or 22 November 1941. Written but not read by Orwell.
        Notes
        No surviving script.

E.009   News review, 29 November 1941. Written but not read by Orwell. No surviving script. Extract in *Talking to India*, the first of 'Five Specimens of Propaganda', pp162–165.

E.010   'Through Eastern Eyes'. News review, written by Orwell, read by Z.A. Bokhari, Indian Programme Organiser. BBC Eastern Service, Indian Section, 20 December 1941. 12 minutes. Surviving typescript.
        Notes
        On continuing instability on all fronts: Germans being beaten back in Russia and Libya; Japanese advancing on Hong Kong and Penang.
        Reprinted in *The War Commentaries* 25–28.

E.011   'Through Eastern Eyes'. News review, written by Orwell, read by Z.A. Bokhari. BBC Eastern Service, Indian Section, 3 January 1942. Surviving fair copy of typescript.

Notes

On solidarity of the free nations: signing of pact to end fascism; Chinese troops to defend Burma.

Reprinted in *The War Commentaries* 28–31.

E.012   'Through Eastern Eyes: Paper is Precious'. News review written by Orwell, read by B. Sahni. BBC Eastern Service, Indian Section, 10 January 1942. 8 minutes 45 seconds. Surviving microfilm version.

E.013   'Through Eastern Eyes'. News review, written by Orwell, read by Z.A. Bokhari. BBC Eastern Service, Indian Section, 10 January 1942. Surviving typescript.

Notes

On Japanese defeat at Changsha, China; Japanese advance on Manila, Kuala Lumpur and Singapore; Germans retreating on Russian and Libyan fronts, but still attacking Malta.

Reprinted in *The War Commentaries* 32–35.

E.014   'We Speak to India: Cable to Chungking'. English version of Hindustani talk, read by Orwell. BBC Eastern Service, Indian Section, 14 January 1942, 1430–1500 GMT.

E.015   'The Meaning of Scorched Earth'. Written by Orwell, read by Balraj Sahni. BBC Eastern Service, Indian Section, 15 January 1942.

Notes

No surviving script.

E.016   'Through Eastern Eyes'. News review, written by Orwell, read by Z.A. Bokhari. BBC Eastern Service, Indian Section, 17 January 1942. Surviving fair copy of typescript.

Notes

On continuing Japanese advances; Russians advance on Kharkov; German defeats in Egypt; the continuing propaganda war.

Reprinted in *The War Commentaries* 35–39.

E.017   'Money and Guns'. Talk written by Orwell, read by B. Sahni. BBC Eastern Service, Indian Section, 20 January 1942. 11 minutes 30 seconds.

Notes

Surviving typescript.

Reprinted in *The War Broadcasts* 71–73.

E.018   'The Maharao of Cutch'. Script taken from *The Times* obituary, 20 January 1942 and read by Orwell. BBC Eastern Service, Indian Section, 20 January 1942, 1455 GMT.

E.019   'Through Eastern Eyes: British Rations and the Submarine War'. Written by Orwell, read by I.B. Sarin. BBC Eastern Service, Indian Section, 22 January 1942. 10 minutes 10 seconds.

Notes

Surviving typescript.

Reprinted in *The War Broadcasts* 74–76.

E.020   'Through Eastern Eyes'. News review written by Orwell, read by Z.A. Bokhari. BBC Eastern Service, Indian Section, 24 January 1942. 11 minutes. Surviving fair copy of typescript.

Notes

On growing strength of Allied air power in Far East, amid continuing Japanese advances; continuing German retreat on Russian front; Central and South American republics turning away from Axis towards Allies.

Reprinted in *The War Commentaries* 39–42.

E.021   'Through Eastern Eyes: The Meaning of Sabotage'. Talk written by Orwell, read by Balraj Sahni. BBC Eastern Service, Indian Section, 29 January 1942. 10 minutes 10 seconds.

Notes
Surviving typescript.
Reprinted in *The War Broadcasts* 77–79.

E.022 'Through Eastern Eyes'. News review written by Orwell, read by Z.A. Bokhari. BBC Eastern Service, Indian Section, 31 January 1942. 10 minutes 50 seconds. Surviving typescript.
Notes
On arrival of British and American reinforcements in the Far East; Japanese losses in Rangoon attacks; Japanese advances in Malaya; Russian advances; North African battle continues; Allies in closer military and political agreement.
Reprinted in *The War Commentaries* 42–46.

E.023 'Through Eastern Eyes: The Next Three Months', BBC Eastern Service, Indian Section, 1 February 1942, 1500 GMT.
Notes
Surviving typescript.

E.024 'Through Eastern Eyes'. News review written by Orwell, read by Z.A. Bokhari. BBC Eastern Service, Indian Section, 7 February 1942. 10 minutes 30 seconds. Surviving fair copy of typescript.
Notes
On the siege of Singapore; British loan to China; delaying actions in Burma, Dutch East Indies and Philippines; Anglo-Ethiopian Treaty signed; Lord Beaverbrook appointed Minister of Production.
Reprinted in *The War Commentaries* 46–50.

E.025 'Through Eastern Eyes'. News review written by Orwell, read by Z.A. Bokhari. BBC Eastern Service, Indian Section, 14 February 1942. 11 minutes. Surviving fair copy of typescript.
Extract in *Talking to India*, the second of 'Five Specimens of Propaganda', pp165–168.
Notes
On continuing struggle for Singapore; possible Japanese naval advances and their effects on Allied shipping; German advances towards Persian Gulf; importance of India; the war economy in Britain.
Reprinted in *The War Commentaries* 50–53.

E.026 'Through Eastern Eyes'. News review written by Orwell, read by Z.A. Bokhari. BBC Eastern Service, Indian Section, 21 February 1942. 10 minutes 45 seconds.
Notes
On the Far East war after the fall of Singapore; offensives against Burma, the Philippines and Java; Australia bombed; new German offensives likely on eastern front; new, smaller British war cabinet.
Reprinted in *The War Commentaries* 54–57.

E.027 'Through Eastern Eyes'. News review written by Orwell, read by Z.A. Bokhari. BBC Eastern Service, Indian Section, 28 February 1942. 10 minutes 30 seconds. Surviving fair copy of typescript.
Notes
On the Allied containment of Japanese advances; the importance of supplies and oil; British political developments.
Reprinted in *The War Commentaries* 57–60.

E.028 Gujarati Newsletter 1. BBC Eastern Service, 2 March 1942. 1515–1530 GMT. 14 minutes. English version written by Orwell, translated and read by R.R. Desai.
Notes
No surviving script.

E.029 Marathi Newsletter 1. BBC Eastern Service, 5 March 1942. 1515–1530 GMT. English version written by Orwell, translated and read by Shridhar M. Telkar.
Notes
No surviving script.

E.030   News review. BBC Eastern Service, 7 March 1942. Written by Orwell, read by Z.A. Bokhari. 10 minutes 30 seconds. Surviving fair copy of typescript.

E.031   Bengali and Hindustani versions of English newsletter, 7 March 1942. 1345–1400 and 1515–1530 GMT. English version written by Orwell.

E.032   Gujarati Newsletter 2. BBC Eastern Service, 9 March 1942. 1515–1530 GMT. English version written by Orwell, translated and read by R.R. Desai.
    Notes
    No surviving script.

E.033   'We Speak to India: The Re-discovery of Europe', No. 1 in the series 'Literature Between the Wars'. BBC Eastern Service, 10 March 1942. 1430–1500 GMT. Written and read by Orwell.
    Notes
    Surviving typescript.
    Shortened version printed in *The Listener* (19 March 1942) [C.305].
    Full length, revised version in *Talking to India* 40–51.

E.034   Marathi Newsletter 2. BBC Eastern Service, 12 March 1942. 1515–1530 GMT. English version written by Orwell, translated by Shridhar M. Telkar, read by Venu Chitale.
    Notes
    No surviving script.

E.035   'Through Eastern Eyes'. News review written by Orwell, read by Z.A. Bokhari. BBC Eastern Service, Indian Section, 14 March 1942. 10 minutes 30 seconds.
    Notes
    Surviving fair copy typescript.
    Reprinted in *The War Commentaries* 60–64.

E.036   Gujarati Newsletter 3. BBC Eastern Service, 16 March 1942. 1515–1530 GMT. English version written by Orwell, translated by R.R. Desai & H.L. Desai, read by R.R. Desai. 12 minutes 30 seconds.
    Notes
    No surviving script.

E.037   Marathi Newsletter 3. BBC Eastern Service, 19 March 1942. 1515–1530 GMT. English version written by Orwell, translated and read by Venu Chitale.
    Notes
    No surviving script.

E.038   'Through Eastern Eyes'. News review written by Orwell, read by Z.A. Bokhari. BBC Eastern Service, Indian Section, 21 March 1942.
    Notes
    Surviving fair copy typescript.
    Reprinted in *The War Commentaries* 64–67.

E.039   Gujarati Newsletter 4. BBC Eastern Service, 23 March 1942. 1515–1530 GMT. English version written by Orwell, translated and read by R.R. Desai.
    Notes
    No surviving script.

E.040   'Through Eastern Eyes'. News review written by Orwell, read by Z.A. Bokhari. BBC Eastern Service, Indian Section, 28 March 1942. 10 minutes.
    Notes
    Surviving fair copy typescript.
    Reprinted in *The War Commentaries* 67–72.

E.041   Gujarati Newsletter 5. BBC Eastern Service, 30 March 1942. 1515–1530 GMT. English version written by Orwell, translated and read by R.R. Desai.
    Notes
    No surviving script.

E.042   'Through Eastern Eyes'. News review written by Orwell, read by Z.A. Bokhari. BBC Eastern Service, Indian Section, 4 April 1942. 10 minutes 30 seconds.

Notes

Surviving original typescript.

Reprinted in *The War Commentaries* 72–75.

Extract in *Talking to India*, the third of 'Five Specimens of Propaganda', pp168–171.

E.043   Gujarati Newsletter 6. BBC Eastern Service, 6 April 1942. 1515–1530 GMT. English version written by Orwell, translated and read by R.R. Desai.

Notes

No surviving script.

E.044   Gujarati Newsletter 7. BBC Eastern Service, 13 April 1942. 1515–1530 GMT. English version written by Orwell, translated and read by R.R. Desai. 10 minutes 30 seconds.

Notes

No surviving script.

E.045   'Through Eastern Eyes'. News review written by Orwell, read by Z.A. Bokhari. BBC Eastern Service, Indian Section, 18 April 1942. 10 minutes 30 seconds.

Notes

Surviving typescript.

Reprinted in *The War Commentaries* 76–80.

Extract in *Talking to India*, the fourth of 'Five Specimens of Propaganda', pp171–173.

E.046   Gujarati Newsletter 8. BBC Eastern Service, 20 April 1942. English version written by Orwell, translated and read by R.R. Desai. 13 minutes.

Notes

No surviving script.

E.047   'Birthdays of the Week', Adolf Hitler. BBC Eastern Service, 24 April 1942. 5 minutes.

Notes

No surviving script.

A half-hour programme in which Shridhar Telkar spoke on Sir Stafford Cripps, William Empson on Shakespeare, and Orwell on Hitler. Marius Goring read from James Murphy's translation of *Mein Kampf*, and a short recording of Hitler speaking was played.

E.048   'Through Eastern Eyes'. News review written by Orwell, read by Z.A. Bokhari. BBC Eastern Service, Indian Section, 25 April 1942. 13 minutes 30 seconds.

Notes

Surviving original typescript.

Reprinted in *The War Commentaries* 80–84.

E.049   Gujarati Newsletter 9. BBC Eastern Service, 27 April 1942. English version written by Orwell, translated and read by R.R. Desai. 13 minutes.

Notes

No surviving script.

E.050   Gujarati Newsletter 10. BBC Eastern Service, 4 May 1942. English version written by Orwell, translated and read by R.R. Desai. 11 minutes.

Notes

No surviving script.

E.051   'Through Eastern Eyes'. News review written by Orwell, read by Z.A. Bokhari. BBC Eastern Service, Indian Section, 9 May 1942. 13 minutes 45 seconds.

Notes

Surviving fair copy typescript.

Reprinted in *The War Commentaries* 87–92.

E.052   Gujarati Newsletter 11. BBC Eastern Service, 11 May 1942. English version written by Orwell, translated and read by R.R. Desai. 13 minutes.

Notes

No surviving script.

E.053   'Through Eastern Eyes'. News review written by Orwell, read by Z.A. Bokhari. BBC Eastern Service, Indian Section, 16 May 1942.
    Notes
    Original surviving typescript.
    Reprinted in *The War Commentaries* 92–96.

E.054   Gujarati Newsletter 12. BBC Eastern Service, 18 May 1942. English version written by Orwell, translated and read by R.R. Desai.
    Notes
    No surviving script.

E.055   Marathi Newsletter 12. BBC Eastern Service, 21 May 1942. English version written by Orwell, translated and read by D.M. Kanekar. 13 minutes 25 seconds.
    Notes
    No surviving script.

E.056   'Through Eastern Eyes'. News review which may have been written by Orwell, read by Dick Wessel. BBC Eastern Service, Indian Section, 23 May 1942. 11 minutes 20secs [or 13 minutes 30 seconds].
    Notes
    Surviving fair copy typescript.
    Reprinted in *The War Commentaries* 96–100.
    West includes two other broadcasts which he attributes to Orwell, but which Ian Angus and Peter Davison discount as his work, saying that he neither wrote nor read them. They are the 'Through Eastern Eyes' news reviews of 2 May 1942 and 11 July 1942.

E.057   Gujarati Newsletter 13. BBC Eastern Service, 25 May 1942. English version written by Orwell, translated and read by R.R. Desai.
    Notes
    No surviving script.

E.058   'Through Eastern Eyes'. News review written by Orwell, read by Z.A. Bokhari. BBC Eastern Service, Indian Section, 30 May 1942. 13 minutes 30 seconds.
    Notes
    No surviving script.

E.059   Gujarati Newsletter 14. BBC Eastern Service, 1 June 1942. English version written by Orwell, translated and read by R.R. Desai.
    Notes
    No surviving script.

E.060   'Through Eastern Eyes'. News review script, written by Orwell but not broadcast. Scheduled for broadcast in the BBC Eastern Service, Indian Section, 6 June 1942.
    Notes
    Surviving original typescript.
    Reprinted in *The War Commentaries* 100–106.

E.061   Gujarati Newsletter 15. BBC Eastern Service, 8 June 1942. English version written by Orwell, translated and read by R.R. Desai. 12 minutes 20 seconds.
    Notes
    No surviving script.

E.062   'Through Eastern Eyes'. News review written by Orwell, read by Z.A. Bokhari. BBC Eastern Service, Indian Section, 13 June 1942.
    Notes
    Reprinted in *The War Commentaries* 106–110.

E.063   Gujarati Newsletter 16. BBC Eastern Service, 15 June 1942. English version written by Orwell, translated and read by R.R. Desai.
    Notes
    No surviving script.

E.064   'Through Eastern Eyes'. News review written by Orwell, read by Z.A. Bokhari. BBC Eastern Service, Indian Section, 20 June 1942.

Notes
No surviving script.

E.065 Gujarati Newsletter 17. BBC Eastern Service, 22 June 1942. English version written by Orwell, translated and read by R.R. Desai. 11 minutes 30 seconds.
Notes
No surviving script.

E.066 'Through Eastern Eyes'. News review written by Orwell, read by Z.A. Bokhari. BBC Eastern Service, Indian Section, 27 June 1942. 13 minutes 30 seconds.
Notes
No surviving script.

E.067 Gujarati Newsletter 18. BBC Eastern Service, 29 June 1942. English version written by Orwell, translated and read by R.R. Desai.
Notes
No surviving script.

E.068 Marathi Newsletter 20. BBC Eastern Service, 16 July 1942. English version written by Orwell, translated and read by M.R. Kothari.
Notes
No surviving script.

E.069 Bengali Newsletter 1. BBC Eastern Service, 18 July 1942. English version written by Orwell, translated and read by S.K. Das Gupta. 1345GMT.
Notes
No surviving script.

E.070 'Through Eastern Eyes'. News review written by Orwell, read by Z.A. Bokhari. BBC Eastern Service, Indian Section, 18 July 1942. 13 minutes 30 seconds.
Notes
Surviving typescript.
Reprinted in *The War Commentaries* 115–118.

E.071 Gujarati Newsletter 21. BBC Eastern Service, 20 July 1942. English version written by Orwell, translated and read by R.R. Desai.
Notes
No surviving script.

E.072 Marathi Newsletter 21. BBC Eastern Service, 23 July 1942. English version written by Orwell, translated and read by M.R. Kothari.
Notes
No surviving script.

E.073 'Through Eastern Eyes'. News review written by Orwell, read by Z.A. Bokhari. BBC Eastern Service, Indian Section, 25 July 1942. 13 minutes 30 seconds.
Notes
Surviving typescript.
Reprinted in *The War Commentaries* 119–123.

E.074 Bengali Newsletter 2. BBC Eastern Service, 25 July 1942. English version written by Orwell, translated and read by Aziz-ul-Huque. 1345GMT.
Notes
No surviving script.

E.075 Gujarati Newsletter 22. BBC Eastern Service, 27 July 1942. English version written by Orwell, translated and read by R.R. Desai.
Notes
No surviving script.

E.076 Marathi Newsletter 22. BBC Eastern Service, 30 July 1942. English version written by Orwell, translated and read by M.R. Kothari.
Notes
No surviving script.

E.077 'Through Eastern Eyes'. News review written by Orwell, read by Shridhar Telkar. BBC Eastern Service, Indian Section, 1 August 1942.

        Notes
        Surviving typescript.
        Reprinted in *The War Commentaries* 123–127.

E.078 Bengali Newsletter 3. BBC Eastern Service, 1 August 1942. English version written by Orwell, translated and read by S.K. Das Gupta. 1345GMT.
        Notes
        No surviving script.

E.079 Gujarati Newsletter 23. BBC Eastern Service, 3 August 1942. English version written by Orwell, translated and read by R.R. Desai.
        Notes
        No surviving script.

E.080 Marathi Newsletter 23. BBC Eastern Service, 6 August 1942. English version written by Orwell, translated and read by M.R. Kothari.
        Notes
        No surviving script.

E.081 'Through Eastern Eyes'. News review written by Orwell, read by J. Bahadur Singh. BBC Eastern Service, Indian Section, 8 August 1942.
        Notes
        Surviving typescript.
        Reprinted in *The War Commentaries* 127–131.

E.082 Bengali Newsletter 4. BBC Eastern Service, 8 August 1942. English version written by Orwell, translated and read by S.K. Das Gupta. 1345GMT.
        Notes
        No surviving script.

E.083 Gujarati Newsletter 24. BBC Eastern Service, 10 August 1942. English version written by Orwell, translated and read by R.R. Desai.
        Notes
        No surviving script.

E.084 'Voice', No. 1, BBC Eastern Service, Indian Section, 11 August 1942, 1115–1145 GMT. 27 minutes 30 seconds.
        Notes
        'Voice' was a poetry magazine in six parts, edited, introduced and with contributions by Orwell, with Mulk Raj Anand, John Atkins, William Empson, Inez Holden, Vida Hope and Herbert Read. Pre-recorded 8 August 1942. Rehearsal 6 August 1942 2.30–4.00pm.
        Surviving prompter's typescript.
        Reprinted in *The War Broadcasts* 80–84.

E.085 'Through Eastern Eyes: Anniversary of the Month'. BBC Eastern Service, Indian Section, 11 August 1942. 1 minute 30 seconds.
        Notes
        No surviving script.
        Pre-recorded.
        Contributions by Orwell, A.L. Bakaya, M.M. Haque, Geoffrey Kenton, Arthur Lewis and Una Marson.

E.086 Marathi Newsletter 24. BBC Eastern Service, 13 August 1942. English version written by Orwell, translated and read by M.R. Kothari.
        Notes
        No surviving script.

E.087 'Through Eastern Eyes'. News review written by Orwell, read by Noel Sircar. BBC Eastern Service, Indian Section, 15 August 1942.
        Notes
        Surviving fair copy typescript.
        Reprinted in *The War Commentaries* 131–135.

E.088 Bengali Newsletter. BBC Eastern Service, 15 August 1942. English version written by Orwell, translated and read by S.K. Das Gupta. 1345GMT.

Notes
No surviving script.

E.089   Gujarati Newsletter 25. BBC Eastern Service, 17 August 1942. English version written by Orwell, translated and read by R.R. Desai.
Notes
No surviving script.

E.090   Marathi Newsletter 25. BBC Eastern Service, 20 August 1942. English version written by Orwell, translated and read by M.R. Kothari.
Notes
No surviving script.

E.091   'Through Eastern Eyes'. News review written by Orwell, read by Homi Bode. BBC Eastern Service, Indian Section, 22 August 1942.
Notes
Surviving typescript.
Reprinted in *The War Commentaries* 135–139.

E.092   Bengali Newsletter. BBC Eastern Service, 22 August 1942. English version written by Orwell, translated and read by S.K. Das Gupta. 1345GMT.
Notes
No surviving script.

E.093   Gujarati Newsletter 26. BBC Eastern Service, 24 August 1942. English version written by Orwell, translated and read by R.R. Desai. 11 minutes 22 seconds.
Notes
No surviving script.

E.094   Marathi Newsletter 26. BBC Eastern Service, 27 August 1942. English version written by Orwell, translated and read by M.R. Kothari. 14 minutes.
Notes
No surviving script.

E.095   'Through Eastern Eyes'. News review, written but not read by Orwell, BBC Eastern Service, Indian Section, 29 August 1942. 11 minutes.
Notes
Reprinted in *The War Commentaries* 139–143.

E.096   Bengali Newsletter. BBC Eastern Service, 29 August 1942. English version written by Orwell, translated and read by S.K. Das Gupta. 1345GMT. 11 minutes.
Notes
No surviving script.

E.097   Gujarati Newsletter 27. BBC Eastern Service, 31 August 1942. English version written by Orwell, translated and read by R.R. Desai. 1345–1355GMT. 9 minutes.
Notes
No surviving script.

E.098   Marathi Newsletter 27. BBC Eastern Service, 3 September 1942. English version written by Orwell, translated and read by M.R. Kothari. 1335. 12 minutes 30 seconds.
Notes
No surviving script.

E.099   'Through Eastern Eyes'. News review written by Orwell, read by Bahadur Singh. BBC Eastern Service, Indian Section, 5 September 1942. 13 minutes 18 seconds.
Notes
Surviving typescript.
Reprinted in *The War Commentaries* 143–147.

E.100   Bengali Newsletter. BBC Eastern Service, 5 September 1942. English version written by Orwell, translated and read by S.K. Das Gupta. 1430 GMT. 13 minutes.
Notes
No surviving script.

E.101   Gujarati Newsletter 28. BBC Eastern Service, 7 September 1942. English version written by Orwell, translated and read by R.R. Desai.

Notes

No surviving script.

E.102   'Voice', No. 2, BBC Eastern Service, Indian Section, 8 September 1942, 1115–1145 GMT. 25 minutes 21 seconds

Notes

Poetry magazine edited, introduced and with contributions by Orwell, with Mulk Raj Anand, Edmund Blunden, William Empson, Godfrey Kenton, Herbert Read, and George Woodcock.

Surviving typescript.

Reprinted in *The War Broadcasts* 84–87.

E.103   Marathi Newsletter 28. BBC Eastern Service, 10 September 1942. English version written by Orwell, translated and read by M.R. Kothari. 1335 GMT. 11 minutes 40 seconds.

Notes

No surviving script.

E.104   'Through Eastern Eyes'. News review written by Orwell, read by Noel Sircar. BBC Eastern Service, Indian Section, 12 September 1942.

Notes

Surviving typescript.

Reprinted in *The War Commentaries* 147–149.

E.105   Bengali Newsletter. BBC Eastern Service, 12 September 1942. English version written by Orwell, translated and read by S.K. Das Gupta. 1430 GMT. 12 minutes 15 seconds.

Notes

No surviving script.

E.106   Gujarati Newsletter 29. BBC Eastern Service, 14 September 1942. English version written by Orwell, translated and read by R.R. Desai.

Notes

No surviving script.

E.107   Marathi Newsletter 29. BBC Eastern Service, 17 September 1942. English version written by Orwell, translated and read by M.R. Kothari. 1335 GMT. 10 minutes 43 seconds.

Notes

No surviving script.

E.108   'Through Eastern Eyes'. News review written by Orwell, read by Homi Bode. BBC Eastern Service, Indian Section, 19 September 1942.

Notes

Surviving typescript.

Reprinted in *The War Commentaries* 150–153.

E.109   Bengali Newsletter. BBC Eastern Service, 19 September 1942. English version written by Orwell, translated and read by S.K. Das Gupta. 1430 GMT. 13 minutes 5 seconds.

Notes

No surviving script.

E.110   Gujarati Newsletter 30. BBC Eastern Service, 21 September 1942. English version written by Orwell, translated and read by R.R. Desai. 11 minutes 5 seconds.

Notes

No surviving script.

E.111   'Through Eastern Eyes'. News review written by Orwell, read by Shridhar Telkar. BBC Eastern Service, Indian Section, 26 September 1942. 11 minutes.

Notes

Surviving typescript.

Reprinted in *The War Commentaries* 153–157.

E.112   Bengali Newsletter. BBC Eastern Service, 26 September 1942. English version written by Orwell, translated and read by S.K. Das Gupta. 1430 GMT. 11 minutes 4 seconds.

Notes
No surviving script.

E.113   Gujarati Newsletter 31. BBC Eastern Service, 28 September 1942. English version written by Orwell, translated and read by R.R. Desai. 9 minutes 40 seconds.
Notes
No surviving script.

E.114   'Through Eastern Eyes'. News review written by Orwell, read by Bahadur Singh. BBC Eastern Service, Indian Section, 3 October 1942. 11 minutes 38 seconds.
Notes
Surviving typescript.
Reprinted in *The War Commentaries* 157–161.

E.115   Bengali Newsletter. BBC Eastern Service, 3 October 1942. English version written by Orwell, translated and read by S.K. Das Gupta. 1430 GMT. 12 minutes 20 seconds.
Notes
No surviving script.

E.116   Gujarati Newsletter 32. BBC Eastern Service, 5 October 1942. English version written by Orwell, translated and read by R.R. Desai. 11 minutes.
Notes
No surviving script.

E.117   'Voice', No. 3, BBC Eastern Service, Indian Section, 6 October 1942, 1115–1145 GMT. c21 minutes 30 seconds.
Notes
Surviving typescript.
Poetry magazine edited, introduced and with contributions by Orwell, with Mulk Raj Anand, William Empson, Herbert Read, and Stephen Spender.
Reprinted in *The War Broadcasts* 87–89.

E.118   'Through Eastern Eyes: Story by Five Authors', Part I by George Orwell, BBC Eastern Service, Indian Section, 9 October 1942, 1115–1130 GMT.
Notes
Surviving typescript.
Reprinted in *The War Broadcasts* 95–98.

E.119   'Through Eastern Eyes'. News review written by Orwell, read by Noel Sircar. BBC Eastern Service, Indian Section, 10 October 1942.
Notes
Surviving typescript.
Reprinted in *The War Commentaries* 161–164.

E.120   Bengali Newsletter. BBC Eastern Service, 10 October 1942. English version written by Orwell, translated and read by S.K. Das Gupta. 1430 GMT. 11 minutes 45 seconds.
Notes
No surviving script.

E.121   Gujarati Newsletter 33. BBC Eastern Service, 12 October 1942. English version written by Orwell, translated and read by R.R. Desai. 10 minutes 11 seconds.
Notes
No surviving script.

E.122   'Through Eastern Eyes'. News review written by Orwell, read by Homi Bode. BBC Eastern Service, Indian Section, 17 October 1942.
Notes
Surviving typescript.
Reprinted in *The War Commentaries* 164–167.

E.123   Bengali Newsletter. BBC Eastern Service, 17 October 1942. English version written by Orwell, translated and read by S.K. Das Gupta. 1430 GMT.
Notes
No surviving script.

E.124   'Answering You', No. 65: No. 4 in the series 'Two-Way', discussion between speakers in London and New York, 18 October 1942 2130–2200 GMT, and 19 October 1942 0200–0230 GMT.
        Notes
        Orwell was one of five speakers in the London studio where the others were Miss Dean, Pauline Gower, George Strauss, and W. Vaughan Thomas.

E.125   Gujarati Newsletter 34. BBC Eastern Service, 19 October 1942. English version written by Orwell, translated and read by R.R. Desai. 10 minutes.
        Notes
        No surviving script.

E.126   'Through Eastern Eyes'. News review written by Orwell, read by Shridhar Telkar. BBC Eastern Service, Indian Section, 24 October 1942. 13 minutes 7 seconds.
        Notes
        Reprinted in *The War Commentaries* 168–172.

E.127   Bengali Newsletter. BBC Eastern Service, 24 October 1942. English version written by Orwell, translated and read by S.K. Das Gupta. 1430 GMT. 13 minutes 32 seconds.
        Notes
        No surviving script.

E.128   Gujarati Newsletter 35. BBC Eastern Service, 26 October 1942. English version written by Orwell, translated and read by R.R. Desai. 12 minutes.
        Notes
        No surviving script.

E.129   'Through Eastern Eyes'. News review written by Orwell, read by Bahadur Singh. BBC Eastern Service, Indian Section, 31 October 1942. 11 minutes 20 seconds.
        Notes
        Reprinted in *The War Commentaries* 172–175.

E.130   Bengali Newsletter. BBC Eastern Service, 31 October 1942. English version written by Orwell, translated and read by S.K. Das Gupta. 1430 GMT.
        Notes
        No surviving script.

E.131   Gujarati Newsletter 36. BBC Eastern Service, 2 November 1942. English version written by Orwell, translated and read by R.R. Desai. 10 minutes 35 seconds.
        Notes
        No surviving script.

E.132   'Jonathan Swift, an Imaginary Interview', BBC African Service, 6 November 1942, 1145–1230 GMT. c13 minutes 30 seconds.
        Notes
        Recorded 2 November 1942.
        Surviving typescript.
        Reprinted as 'Too Hard on Humanity', *The Listener* (26 November 1942) 692–693 [C.322], and in *The War Broadcasts* 112–116.

E.133   'Voice', No. 4, BBC Eastern Service, Indian Section, 3 November 1942.
        Notes
        Surviving typescript.
        Poetry magazine edited, introduced and with contributions by Orwell, with Mulk Raj Anand, William Empson, Una Marson, and Herbert Read.
        Reprinted in *The War Broadcasts* 89–92.

E.134 'Through Eastern Eyes'. News review written by Orwell, read by Noel Sircar. BBC Eastern Service, Indian Section, 7 November 1942. 9 minutes 22 seconds.
Notes
Surviving typescript.
Reprinted in *The War Commentaries* 175–178.

E.135 Bengali Newsletter. BBC Eastern Service, 7 November 1942. English version written by Orwell, translated and read by S.K. Das Gupta. 1430 GMT.
Notes
No surviving script.

E.136 Gujarati Newsletter 37. BBC Eastern Service, 9 November 1942. English version written by Orwell, translated and read by R.R. Desai. 10 minutes.
Notes
No surviving script.

E.137 Introduction to 'Let's Act it Ourselves – 1'. BBC Eastern Service, 13 November 1942.
Notes
Surviving typescript.
Orwell introduced only the first of this six-part series on amateur dramatics, presented by Norman Marshall.

E.138 Bengali Newsletter. BBC Eastern Service, 14 November 1942. English version written by Orwell, translated and read by S.K. Das Gupta. 1430 GMT. 10 minutes 5 seconds.
Notes
No surviving script.

E.139 Gujarati Newsletter 38. BBC Eastern Service, 16 November 1942. English version written by Orwell, translated and read by R.R. Desai. 10 minutes
Notes
No surviving script.

E.140 News Commentary in English for Malaya, 20 November 1942. Written and read by Orwell. 1130 GMT.
Notes
No surviving script.

E.141 'Through Eastern Eyes'. News review written and read by Orwell, BBC Eastern Service, Indian Section, 21 November 1942, 1115–1130 GMT. 13 minutes 15 seconds.
Notes
Surviving typescript.
This was the first weekly newsletter in English for India which Orwell wrote and read.

E.142 Bengali Newsletter. BBC Eastern Service, 21 November 1942. English version written by Orwell, translated and read by S.K. Das Gupta. 1430 GMT.
Notes
No surviving script.

E.143 Gujarati Newsletter 39. BBC Eastern Service, 23 November 1942. English version written by Orwell, translated and read by R.R. Desai.
Notes
No surviving script.

E.144 News Commentary in English for Malaya, 27 November 1942. Written and read by Orwell. 1130 GMT.
Notes
No surviving script.

E.145 'Through Eastern Eyes'. News review written and read by Orwell, BBC Eastern Service, Indian Section, 28 November 1942, 1115–1130 GMT. 12 minutes 15 seconds.
Notes
Surviving typescript.
Reprinted in *The War Commentaries* 179–183.

E.146   Bengali Newsletter. BBC Eastern Service, 28 November 1942. English version written by Orwell, translated and read by S.K. Das Gupta. 1430 GMT. 8 minutes 30 seconds.
    Notes
    No surviving script.

E.147   Gujarati Newsletter 40. BBC Eastern Service, 30 November 1942. English version written by Orwell, translated and read by R.R. Desai. 8 minutes 35 seconds.
    Notes
    No surviving script.

E.148   'Voice', No. 5, BBC Eastern Service, Indian Section, 1 December 1942.
    Notes
    Surviving typescript.
    Poetry magazine edited, introduced and with contributions by Orwell, with Mulk Raj Anand, T.S. Eliot, William Empson, Una Marson, Narayana Menon, Christopher Pemberton, and M.J. Tambimuttu.

E.149   News Commentary in English for Malaya, 4 December 1942. Written and read by Orwell. 1130 GMT.
    Notes
    No surviving script.

E.150   Bengali Newsletter. BBC Eastern Service, 5 December 1942. English version written by Orwell, translated and read by S.K. Das Gupta. 1430 GMT. 11 minutes 30 seconds.
    Notes
    No surviving script.

E.151   'Through Eastern Eyes'. News review written and read by Orwell, BBC Eastern Service, Indian Section, 5 December 1942, 1115–1130 GMT.
    Notes
    No surviving script.

E.152   Gujarati Newsletter 41. BBC Eastern Service, 7 December 1942. English version written by Orwell, translated and read by R.R. Desai.
    Notes
    No surviving script.

E.153   News Commentary in English for Malaya, 11 December 1942. Written and read by Orwell. 1130 GMT.
    Notes
    No surviving script.

E.154   'Through Eastern Eyes'. News review by Orwell, BBC Eastern Service, Indian Section, 12 December 1942, 1115–1130 GMT. 13 minutes.
    Notes
    Reprinted in *The War Commentaries* 183–188.

E.155   Bengali Newsletter. BBC Eastern Service, 12 December 1942. English version written by Orwell, translated and read by S.K. Das Gupta. 1430 GMT. 14 minutes 30 seconds.
    Notes
    No surviving script.

E.156   Gujarati Newsletter 42. BBC Eastern Service, 14 December 1942. English version written by Orwell, translated and read by R.R. Desai. 11 minutes 30 seconds.
    Notes
    No surviving script.

E.157   News Commentary in English for Malaya, 18 December 1942. Written and read by Orwell. 1130 GMT.
    Notes
    No surviving script.

E.158   'Through Eastern Eyes'. News review by Orwell, BBC Eastern Service, Indian Section, 19 December 1942, 1115–1130 GMT. 12 minutes 5 [or 50 seconds].

Notes
Surviving typescript.
Reprinted in *The War Commentaries* 188–192.

E.159 Bengali Newsletter. BBC Eastern Service, 19 December 1942. English version written by Orwell, translated and read by S.K. Das Gupta. 1430 GMT. 9 minutes 20 seconds.
Notes
No surviving script.

E.160 Gujarati Newsletter 43. BBC Eastern Service, 21 December 1942. English version written by Orwell, translated and read by R.R. Desai. 8 minutes 35 seconds.
Notes
No surviving script.

E.161 News Commentary in English for Malaya, 25 December 1942. Written and read by Orwell. 1130 GMT.
Notes
No surviving script.

E.162 'Through Eastern Eyes'. News review by Orwell, BBC Eastern Service, Indian Section, 26 December 1942, 1115–1130 GMT. 13 minutes 8 [or 15 seconds].
Notes
Surviving typescript.
Reprinted in *The War Commentaries* 193–198.

E.163 Bengali Newsletter. BBC Eastern Service, 26 December 1942. English version written by Orwell, translated and read by S.K. Das Gupta. 1430 GMT. 12 minutes.
Notes
No surviving script.

E.164 Gujarati Newsletter 44. BBC Eastern Service, 28 December 1942. English version written by Orwell, translated and read by R.R. Desai. 11 minutes 2 seconds.
Notes
No surviving script.
This was the last Gujarari Newsletter which Orwell wrote.

E.165 'Voice', No. 6, BBC Eastern Service, Indian Section, 29 December 1942, 1115–1145 GMT. 29 minutes 15 seconds.
Notes
Surviving typescript.
Poetry magazine edited, introduced and with contributions by Orwell, with Mulk Raj Anand, Venu Chitale, William Empson, Christopher Pemberton, and Herbert Read, and a pre-recorded contribution by T.S. Eliot.
Reprinted in *The War Broadcasts* 92–94.

E.166 News Commentary in English for Malaya, 1 January 1943. Written and read by Orwell. 1130 GMT.
Notes
No surviving script.

E.167 'Through Eastern Eyes'. News review by Orwell, BBC Eastern Service, Indian Section, 2 January 1943. 1115–1130 GMT. 6 minutes 15 seconds.
Notes
No surviving script.

E.168 Bengali Newsletter. BBC Eastern Service, 2 January 1943. English version written by Orwell, translated and read by S.K. Das Gupta. 1430 GMT. 7 minutes 47 seconds.
Notes
No surviving script.

E.169 Introduction to 'Calling All Students' No. 3. BBC Eastern Service, Indian Section, 8 January 1943, 1115–1145 GMT.
Notes
Programme on Thomas Hardy and *Far From the Madding Crowd* presented by Edmund Blunden.

Surviving typescript.
Reprinted in *The War Broadcasts* 117.

E.170   News Commentary in English for Malaya, 8 January 1943. Written and read by Orwell. 1130 GMT.
Notes
No surviving script.

E.171   'Through Eastern Eyes'. News review by Orwell, BBC Eastern Service, Indian Section, 9 January 1943, 1115–1130 GMT. c12 minutes 10 seconds.
Notes
Surviving typescript.
Reprinted in *The War Commentaries* 198–202.

E.172   Bengali Newsletter. BBC Eastern Service, 9 January 1943. English version written by Orwell, translated and read by S.K. Das Gupta. 1430 GMT. 11 minutes 4 seconds.
Notes
No surviving script.

E.173   News Commentary in English for Malaya, 15 January 1943. Written and read by Orwell. 1130 GMT.
Notes
No surviving script.

E.174   'Through Eastern Eyes'. News review by Orwell, BBC Eastern Service, Indian Section, 16 January 1943, 1115–1130 GMT. 13 minutes.
Notes
Surviving typescript, which shows that this script, although longer, was the basis for the Bengali Newsletter broadcast the same day. [E.176].
Reprinted in *The War Commentaries* 202–206.

E.175   Bengali Newsletter. BBC Eastern Service, 16 January 1943. English version written by Orwell, translated and read by S.K. Das Gupta. 1430 GMT. 9 minutes.
Notes
No surviving script.

E.176   'Bernard Shaw': No. 5 in the series 'Calling All Students', BBC Eastern Service, Indian Section, 22 January 1943, 1115–1145 GMT. 14 minutes 20 seconds.
Notes
On *Arms and the Man*.
Pre-recorded.
Surviving typescript.
Published in BBC Pamphlets No. 2 *Books and Authors* ed. Laurence Brander (Bombay: Oxford University Press, 1946).
Reprinted in *The War Broadcasts* 118–121.

E.177   News Commentary in English for Malaya, 22 January 1943. Written by Orwell, read by D. Prentice. 1130 GMT.
Notes
No surviving script.
Orwell was taken ill before the broadcast.

E.178   Bengali Newsletter. BBC Eastern Service, 23 January 1943. English version written by Orwell, translated and read by S.K. Das Gupta. 1430 GMT.
Notes
No surviving script.

E.179   Bengali Newsletter. BBC Eastern Service, 30 January 1943. English version written by Orwell, translated and read by S.K. Das Gupta. 1430 GMT.
Notes
No surviving script.

E.180   News Commentary in English for Malaya, 19 February 1943. Written and read by Orwell. 1130 GMT.
Notes
No surviving script.

E.181   'Through Eastern Eyes'. News review by Orwell, BBC Eastern Service, Indian Section, 20 February 1943, 1115–1130 GMT. 13 minutes.
       Notes
       Surviving typescript.
       Reprinted in *The War Commentaries* 206–210.

E.182   Bengali Newsletter. BBC Eastern Service, 20 February 1943. English version written by Orwell, translated and read by S.K. Das Gupta. 1430 GMT. 9 minutes 3 seconds.
       Notes
       No surviving script.

E.183   News Commentary in English for Malaya, 26 February 1943. Written and read by Orwell. 1130 GMT.
       Notes
       No surviving script.

E.184   'Through Eastern Eyes'. News review by Orwell, BBC Eastern Service, Indian Section, 27 February 1943, 1115–1130 GMT. 11 minutes 35 seconds.
       Notes
       Surviving typescript.
       Reprinted in *The War Commentaries* 210–215.

E.185   Bengali Newsletter. BBC Eastern Service, 27 February 1943. English version written by Orwell, translated and read by S.K. Das Gupta. 1430 GMT.
       Notes
       No surviving script.
       This was the last Bengali Newsletter which Orwell wrote.

E.186   'Jack London': No. 5 in the series 'Landmarks in American Literature', BBC Eastern Service, Indian Section, 5 March 1943, 1115–1145 GMT. 14 minutes 8 seconds.
       Notes
       Pre-recorded 1 March 1943.
       Narrated by Orwell.
       Surviving typescript.
       Payment £18 18s 0d.
       Published in BBC Pamphlets No. 3 *Books and Authors* ed. Laurence Brander (Bombay: Oxford University Press, 1946).
       Reprinted in *The War Broadcasts* 122–125.

E.187   News Commentary in English for Malaya, 5 March 1943. Written and read by Orwell. 1130 GMT.
       Notes
       No surviving script.

E.188   News Commentary in English for Malaya, 12 March 1943. Written and read by Orwell. 1130 GMT.
       Notes
       No surviving script.

E.189   News review by Orwell, BBC Eastern Service, Indian Section, 13 March 1943, 1115–1130 GMT. 13 minutes 30 seconds.
       Notes
       Surviving typescript.
       Reprinted in *The War Commentaries* 215–219.

E.190   News Commentary in English for Malaya, 19 March 1943. Written by Orwell, read by John Morris. 1130 GMT.
       Notes
       No surviving script.

E.191   News review by Orwell, BBC Eastern Service, Indian Section, 13 March 1943, 1115–1130 GMT.
       Notes
       No surviving script.

E.192   News Commentary in English for Malaya, 2 April 1943. Written and read by
Orwell. 1130 GMT.
Notes
No surviving script.

E.193   News Commentary in English for Malaya, 9 April 1943. Written and read by
Orwell. 1130 GMT.
Notes
No surviving script.

E.194   News Commentary in English for Malaya, 16 April 1943. Written and read by
Orwell. 1130 GMT.
Notes
No surviving script.

E.195   Tamil Newsletter, BBC Eastern Service, 22 April 1943. English version written by
Orwell, translated and read by J.D.S. Paul.
Notes
No surviving script.

E.196   News Commentary in English for Malaya, 16 April 1943. Written and read by
Orwell. 1130 GMT.
Notes
No surviving script.

E.197   Tamil Newsletter, BBC Eastern Service, 29 April 1943. English version written by
Orwell, translated and read by J.D.S. Paul.
Notes
No surviving script.

E.198   News Commentary in English for Malaya, 30 April 1943. Written and read by
Orwell. 1130 GMT.
Notes
No surviving script.

E.199   Tamil Newsletter, BBC Eastern Service, 6 May 1943. English version written by
Orwell, translated and read by J.D.S. Paul.
Notes
No surviving script.

E.200   News Commentary in English for Malaya, 7 May 1943. Written and read by
Orwell. 1130 GMT.
Notes
No surviving script.

E.201   'Marrakech', BBC Radio Newsreel, 10 May 1943. 1830 GMT.
Notes
No surviving script.
No fee.

E.202   News in Tamil, BBC Eastern Service, 13 May 1943. English version written by
Orwell, translated and read by J.D.S. Paul.
Notes
No surviving script.

E.203   News Commentary in English for Malaya, 14 May 1943. Written and read by
Orwell. 1130 GMT.
Notes
No surviving script.

E.204   Tamil Newsletter, BBC Eastern Service, 20 May 1943. English version written by
Orwell, translated and read by J.D.S. Paul.
Notes
No surviving script.

E.205   News Commentary in English for Malaya, 21 May 1943. Written and read by
Orwell. 1130 GMT.

Notes
No surviving script.

E.206 Tamil Newsletter, BBC Eastern Service, 27 May 1943. English version written by Orwell, translated and read by J.D.S. Paul.
Notes
No surviving script.

E.207 News Commentary in English for Malaya, 28 May 1943. Written and read by Orwell. 1130 GMT.
Notes
Surviving script extract.

E.208 Tamil Newsletter, BBC Eastern Service, 3 June 1943. English version written by Orwell, translated and read by J.D.S. Paul.
Notes
No surviving script.

E.209 News Commentary in English for Malaya, 4 June 1943. Written and read by Orwell. 1130 GMT.
Notes
No surviving script.

E.210 Tamil Newsletter, BBC Eastern Service, 10 June 1943. English version written by Orwell, translated and read by J.D.S. Paul.
Notes
No surviving script.

E.211 News Commentary in English for Malaya, 11 June 1943. Written and read by Orwell. 1130 GMT.
Notes
No surviving script.

E.212 'English Poetry Since 1900': No. 1 in the series 'Calling All Students, Literary Series', BBC Eastern Service, Indian Section, 13 June 1943, 1515–1530 GMT. 13 minutes.
Notes
Surviving typescript.
Reprinted in *The War Broadcasts* 126–129.

E.213 Tamil Newsletter, BBC Eastern Service, 17 June 1943. English version written by Orwell, translated and read by J.D.S. Paul.
Notes
No surviving script.

E.214 News Commentary in English for Malaya, 18 June 1943. Written and read by Orwell. 1130 GMT.
Notes
No surviving script.

E.215 Tamil Newsletter, BBC Eastern Service, 24 June 1943. English version written by Orwell, translated and read by J.D.S. Paul.
Notes
No surviving script.

E.216 News Commentary in English for Malaya, 25 June 1943. Written and read by Orwell. 1130 GMT.
Notes
No surviving script.

E.217 Tamil Newsletter, BBC Eastern Service, 1 July 1943. English version written by Orwell, translated and read by J.D.S. Paul.
Notes
No surviving script.

E.218 News Commentary in English for Malaya, 2 July 1943. Written and read by Orwell. 1130 GMT.

   Notes
   No surviving script.
   This was Orwell's last News Commentary in English for Malaya.

E.219 Tamil Newsletter, BBC Eastern Service, 8 July 1943. English version written by Orwell, translated and read by J.D.S. Paul.
   Notes
   No surviving script.

E.220 English Newsletter for Indonesia No. 1, 9 July 1943. Written by Orwell, read by John Morris. 1330 GMT.
   Notes
   No surviving script.

E.221 Tamil Newsletter, BBC Eastern Service, 15 July 1943. English version written by Orwell, translated and read by J.D.S. Paul.
   Notes
   No surviving script.

E.222 English Newsletter for Indonesia No. 2, 16 July 1943. Written and read by Orwell. 1330 GMT.
   Notes
   No surviving script.

E.223 Tamil Newsletter, BBC Eastern Service, 22 July 1943. English version written by Orwell, translated and read by J.D.S. Paul.
   Notes
   No surviving script.

E.224 English Newsletter for Indonesia No. 3, 23 July 1943. Written and read by Orwell. 1330 GMT.
   Notes
   No surviving script.

E.225 Tamil Newsletter, BBC Eastern Service, 29 July 1943. English version written by Orwell, translated and read by J.D.S. Paul.
   Notes
   No surviving script.

E.226 English Newsletter for Indonesia No. 4, 30 July 1943. Written and read by Orwell. 1330 GMT.
   Notes
   No surviving script.

E.227 Tamil Newsletter, BBC Eastern Service, 5 August 1943. English version written by Orwell, translated and read by J.D.S. Paul.
   Notes
   No surviving script.

E.228 English Newsletter for Indonesia No. 5, 6 August 1943. Written and read by Orwell. 1330 GMT.
   Notes
   No surviving script.

E.229 '*Crainquebille* by Anatole France', adapted and narrated by George Orwell, BBC Eastern Service, Indian Section, 11 August 1943, 1000–1030 GMT.
   Notes
   Surviving typescript.
   Reprinted in *The War Broadcasts* 130–138.

E.230 Tamil Newsletter, BBC Eastern Service, 12 August 1943. English version written by Orwell, translated and read by J.D.S. Paul.
   Notes
   No surviving script.

E.231 English Newsletter for Indonesia No. 6, 13 August 1943. Written and read by Orwell. 1330 GMT.

       Notes
       No surviving script.

E.232 Tamil Newsletter, BBC Eastern Service, 19 August 1943. English version written by Orwell, translated and read by J.D.S. Paul.
       Notes
       No surviving script.

E.233 English Newsletter for Indonesia No. 7, 20 August 1943. Written and read by Orwell. 1330 GMT.
       Notes
       No surviving script.

E.234 Tamil Newsletter, BBC Eastern Service, 26 August 1943. English version written by Orwell, translated and read by J.D.S. Paul.
       Notes
       No surviving script.

E.235 English Newsletter for Indonesia No. 8, 27 August 1943. Written and read by Orwell. 1330 GMT.
       Notes
       No surviving script.

E.236 English Newsletter for Indonesia No. 9, 3 September 1943. Written and read by Orwell. 1330 GMT.
       Notes
       No surviving script.

E.237 '*The Fox* by Ignazio Silone', adapted and narrated by George Orwell, BBC Eastern Service, Indian Section, 9 September 1943. 26 minutes 30 seconds.
       Notes
       Surviving typescript.
       Reprinted in *The War Broadcasts* 139–148.

E.238 Tamil Newsletter, BBC Eastern Service, 23 September 1943. English version written by Orwell, translated and read by J.D.S. Paul.
       Notes
       No surviving script.

E.239 English Newsletter for Indonesia No. 12, 24 September 1943. Written and read by Orwell. 1330 GMT.
       Notes
       No surviving script.

E.240 Tamil Newsletter, BBC Eastern Service, 30 September 1943. English version written by Orwell, translated and read by J.D.S. Paul.
       Notes
       No surviving script.

E.241 English Newsletter for Indonesia No. 13, 1 October 1943. Written and read by Orwell. 1330 GMT.
       Notes
       No surviving script.

E.242 '*A Slip Under the Microscope* by H.G. Wells', adapted and narrated by George Orwell, BBC Eastern Service, Indian Section, 6 October 1943.
       Notes
       Surviving typescript.
       Reprinted in *The War Broadcasts* 149–158.

E.243 Tamil Newsletter, BBC Eastern Service, 7 October 1943. English version written by Orwell, translated and read by J.D.S. Paul.
       Notes
       No surviving script.

E.244 English Newsletter for Indonesia No. 14, 8 October 1943. Written and read by Orwell. 1330 GMT.

    Notes
    No surviving script.

E.245 Tamil Newsletter, BBC Eastern Service, 14 October 1943. English version written by Orwell, translated and read by J.D.S. Paul.
    Notes
    No surviving script.

E.246 English Newsletter for Indonesia No. 15, 15 October 1943. Written and read by Orwell. 1330 GMT.
    Notes
    No surviving script.

E.247 '*Macbeth*, A Commentary': No. 1 'William Shakespeare', in the series 'Great Dramatists', BBC Eastern Service, Indian Section, 17 October 1943, 1515–1545 GMT.
    Notes
    Adapted and introduced by Orwell. His talk lasted 9 minutes 26 seconds. Surviving typescript.
    Reprinted in *The War Broadcasts* 159–161.

E.248 Tamil Newsletter, BBC Eastern Service, 21 October 1943. English version written by Orwell, translated and read by J.D.S. Paul.
    Notes
    No surviving script.

E.249 English Newsletter for Indonesia No. 16, 22 October 1943. Written and read by Orwell. 1330 GMT.
    Notes
    No surviving script.

E.250 Tamil Newsletter, BBC Eastern Service, 28 October 1943. English version written by Orwell, translated and read by J.D.S. Paul.
    Notes
    No surviving script.

E.251 English Newsletter for Indonesia No. 17, 29 October 1943. Written and read by Orwell. 1330 GMT.
    Notes
    No surviving script.

E.252 Tamil Newsletter, BBC Eastern Service, 4 November 1943. English version written by Orwell, translated and read by G.J.C. Francis.
    Notes
    No surviving script.

E.253 English Newsletter for Indonesia No. 18, 5 November 1943. Written and read by Orwell. 1330 GMT.
    Notes
    No surviving script.

E.254 Tamil Newsletter, BBC Eastern Service, 11 November 1943. English version written by Orwell, translated and read by J.D.S. Paul.
    Notes
    No surviving script.

E.255 English Newsletter for Indonesia No. 19, 12 November 1943. Written and read by Orwell. 1330 GMT.
    Notes
    No surviving script.

E.256 '*The Emperor's New Clothes* by Hans Andersen', adapted and narrated by George Orwell, BBC Eastern Service, Indian Section, 18 November 1943, 1615–1630 GMT.
    Notes
    Rehearsals 18 November, 10–11am, 11.30am-1pm, 2–4pm.

Surviving fair copy typescript.

Reprinted in *The War Broadcasts* 162–167.

E.257 Tamil Newsletter, BBC Eastern Service, 18 November 1943. English version written by Orwell, translated and read by J.D.S. Paul.

Notes

No surviving script.

E.258 English Newsletter for Indonesia No. 20, 19 November 1943. Written and read by Orwell. 1330 GMT.

Notes

No surviving script.

E.259 '*Lady Windermere's Fan*, A Commentary': No. 6 'Oscar Wilde', in the series 'Calling All Students: Great Dramatists', BBC Eastern Service, Indian Section, 21 November 1943, 1515–1545 GMT.

Notes

Written and read by Orwell.

Surviving typescript.

Reprinted in *The War Broadcasts* 168–171.

E.260 Tamil Newsletter, BBC Eastern Service, 25 November 1943. English version written by Orwell, translated and read by J.D.S. Paul.

Notes

No surviving script.

The day before this broadcast was transmitted Orwell left the BBC.

E.261 English Newsletter for Indonesia No. 21, 26 November 1943. Written by Orwell, read by John Morris. 1330 GMT.

Notes

No surviving script.

Written by Orwell before he left the BBC on 24 November 1943.

E.262 'Your Questions Answered', No. 25, BBC Overseas Service, 2 December 1943, and SOX 23536 Service, 3 December 1943.

Notes

Orwell was one of four panellists and answered questions on Wigan and Wigan Pier.

E.263 'Political Theories and European Literature', BBC Latin American Service, 29 June 1944. Written by Orwell, translated by J. Tuya Videl, read by W.G. Cain. 0245–0300 GMT.

E.264 '*Erewhon* by Samuel Butler', in the series 'Talks for Sixth Forms', BBC Home Service, 8 June 1945, 11.40am-1200pm. Written and read by Orwell.

Notes

Recorded 6 June 1945.

Payment £12 12s.

Surviving fair copy of typescript.

E.265 '*The Way of All Flesh* by Samuel Butler', in the series 'Talks for Sixth Forms', BBC Home Service, 15 June 1945, 11.40am-12.00pm. Written and read by Orwell.

Notes

Payment £12 12s.

Surviving fair copy of typescript.

E.266 'Jack London': Forces Educational Broadcast, BBC Light Programme, 8 October 1945, 10.00–10.30am.

E.267 'The Voyage of the Beagle': No. 2 in the series 'Voyages of Discovery', BBC Home Service, 29 March 1946, 9.30–10.15pm.

Notes

Written by Orwell.

Payment £47 5s 0d plus £5 5s 0d for additional research.

E.268 'Little Red Riding Hood', adapted by Orwell for 'Children's Hour', BBC Home Service, 9 July 1946, 5.00pm.

Notes

Payment £10 10s 0d.

Surviving typescript.

E.269   *Animal Farm*, adapted for broadcasting by Orwell, BBC Third Programme, 14 January 1947, 9.15–10.45pm.

Notes

Music composed and directed by Anthony Hopkins.

Produced by Rayner Heppenstall.

Repeated as another live broadcast on 15 January 1947, 7.25–8.55pm. A recording of the first performance was broadcast on 2 February 1947 at 6.00pm.

In April 1947 Orwell gave permission for a Dutch version of *Animal Farm* to be broadcast.

Another version was broadcast in England on 3 March 1952, 9.15–10.45pm, BBC Home Service. Adapted by P. Duval Smith.

A musical version of the radio broadcast was produced by the National Theatre, first performed at the Cottesloe Theatre, London, on 25 April 1984 and published by Methuen in 1985. Surviving typescript at Orwell Archive.

F: BBC talks organised by Orwell

Talks organisers completed booking forms when arranging for a speaker, giving details of the speaker's name, subject, recording and broadcast dates, contract details and fee. The following are talks initiated, arranged or produced by Orwell, although the booking forms do not always bear his signature. The date is that of the broadcast; subjects are given in brackets; speakers are identified at the end of the entry. Where a broadcast was pre-recorded with no fixed broadcast date, the date of the recording is given. Talks organised by Orwell and with his own written or spoken content are not included in this list but in Section E Radio broadcasts.

F.001 10 October 1941. 'Through Eastern Eyes: The Man in the Street'
       P.B. Seal
F.002 17 October 1941. 'Through Eastern Eyes: The Man in the Street' (reactions to war situation)
       M.J. Tambimuttu
F.003 24 October 1941. 'Through Eastern Eyes: The Man in the Street' (fashions are not rationed)
       Venu Chitale
F.004 26 October 1941. 'Through Eastern Eyes: How it Works' (Rural District Councils).
       P. Chatterjee
F.005 31 October 1941. 'Through Eastern Eyes: The Man in the Street'
       M.J. Tambimuttu
F.006 4 November 1941. 'Through Eastern Eyes: Mind the Doors', (London Underground)
       Shridhar Telkar
F.007 17 November 1941. 'Through Eastern Eyes: Around the Courts'
       H. Umrigar
F.008 27 November 1941. 'Through Eastern Eyes: The Debate Continues' (House of Commons)
       Shridhar Telkar
F.009 30 November 1941. 'Through Eastern Eyes: How it Works' (banking)
       P. Chatterjee
F.010 1 December 1941. 'Through Eastern Eyes: The Debate Continues'
       Shridhar Telkar
F.011 5 December 1941. 'Through Eastern Eyes: The Man in the Street' (street markets)
       Noel Sircar
F.012 8 December 1941. 'Through Eastern Eyes: The Debate Continues'
       Shridhar Telkar
F.013 13 December 1941. 'Through Eastern Eyes: The Debate Continues'
       Shridhar Telkar
F.014 18 December 1941. 'Through Eastern Eyes: The Hand that Rocks the Cradle'
       S. Lall
F.015 17 December 1941. 'Through Eastern Eyes: With the Workers' (Post Office)
       B.N. Mukerjee
F.016 21 December 1941. 'Through Eastern Eyes: How it Works' (the press)
       M.J. Tambimuttu
F.017 22 December 1941. 'Through Eastern Eyes: The Debate Continues'
       Shridhar Telkar

F.018   23 December 1941. 'Through Eastern Eyes' (London Council)
        P. Chatterjee
F.019   25 December 1941. 'Through Eastern Eyes: England on Christmas Day'. Pre-recorded
        Bahadur Singh
F.020   26 December 1941. 'Through Eastern Eyes: The Man in the Street'
        Noel Sircar
F.021   29 December 1941. 'Through Eastern Eyes: The Debate Continues'
F.022   30 December 1941. 'Through Eastern Eyes: The News'
        D.V. Tahmankar
F.023   5 January 1942. 'Through Eastern Eyes: The Debate Continues'
F.024   12 January 1942. 'Through Eastern Eyes: The Debate Continues'
        Shridhar Telkar
F.025   19 January 1942. 'Through Eastern Eyes: The Debate Continues'
        Shridhar Telkar
F.026   21 January 1942. 'Through Eastern Eyes: The Fate of Japan'
        J. Chinna Durai
F.027   26 January 1942. 'Through Eastern Eyes: The Debate Continues'
        Shridhar Telkar
F.028   2 February 1942. 'Through Eastern Eyes: The Debate Continues'
F.029   3 February 1942. 'We Speak to India: Masterpieces of English Literature –
        Ruskin's *Sesame and Lilies*'
        Herbert Read
F.030   5 February 1942. 'Through Eastern Eyes: What It Means to Me' (democracy)
        Sirdar Iqbal'Ali Shah
F.031   5 February 1942. 'We Speak to India' (Moulmein)
        M. Myat Tun
F.032   9 February 1942. 'Through Eastern Eyes: The Debate Continues'
        Shridhar Telkar
F.033   10 February 1942. 'Through Eastern Eyes: These Names Will Live – H.G. Wells'
        Mulk Raj Anand
F.034   10 February 1942. 'We Speak to India: Masterpieces of English Literature –
        Browning's "Abt Vogler"''
        Herbert Read
F.035   12 February 1942. 'Through Eastern Eyes: What It Means to Me' (liberty)
        Shridhar Telkar
F.036   16 February 1942. 'Through Eastern Eyes: The Debate Continues'
F.037   18 February 1942. 'We Speak to India: The World Is Round' (popular geography)
        J.F. Horrabin
F.038   19 February 1942. 'Through Eastern Eyes: What It Means to Me' (nationalism)
        Cedric Dover
F.039   20 February 1942. 'Through Eastern Eyes: The Man in the Street' (Turkish
        Halkevi in London)
        Sirdar Iqbal'Ali Shah
F.040   20 February 1942. 'Through Eastern Eyes' (restaurants). Pre-recorded for use in
        emergency
        Noel Sircar
F.041   23 February 1942. 'Through Eastern Eyes: The Debate Continues'
        Shridhar Telkar
F.042   24 February 1942. 'Through Eastern Eyes: These Names Will Live – Bernard
        Shaw'
        Mulk Raj Anand
F.043   25 February 1942. 'We Speak to India: The World Is Round' (popular geography)
        J.F. Horrabin
F.044   25 February 1942. 'Through Eastern Eyes: Today and Yesterday' (minorities)
        Cedric Dover

F.045 26 February 1942. 'Through Eastern Eyes: What It Means to Me' (Japan and the New Order)
       Hsiao Ch'ien
F.046 2 March 1942. 'Through Eastern Eyes: The Debate Continues'
       Shridhar Telkar
F.047 4 March 1942. 'We Speak to India: Women Generally Speaking'
       Lady Grigg
F.048 4 March 1942. 'Through Eastern Eyes: Today and Yesterday' (federal idea)
       Cedric Dover
F.049 5 March 1942. 'Through Eastern Eyes: What It Means to Me' (Japanese-occupied China)
       Hsiao Ch'ien
F.050 6 March 1942. 'Through Eastern Eyes: The Man in the Street' (film acting)
       Lilla Erulkar
F.051 9 March 1942. 'Through Eastern Eyes: The Debate Continues'
       Princess Indira of Kapurthala
F.052 11 March 1942. 'We Speak to India: The World Is Round' (popular geography)
       J.F. Horrabin
F.053 11 March 1942. 'We Speak to India: Women Generally Speaking'
       Lady Grigg
F.054 15 March 1942. 'Through Eastern Eyes: New Weapons of War, 1 – Fifth Column'
       Mulk Raj Anand
F.055 16 March 1942. 'Through Eastern Eyes: The Debate Continues'
       Princess Indira of Kapurthala
F.056 17 March 1942. 'We Speak to India: Literature Between Wars: Poetry and Tradition'
       Stephen Spender
F.057 18 March 1942. 'We Speak to India: Women Generally Speaking'
       Lady Grigg
F.058 20 March 1942. 'Through Eastern Eyes: The Man in the Street' (Red Cross)
       Sujata Khanna
F.059 22 March 1942. 'Through Eastern Eyes: New Weapons of War, 2 – Living Space'
       Mulk Raj Anand
F.060 23 March 1942. 'Through Eastern Eyes: The Debate Continues'
       Princess Indira of Kapurthala
F.061 24 March 1942. 'Through Eastern Eyes: These Names Will Live' (General Sikorski)
       Shridhar Telkar
F.062 24 March 1942. 'We Speak to India: Literature Between Wars: Science and Literature'
       C.H. Waddington
F.063 25 March 1942. 'We Speak to India: The World Is Round' (popular geography)
       J.F. Horrabin
F.064 25 March 1942. 'We Speak to India: Women Generally Speaking'
       Lady Grigg
F.065 25 March 1942. 'Through Eastern Eyes: The Soviet East. 1 – Economic Reconstruction'
       Krishna S. Shelvankar
F.066 26 March 1942. Marathi Newsletter 4
       Shridhar Telkar
F.067 27 March 1942. 'Through Eastern Eyes: What It Means to Me' (race mixture and world peace). Pre-recorded
       Cedric Dover
F.068 28 March 1942. 'We Speak to India' (Sir Stafford Cripps)
       J. Chinna Durai

F.069   30 March 1942. 'We Speak to India: Discussion on the Federal Idea'. Pre-recorded
         Cedric Dover and C.E.M. Joad

F.070   29 March 1942. 'Through Eastern Eyes: New Weapons of War, 3 – Propaganda'
         Mulk Raj Anand

F.071   31 March 1942. 'We Speak to India: Literature Between Wars: the 1930s'
         Cyril Connolly

F.072   1 April 1942. 'Through Eastern Eyes: The Soviet East. 2 – Cultural Development'
         Krishna S. Shelvankar

F.073   5 April 1942. 'Through Eastern Eyes: New Weapons of War, 4 – New Order'
         Mulk Raj Anand

F.074   5 April 1942. 'We Speak to India: I Speak English'
         Princess Indira of Kapurthala

F.075   6 April 1942. 'Through Eastern Eyes' (Thailand)
         Dr Hingorani

F.076   7 April 1942. 'We Speak to India: Literature Between Wars: the New Romantic
         Movement'. Pre-recorded
         Herbert Read

F.077   7 April 1942. 'Through Eastern Eyes: These Names Will Live' (Paul Robeson)
         Cedric Dover

F.078   8 April 1942. 'We Speak to India: Peace in Wartime'
         Jack Common

F.079   12 April 1942. 'Through Eastern Eyes: New Weapons of War' (propaganda)
         Mulk Raj Anand

F.080   12 April 1942. 'We Speak to India: I Speak English'
         Princess Indira of Kapurthala

F.081   14 April 1942. 'Literature Between Wars: Money and the Artist'
         Arthur Calder-Marshall

F.082   14 April 1942. 'Through Eastern Eyes: These Names Will Live' (J.L. Garvin)
         Shridhar Telkar

F.083   15 April 1942. 'We Speak to India'
         Jack Common

F.084   20 April 1942. 'Through Eastern Eyes: The Debate Continues'
         Princess Indira of Kapurthala

F.085   21 April 1942. 'Through Eastern Eyes: These Names Will Live' (Frank Owen)
         Shridhar Telkar

F.086   21 April 1942. 'The Sick Man Revives' and '43 Years in England'. Two pre-
         recorded talks
         K.K. Ardaschir

F.087   22 April 1942. 'Through Eastern Eyes: China. 1 The Co-operative Movement'
         Krishna S. Shelvankar

F.088   22 April 1942. 'Women Generally Speaking'
         Rebecca West

F.089   23 April 1942. Marathi Newsletter, 'A Day in the Life of a Factory Worker'
         Shridhar Telkar

F.090   24 April 1942. 'Birthdays of the Week' (Sir Stafford Cripps)
         Shridhar Telkar

F.091   25 April 1942. 'The Music I Like: 1 – Folk Songs of Europe'
         Bhupen Mukerjee

F.092   27 April 1942. 'Through Eastern Eyes: The Debate Continues'
         Princess Indira of Kapurthala

F.093   29 April 1942. 'Through Eastern Eyes: China. 2 Education in Wartime'
         Krishna S. Shelvankar

F.094   29 April 1942. 'Some Books'
         E.M. Forster

F.095 29 April 1942. 'Women Generally Speaking'
      Mrs Bentwich

F.096 30 April 1942. 'Through Eastern Eyes: Today and Yesterday' (happiness)
      Shridhar Telkar

F.097 4 May 1942. 'Through Eastern Eyes: The Debate Continues'
      Princess Indira of Kapurthala

F.098 5 May 1942. 'Freedom and Cultural Expression'. Pre-recorded on this date
      Cedric Dover

F.099 5 May 1942. 'These Names Will Live' (Bertrand Russell)
      Cedric Dover

F.100 6 May 1942. 'Women Generally Speaking' (*Time and Tide*)
      Viscountess Rhondda

F.101 11 May 1942. 'Through Eastern Eyes: The Debate Continues'
      Princess Indira of Kapurthala

F.102 12 May 1942. 'Through Eastern Eyes: These Names Will Live' (Aldous Huxley)
      Krishna S. Shelvankar

F.103 13 May 1942. 'Women Generally Speaking'
      Lady Grigg

F.104 15 May 1942. 'The Rebirth of a Nation'
      K.K. Ardaschir

F.105 15 May 1942. 'The Man in the Street: What the Public Wants'
      Kingsley Martin

F.106 16 May 1942. 'The Music I Like' (Moura Lympany)
      Doulat Nanavati

F.107 18 May 1942. 'Through Eastern Eyes: The Debate Continues'
      Princess Indira of Kapurthala

F.108 19 May 1942. 'Through Eastern Eyes: These Names Will Live' (T.S. Eliot)
      M.J. Tambimuttu

F.109 19 May 1942. 'Literature Between Wars: Contemporary Chinese Literature'
      Hsiao Ch'ien

F.110 20 May 1942. 'Women Generally Speaking'
      Lady Grigg

F.111 20 and 21 May 1942 (a visit to Egypt)
      Two broadcasts: 20 May Hindustani, 21 May English
      Aziz-ul-Huque

F.112 22 May 1942 (A.R.P). Pre-recorded
      J.B.S. Haldane

F.113 25 May 1942. 'Through Eastern Eyes: The Debate Continues'
      Princess Indira of Kapurthala

F.114 26 May 1942. 'Through Eastern Eyes: These Names Will Live' (William Walton).
      Pre-recorded
      Narayana Menon

F.115 26 May 1942. 'Literature Between Wars: Contemporary Chinese Literature'
      Hsiao Ch'ien

F.116 27 May 1942. 'Women Generally Speaking'
      Lady Grigg

F.117 27 May 1942. 'Some Books'
      E.M. Forster

F.118 27 May 1942. 'Through Eastern Eyes: Meet My Friend'
      Mulk Raj Anand

F.119 1 June 1942. 'Through Eastern Eyes: The Debate Continues'
      Princess Indira of Kapurthala

F.120 2 June 1942. 'Science and Politics: 1 – The Birth of Science'. Pre-recorded
      V.G. Childe

F.121   3 June 1942. 'Through Eastern Eyes: Meet My Friend'
          Mulk Raj Anand with A.E. Manderson

F.122   3 June 1942. 'Women Generally Speaking'
          Lady Grigg with Clemence Dane

F.123   5 June 1942. 'The Man in the Street: Popular Novels and the Public Taste'
          Shridhar Telkar

F.124   6 June 1942. 'The Music I Like' (Philharmonic Ensemble)
          B.N. Mukerjee

F.125   8 June 1942. 'Through Eastern Eyes: The Debate Continues'
          Princess Indira of Kapurthala

F.126   9 June 1942. 'Through Eastern Eyes: These Names Will Live' (Edwin Muir). Pre-
          recorded
          Narayana Menon

F.127   9 June 1942. 'Science and Politics: 2 – The Beginnings of Modern Science'
          J.A. Lauwerys

F.128   10 June 1942. 'Through Eastern Eyes: Meet My Friend'
          Mulk Raj Anand

F.129   10 June 1942. 'Women Generally Speaking'
          Lady Grigg

F.130   12 June 1942 (prison literature)
          Reginald Reynolds

F.131   15 June 1942. 'Through Eastern Eyes: The Debate Continues'
          Princess Indira of Kapurthala

F.132   16 June 1942. 'Science and Politics: 3 – Experimental and Applied Science'. Pre-
          recorded
          A.C.G. Egerton

F.133   16 June 1942. 'These Names Will Live' (John Gordon)
          Shridhar Telkar

F.134   17 June 1942. 'Through Eastern Eyes: Meet My Friend'
          Mulk Raj Anand with Inez Holden

F.135   17 June 1942. 'Women Generally Speaking'
          Lady Grigg

F.136   19 June 1942 (prison literature)
          Reginald Reynolds

F.137   22 June 1942. 'Through Eastern Eyes: The Debate Continues'
          Princess Indira of Kapurthala

F.138   22 June 1942. 'A Year Ago Today' (Russia's entry into war)
          Shridhar Telkar

F.139   23 June 1942. 'Science and Politics: 4 – The Economic Bases of Science'
          Joseph Needham

F.140   23 June 1942. 'These Names Will Live' (Augustus John)
          M.J. Tambimuttu

F.141   24 June 1942 'Some Books'
          E.M. Forster

F.142   24 June 1942. 'Through Eastern Eyes: Meet My Friend'
          Mulk Raj Anand

F.143   24 June 1942. 'Women Generally Speaking'
          Lady Grigg

F.144   25 June 1942. 'Today and Yesterday: My Escape from France'
          Diana Wong

F.145   26 June 1942 (future of Indian agriculture)
          John Russell

F.146   26 June 1942. 'The Marriage of the Seas' (Suez Canal). Pre-recorded
          K.K. Ardaschir

F.147   27 June 1942. 'The Music I Like' (Luton Band)
        Bhupen Mukerjee
F.148   29 June 1942. 'Through Eastern Eyes: The Debate Continues'
        Princess Indira of Kapurthala
F.149   1 July 1942. 'Through Eastern Eyes: Meet My Friend'
        Mulk Raj Anand with L. Haden-Guest
F.150   1 July 1942. 'Women Generally Speaking'
        Lady Grigg with Clemence Dane
F.151   2 July 1942. 'Through Eastern Eyes: Today and Yesterday – Law and Order'. Pre-
        recorded
        Bahadur Singh
F.152   3 July 1942. 'A.D. 2000: 2 – The Indian Population Problem'
        Richard Titmuss
F.153   6 July 1942. 'Through Eastern Eyes: The Debate Continues'
        Princess Indira of Kapurthala
F.154   7 July 1942. 'Science and Politics: 5 – Science in the USSR'
        J.G. Crowther
F.155   7 July 1942. 'Science and Politics: 6 – The Future of Science'
        C.D. Darlington
F.156   8 July 1942. 'Women Generally Speaking'
        Lady Grigg with Clemence Dane
F.157   8 July 1942. 'Meet My Friend'. Pre-recorded
        Mulk Raj Anand
F.158   10 July 1942. 'A.D. 2000: 3 – India in the Steel Age'. Pre-recorded
        C.D. Darlington
F.159   13 July 1942. 'Through Eastern Eyes: The Debate Continues'
        Princess Indira of Kapurthala
F.160   14 July 1942. 'These Names Will Live' (Lindsay, Master of Balliol)
        Bahadur Singh
F.161   5 July 1942. 'Women Generally Speaking'
        Lady Grigg
F.162   15 July 1942. 'Meet My Friend'. Pre-recorded
        Mulk Raj Anand with André van Gysegham
F.163   20 July 1942. 'Through Eastern Eyes: The Debate Continues'
        Princess Indira of Kapurthala
F.164   22 July 1942. 'Some Books'
        E.M. Forster
F.165   22 July 1942. 'Meet My Friend'. Pre-recorded
        Mulk Raj Anand
F.166   27 July 1942. 'Through Eastern Eyes: The Debate Continues'
        Princess Indira of Kapurthala
F.167   28 July 1942 (current films in India)
        Noel Sircar
F.168   29 July 1942. 'Women Generally Speaking'
        Lady Grigg
F.169   29 July 1942. 'Topic of the Week'
        Shridhar Telkar
F.170   30 July 1942. 'Open Letter to a Chinese Guerilla'
        Mulk Raj Anand
F.171   31 July 1942. 'I'd Like it Explained'. 1 (aviation)
        E.C. Bowyer with Peter Masefield
F.172   31 July 1942. 'A.D. 2000: 6 – East or West? India's Cultural Future'
        Narayana Menon
F.173   31 July 1942 (programme of gramophone records)
        Narayana Menon

F.174   3 August 1942. 'Through Eastern Eyes: The Debate Continues'
         Princess Indira of Kapurthala

F.175   5 August 1942. 'Women Generally Speaking'
         Lady Grigg with Clemence Dane

F.176   5 August 1942. 'Topic of the Week'
         Shridhar Telkar

F.177   6 August 1942. 'Open Letter'. 2 (to a pacifist)
         J. Chinna Durai

F.178   7 August 1942. 'I'd Like it Explained'. 2 (the press)
         Hamilton Fyfe with Wickham Steed

F.179   7 August 1942. 'War of the Three Oceans'
         J.F. Horrabin

F.180   10 August 1942. 'Through Eastern Eyes: The Debate Continues'
         Princess Indira of Kapurthala

F.181   12 August 1942. 'Women Generally Speaking'
         Lady Grigg

F.182   12 August 1942. 'Topic of the Week'
         Shridhar Telkar

F.183   13 August 1942. 'Open Letter: 3 – Open Letter to a Nazi'
         R.R. Desai

F.184   14 August 1942. 'I'd Like it Explained: 3 – Agriculture'. Pre-recorded
         L.F. Easterbrook with John Russell

F.185   14 August 1942. 'War of the Three Oceans'
         J.F. Horrabin

F.186   17 August 1942. 'Through Eastern Eyes: The Debate Continues'
         Princess Indira of Kapurthala

F.187   19 August 1942. 'Topic of the Week'
         Shridhar Telkar

F.188   19 August 1942. 'Some Books'
         E.M. Forster

F.189   19 August 1942. 'Women Generally Speaking'
         Lady Grigg

F.190   20 August 1942. 'Open Letter'. 4 (to a liberal)
         Cedric Dover

F.191   20 August 1942. 'Women Generally Speaking' (books and reading)
         Clemence Dane

F.192   21 August 1942. 'I'd Like it Explained: 4 – Scientific Research'. Pre-recorded
         J.B.S. Haldane with C.H. Waddington

F.193   21 August 1942. 'War of the Three Oceans'
         J.F. Horrabin

F.194   24 August 1942. 'Through Eastern Eyes: The Debate Continues'
         Princess Indira of Kapurthala

F.195   25 August 1942 (current films in India)
         Noel Sircar

F.196   26 August 1942. 'Women Generally Speaking'
         Lady Grigg

F.197   28 August 1942. 'War of the Three Oceans'
         J.F. Horrabin

F.198   28 August 1942. 'Women Generally Speaking'. Pre-recorded in Manchester
         Clemence Dane

F.199   31 August 1942. 'Through Eastern Eyes: The Debate Continues'
         Princess Indira of Kapurthala

F.200   2 September 1942. 'Topic of the Week'
         Shridhar Telkar

F.201   2 September 1942. 'Women Generally Speaking'
        Lady Grigg
F.202   4 September 1942. 'I'd Like it Explained. 6 – The Future of Parliament'
        Harold Laski with Lord Winterton
F.203   7 September 1942. 'Through Eastern Eyes: The Debate Continues'
        Princess Indira of Kapurthala
F.204   9 September 1942. 'Topic of the Week'
        Shridhar Telkar
F.205   9 September 1942. 'Women Generally Speaking'
        Lady Grigg
F.206   10 September 1942. 'Open Letter' (to a Marxist)
        J.M. Tambimuttu
F.207   11 September 1942. 'I'd Like it Explained: Education'
        T.C. Worsley with G.M. Young
F.208   14 September 1942. 'Through Eastern Eyes: The Debate Continues'
        Princess Indira of Kapurthala
F.209   16 September 1942. 'Some Books'
        E.M. Forster
F.210   16 September 1942. 'Topic of the Week'
        Shridhar Telkar
F.211   21 September 1942. 'Through Eastern Eyes: The Debate Continues'
        Princess Indira of Kapurthala
F.212   23 September 1942. 'Topic of the Week'
        Shridhar Telkar
F.213   23 September 1942. 'Women Generally Speaking'
        Lady Grigg
F.214   25 September 1942. (Ram Nahum, an Egyptian undergraduate)
        Narayana Menon
F.215   2 September 1942. 'The Moslem Minorities of Europe'. Pre-recorded
        K.K. Ardaschir
F.216   4 September 1942. 'In Black and White'
        Sidney Horniblow
F.217   8 September 1942. 'Anniversaries of the Month' 2
        Cedric Dover, Lilla Erulkar, Noel Sircar
F.218   9 September 1942. 'In Black and White'
        Sidney Horniblow
F.219   9 September 1942 (Anti-fascist youth rally)
        Narayana Menon
F.220   11 September 1942. 'In Black and White'
        Sidney Horniblow
F.221   12 September 1942. 'Great Cellists'
        Princess Indira of Kapurthala
F.222   17 September 1942. 'Books that Changed the World: *Gulliver's Travels*'
        Narayana Menon
F.223   18 September 1942. 'In Black and White'
        Sidney Horniblow
F.224   18 September 1942 (rebirth of the Egyptian nation)
        K.K. Ardaschir
F.225   19 September 1942. 'Great Cellists'
        Princess Indira of Kapurthala
F.226   22 September 1942. Film commentary
        Noel Sircar
F.227   22 September 1942. 'The Highway of the World'. Pre-recorded
        K.K. Ardaschir

F.228   24 September 1942. 'Books that Changed the World: *The Social Contract*'
         Krishna S. Shelvankar
F.229   25 September 1942. 'In Black and White'
         Sidney Horniblow
F.230   25 September 1942. 'I'd Like it Explained' (female emancipation)
         Ethel Mannin
F.231   26 September 1942. 'Great Cellists'
         Princess Indira of Kapurthala
F.232   28 September 1942. 'Through Eastern Eyes: The Debate Continues'
         Princess Indira of Kapurthala
F.233   29 September 1942. 'Women Generally Speaking – More Books' (*The Wife of Bath*)
         Clemence Dane
F.234   30 September 1942. 'Topic of the Week'
         Shridhar Telkar
F.235   30 September 1942. 'Women Generally Speaking'
         Lady Grigg
F.236   1 October 1942. 'Books that Changed the World: *The Descent of Man*'
         Cedric Dover
F.237   2 October 1942. 'In Black and White'
         Sidney Horniblow
F.238   2 October 1942. 'I'd Like it Explained' (basic English)
         Zahra Taki
F.239   3 October 1942. 'Women Generally Speaking'
         Lady Grigg
F.240   5 October 1942. 'Through Eastern Eyes: The Debate Continues'
         Princess Indira of Kapurthala
F.241   5 October 1942. 'China and the Chinese'. Pre-recorded
         R.U. Hingorani
F.242   5 October 1942. 'Japanese Impressions'. Pre-recorded
         R.U. Hingorani
F.243   5 October 1942. 'Turkey'. Pre-recorded
         R.U. Hingorani
F.244   6 October 1942 (reading book extract)
         Herbert Read
F.245   7 October 1942. 'Topic of the Week'
         Shridhar Telkar
F.246   8 October 1942. 'Books that Changed the World: *Uncle Tom's Cabin*'
         Cedric Dover
F.247   9 October 1942. 'I'd Like it Explained: Air Transport'
         C.H. Desch
F.248   10 October 1942. 'Women Generally Speaking'
         Lady Grigg
F.249   12 October 1942. 'Through Eastern Eyes: The Debate Continues'
         Princess Indira of Kapurthala
F.250   14 October 1942. 'Some Books'
         E.M. Forster
F.251   14 October 1942. 'Topic of the Week'
         Shridhar Telkar
F.252   14 October 1942. 'Women Generally Speaking – The House of Commons'
         Ellen Wilkinson
F.253   15 October 1942. 'Books that Changed the World: *War and Peace*'
         Mulk Raj Anand
F.254   16 October 1942. 'I'd Like it Explained: Land Reclamation'
         J.F. Horrabin

F.255   16 October 1942 (story by five authors)
        L.A.G. Strong
F.256   17 October 1942. 'Women Generally Speaking'
        Lady Grigg
F.257   19 October 1942. 'Through Eastern Eyes: The Debate Continues'
        Princess Indira of Kapurthala
F.258   20 October 1942. Film commentary
        Noel Sircar
F.259   20 October 1942. 'Women of the West'
        K.K. Ardaschir
F.260   20 October 1942. 'Science and the People: 1 – Dehydration'. Pre-recorded
        Franklin Kidd
F.261   21 October 1942. 'Topic of the Week'
        Shridhar Telkar
F.262   22 October 1942. 'Books that Changed the World: *Das Kapital*'
        Krishna S. Shelvankar
F.263   23 October 1942. 'I'd Like it Explained: Air Transport'
        E.C. Bowyer
F.264   23 October 1942 (story by five authors)
        Inez Holden
F.265   24 October 1942. 'Women Generally Speaking'
        Lady Grigg
F.266   26 October 1942. 'Through Eastern Eyes: The Debate Continues'
        Princess Indira of Kapurthala
F.267   28 October 1942. 'Topic of the Week'
        Shridhar Telkar
F.268   29 October 1942. 'Books that Changed the World: *Mein Kampf*'
        R.R. Desai
F.269   30 October 1942 (story by five authors)
        Martin Armstrong, Inex Holden
F.270   31 October 1942. 'Women Generally Speaking'
        Lady Grigg
F.271   2 November 1942. 'Through Eastern Eyes: The Debate Continues'
        Princess Indira of Kapurthala
F.272   3 November 1942 (poetry reading). Pre-recorded
        Henry Treece
F.273   4 November 1942. 'Women Generally Speaking'
        Lady Grigg
F.274   4 November 1942. 'Behind the Headlines'
        Shridhar Telkar
F.275   5 November 1942. 'History of Fascism. No. 1 – The March on Rome'
        Cedric Dover
F.276   6 November 1942. 'A Day in My Life'
        Mulk Raj Anand
F.277   6 November 1942. 'Story by Five Authors'
        E.M. Forster
F.278   9 November 1942. 'Through Eastern Eyes: The Debate Continues'
        Princess Indira of Kapurthala
F.279   10 November 1942. 'Indians in Great Britain'
        Aziz-ul-Huque
F.280   11 November 1942 (President Inonu)
        K.K. Ardaschir
F.281   11 November 1942. 'Some Books'
        E.M. Forster

F.282   11 November 1942. 'Behind the Headlines'
        Shridhar Telkar

F.283   11 November 1942. 'Women Generally Speaking'
        Lady Grigg

F.284   12 November 1942. 'History of Fascism. No. 2 – Rise of the Nazi Party'
        Krishna S. Shelvankar

F.285   13 November 1942. 'A Day in My Life'
        Mulk Raj Anand with Keidrych Rhys

F.286   13 November 1942. 'French North Africa'
        K.K. Ardaschir

F.287   16 November 1942. 'Through Eastern Eyes: The Debate Continues'
        Princess Indira of Kapurthala

F.288   17 November 1942. 'Science and the People' (microfilms)
        Ritchie Calder

F.289   17 November 1942. Film commentary
        Noel Sircar

F.290   18 November 1942. 'Women Generally Speaking'
        Lady Grigg

F.291   18 November 1942. 'Behind the Headlines'
        Shridhar Telkar

F.292   19 November 1942. 'History of Fascism. No. 3 – The June Purge'
        R.R. Desai

F.293   20 November 1942. 'A Day in My Life'
        Mulk Raj Anand

F.294   20 November 1942. 'Let's Act it Ourselves – 2' (amateur dramatics)
        Norman Marshall

F.295   23 November 1942. 'Through Eastern Eyes: The Debate Continues'
        Princess Indira of Kapurthala

F.296   25 November 1942. 'Women Generally Speaking'
        Lady Grigg

F.297   25 November 1942. 'Behind the Headlines'
        Shridhar Telkar

F.298   27 November 1942. 'A Day in My Life'
        Mulk Raj Anand

F.299   27 November 1942. 'Let's Act it Ourselves – 3' (amateur dramatics)
        Norman Marshall

F.300   30 November 1942. 'Through Eastern Eyes: The Debate Continues'
        Princess Indira of Kapurthala

F.301   2 December 1942. 'Women Generally Speaking'
        Lady Grigg

F.302   2 December 1942. 'Behind the Headlines'
        Shridhar Telkar

F.303   3 December 1942. 'History of Fascism. No. 5 – The Spanish Civil War'
        Mulk Raj Anand

F.304   4 December 1942. 'A Day in My Life'
        Mulk Raj Anand

F.305   4 December 1942. 'Let's Act it Ourselves – 4' (amateur dramatics)
        Norman Marshall

F.306   5 December 1942. 'Favourite Moments' (talk and gramophone records)
        Princess Indira of Kapurthala

F.307   7 December 1942. 'The Debate Continues'
        Princess Indira of Kapurthala

F.308   8 December 1942. 'Indians in Great Britain'
        Aziz-ul-Huque

F.309   9 December 1942. 'Some Books'
        E.M. Forster

F.310   9 December 1942. 'Women Generally Speaking'
        Lady Grigg

F.311   9 December 1942. 'Behind the Headlines'
        Shridhar Telkar

F.312   11 December 1942. 'A Day in My Life'
        Mulk Raj Anand

F.313   11 December 1942. 'Let's Act it Ourselves – 5' (amateur dramatics)
        Norman Marshall

F.314   12 December 1942. 'Favourite Moments' (talk and gramophone records)
        Princess Indira of Kapurthala

F.315   14 December 1942. 'The Debate Continues'
        Princess Indira of Kapurthala

F.316   15 December 1942. Film commentary
        Noel Sircar

F.317   15 December 1942. 'Science and the People. No. 3 – Plastics'
        V.E. Yarsley

F.318   16 December 1942. 'Women Generally Speaking'
        Lady Grigg

F.319   16 December 1942. 'Behind the Headlines'
        Shridhar Telkar

F.320   17 December 1942. 'History of Fascism. No. 7 – The Invasion of the USSR'
        Krishna S. Shelvankar

F.321   18 December 1942. 'A Day in My Life'
        Mulk Raj Anand with Lady Peel

F.322   18 December 1942. 'Let's Act it Ourselves – 6' (amateur dramatics)
        Norman Marshall

F.323   19 December 1942. 'Favourite Moments' (talk and gramophone records)
        Princess Indira of Kapurthala

F.324   21 December 1942. 'The Debate Continues'
        Princess Indira of Kapurthala

F.325   21 December 1942. Gujarati Newsletter
        R.R. Desai

F.326   23 December 1942. 'Women Generally Speaking'
        Lady Grigg

F.327   23 December 1943. 'In the Public Eye'
        Noel Sircar

F.328   24 December 1942. 'Behind the Headlines'
        Shridhar Telkar

F.329   25 December 1942. 'Calling All Students' (English literature). Pre-recorded
        Edmund Blunden with E.M. Forster

F.330   26 December 1942. 'Favourite Moments' (talk and gramophone records)
        Princess Indira of Kapurthala

F.331   28 December 1942. 'The Debate Continues'
        Princess Indira of Kapurthala

F.332   29 December 1942. 'The High Commissioner Talks to You'
        Aziz-ul-Huque

F.333   30 December 1942. 'Women Generally Speaking'
        Lady Grigg

F.334   30 December 1942. 'In the Public Eye'
        Noel Sircar

F.335   31 December 1942. 'Behind the Headlines'
        Shridhar Telkar

F.336   1 January 1943. 'Calling All Students' (English literature)
            Edmund Blunden
F.337   6 January 1943. 'Some Books'
            E.M. Forster
F.338   6 January 1943. 'Women Generally Speaking'
            Lady Grigg
F.339   7 January 1943. 'Behind the Headlines'
            Shridhar Telkar
F.340   8 January 1943. 'Calling All Students' (Thomas Hardy)
            Edmund Blunden
F.341   12 January 1943. Indian Play No. 1 *Malati Madhav*. Pre-recorded
            Lilla Erulkar with Princess Indira of Kapurthala
F.342   13 January 1943. 'Women Generally Speaking'
            Lady Grigg with Marjorie Leaf
F.343   13 January 1943. 'In the Public Eye'
            Bahadur Singh
F.344   14 January 1943. 'Behind the Headlines'
            Shridhar Telkar
F.345   15 January 1943. 'Calling All Students' (English literature)
            Edmund Blunden
F.346   20 January 1943. 'Women Generally Speaking'
            Lady Grigg with Marjorie Leaf
F.347   20 January 1943. 'In the Public Eye'
            Bahadur Singh
F.348   21 January 1943. 'Behind the Headlines'
            Shridhar Telkar
F.349   22 January 1943. 'Calling All Students' (English literature)
            Edmund Blunden
F.350   22 January 1943. 'Modern Aircraft'
            E.C. Bowyer
F.351   25 January 1943. 'The Debate Continues'
            Princess Indira of Kapurthala
F.352   25 January 1943. Bengali Newsletter
            P. Chatterjee
F.353   26 January 1943. 'The High Commissioner Talks to You'
            Aziz-ul-Huque
F.354   27 January 1943. 'Women Generally Speaking'
            Lady Grigg with Evangeline Dora Edwards
F.355   28 January 1943. 'Behind the Headlines'
            Shridhar Telkar
F.356   29 January 1943. 'Calling All Students' (The Book of Job)
            Edmund Blunden with W.J. Turner
F.357   29 January 1943. 'Modern Aircraft'
            E.C. Bowyer
F.358   1 February 1943. 'The Debate Continues'
            Princess Indira of Kapurthala
F.359   3 February 1943. 'Some Books'
            E.M. Forster
F.360   3 February 1943. 'Women Generally Speaking'
            Lady Grigg
F.361   3 February 1943. 'In Your Kitchen'
            N. Gangulee
F.362   4 February 1943. 'Behind the Headlines'
            Shridhar Telkar

F.363   5 February 1943. 'Modern Aircraft'
        E.C. Bowyer
F.364   5 February 1943. 'Landmarks in American Literature' (Nathaniel Hawthorne)
        Herbert Read
F.365   8 February 1943. 'The Debate Continues'
        Princess Indira of Kapurthala
F.366   9 February 1943. Indian Play No. 2 *The Little Clay Cart*
        Indira Roy with Lilla Erulkar
F.367   10 February 1943. 'Women Generally Speaking'
        Lady Grigg with Catherine Lacey
F.368   10 February 1943. 'In Your Kitchen'
        K.C. Roy
F.369   10 February 1943. 'In the Public Eye'
        Bahadur Singh
F.370   11 February 1943. 'Behind the Headlines'
        Shridhar Telkar
F.371   12 February 1943. 'Modern Aircraft'
        E.C. Bowyer
F.372   12 February 1943. 'Landmarks in American Literature' (Edgar Allan Poe)
        T.S. Eliot
F.373   15 February 1943. 'The Debate Continues'
        Princess Indira of Kapurthala
F.374   17 February 1943. 'Women Generally Speaking'
        Lady Grigg with Naomi Royd-Smith
F.375   17 February 1943. 'In Your Kitchen'
        N. Gangulee
F.376   18 February 1943. 'Behind the Headlines'
        Shridhar Telkar
F.377   19 February 1943. 'Modern Aircraft'
        E.C. Bowyer
F.378   19 February 1943. 'Landmarks in American Literature'
F.379   22 February 1943. 'The Debate Continues'
        Princess Indira of Kapurthala with Stephen King-Hall
F.380   23 February 1943. 'The High Commissioner Talks to You'
        Aziz-ul-Huque
F.381   24 February 1943. 'Women Generally Speaking: Films of the Month'
        Lady Grigg with Oliver Bell
F.382   24 February 1943. 'In Your Kitchen'
        K.C. Roy
F.383   24 February 1943. 'In the Public Eye: Madame Chiang Kai-Shek'
        Bahadur Singh
F.384   25 February 1943. 'Behind the Headlines'
        Shridhar Telkar
F.385   26 February 1943. 'Modern Aircraft'
        E.C. Bowyer
F.386   26 February 1943. 'Landmarks in American Literature' (Mark Twain)
        V.S. Pritchett
F.387   1 March 1943. 'The Debate Continues'
        Princess Indira of Kapurthala
F.388   2 March 1943. 'Anniversary of the Month'
        Desmond Hawkins
F.389   3 March 1943. 'In Your Kitchen'
        N. Gangulee
F.390   3 March 1943. 'Some Books'
        E.M. Forster

F.391   3 March 1943. 'Women Generally Speaking'
         Lady Grigg
F.392   3 March 1943. 'In the Public Eye'
         Bahadur Singh
F.393   4 March 1943. 'Behind the Headlines'
         Shridhar Telkar
F.394   8 March 1943. 'The Debate Continues'
         Princess Indira of Kapurthala with Tom Driberg
F.395   10 March 1943. 'Women Generally Speaking'
         Lady Grigg with Catherine Lacey
F.396   10 March 1943. 'In Your Kitchen'
         K.C. Roy
F.397   10 March 1943. 'In the Public Eye'
         Bahadur Singh
F.398   11 March 1943 (Indian Red Cross)
         Lester Powell
F.399   12 March 1943. 'Landmarks in American Literature'
F.400   12 March 1943. 'Victoria Station Bombay to Victoria Station London'
         K.K. Ardaschir
F.401   15 March 1943. 'The Debate Continues'
         Princess Indira of Kapurthala
F.402   17 March 1943. 'Women Generally Speaking'
         Lady Grigg with Naomi Royd-Smith
F.403   17 March 1943. 'In Your Kitchen'
         N. Gangulee with Shridhar Telkar
F.404   18 March 1943. 'Behind the Headlines'
         Shridhar Telkar
F.405   22 March 1943. 'The Debate Continues'
         Princess Indira of Kapurthala
F.406   24 March 1943. 'Women Generally Speaking: Films of the Month'
         Lady Grigg with Oliver Bell
F.407   24 March 1943. 'In Your Kitchen'
         Shridhar Telkar
F.408   25 March 1943. 'Behind the Headlines'
         Shridhar Telkar
F.409   26 March 1942. 'Books That Changed the World: The Koran'
         Sirdar Ikbal Ali Shah
F.410   29 March 1943. 'The Debate Continues'
         Princess Indira of Kapurthala
F.411   31 March 1943. 'Women Generally Speaking: Everyday Chinese Heroes'
         Lady Grigg with E.D. Edwards
F.412   31 March 1943. 'Some Books'
         E.M. Forster
F.413   1 April 1943. 'Calling All Students: Great Dramatists' (John Dryden)
         T.S. Eliot
F.414   1 April 1943. 'Behind the Headlines'
         Shridhar Telkar
F.415   5 April 1943. 'Work of Indian Troops in the Libyan Campaign'
         Quintin Hogg
F.416   5 April 1943. 'The Debate Continues'
         Princess Indira of Kapurthala
F.417   6 April 1943. Indian Play No. 4 *The Post Office*
         Indira Roy
F.418   7 April 1943. 'In Your Kitchen'
         N. Gangulee with K.C. Roy and Shridhar Telkar

F.419   7 April 1943. 'Women Generally Speaking'
        Lady Grigg
F.420   8 April 1943. 'Behind the Headlines'
        Shridhar Telkar
F.421   9 April 1943. 'Books That Changed the World: *Bhagavat Gita*'
        G.V. Desani
F.422   12 April 1943. 'The Debate Continues'
        Princess Indira of Kapurthala
F.423   14 April 1943. 'Women Generally Speaking'
        Lady Grigg
F.424   14 April 1943. 'In Your Kitchen'
        N. Gangulee with Shridhar Telkar
F.425   15 April 1943. 'Behind the Headlines'
        Shridhar Telkar
F.426   19 April 1943. 'The Debate Continues'
        Princess Indira of Kapurthala
F.427   21 April 1943. 'Women Generally Speaking'
        Lady Grigg with Naomi Royd-Smith
F.428   21 April 1943. 'In Your Kitchen'
        N. Gangulee with K.C. Roy and Shridhar Telkar
F.429   22 April 1943. 'The Second Discovery of America'. Pre-recorded
        Reginald Reynolds
F.430   22 April 1943. 'Behind the Headlines'
        Shridhar Telkar
F.431   26 April 1943. 'The Debate Continues'
        Princess Indira of Kapurthala
F.432   26 April 1943. 'Women Generally Speaking'
        Lady Grigg
F.433   28 April 1943. 'Women Generally Speaking'
        Lady Grigg with Oliver Bell
F.434   28 April 1943. 'Some Books'
        E.M. Forster
F.435   29 April 1943. 'Behind the Headlines'
        Shridhar Telkar
F.436   3 May 1943 (agriculture)
        Lord Winterton
F.437   3 May 1943. 'The Debate Continues'
        Princess Indira of Kapurthala
F.438   3 May 1943. Indian Play: *The Jasmine Garland*. Pre-recorded
        Lilla Erulkar
F.439   5 May 1943. 'Women Generally Speaking'
        Lady Grigg
F.440   5 May 1943. 'In Your Kitchen'
        N. Gangulee with K.C. Roy and Shridhar Telkar
F.441   6 May 1943 (Turkish University)
        K.K. Ardaschir
F.442   6 May 1943. 'Behind the Headlines'
        Shridhar Telkar
F.443   7 May 1943. 'Books That Changed the World: The Analects of Confucius'
        Dr Edwards
F.444   10 May 1943. 'The Debate Continues'
        Princess Indira of Kapurthala with Arthur Greenwood
F.445   11 May 1943. 'The Panama Canal'
        K.K. Ardaschir

F.446   12 May 1943. 'In Your Kitchen'
         N. Gangulee with Shridhar Telkar and D. Nanavati
F.447   12 May 1943. 'Women Generally Speaking'
         Lady Grigg with Catherine Lacey
F.448   13 May 1943. 'Calling All Students – Great Dramatists' (Oscar Wilde and *The
         Importance of Being Ernest*)
         Raymond Mortimer
F.449   13 May 1943. 'Behind the Headlines'
         Shridhar Telkar
F.450   17 May 1943. 'The Debate Continues'
         Princess Indira of Kapurthala with George Strauss
F.451   19 May 1943. 'Women Generally Speaking'
         Lady Grigg with Naomi Royde-Smith
F.452   19 May 1943. 'In Your Kitchen'
         N. Gangulee with K.C. Roy and Shridhar Telkar
F.453   20 May 1943. 'Behind the Headlines'
         Shridhar Telkar
F.454   24 May 1943. 'The Debate Continues'
         Princess Indira of Kapurthala with Wilfrid Roberts
F.455   26 May 1943. 'Some Books'
         E.M. Forster
F.456   26 May 1943. 'Women Generally Speaking. Films of the Month'
         Lady Grigg with Oliver Bell
F.457   27 May 1943. 'Calling All Students – Great Dramatists No. 6: W.B. Yeats and *The
         Glass Hour*'
         James Stephens
F.458   27 May 1943. 'Behind the Headlines'
         Shridhar Telkar
F.459   28 May 1943. 'Books That Changed the World: The New Testament'
         John Macmurray
F.460   31 May 1943. 'The Debate Continues'
         Princess Indira of Kapurthala
F.461   1 June 1943. Malay News Commentary
         Richard Winstedt
F.462   2 June 1943. 'Women Generally Speaking'
         Lady Grigg
F.463   2 June 1943. 'In Your Kitchen'
         N. Gangulee with K.C. Roy
F.464   7 June 1943. 'The Debate Continues'
         Eleanor Rathbone
F.465   8 June 1943. Malay News Commentary
         Richard Winstedt
F.466   9 June 1943. 'Women Generally Speaking'
         Lady Grigg
F.467   9 June 1943. 'In Your Kitchen'
         N. Gangulee with Shridhar Telkar and D. Nanavati
F.468   9 June 1943. 'My Visit to the Indian Contingent in Great Britain'. Pre-recorded
         Roger Falk
F.469   10 June 1943. 'Great Dramatists. No. 7 – Shakespeare's *Measure For Measure*'
         W.J. Turner
F.470   15 June 1943. Malay News Commentary
         Richard Winstedt
F.471   16 June 1943. 'Women Generally Speaking'
         Lady Grigg with Naomi Royde-Smith

F.472   17 June 1943. 'In Your Kitchen'
         N. Gangulee with K.C. Roy

F.473   19 June 1943. 'The Debate Continues'. Pre-recorded
         Kingsley Martin

F.474   22 June 1943. Malay News Commentary
         Richard Winstedt

F.475   23 June 1943. 'Women Generally Speaking'
         Lady Grigg with Oliver Bell

F.476   24 June 1943. 'In Your Kitchen'
         N. Gangulee

F.477   24 June 1943. 'Calling All Students. No. 4 T.S. Eliot'
         David Cecil

F.478   26 June 1942 (Indian Air Cadets)
         Roger Falk

F.479   29 June 1943. Malay News Commentary
         Richard Winstedt

F.480   30 June 1943. 'Women Generally Speaking'
         Lady Grigg with E.D. Edwards

F.481   1 July 1943. 'In Your Kitchen'
         N. Gangulee

F.482   4 July 1943. 'Calling All Students – Literary Series No. 2: Georgian Poets'
         L.A.G. Strong

F.483   6 July 1943
         Kingsley Martin

F.484   8 July 1943. 'In Your Kitchen'
         N. Gangulee

F.485   11 July 1943. 'Calling All Students. No. 5 War Poets of 1914–1918'. Pre-recorded
         Alan Rook

F.486   14 July 1943. 'Great Poetry'
         Cherry Cottrell

F.487   15 July 1943. 'Calling All Students – Scientific Series: Malnutrition'
         J.C. Drummond

F.488   21 July 1943. 'Women Generally Speaking'
         Naomi Royde-Smith

F.489   28 July 1943. 'Women Generally Speaking – Films of the Month'
         Oliver Bell

F.490   29 July 1943. 'Calling All Students – Scientific Series. No. 3: Soil Erosion and Soil
         Deterioration'
         John Russell

F.491   1 August 1943. 'Calling All Students – Literary Series No. 5' (W.H. Auden)
         John Lehmann

F.492   3 August 1943. 'Topic of the Month'
         Kingsley Martin

F.493   7 August 1943. 'The Debate Continues'. Pre-recorded
         Edith Summerskill

F.494   19 August 1943. 'Calling All Students – Scientific Series. No. 6: Drinking Water'
         E.F.W. MacKenzie

F.495   22 August 1943. 'Modern Men of Letters No. 1 – H.G. Wells'. Pre-recorded
         V.S. Pritchett

F.496   25 August 1943. 'Film Talk'
         Oliver Bell

F.497   26 August 1943. 'Calling All Students – Second Scientific Series. No. 1 –
         Sulphonomide Group'
         L.P. Garrod

F.498   31 August 1943. 'Topic of the Month'
        Kingsley Martin

F.499   2 September 1943. 'Calling All Students – Second Scientific Series. No. 2 – Penicillin'
        C.M. Fletcher

F.500   4 September 1943. 'The Debate Continues'. Pre-recorded
        Quintin Hogg

F.501   5 September 1943. 'Modern Men of Letters No. 3 – Bernard Shaw'
        James Stephens

F.502   9 September 1943. 'Calling All Students – Second Scientific Series. No. 3 – Plasma'
        Bryan Brooke

F.503   18 September 1943. Bengali Newsletter
        P. Chatterjee

F.504   19 September 1943. 'Modern Men of Letters No. 4 – E.M. Forster'
        Stephen Spender

F.505   20 September 1943. 'The World I Hope For'
        George Yeh

F.506   22 September 1943. 'Monthly Film Talk'
        Oliver Bell

F.507   26 September 1943 (4th Indian Division)
        Roger Falk

F.508   14 October 1943. 'Calling All Students – Third Scientific Series: Psychology'
        T.H. Pear

F.509   20 October 1943. Monthly Film Talk
        Oliver Bell

F.510   21 October 1943. 'Calling All Students – Third Scientific Series: Psychology'
        J.C. Flugel

F.511   28 October 1943. 'Calling All Students – Third Scientific Series: Psychology'. Pre-recorded
        C.W. Valentine

F.512   31 October 1943. 'Great Dramatists: *The Taming of the Shrew*'
        L.A.G. Strong

F.513   4 November 1943. 'Calling All Students: Psychology – Mental Tests'
        D.W. Harding

F.514   7 November 1943. 'Great Dramatists No. 4: Anton Chekov *The Cherry Orchard*'
        André van Gysegham

F.515   8 November 1943. 'Calling All Students – Third Scientific Series: Psychology'
        Susan Isaacs

F.516   14 November 1943. 'Great Dramatists: Karel Capek *R.U.R.*'
        W.J. Turner with Noel Iliffe

F.517   17 November 1943. 'Films of the Month'
        Oliver Bell

F.518   5 December 1943. 'Great Dramatists No. 8: *Strife*'
        H.J. Laski

F.519   15 December 1943. 'Monthly Film Talk'
        Oliver Bell

G: Published letters

People who don't write think that writing isn't work.[1]

There are also fragments of letters quoted in the major biographies of Orwell by Crick and Shelden, and in other reminiscences by his contemporaries, none of which are listed here. Orwell's 'London Letter' series to *The Partisan Review* is not included here, nor are letters published in newspapers and magazines. Correspondence is by letter unless otherwise noted as, for example, postcard. The first four lines of the entries below show to whom the letter was addressed, Orwell's address as written in the letter, the date as shown in the letter with editorial additions in square brackets, and the form of the closing and signature. This is followed by very brief details of any reference in the letter to Orwell's work, and finally by the published source. Cross references are given to works in Section C Contributions to periodicals, but not to Orwell's book publications.

1911

G.001   To Ida Blair[2]
from St Cyprian's Eastbourne
September 14 [1911]
from E. Blair
    Crick 17

G.002   To Ida Blair
from St Cyprian's Eastbourne
October 8 1911 Sunday
from E. Blair
    Crick 17–18

G.003   To Ida Blair
from St Cyprian's Eastbourne
Nov. 5 [1911]
lots of love from E. Blair
    Crick 18

G.004   To Ida Blair
from St Cyprian's Eastbourne
Nov. 12 [1911]
Much love from E. Blair
    Crick 18

G.005   To Ida Blair
from St Cyprian's Eastbourne
[November 1911]
Much love from your son. Eric Blair xxxxx
    Crick 18

G.006   To Ida Blair
from St Cyprian's Eastbourne
[26 November? 1911]
from your loving son E. Blair
    Crick 19

G.007   To Ida Blair
from St Cypriann's [sic] Eastbourne
Dec. 2 [1911]
from your loveing [sic] son, E.A. Blair
    Crick 19

1912

G.008   To Ida Blair
        from St Cyprians [sic] Eastbourne
        30th of June 1912
        With lots of love from Eric Blair
            Crick 19
G.009   To Ida Blair
        from St Cyprians Eastbourne
        21st July [1912]
        With lots of love from Eric Blair
            Crick 34
G.010   To Ida Blair
        from St Cyprians
        [8 December 1912]
        With lots of love from Eric Blair
            Crick 34–35
G.011   To Ida Blair
        undated [mid-July or September? 1914]
        Your loving son Eric
            Crick 37

1920

G.012   To Mrs Buddicom[3]
        from Eton College, Windsor
        27/6/20
        Yours sincerely, Eric Blair
            Buddicom 102–103. Photograph in Buddicom
G.013   To Stephen Runciman[4]
        from Grove Terrace, Polperro RSO, Cornwall
        undated [August 1920]
        Yours sincerely, E.A. Blair
            Account of 'my first adventure as an amateur tramp'
            CEJL I 11–12; Crick 66
G.014   To Prosper Buddicom[5]
        28 [December 1920]
        Yours, Eric
            Buddicom 109

1921

G.015   To Prosper Buddicom
        from Walnut Tree House, Burstall
        Monday [10 January 1921 from postmark]
        Yours, Eric
            Buddicom 110–111
G.016   To Prosper Buddicom
        from 23 Mall Chambers, Nottinghill Gate W.8
        Wednesday [19 January 1921]
        Yours, Eric
            Buddicom 111

1929

G.017 To the Editor of *The New Adelphi*[6]
from 6 Rue du Pot de Fer, Paris 5
22 September 1929
Yours faithfully, E.A. Blair
    Enquiry about an article sent in August [later published in revised form as
    'The Spike'].
    CEJL I 15
G.018 Postcard to Max Plowman
from 6 Rue du Pot de Fer, Paris 5
[12 December 1929]
Yours faithfully, E.A. Blair
    On the tramps article
    Shelden 133

1929

G.019 To Max Plowman
from 3 Queen Street, Southwold, Suffolk
1 November 1930
Yours sincerely, Eric A. Blair
    On *The Adelphi*, his forthcoming review of *The Horrors of Cayenne* [See
    C.037], enclosing 'The Spike', and on the MS of an early version of *Down and
    Out in Paris and London*
    CEJL I 27–29

1931

G.020 Lettercard to Max Plowman
Monday [12 January 1931, Golders Green NW11]
Yours sincerely, Eric A Blair
    On an article, probably 'A Hanging', and a review of *The Two Carlyles*, both
    later published in *The Adelphi*
    CEJL I 33
G.021 To Dennis Collings[7]
from 1b Oakwood Road, Golders Green NW
16 August 1931
Yours, Eric A Blair
    CEJL I 49–50
G.022 To Dennis Collings
from 2 Windsor Street, London W9
Monday night [12 October 1931]
Yours, Eric A Blair
    Enclosing 'Hop-Picking'
    CEJL I 51
G.023 To T.S. Eliot[8]
from 2 Windsor Street, London W9
30 October 1931
Yours truly, Eric Blair
    Offering to translate *A la Belle de Nuit*
    CEJL I 72
G.024 To T.S. Eliot
from 2 Windsor St, W9
4 November 1931

Yours truly, Eric A Blair
   About translation of *A la Belle de Nuit*
   CEJL I 73

1932

G.025   To Leonard Moore[9]
   from The Hawthorns, Station Rd, Hayes, Middlesex
   26 April 1932
   Yours truly, Eric A. Blair
      On MS of 'Days in London and Paris'
      CEJL I 77–78
G.026   To Eleanor Jaques[10]
   from The Hawthorns, Hayes, Middlesex
   Tuesday [14 June 1932]
   Yours, Eric A Blair
      Mentions *Burmese Days*
      CEJL I 81–83
G.027   To Eleanor Jaques
   from The Hawthorns, Station Road, Hayes, Middlesex
   Sunday [19 June 1932]
   Yours, Eric A. Blair
      CEJL I 83
G.028   To Leonard Moore
   from The Hawthorns, Church Road, Hayes, Middlesex
   1 July 1932
   Yours truly, Eric A. Blair
      On Gollancz's required alterations to *Down and Out in Paris and London*
      CEJL I 84
G.029   To Leonard Moore
   from The Hawthorns, Church Road, Hayes, Middlesex
   6 July 1932
   Yours truly, Eric A Blair
      On revisions to *Down and Out in Paris and London*, and his decision to use
      a pseudonym
      CEJL I 84–85
G.030   To Eleanor Jaques
   from The Hawthorns, Church Road, Hayes, Middlesex
   Friday [8 July 1932]
   Yours, Eric A Blair
      CEJL I 85–86
G.031   To Brenda Salkeld[11]
   from The Hawthorns, Church Rd, Hayes, Middlesex
   Sunday [September 1932]
      Mentions rough draft of *Burmese Days*
      Extract *CEJL* I 100–101
G.032   To Eleanor Jaques
   from The Hawthorns, Church Road, Hayes, Mdx
   Monday [19 September 1932]
   With all my love, Eric
      CEJL I 101–102
G.033   To Eleanor Jaques
   from The Hawthorns, Church Road, Hayes, Middlesex
   Wed. night [19 October 1932]
   With love, Eric

Mentions MS of 'Clink' and *Burmese Days*
CEJL I 102–104

G.034   To Leonard Moore
from The Hawthorns, Church Road, Hayes, Middlesex
15 November 1932
Yours sincerely, Eric A Blair
On proofs of *Down and Out in Paris and London*, and progress with *Burmese Days*
CEJL I 104–105

G.035   To Eleanor Jaques
from The Hawthorns, Church Rd, Hayes, Mdx
18 November 1932
With love, Eric
Mentions *Down and Out in Paris and London*
CEJL I 105–106

G.036   To Leonard Moore
from The Hawthorns, Church Rd, Hayes, Mdx
Sat. [19 November 1932]
Yours sincerely, Eric A. Blair
On proofs of *Down and Out in Paris and London*, progress with *Burmese Days*, and choice of pseudonym 'George Orwell'
CEJL I 106–107

G.037   To Eleanor Jaques
from The Hawthorns, Church Rd, Hayes, Mdx
Wed. [30 November 1932]
With much love, Eric
CEJL I 107–108

G.038   To Eleanor Jaques
from The Hawthorns, Church Rd, Hayes, Mdx
Tue. [13 December 1932]
With much love, Eric
CEJL I 108–109

G.039   To Leonard Moore
from 36 High St, Southwold, Suffolk
Friday [23 December 1932]
Yours very sincerely, Eric A Blair
On advance copies of *Down and Out in Paris and London*, and progress with *Burmese Days*
CEJL I 109–110

1933

G.040   To Leonard Moore
from The Hawthorns, Church Rd, Hayes, Mdx
1 February 1933
Yours sincerely, Eric A. Blair
On *Burmese Days*
CEJL I 115

G.041   To Eleanor Jaques
from The Hawthorns, Church Rd, Hayes, Mdx
Sunday [26 February 1933]
With much love, Eric
Mentions *Down and Out in Paris and London* and *Burmese Days*
CEJL I 117

G.042 To Brenda Salkeld
       from The Hawthorns, Church Rd, Hayes, Mdx
       Friday night [10? March 1933]
              Extract *CEJL* I 119
G.043 To Eleanor Jaques
       from The Hawthorns, Church Rd, Hayes, Mdx
       Thursday [25 May 1933]
       With love from Eric
              CEJL I 119–120
G.044 To Brenda Salkeld
       from The Hawthorns, Church Rd, Hayes, Mdx
       Saturday [June? 1933]
              Mentions *Burmese Days*
              Extract *CEJL* I 120–121
G.045 To Eleanor Jaques
       from The Hawthorns, Church Rd, Hayes, Mdx
       7 July 1933
       With much love, Eric
              CEJL I 122
G.046 To Eleanor Jaques
       from The Hawthorns, Church Rd, Hayes, Mdx
       Thursday [20 July 1933]
       Much love from Eric
              CEJL I 122–123
G.047 To Leonard Moore
       from Frays College, Harefield Road, Uxbridge, Mdx
       Sunday [26 November 1933]
       Yours sincerely, Eric A. Blair
              On *Burmese Days*
              CEJL I 125
G.048 To Brenda Salkeld
       from Frays College, Harefield Road, Uxbridge, Mdx
       Sunday [10? December 1933]
              Mentions *Burmese Days* and *A Clergyman's Daughter*
              Extract *CEJL* I 125–129
G.049 To Leonard Moore
       from Uxbridge Cottage Hospital
       Thursday [28 December 1933]
       Yours sincerely, Eric A. Blair
              Mentions *A Clergyman's Daughter*
              CEJL I 129–130

1934

G.050 To Leonard Moore
       from 36 High St, Southwold, Suffolk
       Saturday [27 January 1934]
       Yours sincerely, Eric A. Blair
              On rejection of *Burmese Days* and royalties from *Down and Out in Paris and
              London*
              CEJL I 133
G.051 To Leonard Moore
       from 36 High St, Southwold, Suffolk
       Thursday [8 February 1934]
       Yours sincerely, Eric A. Blair

On revisions to *Burmese Days*
CEJL I 134

G.052 To Leonard Moore
from 36 High Street, Southwold, Suffolk
11 April 1934
Yours sincerely, Eric A. Blair
On *Burmese Days* and *A Clergyman's Daughter*
CEJL I 135–136

G.053 To Brenda Salkeld
from 36 High Street, Southwold, Suffolk
27 July 1934
Mentions *A Clergyman's Daughter*
Extract *CEJL* I 136–137

G.054 To Brenda Salkeld
from 36 High St, Southwold, Suffolk
Tuesday night [late August? 1934]
Mentions *A Clergyman's Daughter*
Extract *CEJL* I 137–139

G.055 To Brenda Salkeld
from 36 High St, Southwold, Suffolk
Wed. night [early September? 1934]
Mentions *A Clergyman's Daughter*
Extract *CEJL* I 139–140

G.056 To Leonard Moore
from 36 High St, Southwold, Suffolk
3 October 1934
Yours sincerely, Eric A. Blair
On *A Clergyman's Daughter* and *Burmese Days*
CEJL I 141

G.057 To Leonard Moore
from 3 Warwick Mansions, Pond St, Hampstead NW3
14 November 1934
Yours sincerely, Eric A. Blair
On *A Clergyman's Daughter* and *Burmese Days*
CEJL I 142–143

1935

G.058 To Leonard Moore
from 3 Warwick Mansions, Pond Street, Hampstead NW3
22 January 1935
Yours sincerely, Eric A. Blair
On *A Clergyman's Daughter* and *Burmese Days*
CEJL I 147

G.059 To Brenda Salkeld
from Booklovers' Corner, 1 South End Road, Hampstead NW3
16 February 1935
On *A Clergyman's Daughter*, *Burmese Days*, and *Keep the Aspidistra Flying*
Extract *CEJL* I 147–148

G.060 To Brenda Salkeld
from 77 Parliament Hill, Hampstead NW3
7 March 1935
On *A Clergyman's Daughter* and *Burmese Days*
Extract *CEJL* I 150–151; additional fragment Shelden 205

G.061   To Rayner Heppenstall[12]
         from 50 Lawford Road, Kentish Town NW
         Tuesday night [September? 1935]
         Yours, Eric A. Blair
             Mentions *Keep the Aspidistra Flying*
             CEJL I 152–153
G.062   To Rayner Heppenstall
         50 Lawford Rd, Kentish Town NW
         5 October 1935
         Yours, Eric
             Mentions *Keep the Aspidistra Flying*
             CEJL I 153–154

1936

G.063   To Cyril Connolly[13]
         from Warrington Lane, Wigan, Lancashire
         14 February 1936
         Yours, Eric A. Blair
             Mentions *Keep the Aspidistra Flying*
             Encounter (January 1962) 55; *CEJL* I 162–163
G.064   To Norman Collins[14]
         [from Wigan]
         [18 February 1936]
             On proofs of *Keep the Aspidistra Flying*
             Extract Shelden 225
G.065   To Leonard Moore
         from 22 Darlington Street, Wigan, Lancs
         24 February 1936
         Yours sincerely, Eric A. Blair
             On changes to *Keep the Aspidistra Flying*
             TLS (January 1984) 15
             Extract Shelden 225–226
G.066   To Richard Rees[15]
         from Darlington Street, Wigan, Lancs.
         29 February 1936
         Yours, Eric A. Blair
             Mentions *Keep the Aspidistra Flying*
             Encounter (January 1962) 55 [letter wrongly dated 29 March 1936]; *CEJL* I
             163–165
G.067   To Jack Common[16]
         from Agnes Terrace, Barnsley, Yorks.
         17 March 1936
         Yours, Eric A. Blair
             Offers a review of *The Fate of the Middle Classes* [See C.078]. Mentions *The
             Road to Wigan Pier* and *Keep the Aspidistra Flying*
             CEJL I 168–169
G.068   To Jack Common
         from The Stores, Wallington
         3 April 1936
         Yours, Eric A. Blair
             Mentions review of *The Fate of the Middle Classes* [See C.078], *Keep the
             Aspidistra Flying*, and *The Road to Wigan Pier*
             CEJL I 214–215

G.069 To Jack Common
      from The Stores, Wallington, Nr Baldock
      Thursday [16? April 1936]
      Yours, Eric A. Blair
          Mentions *The Road to Wigan Pier*
          CEJL I 215–216

G.070 To Richard Rees
      from The Stores, Wallington, Nr Baldock, Herts.
      20 April 1936
      Yours, Eric A. Blair
          Mentions *The Road to Wigan Pier* and *Keep the Aspidistra Flying*
          Encounter (January 1962) 56–57; *CEJL* I 217–218

G.071 To John Lehmann[17]
      from The Stores, Wallington, Near Baldock, Herts.
      27 May 1936
      Yours very truly, George Orwell
          On 'Shooting an Elephant' [See C.087].
          CEJL I 221

G.072 To Geoffrey Gorer[18]
      from The Stores, Wallington, Nr Baldock, Herts.
      Sat. [May? 1936]
      Yours, Eric A. Blair
          Mentions *The Road to Wigan Pier*
          CEJL I 221–223

G.073 To Anthony Powell[19]
      from The Stores, Wallington, Nr Baldock, Herts.
      8 June 1936
      Yours truly, George Orwell
          CEJL I 223

G.074 To Denys King-Farlow[20]
      from The Stores, Wallington, Nr Baldock, Herts.
      9 June 1936
      Yours, Eric A. Blair
          Encounter (January 1962) 57; *CEJL* I 224–225

G.075 To Henry Miller[21]
      from The Stores, Wallington, Nr Baldock, Herts.
      26–27 August 1936
      Yours, Eric. A. Blair
          Mentions review of *Black Spring* [See C.086], *Down and Out in Paris and London*, *Burmese Days*, *A Clergyman's Daughter*, *Keep the Aspidistra Flying*, and *The Road to Wigan Pier*
          CEJL I 227–229

G.076 To Jack Common
      from The Stores, Wallington, Nr Baldock, Herts.
      5 October 1936
      Yours, Eric A. Blair
          Mentions review of *Walls Have Mouths* [See C.089], and 'A happy vicar I might have been' [See C.095].
          CEJL I 233–234

G.077 To Leonard Moore
      from The Stores, Wallington, Nr Baldock, Herts.
      15 December 1936
      Yours sincerely, Eric A. Blair
          On *The Road to Wigan Pier*
          CEJL I 256

1937

G.078   Postcard to James Hanley[22]
from Juventud Communist Iberica, Monte Oscurio, Alcubierre, Huesca, Commandante Kopp
[13 February 1937 from postmark]
Yours sincerely, Eric Blair ("George Orwell")
    Mentions *The Road to Wigan Pier*
    CEJL I 263

G.079   To Eileen Blair[23]
[Hospital, Monflorite]
[5? April 1937]
With all my love, Eric
    Mentions reviews of *The Road to Wigan Pier*
    CEJL I 264–266

G.080   To Victor Gollancz[24]
from Hotel Continental, Barcelona
9 May 1937
Yours sincerely, Eric A. Blair
    On *The Road to Wigan Pier*
    CEJL I 267

G.081   To Mr Thompson [unidentified]
from Sanatori Maurin, Sarria, Barcelona
8 June 1937
Yours sincerely, George Orwell
    Mentions *The Road to Wigan Pier*
    CEJL I 268

G.082   To Cyril Connolly
from Sanatori Maurin, Sarria, Barcelona
8 June 1937
Yours, Eric Blair
    Encounter (January 1962) 57–58; *CEJL* I 268–269

G.083   To Leonard Moore
from 24 Croom's Hill, Greenwich, S.E. 10
8 July 1937
Yours sincerely, Eric A. Blair
    TLS (January 1984) 15

G.084   To Rayner Heppenstall
from The Stores, Wallington, Nr Baldock, Herts.
31 July 1937
Yours, Eric
    Mentions review of *The Spanish Cockpit* [See C.101], and *Homage to Catalonia*
    CEJL I 278–280

G.085   To Geoffrey Gorer
from The Stores, Wallington, Nr Baldock, Herts.
16 August 1937
Yours, Eric A. Blair
    Mentions review of *The Spanish Cockpit* [See C.101] and *Homage to Catalonia*
    CEJL I 280–282

G.086   To Geoffrey Gorer
from The Stores, Wallington, Nr Baldock, Herts.
15 September 1937
Yours, Eric

Mentions *Homage to Catalonia*
CEJL I 283–285

G.087 To Jack Common
from The Stores, Wallington, Nr Baldock, Herts.
Tuesday [October? 1937]
Yours, Eric Blair
Mentions *Homage to Catalonia*
CEJL I 288–290

G.088 To Cyril Connolly
from 36 High Street, Southwold, Suffolk
12 October 1937
Yours, Eric Blair
Encounter (January 1962) 58

G.089 Lettercard to Cyril Connolly
from 56 Upper Park Rd, Hampstead NW3
1 December 1937 from postmark
Yours, Eric Blair
Encounter (January 1962) 58; CEJL I 290

1938

G.090 To Jack Common
from The Stores, Wallington, Nr Baldock, Herts.
5 February 1938
Yours, Eric Blair
Mentions *Homage to Catalonia*
CEJL I 296

G.091 To Raymond Mortimer[25]
from The Stores, Wallington, Nr Baldock, Herts.
9 February 1938
Yours sincerely [George Orwell]
On rejection of review of *The Spanish Cockpit* [See C.101]
CEJL I 299–302

G.092 To Alec Houghton Joyce[26]
from The Stores, Wallington, Nr Baldock, Herts.
12 February 1938
Yours sincerely, Eric Blair
On possible appointment to the Lucknow *Pioneer*. Mentions *Down and Out in Paris and London, Burmese Days, A Clergyman's Daughter, Keep the Aspidistra Flying, The Road to Wigan Pier*, and *Homage to Catalonia*
CEJL I 302–303.

G.093 To Jack Common
from The Stores, Wallington, Nr Baldock, Herts.
16 February 1938
Yours, Eric Blair
Mentions *Coming Up for Air*
CEJL I 303–304

G.094 To Cyril Connolly
from The Stores, Wallington, Nr Baldock, Herts.
14 March 1938
Yours, Eric Blair
Mentions *Homage to Catalonia*
Encounter (January 1962) 58; CEJL I 309

G.095 To Jack Common
from Jellico Ward, Preston Hall, Aylesford, Kent

Wed. [late March? 1938]
Yours, Eric Blair
    Mentions *Homage to Catalonia* and *Coming Up for Air*
    CEJL I 310–311

G.096   To Stephen Spender[27]
from Jellico Ward, Preston Hall, Aylesford, Kent
2 April 1938
Yours, Eric Blair
    Mentions *Homage to Catalonia*
    Encounter (January 1962) 58–59; *CEJL* I 311–312

G.097   To Stephen Spender
from Jellico Pavilion, Preston Hall, Aylesford, Kent
Friday [15? April 1938]
Yours, Eric Blair
    Mentions *Homage to Catalonia*
    Encounter (January 1962) 59–60; *CEJL* I 312–313

G.098   To Geoffrey Gorer
from Jellico Pavilion, Preston Hall, Aylesford, Kent
18 April 1938
Yours, Eric Blair
    On review of *Homage to Catalonia*
    CEJL I 315

G.099   To Jack Common
from Jellico Pavilion, Preston Hall, Aylesford, Kent
20 April 1938
Love to all, Yours, Eric Blair
    Mentions *Homage to Catalonia*
    CEJL I 314

G.100   To Cyril Connolly
from Jellico Pavilion, Preston Hall, Aylesford, Kent
27 April 1938
Yours, Eric Blair
    Mentions *Homage to Catalonia*
    Encounter (January 1962) 60; *CEJL* I 328–329

G.101   To Jack Common
from Jellico Pavilion, Preston Hall, Aylesford, Kent
Sunday [22 May? 1938]
Yours, Eric Blair
    On review of *The Freedom of the Streets* [See C.127], and *Homage to Catalonia*. Mentions *Coming Up for Air*
    CEJL I 329–330

G.102   To Jack Common
from New Hostel, Preston Hall, Aylesford, Kent
5 July 1938
Yours, Eric Blair
    CEJL I 338–339

G.103   To Cyril Connolly
from New Hostel, Preston Hall, Aylesford, Kent
8 July 1938
Yours, Eric Blair
    Mentions *Homage to Catalonia* and *Coming Up for Air*
    Encounter (January 1962) 60; *CEJL* I 343–344

G.104   To Ida Mabel Blair
from New Hostel, Preston Hall, Aylesford, Kent
8 August 1938

Much love to all, Eric
  Mentions *Coming Up for Air*
  CEJL I 347–348

G.105 To Jack Common
from Chez Madame Vellat, Rue Edmond Doutte, Medinah, Marrakech, French Morocco
26 September 1938
Yours, Eric
  CEJL I 351–352

G.106 To Jack Common
from Chez Madame Vellat, Rue Edmond Doutte, Marrakech, French Morocco
29 September 1938
Yours, Eric
  Mentions *Coming Up for Air*
  CEJL I 352–354

G.107 To Jack Common
from Chez Madame Vellat, Rue Edmond Doutte, Medinah, Marrakech, French Morocco
12 October 1938
Yours, Eric
  Mentions *The Road to Wigan Pier* and *Coming Up for Air*
  CEJL I 355–357

G.108 To John Sceats[28]
from Boite Postale 48, Gueliz, Marrakech, French Morocco
26 October 1938
Yours, Eric Blair
  On *Coming Up for Air*
  CEJL I 357–359

G.109 To John Sceats
from Boite Postale 48, Gueliz, Marrakech, French Morocco
24 November 1938
Yours E.A. Blair
  Mentions *Coming Up for Air*
  CEJL I 360–361

G.110 To Cyril Connolly
from Boite Postale 48, Gueliz, Marrakech, French Morocco
14 December 1938
Yours, E.A. Blair
  Mentions *Coming Up for Air*
  Encounter (January 1962) 60–61; *CEJL* I 362–363

G.111 To Jack Common
from Boite Postale 48, Gueliz, Marrakech, French Morocco
26 December 1938
Yours, Eric
  Mentions *Coming Up for Air*, *Down and Out in Paris and London*
  CEJL I 367–371

G.112 To Frank Jellinek[29]
from Boite Postale 48, Gueliz, Marrakech, French Morocco
29 December 1938
Yours, Eric Blair ("George Orwell")
  Mentions *Homage to Catalonia*, and a letter he was writing to *The New Leader* about an error. See 'A Mistake Corrected', *New Leader* (13 January 1939) [See C.144].
  CEJL I 363–367

1939

G.113   To Herbert Read[30]
    from Boite Postale 48, Gueliz, Marrakech, French Morocco
    4 January 1939
    Yours, Eric Blair
        Mentions *Coming Up for Air*
        CEJL I 377–378
G.114   To Geoffrey Gorer
    from Boite Postale 48, Gueliz, Marrakech, French Morocco
    20 January 1939
    Yours, Eric
        Mentions *Coming Up for Air*
        CEJL I 381–383
G.115   To Lady Rees[31]
    from Boite Postale 48, Gueliz, Marrakech, French Morocco
    23 February 1939
    Yours sincerely, E.A. Blair
        Mentions *Coming Up for Air*
        Encounter (January 1962) 61
G.116   To Herbert Read
    from Boite Postale 48, Gueliz, Marrakech, French Morocco
    5 March 1939
    Yours, Eric Blair
        CEJL I 385–387
G.117   To Jack Common
    from 36 High St, Southwold, Suffolk
    Sunday [9 April 1939]
    Yours, Eric
        Mentions *Coming Up for Air*
        CEJL I 393–394
G.118   To Leonard Moore
    from The Stores, Wallington, Nr Baldock, Herts
    25 April 1939
    Yours sincerely, Eric Blair
        TLS (January 1984) 15–16

1940

G.119   To Victor Gollancz
    from The Stores, Wallington, Nr Baldock, Herts.
    8 January 1940
    Yours sincerely, Eric Blair
        On *Inside the Whale*
        CEJL I 409–410
G.120   To Geoffrey Gorer
    from The Stores, Wallington, Nr Baldock, Herts.
    10 January 1940
    Yours, Eric
        Mentions *Inside the Whale*
        CEJL I 410–411
G.121   To David H. Thomson[32]
    from The Stores, Wallington, Nr Baldock, Herts.
    8 March 1940
    Yours sincerely, George Orwell

Mentions 'Boys' Weeklies' [See C.163] and *Inside the Whale*
CEJL I 413

G.122   To Geoffrey Gorer
from The Stores, Wallington, Nr Baldock, Herts.
3 April 1940
Yours, Eric
Mentions *Inside the Whale*, 'Boys' Weeklies' [See C.163], and 'Charles Dickens'.
CEJL I 527–529

G.123   To Humphry House[33]
from The Stores, Wallington, Nr Baldock, Herts.
11 April 1940
Yours sincerely, George Orwell
Mentions 'Charles Dickens' and *Inside the Whale*
CEJL I 529–532

G.124   To Rayner Heppenstall
from The Stores, Wallington, Nr Baldock, Herts.
11 April 1940
Yours, Eric
Mentions entry in *Twentieth Century Authors*.
CEJL II 18–19

G.125   To Rayner Heppenstall
from The Stores, Wallington, Nr Baldock, Herts.
16 April 1940
Yours, Eric
CEJL II 22

G.126   To John Lehmann
from 18 Dorset Chambers, Chagford Street, Ivor Place, NW1
6 July 1940
Yours, George Orwell
Mentions 'Shooting an Elephant' [See C.087].
CEJL II 29

G.127   To Sir Sacheverell Sitwell[34]
from 18 Dorset Chambers, Chagford Street, Ivor Place, NW1
6 July 1940
Yours sincerely, George Orwell
Extract Shelden 141

G.128   To James Laughlin[35]
from 18 Dorset Chambers, Chagford Street, Ivor Place, NW1, England
16 July 1940
Yours sincerely, George Orwell
Mentions 'Inside the Whale' and *Inside the Whale*
CEJL II 33–34

1941

G.129   To the Reverend Iorwerth Jones[36]
from 111 Langford Court, Abbey Road, London NW8
8 April 1941
Yours sincerely, George Orwell
On *The Lion and the Unicorn*
CEJL II 109–112

G.130   To Dorothy Plowman[37]
from 111 Langford Court, Abbey Road, London NW8
20 June 1941

Yours, Eric Blair
          CEJL II 138–139
G.131   To M.J. Tambimuttu[38]
          from P[ortland] P[lace] [ie the BBC]
          25 November 1941
          Yours sincerely, Eric Blair
              The War Broadcasts 175
G.132   To J. Bahadur Singh[39]
          from P[ortland] P[lace]
          26 November 1941
          Yours sincerely, Eric Blair
              The War Broadcasts 176
G.133   To Mulk Raj Anand[40]
          from P[ortland] P[lace]
          22 December 1941
          Yours sincerely, Eric Blair
              The War Broadcasts 176

1942

G.134   To Hsiao Ch'ien[41]
          from P[ortland] P[lace]
          14 January 1942
          Yours sincerely, Eric Blair
              The War Broadcasts 176–177
G.135   To Mulk Raj Anand
          from P[ortland] P[lace]
          19 January 1942
          Yours sincerely, Eric Blair
              The War Broadcasts 177
G.136   To Hsiao Ch'ien
          from P[ortland] P[lace]
          24 January 1942
          Yours sincerely, Eric Blair
              The War Broadcasts 177–178
G.137   To T.S. Eliot
          from P[ortland] P[lace]
          2 February 1942
          Yours sincerely, Eric Blair
              The War Broadcasts 178
G.138   To J.F. Horrabin[42]
          from P[ortland] P[lace]
          3 February 1942
          Yours sincerely, Eric Blair
              The War Broadcasts 27–28
G.139   To J.F. Horrabin,
          from P[ortland] P[lace]
          13 February 1942
          Yours sincerely, Eric Blair
              The War Broadcasts 179
G.140   To Arthur Calder-Marshall[43]
          from E[astern] S[ection] [BBC]
          17 February 1942
          Yours sincerely, George Orwell
              The War Broadcasts 31

G.141 To Cyril Connolly
       from P[ortland] P[lace]
       27 February 1942
       Yours, Eric Blair
       The War Broadcasts 180

G.142 To Mulk Raj Anand
       from E[astern] S[ection] [BBC]
       27 February 1942
       Yours, Eric Blair
       The War Broadcasts 24–25

G.143 To C.H. Waddington[44]
       from P[ortland] P[lace]
       28 February 1942
       Yours sincerely, George Orwell
       The War Broadcasts 180

G.144 To Stephen Spender
       from P[ortland] P[lace]
       5 March 1942
       Yours, Eric Blair
       The War Broadcasts 181

G.145 To Princess Indira of Kapurthala[45]
       from P[ortland] P[lace]
       5 March 1942
       Yours sincerely, Eric Blair
       The War Broadcasts 181

G.146 To J.D. Bernal[46]
       from E[astern] S[ection] [BBC]
       6 March 1942
       Yours sincerely, George Orwell
       The War Broadcasts 28–29

G.147 To Herbert Read
       from E[astern] S[ection] [BBC]
       6 March 1942
       Yours sincerely, Eric Blair
       The War Broadcasts 32

G.148 To Hsiao Ch'ien
       from E[astern] S[ection] [BBC]
       13 March 1942
       Yours sincerely, Eric Blair
       The War Broadcasts 25–26

G.149 To Hsiao Ch'ien
       from P[ortland] P[lace]
       19 March 1942
       Yours sincerely, Eric Blair
       The War Broadcasts 182

G.150 To Hsiao Ch'ien
       from P[ortland] P[lace]
       25 March 1942
       Yours sincerely, Geo. Orwell
       The War Broadcasts 182–183

G.151 To Joseph Needham[47]
       from P[ortland] P[lace]
       26 March 1942
       Yours truly, Eric Blair
       The War Broadcasts 183

G.152   To Lady Grigg[48]
        from P[ortland] P[lace]
        27 March 1942
        Yours sincerely, Eric Blair
            The War Broadcasts 183–184
G.153   To BBC Eastern Services Director[49]
        from 200 Oxford Street
        undated
        from Eric Blair
            The War Broadcasts 184
G.154   To J.D. Bernal
        from P[ortland] P[lace]
        27 March 1942
        Yours sincerely, Eric Blair
            The War Broadcasts 185
G.155   To Joseph Needham
        from P[ortland] P[lace]
        31 March 1942
        Yours sincerely, Eric Blair
            The War Broadcasts 185–186
G.156   To Hsiao Ch'ien
        from P[ortland] P[lace]
        31 March 1942
        Yours
            The War Broadcasts 186
G.157   To Amabel Williams-Ellis[50]
        from P[ortland] P[lace]
        31 March 1942
        Yours sincerely, George Orwell
            The War Broadcasts 186
G.158   To E.M. Forster[51]
        from P[ortland] P[lace]
        10 April 1942
        Yours sincerely, George Orwell
            The War Broadcasts 187
G.159   To E.M. Forster
        no address
        14 April 1942
        Yours, George Orwell
            The War Broadcasts 188
G.160   To J.D. Bernal
        from P[ortland] P[lace]
        27 April 1942
        Yours sincerely, George Orwell
            The War Broadcasts 189–190
G.161   To E.M. Forster
        from P[ortland] P[lace]
        27 April 1942
        Yours sincerely, George Orwell
            The War Broadcasts 190
G.162   To J.D. Bernal
        from P[ortland] P[lace]
        5 May 1942
        Yours sincerely, George Orwell
            The War Broadcasts 190–191

G.163   To Reginald Reynolds[52]
        from P[ortland] P[lace]
        5 May 1942
        Yours
            The War Broadcasts 191
G.164   To J.B.S. Haldane[53]
        from P[ortland] P[lace]
        7 May 1942
        Yours sincerely, George Orwell
            The War Broadcasts 191–192
G.165   To Mulk Raj Anand
        from P[ortland] P[lace]
        8 May 1942
        Yours
            The War Broadcasts 192
G.166   To J.F. Horrabin
        from P[ortland] P[lace]
        11 May 1942
        Yours sincerely, George Orwell
            The War Broadcasts 192–193
G.167   To Hsiao Ch'ien
        from P[ortland] P[lace]
        11 May 1942
        Yours sincerely, George Orwell
            The War Broadcasts 193
G.168   To Mulk Raj Anand
        from P[ortland] P[lace]
        14 May 1942
        Yours
            The War Broadcasts 194
G.169   To C.D. Darlington[54]
        from P[ortland] P[lace]
        15 May 1942
        Yours truly, George Orwell
            The War Broadcasts 194–196
G.170   Memorandum to E. Rowan-Davies[55]
        no address
        16 May 1942
        Eric Blair
            The War Broadcasts 34–35
G.171   To Richard Titmuss[56]
        from P[ortland] P[lace]
        19 May 1942
        Yours truly, George Orwell
            The War Broadcasts 196
G.172   To E.M. Forster
        from P[ortland] P[lace]
        10 June 1942
        Yours, George Orwell
            The War Broadcasts 197
G.173   To Princess Indira of Kapurthala
        from P[ortland] P[lace]
        10 June 1942
        Yours sincerely, Eric Blair
            The War Broadcasts 198

G.185 To Vida Hope[62]
       from P[ortland] P[lace]
       18 July 1942
       Yours truly, George Orwell
         The War Broadcasts 204–205
G.186 To G.M. Young
       from P[ortland] P[lace]
       23 July 1942
       Yours sincerely, George Orwell
         The War Broadcasts 205
G.187 To Cyril Connolly
       from E[astern] S[ection] [BBC]
       23 July 1942
       Yours, George Orwell
         The War Broadcasts 38
G.188 To T.S. Eliot
       from P[ortland] P[lace]
       23 July 1942
       Yours sincerely, George Orwell
         The War Broadcasts 206
G.189 To Henry Treece[63]
       from P[ortland] P[lace]
       25 July 1942
       Yours sincerely, George Orwell
         The War Broadcasts 206
G.190 To Herbert Read
       from P[ortland] P[lace]
       25 July 1942
       Yours, George Orwell
         The War Broadcasts 207
G.191 To Inez Holden[64]
       from P[ortland] P[lace]
       25 July 1942
       Yours, George Orwell
         The War Broadcasts 207
G.192 To T.C. Worsley
       from P[ortland] P[lace]
       27 July 1942
       Yours, George Orwell
         The War Broadcasts 208
G.193 To Henry Treece
       from P[ortland] P[lace]
       30 July 1942
       Yours sincerely, George Orwell
         The War Broadcasts 208
G.194 To Herbert Read
       from P[ortland] P[lace]
       31 July 1942
       Yours, George Orwell
         The War Broadcasts 39
G.195 To Narayana Menon[65]
       from P[ortland] P[lace]
       6 August 1942
       Yours sincerely, Eric Blair
         The War Broadcasts 209

G.196   To E.M. Forster
         from P[ortland] P[lace]
         10 August 1942
         Yours sincerely, George Orwell
             The War Broadcasts 209
G.197   To Lord Winterton[66]
         from P[ortland] P[lace]
         10 August 1942
         Yours sincerely, George Orwell
             The War Broadcasts 210
G.198   To Vida Hope
         from P[ortland] P[lace]
         11 August 1942
         Yours sincerely, George Orwell
             The War Broadcasts 211
G.199   To Henry Treece
         from P[ortland] P[lace]
         11 August 1942
         Yours sincerely, George Orwell
             The War Broadcasts 210–211
G.200   To Peggotty Freeman[67]
         from P[ortland] P[lace]
         18 August 1942
         Yours sincerely, Eric Blair
             The War Broadcasts 211
G.201   To Peggotty Freeman
         from P[ortland] P[lace]
         24 August 1942
         Yours sincerely, Eric Blair
             The War Broadcasts 212
G.202   To G.M. Young
         from P[ortland] P[lace]
         24 August 1942
         Yours sincerely, George Orwell
             The War Broadcasts 212
G.203   To C.H. Waddington
         from P[ortland] P[lace]
         28 August 1942
         Yours sincerely, George Orwell
             The War Broadcasts 212–213
G.204   To Harold Laski[68]
         from E[astern] S[ection] [BBC]
         31 August 1942
         Yours sincerely, George Orwell
             The War Broadcasts 40–41
G.205   To Inez Holden
         from P[ortland] P[lace]
         9 September 1942
         Yours sincerely, George Orwell
             The War Broadcasts 213
G.206   To L.A.G. Strong[69]
         from P[ortland] P[lace]
         9 September 1942
         Yours sincerely, George Orwell
             The War Broadcasts 213–214

G.207   To Martin Armstrong[70]
from P[ortland] P[lace]
9 September 1942
Yours sincerely, George Orwell
The War Broadcasts 214

G.208   To J.A. Lauwerys[71]
from P[ortland] P[lace]
15 September 1942
Yours sincerely, George Orwell
The War Broadcasts 215

G.209   To Ritchie Calder[72]
from P[ortland] P[lace]
22 September 1942
Yours, George Orwell
The War Broadcasts 215

G.210   To Herbert Read
from P[ortland] P[lace]
28 September 1942
Yours, George Orwell
The War Broadcasts 216

G.211   To Mulk Raj Anand
from P[ortland] P[lace]
1 October 1942
Yours, George Orwell
The War Broadcasts 216

G.212   To Princess Indira of Kapurthala
from P[ortland] P[lace]
1 October 1942
Yours sincerely, Eric Blair
The War Broadcasts 216–217

G.213   To E.M. Forster
from P[ortland] P[lace]
1 October 1942
Yours, George Orwell
The War Broadcasts 217

G.214   To Mulk Raj Anand
from P[ortland] P[lace]
7 October 1942
Yours, Eric Blair
The War Broadcasts 217

G.215   To Mulk Raj Anand
from P[ortland] P[lace]
7 October 1942
Yours sincerely, George Orwell
The War Broadcasts 218

G.216   To L.A.G. Strong
from P[ortland] P[lace]
7 October 1942
Yours sincerely, George Orwell
The War Broadcasts 218–219

G.217   To E.M. Forster
from P[ortland] P[lace]
10 October 1942
Yours, George Orwell
The War Broadcasts 219–220

G.218   To the Editor of *The Times*
         from 10a Mortimer Crescent, NW6
         12 October 1942
         Yours truly
             Unpublished. *CEJL* text from carbon copy.
             CEJL II 243–244
G.219   BBC Internal Memorandum
         Confidential, 15 October 1942
         Eric Blair, Indian Section
             CEJL II 244–245
G.220   To T.S. Eliot
         [from the BBC, Broadcasting House, London, W1]
         16 October 1942
         Yours sincerely, George Orwell
             CEJL text from carbon copy
             CEJL II 245–246
             The War Broadcasts 220
G.221   To Martin Armstrong
         from P[ortland] P[lace]
         17 October 1942
         Yours sincerely, George Orwell
             The War Broadcasts 220–221
G.222   To Desmond Hawkins[73]
         from P[ortland] P[lace]
         19 October 1942
         Yours, George Orwell
             The War Broadcasts 221
G.223   To Mulk Raj Anand
         from P[ortland] P[lace]
         20 October 1942
         Yours, George Orwell
             The War Broadcasts 221–222
G.224   To Herbert Read
         from P[ortland] P[lace]
         20 October 1942
         Yours sincerely, George Orwell
             The War Broadcasts 222
G.225   To E.M. Forster
         from P[ortland] P[lace]
         24 October 1942
         Yours, George Orwell
             The War Broadcasts 222–223
G.226   To Henry Treece
         from P[ortland] P[lace]
         27 October 1942
         Yours sincerely, George Orwell
             The War Broadcasts 223–224
G.227   To Keidrych Rhys[74]
         from P[ortland] P[lace]
         27 October 1942
         Yours sincerely, George Orwell
             The War Broadcasts 224
G.228   Memorandum to Miss Alexander[75]
         from 200 Oxford Street
         28 October 1942

Yours sincerely, Eric Blair
The War Broadcasts 231

G.240 To Norman Marshall
from P[ortland] P[lace]
30 November 1942
Yours sincerely, George Orwell
The War Broadcasts 231–232

G.241 To George Woodcock[76]
from 10a Mortimer Crescent, NW6
2 December 1942
Yours, Geo. Orwell
Mentions 'Pacifism and the War' [See C.317] and *Talking to India*
CEJL II 267–268

G.242 To Edmund Blunden[77]
from E[astern] S[ection] [BBC]
3 December 1942
Yours sincerely, George Orwell
The War Broadcasts 45

G.243 To Herbert Read
from P[ortland] P[lace]
4 December 1942
Yours, George Orwell
The War Broadcasts 232

G.244 To T.S. Eliot
from P[ortland] P[lace]
4 December 1942
Yours sincerely, George Orwell
The War Broadcasts 233

G.245 To Edmund Blunden
from P[ortland] P[lace]
5 December 1942
Yours sincerely, George Orwell
The War Broadcasts 233–234

G.246 To Edmund Blunden
from E[astern] S[ection] [BBC]
10 December 1942
Yours sincerely, George Orwell
The War Broadcasts 234–235

G.247 Memorandum to Miss Boughen
200 Oxford Street
10 December 1942
Eric Blair
The War Broadcasts 44

G.248 To E.M. Forster
from E[astern] S[ection] [BBC]
14 December 1942
Yours, George Orwell
The War Broadcasts 235

G.249 To Edmund Blunden
from E[astern] S[ection] [BBC]
14 December 1942
Yours sincerely, George Orwell
The War Broadcasts 235

G.250 To C.K. Ogden[78]
from E[astern] S[ection] [BBC]

16 December 1942
Yours sincerely, George Orwell
The War Broadcasts 47–48

G.251 To Edmund Blunden
from E[astern] S[ection] [BBC]
30 December 1942
Yours sincerely, George Orwell
The War Broadcasts 236–237

G.252 To Desmond Hawkins
from E[astern] S[ection] [BBC]
30 December 1942
Yours sincerely, George Orwell
The War Broadcasts 237

G.253 To John Beavan[79]
from E[astern] S[ection] [BBC]
30 December 1942
Yours sincerely, George Orwell
The War Broadcasts 237–238

G.254 To T.S. Eliot
from E[astern] S[ection] [BBC]
30 December 1942
Yours sincerely, George Orwell
The War Broadcasts 238

1943

G.255 To Desmond Hawkins
from E[astern] S[ection] [BBC]
6 January 1943
Yours sincerely, George Orwell
The War Broadcasts 239

G.256 To Herbert Read
from E[astern] S[ection] [BBC]
18 January 1943
Yours, George Orwell
The War Broadcasts 239–240

G.257 To A.L.C. Bullock[80]
from E[astern] S[ection] [BBC]
25 January 1943
Yours sincerely, George Orwell
The War Broadcasts 240

G.258 To E.M. Forster
from E[astern] S[ection] [BBC]
4 February 1943
Yours sincerely, Eric Blair
The War Broadcasts 241

G.259 To Harry W. Todd[81]
from E[astern] S[ection] [BBC]
10 February 1943
Yours truly, Eric Blair
The War Broadcasts 241

G.260 To Norman Collins
from 200 Oxford Street
13 February 1943
Eric Blair
The War Broadcasts 241–242

G.261   To H.D. Graves-Law[82]
from E[astern] S[ection] [BBC]
16 February 1942
Yours faithfully, Eric Blair
The War Broadcasts 242

G.262   To E.M. Forster
from E[astern] S[ection] [BBC]
22 February 1943
Yours sincerely, Eric Blair
The War Broadcasts 242

G.263   To Norman Collins
from 200 Oxford Street
24 February 1943
Eric Blair
The War Broadcasts 49

G.264   To James Stephens[83]
from E[astern] S[ection] [BBC]
24 February 1943
Yours sincerely, George Orwell
The War Broadcasts 242–243

G.265   To Arthur Wynn[84]
from E[astern] S[ection] [BBC]
24 February 1943
Yours sincerely, George Orwell
The War Broadcasts 243–244

G.266   To T.S. Eliot
from E[astern] S[ection] [BBC]
24 February 1943
Yours sincerely, George Orwell
The War Broadcasts 244

G.267   To Desmond Hawkins
from E[astern] S[ection] [BBC]
27 February 1943
Yours sincerely, George Orwell
The War Broadcasts 244–245

G.268   To T.S. Eliot
from E[astern] S[ection] [BBC]
4 March 1943
Yours sincerely, George Orwell
The War Broadcasts 245

G.269   To T.S. Eliot
from E[astern] S[ection] [BBC]
11 March 1943
Yours sincerely, Eric Blair
The War Broadcasts 246

G.270   To T.S. Eliot
from E[astern] S[ection] [BBC]
15 March 1943
Yours sincerely, George Orwell
The War Broadcasts 247

G.271   To James Stephens
from E[astern] S[ection] [BBC]
18 March 1943
Yours sincerely, George Orwell
The War Broadcasts 247

G.272   To Reginald Reynolds
        from E[astern] S[ection] [BBC]
        29 March 1943
        Yours, Eric Blair
        The War Broadcasts 247–248

G.273   To Osbert Sitwell[85]
        from E[astern] S[ection] [BBC]
        1 April 1943
        Yours sincerely, George Orwell
        The War Broadcasts 248–249

G.274   To E.M. Forster
        from E[astern] S[ection] [BBC]
        5 April 1943
        Yours, George Orwell
        The War Broadcasts 249

G.275   To E.M. Forster
        from E[astern] S[ection] [BBC]
        6 April 1943
        Yours, George Orwell
        The War Broadcasts 250

G.276   To Lord Winterton
        from E[astern] S[ection] [BBC]
        7 April 1943
        Yours sincerely, Eric Blair
        The War Broadcasts 250

G.277   To J.F. Horrabin
        from E[astern] S[ection] [BBC]
        7 April 1943
        Yours sincerely, George Orwell
        The War Broadcasts 50–51

G.278   To Lord Winterton
        from E[astern] S[ection] [BBC]
        9 April 1943
        Yours sincerely, Eric Blair
        The War Broadcasts 250–251

G.279   To John Lehmann
        from E[astern] S[ection] [BBC]
        13 April 1943
        Yours sincerely, George Orwell
        The War Broadcasts 251

G.280   To John Lehmann
        from E[astern] S[ection] [BBC]
        15 April 1943
        Yours sincerely, George Orwell
        The War Broadcasts 252

G.281   To E.M. Forster
        from E[astern] S[ection] [BBC]
        20 April 1943
        Yours, George Orwell
        The War Broadcasts 252–253

G.282   To Desmond Hawkins
        from E[astern] S[ection] [BBC]
        22 April 1943
        Yours, George Orwell
        The War Broadcasts 253

G.283   To Eleanor Rathbone[86]
from E[astern] S[ection] [BBC]
18 May 1943
Yours sincerely, Eric Blair
The War Broadcasts 254

G.284   To Wilfrid Roberts[87]
from E[astern] S[ection] [BBC]
18 May 1943
Yours sincerely, Eric Blair
The War Broadcasts 255

G.285   To C.D. Darlington
from E[astern] S[ection] [BBC]
19 May 1943
Yours sincerely, George Orwell
The War Broadcasts 255–256

G.286   To E.M. Forster
from E[astern] S[ection] [BBC]
4 June 1943
Yours sincerely, George Orwell
The War Broadcasts 257

G.287   To T.S. Eliot
from E[astern] S[ection] [BBC]
17 June 1943
Yours sincerely, George Orwell
The War Broadcasts 257–258

G.288   To T.S. Eliot
from E[astern] S[ection] [BBC]
18 June 1943
Yours sincerely, George Orwell
The War Broadcasts 258

G.289   To William Plomer[88]
from E[astern] S[ection] [BBC]
18 June 1943
Yours sincerely, George Orwell
The War Broadcasts 258–259

G.290   To T.S. Eliot
from E[astern] S[ection] [BBC]
25 June 1943
Yours sincerely, George Orwell
The War Broadcasts 259

G.291   To Desmond Hawkins
from E[astern] S[ection] [BBC]
25 June 1943
Yours, George Orwell
The War Broadcasts 259–260

G.292   To Stephen Spender
from E[astern] S[ection] [BBC]
25 June 1943
Yours, Eric Blair
The War Broadcasts 260

G.293   To E.M. Forster
from E[astern] S[ection] [BBC]
28 June 1943
Yours, George Orwell
The War Broadcasts 261

G.294   To E.M. Forster
        from E[astern] S[ection] [BBC]
        1 July 1943
        Yours sincerely, George Orwell
            The War Broadcasts 261
G.295   To E.M. Forster
        from E[astern] S[ection] [BBC]
        2 July 1943
        Yours sincerely, George Orwell
            The War Broadcasts 262
G.296   To E.M. Forster
        from E[astern] S[ection] [BBC]
        2 July 1943
        Yours sincerely, George Orwell
            The War Broadcasts 262–263
G.297   To E.M. Forster
        from E[astern] S[ection] [BBC]
        5 July 1943
        Yours, George Orwell
            The War Broadcasts 263–264
G.298   To E.C. Bowyer[89]
        from E[astern] S[ection] [BBC]
        9 July 1943
        Yours sincerely, George Orwell
            The War Broadcasts 264
G.299   To Alex Comfort[90]
        from 10a Mortimer Crescent, London, NW6
        Sunday [11? July 1943]
        Yours sincerely, Geo, Orwell
            Mentions 'As One Non-Combatant to Another' [See C.347], and review of
            Beggar My Neighbour [See C.353]
            CEJL II 303–305
G.300   To C.D. Darlington
        from E[astern] S[ection] [BBC]
        13 July 1943
        Yours sincerely, George Orwell
            The War Broadcasts 264
G.301   To James Stephens
        from E[astern] S[ection] [BBC]
        16 July 1943
        Yours sincerely, George Orwell
            The War Broadcasts 265
G.302   To James Stephens
        from E[astern] S[ection] [BBC]
        23 July 1943
        Yours sincerely, George Orwell
            The War Broadcasts 265
G.303   To C.M. Fletcher[91]
        from E[astern] S[ection] [BBC]
        29 July 1943
        Yours truly, Eric Blair
            The War Broadcasts 266
G.304   To B.H. Alexander
        from E[astern] S[ection] [BBC]
        2 August 1943

Yours sincerely, George Orwell
The War Broadcasts 271–272

G.316 To L.F. Rushbrook-Williams
from BBC
24 September 1943
Yours sincerely, Eric Blair
CEJL II 315–316; *The War Broadcasts* 57–58

G.317 To E.M. Forster
from E[astern] S[ection] [BBC]
27 September 1943
Yours sincerely, George Orwell
The War Broadcasts 273

G.318 To Stephen Spender
from E[astern] S[ection] [BBC]
28 September 1943
Yours sincerely, George Orwell
The War Broadcasts 273

G.319 To Norman Collins
from E[astern] S[ection] [BBC]
4 October 1943
Eric Blair
The War Broadcasts 274

G.320 To T.S. Eliot
from E[astern] S[ection] [BBC]
8 October 1943
Yours sincerely, George Orwell
The War Broadcasts 274

G.321 To Philip Rahv[92]
from 10a Mortimer Crescent, London NW6
14 October 1943
Yours, Geo. Orwell
CEJL II 317–319

G.322 To Desmond Hawkins
from E[astern] S[ection] [BBC]
16 October 1943
Yours truly, George Orwell
The War Broadcasts 275

G.323 Memorandum to Norman Collins
no address
19 October 1943
EB
The War Broadcasts 275

G.324 To Ivor Brown[93]
from E[astern] S[ection] [BBC]
11 November 1943
Yours sincerely, George Orwell
The War Broadcasts 276

G.325 To Philip Rahv
from 10a Mortimer Crescent, London NW6
9 December 1943
Yours Geo. Orwell
Mentions review of *Beggar My Neighbour* [See C.353], *Animal Farm*, and
Talking to India
CEJL III 53–54

1944

G.326   To Leonard Moore
from 10a Mortimer Crescent, London NW6
9 January 1944
Yours sincerely, Eric Blair
Concerning *Animal Farm*
Ten Animal Farm Letters

G.327   To Gleb Struve[94]
from 10a Mortimer Crescent, London NW6
17 February 1944
Yours sincerely, Geo. Orwell
Mentions *Animal Farm* and the idea for *Nineteen Eighty-Four*
CEJL III 95–96

G.328   To Roy Fuller[95]
from 10a Mortimer Crescent, London NW6
7 March 1944
Yours truly, Geo. Orwell
CEJL III 104–105

G.329   To Leonard Moore
from 10a Mortimer Crescent, NW6
19 March 1944
Yours sincerely, Eric Blair
TLS (January 1984) 16

G.330   To Leonard Moore
from 10a Mortimer Crescent, London NW6
23 March 1944
Yours sincerely, Eric Blair
Concerning *Animal Farm*
Ten Animal Farm Letters

G.331   To Leonard Moore
from 10a Mortimer Crescent, London NW6
25 March 1944
Yours sincerely, Eric Blair
Concerning *Animal Farm*
Ten Animal Farm Letters

G.332   To Leonard Moore
from 10a Mortimer Crescent, London NW6
5 April 1944
Yours sincerely, Eric Blair
Concerning *Animal Farm*
Ten Animal Farm Letters

G.333   To Leonard Moore
from 10a Mortimer Crescent, London NW6
15 April 1944
Yours sincerely, Eric Blair
Concerning *Animal Farm*
Ten Animal Farm Letters

G.334   To Philip Rahv
from 10a Mortimer Crescent, London NW6
1 May 1944
Yours, Geo. Orwell
Mentions 'London Letter' [See C.438] and *Animal Farm*

G.335   To Leonard Moore
from 10a Mortimer Crescent, London NW6

9 May 1944
Yours sincerely, Eric Blair
    Concerning *Animal Farm*
    Ten Animal Farm Letters

G.336 To Mr Willmett [unidentified]
from 10a Mortimer Crescent, London NW6
18 May 1944
Yours sincerely, Geo. Orwell
    Mentions *The Lion and the Unicorn*
    CEJL III 148–150

G.337 To Leonard Moore
from 10a Mortimer Crescent, London NW6
24 May 1944
Yours sincerely, Eric Blair
    Concerning *Animal Farm*
    Ten Animal Farm Letters

G.338 To Leonard Moore
from 10a Mortimer Crescent, London NW6
8 June 1944
Yours sincerely, Eric Blair
    Ten Animal Farm Letters
    TLS (January 1984) 16

G.339 To Leonard Moore
from 10a Mortimer Crescent, London NW6
24 June 1944
Yours sincerely, Eric Blair
    Ten Animal Farm Letters
    TLS (January 1984) 16

G.340 To T.S. Eliot
from 10a Mortimer Crescent, NW6, (Or "Tribune" CEN 2572)
28 June 1944
Yours sincerely, Geo. Orwell
    On *Animal Farm*
    CEJL III 176

G.341 To John Middleton Murry[96]
from The Tribune, 222 Strand, London WC2
14 July 1944
Yours Geo. Orwell
    Mentions review of *Adam and Eve* [See C.477]
    CEJL III 184–185

G.342 To Rayner Heppenstall
from The Tribune, 222 Strand, London WC2
17 July 1944
Yours, Eric
    CEJL III 185–186

G.343 To Leonard Moore
from "Tribune", 222 Strand, WC2
18 July 1944
Yours sincerely, E.A. Blair
    On *Animal Farm*
    Extract *CEJL* III 186–187

G.344 To John Middleton Murry
from The Tribune, 222 Strand, London, WC2
21 July 1944
Yours sincerely, Geo. Orwell

Mentions reviews of *Beggar My Neighbour* [See C.353] and *No Such Liberty* [See C.295]
CEJL III 190–191

G.345 To John Middleton Murry
from the "Tribune", The Outer Temple, 222 Strand, WC2
5 August 1944
Yours sincerely, Geo. Orwell
CEJL III 202–204

G.346 To John Middleton Murry
from the "Tribune", The Outer Temple, 222 Strand, WC2
11 August 1944
Yours sincerely, Geo. Orwell
Mentions review of *Adam and Eve* [See C.477]
CEJL III 206–207

G.347 To Leonard Moore
Care of the "Tribune", 222 Strand, WC2
15 August 1944
Yours sincerely, Eric Blair
TLS (January 1984) 16

G.348 To Leonard Moore
from 10a Mortimer Crescent, London NW6
29 August 1944
Yours sincerely, Eric Blair
Concerning *Animal Farm*
Ten Animal Farm Letters

G.349 To Frank Barber[97]
from 27B Canonbury Square, Islington, London N1
15 December 1944
Yours sincerely, Geo. Orwell
CEJL III 291–293

1945

G.350 To Leonard Moore
from 27B Canonbury Square, Islington, N1
15 February 1945
Yours sincerely, Eric Blair
On *Animal Farm*
Extract *CEJL* III 358

G.351 To Roger Senhouse[98]
from Room 329, Hotel Scribe, Rue Scribe, Paris, 9e
17 March 1945
Yours, George
Mentions *Homage to Catalonia* and *Animal Farm*
CEJL III 358–359

G.352 To Anthony Powell
from Hotel Scribe, Rue Scribe, Paris, 9e
13 April 1945
Yours, George
CEJL III 359–360

G.353 To Lydia Jackson[99]
Hotel Scribe, Rue Scribe, Paris, 9e
11 May 1945
Yours, George
CEJL III 360–361

G.354   To F.J. Warburg[180]
from London N1
13 June 1945
Yours, George
> On *Animal Farm*
> *CEJL* III 386–387

G.355   To the Editor of *Tribune*
[26?] June 1945
George Orwell
> Not published in *Tribune*.
> *CEJL* III 389–391

G.356   To Leonard Moore
from 27B Canonbury Square, Islington, London N1
3 July 1945
Yours sincerely, Eric Blair
> Mentions *The English People*, *Animal Farm*, *Nineteen Eighty-Four*, *Homage to Catalonia*, and *Critical Essays*
> *CEJL* III 392–393

G.357   To Herbert Read
from 27B Canonbury Square, Islington, London N1
18 August 1945
Yours, George
> Mentions *Animal Farm*
> *CEJL* III 400–401

G.358   To Frank Barber
from 27B Canonbury Square, Islington, London N1
3 September 1945
Yours sincerely, Geo. Orwell
> Mentions *Animal Farm*
> *CEJL* III 402

G.359   To the Duchess of Atholl[181]
from 27B Canonbury Square, Islington, London N1
15 November 1945
Yours truly
> Mentions 'As I Please' article [See C.387]
> *CEJL* text from carbon copy
> *CEJL* IV 30

1946

G.360   To Arthur Koestler[182]
from 27B Canonbury Square, Islington, London N1
10 January 1946
Yours, George
> Mentions *Animal Farm* and *Critical Essays*
> *CEJL* IV 76–77

G.361   To Geoffrey Gorer
from 27B Canonbury Square, Islington, London N1
22 January 1946
Yours, George
> Mentions articles for the *Evening Standard*, *Nineteen Eighty-Four*, and *Dickens, Dali and Others*
> *CEJL* IV 86–88

G.362   To the Reverend Herbert Rogers[183]
from 27B Canonbury Square, Islington, London N1

18 February 1946
Yours sincerely, Geo. Orwell
    On review of *The Democrat at the Supper Table* [See C.656]
    CEJL IV 102–103

G.363 To Dorothy Plowman
from 27B Canonbury Square, Islington, London N1
19 February 1946
Yours, Eric Blair
    Mentions review of *Bridge into the Future: The Letters of Max Plowman* [See
    C.498], *Animal Farm*, *Critical Essays*, and *Nineteen Eighty-Four*
    CEJL IV 104–105

G.364 To Leonard Moore
from 27B Canonbury Square, Islington, London N1
23 February 1946
Yours sincerely, Eric Blair
    On *Animal Farm*. Mentions *Nineteen Eighty-Four*
    CEJL IV 109–111

G.365 To F. Tennyson Jesse[184]
from 27B Canonbury Square, Islington, London N1
4 March 1946
Yours sincerely, George Orwell
    On review of *The Story of Burma* [See C.661]. Mentions *Burmese Days*
    CEJL text from typed copy
    CEJL IV 113–114

G.366 To F. Tennyson Jesse
from 27B Canonbury Square, Islington, London N1
14 March 1946
Yours sincerely, George Orwell
    On review of *The Story of Burma*
    CEJL text from typed copy
    CEJL IV 114

G.367 To Arthur Koestler
from 27B Canonbury Square, Islington, London N1
16 March 1946
Yours, George
    CEJL IV 120–122

G.368 To Arthur Koestler
from 27B Canonbury Square, Islington, London N1
31 March 1946
Yours, George
    CEJL IV 126–127

G.369 To Philip Rahv
from 27B Canonbury Square, Islington, London N1
9 April 1946
Yours, Geo. Orwell
    Mentions *Animal Farm* and 'Second Thoughts on James Burnham' [See C.694]
    CEJL IV 140–141

G.370 To Arthur Koestler
from 27B Canonbury Square, Islington, London N1
13 April 1946
Yours, George
    Mentions review of *Freedom of Expression*
    CEJL IV 145–146

G.371 To A.S.F. Gow[185]
from 27B Canonbury Square, Islington, London N1

13 April 1946
Yours, Eric Blair
    Mentions 'Boys' Weeklies', *Nineteen Eighty-Four* and *Animal Farm*
    CEJL IV 146–148

G.372 To Stafford Cottman[186]
from 27B Canonbury Square, Islington, London N1, CAN 3751
25 April 1946
Yours, Eric Blair
    Mentions *Nineteen Eighty-Four*
    CEJL IV 148–149

G.373 To F.J. Warburg
from 27B Canonbury Square, Islington, London N1
4 May 1946
Yours, George
    CEJL IV 194–196

G.374 To Michael Meyer[187]
from Barnhill, Isle of Jura, Argyllshire
23 May 1946
All the best, George
    CEJL IV 196–197

G.375 To Richard Rees
from Barnhill, Isle of Jura
5 July 1946
Yours, G
    Encounter (January 1962) 62

G.376 To Vernon Richards[188]
from Barnhill, Isle of Jura, Argyllshire
6 August 1946
Yours sincerely, Geo. Orwell
    CEJL IV 197–198

G.377 To Celia Kirwan[189]
from Barnhill, Isle of Jura, Argyllshire
17 August 1946
With love, George
    Mentions 'Politics vs. Literature' [See C.710]
    CEJL IV 198–200

G.378 To George Woodcock
from Barnhill, Isle of Jura, Argyllshire
2 September 1946
Yours, George
    CEJL IV 203–204

G.379 To George Woodcock
from Barnhill, Isle of Jura, Argyllshire
28 September 1946
Yours, George
    Mentions 'James Burnham and the Managerial Revolution', *Keep the Aspidistra Flying* and *A Clergyman's Daughter*
    CEJL IV 204–205

G.380 To Leonard Moore
from 27B Canonbury Square, Islington, London N1
2 November 1946
Yours sincerely, E.A. Blair
    CEJL IV 233–234

G.381 To Dr W.M.C. Harrowes[190]
from 27B Canonbury Square, Islington, London N1

15 November 1946
Yours truly [unsigned]
   Extract Shelden 182–183

1947

G.382 To Rayner Heppenstall
      from 27B Canonbury Square, Islington, N1
      25 January 1947
      Yours, Eric
         On *Animal Farm*
         CEJL IV 275–276

G.383 To Victor Gollancz
      from 27B Canonbury Square, Islington, N1
      14 March 1947
      Yours sincerely, Geo. Orwell
         Mentions *Keep the Aspidistra Flying*, *Coming Up for Air*, and *Animal Farm*
         CEJL IV 307–308

G.384 To Victor Gollancz
      from 27B Canonbury Square, Islington, London N1
      25 March 1947
      Yours sincerely, Geo. Orwell
         Mentions *Nineteen Eighty-Four*
         CEJL IV 308–309

G.385 To Victor Gollancz
      from 27B Canonbury Square, Islington, N1
      9 April 1947
      Yours sincerely, Geo. Orwell
         CEJL IV 326

G.386 To Sonia Brownell[191]
      from Barnhill, Isle of Jura, Argyllshire
      12 April 1947
      With much love, George
         CEJL IV 326–329

G.387 To F.J. Warburg
      from Barnhill, Isle of Jura, Argyllshire
      31 May 1947
      Yours, George
         Mentions *Nineteen Eighty-Four* and 'Such, Such Were the Joys'
         CEJL IV 329–330

G.388 To George Woodcock
      from Barnhill, Isle of Jura, Argyllshire
      18 June 1947
      Yours, George
         Mentions 'How the Poor Die' [See C.714]
         CEJL IV 369–370

G.389 To George Woodcock
      from Barnhill, Isle of Jura, Argyllshire
      9 August 1947
      Yours, George
         Mentions *Nineteen Eighty-Four*
         CEJL IV 376–377

G.390 To Anthony Powell
      from Barnhill, Isle of Jura, Argyllshire
      8 September 1947

Yours, George
> Mentions *Nineteen Eighty-Four*
> *CEJL* IV 377–379

G.391   To Arthur Koestler
from Barnhill, Isle of Jura, Argyllshire
20 September 1947
Yours, George
> Mentions *Animal Farm* and *Nineteen Eighty-Four*
> *CEJL* IV 379–380

G.392   To Julian Symons[192]
from Barnhill, Isle of Jura, Argyllshire
9 October 1947
Yours, Geo. Orwell
> Mentions *The English People*
> *CEJL* IV 380–381

G.393   To Roger Senhouse
from Barnhill, Isle of Jura, Argyllshire
22 October 1947
Yours, George
> On *Coming Up for Air* and *Nineteen Eighty-Four*
> *CEJL* IV 381–382

G.394   To Anthony Powell
from Barnhill, Isle of Jura, Argyllshire
23 October 1947
Yours, George
> Mentions *Nineteen Eighty-Four*
> *CEJL* IV 382–383

G.395   To Julian Symons
from Barnhill, Isle of Jura, Argyllshire
25 October 1947
Yours, George
> *CEJL* IV 383–384

G.396   To Anthony Powell
from Barnhill, Isle of Jura, Argyllshire
29 November 1947
Yours, George
> Mentions *Nineteen Eighty-Four*
> *CEJL* IV 384–385

G.397   To Celia Kirwan
from Barnhill, Isle of Jura, Argyllshire
7 December 1947
With much love, George
> *CEJL* IV 385–386

G.398   To T.R. Fyvel[193]
from Ward 3, Hairmyres Hospital, East Kilbride, Lanarkshire
31 December 1947
Yours, George
> Mentions *Nineteen Eighty-Four*
> *Encounter* (January 1962) 62–63; *CEJL* IV 386–387

1948

G.399   To Gwen O'Shaughnessy[194]
from Ward 3, Hairmyres Hospital, East Kilbride, Nr Glasgow
1 January 1948

Yours, George
CEJL IV 391–392

G.400   To Julian Symons
from Ward 3, Hairmyres Hospital, East Kilbride, Lanarkshire
2 January 1948
Yours, George
Mentions *Nineteen Eighty-Four* and 'In Defence of Comrade Zilliacus' [See I.1001]
CEJL IV 393–394

G.401   To George Woodcock
from Ward 3, Hairmyres Hospital, East Kilbride, Lanarkshire
4 January 1948
Yours, George
CEJL IV 401

G.402   To Celia Kirwan
from Ward 3, Hairmyres Hospital, East Kilbride, Lanarkshire
20 January 1948
With much love, George
CEJL IV 402–403

G.403   To Anthony Powell
from Ward 3, Hairmyres Hospital, East Kilbride, Lanarkshire
25 January 1948
Yours, George
CEJL IV 403–404

G.404   To F. J. Warburg
from Ward 3, Hairmyres Hospital, East Kilbride, Lanarkshire
4 February 1948
Yours, George
Mentions *Nineteen Eighty-Four*
CEJL IV 404

G.405   To John Middleton Murry
from Ward 3, Hairmyres Hospital, East Kilbride, Lanarkshire
5 March 1948
Yours sincerely, Geo. Orwell
CEJL IV 405

G.406   To Julian Symons
from Ward 3, Hairmyres Hospital, East Kilbride, Lanarkshire
21 March 1948
Yours, George
Mentions 'Writers and Leviathan' [See C.783]
CEJL IV 406–407

G.407   To George Woodcock
from Ward 3, Hairmyres Hospital, East Kilbride, Lanarkshire
23 March 1948
Yours, George
CEJL IV 414–415

G.408   To Julian Symons
from Ward 3, Hairmyres Hospital, East Kilbride, Lanarkshire
20 April 1948
Yours, George
Mentions 'George Gissing' [See C.837], *Coming Up for Air*, *Burmese Days* and *Animal Farm*
CEJL IV 415–417

G.409   To Gleb Struve
from Ward 3, Hairmyres Hospital, East Kilbride, Lanarkshire

21 April 1948
Yours sincerely, Geo. Orwell
  Mentions *Burmese Days*
G.410 To George Woodcock
from Ward 3, Hairmyres Hospital, East Kilbride, Lanarkshire
24 April 1948
Yours, George
  Mentions review of *The Soul of Man Under Socialism*
  CEJL IV 418–419
G.411 To Roger Senhouse
[from Hairmyres Hospital]
3 May 1948
Yours, George
  Mentions *Burmese Days*
  CEJL IV 419–420
G.412 To Roger Senhouse
[from Hairmyres Hospital]
Thursday [6? May 1948]
Yours, George
  Mentions *Nineteen Eighty-Four*
  CEJL IV 420–421
G.413 To Julian Symons
from Ward 3, Hairmyres Hospital, East Kilbride, Lanark
10 May 1948
Yours, George
  Mentions *Coming Up for Air*
  CEJL IV 421–423
G.414 To George Woodcock
[from Hairmyres Hospital]
24 May 1948
Yours, George
  CEJL IV 423–424
G.415 To Celia Kirwan
from Ward 3, Hairmyres Hospital, East Kilbride, Lanarkshire
27 May 1948
With love, George
  Mentions *Nineteen Eighty-Four*
  CEJL IV 425–426
G.416 To Anthony Powell
from Ward 3, Hairmyres Hospital, East Kilbride, Lanarkshire
25 June 1948
Yours, George
  Mentions reviews of *The Heart of the Matter*, *The Dawn's Delay*, and
  Nineteen Eighty-Four
  CEJL IV 436–437
G.417 To Julian Symons
from Ward 3, Hairmyres Hospital, East Kilbride, Lanarkshire
10 July 1948
Yours, George
  Mentions review of *Coming Up for Air*, and *Nineteen Eighty-Four*, 'George
  Gissing' [See C.837]
  CEJL IV 437–439
G.418 To F.J. Warburg
from Barnhill, Isle of Jura, Argyllshire
29 October 1948

Yours, George
> Mentions *Nineteen Eighty-Four*
> *CEJL* IV 449–452

G.419   To Anthony Powell
from Barnhill, Isle of Jura, Argyllshire
15 November 1948
Yours, George
> Mentions *Nineteen Eighty-Four*
> *CEJL* IV 454–455

G.420   To Gwen O'Shaughnessy
from Barnhill, Isle of Jura, Argyllshire
28 November 1948
Yours, George
> Mentions *Nineteen Eighty-Four*
> *CEJL* IV 458

G.421   To T.R. Fyvel
from Barnhill, Isle of Jura, Argyllshire
18 December 1948
Yours, George
> *Encounter* (January 1962) 63

G.422   To F.J. Warburg
from Barnhill
21 December 1948
Love to all, George
> Mentions *Nineteen Eighty-Four*
> *CEJL* IV 459

G.423   To Roger Senhouse
from Barnhill, Isle of Jura, Argyll.
26 December 1948
Love to all, George
> Mentions *Nineteen Eighty-Four*
> *CEJL* IV 460

1949

G.424   To Reginald Reynolds
from The Cotswold Sanatorium, Cranham, Glos.
17 January 1949
Yours, George
> *CEJL* IV 471

G.425   To Richard Rees
from Cranham
28 January 1949
Yours, Eric
> Mentions *Nineteen Eighty-Four*
> *CEJL* IV 472–473

G.426   To Julian Symons
from The Cotswold Sanatorium, Cranham, Glos.
2 February 1949
Yours, George
> Mentions *Nineteen Eighty-Four* and 'George Gissing' [See C.837]
> *CEJL* IV 474–475

G.427   To Julian Symons
from The Cotswold Sanatorium, Cranham, Glos.
4 February 1949

Yours, George
Mentions *Nineteen Eighty-Four*
CEJL IV 475–476

G.428   To Richard Rees
from The Cotswold Sanatorium, Cranham, Glos.
4 February 1949
Yours, Eric
CEJL IV 476–477

G.429   To Jacintha Buddicom[195]
from The Cotswold Sanatorium, Cranham, Glos
14.2.49
Yours, Eric Blair
Typewritten
Buddicom 149–151

G.430   To Jacintha Buddicom
from Cranham
Tuesday [15 February 1949 from postmark Gloucester]
Farewell and Hail, Eric
Buddicom 151–152. Photograph in Buddicom

G.431   To Richard Rees
from Cranham
3 March 1949
Yours, Eric
Mentions review of *Dickens: His Character, Comedy and Career* [See C.817]
Encounter (January 1962) 63–64; *CEJL* IV 478–479

G.432   To Michael Meyer
from The Cotswold Sanatorium, Cranham, Glos.
12 March 1949
Yours, George
Mentions *Nineteen Eighty-Four*
CEJL IV 480–481

G.433   To Julian Symons
from Cranham
15 March 1949
Yours, George
CEJL IV 481–482

G.434   To Richard Rees
from Cranham
16 March 1949
Yours, Eric
Mentions *Nineteen Eighty-Four*
CEJL IV 482–483

G.435   To Leonard Moore
from The Cotswold Sanatorium, Cranham, Glos.
17 March 1949
Yours sincerely, Eric Blair
On *Nineteen Eighty-Four*
CEJL IV 483–484

G.436   To Richard Rees
from Cranham
18 March 1949
Yours, Eric
Mentions 'Reflections on Gandhi' [See C.808]
CEJL IV 484–485

G.437   To F.J. Warburg
        from Cranham
        30 March 1949
        Yours, George
            CEJL IV 485–486

G.438   To Richard Rees
        from Cranham
        31 March 1949
        Yours, Eric
            Mentions 'Reflections on Gandhi' [See C.808] 'Lear, Tolstoy and the Fool' [See
            C.753], and *Nineteen Eighty-Four*

G.439   To Richard Rees
        from Cranham
        8 April 1949
        Love to all, Eric
            Mentions *Nineteen Eighty-Four*
            CEJL IV 487–488

G.440   To Robert Giroux[196]
        from The Cotswold Sanitorium, Cranham, Glos.
        14 April 1949
        Yours sincerely, Geo. Orwell
            Mentions *Nineteen Eighty-Four* and 'Lear, Tolstoy and the Fool' [See C.753]
            CEJL IV 495

G.441   To T.R. Fyvel
        from Cranham
        15 April 1949
        Yours, George
            Encounter (January 1962) 64–65; *CEJL* IV 496–497

G.442   To Richard Rees
        from Cranham
        25 April 1949
        Yours, Eric
            CEJL IV 498

G.443   To Anthony Powell
        from Cranham
        11 May 1949
        Yours, George
            CEJL IV 499

G.444   To F.J. Warburg
        from Cranham
        16 May 1949
        Yours, George
            Mentions *Nineteen Eighty-Four*
            CEJL IV 500

G.445   To Jacintha Buddicom
        from Cranham Lodge, Cranham, Gloucestershire
        22 May 1949
        Yours, [indecipherable]
            Buddicom 156. Photograph in Buddicom

G.446   To Richard Rees
        from Cranham Lodge, Cranham, Gloucestershire
        1 June 1949
        Yours, G
            Encounter (January 1962) 65

G.447 To Anthony Powell
from Cranham Lodge, Cranham, Gloucester
6 June 1949
Yours, George
CEJL IV 501

G.448 To Francis A. Henson[197]
[16 June 1949]
On *Nineteen Eighty-Four*
Extract from two letters *CEJL* IV 502

G.449 To Julian Symons
from Cranham Lodge, Cranham, Gloucester
16 June 1949
Yours, George
Mentions *Nineteen Eighty-Four*
CEJL IV 502–503

G.450 To Vernon Richards
from Cranham Lodge, Cranham, Gloucester
22 June 1949
Yours, George
Mentions *Nineteen Eighty-Four*
CEJL IV 503–504

G.451 To Richard Rees
from Cranham Lodge, Cranham, Gloucester
28 July 1949
Yours, Eric
Mentions *Nineteen Eighty-Four*
Encounter (January 1962) 65; *CEJL* IV 504–505

G.452 To F.J. Warburg
from Cranham Lodge, Cranham, Gloucester
22 August 1949
Love to all, George
Mentions *Burmese Days*, *Coming Up for Air* and 'George Gissing' [See C.837]

G.453 To Philip Rahv
from Room 65, Private Wing, University College Hospital, Gower Street, London WC1
17 September 1949
Yours sincerely, Geo. Orwell
Mentions review of *Nineteen Eighty-Four*
CEJL IV 163

G.454 To Julian Symons
from Room 65, Private Wing, UC Hospital, Gower Street, WC1
[17? September 1949]
Yours, George
CEJL IV 507–508

G.455 To Leonard Moore
from Room 65, Private Wing, UC Hospital
11 October 1949
Yours sincerely, Eric Blair
Mentions *Nineteen Eighty-Four*
CEJL IV 508

G.456 To T.R. Fyvel
from Room 65, Private Wing, UC Hospital
25 October 1949
Yours, George
CEJL IV 508–509

Notes to G

1 Letter to Jack Common, 29 September 1938. *CEJL* I 354.
2 Ida Mabel Blair, née Limouzin (1875–1943), Orwell's mother.
3 The mother of Orwell's childhood friends Jacintha, Guinever and Prosper Buddicom.
4 Later Sir Steven Runciman, the historian. He was at Eton with Orwell.
5 Jacintha's brother, and Orwell's childhood friend.
6 Max Plowman (1883–1941) was currently the Editor. He worked on *The Adelphi* from 1929–1941.
7 Orwell had known Collings since 1921 in Southwold, where his father was the Blairs' family doctor.
8 T.S. Eliot was a director of Faber & Faber, the publishers, at this time.
9 Leonard Moore, of Christy and Moore, was Orwell's literary agent from this time until Orwell's death.
10 Eleanor Jaques (1906–1962) had moved to Southwold, with her family, from Canada in 1921. At one time they lived next door to the Blairs. She and Orwell had a brief affair in 1932. She married Dennis Collings in 1934.
11 Brenda Salkeld worked as a teacher in a girls' school at Southwold, where she and Orwell met in 1928. They remained friends until his death.
12 Rayner Heppenstall, novelist, poet and critic, met Orwell in 1935 through Richard Rees. He and Orwell shared a flat at this address in Lawford Road in 1935.
13 Orwell and Cyril Connolly met at St Cyprian's School at Eastbourne, and they were later at Eton together. Connolly became an author and critic, and editor of *Horizon*. Orwell once said, 'Without Connolly's help I don't think I would have got started as a writer when I came back from Burma.' [*CEJL* I 162].
14 Norman Collins was a popular novelist; from 1934–1941 he was Deputy Chairman of Victor Gollancz Ltd, the publishers; and Controller of the BBC Light Programme 1946–1947.
15 Later Sir Richard Rees, painter, author and critic. He and Orwell met while he was editor of *The Adelphi* from 1930–1936, and they remained close friends until Orwell's death. He was Orwell's literary executor.
16 Jack Common was a writer and editor. He joined *The Adelphi* in 1930 as a sales promoter. He was assistant editor in 1932 and editor from 1935–1936. He and Orwell remained friends until Orwell's death.
17 John Lehmann, writer and publisher, was younger than Orwell but they were at Eton for a while together. He founded the anti-Fascist *New Writing*.
18 Geoffrey Gorer, social anthropologist and writer. He admired *Burmese Days* and wrote to Orwell. They remained friends until Orwell's death.
19 Anthony Powell, novelist. He wrote to Orwell about *Keep the Aspidistra Flying*. They met in 1941 and remained friends.
20 Denys King-Farlow was at Eton with Orwell. Together they produced the *Election Times*. He became a successful international businessman.
21 Henry Miller, novelist and friend of Orwell's.
22 James Hanley, novelist and short story writer.
23 Eileen Blair (1905–1945), née O'Shaughnessy, Orwell's first wife. They met while she was studying for her MA in psychology at University College, London. They were married in 1936. She died in 1945, less than a year after they had adopted their son, Richard.
24 Victor Gollancz (1893–1967), the publisher.
25 Raymond Mortimer, critic. He was at this time literary editor of the *New Statesman and Nation*.
26 Alec Houghton Joyce, Information Officer at the Indian Office.
27 Stephen Spender, the poet and critic.
28 John Sceats was an insurance agent who also wrote for the socialist magazine *Controversy*, which later became *Left Forum*, then *Left*.
29 Jellinek had written a book about the Spanish civil war, which Orwell had reviewed [See C.131].
30 Herbert Read, poet and critic of art and literature.
31 Wife of Richard Rees.
32 David H. Thomson, Deputy Regional Officer, National Council of Social Service.
33 Humphry House (1908–1955), literary scholar, Fellow of Wadham College, Oxford.
34 Sacheverell Sitwell, brother of Edith and Osbert. Poet.
35 James Laughlin, American writer and editor, and publisher of New Directions books.
36 A Congregationalist minister. See A.9.
37 Widow of Max Plowman, who had just died.
38 M.J. Tambimuttu, Sinhalese poet, founded and edited *Poetry London*.

39 Bahadur Singh, from Trinidad, had been President of the Oxford Union Society and he was this time broadcasting for the BBC.
40 Mulk Raj Anand, Indian novelist and critic, broadcast for the Indian Section of the BBC.
41 Hsiao Ch'ien, Chinese writer and critic, was broadcasting for the BBC at this time.
42 J.F. Horrabin (1884–1962), journalist, illustrator, map-maker and left-wing Socialist. He was broadcasting for the BBC at this time.
43 Arthur Calder-Marshall worked at the Film Division of the Ministry of Information, and was then broadcasting for the BBC.
44 C.H. Waddington (1901–1975) was currently broadcasting for the BBC. He was later Professor of Animal Genetics at the University of Edinburgh.
45 Parliamentary Correspondent of the Indian Section of the BBC.
46 Professor at Birkbeck College, broadcasting for the BBC at this time on science and Soviet topics.
47 Joseph Needham, Cambridge scientist, currently broadcasting for the BBC.
48 Lady Grigg, wife of Sir James Grigg Secretary of State for War, was broadcasting for the BBC at this time.
49 L.F. Rushbrook-Williams, Eastern Services Director at the BBC.
50 Amabel Williams-Ellis, writer and broadcaster on women and war work.
51 E.M. Forster, the novelist, was currently broadcasting for the BBC Eastern Section.
52 Reginald Reynolds (1905–1958) writer and broadcaster on India. He edited *British Pamphleteers* with Orwell [See B.31].
53 J.B.S. Haldane (1892–1964), geneticist, was then broadcasting for the BBC.
54 C.D. Darlington, scientist, was currently broadcasting for the BBC.
55 E. Rowan-Davies worked for the BBC Eastern Section.
56 Richard Morris Titmuss (1907–1973), writer on social issues, including poverty, was at this time broadcasting for the BBC. He later became Professor of Social Administration at the London School of Economics.
57 Frank Brown had edited the *Indian Daily Telegraph*. He was at this time on the editorial staff of *The Times*, and also broadcasting for the BBC.
58 Michael Foot, later a socialist politician, was at this time editor of the *Evening Standard*.
59 T.C. Worsley, schoolmaster and writer, occasionally broadcast for the BBC at this time.
60 Laurence F. Easterbrook, writer on agriculture, occasionally broadcast for the BBC.
61 G.M. Young (1882–1959) historian and educationalist, occasionally broadcast for the BBC at this time.
62 Vida Hope, actress, who read poems and did other recitations on the BBC at this time.
63 Henry Treece (1911–1966) poet and editor of *Kingdom Come*, a wartime poetry magazine.
64 Inez Holden (1906–1974) novelist.
65 Vatake Kurnpath Narayana Menon, author, occasionally broadcast for the BBC.
66 Lord Winterton (1883–1962) politician, formerly Under-Secretary for India.
67 Peggotty Freeman worked for the University Labour Federation in Cambridge.
68 Harold Laski (1893–1950), Professor of Political Science at the London School of Economics.
69 L.A.G. Strong, writer and poetry editor, occasionally broadcast for the BBC at this time.
70 Martin Armstrong, writer and occasional broadcaster for the BBC.
71 Joseph Albert Lauwerys (1902–1981) writer on education and the use of English.
72 Ritchie Calder (1906–1982) scientific journalist and broadcaster. Orwell had edited his *Searchlight* book, *The Lesson of London*. [See B.7].
73 Desmond Hawkins, BBC writer and broadcaster.
74 Keidrych Rhys, poet, occasionally broadcast for the BBC at this time.
75 Miss B.H. Alexander worked for the BBC Copyright department.
76 Norman Marshall (1901–1980) writer and broadcaster on the theatre.
77 Edmund Blunden, poet, man of letters and editor, occasionally broadcast for the BBC.
78 C.K. Ogden, inventor of the 'Basic English' language.
79 John Beavan, News Editor of *The Observer*.
80 A.L.C. Bullock, BBC European Talks Director.
81 Harry W. Todd worked for the Film Department at the British Council in London.
82 H.D. Graves-Law worked for the Middle East section of the Ministry of Information. Orwell needed their permission to broadcast a script.
83 James Stephens (1880–1950), the Irish writer, broadcast for the BBC.
84 Arthur Wynn, Musical Bookings Manager at the BBC.
85 Osbert Sitwell (1892–1969), novelist and poet, occasionally broadcast for the BBC at this time.
86 Eleanor Florence Rathbone (1872–1946), MP and social activist, occasionally broadcast for the BBC.

87 Wilfrid Roberts, MP, occasionally broadcast for the BBC at this time.
88 William Plomer, writer and editor, occasionally broadcast for the BBC at this time.
89 E.C. Bowyer worked for the Aircraft Manufacturers' Association, and occasionally broadcast for the BBC.
90 Alexander Comfort, medical biologist, poet, novelist and editor.
91 Dr C.M. Fletcher occasionally broadcast for the BBC at this time on medical and scientific subjects.
92 Philip Rahv, American critic, and founding editor of the *Partisan Review*.
93 Ivor Brown (1891–1974), author and journalist, editor of *The Observer*.
94 Gleb Struve, Russian writer and critic, later Professor of Slavic Languages, University of California at Berkeley.
95 Roy Fuller, poet and novelist.
96 John Middleton Murry (1889–1957), writer, critic, founder of *The Adelphi*, and later editor of *Peace News*.
97 Frank Barber, journalist, at this time assistant editor of the *Leeds Weekly Citizen*.
98 Roger Senhouse, a director of Secker & Warburg.
99 Lydia Jackson, writer under the name Elisaveta Fen.
100 Fredric J. Warburg, the publisher.
101 The Duchess of Atholl (1874–1960), Unionist MP and government minister.
102 Arthur Koestler, the essayist and novelist.
103 The Rev. Herbert Rogers, Chaplain to St Mungo's School, Ayrshire.
104 Miss F. Tennyson Jesse, novelist and journalist.
105 A.S.F. Gow, classical scholar, Orwell's teacher at Eton, later a Fellow of Trinity College, Cambridge.
106 Stafford Cottman, local government clerk, had fought in Spain with Orwell.
107 Michael Meyer, author and translator.
108 Vernon Richards, civil engineer, journalist and anarchist. Editor of magazines including *War Commentary* which later became *Freedom*, the anarchist newspaper.
109 Celia Kirwan was at this time editorial assistant on *Polemic*.
110 Dr W.M.C. Harrowes was an interested reader who had written to Orwell about *Burmese Days*.
111 Sonia Brownell was at this time editorial secretary of *Horizon*. She became Orwell's second wife in 1949.
112 Julian Symons, the poet, novelist and editor.
113 Tosco Fyvel, editor and journalist, at this time literary editor of *Tribune*. He was joint editor of the *Searchlight* books with Orwell.
114 Dr Gwen O'Shaughnessy was the widow of Eileen Blair's brother, Laurence.
115 Jacintha Buddicom, Orwell's childhood friend.
116 Robert Giroux, an editor at Harcourt, Brace, the American publishers.
117 Francis A. Henson, an American who worked for the United Automobile Workers and wrote to Orwell about *Nineteen Eighty-Four*. The original of the letter is lost but two extracts were published in *Life* (25 July 1949) and the *New York Times Book Review* (31 July 1949) [See C.821 and C.822]. *CEJL* prints an amalgam of the two.

H: Poems

I dreamed I dwelt in Marble halls,
And woke to find it true;
I wasn't born for an age like this;
Was Smith? Was Jones? Were you?[1]

A few of Orwell's poems were published in his lifetime and therefore also appear in other sections of this bibliography, for example, as periodical publications, as noted, and further publication notes are given there. Others appear either in whole or in part in biographies and various secondary works.

H.001   'Awake! Young Men of England', *The Henley and South Oxfordshire Standard* (2 October 1914) [See C.001].
    Notes
    Written September 1914.
    Stansky and Abrahams[2] 61, Buddicom[3] 36, Crick[4] 36, fragment in Shelden[5] 42.

H.002   'Kitchener', *The Henley and South Oxfordshire Standard* (21 July 1916) [See C.002].
    Notes
    Stansky & Abrahams 75–76, Buddicom 37, Crick 38, fragment in Shelden 47.

H.003   'The Pagan'
    Notes
    Written autumn 1918 and sent to Jacintha Buddicom.
    Autograph rough copy in Orwell Archive. Photograph of rough copy in Buddicom. Jacintha's copy was destroyed by a land mine in Chelsea in October 1940.
    Surviving MS 2ff – 1 blank [1918–1919]. Orwell Archive.
    Buddicom 71, Crick 57, and Shelden 66.

H.004   [fragment of ribald song] 'Then up waddled Wog'
    Notes
    Written c. 1918.
    In Denys King-Farlow, 'College Days with George Orwell', MS c1967. Five typed pages in Orwell Archive, Reminiscences.
    Crick 58.

H.005   'The Wounded Cricketer (Not by Walt Whitman)', *The Election Times* No. 4 (3 June 1918) 61 [See C.007].
    Notes
    Unsigned.
    Handwritten by Eric Blair.
    Reprinted in *College Days* No. 5 (9 July 1920) 136. Unsigned.

H.006   Two stanzas of 'The Youthful Mariner', *The Election Times* No. 4 (3 June 1918) 62 [See C.008].
    Notes
    Unsigned.
    Handwritten by Eric Blair.
    Reprinted in *College Days* No. 5 (9 July 1920) 156, 158. Unsigned.

H.007   'Our minds are married, but we are too young'
    Notes
    Given to Jacintha Buddicom, Christmas 1918.
    Buddicom 87, Crick 61, fragment in Shelden 67.

H.008   'After Twelve', *College Days* No. 4 (1 April 1919) 104 [See C.015].
         Notes
         Unsigned.
H.009   'Ode to Field Days', *College Days* No. 4 (1 April 1919) 114 [See C.016].
         Notes
         Fragment in Crick 70.
H.010   'To A.R.H.B.', *College Days* No. 2 (27 June 1919) 42 [See C.009].
         Notes
         Unsigned.
         College Days was a printed publication produced by Eton scholars.
         A.R.H.B. was A. Roland Hanbury Bateman, an Eton scholar.
H.011   'Wall Game', *College Days* No. 3 (29 November 1919) 78 [See C.011].
         Notes
         Unsigned.
H.012   'The Photographer', *College Days* No. 5 (9 July 1920) 130 [See C.020].
         Notes
         College Days was an Eton College magazine, sometimes published by Eric
         Blair and Denys King-Farlow.
         Fragment in Crick 70.
H.013   'Friendship and love are closely intertwined'
         Notes
         Given to Jacintha Buddicom summer 1921.
         Buddicom 117, Crick 72, Shelden 84.
H.014   'The Lesser Evil'
         Notes
         Written between 1922 and 1927 in Burma, or shortly after his return to
         England in 1927, on Burma Government writing paper.
         Crick 92.
         Typescript with MS corrections in Orwell Archive, 2ff.
H.015   'Romance'
         Notes
         Written between 1922 and 1927 in Burma, or shortly after his return to
         England in 1927, on Burma Government writing paper.
         Crick 93, and Shelden 99.
         Typescript with MS corrections in Orwell Archive, 1f.
H.016   'When the Franks have lost their sway'
         Notes
         Written between 1922 and 1927 in Burma, or shortly after his return to
         England in 1927, on Burma Government writing paper.
         Crick 99–100.
         MS in Orwell Archive, 1f.
H.017   'Here lie the bones of poor John Flory'.
         Notes
         Written winter 1927–28 or 1928–29 [See Crick 118].
         In a fragment of twenty-one pages of manuscript, perhaps an early draft of a
         version of what became *Burmese Days*.
         Crick 119.
H.018   'Sometimes in the middle autumn days', *The Adelphi* Vol. 5, No. 6 (March 1933)
         410 [See C.053].
         Notes
         Signed: Eric Blair.
         CEJL I 118.
H.019   'Summer-like for an instant the autumn sun bursts out', *The Adelphi* Vol. 6, No.
         2 (May 1933) 102 [See C.055].

> *Notes*
> Signed: Eric Blair.

H.020 'A dressed man and a naked man', *The Adelphi* Vol. 7, No. 1 (October 1933) 47–48 [See C.057].

> *Notes*
> Signed: Eric Blair.
> *CEJL* I 123–125.

H.021 'On a Ruined Farm near the His Master's Voice Gramophone Factory', *The Adelphi* Vol. 8, No. 1 (April 1934) 35–36 [See C.060].

> *Notes*
> Signed: Eric Blair.
> Thomas Moult, ed. *The Best Poems of 1934* 113–114 [B.1].
> *CEJL* I 134–135.
> Fragment in Crick 152.

H.022 'St Andrew's Day, 1935', *The Adelphi* Vol. 11, No. 2 (November 1935) 86 [See C.071].

> *Notes*
> Also published, without title and with six minor changes, in *Keep the Aspidistra Flying*, Chapter 7.

H.023 'A happy vicar I might have been', *The Adelphi* Vol. 13, No. 3 (December 1936) 173 [See C.095].

> *Notes*
> Written at the end of 1935 [See *CEJL* I 4].
> Quoted in full in the essay, 'Why I Write', first published in *Gangrel* No. 4 (Summer 1946), which was reprinted as follows:
> *Such, Such Were the Joys*
> *England Your England*
> *The Orwell Reader*
> *Collected Essays*
> *CEJL* I 4–5.
> Fragments in Crick 193, and Shelden 221–222.

H.024 'The Italian soldier shook my hand', in 'Looking Back on the Spanish War', sections of which were first published in *New Road* (1943) [See B.20].

> *Notes*
> Written late 1930s.
> 'Looking Back on the Spanish War' reprinted as follows:
> *Such, Such Were the Joys*
> *England Your England*
> *Collected Essays*
> *CEJL* II 249–267
> Last stanza in Shelden 199.

H.025 'As One Non-Combatant To Another: A Letter to "Obadiah Hornbooke"', *Tribune* (18 June 1943) 18–19 [See C.347].

> *Notes*
> In reply to Alex Comfort's poem, 'Letter to An American Visitor', *Tribune* (4 June 1943) 18–19.
> Both poems are reprinted in *CEJL* II 294–303.
> Fragment in Crick 300.

H.026 'Memories of the Blitz', *Tribune* (21 January 1944) 18 [See C.381].

> *Notes*
> Completed 17 January 1944.
> Payment 10s 6d.

H.027 'The Little Apocalypse of Obadiah Hornbrook', *Tribune* (30 June 1944) 19 [See C.437].

H.028   "'Twas on a Tuesday morning'
       Notes
       Fragments of an unfinished poem in a 1948 notebook, first published in Crick
       4–5.

Notes to H

1 See H.023.
2 Peter Stansky and William Abrahams *The Unknown Orwell* (New York: Alfred A. Knopf, 1972).
3 Jacintha Buddicom *Eric and Us A Remembrance of George Orwell* (London: Leslie Frewin, 1974).
4 Bernard Crick *George Orwell A Life* (London: Secker & Warburg, 1980).
5 Michael Shelden *Orwell The Authorised Biography* (London: Heinemann, 1991).

I: Unpublished materials

... there has literally been not one day in which I did not feel that I was idling, that I was behind with the current job, and that my total output was miserably small. Even at periods when I was working ten hours a day on a book, or turning out four or five articles a week, I have never been able to get away from this neurotic feeling, that I was wasting time! (Extract from manuscript notebook written in 1949. *CEJL* IV 510–511.)

The publication of the concluding volumes of the *Complete Works* will remove most of the following items from the 'Unpublished' category. Ian Angus and Peter Davison generously allowed me to see the proofs of those volumes, and I therefore include here Davison's enumeration at the end of each line: D=Davison followed by the number he has assigned to the item. These numbers run on from volume to volume and I have not, therefore, noted his volume breaks. Where not otherwise noted, originals or copies of items are in the Orwell Archive.

I.001	Letter to Ida Blair, 14 September 1911. D2
I.002	Letter to Ida Blair, 8 October 1911. D3
I.003	Letter to Ida Blair, 5 November 1911. D4
I.004	Letter to Ida Blair, 12 November [1911]. D5
I.005	Letter to Ida Blair, [November 1911?]. D6
I.006	Letter to Ida Blair, [November 1911?]. D7
I.007	Letter to Ida Blair, 2 December [1911]. D8
I.008	Letter to Ida Blair, 4 February 1912. D9
I.009	Letter to Ida Blair, 11 February 1912. D10
I.010	Letter to Ida Blair, 3 March 1912. D12
I.011	Letter to Ida Blair, 10 March 1912. D13
I.012	Letter to Ida Blair, 17 March 1912. D14
I.013	Letter to Ida Blair, 12 May 1912. D15
I.014	Letter to Ida Blair, 2 June 1912. D16
I.015	Letter to Ida Blair, 23 June 1912. D17
I.016	Letter to Ida Blair, 30 June 1912. D18
I.017	Letter to Ida Blair, 21 July 1912. D19
I.018	Letter to Ida Blair, 17 November 1912. D20
I.019	Letter to Ida Blair, 1 December 1912. D21
I.020	Letter to Ida Blair, 8 December 1912. D22
I.021	Criticism of Cyril Connolly's Poem 'Kitchener', [c10–16 July 1916]. D25
I.022	Letter to Ida Blair, [mid-July 1916?]. D26
I.023	Short story, 'The Vernon Murders' [1916–1918?]. D27. MS in ink and pencil in green notebook. 32 pp.
I.024	Play, 'The Man and the Maid' [1916–1918?]. D28. MS marked by Orwell: masterpiece ii. 26ff.
I.025	Inscription in *Paradise Lost*, 'E.A. Blair K.S.' [c1919]. D36
I.026	Letter to Mrs Laura Buddicom, 27 June 1920. D48
I.027	Letter to Steven Runciman, August 1920. D56
I.028	Letter to Prosper Buddicom, 28 [December 1920]. D57
I.029	Letter to Prosper Buddicom, [10 January 1921]. D58
I.030	Letter to Prosper Buddicom, 19 January 1921. D59
I.031	Extract from letter to Cyril Connolly, Easter 1921.
I.032	'Mrs Puffin and the Missing Matches', [c1919–22]. D60. Short story. MS 2ff.

I.033   Poem, 'Dear Friend: allow me for a little while'. [1922– 1927?]. D63. MS 1f.

I.034   Poem, 'Romance', [1922–1927?]. D64

I.035   Poem, 'When the Franks have lost their sway', [1922–1927?]. D65

I.036   Poem, 'My love and I walked in the dark', [1922–1927?]. D66, MS 1f.

I.037   Poem, 'Suggested by a toothpaste advertisement', [1922–1927?]. D67. Surviving typescript. 1f [1918–1919].

I.038   Poem, 'The lesser evil' [1922–1927?]. D68

I.039   Preliminary sketch for Burmese Days, [John Flory: My Epitaph], [1927–1930?] D70

I.040   Preliminary sketch for *Burmese Days*. [Preliminary to Autobiography, beginning:] 'I said at the end of the last chapter', [1927–1930?]. D71

I.041   Preliminary sketch for *Burmese Days*, [The Autobiography of John Flory], [1925–1930?]. D72

I.042   Preliminary sketch for *Burmese Days*, [An Incident in Rangoon, beginning:] 'Here for awhile [sic] I abandon autobiography', [1927–1930?]. D73

I.043   Preliminary sketch for *Burmese Days*. [A Rebuke to the Author, John Flory], [1927–1930?]. D74

I.044   Scenario and Dialogues from play associated with *Burmese Day*, ['Francis Stone'], [c1927–1928]. D75

I.045   'A Short Story', [c1928–1929?]. D77. Typescript in Orwell Archive, 2ff.

I.046   Letter to the Editor, *The New Adelphi*, 22 September 1929. D86
        (Max Plowman (1883–1941), journalist and author, worked at *The Adelphi* from 1929 until his death, and encouraged Orwell in his early professional writing career.)

I.047   Letter to the Editor, *The New Adelphi*, 12 December 1929. D87

I.048   Letter to Max Plowman, 24 October 1930. D92

I.049   Letter to Max Plowman, 1 November 1930. D93

I.050   Letter to Max Plowman, [12 January 1931]. D95

I.051   Letter to Brenda Salkeld, [July 1931]. D100

I.052   Letter to Dennis Collings, 16 August 1931. D102

I.053   Letter to Dennis Collings, [27 August 1931]. D104

I.054   Diary 27 August-9 September 1931. D105

I.055   Letter to Dennis Collings, 4 September 1931. D106

I.056   Diary 9 September 1931. D107

I.057   Letter to Dennis Collings, [12 October 1931]. D108

I.058   Letter to Christy & Moore, [after 12 October 1931]. D109

I.059   Extract from letter to Brenda Salkeld, [October 1931?]. D110

I.060   Letter to T.S. Eliot, 30 October 1931. D112

I.061   Letter to T.S. Eliot, 4 November 1931. D113

I.062   Letter to Brenda Salkeld, [November or December 1931]. D114

I.063   Letter to Leonard Moore, 6 January 1932. D115

I.064   Postcard to T.S. Eliot, [17 February 1932]. D116

I.065   Letter to Leonard Moore, 26 April 1932. D118

I.066   Letter to Leonard Moore, 10 June 1932. D122

I.067   Letter to Eleanor Jaques, [14 June 1932]. D123

I.068   Letter to Eleanor Jaques, [19 June 1932]. D124

I.069   Letter to Leonard Moore, 1 July 1932. D126

I.070   Letter to Leonard Moore, 6 July 1932. D127

I.071   Letter to Eleanor Jaques, [8 July 1932]. D128

I.072   Letter to Leonard Moore, 4 August 1932. D130

I.073   Letter to Leonard Moore, 12 August 1932. D131

I.074   Letter to Eleanor Jaques, [18 August 1932]. D132

I.075   Letter to Brenda Salkeld, [September 1932]. D136

I.076   Letter to Eleanor Jaques, [19 September 1932]. D137

I.077   Letter to Eleanor Jaques, [19 October 1932]. D139

I.078   Letter to Leonard Moore, 15 November 1932. D140

I.079   Letter to Eleanor Jaques, 18 November 1932. D141

I.080   Letter to Leonard Moore, [19 November 1932]. D142
I.081   Postcard to Leonard Moore, 21 November 1932. D143
I.082   Letter to Eleanor Jaques, [22 November 1932]. D144
I.083   Letter to Eleanor Jaques, [30 November 1932]. D145
I.084   Letter to Eleanor Jaques, [13 December 1932]. D146
I.085   Letter to Eleanor Jaques, [19 December 1932]. D147
I.086   Play, 'King Charles II', [September-December 1932]. D148
I.087   Letter to Leonard Moore, [23 December 1932]. D149
I.088   Letter to Leonard Moore, 24 December 1932. D150
I.089   Letter to Leonard Moore, 17 January 1933. D158
I.090   Letter to Eleanor Jaques, 18 February 1933. D161
I.091   Letter to Leonard Moore, 21 February 1933. D162
I.092   List of books recommended to Brenda Salkeld in the 1930s. D166
I.093   Letter to Leonard Moore, 25 March 1933. D167
I.094   Letter to Leonard Moore, 7 April 1933. D169
I.095   Letter to Leonard Moore, [29 April 1933]. D170
I.096   Letter to Leonard Moore, [4 May 1933]. D172
I.097   Letter to Eleanor Jaques, [6 June 1933]. D175
I.098   Letter to Leonard Moore, [16 June 1933]. D177
I.099   Letter to Leonard Moore, [1 August 1933]. D181
I.100   Letter to Leonard Moore, 17 October 1933. D183
I.101   Letter to Leonard Moore, 4 January 1934. D188
I.102   Letter to Leonard Moore, 16 January 1934. D189
I.103   Letter to Leonard Moore, 2 February 1934. D191
I.104   Letter to Leonard Moore, [15 February 1934]. D193
I.105   Letter to Leonard Moore, 12 March 1934. D195
I.106   Letter to Leonard Moore, 25 April 1934. D199
I.107   Letter to Leonard Moore, 2 May 1934. D200
I.108   Letter to Leonard Moore, 10 September 1934. D206
I.109   Letter to Brenda Salkeld, [11 September? 1934]. D207
I.110   Letter to Leonard Moore, [23 September 1934]. D208
I.111   Letter to Leonard Moore, 9 October 1934. D210
I.112   Letter to Leonard Moore, [20 October 1934]. D213
I.113   Letter to Leonard Moore, 20 November 1934. D216
I.114   Letter to Leonard Moore, 10 December 1934. D218
I.115   Letter to Victor Gollancz, 17 December 1934. D219
I.116   Letter to Leonard Moore, 24 December 1934. D220
I.117   Letter to Leonard Moore, 28 December 1934. D221
I.118   Letter to Leonard Moore, 9 January 1935. D222
I.119   Letter to Victor Gollancz, 10 January 1935. D223
I.120   Letter to Brenda Salkeld, [15 January 1935]. D224
I.121   Letter to Leonard Moore, 31 January 1935. D226
I.122   Letter to Victor Gollancz, 1 February 1935. D227
I.123   Letter to Victor Gollancz, 1 February 1935. D228
I.124   Postcard to Victor Gollancz, 2 February 1935. D229
I.125   Postcard to Leonard Moore, 2 February 1935. D230
I.126   Postcard to Victor Gollancz, 4 February 1935. D231
I.127   Postcard to Victor Gollancz, [6 February 1935]. D232
I.128   Letter to Victor Gollancz, 14 February 1935. D233
I.129   Letter to Leonard Moore, 14 February 1935. D234
I.130   Telegram to Victor Gollancz, 19 February 1935. D236
I.131   Letter to Leonard Moore, 22 February 1935. D238
I.132   Letter to Victor Gollancz, 28 February 1935. D239
I.133   Postcard to Christy & Moore Ltd, 1 March 1935. D241
I.134   Letter to Leonard Moore, 27 March 1935. D243

I.135   Letter to Leonard Moore, 13 April 1935. D244
I.136   Letter to Brenda Salkeld, 7 May [1935]. D245
I.137   Letter to Leonard Moore, 14 May 1935. D246
I.138   Letter to Leonard Moore, 15 July 1935. D247
I.139   Letter to Christy & Moore, 4 August 1935. D150
I.140   Letter to Leonard Moore, 6 September 1935. D251
I.141   Letter to Leonard Moore, 12 September 1935. D252
I.142   Letter to Leonard Moore, 30 September 1935. D255
I.143   Report on lecture 'Confessions of a Down and Out'. Lecture to the South Woodford Literary Society, 16 October 1935. Report is in *The Woodford Times* (25 October 1935). D258
I.144   Letter to Rayner Heppenstall, [18 October 1935]. D259
I.145   Letter to Leonard Moore, [26 October 1935]. D260
I.146   Letter to Leonard Moore, 8 November 1935. D262
I.147   Postcard to Leonard Moore, 17 January 1936. D264
I.148   Letter to Victor Gollancz, 23 January 1936. D268
I.149   Letter to Dorothy Horsman, [31 January 1936]. D269
I.150   *The Road to Wigan Pier* Diary, 31 January-25 March 1936. D272, 274, 276, 278, 282, 285, 287, 289, 291, 294, 296
I.151   Letter to Christy & Moore, 11 February 1936. D273
I.152   Letter to Leonard Moore, 13 February 1936. D275
I.153   Telegram to Gollancz Ltd, 19 February 1936. D281
I.154   Letter to Victor Gollancz, 24 February 1936. D283
I.155   Letter to Christy & Moore, 27 February 1936. D286
I.156   Letter to Victor Gollancz, 11 March 1936. D292
I.157   Letter to Leonard Moore, 11 March 1936. D293
I.158   Letter to Leonard Moore, 1 April 1936. D297
I.159   Letter to Leonard Moore, 11 April 1936. D299
I.160   Letter to Cyril Connolly, [17? April 1936]. D301
I.161   Letter to Leonard Moore, [18 April 1936]. D302
I.162   Letter to Leonard Moore, [25 April 1936]. D306
I.163   Letter to Leonard Moore, 2 May 1936. D309
I.164   Letter to Leonard Moore, 8 June 1936. D313
I.165   Letter to Anthony Powell, 8 June 1936. D314
I.166   Letter to John Lehmann, 12 June 1936. D317
I.167   Lecture: 'An Outsider Sees the Distressed Areas', The Adelphi Summer School, 4 August 1936, Langham, near Colchester. D322
I.168   Letter to Leonard Moore, 19 October 1936. D329
I.169   Letter to Leonard Moore, 10 December 1936. D337
I.170   Letter to Christy & Moore, 11 December 1936. D338
I.171   Postcard to Leonard Moore, [19 December 1936]. D340
I.172   Letter to Victor Gollancz, 19 December 1936. D341
I.173   Orwell's notes for *The Road to Wigan Pier*, 1936. D345
I.174   Letter to Frederick Bardford, 10 June 1937. D372
I.175   Letter to John Lehmann, 8 July 1937. D376
I.176   Letter to Leonard Moore, 17 July 1937. D377
I.177   Letter to Leonard Moore, 31 July 1937. D380
I.178   Letter to Miss Charlesworth, 1 August 1937. D384
I.179   Letter to Charles Doran, 2 August 1937. D388 [sic, but probably 386]
I.180   Letter to Leonard Moore, 19 August 1937. D388
I.181   Letter to Yvonne Davet, 19 August 1937. D389
I.182   Letter to Victor Gollancz, 20 August 1937. D390
I.183   Letter to Leonard Moore, 27 August 1937. D391
I.184   Letter to Miss Charlesworth, 30 August 1937. D393
I.185   Letter to Leonard Moore, 1 September 1937. D395

I.560   Letter to A. Morley, 5 March 1943. D1933
I.561   Letter to BBC Talks Booking Manager, 5 March 1943. D1934
I.562   Letter to L.F. Rushbrook Williams, 5 March 1943. D1935
I.563   Letter to Philip Unwin, 5 March 1943. D1936
I.564   Letter to K.K. Ardaschir, 8 March 1943. D1939
I.565   Letter to Lester Powell, 8 March 1943. D1940
I.566   Letter to Arthur Wynn, 8 March 1943. D1941
I.567   Letter to Penguin Books, 8 March 1943. D1942
I.568   Letter to Ikbar Ali Shah, 10 March 1943. D1946
I.569   Letter to L.F. Rushbrook Williams, 5 March 1943. D1947
I.570   Letter to Penguin Books, 11 March 1943. D1949
I.571   Note to Norman Collins, c16 March 1943, D1954
I.572   Note to Norman Collins, 17 March 1943. D1960
I.573   Memorandum to Arthur Wynn, [17 March 1943]. D1961
I.574   Letter to Arthur Wynn, 22 March 1943. D1966
I.575   Letter to P. Chatterjee, 23 March 1943. D1967
I.576   Letter to Quintin Hogg, 24 March 1943. D1969
I.577   Letter to G.V. Desani, 25 March 1943. D1970
I.578   Letter to Paul Potts, 25 March 1943. D1971
I.579   Letter to Philip Unwin, 26 March 1943. D1973
I.580   Letter to E.W.D. Boughen, 27 March 1943. D1975
I.581   Letter to Philip Unwin, 31 March 1943. D1983
I.582   Postcard to Reginald Reynolds, [31 March 1943]. D1984
I.583   Letter to R.R. Desai, [31 March 1943]. D1985
I.584   Letter to Noel Sircar, 2 April 1943. D1990
I.585   Memorandum to Arthur Wynn, 2 April 1943. D1991
I.586   Postcard to Reginald Reynolds [5 April 1943?]. D1993
I.587   Letter to Benjamin Musgrave, 5 April 1943. D1995
I.588   Letter to Philip Unwin, 5 April 1943. D1996
I.589   Letter to J.B.S. Haldane, 7 April 1943. D1998
I.590   Letter to John Russell, 12 April 1943. D2004
I.591   Letter to K.K. Ardaschir, 13 April 1943. D2005
I.592   Letter to Desmond Hawkins, with BBC speakers' schedule notes to John Lehmann, Herbert Read and Osbert Sitwell, 13 April 1943. D2006
I.593   Letter to R.U. Hingorani, 13 April 1943. D2007
I.594   Letter to Michael Meyer, 13 April 1943. D2008
I.595   Letter to P.A. Buxton, 15 April 1943. D2010
I.596   Letter to Penguin Books, 16 April 1943. D2013
I.597   Letter to John Russell, 16 April 1943. D2014
I.598   Letter to Raymond Mortimer, 20 April 1943. D2022
I.599   Letter to J. Elizabeth Jermyn, 22 April 1943. D2026
I.600   Letter to Alan Rook, 22 April 1943. D2027
I.601   Letter to V.B. Wigglesworth, 22 April 1943. D2028
I.602   Letter to David Cecil, 23 April 1943. D2035
I.603   Letter to E.D. Edwards, 23 April 1943. D2036
I.604   Letter to Malcolm Darling, 23 April 1943. D2037
I.605   Letter to N. Gangulee, 23 April 1943. D2038
I.606   Letter to Alan Rook, 23 April 1943. D2039
I.607   Letter to K.K. Ardaschir, 27 April 1943. D2041
I.608   Letter to David Cecil, 27 April 1943. D2042
I.609   Postcard to Alan Rook, [27 April 1943?]. D2043
I.610   Postcard to John Russell, [27 April 1943?]. D2044
I.611   Letter to Secretaries, Students Unions, University of Cambridge, 3 May 1943. D2058
I.612   Letter to Elizabeth Jermyn, 5 May 1943. D2059

I.613   Letter to Director, London School of Hygiene and Tropical Medicine, 5 May 1943. D2060
I.614   Letter to F.W. Mackenzie, 7 May 1943. D2067
I.615   Letter to L.A.G. Strong, 7 May 1943. D2068
I.616   Letter to V.B. Wigglesworth, 7 May 1943. D2069
I.617   Letter to John Macmurray, 10 May 1943. D2071
I.618   Letter to V.B. Wigglesworth, 11 May 1943. D2074
I.619   Letter to K.K. Ardaschir, 13 May 1943. D2077
I.620   Letter to Royal Literary Fund, 13 May 1943. D2078
I.621   Letter to Norman Collins, 18 May 1943. D2084
I.622   Letter to E.F.W. Mackenzie, 24 May 1943. D2097
I.623   Letter to John Russell, 27 May 1943. D2101
I.624   Letter to N. Gangulee, 28 May 1943. D2103
I.625   Letter to John Atkins, 31 May 1943. D2110
I.626   Letter to K.K. Ardaschir, 3 June 1943. D2116
I.627   Memorandum to Norman Collins, 3 June 1943. D2117
I.628   Letter to Mrs Milton, 3 June 1943. D2118
I.629   Letter to Mrs Milton, 5 June 1943.
I.630   Letter to Arthur Wynn, 7 June 1943. D2126
I.631   Letter to Alan Rook, 8 June 1943. D2127
I.632   Letter to Professor Joad, 9 June 1943. D2128
I.633   Letter to Balachandra Rajan, 11 June 1943. D2131
I.634   Letter to C.E.M. Joad, 14 June 1943. D2134
I.635   Letter to Raymond Mortimer, 18 June 1943. D2142
I.636   Letter to V.S. Pritchett, 18 June 1943. D2143
I.637   Letter to Philip Unwin, 21 June 1943. D2145
I.638   Letter to J.C. Drummond, [25/26] June 1943. D2153
I.639   Letter to R.R. Desai, 29 June 1943. D2164
I.640   Postcard to Desmond Hawkins, 29 June 1943. D2163
I.641   Letter to John Russell, 30 June 1943. D2166
I.642   Letter to Alan Rook, 1 July 1943. D2169
I.643   Letter to V.S. Pritchett, 2 July 1943. D2172
I.644   Letter to P. Chatterjee, 6 July 1943. D2178
I.645   Letter to Alan Rook, 12 July 1943. D2184
I.646   Letter to Alex Comfort, 13 July 1943. D2185
I.647   Letter to Samuel Runganadhan, 13 July 1943. D2187
I.648   Letter to C.E.M. Joad, 16 July 1943. D2191
I.649   Letter to Bryan Brooke, 19 July 1943. D2192
I.650   Postcard to George Allen & Unwin, 21 July 1943. D2193
I.651   Letter to Bryan Brooke, 23 July 1943. D2197
I.652   Letter to R.R. Desai, 23 July 1943. D2198
I.653   Letter to Indian Programme Organiser, 26 July 1943. D2200
I.654   Letter to L.P. Garrod, 29 July 1943. D2207
I.655   Letter to Ronald Boswell, 30 July 1943. D2210
I.656   Letter to L.P. Garrod, 3 August 1943. D2214
I.657   Letter to Diana Wong, 3 August 1943. D2215
I.658   Letter to V.S. Pritchett, 4 August 1943. D2218
I.659   Letter to Oliver Bell, 6 August 1943. D2225
I.660   Letter to Oliver Bell, 12 August 1943. D2232
I.661   Letter to F.R. Daruvala, 12 August 1943. D2233
I.662   Postcard to L.P. Garrod, [c12 August 1943]. D2234
I.663   Letter to Oliver Bell, 17 August 1943. D2238
I.664   Letter to Bryan Brooke, 18 August 1943. D2239
I.665   Postcard to G.E. Harvey, 18 August 1943. D2240
I.666   Letter to L.P. Garrod, 20 August 1943. D2244

I.667   Postcard to C.E.M. Joad, [c. 24 August 1943]. D2248
I.668   Letter to Ivor Brown, 31 August 1943. D2255
I.669   Letter to Samuel Runganadhan, 31 August 1943. D2256
I.670   Letter to C.E.M. Joad, 2 September 1943. D2262
I.671   Letter to R.R. Desai, 24 September 1943. D2280
I.672   Letter to V.S. Pritchett, 24 September 1943. D2281
I.673   Letter to Herbert Read, 24 September 1943. D2282
I.674   Letter to W.J. Turner, 24 September 1943. D2284
I.675   Letter to T.H. Pear, 4 October 1943. D2294
I.676   Letter to T.H. Pear, 5 October 1943. D2296
I.677   Letter to J.C. Flugel, 6 October 1943. D2298
I.678   Letter to Leonard Moore, 6 October 1943. D2299
I.679   Letter to W.J. Turner, 6 October 1943. D2300
I.680   Letter to Susan Isaacs, 7 October 1943. D2303
I.681   Letter to C.W. Valentine, 8 October 1943. D2306
I.682   Letter to Frederick Laws, [8/10 October 1943?]. D2307
I.683   Letter to C.W. Valentine, 14 October 1943. D2315
I.684   Letter to J.C. Flugel, 15 October 1943. D2317
I.685   Letter to Frederick Laws, 18 October 1943. D2320
I.686   Letter to George Bernard Shaw, 18 October 1943. D2321
I.687   Letter to André Van Gysegham, 20 October 1943. D2323
I.688   Letter to Susan Isaacs, 22 October 1943. D2330
I.689   Letter to Blanche Patch, 22 October 1943. D2331
I.690   Letter to André Van Gysegham, 22 October 1943. D2333
I.691   Letter to D.W. Harding, [28/29 October 1943]. D2341
I.692   Letter to Reginald Reynolds, 5 November 1943. D2346
I.693   Letter to Harold Laski, 11 November 1943. D2350
I.694   Letter to Reginald Reynolds, 12 November 1943. D2352
I.695   Letter to Edmund Blunden, 16 November 1943. D2354
I.696   Letter to H.J. Laski, 16 November 1943. D2355
I.697   Letter to S. Moos, 16 November 1943. D2356
I.698   Letter to V.S. Pritchett, 19 November 1943. D2364
I.699   Letter to Penguin Books, 21 November 1943. D2367
I.700   Letter to Allen & Unwin, 23 November 1943. D2368
I.701   Letter to Cecil Day Lewis, 23 November 1943. D2369
I.702   Notebook for 'The Quick & the Dead' and 'The Last Man in Europe'. D2376 and
        D2377.
I.703   Letter to Alex Comfort, 29 November 1943. D2381
I.704   Letter to T.S. Eliot, 29 November 1943. D2382
I.705   Letter to Henry Treece, 29 November 1943. D2383
I.706   Letter to Leonard Moore, 6 December 1943. D2386
I.707   Letter to Henry Treece, 7 December 1943. D2387
I.708   Letter to Dwight Macdonald, 11 December 1943. D2392
I.709   Letter to Dwight Macdonald, 25 January 1944. D2411
I.710   Letter to R.S.R. Fitter, 31 January 1944. D2414
I.711   Letter to R.S.R. Fitter, 17 February 1944. D2420
I.712   Letter to Dwight Macdonald, 21 February 1944. D2423
I.713   Letter to Rayner Heppenstall, 28 February 1944. D2426
I.714   Letter to C.K. Ogden, 1 March 1944. D2427
I.715   Rejected review for *Manchester Evening News*, on Harold J. Laski *Faith, Reason
        and Civilisation*, submitted 13 March 1944. D2434
I.716   Letter to Victor Gollancz, 19 March 1944. D2437
I.717   Fragment of letter to Victor Gollancz, 25 March 1944. D2442
I.718   Postcard to Leonard Moore, 31 March 1944. D2446
I.719   Telegram to Leonard Moore, 5 April 1944. D2447

I.720   Letter to W.J. Strachan, 20 April 1944. D2456
I.721   Letter to Charles Hamblett, 8 May 1944. D2465
I.722   Letter to W.F. Stirling, 16 May 1944. D2469
I.723   Letter to A.S. Umpleby, 25 May 1944. D2477
I.724   Letter to Royal Literary Fund, 26 May 1944. D2479
I.725   Letter to Leonard Moore, 27 May 1944. D2480
I.726   Letter to C. Hopkins, 14 June 1944. D2488
I.727   Letter to W.F. Stirling, 19 June 1944. D2491
I.728   Letter to Mrs Gerry Byrne, 23 June 1944. D2493
I.729   Letter to Rayner Heppenstall, 11 July 1944. D2503
I.730   Letter to Z.A. Bokhari, 18 July 1944. D2512
I.731   Letter to Rayner Heppenstall, 21 July 1944. D2515
I.732   Letter to Dwight Macdonald, 23 July 1944. D2518
I.733   Letter to Ivor Brown, 24 July 1944. D2520
I.734   Letter to Rayner Heppenstall, 2 August 1944. D2524
I.735   Letter to W.J. Strachan, 2 August 1944. D2525
I.736   Letter to T.S. Eliot, 5 September 1944. D2543
I.737   Letter to R.S.R. Fitter, 5 September 1944. D2544
I.738   Letter to Dwight Macdonald, 5 September 1944. D2545
I.739   Letter to Dwight Macdonald, 15 September 1944. D2550
I.740   Letter to T.S. Eliot, 3 October 1944. D2555
I.741   Letter to Leonard Moore, 3 October 1944. D2556
I.742   Letter to Stanley Unwin, 3 October 1944. D2557
I.743   Letter to Rayner Heppenstall, 4 October 1944. D2558
I.744   Letter to Daniel George, [9 October 1944]. D2561
I.745   Letter to Rayner Heppenstall, 13 October 1944. D2563
I.746   Unpublished review for *The Observer* on C.S. Lewis *Beyond Personality*, written mid-October 1944.
I.747   Letter to Mrs G. Byrne, 28 October 1944. D2569
I.748   Letter to Tom Driberg, 30 October 1944. D2571
I.749   Letter to Tom Driberg, 4 November 1944. D2579
I.750   Letter to Gleb Struve, 28 November 1944. D2583
I.751   Letter to F.D. Barber, 5 December 1944. D2587
I.752   Letter to Ralph C. Elsley, 5 December 1944. D2588
I.753   Letter to Sunday Wilshin, 10 January 1945. D2600
I.754   Letter to Gleb Struve, 23 January 1945. D2606
I.755   Letter to Leonard Moore, 23 January 1945. D2607
I.756   Letter to W.J. Strachan, 7 February 1945. D2614
I.757   Letter to Kay Dick, 15 February 1945. D2618
I.758   Letter to Royal Literary Fund, 15 February 1945. D2620
I.759   Letter to Roger Senhouse, 15 February 1945. D2621
I.760   Letter to Roger Senhouse, 28 February 1945. D2628
I.761   Letter to Sally McEwan, 12 March 1945. D2634
I.762   Orwell's notes for his literary executor, 31 March 1945. D2648
I.763   Orwell's notes on possibly reprintable fragments of his writings, compiled 1945–1949. D2649
I.764   Letter to Lydia Jackson, 1 April 1945. D2650
I.765   Letter to Leonard Moore, 1 April 1945. D2651
I.766   Letter to Dwight Macdonald, 4 April 1945. D2652
I.767   Letter to Leonard Moore, 23 June 1945. D2682
I.768   Letter to Gerry Byrne, 28 June 1945. D2687
I.769   Letter to Ronald Boswell, 29 June 1945. D2688
I.770   Letter to C.E. de Salis, 29 June 1945. D2689
I.771   Letter to Leonard Moore, 4 July 1945. D2696
I.772   Postcard to Michael Meyer, 5 July 1945. D2698

I.773   Letter to Maurice Hussey, 10 July 1945. D2700
I.774   Postcard to George Woodcock, 13 July 1945. D2702
I.775   Letter to Kathleen Raine, 24 July 1945. D2707
I.776   Unpublished review for *Manchester Evening News*, c25 July 1945. Payment £8 8s. D2709
I.777   Letter to Mrs Belloc Lowndes, 31 July 1945. D2711
I.778   Letter to Lydia Jackson, 1 August 1945. D2712
I.779   Letter to Geoffrey Earle, 8 August 1945. D2715
I.780   Letter to Leonard Moore, 8 August 1945. D2716
I.781   Letter to Eric Warman, 11 August 1945. D2718. Sold at Sotheby's on 21 February 1978 but not now traceable.
I.782   Letter to Geoffrey Earle, 17 August 1945. D2722
I.783   Letter to Roger Senhouse, 17 August 1945. D2723
I.784   Letter to Leonard Moore, 18 August 1945. D2724
I.785   Postcard to Leonard Moore, 20 August 1945. D2727
I.786   Postcard to Leonard Moore, 23 August 1945. D2730
I.787   Letter to Leonard Moore, 24 August 1945. D2731
I.788   Letter to Roger Senhouse, 26 August 1945. D2732
I.789   Letter to Geoffrey Earl, 29 August 1945. D2733
I.790   Letter to Leonard Moore, 1 September 1945. D2736
I.791   Letter to Gleb Struve, 1 September 1945. D2737
I.792   Letter to Leonard Moore, 8 September 1945. D2747
I.793   Letter to George Woodcock, 8 September 1945. D2748
I.794   Letter to S. McGrath, 9 September 1945. D2750
I.795   Letter to George Woodcock, 9 September 1945. D2751
I.796   Letter to Leonard Moore, 24 September 1945. D2753
I.797   Letter to Kay Dick, 26 September 1945. D2754
I.798   Letter to Leonard Moore, 29 September 1945. D2756
I.799   Letter to Leonard Moore, 6 October 1945. D2759
I.800   Letter to Leonard Moore, 10 October 1945. D2762
I.801   Letter to Fredric Warburg, 17 October 1945. D2766
I.802   Letter to Roger Senhouse, 17 October 1945. D2767
I.803   Letter to Eric Warman, 30 October 1945. D2776
I.804   Letter to Roger Senhouse, 6 November 1945. D2782
I.805   Letter to Leonard Moore, 9 November 1945. D2787
I.806   Letter to J.G. Manton, 10 November 1945. D2788
I.807   Letter to Frank Barber, 10 November 1945. D2789
I.808   Letter to Leonard Moore, 14 November 1945. D2793
I.809   Letter to Leonard Moore, 17 November 1945. D2797
I.810   Letter to Fredric Warburg, 24 November 1945. D2803
I.811   Letter to E. Lyon Young, 24 November 1945. D2804
I.812   Letter to Leonard Moore, 29 November 1945. D2806
I.813   Letter to Leonard Moore, 1 December 1945. D2810
I.814   Notes for 'Politics and the English Language', [February–October 1945?]. D2816
I.815   Fragments of letter to G.H. Bantock [late 1945–early 1946]. D2825
I.816   Letter to Dudley Cloud, 2 January 1946. D2792
I.817   Letter to B.J. Brooke, 2 January 1946. D2835
I.818   Letter to Arthur Koestler, 2 January 1946. D2836
I.819   Letter to Dwight Macdonald, 3 January 1946. D2839
I.820   Letter to John Beavan, 7 January 1946. D2844
I.821   Letter to Philip Rahv, 7 January 1946. D2845
I.822   Letter to Kay Dick, 7 January 1946. D2846
I.823   Letter to Gleb Struve, 7 January 1946. D2847
I.824   Letter to Leonard Moore, 9 January 1946. D2848
I.825   Letter to Gleb Struve, 9 January 1946. D2849

I.879   Letter to unknown correspondent, 31 May 1946. D3006. Sold by Kingston Galleries, November or December 1969, but not now traceable.
I.880   Letter to David Astor, 4 June 1946. D3012
I.881   Letter to Rayner Heppenstall, 4 June 1946. D3013
I.882   Letter to Leonard Moore, 4 June 1946. D3014
I.883   Letter to Rayner Heppenstall, 16 June 1946. D3016
I.884   Letter to Rayner Heppenstall, 22 June 1946. D3018
I.885   Letter to Leonard Moore, 22 June 1946. D3019
I.886   Letter to Fredric Warburg, 22 June 1946. D3020
I.887   Letter to Terence Cooper, 29 June 1946. D3022
I.888   Letter to Leonard Moore, 30 June 1946. D3024
I.889   Lettercard to Rayner Heppenstall, 3 July 1946. D3027
I.890   Letter to Sally McEwan, 5 July 1946. D3028
I.891   Letter to Fredric Warburg, 8 July 1946. D3031
I.892   Letter to Dwight Macdonald, 20 July 1946. D3035
I.893   Letter to Yvonne Davet, 29 July 1946. D3037
I.894   Letter to Leonard Moore, 29 July 1946. D3038
I.895   Letter to P.G. Walford, 2 August 1946. D3040
I.896   Letter to Leonard Moore, 6 August 1946. D3042
I.897   Letter to Lydia Jackson, 7 August 1946. D3045
I.898   Letter to Anne Popham, 7 August 1946. D3046
I.899   Letter to Leonard Moore, 12 August 1946. D3048
I.900   Letter to George Woodcock, 12 August 1946. D3049
I.901   Letter to Michael Meyer, 14 August 1946. D3051
I.902   Letter to Fredric Warburg, 23 August 1946. D3054
I.903   Letter to Leonard Moore, 26 August 1946. D3056
I.904   Letter to Rayner Heppenstall, 5 September 1946. D3060
I.905   Letter to Leonard Moore, 5 September 1946. D3061
I.906   Letter to Miss Shaw, 5 September 1946. D3062
I.907   Letter to Yvonne Davet, 6 September 1946. D3064
I.908   Letter to Leonard Moore, 6 September 1946. D3065
I.909   Letter to Michael Meyer, 9 September 1946. D3067
I.910   Letter to Philip Rahv, 16 September 1946. D3071
I.911   Letter to Leonard Moore, 17 September 1946. D3073
I.912   Letter to Rayner Heppenstall, 19 September 1946. D3075
I.913   Letter to Leonard Moore, 21 September 1946. D3077
I.914   Letter to Herbert W. Simpson, 21 September 1946. D3078
I.915   Letter to Yvonne Davet, 23 September 1946. D3080
I.916   Letter to K.A.G.S. Lane, 24 September 1946. D3082
I.917   Letter to Helmut Klose, 26 September 1946. D3084
I.918   Letter to Humphrey Slater, 26 September 1946. D3085
I.919   Letter to Leonard Moore, 28 September 1946. D3087
I.920   Letter to K.A.G.S. Lane, 1 October 1946. D3092
I.921   Letter to K.A.G.S. Lane, 5 October 1946. D3094
I.922   Letter to Rayner Heppenstall, 13 October 1946. D3096
I.923   Letter to the Controller, BBC European Service, 14 October 1946. D3097
I.924   Letter to Dwight Macdonald, 15 October 1946. D3098
I.925   Letter to Leonard Moore, 17 October 1946. D3099
I.926   Letter to Leonard Moore, 18 October 1946. D3100
I.927   Letter to Leonard Moore, 23 October 1946. D3101
I.928   Letter to Harcourt, Brace & Co., 30 October 1946. D3103
I.929   Letter to BBC Copyright Director, 6 November 1946. D3106
I.930   Letter to D. Ross, 11 November 1946. D3110
I.931   Letter to Julian Symons, 11 November 1946. D3111
I.932   Letter to Leonard Moore, 14 November 1946. D3113

I.933 Letter to unnamed correspondent, 14 November 1946. D3114. Advertised in a catalogue issued by R.A. Gekosi in 1983, but not now traceable.
I.934 Letter to Sheila Hodges, 15 November 1946. D3116
I.935 Letter to Helmut Klose, 18 November 1946. D3118
I.936 Letter to Graham Greene, 20 November 1946. D3119
I.937 Letter to Leonard Moore, 20 November 1946. D3120
I.938 Letter to Fredric Warburg, [20 November 1946]. D3121
I.939 Letter to Edward R. Ward, 26 November 1946. D3125
I.940 Letter to Helmut Klose, 29 November 1946. D3127
I.941 Letter to Dwight Macdonald, 5 December 1946. D3128
I.942 Letter to Leonard Moore, 5 December 1946. D3129
I.943 Letter to Stanley Unwin, 5 December 1946. D3130
I.944 Letter to Leonard Moore, 7 December 1946. D3132
I.945 Letter to M.C. Plummer, 9 December 1946. D3133
I.946 Letter to Grace Wyndham Goldie, 13 December 1946. D3135
I.947 Letter to Paul Tabori, 13 December 1946. D3136
I.948 Letter to John Gawsworth, 20 December 1946. D3138
I.949 Letter to Dmitrii Fedotoff-White, 20 December 1946. D3139
I.950 Note to Dwight Macdonald, [c27 December 1946]. D3141
I.951 Letter to Leonard Moore, 27 December 1946. D3142
I.952 Letter to Gleb Struve, 27 December 1946. D3143
I.953 Domestic diary 1947. D3147
I.954 Letter to Leonard Moore, 9 January 1947. D3148
I.955 Letter to Helmut Klose, 10 January 1947. D3149
I.956 Letter to Leonard Moore, 17 January 1947. D3154
I.957 Letter to Mamaine Koestler, 24 January 1947. D3159
I.958 Letter to Leonard Moore, 24 January 1947. D3161
I.959 Letter to Fredric Warburg, 24 January 1947. D3162
I.960 Letter to Dudley Cloud, 27 January 1947. D3164
I.961 Letter to Fredric Warburg, 30 January 1947. D3166
I.962 Letter to Leonard Moore, 11 February 1947. D3170
I.963 Letter to Leonard Moore, 21 February 1947. D3173
I.964 Letter to Leonard Moore, 23 February 1947. D3174
I.965 Letter to Dwight Macdonald, 26 February 1947. D3175
I.966 Letter to Emilio Cecchi, 28 February 1947. D3178
I.967 Letter to Fredric Warburg, 28 February 1947. D3179
I.968 Letter to George Woodcock, 28 February 1947. D3180
I.969 Letter to Leonard Moore, 7 March 1947. D3183
I.970 Letter to Leonard Moore, 7 March 1947. D3184
I.971 Letter to George Woodcock, 7 March 1947. D3185
I.972 Cable to *New Leader* (New York), 12 March 1947. D3186
I.973 Letter to Ihor Szewczenko, 13 March 1947. D3188
I.974 Letter to A.S.B. Glover, 19 March 1947. D3192
I.975 Letter to Leonard Moore, 19 March 1947. D3193
I.976 Letter to Emilio Cecchi, 20 March 1947. D3194
I.977 Letter to Brenda Salkeld, 20 March 1947. D3195
I.978 Letter to Ihor Szewczenko, 21 March 1947. D3197
I.979 Letter to Leonard Moore, 25 March 1947. D3199
I.980 Letter to Leonard Moore, 28 March 1947. D3202
I.981 Postcard to Secker & Warburg, 28 March 1947. D3203
I.982 Letter to Leonard Moore, 29 March 1947. D3205
I.983 Letter to Leonard Moore, 2 April 1947. D3207
I.984 Letter to Yvonne Davet, 7 April 1947. D3209
I.985 Letter to George Woodcock, 9 April 1947. D3210
I.986 Letter to Frank D. Barber, 15 April 1947. D3214

I.987   Letter to Leonard Moore, 15 April 1947. D3216
I.988   Letter to George Woodcock, 19 April 1947. D3219
I.989   Letter to Janamanci Ramakrisna, 30 April 1947. D3221
I.990   Letter to Sunday Wilshin, 30 April 1947. D3222
I.991   Letter to Leonard Moore, 21 May 1947. D3226
I.992   Letter to George Woodcock, 26 May 1947. D3228
I.993   Letter to Leonard Moore, 29 May 1947. D3230
I.994   Letter to John Gawsworth, 2 June 1947. D3234
I.995   Letter to Leonard Moore, 9 June 1947. D3238
I.996   Letter to George Woodcock, 9 June 1947. D3239
I.997   Letter to Leonard Moore, 7 July 1947. D3246
I.998   Letter to Leonard Moore, 14 July 1947. D3248
I.999   Letter to Lydia Jackson, 28 July 1947. D3250
I.1000   Letter to Leonard Moore, 28 July 1947. D3251
I.1001   Unpublished article for *Tribune*, 'In Defence of Comrade Zilliacus', [August–September 1947?]. D3254
I.1002   Letter to Leonard Moore, 25 August 1947. D3258
I.1003   Letter to William Phillips, 25 August 1947. D3259
I.1004   Letter to Leonard Moore, 1 September 1947. D3261
I.1005   Letter to Brenda Salkeld, 1 September 1947. D3262
I.1006   Letter to Fredric Warburg, 1 September 1947. D3263
I.1007   Letter to Leonard Moore, 8 September 1947. D3265
I.1008   Letter to Stanley Unwin, 8 September 1947. D3266
I.1009   Letter to George Woodcock, 8 September 1947. D3268
I.1010   Letter to Helmut Klose, 19 September 1947. D3273
I.1011   Letter to Christy & Moore, 20 September 1947
I.1012   Letter to David Astor, 29 September 1947. D3277
I.1013   Letter to Leonard Moore, 4 October 1947. D3282
I.1014   Letter to D.F. Boyd, 12 October 1947. D3286
I.1015   Letter to Leonard Moore, 25 October 1947. D3294
I.1016   Letter to George Woodcock, 25 October 1947. D3296
I.1017   Letter to Celia Kirwin, 27 October 1947. D3298
I.1018   Letter to Leonard Moore, 31 October 1947. D3300
I.1019   Letter to Leonard Moore, 7 November 1947. D3303
I.1020   Letter to Leonard Moore, 8 November 1947. D3304
I.1021   Letter to Roger Senhouse, 14 November 1947. D3305
I.1022   Letter to Arthur Koestler, 24 November 1947. D3306
I.1023   Letter to Frederick Tomlinson, 24 November 1947. D3307
I.1024   Letter to Leonard Moore, 30 November 1947. D3310
I.1025   Letter to Celia Kirwin, 7 December 1947. D3312
I.1026   Letter to Leonard Moore, 7 December 1947. D3313
I.1027   Letter to Leonard Moore, 17 December 1947. D3314
I.1028   Letter to Frederick Tomlinson, 23 December 1947. D3315
I.1029   Letter to Leonard Moore, 26 December 1947. D3317
I.1030   Letter to Julian Symons, 26 December 1947. D3318
I.1031   Letter to David Astor, 31 December 1947. D3320
I.1032   Letter to Ivor Brown, 31 December 1947. D3321
I.1033   Letter to Tosco Fyvel, 31 December 1947. D3322
I.1034   Letter to Humphrey Dakin, 3 January 1948. D3326
I.1035   Letter to Leonard Moore, 3 January 1948. D3327
I.1036   Letter to Edmund Wilson, 3 January 1948. D3328
I.1037   Letter to Helmut Klose, 12 January 1948. D3330
I.1038   Letter to Mary Fyvel, 16 January 1948. D3331
I.1039   Letter to Eugene Reynal, 28 January 1948. D3335
I.1040   Letter to David Astor, 1 February 1948. D3337

I.1041   Letter to Philip Rahv, 4 February 1948. D3338
I.1042   Telegram to Fredric Warburg, 4 February 1948. D3340
I.1043   Letter to Leonard Moore, 5 February 1948. D3341
I.1044   Letter to David Astor, [9 February 1948]. D3342
I.1045   Letter to Edmund Wilson, 12 February 1948. D3343
I.1046   Letter to David Astor, [14 February 1948]. D3344
I.1047   Letter to Edmund Wilson, 14 February 1948. D3345
I.1048   Notes for 'Marx and Russia'. D3347
I.1049   Letter to Helmut Klose, 15 February 1948. D3348
I.1050   Letter to David Astor, [16 February 1948]. D3349
I.1051   Letter to John Middleton Murry, 20 February 1948. D3350
I.1052   Letter to Fredric Warburg, 20 February 1948. D3351
I.1053   Orwell's notes of Hairmyres Hospital Timetable. D3352
I.1054   Letter to Fredric Warburg, 22 February 1948. D3353
I.1055   Letter to Gleb Struve, 25 February 1948. D3354
I.1056   Letter to Hermon Ould, 28 February 1948. D3355
I.1057   Letter to Emilio Cecchi, 3 March 1948. D3357
I.1058   Letter to Dwight Macdonald, 7 March 1948. D3359
I.1059   Letter to Anthony Powell, 8 March 1948. D3360
I.1060   Letter to Leonard Moore, 19 March 1948. D3362
I.1061   Preparatory notes for 'Writers and Leviathan'. D3365
I.1062   Preparatory notes for 'Britain's Left-Wing Press'. D3367
I.1063   Letter to Leonard Moore, 23 March 1948. D3368
I.1064   Letter to Celia Kirwin, 24 March 1948. D3370
I.1065   Letter to Fredric Warburg, [26 March or 2 April 1948]. D3371
I.1066   Letter to Ivor Brown, 27 March 1948. D3372
I.1067   Letter to Sally McEwan, 27 March 1948. D3373
I.1068   Diary 1948. D3374
I.1069   Letter to David Astor, 31 March 1948. D3375
I.1070   Letter to Mrs David Astor, 5 April 1948. D3376
I.1071   Letter to David Astor, [7 April 1948]. D3377
I.1072   Diary 1949. D3378
I.1073   Letter to David Astor, [14 April 1948]. D3379
I.1074   Preparatory notes for review of *Spearhead*. D3381
I.1075   Letter to Leonard Moore, 17 April 1948. D3382
I.1076   Letter to Philip Rahv, 17 April 1948. D3383
I.1077   Letter to Roger Senhouse, 19 April 1948. D3385
I.1078   Letter to Leonard Moore, 26 April 1948. D3389
I.1079   Letter to John Middleton Murry, 28 April 1948. D3390
I.1080   Letter to Leonard Moore, 1 May 1948. D3391
I.1081   Letter to Dwight Macdonald, 2 May 1948. D3392
I.1082   Letter to David Astor, 4 May 1948. D3394
I.1083   Preparatory notes for review of *The Soul of Man Under Socialism*. D3396
I.1084   Letter to Leonard Moore, 12 May 1948. D3398
I.1085   Letter to Roger Senhouse, [13 or 20 May 1948]. D3399
I.1086   Letter to Leonard Moore, 15 May 1948. D3400
I.1087   Letter to Evelyn Waugh, 16 May 1948. D3401
I.1088   Letter to Michael Kennard, 25 May 1948. D3404
I.1089   Preparatory notes for 'George Gissing'. D3407
I.1090   Letter to S.N. Levitas, 4 June 1948. D3410
I.1091   Letter to Michael Kennard, 7 June 1948. D3412
I.1092   Letter to Leonard Moore, 8 June 1948. D3413
I.1093   Letter to Leonard Moore, 12 June 1948. D3414
I.1094   Letter to Leonard Moore, 25 June 1948. D3415
I.1095   Letter to George Woodcock, 30 June 1948. D3417

I.1208   Letter to Tosco Fyvel, 26 May 1949. D3634
I.1209   Letter to Fredric Warburg, [27 May 1949]. D3635
I.1210   Letter to Leonard Moore, 31 May 1949. D3637
I.1211   Letter to Fredric Warburg, 2 June 1949. D3639
I.1212   Letter to Robert Giroux, 3 June 1949. D3640
I.1213   Letter to Fredric Warburg, 6 June 1949. D3642
I.1214   Letter to William Phillips, 8 June 1949. D3644
I.1215   Letter to Leonard Moore, 18 June 1949. D3648
I.1216   Letter to Tosco Fyvel, 20 June 1949. D3649
I.1217   Letter to Mr Shaw, 20 June 1949. D3650
I.1218   Letter to Leonard Moore, 22 June 1949. D3651
I.1219   Letter to Mamaine Koestler, 27 June 1949. D3653
I.1220   Letter to Celia Kirwan, 27 June 1949. D3654
I.1221   Letter to Leonard Moore, 27 June 1949. D3655
I.1222   Letter to S.M. Levitas, 11 July 1949. D3656
I.1223   Letter to Leonard Moore, 13 July 1949. D3657
I.1224   Letter to David Astor, 14 July 1949. D3658
I.1225   Letter to Ruth Fischer, 15 July 1949. D3659
I.1226   Letter to David Astor, 15 July 1949. D3660
I.1227   Letter to David Astor, 18 July 1949. D3661
I.1228   Letter to Leonard Moore, 20 July 1949. D3662
I.1229   Letter to Leonard Moore, 21 July 1949. D3663
I.1230   Letter to Leonard Moore, 24 July 1949. D3665
I.1231   Letter to Jack Common, 27 July 1949. D3666
I.1232   Letter to Gleb Struve, 27 July 1949. D3667
I.1233   Letter to Leonard Moore, 28 July 1949. D3668
I.1234   Letter to Leonard Moore, 30 July 1949. D3670
I.1235   Letter to Leonard Moore, 4 August 1949. D3671
I.1236   Letter to Fredric Warburg, 4 August 1949. D3672
I.1237   Letter to Tosco Fyvel, 11 August 1949. D3674
I.1238   Letter to Leonard Moore, 12 August 1949. D3675
I.1239   Letter to Leonard Moore, 16 August 1949. D3676
I.1240   Letter to Leonard Moore, 22 August 1949. D3677
I.1241   Letter to Fredric Warburg, 24 August 1949. D3679
I.1242   Letter to David Astor, 25 August 1949. D3680
I.1243   Letter to Leonard Moore, 30 August 1949. D3683
I.1244   Letter to Richard Rees, 30 August 1949. D3684
I.1245   Letter to David Astor, 5 September 1949. D3687
I.1246   Postcard to Leonard Moore, [7] September 1949. D3689
I.1247   Letter to Philip Rahv, 17 September 1949. D3691
I.1248   Letter to Richard Rees, 17 September 1949. D3692
I.1249   Letter to Melvin Lasky, 21 September 1949. D3695
I.1250   Letter to Leonard Moore, 2 October 1949. D3697
I.1251   Letter to Roger Senhouse, 12 October 1949. D3701
I.1252   Letter to Leonard Moore, 4 November 1949. D3707
I.1253   Letter to Robert Giroux, 17 November 1949. D3708
I.1254   Telegram to Harry Roskolenko, 13 December 1949. D3714
I.1255   Orwell's last will, 18 January 1950.
I.1256   'A Smoking Room Story', draft and notes of work in progress, and presumed fair
          copy, 1949.
I.1257   Statement of assets.
I.1258   Orwell's reading list for 1949.
I.1259   Orwell's notes on his books and essays.
I.1260   Names in Orwell's address book.
I.1261   List of communists.
I.1262   List of books in Orwell's collection.

Appendix I: Payments and royalties

I gave in my resignation [from the Indian Imperial Police] in the hopes of being able to earn my living by writing. I did just about as well at it as do most young people who take up a literary career – that is to say, not at all. My literary efforts in the first year barely brought me in twenty pounds.[1]

The following notes on Orwell's income are not meant to constitute a full account of his earnings. His annual and total earnings from his writing are difficult to calculate, mainly because they came from so many different sources.[2] In the early 1930s he was workng as a teacher in private schools, and any income from his writing was purely incidental. He was writing mainly to gain practice in writing. Nonetheless his £40 advice for *Down and Out in Paris and London*, upon signing the contact for the book with Victor Gollancz, must not have been unwelcome. In 1934, for the same book, he suspected that Harper's owed him £20 or £30 for the American publication. In January 1936, Victor Gollancz commissioned Orwell to write a book about the condition of the working classes and unemployed in the north of England. It became *The Road to Wigan Pier*. Gollancz's offer of a £500 advance, payable in instalments over two years, convinced Orwell to take on the work. On 18 April 1936 he recorded earning '£30 odd' in half-yearly royalties from his books, and then on 19 October 1936, another £8 9s 0d. Writing *Coming Up for Air* in Marrakech in 1938 he was concerned to keep his home in England in good order in his absence since, as he pointed out, 'I don't know what my financial situation will be next year … and if I have to come back to England and start on yet another book with only £50 in the world I would rather have a roof over my head from the start.'[3]

In August 1941 Orwell joined the BBC, first as a Talks Assistant and later as a Talks Producer, at a salary of £640 a year. It was full-time work, although he continued to write for a few newspapers and magazines. In a letter to Leonard Moore on 4 September 1942 Orwell thanks him for a cheque for £10 17s 1d. He adds, 'I am unfortunately far too busy to write anything except casual journalism', because he was at that time working full-time at the BBC and volunteering in the Home Guard. His total royalties from his books in 1943 amounted to £154 19s 0d. In other words he was not making a huge income from his writing, or even an income on which he could live comfortably at this time. On 14 July 1945 he received a £20 advance for *The English People* against the final total payment of £50. Occasionaly he received payment for work not published. For example, he recorded in his payments notebook an 800-word article written for *The Observer*, completed on 7 September 1945. The payment was £10 0s 0d for an 800-word article completed on this date, but now untraceable. It was really not until the publication of *Animal Farm* in 1945 and, all but too late for his benefit, *Nineteen Eighty-Four* in 1949 that Orwell began to make large amounts of money from his books. In 1945 he received a £100 advance against the American royalties of *Animal Farm*, and later £6,500 in advance royalties for the Book-of-the-Month Club edition, albeit subject to American and British tax and even supertax.

It was only with the imminent publication and then the actual publication of *Nineteen Eighty-Four* that Orwell's income increased significantly. For example, Fredric Warburg told him that by refusing to cut 'The Principles of Newspeak', he risked losing Book-of-the-Month publication in the United States, and hence at least £40,000 in their royalties alone. The sheer numbers of copies printed guaranteed significant royalties.

1 Introduction to *La Vache Enragé*, the French Edition of *Down and Out in Paris and London*, 1935. A.1.T5a
2 For a detailed analysis of Orwell's income see Peter Davison, 'Orwell: Balancing the Books', *The Library* Vol. XVI, No. 2 (June 1994) 77–100; and summaries of the tables and further discussion in Peter Davison, *George Orwell: A Literary Life* (London: Macmillan, 1996).
3 Letter to Jack Common (12 October 1938). *CEJL* I 355–356.

In the following list of payments received by Orwell for various kinds of work, including essays, reviews and contributions to books, the dates are publication dates unless otherwise noted. I have not attempted to calculate yearly totals, since payments often overlapped calendar years. Nor does the list go beyond the beginning of 1947, when the amounts he earned become more difficult to trace. Orwell's payments book, in which he kept detailed, although not necessarily comprehensive accounts of his earnings, ends in 1945. Also not included here is Eileen Blair's income from the time of their marriage in June 1936 until she gave up her work as a Civil Servant in June 1944.

1922   £444 a year, plus bonuses, Burma Police.

1925–1927   £696 a year, plus bonuses, Burma Police.

1928–1931   Tutor, dishwasher, odd jobs, £10–25 each.
            7 published articles 1928–29, total £14.
            4 published articles 1930, total £8.
            6 published articles 1931, total £12.

1932–1933   Teacher in private schools, £30–60 a year.
            6 published articles 1932, total £10.
            6 published articles 1933, total £12.
            Down and Out in Paris and London:
                Advance August 1932, £40.
                Royalties £100.
                US royalties £95.

1934–1935   Part-time work at Booklovers' Corner 15s 0d per week, October 1934–January 1936, total £48.
            7 published articles 1934, total £14.
            7 published articles 1935, total £8.
            Burmese Days:
                Advance £50.
                US royalties £116.
            A Clergyman's Daughter:
                Royalties £74.
                French royalties £5.

1936   25 published articles, total £35.
            Down and Out in Paris and London:
                French royalties £5.
            A Clergyman's Daughter:
                US royalties £33.
            Keep the Aspidistra Flying:
                Advance £75.

1937   13 published articles, total £20.
            Down and Out in Paris and London:
                French royalties £5.
            The Road to Wigan Pier:
                Advance £100.
                Royalties £494.

1938   £300 loan.
            Down and Out in Paris and London:
                French royalties £5.
            Homage to Catalonia:
                Advance £150.

1939	16 published articles, total £25. *Coming Up for Air*: Royalties £100.
1940	75 published articles £159. *Down and Out in Paris and London*: Penguin royalties £91. *Inside the Whale:* Advance £20. Royalties £10.
1941	BBC Talks Assistant, later Talks Producer £267. 61 published articles, total £156. *The Lion and the Unicorn*: Royalties £150.
1942	BBC Talks Producer £640. 18 published articles, total £60. *Keep the Aspidistra Flying*: Royalties £6
1943	BBC Talks Producer £580. Literary Editor *Tribune* £33. 12 published articles £40.
1944	Literary Editor *Tribune* c. £400. Other journalism £154. *Burmese Days*: Penguin royalties £148. *Animal Farm*: Advance £90.
1945	Literary Editor *Tribune* £66. Journalism for *The Observer* £500. Journalism for the *Manchester Evening News* c. £42. Other journalism £782. *Animal Farm*: Royalties £88. *The English People*: Royalties £20. *Talking to India*: Royalties £16.
1946	Journalism £134. BBC broadcasts £63. *Love of Life Introduction* £21. *Animal Farm*: Abridged version royalties £26.
1947	Journalism £26.

Appendix II: Some archival materials

This section makes no pretensions to be comprehensive. It is merely a list of the repositories and materials I have consulted in writing this bibliography. Undoubtedly, there are other libraries and archives around the world with Orwell holdings. But the Orwell Archive at University College, London, has such a full collection, attempting to obtain copies of all known materials, that the deficiencies of the following list are undoubtedly filled by its comprehensiveness.

BOSTON UNIVERSITY
The Mugar Memorial Library has 14 Orwell letters in the Partisan Review Collection. There are additional letters in the collection referring to Orwell. There are copies of letters in the Ethel Mannin collection, and a few Sonia Orwell letters and cards in the Terence de Vere White Collection.

UNIVERSITY OF BRISTOL
The University Library holds the editorial correspondence relating to the Penguin publication of Orwell's books, including letters from Orwell. There are also Orwell letters in the Hamish Hamilton editorial archive, although the publishing files were apparently not preserved. Neither of these collections is fully catalogued, although even uncatalogued materials are available for users.

BRITISH BROADCASTING CORPORATION
The BBC Written Archive at Caversham Park, Reading, holds correspondence between Orwell and members of the BBC staff as well as letters to broadcasters. They include autograph letters, typescripts and memos from Orwell to Martin Armstrong, Edmund Blunden, T.S. Eliot, E.M. Forster and George Bernard Shaw. There are also surviving scripts from Orwell's broadcasts in the Eastern Service of the BBC, and details of programme he organised, arranged and produced.

BRITISH LIBRARY
The British Library has two Orwell letters and a typescript copy of Orwell's autobiographical sketch for *Twentieth Century Authors*.

CAMBRIDGE UNIVERSITY LIBRARY
Cambridge University Library has copyright deposit copies of every edition of Orwell's books, as well as some reissues, and editions of books which he edited or to which he contributed. It is worth noting that while books ordered in the West Room arrive without jackets, writing 'WITH JACKET' on the requisition slip means that, where available, the jackets will be fetched. Although there are no Orwell manuscripts in the CUL collection, there is an interesting note in the 'Femina Vie Heureuse' Prize collection. This was a literary prize, for an English imaginative work, awarded annually between 1920 and 1939. *Keep the Aspidistra Flying and The Road to Wigan Pier* were considered in 1936 and 1937, but neither was short-listed.

KING'S COLLEGE, CAMBRIDGE
The College Library has a few letters relating to Orwell, including one from Sonia Orwell to Rosamond Lehmann, in the Lehmann papers, and the draft of a letter of 5 October 1949 from John Hayward to the Archbishop of Canterbury asking on Orwell's behalf for a special licence to marry Sonia Brownell.

CASE WESTERN RESERVE UNIVERSITY
Letter from Orwell to Edward R. Ward, 26 November 1949.

COLUMBIA UNIVERSITY LIBRARY
The Butler Library has two letters from Orwell, and one from Sonia Orwell.

CORNELL UNIVERSITY
Letter from Orwell to J.C. Hodgart, 25 October 1946.

UNIVERSITY OF EDINBURGH
The University Library has the extensive Arthur Koestler Archive. It includes 15 letters from Orwell to Koestler and 8 from Koestler to Orwell. In additions, there are references to Orwell in other correspondence in the collection.

ETON COLLEGE
Letter from Orwell to Graham Greene, 1946.

GEORGETOWN UNIVERSITY
The University Library contains a few letters from Evelyn Waugh to Orwell, in the Christopher Sykes Papers.

HARVARD UNIVERSITY
The Houghton Library has two letters from Orwell to Ruth Fischer and three from Fischer to Orwell.

INDIANA UNIVERSITY
The Lilly Library holds 99 Orwell items, chiefly correspondence with his literary agent, Leonard Moore. There are also letters from Eileen Blair to Moore during the time she was conducting Orwell's business affairs while he was fighting in Spain. There is also correspondence from Orwell's publishers, Victor Gollancz and Fredric Warburg, to Orwell.

KING'S COLLEGE, LONDON
The Liddell Hart Centre for Military Archives at King's College contains a brief correspondence between Orwell and Captain Sir Basil Liddell Hart in 1942.

UNIVERSITY COLLEGE, LONDON
The Department of Rare Books and Manuscripts houses the Orwell Archive. The Archive consists of manuscripts, typescripts, carbon copies, proofs and many other materials as described throughout the bibliography. There are also editions of most of Orwell's books, some in multiple copies, copies of reissues, and translations. There are runs of some of the journals to which Orwell contributed, and copies of all his published journalism. There is an extensive collection of secondary, critical material on Orwell. There are also books from Orwell's library. In addition there is a collection of related materials, including posters, newspaper cuttings, cassette tapes, cartoons, advertising materials etc.

UNIVERSITY OF MANCHESTER
The John Rylands Library has correspondence to and from Orwell in the files of the *Manchester Guardian*.

UNIVERSITY OF NEWCASTLE UPON TYNE
The Robinson Library has five letters from Orwell to Jack Common. There are also letters from Eileen Blair to Common and one from Mary Common to Eileen.

NEW YORK PUBLIC LIBRARY
The Berg Collection holds 205 Orwell letters to his literary agent, Leonard Moore, in addition to correspondents including John Middleton Murry, Jack Common, Julian Symonds and A.P. Watt and Son.

OHIO STATE UNIVERSITY
The University Library holds correspondence between Jessica Mitford and Sonia Orwell.

CHRIST CHURCH COLLEGE, OXFORD
The College Library has Orwell correspondence in the Tom Driberg collection.

PRINCETON UNIVERSITY
Letter from Orwell to Mr Lynn, undated.

UNIVERSITY OF READING
The extensive publishing archives at the University Library include the Secker & Warburg Archive and the Routledge Archive, both of which contain Orwell material.

HOOVER INSTITUTION, STANFORD
The Hoover Institution Archive has papers of Harry Milton, some of which relate to Orwll. Milton was with the Patido Obrero de Unificaci on Marxista (POUM) during the Spanish Civil War at the same time as Orwell.

UNIVERSITY OF TEXAS
The Harry Ransom Humanities Research Center at Austin holds correspondence to and from Orwell. Correspondents include John Lehmann, Henry Treece, Rayner Heppenstall, Edmund Blunden, Kay Dick and Stephen Spender. A few of the 48 letters are copies, but most are original manuscripts and typescripts.

UNIVERSITY OF TULSA
The McFarlin Library has copies of letters from Orwell in the Cyril Connolly collection, as well as a postcard from Marrakech from Orwell to Connolly. There are also Sonia Orwell letters, and correspondence in the Stevie Smith collection which discusses Orwell.

YALE UNIVERSITY
The Beinecke Library holds two letters from Orwell as well as a telegram from Sonia Orwell.

Appendix III: Some books and articles about Orwell and his writings

Keith Alldritt, *The Making of George Orwell: An Essay in Literary History*. London: Arnold, 1969.

John Atkins, *George Orwell: A Literary Study*. London: Calder & Boyars, 1954.

Laurence Brander, *George Orwell*. London: Longmans, Green & Co., 1954.

Jacintha Buddicom, *Eric and Us: A Remembrance of George Orwell*. London: Leslie Frewin, 1974.

Anthony Burgess, *1985*. London: Hutchinson, 1978.

Jenni Calder, *Chronicles of Conscience: A Study of George Orwell and Arthur Koestler*. London: Secker & Warburg, 1968.

Cyril Connolly, *Enemies of Promise*. London: Routledge & Kegan Paul, 1938.

James Connors, 'Zamyatin's *We* and the Genesis of *1984*', *Modern Fiction Studies* Vol. XXI (Spring 1975) 107–124.

Audrey Coppard and Bernard Crick, eds., *Orwell Remembered*. London: BBC Ariel Books, 1984.

Bernard Crick, 'How the Essay Came to be Written', *Times Literary Supplement* (15 September 1972) 1039–1040 [See C.839].

——, *George Orwell: A Life*. London: Secker & Warburg, 1980.

——, ed., *Nineteen Eighty-Four*. Oxford: Clarendon Press, 1984.

David Crompton, 'False Maps of the World: George Orwell's Autobiographical Writings and Early Writings', *Critical Quarterly* Vol. XVI (1974) 149–169.

Peter Davison, 'Editing Orwell: Eight Problems', *The Library* Vol. VI, No. 6 (September 1984) 217–228.

——, 'What Orwell Really Wrote', *George Orwell and 'Nineteen Eighty-Four': The Man and the Book*. Washington: Library of Congress, 1985.

——, 'George Orwell: Dates and Origins', *The Library* Vol. VI, No. 13 (June 1991) 137–150.

——, 'Orwell: Balancing the Books', *The Library* Vol. VI, No. 16 (June 1994) 77–100.

——, *George Orwell: A Literary Life*. London: Macmillan, 1996.

Avril Dunn, 'My Brother, George Orwell', *Twentieth Century* Vol. 169 (March 1961) 255–261.

Ruth Dudley Edwards, *Victor Gollancz: A Biography*. London: Gollancz, 1987.

Valerie Eliot, 'T.S. Eliot and *Animal Farm*: Reasons for Rejection', *The Times* (6 January 1969) 9.

William Empson, 'Orwell at the BBC', *The Listener* Vol. 85 (4 February 1971) 129–131, 144–145, 149–150.

Elisaveta Fen, 'George Orwell's First Wife', *Twentieth Century* Vol. 168 (August 1960) 115–126.

E.M. Forster, *Two Cheers for Democracy*. London: Edward Arnold, 1951.

Tosco Fyvel, 'A Writer's Life', *World Review* Vol. 16 (June 1950) 7–20.

——, 'George Orwell and Eric Blair: Glimpses of a Dual Life', *Encounter* Vol 13 (July 1959) 60–65.

——, *George Orwell: A Personal Memoir*. London: Weidenfeld and Nicolson, 1982.

John Gross, *The Rise and Fall of the Man of Letters: Aspects of English Literary Life Since 1800*. London: Weidenfeld and Nicolson, 1969.

Miriam Gross, *The World of George Orwell*. London: Weidenfeld and Nicolson, 1971.

J.R. Hammond, *A George Orwell Companion*. London: Macmillan, 1982.

Rayner Heppenstall, 'Memoirs of George Orwell: The Shooting Stick', *Twentieth Century* Vol. 157 (April 1955) 367–373.

——, 'Orwell Intermittent', *Twentieth Century* Vol. 157 (May 1955) 470–483.

——, *Four Absentees*. London: Barrie and Rockliff, 1960.

Sheila Hodges, *Gollancz: The Story of a Publishing House, 1928–1978*. London: Gollancz, 1978.

Richard Hoggart, 'George Orwell and *The Road to Wigan Pier*', *Critical Quarterly* Vol. 7 (1965) 72–85.

Christopher Hollis, 'George Orwell and his Schooldays', *The Listener* Vol. 51 (4 March 1954) 382–383.

——, *A Study of George Orwell: The Man and his Works*. London: Hollis & Carter, 1956.

Tom Hopkinson, *George Orwell*. London: Longman, 1953.

——, 'George Orwell: Dark Side Out', *Cornhill* Vol. 166 (1953) 450–470.

Irving Howe, ed., *Orwell's Nineteen Eighty-Four: Text, Sources, Criticism*. New York: Harcourt, Brace, 1982.

——, ed., *'1984' Revisited*. New York: Harper & Row, 1983.

Maung Htin Aung, 'Orwell of the Burma Police', *Asian Affairs* Vol. 60 (1973) 181–186.

Stefan Kanfer, 'Orwell 25 Years Later: Future Imperfect', *Time* (24 March 1975) 77–78.

Q.D. Leavis, 'The Literary Life Respectable', *Scrutiny* Vol. 9 (1940) 173–176.

Peter Lewis, *George Orwell: The Road to 1984*. London: Heinemann, 1981.

Lawrence Malkin, 'Halfway to 1984', *Horizon* Vol. 12 (1970) 33–39.

Roger Manvell, *The Animated Film, with Pictures from the Film "Animal Farm"*. London: 1954.

Jennifer McDowell, 'George Orwell: Bibliographical Addenda', *Bulletin of Bibliography* Vol. XXIII (1963) 19–24, 36–40, 224–229.

Jeffrey Meyers, 'George Orwell, the Honorary Proletarian', *Philological Quarterly* Vol. 47 (1969) 526–549.

——, 'George Orwell: A Bibliography', *Bulletin of Bibliography* Vol. XXXI (July–September 1974) 117–121.

——, 'George Orwell: A Selected Checklist', *Modern Fiction Studies* Vol. XXI (Spring 1975) 133–136.

——, *A Reader's Guide to George Orwell*. London: Thames & Hudson, 1975.

—— ed., *George Orwell: The Critical Heritage*. London: Routledge & Kegan Paul, 1975.

Jeffrey and Valerie Meyers, *George Orwell: An Annotated Bibliography of Criticism*. New York: Garland, 1977.

Modern Fiction Studies Vol. XXI (Spring 1975) 1–136. Special Orwell issue.

Gordon Barrick Neavill, 'Victor Gollancz and the Left Book Club', *The Library Quarterly* Vol. 41 (1971) 197–215.

Christopher Norris, ed., *Inside the Myth; Orwell: Views from the Left*. London: Lawrence & Wishart, 1984.

Bernard Oldsey and Joseph Browne, eds., *Critical Essays on George Orwell*. Boston: G.K. Hall, 1986.

Sonia Orwell, 'Unfair to George', *Nova* (June–July 1969) 18, 20, 22, 27, 29, 31.

David Plante, *Difficult Women: A Memoir of Three*. London: Gollancz, 1983.

Anthony Powell, 'George Orwell: A Memoir', *Atlantic Monthly* Vol. 220 (October 1967) 62–68.

V.S. Pritchett, 'George Orwell', *New Statesman* Vol. 39 (28 January 1950) 96.

Alok Rai, *Orwell and the Politics of Despair: A Critical Study of the Writings of George Orwell*. Cambridge: Cambridge University Press, 1988.

Simon Raven, 'Portrait of a Gentleman', *Sunday Times Magazine* (18 August 1968) 20–25, 27–29.

Richard Rees, 'George Orwell', *Scots Chronicle* Vol. 26 (1951) 7–14.

——, *George Orwell: Fugitive from the Camp of Victory*. London: Secker & Warburg, 1961.

Patrick Reilly, *George Orwell: The Age's Adversary*. London: Macmillan, 1986.

Bertrand Russell, 'George Orwell', *World Review* Vol. 16 (June 1950) 5–7.

Michael Shelden, *Orwell: The Authorised Biography*. London: Heinemann, 1991.

Peter Stansky, ed., *On Nineteen Eighty-Four*. New York: W.H. Freeman & Co., 1983.

Peter Stansky and William Abrahams, *The Unknown Orwell*. London: Constable, 1972.

——, *Orwell: The Transformation*. London: Constable, 1979.

William Steinhoff, *George Orwell and the Origins of '1984'*. Ann Arbor: University of Michigan Press, 1975.

Julian Symons, 'Orwell – A Reminiscence', *London Magazine* Vol. 3 (September 1963) 35–49.

Edward M. Thomas, *Orwell*. Edinburgh and London: Oliver and Boyd, 1965.

John Thompson, *Orwell's London*. London: Fourth Estate, 1984.

Peter Viereck, 'Bloody-Minded Professors', *Confluence* Vol 1 (September 1952) 36–37.

Richard Voorhees, 'Some Recent Books on Orwell: An Essay Review', *Modern Fiction Studies* Vol. 21 (Spring 1975) 125–131.

Stephen Wadhams, *Remembering Orwell*. Harmondsworth: Penguin, 1984.

John Wain, 'Orwell in Perspective', *New World Writing* Vol. 12 (1957) 84–96.

Fredric Warburg, 'George Orwell', *Bookseller* (11 February 1950) 200.

——, *An Occupation for Gentlemen* London: Secker & Warburg, 1960.

——, *All Authors are Equal: The Publishing Life of Fredric Warburg 1936–1971*. London: Hutchinson, 1973.

Raymond Williams, *Culture and Society* Harmondsworth: Penguin, 1961.

——, *Orwell*. London: Fontana, 1971.

——, ed., *George Orwell: A Collection of Critical Essays*. Englewood Cliffs, NJ: Prentice-Hall, 1974.

Ian Willison, *George Orwell: Some Materials for a Bibliography*. Librarianship Diploma Thesis, University College London, 1953.

——, 'Orwell's Bad Good Books', *Twentieth Century* Vol. 157 (April 1955) 354–366.

Ian Willison and Ian Angus, 'George Orwell: Bibliographical Addenda', *Bulletin of Bibliography* Vol. XXIV (1965) 180–187.

George Woodcock, 'Recollections of George Orwell', *Northern Review* Vol. 6 (1953) 17–27.

——, *The Crystal Spirit: A Study of George Orwell*. London: Jonathan Cape, 1967.

Gillian Workman, 'Orwell Criticism', *Ariel* Vol. 3 (1972) 62–73.

World Review Vol. 16 (June 1950) 3–60. Special Orwell issue.

David Wykes, *A Preface to Orwell*. London: Longman, 1987.

Zoltand Zeke and William White, 'George Orwell: A Selected Bibliography', *Bulletin of Bibliography* Vol. XXIII (May 1961) 110–114.

——, 'Orwelliana', *Bulletin of Bibliography* Vol. XXIII (September 1961) 140–144.

——, 'Orwelliana', *Bulletin of Bibliography* Vol. XXIII (January 1962) 166–168.

Index

The Index covers Sections **A** to **H** of the text. References are to section-numbers; subsection-numbers in **bold type** denote main references. The following abbreviations have been used:

A/E: article or essay; *bdcstr*: broadcaster; *ed*.: editor; *edn*: edition; G. O.: George Orwell (Eric Blair); *J*: journal/magazine; *L*: letter (to newspaper etc.); *N*: newspaper; *P*: publishers; *pm*: poem; *ps*: pseudonym; *Q*: questionnaire; *R*: review; *rad*: radio broadcast; vol.: volume